Child & Adolescent
Psychology
BEHAVIOR AND DEVELOPMENT

Child & Adolescent Psychology

BEHAVIOR AND DEVELOPMENT

Gene R. Medinnus
SAN JOSE STATE COLLEGE

Ronald C. Johnson
UNIVERSITY OF COLORADO

John Wiley & Sons, Inc.
New York · London · Sydney · Toronto

Preface

Developmental psychology is inextricably linked with other psychological fields, such as experimental psychology, the psychology of individual differences, social psychology, learning, and personality. It is also multidisciplinary, since it draws on data gathered in such diverse fields as sociology, anthropology, behavioral genetics, pediatrics, and some areas of home economics. From these different areas of specialization we have gathered data dealing with two major aspects: first, those ways in which all humans are similar to one another in their potentialities, patterns of development, and behavior; and, second, the differences between human beings in capabilities and in behavior as these differences are manifested within the basic core of similarity.

We see two forces operating to produce similarity. The first is our biological nature, which makes humans the moderately large, omnivorous, tough, stimulation-seeking, problem-solving, symbol-using organisms that we are. The second is that necessary core of culture based on such aspects of the human condition as a long period of dependency that in turn demands a stable family structure, considerable instruction, and considerable psychological support if the immature organism is to survive. Within the limits imposed by these two forces, individual differences in behavior occur as a result of hereditary and environmental variability.

We have attempted to present a sound body of facts within the context of those ideas and theories that influence our view of development. We can discuss and raise questions, but the reader must interact with real children to understand the reasons for our interest, our discussion, and our questions.

The basic motivation of any science is to understand fully and accurately those natural phenomena that are the object of study within that science. We have tried to present data that will help the reader in the task of understanding the processes involved in human development. We have tried as best we could to weight the evidence in our interpretations and explanations of psychological phenomena. There are matters on which our position is not the only one available, and future research may demonstrate that we are clearly wrong, but at this time we believe our view to be supported by a preponderance of evidence. Perhaps some reader will provide the crucial experimental data that will resolve some of the still unanswered questions concerning the psychology of human development.

The present text, *Child and Adolescent Psychology*, is basically an extension of the second edition of *Child Psychology: Behavior and Development*. Except for minor changes, the child psychology chapters are the same. The three adolescence chapters came into being partly to meet the demands of courses covering both childhood and adolescence and partly as an effort on our part to come to understand adolescent behavior more adequately, since some of our own children are moving into that stage of development.

Our contributions to this book have been equal. Since there is no "first" or "second" author, except alphabetically, we have taken this opportunity to name G. R. M. first and R. C. J. second, thus reversing the order of seniority that appears in our child psychology text.

We wish to express our gratitude to our teachers, our colleagues, our critics, and our students. We wish to thank the authors whose research has contributed so greatly to this book and the publishers who granted us permission to quote some of these research findings. We are grateful to each other for the comments and encouragement that shaped the structure of this book and brought it to completion.

Gene R. Medinnus

November 1968

Ronald C. Johnson

Contents

Child & Adolescent Psychology

Psychology

BEHAVIOR AND DEVELOPMENT

SECTION I
INTRODUCTION

All sciences attempt to understand the phenomena with which they deal. Some of them control these phenomena. All of them make predictions. Whether physics, biochemistry, psychology, or any other science, the aims and methods of procedure are basically alike. Some sciences may have progressed further than others in achieving these aims. However, it is believed that all of them can ultimately reach the same level of accuracy in explanation and prediction if they employ what is universally known as the scientific method.

This opening section of the book, consisting of a single chapter, considers the scientific method and how child psychologists have developed techniques for observation and experimentation that have yielded a clearer, less biased, and more systematic understanding of human behavior and have enhanced predictive powers. A review of these processes also discloses the historical development of child psychology as a scientific discipline. It is to that review that the next several pages pay close attention.

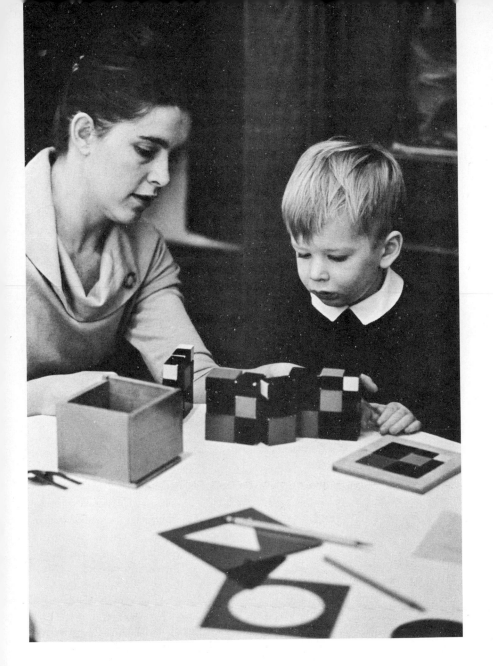

Scientific Method and Child Psychology

One of the many reasons a person seeks knowledge is to understand the world around him. By learning the *why* of what he sees, he acquires some proficiency at discerning orderly sequences of events and predicting the future from the present. Through understanding the causes of events, an individual may at times change the sequence and produce a different end result. Understanding leads to prediction and often, ultimately, to control of the environment. But there is a great difference between common, ordinary, everyday understanding and scientific understanding. The latter is achieved by application of what is widely known as the scientific method. Let us therefore explore this method to learn how scientific understanding, prediction, and control develop, in distinction to the more personal, day-to-day understanding of the universe that is shared by all manner of men. And then let us see how scientific techniques develop valuable findings in child development.

SCIENTIFIC METHOD

Observation

The raw data of scientific knowledge are facts, and scientific undertakings usually begin with observation. Astronomy, the first of the sciences, grew out of the keen observations of Egyptian and Babylonian priests. To them, the orderly sequences of day and night and of the seasons might have suggested an orderliness, that is, a predictability, in the physical world. Careful observation led to knowledge of planetary movement and of fixed stars; this knowledge enabled these priestly astronomers to make practical predictions, such as the time at which the Nile would flood. Because they also believed in astrology, they made less valid predictions too—such as "Beware of a dark-haired man next Tuesday." In all probability, the science of astronomy resulted from false notions about the influence of celestial bodies on human behavior as much as from a belief in an orderly universe. Yet the information collected by these early observers was substantially correct, even when their interpretations fell short of the mark.

Since these initial probings of the unknown, knowledge of the world has progressed a long way to its present state. In this advance, observation has played a major role: *knowledge, in fact, has depended on observation.* Although the ability to observe is widespread, scientific observation differs from ordinary observation in several respects. Scientific observation is systematic; it dwells on a particular phenomenon. This phenomenon may be the movement of the planets as observed by the ancients, or it may be the social relations of two-year-olds as observed by child psychologists. In either instance, as in any scientific undertaking, the observation is restricted to one or, at the most, a few kinds of object or event; it does not extend to all things. Moreover, this kind of observation concentrates on *all* aspects of the particular kinds of event, whereas everyday observation may take in only part of many events.

Take the bias found in the casual observation of the relation between physical characteristics and behavior. Redheads have hot tempers, we hear; people with big ears are generous; long fingers denote the artist. If these views were valid, we could easily predict appropriate behavior toward redheads, whom to approach for a loan, and which child would perform in Carnegie Hall. This is hazardous terrain. It leads from fallacies concerning the most observable characteristics of people with big ears to the quicksand of characteristics believed to be evident among members of racial or religious groups. These questionable beliefs result from the human tendency *not* to observe negative manifestations. People prefer to notice only those things that confirm their beliefs; if an event runs counter to a belief, they are more likely to forget or distort the event than to change the belief. This tendency may be seen in a vast number of studies cited by Rapaport (1942), and more recently in the work of Festinger (1957), centered in his theory of cognitive dissonance. Scientific method, in contrast, is aimed at ensuring complete, accurate observation and inclusion of even negative findings. The observation of these instances—the cases that do not fit the expectation—is the very essence of science.

Observation leads to the formation of hypotheses, which may be considered educated guesses or suppositions. If these hypotheses are so linked that a test of any one of them yields information not only about itself but also about the other hypotheses dependent in whole or in part upon it, a theory exists. Sometimes the information bears no essential relation to any specific hypothesis and hence no essential relation to the theory. For example, the difference in average sentence length in the speech of two-year-olds and three-year-olds may have some value for other purposes, but it suggests no new ideas and leads no further to basic understanding of the child. Other data, however, may help to find out whether a hypothesis conforms to reality; such data permit new predictions, which in turn provide new insights about the world. Scientific procedure benefits greatly from findings of this kind and the experimental processes uncovering them, but all scientific investigations must start with the accumulation of facts from observation and then test hypotheses aginst these facts.

If a theory or a hypothesis does not fit the observed facts, it must be discarded, whether it concerns a folk belief like the temper of redheads or a cosmological issue such as the question of whether the universe is expanding or standing still. The rejection of a theory generally results from systematic, close observation of *all* cases. Sometimes the facts fit the theory fairly well, but not well enough. Here, the negating instances indicate where a theory is weak and where it must be revised promptly to improve its accuracy. The next result is a fuller, clearer understanding of the world, which sharpens the skill of predicting the future more precisely.

Prediction

All scientific endeavor is concerned with making observations that lead to accurate predictions—predictions ranging from what may result from a change in the structure of a molecule to what new attitudes may develop among race-prejudiced persons exposed to close contact with another race, as in an integrated teen-aged boys' camp.

Prediction, however, is never certain. It is merely a statement of probability. The form in which it is used in all sciences is often called *actuarial prediction.* This term is borrowed from the insurance field, whose actuaries can tell—barring great, unexpected catastrophes such as wars—the number of individuals in a given age group who will die in a particular year. An actuarial statement sets forth the odds, the chances that a specific thing will happen. In child psychology, for example, an actuarial statement might hold that "a child of IQ 70 at age 12 has less than one chance in 100 of completing a conventional high-school course curriculum by age 20." The chance is there (Baller, 1936), but it is a long shot.

This form of prediction is also known as *nomothetic prediction*—that is, arising from or based on law—a distinction noted by Allport (1937). A nomothetic statement, like an actuarial statement, asserts the odds; it is a statement of probability. A statement like "Republicans worry more about a balanced budget than do Democrats" is a nomothetic statement. It may very well be true, based on a theory of budgeting that has influenced many Democrats, but it is only a matter of probability for any individual member of either party. Even though the odds in its favor are excellent, the statement is still not a certainty.

A second type of prediction, limited almost entirely to the social sciences, applies to the individual case. This is *idiographic prediction,* roughly a "drawing or graphing of an individual," and it is aimed at understanding a particular individual. Idiographic prediction makes use of nomothetic knowledge, but is concerned only with one individual. To the applied psychologist, it is the predictive technique *par excellence:* "Mr. X will not commit suicide"; "Miss A will do better in group therapy than in analysis"; "Mr. K is not a good parole risk." Such predictions are often wrong. They are based on knowledge acquired by nomothetic means which only imply the odds. Nevertheless, the social scientist must make these predictions, for, although they often prove inaccurate, they are frequently more precise than the predictions made by others. Indeed, considering the present state of knowledge and the complexity of subject matter, the proportion of accuracy in prediction is remarkable.

Whether nomothetic or idiographic, the accuracy of a prediction supplies cues to the truth of a belief. The most wonderful thing about science, believed M. R. Cohen (1949), is that built into it is the notion that unless ideas accurately portray reality, they must be changed. If, for example, one of two theories makes more accurate predictions about the phenomena with which both deal, the more accurate theory is accepted and the other is rejected. If the two predict equally well, the more *parsimonious* theory, the one making fewer assumptions, takes precedence. Should a new theory be developed that outshines either of the other two, both prior theories are discarded. No truth is sacred, universal, or immutable to science or the scientist. This attitude of disrespect for any authority other than nature, observed systematically and without bias, is what has enabled science to change rapidly and relinquish old ideas for better—that is, more accurate or more truthful—new ones. Certainly this applies to many of the ideas discussed in this book; they are likely to be superseded in time by more reliable interpretations.

If the goal of psychology is highly accurate prediction, how closely has this been approached? Not very closely, but progress is being made. There are several reasons why success in psychological prediction has only been moderate. First, the subject matter of psychology is more complex than the subject matter of many other sciences; at least psychologists claim this to be so. Second, psychology is a comparatively young science. One of the early American students of Wilhelm Wundt, a founder of modern psychology, died only recently. This makes one realize, as does nothing else, how young this science is. Psychology may not mature for hundreds of years, and it must suffer the problems of growing up; but there are aspects of the young science that can be changed, aspects that at present contribute to a deficiency in skill.

One change desired by most psychologists and toward which they are working is an increase in the reliability and validity of measuring devices. In its simplest form, reliability means that a device used to measure a stable characteristic, such as the height of an adult, will give the same information on every occasion. If a yardstick expanded or contracted capriciously, what would measure five feet, 10 inches today might measure three feet, six inches or nine feet, eight inches at some future date. Obviously this yardstick would be unreliable as a measuring device, and because of its unreliability growth trends could not be predicted with any accuracy over intervals of time. The reliability of many measuring instruments is indeed low, especially the tests for measuring personality. Perhaps personality characteristics are basically unstable and individual personality varies greatly at different points in time. If, however, this lack of reliability is largely the fault of inadequate tests rather than of actual personality change, continued efforts to increase the reliability of psychological tests should make their results more dependable and therefore better instruments for predicting behavior.

A test is valid if it measures what it set out to measure. It is invalid if it measures other things and not what it was designed to test. Suppose we measured the height of members of a psychology class and graded them on the basis of height. The measurements would be highly reliable on the subject of height, but they would not be valid for achievement, since tallness is hardly a good measure of ability. Whereas a reliable measure may not be valid, as in the foregoing example, a measure cannot be highly valid unless it is highly reliable. As better testing methods are used and reliability grows, the validity of measurements increases. But more important, the validity of the measuring device can be checked by comparing its findings with reality. Does the person who does well in a test of creativity, for example, actually behave creatively? Only when behavior in the real world is predictable from test results does a test become a valid predictive device. Development of tests at once reliable and valid increases the power to predict.

Phenotype and Genotype. Psychology also stands to gain in both understanding and predictability from an increasing awareness of *genotypic* variation as opposed to *phenotypic* variation between individuals. (It should be noted that the words genotype and phenotype are used here, as among psychologists, in a way similar to that first introduced by Kurt Lewin. The words are used differently by geneticists, with *genotype* referring only to genetic forces.)

Genotype refers to the similarity in background forces that produce behavior. One young man steals an automobile. Another holds down two jobs to pay for an automobile. Both are motivated chiefly by a desire to impress some young woman. They are genotypically alike in this specific aspect of their motivation even though their outward behavior differs. *Phenotype,* on the other hand, concerns the phenomenal or observable world. Phenotypically, or observably, these young men differ greatly.

Psychologists, and social scientists in general, have dwelt on phenotypes rather than genotypes and, further, have not done as good a job as they might on distinguishing between phenotypes. Consider the problem as it relates to the diagnosis and treatment of physical and psychological disorders. A physical disorder entailing an increase in temperature is called a fever. Although various fevers differ in a number of secondary aspects, their major phenotypical or observable feature is the heightened temperature they all share. If physicians had paid attention only to the temperature, no effective methods of treatment would have been developed, since a therapeutic aid for reducing one fever, such as quinine for malarial fever, is utterly useless in the treatment of many other fevers. Astute physicians managed, however, through keen observation, to distinguish several *sub*phenotypes within the general phenotype *fever.* These subphenotypes differed in genotype—or cause—and, once separated from one another, also differed in the treatment effective for each of them. This knowledge enabled development of individual treatments. By carefully examining subjects manifesting a common genotype, one can often discern systematic variations in their observable characteristics. Though superficially resembling one another, subjects in each group actually fall into distinct subgroups, each a result of another genotype. This distinction will be discussed at some length in Chapter 16.

How successful is this approach in psychology? Individuals with severe mental defects—say, below IQ 50—are phenotypically alike in being defective. Yet there are several rather easily observable distinctions among them. Some of these individuals have clearly suffered brain damage during prenatal development, in a difficult birth process, or after birth itself. Others form the low end of the normal distribution of intelligence. For every IQ of 160, presumably, there is another of 40, and its possessor is defective as a result of multiple genetic variation. Still others are defective from the effects of a single gene or of a chromosomal abnormality rather than the multiple-genetic deficiency responsible for the IQ of 40. More careful scrutiny divides these individuals into additional subphenotypes, suggesting the existence of still more genotypes than are casually perceived. One variety of defectiveness resembles any other *until* the individual's urine is subjected to chemical analysis. This particular disorder with the formidable name of *phenylpyruvic oligophrenia* or *phenylketonuria* has an observable symptom in the excretion of phenylpyruvic acid in the urine when phenylalanine, an amino acid, is incompletely oxidized. When this acid is found in the urine, the individual is nearly always defective, presumably because of the unmetabolized amino acid in the system. The condition results from a double recessive genetic characteristic. Anyone may be a carrier of the disorder, although the probabilities are slight. The carrier who transmits the disorder has one recessive and one dominant gene, whereas the defective child has a double recessive pair of genes. If married, by chance, to another carrier, the original carrier has one chance in four of having a child with this affliction, two chances in four of having children who do not have it but who are carriers, and one chance in four of having a child who is neither defective nor a carrier.

Here is an instance in which careful phenotypical observation led to the discovery of a specific genotype. Once the genotype was found, effective treatment was soon developed. With a phenylalanine-free diet, especially during the first year of life, a child generally could overcome the hereditary disposition toward idiocy (Armstrong & Tyler, 1955; Woolf, Griffiths, & Moncrieff, 1955) and be, on the average, dull normal in ability. Without doubt, there are a number of genotypes of this sort hidden within the larger phenotypical category severely mentally defective, as there are in such widely inclusive phenotypes as juvenile delinquency, schizophrenia, or even shyness. But as long as psychologists continue to study individuals on the basis of broad phenotypes, there is scant likelihood for additional success in diagnosis, prediction of outcome, and treatment. A shift in interest to genotypes may very well improve the predictive powers of the child psychologist.

Control

A basic purpose of prediction is control. However, prediction and control are separate aspects of science. In fact, control is not a necessary part of science, since some sciences exist for which control is clearly impossible. Many sciences such as astronomy, cosmology, volcanology, and seismology, for example, are reasonably adequate at predicting events, but they obviously have no control over the phenomena to which they attend. Predicting an eclipse is a simple matter for an astronomer, whereas causing or controlling one is indeed beyond human capability.

One might contend that ability to predict without ability to control is essentially useless. The argument depends on the definition of utility. If immediate, demonstrable usefulness is necessary, then, as Bugelski (1960, p. 20) said, "Such a viewpoint might limit the work of astronomers to observations of the moon and the navigational stars since outside of these might be little of an immediately practical nature in astronomy." Most scientists, however, are unconcerned with practical utility. For them, knowledge is an end in itself. More cogently and more practically, knowledge that does not have immediate utility might be of value in the future. Bugelski (1960) noted that Faraday once demonstrated an elementary form of a dynamo to Disraeli. "What good is it?" Disraeli asked. Faraday retorted, "Someday you may tax it." The practical and concrete fact often arises from the impractical and abstract theory. From an interesting set of ideas proposed by a young man named Einstein evolved the atomic bomb. The justification for seeking knowledge clearly does not depend on the practical utility of the knowledge for controlling the surrounding world.

In certain areas of psychology, notably clinical psychology, control of behavior is often considered to be a major aim. As used in this sense, control does not mean forcing the individual to act in a desired manner. It rather means increasing the frequency of certain behaviors and decreasing the frequency of other behaviors through a manipulation of the environment. Suppose it is believed that a boy who sets fires does so because of neurotic difficulties stemming from his acceptance of the masculine sex role. The clinical psychologist, using some form of therapy, tries to bring these problems into the open where they can be treated. If given some insight into the roots of his problems, plus, perhaps, some form of training and support, the boy may indeed cease his arsonous activities. If successful, the clinician has controlled behavior. Certain behaviors, such as setting fires, decrease in frequency whereas other behaviors, such as dating, increase. Even if the boy now starts stealing cars to provide himself and his young lady friend with transportation, the therapy quite likely has been successful. It has discovered the sources of the arsonous conduct, and certain hypotheses have been formed regarding the efficacy of various treatment techniques. Behavior has been controlled.

Very often the child psychologist is asked questions pertaining to control. How does one increase a behavior such as eating everything on the plate, or decrease a behavior such as having temper tantrums?

Psychology has some answers to these questions, and this book attempts to deal with them. The scientist may not be sure that control should be attempted because he is not certain that control is desirable for human beings. The parent, on the other hand, controls his children's present and attempts to control their future through manipulating the environment. Good or bad, this is parenthood. All any parent can do is to try to increase those behaviors that he values as "good" in a child and decrease those deemed "bad." Like the clinician and the parent, the teacher, too, must act. Since these acts have far-reaching consequences, parent and teacher, again like the clinician, should use what scientific understanding is available. Although much remains to be known, this book endeavors to discuss what is understood, what is predictable, and what forms control may take.

RESEARCH METHODS IN CHILD PSYCHOLOGY

There are several reasons why knowledge of research methods is important for the beginning student in child development. Like other areas of the social sciences, child psychology is imprecise as compared with the more exact physical sciences. Yet in a relatively brief interval of time the precision of research and hence the reliability and validity of conclusions have shown a remarkable advance.

The volume dealing with research methods in child development (Mussen, 1960) illustrates the tremendous concern with research methodology in a wide range of areas including physical growth, intellectual development, language and communication, personality development, and social behavior.

The study of research methods tends to foster a critical faculty in a student; he is better able to judge the value of research data and the conclusions by examining the methods that produce them. This ability is perhaps more necessary in the field of child psychology than in any other scientific area. Here every layman considers himself an expert and is quite willing to proffer advice in such matters as child discipline, juvenile delinquency, and child growth. It is therefore of particular importance that the student of child psychology be well grounded in scientific methods. Only then can he judge, not on the basis of apparent meaningfulness and plausibility of statements, but by examining the source of the data, the correctness and appropriateness of the techniques employed, and the justifiability of the conclusion drawn.

Four main questions will guide the inquiry into research methods in child psychology: (1) When is the particular method applicable?

(2) What are its advantages? (3) What are its disadvantages? (4) What does the method tell, and what kinds of information can it not provide?

Naturalistic Observation

The scientist, like the novelist, can gain his raw data from observing organisms in nature—that is, in their natural habitat—and not in any controlled or experimentally manipulated environment. Many psychologists believe that such naturalistic observation, which is relatively objective, will ultimately yield more information than better controlled but more limited techniques—limited in the sense of the amount of behavior observed—such as experimentation.

Baby Biographies. Among the types of naturalistic observation, the early diary accounts describing child behavior have been of both historical and methodological importance. The biographer, usually an interested parent or relative, has observed the behavior of a single child and recorded the observations in diary style. Often the biographers have been scientists in fields other than child behavior. Charles Darwin, for example, was a biologist. Thus an individual of scientific bent, curious, yearning to know, to understand, to find out, approaches each new, unexplored area with a desire to observe and record the phenomena under study. Many criticisms may be voiced over the trustworthiness of the information contained in these early biographies. The following excerpt from Darwin's biography of his infant son illustrates several points.

> It was difficult to decide at how early an age anger was felt; on his eighth day he frowned and wrinkled the skin round his eyes before a crying fit, but this may have been due to pain or distress, and not to anger. When about ten weeks old, he was given some rather cold milk and he kept a slight frown on his forehead all the time that he was sucking, so that he looked like a grown-up person made cross from being compelled to do something which he did not like. When nearly four months old, and perhaps much earlier, there could be no doubt, from the manner in which the blood gushed into his whole face and scalp, that he easily got into a violent passion. A small cause sufficed; thus, when a little over seven months old, he screamed with rage because a lemon slipped away and he could not seize it with his hands. When eleven months old, if a wrong plaything was given him, he would push it away and beat it; I presume that the beating was an instinctive sign of anger, like the snapping of the jaws by a young crocodile just out of the

egg, and not that he imagined he could hurt the plaything. When two years and three months old, he became a great adept at throwing books and sticks, and the like at anyone who offended him; and so it was with some of my other sons. On the other hand, I could never see a trace of such aptitude in my infant daughters (Darwin, 1881).

Darwin's attempts to separate the facts of observation from an interpretation of them were not always successful. A common weakness of such observations is the tendency to project onto the child the emotions, motives, and attitudes of the adult. Besides, there are other disadvantages and limitations to the biographical approach. First, the relevance of the observations depends in part on the adequacy of the observer's background and training. Since such observations are highly subjective, the biases of the observer may very well influence the types of behavior recorded and the interpretations of these behaviors. Second, it is immediately apparent that the child cannot be considered truly representative of all children of his age and sex. This limits the extent to which the data can apply to other children. Third, the type of parent who would engage in such painstaking observation and recording would not be likely to represent parents in general.

So much for the observer and the observed. Several things may also be said about the information itself. Since the baby biographies were usually initiated with no specific purpose in mind, no single type of behavior was examined systematically. How representative any of these sampled behaviors might be is a matter for debate. Representativeness is imperative in research if the investigator attempts to conclude from his observations that a certain behavior is typical or characteristic of a particular child. As a final caution, the observer must remain alert to the danger of the observation itself interfering with the behavior of the child under observation. More recent research, to be discussed in the next section, has dealt with this problem through a similar observational method.

Case-Study Method. A modern approach that shows much similarity to the baby biography is the case study. This technique collects a great variety of information about a single child, usually to help a professional person understand the child's behavior. Delinquency, school failure, problem behavior are common subjects studied through the case method. School records, accounts obtained from parents, relatives, other interested adults, and the child himself, as well as the results of psychological examinations are among the sources of information consulted. The following case study was undertaken to obtain clinical evaluation of one child's behavior problems.

CASE-STUDY REPORT

Name: ANDREWS, James
Age: 10 years, 6 months   *Examined by:* L. S. Martin, Ph.D.

Reason for Referral

Mr. and Mrs. Andrews requested an evaluation of their son, James, because they have become increasingly upset by his behavior and have been unable to handle him at times.   They are especially frightened of his rage reactions and are concerned about his lack of self-discipline and his inability to accept limits.

Interview with Parents

The parents describe Jim as an intelligent boy who is overweight, has a quick temper, and is a chronic "tease."   They believe that he is sensitive about his obesity and that this prevents him from taking an active part in sports.   They also noted that his rudeness, his unwillingness to cooperate, and his inability to accept criticism help to prevent his participation in organized sports.

The Andrews feel that Jim hates to be frustrated, is rebellious, disorderly, and that he refuses to dress up.   He likes to work with mechanical things and is very interested in "hot rods."   Jim shows a great deal of animosity toward his eight-year-old sister.   He becomes profane when angry and constantly threatens to leave home.

The parents remember Jim to have been a relaxed and happy baby.   They are rather vague about developmental history, but believe that he did everything early.   Mrs. Andrews holds certain beliefs about food which do not have their basis in religious ideas.   Hence, she has raised Jim as a vegetarian and he was fed soy-bean milk for approximately the first three years of life. Mrs. Andrews could not recall when he stopped taking the bottle, nor could she describe how weaning occurred.   She thought that Jim walked at nine months and talked at one year, but she could not recall his first words.   She thought she began toilet training at about a year and a half and that Jim was easy to train.

Jim fell out of a crib before age two, fell off a tricycle and hurt his chin at age four or five and he fell out of a car when he was four or five years old.   His ears bother him; he feels as if there is wax in them and has had X-ray treatment for this irritation.   He does not report hearing difficulties, however, nor does he hear peculiar sounds.

Jim never sucked his fingers or showed evidence of masturbatory activity. Nightmares, sleepwalking, or enuresis were not present according to the parents.   Sexual information has been obtained largely from other boys, although he is able to talk with his father about sexual matters.

The Andrews have moved around a good deal; hence, Jim has attended a variety of schools.   There were no apparent difficulties about starting to school and no academic problems until recently.   He attended Broadhurst

Elementary School, beginning two years ago, but was about to be expelled when his parent contacted the clinic. They transferred him to Edgewater Elementary School but Jim does not like this school. His recent school history indicates that he constantly disrupts the classroom with various kinds of attention-getting behavior.

The parents also described Jim as being somewhat belligerent toward younger children and as somewhat blustering in his approach to other children. He has to have his own way, and at times it seems that he deliberately antagonizes his playmates.

Mr. Andrews feels that he has always been "too indulgent" toward Jim. He has always found it difficult to set limits on Jim's behavior or to attempt to discipline him. Mrs. Andrews, on the other hand, feels that Jim should be made to conform to certain standards; she keeps after him to see that he does.

Psychological Evaluation

TESTS ADMINISTERED.   (1) Wechsler Intelligence Scale for Children (WISC); (2) Rorschach Inkblot Test; (3) Thematic Apperception Test (TAT).

BEHAVIOR AND APPEARANCE.   Jim is an obese ten-and-a-half-year-old boy who was quite belligerent toward the interviewer when first seen. At the same time, he seemed frightened about coming. On his first visit, he ran out of the building and across the street, and on his second visit, he sat in the car refusing to come into the building. On the third and last visit, however, he was able to talk about his anger toward the clinician, including his feelings that "what he was like was his business," and that he couldn't be helped anyway. He denied any fears about coming to the clinic, although he was able to talk about his concern with what his friends would think if they knew he was coming to see a "head shrinker." Initially, he denied having any problems, but as the session progressed, he was able to admit that he was not very satisfied with his family. He claimed that his mother always nags him, especially about eating and about getting his hair cut. He said he likes his father and that they get along fine together when they are away from the rest of the family. He describes his sister as a pest who always gets her own way.

In general, Jim's behavior was quite ambivalent. He vacillated between ingratiation and direct criticism and between joviality and hostility. He seemed to utilize blandness and denial in attempts to handle his anger and fear.

TEST RESULTS AND IMPRESSIONS.   On the Wechsler Intelligence Scale for Children, Jim attained the following scores:

Verbal Scale IQ   = 123 (Superior)
Performance Scale IQ = 114 (Bright-Normal)
Full Scale IQ   = 120 (Superior)

Despite Jim's superior intellectual abilities, he frequently does not function at this level because of his negativistic approach to tasks and his tendencies to put forth minimally adequate efforts.   Such tendencies reflect a lack of stamina and of enduring goals and are sufficient to prevent constructive planning for the future.

Jim is able to see things as most people do; he is aware of conventionally approved standards of behavior.   However, he maintains an active independence of thought and a stubborn insistence on the right to make up his own mind.   Hence he finds it difficult to accept many conventional standards as being the appropriate ones for him to follow.   Instead, his behavior is most apt to be governed by his needs for immediate gratification.

Jim has a great deal of anxiety about dealing with people and is unable to satisfy his needs by manipulating his environment in a socially acceptable manner.   Hence he tends to avoid situations which require social conformity, despite his interest in achieving social adequacy.   Furthermore, he has difficulties in forming close emotional relationships, and seems to vacillate between superficial emotional responsiveness and uncontrolled explosive outbursts.

The test protocols suggest rather intense feelings of hostility which are not very well defended.   It appears that Jim's hostility stems largely from concerns about frustration of impulse gratification and particularly about frustration of oral-dependent needs.   He is resentful of restrictions in general, and feels that social rules and regulations are unfair for the most part.   For example, he told TAT stories about people who were put in jail or kicked out of school because they did not conform to certain standards, e.g., getting a license for a bicycle or getting a haircut.

These attitudes appear to be related to Jim's attitudes toward parental figures.   He sees mother figures as depriving, restricting, and making demands upon their children.   He sees father figures as intervening in such situations, siding with the child and talking the mother into giving in to the child's wishes.   At the same time, he maintains strong underlying feelings of hostility toward father figures.   For example, to TAT Card 8BM he told a story about a "foolish" boy who shot a man accidentally and the man died; then the boy wasn't foolish anymore and lived happily ever after.   Then, too, in the story to Card 12M, the Lilliputians kill the giant.   Jim's ambivalent feelings toward father figures as well as his apprehensiveness toward them is probably best illustrated in his story to TAT Card 13MF: "This guy came in drunk, and he's wipin' his eyes, 'cause he can't see.   And he's an alcoholic and a dope fiend.   And he's a teacher (laughs), and well—he started all his pupils out on the dope and the alcohol and the principal found that out, so he shot him and then he shot himself and everybody laughed—no—that's not a good ending.   They died happily ever after."   It appears that Jim is confused about the motivations of father figures and views them as destructive.

Jim's sexual identification is primarily a passive, feminine one.   However, he struggles diligently to maintain a façade of masculine assertiveness and becomes very anxious if others think of him as feminine or refer to him as a "sissy."

Summary Impression

Jim is an emotionally disturbed boy who is currently functioning at a superior level of intelligence. However, his motivation for achievement is sporadic and his behavior is governed strongly by his needs for immediate gratification and his apprehensiveness about forming close atttachments to others. Hence consistent intellectual efforts and effective achievement are minimal. The test records contain evidence of a passive, dependent orientation with hostility stemming largely from feelings of frustration. Ambivalent feelings toward parental figures are pronounced. Although reality awareness is adequate, there appears to be a lack of integration of conventional standards as guides for his own behavior.

Diagnostic Impression

This appears to be the record of a primary behavior disorder, passive-aggressive type. Although the test record is not suggestive of brain damage, in view of the history of falls, etc., as well as the uncontrolled outbursts of rage, neurological and electroencephalographic studies would seem warranted.

Some branches of child psychology have used the case study more frequently than others. Clinically oriented child psychologists employ it to a great extent. Although the case study helps to understand a single child, the method unfortunately suffers from some of the same defects as the early baby biographies. For example, the reliability of the information gained from informants may be questioned. Does the informant's relationship to the child color his report? Do biases and emotional involvement cloud his memory of past events? Furthermore, how reliable are the test results in the case study? Often the very factors contributing to a child's failure at school also prevent him from scoring at his *true* level in an intellectual examination. The IQ score on the test tells very little about his intellectual potential; it does not contribute to an understanding of the child's school difficulty. Perhaps an even more important consideration in evaluating the case study is the professional who interprets and assesses the data. His experience, theoretical biases, knowledge of research findings, and psychological understanding and skill all influence the value of the study.

Finally, caution has to be exercised whenever one attempts to identify causes and effects. Was a child's rejection by his father the reason for his delinquent behavior? Is rivalry with a year-older sister the basis for a young girl's underachievement in school? Sweeping generalizations and explanations are often made and conclusions drawn from unreliable, sketchy information. *A child's past can never be completely reconstructed.* Rigorous safeguards are required in interpretation, and the person using case-study material must view his conclusions as *tenta-*

tive and subject to modification. Since the case study lacks many of the controls present in the experimental method (to be discussed shortly), generalization of the data tends to be hazardous. No child's heredity or environment is identical to another child's. For this reason, factors causing a certain type of behavior in one case may or may not produce the same result in others.

Psychological Ecology. Two psychologists, Robert Barker and Herbert Wright, have organized a Midwest Field Station in a small Kansas community, which they liken to a weather outpost or a biological field station. It has the purpose of collecting data about children and their daily lives, where they go, what they do, what they say, and with whom they interact. These two men argue that psychology, unlike many other sciences, began early and perhaps somewhat prematurely to gather data in laboratory situations. Psychologists manipulate and experiment with small isolated units of behavior and with specific behavior variables without first describing in detail some of the basic information of human life. They ignore such things as the frequency with which certain behaviors occur and the settings in which these take place.

It is different in other sciences. Geologists, biologists, chemists, and physicists know in considerable detail about the distribution in nature of the materials and processes with which they deal. Chemists know something about the laws governing the interaction of oxygen and hydrogen, and they also know how the elements are distributed in nature. Entomologists know the biological vectors of malaria, and they also know about the occurrence of these vectors over the earth. In contrast, psychologists know little more than laymen about the frequency and degree of occurrence of their basic phenomena in the lives of men—of deprivation, of hostility, of freedom, of friendliness, of social pressure, of rewards and punishments. Although we have daily records of the behavior of volcanoes, of the tides, of sun spots, and of rats and monkeys, there have been few scientific records of how a human mother cared for her young, how a particular teacher behaved in the classroom and how the children responded, what a family actually did and said during a mealtime, or how any boy lived his life from the time he awoke in the morning until he went to sleep at night (Barker & Wright, 1954, p. 2).

The study of behavior in natural situations is given the name *psychological ecology*. This distinguishes it, say Barker and Wright, from experimental psychology which studies behavior in artificially planned situations. Tests, interviews, questionnaires, and experiments distort and destroy the natural stream of behavior (Barker, 1963). Unlike experiments that impose conditions upon the phenomena investigated, ecological methods reveal and discover natural occurrences (Willems,

1965). The Kansas work involves primarily observation and recording of everyday behavior. To maintain some scientific precision and give some purpose to the observations, the psychological ecologists developed several categories. They call the stable parts of the physical and social milieu of a community, which by their very nature lead to standard and distinctive patterns of behavior, *behavior settings*. In their community, Midwest, U.S.A., these settings include the drug store, second-grade classroom, tavern, Methodist Regular Worship Service, cemetery, library, and Brownie's Regular Meeting (Wright & Barker, 1949). They designate the part of a stream of behavior that describes a separate action and the situation in which it occurs a *behavior episode*. Such episodes might include "painting the lips," "wiping paint off face," "moving crate across pit" (Wright & Barker, 1949, 1950). A third category, the *specimen record,* is a collection of behavior episodes. It is "a detailed, sequential, narrative account by skilled observers of an individual child's behavior through a more or less extended time" (Wright & Barker, 1949). A book entitled *One Boy's Day* describes a day in the life of seven-year-old Raymond Birch. Eight observers took turns throughout the day observing and recording the boy's activities. Their objective was to include everything he did. The following paragraphs typify their report.

> *Some cars were resting on a ledge part way up the sloping side of the pit. The ledge consisted of an old shingle and resembled a bridge, supported at each end by dirt. Stewart started undermining the ledge to make the cars fall into the pit. It seemed to me that his action copied Raymond's very closely, although his purpose differed.*
>
> Raymond suddenly stood up and brushed off the dirt which he had carelessly flipped upon his legs and lap.
>
> He knelt down and smoothed the dirt from the rock.
>
> Then he started chopping rhythmically. Time after time he shoved the stick into the damp dirt, and pulled sideways, flipping the dirt away. The stick bent under his vigorous efforts.
>
> *Inadvertently and unnoticed by Raymond, one of the flying clods of dirt happened to hit Clifford. Clifford didn't complain; he was too busy watching what Stewart was doing.*
>
> Finally a car fell off the ledge which Stewart was tearing down. Stewart shouted, "Look at it roll on down below in the canyon."
>
> Raymond looked over and watched the rolling car with mild interest.
>
> He returned immediately to his own digging, not even looking up to see the second car roll down (Barker & Wright, 1951, pp. 356–357).

With some exceptions, the advantages, disadvantages, and usefulness of psychological ecology are the same as those of the baby biographies. One is impressed by the ability of a specimen record to capture the richness and complexity of the environment, the multitude of interactions that influence and shape a child's approach to people and situations, and the repetitiveness but apparent randomness of child behavior. Moreover, the psychological ecologists seem to have avoided some of the shortcomings of the baby biographies. Well trained in observation and well grounded in the basic notions of psychology, the ecologists have deliberately attempted to separate the content of observation from interpretation; in fact, interpretation is indented and set off from observed data in a specimen record. There is also the question of the extent to which the observer, as a result of his observation, changes or influences the individual being observed. Wright and Barker hold that children under the age of nine show neither sensitivity nor self-consciousness when being observed and soon adjust or adapt to the presence of an observer. This view seems to be supported by the relatively small effect an observer has on those being observed, especially when the observation continues over an extended period. Children tend not to act very long in ways differing from their usual behavior. Finally, how representative is the group of children investigated? Although the community chosen was small enough to include all its children in the study, and its environment was undoubtedly less complex than that of a large urban area, it remains to be shown whether environmental complexity has psychological significance in the lives of children.

Controlled Approaches to Observation

Although observation lies at the base of all scientific research, "uncontrolled" observation, as we have seen, has many disadvantages. There is clearly a need for "controlled" observation of phenomena if meaningful comparisons and determinations are to be made. Scientists have developed many techniques for a controlled approach to observation, and in the following several pages we shall examine some of them.

Time Sampling. Arrington (1943) has defined time sampling as a method of observing the behavior of human beings "under the ordinary conditions of everyday life in which observations are made in a series of short time periods so distributed as to afford a representative sampling of the behavior under observation." The method was developed in order to overcome many of the weaknesses in the anecdotal descriptions of child behavior. It was first used by Willard Olson (1929) to record the incidence of "nervous habits" in school children. Briefly, Olson marked off a record blank into five-minute intervals and entered a check whenever a designated behavior occurred within each time interval among a classroom of children he was observing. As originally conceived, time sampling yielded a score indicating *the number of time intervals* in which a specific behavior manifested itself.

Over the years the technique has undergone a great number of modifications. Most of them have resulted from a desire for finer precision in the sampling and recording of behavior. The time interval has been shortened, often consisting of periods from 30 seconds to one minute. Only one child is observed at a time, with the observations distributed at random throughout the day as well as over a term of a week to several months. Symbols have been developed to record continuous behavior instead of the occurrence or nonoccurrence of specific acts. For example, an elaborate set of such symbols has been devised to facilitate the objective description and recording of interaction between adults and children (Moustakas, Sigel, & Schalock, 1956). This set uses five-second time intervals and enters a series of category code letters on a prepared scoring sheet covering 16 minutes of continuous recording. Each square on the sheet represents five seconds of time, and the main categories symbolized by the code letters in this particular recording system include: nonattention, attentive observation, recognition, statement of condition or action, joint participation in activity, offering information, giving help, reassurance, seeking information, restricting, forbidding, disciplinary action, affection, compliance.

Most of the time-sampling studies have been concerned with the social behavior and social interactions of the young child. Among the specific behaviors studied have been language frequency or content, ascendant behavior, physical contacts, quarrels, conflict, resistance, friendship patterns, cooperative and competitive behavior, rivalry, and aggression. The principal advantages of this technique are the reliability and objectivity of recording. Attention is centered on a specific well-defined behavior so that agreement about it among different observers can be achieved. Since scores are obtained usually in terms of frequency, the results can be treated statistically. For example, the frequency of quarrels can be related to age, sex, IQ, ratings of adjustment, and many similar factors.

Time sampling will not work when the behavior under study is neither overt nor readily observable. It is not feasible, either, for observing infrequent behavior, such as the display of sympathy, compliance, or rare, private child behaviors like fire setting. Because time-sampling studies are restricted to the investigation of a specific behavior, much of the richness and meaningfulness of child interaction goes unrecorded. Precision may be obtained at the cost of under-standing. Moreover, data thus obtained can never of themselves yield information about cause and effect. If it were found that one child quarreled more frequently than others, it would be necessary to draw on methods other than time sampling to determine the cause.

Psychometric Instruments. Although intelligence and personality tests are not customarily considered as vehicles for observation, they are, in fact, very short samples of behavior and are extremely important in terms of their ability to disclose useful information. Knowledge of the results of an intelligence test provides insights into a child's ability in comparison with other children and into his level of intellectual per-formance. It also permits one to make predictions about how the child will cope with other tasks and other situations. The usefulness of a score on such *psychometric* tests—tests that measure the speed and precision of mental processes—depends on the meaningfulness of the theory on which the test is based, on the rigor of the procedure, and on the appropriateness of what is measured.

The object of a psychometric test is to provide in a brief interval of time information that would otherwise require hours of intimate con-tact to obtain. Tests, therefore, are shorthand observational techniques that enable us to make inferences about a larger body of data. For example, in administering a standard intelligence test to a five-year-old, we are not interested in his ability to answer the specific questions as such but in how these questions sample his general intelligence. Specific intelligence and personality tests will be discussed in subse-quent chapters.

Questionnaires. Like intelligence and personality tests, the question-naire is a shorthand method for gaining a considerable amount of in-formation on a specific problem in a brief interval of time. Its use, either written or oral, to obtain information about children has a long history. G. Stanley-Hall is often credited with being the first to use this approach in child psychology. Under his supervision school-teachers in the Boston area administered a general information question-naire to beginning first-grade children. Although such a procedure seems commonplace today, it was a marked contribution at a time when unscientific speculation often substituted for the collection of data.

One result of Hall's study was the realization that children's think-ing did indeed differ from that of adults in terms not only of the quantity of information but also of its quality. The following excerpt from Hall's original paper gives the content of the children's responses to certain questions included in the questionnaire.

The chief field for such fond and often secret childish fancies is the sky. About three fourths of all questioned thought the world a plain, and many described it as round like a dollar, while the sky is like a flattened bowl turned over it. The sky is often thin, one might easily break through; half the moon may be seen through it, while the other half is this side; it may be made of snow, but is so large that there is much floor-sweeping to be done in heaven. Some thought the sun went down at night into the ground or just behind certain houses, and went across on or under the ground to go up out of or off the water in the morning, but 48 per cent of all thought that at night it goes or rolls or flies, is blown or walks, or God pulls it up higher out of sight. He takes it into heaven, and perhaps puts it to bed, and even takes off its clothes and puts them on in the morning, or again it lies under the trees where the angels mind it, or goes through and shines on the upper side of the sky, or goes into or behind the moon, as the moon is behind it in the day. It may stay where it is, only we cannot see it, for it is dark, or the dark rains down so, and it comes out when it gets light so it can see. More than half the children questioned conceived the sun as never more than 40 degrees from the zenith, and, naturally enough, city children knew little of the horizon. So the moon comes around when it is a bright night and people want to walk, or forget to light some lamps; it follows us about and has nose and eyes, while it calls the stars into, under, or behind it at night, and they may be made of bits of it. Sometimes the moon is round a month or two, then it is a rim, or a piece is cut off, or it is half stuck or half buttoned into the sky. The stars may be sparks from fire-engines or houses, or, with higher intelligence, they are silver, or God lights them with matches and blows them out or opens the door and calls them in in the morning. Only in a single case were any of the heavenly bodies conceived as openings in the sky to let light or glory through, or as eyes of supernatural beings—a fancy so often ascribed to children and so often found in juvenile literature. Thunder, which anthropologists tell us is or represents the highest God to most savage races, was apperceived as God groaning or kicking, or rolling barrels about, or turning a big handle, or grinding snow, walking loud, breaking something, throwing logs, having coal run in, poundng about with a big hammer, rattling houses, hitting the clouds, or clouds bumping or clapping together or bursting, or else it was merely ice sliding off lots of houses or cannon in the city or sky, hard rain down the chimney, or big rocks pounding, or piles of boards falling down, or very hard rain, hail, or wind. Lightning is God putting out his finger or opening a door, or turning on gas quick, or (very common) striking many matches at once, throwing stones and iron for sparks, setting paper afire, or it is light going outside and inside the sky, or stars falling. God keeps rain in heaven in a big sink, rows of buckets, a big tub or barrels, and they run over or he lets it down with a water hose through a sieve, a dipper with holes, or sprinkles or tips it down or turns a faucet. God makes it in heaven out of nothing or out of water, or it gets up by splashing up, or he dips it up off the roof, or it rains up off the ground when we don't see it. The clouds are close to the sky; they move because the earth moves and makes them. They are dirty, muddy things, or blankets, or doors of heaven, and are made of fog, of steam that makes the sun go, of smoke, of white wool or feathers and birds, or lace or cloth. In their changing forms very many children, whose very life is fancy, think they see veritable men, or more commonly, because they have so many more forms, animals, faces, and very often God, Santa Claus, angels, etc., are also seen. Closely connected with the above are the religious concepts so common with children. God is a big, perhaps blue, man, very often seen in the sky on or in clouds, in the church, or even street. He came in our gate, comes to see us sometimes. He lives in a big palace or a big brick or stone house on the sky. He makes lamps, babies, dogs, trees, money, etc., and the angels work for him. He looks like the priest, Frobel, papa, etc., and they like to look at him, and a few would like to be God. He lights the stars so he can see to go on the sidewalk or into the church. Birds, children, Santa Claus, live with him, and most but not all like him better than they do the latter. When people die they just go, or are put in a hole, or a box or a black wagon that goes to heaven, or they fly up or are drawn or slung up into the sky where God catches them. They never can get out of the hole, and yet all good people somehow get where God is. He lifts them up, they go up on a ladder or rope, or they carry them up, but keep their eyes shut so they do not know the way, or they are shoved up through a hole. When children get there they have candy, rocking-horses, guns, and everything in the toy-shop or picture-book, play marbles, top, ball, cards, hookey, hear brass bands, have nice clothes, gold watches, and pets, ice-cream and soda-water, and no school. There are men there who died in the war made into angels, and dolls with broken heads go there. Some think they must go through the church to get there, a few thought the horse-cars run there, and one said that the birds that grow on apple-trees are drawn up there by the moon. The bad place is like an oven or a police-station, where it burns, yet is all dark, and folks want to get back, and God kills people or beats them with a cane. God makes babies in heaven, tho the holy mother and even Santa Claus makes some. He lets them down or drops them, and the women or doctors catch them, or he leaves them on the sidewalk, or brings them down a wooden ladder backwards and pulls it up again, or mamma or the doctor or the nurse go up and fetch them sometimes in a balloon, or they fly down and lose off their wings in some place or other and forget it, or jump down to Jesus, who gives them around. They were also often said to be found in flour-barrels, and the flour sticks ever so long, you know, or they grow in cabbages, or God puts them in water, perhaps in the sewer, and the doctors gets them out and takes them to sick folks that want them, or the milk-man brings them early in the morning, they are dug out of the ground, or bought at the baby-store. Sometimes God puts on a few things or else sends them along if he don't forget it; this shows that no one since Basedow believes in telling children the truth in all things (Hall, in Dennis, 1948, pp. 267–269).

The questionnaire has several methodological advantages over the earlier baby biographies. Since questionnaires are designed to obtain information for specific purposes, their questions concentrate on a well-defined area. Besides, the researcher who uses them can obtain data from a large and representative sample in a relatively short time as compared with the baby biographies, which were concerned with an individual child. These data can be related to several variables. For example, several researchers have administered Hall's questionnaire, with modifications, to children of various ages, and related the subjects' scores to chronological age, mental age, IQ, socioeconomic class, and sex, noting the differences in total scores as well as in answers to specific questions.

A wide variety of questionnaires has been employed with children and their parents, but one further example will suffice. This questionnaire is directed to parents because knowledge of their attitudes and values is often essential to understanding the child's behavior and personality. Questionnaires of this type may deal with statements of fact, such as the age of weaning the child, or with statements that tap attitudes and values that often relate to child-rearing procedures. In the following items excerpted from the Parent Attitude Research Instrument developed at the National Institute of Mental Health, the parent is asked to check the response that best represents his point of view for each statement.

	Strongly Agree	Mildly Agree	Mildly Disagree	Strongly Disagree
Children should be allowed to disagree with their parents if they feel their own ideas are better.	A	a	d	D
It is frequently necessary to drive the mischief out of a child before he will behave.	A	a	d	D
A wise parent knows better than to pick up the baby whenever he cries.	A	a	d	D
The experience of being on their own is often good for children.	A	a	d	D
Most parents prefer a quiet child to a "scrappy" one.	A	a	d	D

(Schaefer & Bell, 1958)

Complete reliance on questionnaire responses has its weaknesses. Both "truthfulness" and unconscious falsification have to be considered. Some questionnaires contain a "lie scale" designed to assess the respondent's willingness to falsify his replies. There are researchers who believe that in assessing a parent's attitude toward certain topics, falsification as such becomes unimportant. Moreover, parents differ in willingness to divulge various kinds of information. Whether the parent comprehends the question as it was intended by the creator of the questionnaire is another matter of concern. In evaluating the findings emerging from a questionnaire, critical note must be taken of all these points.

Experimental Method. One of the outstanding characteristics of this method is its control over the phenomena under investigation and the variables being observed. Scientific experiments are often called "questions put to nature," and the more precisely the questions are stated—that is, the more carefully the experiment is designed—the more exact and unambiguous the answers will be. Tracing a hypothetical problem of the kind a child-development researcher might face may clarify various points.

Shortly before World War II, the effect of nursery-school experience on intelligence provoked an important controversy. Some say that more heat than light was generated over the issue; if so, the fault lay with the methods used to examine it. Suppose we consider this problem. To begin with, the problem must be stated clearly and precisely or else the research will be neither well defined nor definitive. The problem is usually presented in the form of a hypothesis: nursery-school experience raises the IQ. Now the hypothesis needs to be tested.

First, the IQs are tested of a group of children who have had a year of nursery school. If their IQs are above 100 (average) the hypothesis would seem confirmed. But the group chosen might have been well above average intelligence before going to nursery school. It might have been a *biased sample.* Therefore the above-average IQs cannot be attributed to the nursery-school experience. Something has been learned, but it is necessary to test again.

This time the children to be tested are selected at random from a large group of five-year-olds to ensure an *un*biased sample. The children are tested for intelligence and then retested after a year of nursery school. If the measure of intelligence increases after the second test, the hypothesis would again seem confirmed. However, other factors than nursery-school experience might have improved the children's intelligence; in other words, the effects of other variables have not been controlled. The need is apparent for testing a similar group of children who are *not* exposed to nursery school.

This leads to selection of a *control group,* which does not undergo special treatment. The group accorded special treatment is called the *experimental group.* Subjects for both groups are drawn from a large pool of children and assigned at random to either one. Often, to ensure that no features are present that differentiate the two groups, both are matched on relevant variables, that is, other factors that might influence the results. These might include such things as initial level of ability, sex of the child, or occupational status of the parent. Thus only the one variable under investigation, the *independent variable* (in this illustration, nursery-school experience), is left to be systematically altered. Its effect on the *dependent variable* (intelligence scores) is then measured.

To return to the problem at hand, the intellectual level of both control and experimental groups is measured by administration of a standard intelligence test. The experimental group is then given nursery-school training while the control group is not. Once again, intelligence tests are administered after a period of time. If the scores in the experimental group are significantly higher than those in the control group, the hypothesis is accepted. If no difference in scores exists, the hypothesis is presumably invalid.

This method, then, holds all possibly relevant variables constant while identifying *the effects of the systematic manipulation of the single variable under investigation.* Although it is the most valuable method for research, this technique does not always apply in child development. In many important problems the researcher cannot manipulate the independent variable. For example, rejection or acceptance by parents is thought to have important bearing on child personality and adjustment. Yet it is manifestly impossible to manipulate this variable for research purposes. Under the circumstances, researchers turn to "experiments in nature." They assess the adjustment of children who are thought to have suffered from parental rejection in the past and contrast this with the adjustment of a group of children thought to be accepted. Even so, they can never be sure that the two groups do not differ in other variables that perhaps help to account for the difference in adjustments. Nor can they ever be sure that parental rejection or acceptance does, in fact, affect adjustment, because they are unable to set up an "experimental control," that is, a control group in distinction to an experimental group. The same criticism may be made of any studies that attempt to tie parental attitudes to a type of behavior in the child when the parental attitudes are sought *after* the behavior has appeared.

Experimenter Influences. The relationship between the experimenter and his subjects is an aspect of the experimental method that has received a great deal of attention only recently. Although much effort is made in any experiment to standardize and objectify the procedure employed, there is evidence that the experimenter influences the outcome of the research through his own expectations concerning the organism's behavior (Rosenthal, 1963, 1966) either through experimenter behavior toward the organism or through errors in observation.

In conducting an experiment, the researcher begins with certain hypotheses, expectancies, or biases concerning the results. These are communicated to the subject through various visual and auditory cues such as gestures and tone of voice.

Research has identified a number of characteristics of experimenter and subject that affect the results of an investigation. These include sex, race, need for social approval, status of the experimenter, and prior acquaintance between the experimenter and the subject. Two examples drawn from research with children will serve to illustrate this general phenomenon.

A methodological study (Cowan, Weber, Hoddinott, & Klein, 1967) was designed to examine the effects on mean length of response (MLR) of the stimulus used, the socioeconomic status, age, and sex of the child, and the sex of the experimenter. Approximately 250 children, aged five, seven, nine, and 11, were shown 10 colored pictures with the request that they tell a story about each picture. An MLR score was computed for each story. In general the results showed an increase in MLR with age, and highly significant differences in MLR were obtained depending upon the pictures used to elicit the response. Further, one experimenter elicited longer responses from the five- and seven-year-olds, whereas the seven- and nine-year-olds performed better with the other experimenter. Similar differences were found to depend on the sex of the child; one experimenter elicited higher MLR scores from males and the other from females.

In the second study (Allen, Dubanoski, & Stevenson, 1966), the effects of race of experimenter were examined, comparing praise and criticism in a simple marble-dropping task. In agreement with earlier findings, which suggested that a familiar person is less effective as a social reinforcer than a more remote person, those subjects (all white) who received praise from a Negro experimenter showed an increase in rate of response whereas those receiving praise from a white adult showed a decrease in rate of response.

Two points concerning the interaction between experimenter and subject require emphasis. First, results of research should be interpreted with some caution because they may be affected by experimenter biases and by various experimenter and subject characteristics. Second, the fact that the experimenter influences the subject in subtle and covert ways, even in a situation that is standardized, controlled, and arranged to eliminate such influences as much as possible, should give us pause for thought. How much greater are the mutual influences in parent-child and teacher-child interactions, in which one of the established goals of the relationship is the modification by the adult of child behavior and attitudes. No human interaction leaves the participants unaffected.

Interview Method. Although the interview has been used most frequently as a clinical tool for understanding an individual case, it is now being employed increasingly as a research device for gaining information about a specific question under investigation. An interview is made up of several questions designed to elicit certain kinds of information. Often the questions are tested beforehand to find out if they do, in fact, obtain the information desired. Frequently the interview is tape-recorded so that the interviewer need not rely on memory or sketchily written notes. The information acquired from the interview is evaluated in various ways on a rating scale, with ratings usually made independently by two persons to check on inter-rater agreement. In the following replies of two mothers to the question: "Some people feel that it is very important for a child to learn not to fight with other children; and others feel that there are times when a child has to learn to fight. How do you feel about this?" the first reply was rated as indicating no demand for the child to be aggressive toward her peers, whereas the second reply was considered a high demand to have the child fight.

A

Mother. I go out and ask other mothers what happened and when I find out, I say "All right come in the house now." Sooner than go to their mothers and fight with them, I bring her in the house and keep her in for a while and talk it all over with her and tell her where she's wrong or where the other child is wrong and then after a while I let her out again and tell her to go—either she'll end up probably playing with the same child again, anyway—to go play with somebody else.

B

Mother. Well, I believe that a child has to fight and to stick up for his own rights. I hate to see a kid that is always—well—I think if they don't they are whining babies and are always home with their mothers; and we have always taught Bill to hit them right back and to give them one better than what he got. And there are a few children, in this neighborhood, that Bill is afraid of and he will come home and tell me what they have done to him—but the only satisfaction that he has ever got was that, "We have told you if he hits you to hit him back, and until then don't tell me your stories" (Sears, Maccoby, & Levin, 1957, pp. 246–247).

Some of the disadvantages of the questionnaire pervade the interview technique, but others are eliminated. A mother's need to portray herself in a certain way affects her report. Moreover, the success of the interview depends on her willingness to divulge various sorts of information and on her memory. Several studies have found many inaccuracies in mothers' recall of earlier events related to child-rearing attitudes and practices. One investigation compared information obtained in three interviews with mothers with data from a final interview (Haggard, Brekstad, & Skard, 1960). The interviews spread over a period beginning about a month before delivery and ending when the child was between seven and eight years of age. As a rule, the final interviews were more a reflection of the mother's current recollections of the past than of accurate accounts of past events themselves. The accuracy of recall was related to the type of information requested. Specific facts, such as the length of the child at birth, were recalled best, whereas information on general wishes and attitudes was recalled next best. Data based on earlier anxieties of mothers were recalled least accurately. Furthermore, the lack of independence of the data poses another problem in interviews, especially when the person interviewed is a mother or someone else who is not the actual subject of the investigation. The information so gathered may reflect the personality of the mother rather than the actual facts.

On the other side of the ledger, the face-to-face relationship between interviewer and interviewee enables a skilled interviewer to gauge the earnestness and sincerity of the respondent. This is not possible in a questionnaire.

Longitudinal versus Cross-Sectional Approaches

Although there is a multitude of "facts" one might wish to learn about child behavior, probably one of the most persistent objectives of child research is the study of development. This is the emphasis in child psychology: the changes that take place over time in the behavior and characteristics of children. Thus, if we know enough about development in general and about a particular child's past development, we can predict his future development, his adult personality, his adult adjustment, and the values and purpose he will have as an adult.

Because of this concern of child psychology with development, much research has been devoted to the description of children at various ages. Data are available in the areas of motor development, language development, intellectual development, social development, emotional development, and physical development. These have been acquired through two approaches, the longitudinal and the cross-sectional.

Longitudinal Method. This approach is suited to the study of development because the same children are studied over a period of time. Munn (1955, p. 8) has likened it to time-lapse photography, in which a single object is photographed at periodic intervals, providing a picture of continuous growth. Longitudinal study provides a knowledge of the patterns and processes of change over the long run; thus individual growth curves can be plotted in such areas as language and physical development. With this knowledge of changes in a single individual, one can relate them to the presence or absence of other factors. For example, the changes in IQ in an individual case can be shown to relate to various environmental circumstances (Honzik, Macfarlane, & Allen, 1948). But this does not necessarily mean there is a cause-and-effect relationship.

The early baby biographies discussed above used a longitudinal approach to record and describe the behavior of a single child over a certain time period. The first such study was that by Buffon, in which the height measurements of a child were reported for the 17-year period from 1759 to 1776.

Some research topics require use of the longitudinal approach. It is essential in investigating the effects on development of instituted procedures. It is also useful for gathering data on generational differences and consistency in child-rearing practices. A number of longitudinal studies have been conducted; for a report of them until 1954, see Stone and Onque (1959). More recently, a description of 10 long-term longitudinal studies has been presented by Kagan (1964). The sample, methods, and goals of each project are discussed and bibliographies of published research are included. The longitudinal studies described are the Oakland Growth Study (Adolescent Study), the Berkeley Growth Study, and the Guidance Study at the University of California, Berkeley; the Child Research Council's Study in Human Development at the University of Colorado Medical School; the Study of Human Development at the Fels Research Institute; the Child-to-Adult Study, University of Minnesota; the Longitudinal Study of Child Health and Development, Harvard School of Public Health; the Study of Gifted Children, Stanford

University; the Infancy, Coping, and Mental Health Studies, Menninger Foundation; and the Study of Behavioral Development, New York University. Before considering some of the obstacles to this kind of research, let us briefly examine three longitudinal studies.

One of the first of its kind was the short-term longitudinal study by Shirley (1931, 1933a, b) of motor, intellectual, and personality development, which followed 25 infants from birth to two years of age. During the first week in the hospital, the infants were examined daily. During the second week they were examined every other day. For the remainder of their first year, they were seen at weekly intervals in their homes, and throughout their second year at biweekly intervals. All this time the infants' responses to simple tests were recorded in descriptive, qualitative terms, and mothers' records supplemented the examination data. With respect to motor development, Shirley concentrated on the sequence of development and concluded: (1) there is a consistency in the sequence, with few reversals in the appearance of such items as chest up, sit alone, stand with help, and creep; and (2) motor development is in line with the anatomical law of the direction of growth, which states that growth proceeds from the head to the feet (*cephalocaudal*). The data collected in the intensive study of the 25 infants have been of considerable interest and value in laying the basis for certain areas of developmental research and in providing information obtained by careful, scientific methods.

The second study deals with the long-term prediction of adjustment. In 1950 a wide variety of information was obtained from the entire school population—3200 children—in the fourth grade and above in Nobles County, Minnesota.

There were scales measuring the child's attitudes toward his family, his sense of responsibility, his work and attitudes toward work based on his experience in home duties and chores, his interests and play activities, and his favorable attitudes toward experience. There was also a scale made up of items that in previous studies had been answered differently by delinquent and by nondelinquent children. The items had to do with personal-social attitudes, and with the child's fears and worries. From school records, we obtained the Intelligence Quotients of the children. In addition to information about the education and occupation of each parent, we also had several measures of socio-economic or cultural status. On the basis of a check against the current adjustment of the children, five scores were selected from the inventories given the children to be combined into a Pupil Index, which is used as a general score to predict future adjustment.

Because we wished to see how well ratings made by teachers would predict future adjustment of children, three rating forms were filled out by the teachers in 1950. These ratings concerned the child's responsibility, his personality traits, and his adjustment in the classroom or home room. Scores on these were combined to form the 1950 Teacher Index (Anderson, 1959, pp. 8–9).

Several follow-up studies were conducted and the final assessment of adjustment was made seven years later, in 1957. Again various kinds of information were obtained to measure the adjustment.

> In designing measures of outcomes in terms of later adjustment, the type of information that can be secured about a person's relation to the demands of life must be considered. There is first the record made by the person in school, community, and on the job, which is the most obvious sign of his success. Such information may be regarded as the objective aspect of the person's life and can be obtained from various records. Next, there are the person's own feelings about himself and his view of his relation to others. Does he feel happy and satisfied with his life? Does he think he gets along well? Such information may be regarded as more subjective evidence of the person's life adjustment and is obtained from the person himself. Last, there are the impressions made by the person upon other people. How is he seen by others who know him? Some who know him very well are likely to balance his traits and feelings against his objective record. Finally, an interview with the person himself secures information about his accomplishments and feelings. The psychologically trained interviewer may thus balance the objective and the subjective aspects of the process of adjustment. In our follow-up studies we attempted to secure information about the person for each aspect of his life, such as work, recreation, education, and family life, from each of the sources, that is, from the records, the person's own statement about himself, the impressions others had of him, and the judgment of skilled psychological interviewers with psychological training (Anderson, 1959, pp. 9–10).

In general, the investigators predicted good adjustment more readily and more accurately than poor adjustment. Although separate criteria proved useful for predicting adjustment by sex, IQ predicted equally well for boys and girls. The investigators concluded that "it seems unlikely that a very short screening instrument that will predict well into the future can be developed from our personality measures on the children" (Anderson, 1959, p. 36).

The Berkeley Growth Study was initiated in 1928 (Bayley, 1965). Sixty-one infants were enrolled in the study within their first two months of life. Intelligence tests, anthropometric measures, physical examinations, and X-rays were administered to the subjects at periodic intervals. Assessment was made of manual skills and gross motor performance, and data were collected from projective tests, interest questionnaires, and incidental records. In addition, maternal behaviors toward the child were observed and rated. Data are still being gathered from the original subjects, who are entering their fifth decade of life.

Findings with regard to sex differences will illustrate some of the interesting results obtained in this longitudinal study. The correlations between IQ and several scioeconomic measures (family income, father's occupation, education of parents, and a rating of the home and neighborhood) were established earlier for girls than for boys. This was true also for the relation between the height of parent and child. These trends reflect sex differences in rate of maturing as well as differential effects of maternal behavior. The latter is suggested by the pattern of correlations between various maternal behaviors and the children's IQ level through adolescence. Boys with democratic, loving mothers in infancy scored higher on the IQ measures than boys with hostile, rejecting mothers. However, few such relationships were obtained for girls. Bayley concluded that girls' IQs tend to be related to parental ability, whereas IQs of boys are more closely related to early maternal behaviors.

Several characteristics of the longitudinal approach make it costly in terms of time and effort as well as difficult to carry out. First is the matter of turnover in research personnel. Much time is lost if it becomes necessary to change research directors or other personnel during the investigation. Next is the problem of subjects dropping out. Often the data cannot be analyzed until the very end of the investigation; consequently, if a subject drops out during the study, considerable information involving many hours of research effort is lost. Moreover, the final sample may depart from the original group of subjects so markedly that it may affect the results of the research. Often, too, new insights are achieved and new measuring instruments are developed in the course of a longitudinal study, yet it is never possible to "go back" and obtain previously unsolicited information. Once the plan of research has been established and the subjects and procedure have been selected it is difficult if not hazardous to attempt to alter them without jeopardizing the entire investigation.

Cross-Sectional Method. Because of the foregoing disadvantages of the longitudinal approach, researchers have predominantly used the cross-sectional method in child-development research. This method consists of studying children of different ages. For example, to study language development in the young child, Templin (1957) selected 60 children at each of the following age levels: three, three-and-a-half, four, four-and-a-half, five, six, seven, and eight. This selection furnished norms for four measures of language: speech sound articulation, sound discrimination ability, sentence structure, and vocabulary. Obviously this approach is easier to pursue and saves more time than the longitudinal. The investigator does not have to wait for subjects to pass through various age periods; eight-year-olds, nine-year-olds, and 10-year-olds can all be studied simultaneously. A large number of subjects representative of the population is readily available in the public schools. Furthermore, the plan of research can be modified without a necessary loss of time.

Yet there are some types of information that cross-sectional studies, by their very nature, cannot provide. They teach very little about causation: why does a certain behavior appear at a certain age level? Why are there individual differences at every level? These cross-sectional data do not explain. Nor do they reveal the effect on personality of deviations in development: what effect does retardation in language development have on a child's social adjustment at school? How does an infant's accelerated motor development influence his father's attitude toward him? Finally, the cross-sectional approach does not illuminate the patterning of behavior over the long run for any single child because it studies different children at different age levels at one time.

Some of the advantages of both longitudinal and cross-sectional methods are incorporated in the accelerated longitudinal or convergence approach (Bell, 1953, 1954). Subjects of different ages are retested with some overlapping of age level for younger and older children. For example, four groups of children, aged six, eight, 10, and 12, are each measured over a three-year term. This provides data for 12 points in time rather than only three, and since there is an overlapping of ages tested during the three-year interval, information is obtained that permits the comparison of different groups at the same ages. Note the overlaps in the following illustration.

Group	Ages Tested
A	6, 7, 8
B	8, 9, 10
C	10, 11, 12
D	12, 13, 14

Normative Studies

A brief mention of normative studies or surveys should be made. Although these may be longitudinal, normative data are usually obtained from cross-sectional investigations. In this sense norms are stages related to the age at which various skills or characteristics "normally" appear, or the ages at which they appear among "normal" children. *Norms do*

TABLE 1-1 Developmental Schedules

	15 Months	KEY AGE: 18 Months	21 Months
Motor	Walks: few steps, starts, stops Walks: falls by collapse (*18m) Walks: creeping discarded Stairs: creeps up (*18m) M. Cubes: tower of 2 Pellets: (no dem.) places in bottle Book: helps turn pages (*18m)	Walks: seldom falls Walks: fast, runs stiffly (*24m) Stairs: walks up, 1 hand held (*21m) Small chair: seats self Adult chair: climbs into (*...) Ball: hurls (*48m) Large ball: walks into (*21m) Book: turns pages, 2–3 at once (*24m)	Walks: squats in play (*...) Stairs: walks down, 1 hand held (*24m) Stairs: walks up, holds rail (*24m) Large ball: (dem.) kicks (*24m) M. Cubes: tower of 5–6
Adaptive	M. Cubes: tower of 2 Cup-cu: 6 in & out cup (*18m) Drawing: incip. imitation stroke (*18m) Formbd: (no dem.) places round block Formbd: adapts round block promptly	M. Cubes: tower of 3–4 Cup-cu: 10 into cup Pellet & bo: dumps responsively Drawing: scribbles spontan. (*36m) Drawing: makes stroke imitatively Formbd: piles 3 blocks (*24m)	M. Cubes: tower of 5–6 M. Cubes: imitates pushing train (*24m) Formbd: places 2–3 blocks Perf. box: inserts corner of sq. (*24m) Perf. box: retrieves ball
Language	Vo: 4–5 words includ. names Vo: uses jargon (*24m) Book: pats pictures (*18m)	Book: looks selectively Vo: 10 words includ. names Picture cd: names or points 1 Test obj: names ball Ball: 2 directions	Vo: 20 words Speech: combines 2–3 words spontan. (*24m) Ball: 3 directions
Personal-Social	Feeding: bottle discarded Feeding: inhib. grasp of dish Toilet: partial regulation (*24m) Toilet: bowel control Toilet: indicates wet pants (*18m) Commun: says "ta-ta", or equiv. Commun: points, voc. wants (*21m) Play: shows or offers toy (*21m) Play: casts obj. in play or refus. (*18m)	Feeding: hands empty dish (*...) Feeding: feeds self in part, spills (*36m) Toilet: regulated daytime (*24m) Play: pulls a toy (*30m) Play: carries or hugs doll (*24m)	Feeding: handles cup well Commun: asks for food, toilet, drink Commun: echoes 2 or more last words (*24m) Commun: pulls person to show (*24m)

* Temporary patterns are indicated on the schedules by an asterisk followed by the age at which the pattern is replaced by a more mature pattern of the same nature (Gesell & Amatruda, 1941, p. 24).

1. Walks alone; seldom falls

4. Builds tower of three

2. Seats self in small chair

5. Fills cup with cubes

3. Turns pages two or three at a time

6. Dumps pellet from bottle

FIGURE 1-1   Behavior characteristics of an 18-month-old child (adapted from Gesell & Amatruda, 1941).

not, however, tell what is "normal" for an individual child. Many aspects of development are related only loosely to chronological age. For example, at one time only norms of weight were listed for various ages. Then, as the importance of other variables affecting weight was recognized, weight norms began taking height into account also; and more recently, body build and structure have been added.

However, there has been an overemphasis on norms, especially in

7. Imitates stroke

10. On command puts ball on chair

8. Identifies one picture

11. Walks into ball

9. Hurls ball

12. Pulls toy

FIGURE 1-1 (*Continued*)

books and periodicals available to laymen. Such norms are misunderstood and have been the source of much unnecessary worry and concern, on the part of mothers particularly. Arnold Gesell, an early worker in child growth and development, has published norms for many aspects of development. Table 1-1 contains schedules describing the behavior characteristic of an 18-month-old child. Many of these items are presented pictorially in Figure 1-1. Such books by Gesell as *Infant and*

Child in the Culture of Today (Gesell & Ilg, 1943), *The Child from Five to Ten* (Gesell & Ilg, 1946), and *Youth: the Years from Ten to Sixteen* (Gesell, Ilg, & Ames, 1956) have been criticized for stressing ages and stages of normal development. Entire chapters of these books are devoted to descriptions of the "one-year-old," "two-year-old," and so forth. Perhaps the fault lies not so much with the books as with those who seek too eagerly for early indications of normality or precocity in their children.

Misconceptions about norms have also arisen because of the emphasis on the mean or "average" time of appearance of a certain skill or behavior. Too often, however, the age *range* at which the skill appears in the subjects sampled has not been described. Although the norm for walking alone may be 59 weeks, the *normal range* may be from eight to eighteen months. Few if any developmental skills can be considered to suggest a pathological condition if they do not appear at a *precise* age. Norms do provide some basis for comparison, however, and aid in understanding normal behavior and development.

SUMMARY

In this chapter we have explored techniques of observation, prediction, and control and have described various ways for obtaining information about children. Noting some of the advantages and disadvantages of each, we have seen the research areas in which each method of gaining information is most appropriate. In addition, we have stressed the cautions that must be observed in making statements about cause and effect. The identification of cause-and-effect relationships is most valuable, for it permits predictions about behavior, and predictability is the aim of all scientific research. Only through carefully designed and carefully controlled scientific experiments can safe statements about causation perhaps be made. Yet the basis for formulating "fruitful" experimental hypotheses—that is, hypotheses leading to new hypotheses— may be the use of other research methods.

Much has been learned and much else remains to be learned from use of case studies, questionnaires, broad observational techniques, and psychometric tests. Some research requires the judicious combination of several of these methods. Only when students and researchers recognize the safeguards that must be taken and the shortcomings and weaknesses of a given research method can they show adequate caution in accepting the findings and claims of research. How information is obtained determines the extent to which we can rely on its validity.

REFERENCES

Allen, S., Dubanoski, R., & Stevenson, H. Children's performance as a function of race of E, race of S, and type of verbal reinforcement. *Journal of Experimental Child Psychology,* 1966, **4**, 248–256.

Allport, G. W. *Personality; a psychological interpretation.* New York: Holt, 1937.

Anderson, J. E. *A survey of children's adjustment over time.* Minneapolis: Institute of Child Development, 1959.

Armstrong, M. D., & Tyler, F. H. Studies in phenylketonuria. I. Restricted phenylalanine intake in phenylketonuria. *Journal of Clinical Investigation,* 1955, **34**, 565–580.

Arrington, R. Time sampling in studies of social behavior: A critical review of techniques and results with research suggestions. *Psychological Bulletin,* 1943, **40**, 81–124.

Baller, W. R. A study of the present social status of a group of adults who, when they were in elementary schools, were classified as mentally deficient. *Genetic Psychology Monographs,* 1936, **18**, No. 3.

Barker, R. G. The stream of behavior as an empirical problem. In R. G. Barker (Ed.), *The stream of behavior.* New York: Appleton-Century-Crofts, 1963.

Barker, R. G., & Wright, H. F. *One boy's day.* New York: Harper, 1951.

Barker, R. G., & Wright, H. F. *Midwest and its children.* Evanston, Ill.: Row, Peterson, 1954.

Bayley, N. Research in child development: A longitudinal perspective. *Merrill-Palmer Quarterly,* 1965, **11**, 183–208.

Bell, R. Q. Convergence: An accelerated longitudinal approach. *Child Development,* 1953, **24**, 145–152.

Bell, R. Q. An experimental test of the accelerated longitudinal approach. *Child Development,* 1954, **25**, 281–286.

Bugelski, B. R. *An introduction to the principles of psychology.* New York: Rinehart, 1960.

Cohen, M. R. *Studies in philosophy and science.* New York: Holt, 1949.

Cowan, P., Weber, J., Hoddinott, B., & Klein, J. Mean length of spoken response as a function of stimulus, experimenter, and subject. *Child Development,* 1967, **38**, 191–203.

Darwin, C. A biographical sketch of an infant. *Mind,* 1881, **6**, 104–107. In W. Dennis (Ed.), *Readings in child psychology.* New York: Prentice-Hall, 1951.

Festinger, L. *A theory of cognitive dissonance.* Evanston, Ill.: Row, Peterson, 1957.

Gesell, A., & Amatruda, C. *Developmental diagnosis.* New York: Hoeber, 1941.

Gesell, A., & Ilg, F. L. *Infant and child in the culture of today.* New York: Harper, 1943.

Gesell, A., & Ilg, F. L.   *The child from five to ten.* New York: Harper, 1946.

Gesell, A., Ilg, F. L., & Ames, L. B.   *Youth: The years from ten to sixteen.* New York: Harper, 1956.

Haggard, E. A., Brekstad, A., & Skard, A. On the reliability of the anamnestic interview. *Journal of Abnormal and Social Psychology,* 1960, **61,** 311–318.

Hall, G. S. The contents of children's minds. *Princeton Review,* 1883, 249–272. Reprinted in W. Dennis (Ed.), *Readings in the history of psychology.* New York: Appleton, 1948. Pp. 255–276.

Honzik, M. P., Macfarlane, J. W., & Allen, L. The stability of mental test performance between two and eighteen years. *Journal of Experimental Education,* 1948, **17,** 320.

Kagan, J. American longitudinal research on psychological development. *Child Development,* 1964, **35,** 1–32.

Moustakas, C. E., Sigel, I. E., & Schalock, H. D. An objective method for the measurement and analysis of child-adult interaction. *Child Development,* 1956, **27,** 109–134.

Munn, N. L. *The evolution and growth of human behavior.* Cambridge, Mass.: Riverside, 1955.

Mussen, P. H. (Ed.). *Handbook of research methods in child development.* New York: Wiley, 1960.

Olson, W. C. *The measurement of nervous habits in normal children.* Minneapolis: University of Minnesota Press, 1929.

Rapaport, D. *Emotions and memory.* Baltimore: Williams & Wilkins, 1942.

Rosenthal, R. On the social psychology of the psychological experiment. *American Scientist,* 1963, **51,** 268–283.

Rosenthal, R. *Experimenter effects in behavioral research.* New York: Appleton-Century-Crofts, 1966.

Schaefer, E. S., & Bell, R. Q. Development of a parental attitude research instrument. *Child Development,* 1958, **29,** 339–361.

Sears, R. R., Maccoby, E. E., & Levin, H. *Patterns of child rearing.* Evanston, Ill.: Row, Peterson, 1957.

Shirley, M. M. *The first two years: A study of twenty-five babies, Vol. I. Postural and locomotor development.* Institute of Child Welfare Monograph Series, No. 6. Minneapolis: University of Minnesota Press, 1931.

Shirley, M. M. *The first two years: A study of twenty-five babies, Vol. II. Intellectual development.* Institute of Child Welfare Monograph Series, No. 7. Minneapolis: University of Minnesota Press, 1933. (a)

Shirley, M. M. *The first two years: A study of twenty-five babies, Vol. III. Personality manifestations.* Institute of Child Welfare Monograph Series, No. 8. Minneapolis: University of Minnesota Press, 1933. (b)

Stone, A. A., & Onque, G. C. *Longitudinal studies of child personality.* Cambridge, Mass.: Harvard University Press, 1959.

Templin, M. C. *Certain language skills in children.* Institute of Child Welfare Monograph Series, No. 26. Minneapolis: University of Minnesota Press, 1957.

Willems, E. P.   An ecological orientation in psychology.   *Merrill-Palmer Quarterly*, 1965, **11**, 317–343.

Woolf, L. I., Griffiths, R., & Moncrieff, A.   Treatment of phenylketonuria with a diet low in phenylalanine.   *British Medical Journal*, 1955 (4905), 57–64.

Wright, H. Psychological development in Midwest.   *Child Development*, 1956, **27**, 265–286.

Wright, H., & Barker, R.   Psychological ecology and the problem of psychosocial development.   *Child Development*, 1949, **20**, 131–143.

Wright, H., & Barker, R.   *Methods in psychological ecology.*   Lawrence, Kan.: Department of Psychology, University of Kansas, 1950.

SECTION II
BASIC FACTORS
IN DEVELOPMENT

For the most part, five areas of development provide a basis for the common qualities of human beings. These five—heredity, growth and maturation, learning and motivation, language, and intelligence—each explored in an individual chapter, form the substance of this section.

Heredity serves all species in the same way, providing human beings with a basic similarity. Regardless of individual differences, all human beings are moderately large primates who manipulate the environment with well-developed hands, who show much curiosity, and who seek experience and variation in their surroundings. All human beings follow a similar pattern of growth and maturation. Although human learning capacities and responses to various motivating forces in the environment in many ways resemble those of all other animals, in some forms of learning, especially those involving formation of concepts, solving of problems, and creativity, man excels. This is because of man's high intellectual capacity as a species; and although individual differences are marked, these differences conceal the basic similarity of one human being to another as compared with other species.

Superiority in learning ability and in retaining information appears largely to result from the fact that man is unique in being able to communicate symbolically. Mediated by common capacities, individual differences, whether hereditary or based on environmental forces, come into being. The hereditary forces producing these differences occupy attention in this section, whereas the environmental influences are discussed later in the book.

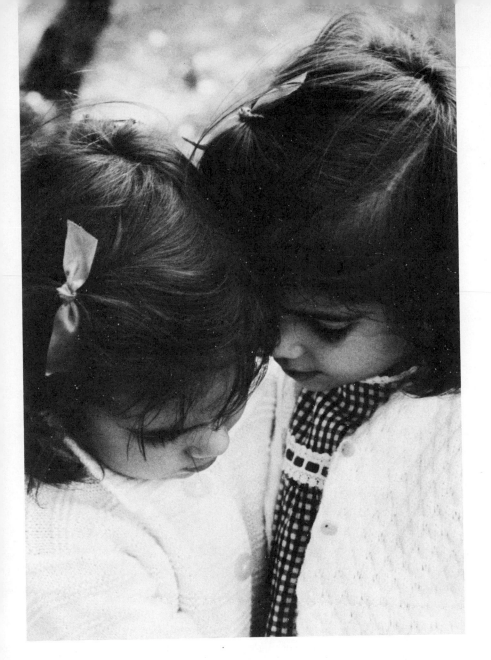

2

Heredity

How mutable or changeable is human nature? This question is implicit in any study of the influence of heredity—biological inheritance—on growth and behavior. Anyone who believes that only a minor portion of an organism's capacities and patterns of response are inherited must also believe that the organism can be molded in large part by its surroundings —its environment. Subscribers to this view are called environmentalists. To paraphrase a distinguished exponent of environmentalism, John B. Watson (1919), "Give me a dozen children and full control of the environment, and I will make of them what I wish—atomic scientists, commissars, professors, or hippies." If this assertion is correct, human nature is indeed changeable and future generations of mankind can be made to differ in basic character from the present generation. Yet the hereditarian insists that man is what he is, and that no amount of manipulation of the environment, unless it is accompanied by some form of selective breeding, can change him greatly.

Following World War II, the science of genetics—the study of heredity —received a setback in the U.S.S.R. The Soviets felt that a belief in genetics implied that human character was determined, in part, by biological inheritance; to that extent, human nature was immutable (Zirkle, 1949). Legislating out of existence one set of views about the nature of the world, the Soviets supported another (Lysenkoism-Michurianism), which holds that changes in the environment of an organism alter the genetic characteristics transmitted to the organism's offspring. This belief, known to the Western world long ago as Lamarck-ianism, was accepted in the West as a means of explaining variation among offspring (see Darwin, 1890), but was fairly well disproved by the 1920's. As a scientific theory it has little to recommend it, although it is most useful as a scientific rationalization for those who believe they can change the basic character of mankind. Yet even now, Soviet scientists are attempting to restore Soviet genetics to a Western point of view.

The belief espoused by the Soviets in the inheritance of acquired characteristics may seem, at first sight, an optimistic one. It holds that any efforts at self-improvement live on in one's offspring. But Herman Muller (1948), America's Nobel Prize-winning geneticist, suggested that this concept might not be as optimistic as it first seemed. If it were true, he noted, then individuals in a backward environment—an environment that allowed little growth in intellect or development of potentialities—should become *genetically inferior*. As Muller pointed out, this is not so. It certainly is not true, for example, of Chinese peasants. Assuming the same form of breeding in two differing environments, individuals from environments that have been depressed for generations

48

display, as a group, when placed in an adequate setting, the same level of abilities as any other group. Those who stress that heredity—as defined in Western culture—is the significant determinant of human capacities would maintain that just as a fine environment cannot make men into angels so a degraded one cannot make them like beasts.

These, then, are the issues involved in the study of heredity and environment as they affect human nature. Although a lengthy discussion of the mechanisms of heredity may belong more appropriately in a course in genetics, the foregoing philosophical considerations are clearly a part of child psychology. How they are regarded determines to a considerable degree the way the child is viewed.

THE HEREDITARY PROCESS

The mechanisms of heredity are essentially the same for all species of plants and animals, although they may be more easily investigated in an ear of corn or a fruit fly than in humans. What is discovered about hereditary transmission in one species can apply, with few qualifications, to all others.

Among humans a sperm cell of the male penetrates the ovum (egg) of the female and thus fertilizes the ovum. Each normal male and female cell has 46 chromosomes. As a result of cell division, any single sperm or ovum contains approximately half the number of chromosomes of its parent cell—usually one-half of 46, or 23. In the fertilized egg, known as a *zygote*, the chromosomes of sperm and ovum combine to give the fertile egg 23 *pairs* of chromosomes; this restores the normal complement of 46, with half inherited from each parent. Each of these chromosomes is composed, in turn, of many genes.

The sperm and the ovum are *germ cells*. Their substance, the chains of genes formed into chromosomes, is called *germ plasm*, which is quite distinct from the plasm of the body, called *somatoplasm*. Through the germ plasm parents transmit their genes to their children. The offspring in turn pass on these genes to their progeny. In a sense, germ plasm, transmitting characteristics as it does across generations and generally unaltered by environmental influences, is immortal. Genetic inheritance determines in large part the physical structure and behavioral potentialities of human organisms. Gene changes occur in the case of mutations caused by factors in the environment. These mutations are sudden changes in the gene structure that result from X-ray, cosmic ray, or fallout irradiation, or from exposure to mustard gas.

What any individual is genetically is determined largely by chance. Half of his genes come from the one sperm cell, among millions of possible sperm cells, that penetrates one of the hundreds of egg cells produced by a female during her reproductive life. Each parent contributes one member of each pair of the many thousands of pairs of genes that affect human inheritance. Each sperm cell and each egg cell differs in the genes it contains from all other sperm and egg cells produced by the same individual. By the random combination of the genes from a particular sperm with the genes of a particular ovum, a human is formed. This human is unique from other humans and yet like fellow men in many respects.

Every individual, as we now know, contains thousands of genes. In some cases one gene is dominant and another is recessive. Those who receive one of each kind from their parents manifest the dominant characteristic, but stand an even chance of passing along the recessive gene to their offspring. Since genes are acquired from parents, it is very likely that individuals are more like their parents genetically, and hence in observable characteristics, than like people in general. However, many characteristics that are recessive in both parents, and therefore not visible, may turn up in the individual. This is one reason why children do not always resemble their parents as closely as might be expected.

Although some characteristics are determined by a single pair of genes, many more characteristics result from the interactive effect of a large number of gene pairs. Suppose that intellectual ability were determined by nine pairs of genes, which is certainly far less than the actual number. Suppose further that there could be only two possible genes in each pair —one that disposed toward "brightness" and the other toward "dullness." Now suppose that the genes disposing toward brightness were dominant in two particular parents, whereas those disposing toward dullness were recessive. Since brightness is dominant in this case any of the nine pairs of genes containing one or both bright genes would dispose the offspring toward being intelligent. Table 2-1 presents several possibilities. Because of the many potential combinations, numerous differences may result. A pair of morons, for example, might produce a genius, and vice versa; this is not impossible but highly improbable.

INHERITED SIMILARITIES

Most psychological research into the influence of heredity has been directed toward determining its role in producing differences among humans. But the overwhelming significance of heredity is not really in this area; rather it is in the area of achieving similarities between individuals.

TABLE 2-1   A Hypothetical Case of Multiple Gene Determination of a Trait *

Gene Pair	Father's Genes	Mother's Genes
1	bright-bright	bright-dull
2	bright-bright	bright-bright
3	bright-dull	dull-dull
4	bright-dull	dull-dull
5	bright-dull	bright-dull
6	dull-dull	bright-bright
7	bright-dull	dull-dull
8	dull-dull	bright-dull
9	dull-dull	bright-dull

Each parent can contribute only one gene out of any gene pair. Possible contributions include the following combinations.

Offspring No. 1		Offspring No. 2	
Offspring Gene Pair	Father-Mother	Offspring Gene Pair	Father-Mother
1	bright-dull	1	bright-dull
2	bright-bright	2	bright-bright
3	bright-dull	3	dull-dull
4	bright-dull	4	dull-dull
5	bright-bright	5	dull-dull
6	dull-bright	6	dull-bright
7	bright-dull	7	dull-dull
8	dull-bright	8	dull-dull
9	dull-bright	9	dull-dull

This offspring has nine of nine pairs of genes with one or more bright genes in the pair. The offspring, then, is brighter than either parent.

This offspring, on the other hand' has only three gene pairs disposing toward brightness and six double recessive pairs of genes disposing him toward dullness. He is less able than his parents.

* We have decided to call bright genes dominant.

Humanness is the result of a number of genetically determined characteristics that, interacting with one another, produce the portion of behavior that is not common with other species. La Barre (1954) argued that the characteristics that made humans unique, except for resemblance to other higher primates, were bipedal locomotion, stereoptic vision, hands, and a fairly high capacity for learning.

When man, heir of four limbs, uses only two of them for walking, his clever primate hands are then finally freed from use in any kind of locomotion whatever. They can now be used for purely exploratory grasping. The advantages of this are not to be underestimated.

Emancipated hands are not enough: many dinosaurs had them, but they lacked sufficient brains. Intelligence is not enough: elephants have a great deal of intelligence behind their trunks, but they do not have stereoscopic sight; the prehensile-tailed monkeys are intelligent too, and they have stereoscopic vision as well, but they do not ordinarily see their tails. Stereoscopic eyes are not enough either: for the intelligent, tree-living apes have them, with color vision and the yellow spot in the retina to boot. It is the combination that counts. Man has paired grasping organs, fully in his field of vision and wholly freed from locomotor duties, in a stereoscopic-sighted, big-brained mammal—and these add up to the answer.

Anaxagoras claimed that man had brains because he had hands, but Aristotle argued that man had hands because he had brains. When the implications of these statements are better understood and the dust of battle has settled a bit, modern anthropologists are inclined to give the decision to Anaxagoras rather than to Aristotle. But hands, brains, and eyes are a case, really, of hens-and-eggs causality; nor did it all begin, strictly speaking, with man. For in all primate evolution they influence each other mutually and develop progressively together; and the ability to "monkey with things" that man got from his primate ancestors is still one of the keystones of human nature. Certainly such hands and eyes and brains put an animal into closer object-relationship with reality and enlarge the animal ego in the technical sense of increasing awareness and testing of reality. Very literally, such an animal as man has more contacts with reality (La Barre, 1954, pp. 86–87).

La Barre's views were supported by Butler (1953, 1954) and others working with Harlow at the University of Wisconsin on experiments dealing with curiosity drive. Butler described his work as follows.

. . . I was testing monkeys on a food-rewarded problem. The monkey worked behind a screen where it could not see the experimenter. By the same token, the experimenter could not see the monkey, and there was a great temptation to peek to find out what the animal was doing. I first made a small peephole in the panel, but the monkey quickly discovered it and thereafter spied on me as often as I did on him. I next tried placing a small mirror in a position that enabled me to watch the animal constantly. The monkey turned the tables by dropping its work and watching me through the mirror!

Taking advantage of this lead, we designed an experiment to investigate monkey's visual exploratory behavior. The apparatus was essentially an enclosure with a built-in color discrimination problem. Monkeys were rewarded by a view of the surroundings outside the enclosure, provided they responded correctly on the problem.

The results of the experiment left no doubt about the strength of the monkey's curiosity or its power in promoting learning. Throughout the 20 days of testing the animals worked away eagerly at the problem. . . . Without tiring of the game, they went on pushing the doors enthusiastically to get a look at the people working in the laboratory outside the box. In a second study that ran for 57 days and presented various color-discrimination problems, the subjects worked just as unflaggingly.

These data strongly suggest that the drive to explore visually is indeed a fundamental drive in monkeys. To measure its strength and persistence further, two monkeys were tested for four continuous hours each day for five days. The animals worked as fast on Day Five as they did on Day One. A second experiment yielded still more surprising results. Three monkeys were put to the door-opening test hour after hour, with 30 seconds between trials, until they quit. One monkey performed for nine continuous hours, another worked for 11 and the third for more than 19 hours! The response time of this marathon performer was actually shortest during the final hour of the test. That the monkeys would work as long and as persistently for a food reward is highly unlikely . . . (Butler, 1954).

Through producing a better understanding of the environment, this primate trait, curiosity, has so much value for survival that natural selection has made it a human characteristic inherited in much the same manner as the opposable thumb. The existence of the curiosity drive and the need it may arouse for stimulation probably produces fundamental differences in learning between primates and nonprimates. This is shown, for example, in the work of Harlow and others who have found that primates attack problems involving manipulation, such as unlocking doors and solving problems, without any special reward. If such a reward is introduced, the primate does *less* well in these tasks (Harlow, 1950). Yet there seems to be little doubt that intrinsic reward hastens learning. Since all responses that satisfy curiosity are rewarding to primates, it seems reasonable to believe that the primate will learn a wide variety of behaviors, some of which will have survival value.

In contrast, the learning of nonprimates seems largely restricted to techniques to reduce such drives as hunger and thirst.

Through an interplay of environment and biological inheritance, the primate—and especially man—has developed physical characteristics that enable an active, manipulative approach to the environment. As a consequence, genetically determined structure and behavior produce a basic similarity among all men. Within this similarity heredity helps to establish variations, or individual differences.

INHERITANCE OF INDIVIDUAL DIFFERENCES

All humans differ from one another. How much of these differences may be imputed to heredity? Although this is not an easy question to answer, since heredity and environment interact, data are available that can tell something about the relative contribution of each to human variability.

The idea that abilities are inherited certainly is not new. Long before there was a science of behavior, the belief in the inheritance of traits formed the basis for class distinction. A knight, no matter how impoverished, could not marry a merchant's daughter, no matter how substantial her dowry, without feeling he had married beneath his station. During the late Middle Ages people believed that there were vast differences between the nobility and the merchant class and between the merchant class and the peasantry. Those in superior positions considered themselves somehow transcendentally different, and held that this superiority was transmitted to their progeny. Even though such ideas, like subsequent notions of racial purity, rested on value judgments about the relative worth of individuals and on rather dubious principles, they indicate that man long has believed in heredity as a determinant of personality.

The first scientific study of the inheritance of ability was undertaken by Sir Francis Galton in *English Men of Science* (1874), *Hereditary Genius* (1869), and *Inquiries into Human Faculty* (1883). The first of these books had to do with the inheritance of scientific ability. A cousin of Darwin and a member of the brilliant but eccentric Darwin-Wedgewood-Galton family, Sir Francis may have been drawn to this area of research by his ponderings over his extensive family and its rich contribution to English science and industry. His discovery that a relatively small number of English families produced most of England's scientists suggested to him that genius was inherited. The difficulty in interpreting his work is the same one encountered in interpreting much of the research into the inheritance of characteristics conducted since his time. Some English families certainly produced many scientific geniuses—but can this be attributed to heredity? The child of a genius may inherit genius or, just as likely, may acquire it through association with a dedicated, brilliant parent—or both. This same contamination of heredity by environment pervades more recent studies, which nevertheless have some bearing on the inheritance of individual differences. *Hereditary Genius* was broader in scope, dealing with such diverse talents as mathematics, poetry, and wrestling, and concluding, on the basis of the same flawed type of evidence that the majority of these talents were inherited. The third book, *Inquiries into Human Faculty,* includes a chapter that opens a new approach to the inheritance of temperament and ability—the twin study, which is discussed later in this chapter.

The United States has an open class society, within which individuals of great ability may rise and those of slight ability may descend in occupational level. Although there is considerable variation in ability within any social class, marked IQ differences are still found to exist among various classes when large samples of individuals are measured in each. If intelligence is inherited, these differences, though attenuated, should also appear in the children of tested individuals. Table 2-2 shows results of studies aimed at testing this hypothesis.

Individual differences do exist. Although superior environment in upper occupational levels probably plays a part in producing them, the similarity in the size of the gaps over a 20-year span during which class distinctions have markedly decreased suggests that heredity figures strongly in intelligence. As in the case of Galton's work, however, the relative influence of heredity and environment and the effects of their

TABLE 2-2 Mean IQs of Preschool Children Classified by Father's Occupation According to the Minnesota Occupational Scale (Goodenough & Anderson, 1931)

	Study		
Father's Occupation	Goodenough (1928)	Terman & Merrill (1937)	Johnson (1948)
Professional	116	116	116
Semiprofessional and managerial	112	112	112
Clerical and skilled trades	108	108	107
Rural owners, farmers		99	95
Semiskilled, minor clerical	105	104	105
Slightly skilled	104	95	98
Unskilled	96	94	96

interaction with one another are difficult, although not impossible, to disentangle (see Loehlin and Vandenberg, 1966).

Family Resemblances

Many studies have measured family resemblances in intelligence. Figure 2-1 presents typical results of such studies. Even though higher correlations among identical (one-egg, monozygotic, or MZ) than fraternal (two-egg, dizygotic, or DZ) twins suggest the impact of heredity on similarity of intelligence, the correlation of fraternal twins in contrast to ordinary siblings or to parents and children implies that similarity of environment increases the degree of resemblance, since fraternal twins are no more alike, genetically, than the other two groups.

The foregoing studies of family resemblances in intelligence shed some light on the inheritance of characteristics. However, these studies do not provide adequate controls for testing similarity of environment. Other experimental procedures are needed if we wish to identify more accurately the relative contributions of heredity and environment. Pro-

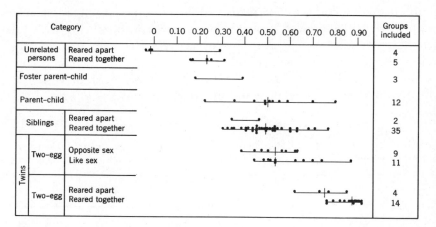

FIGURE 2-1 Correlation coefficients for "intelligence" test scores from 52 studies. Some studies reported data for more than one relationship category; some included more than one sample per category, giving a total of 99 groups. Over two-thirds of the correlation coefficients were derived from IQs, the remainder from special tests (for example, Primary Mental Abilities). Mid-parent-child correlation was used when available, otherwise mother-child correlation. Correlation coefficients obtained in each study are indicated by dark circles; medians are shown by vertical lines intersecting the horizontal lines, which represent the ranges (from Erlenmeyer-Kimling & Jarvik, 1963).

cedures employed to accomplish this task include comparisons of identical and fraternal twins, studies of separated identical twins, investigations of adopted children, and selective breeding.

What evidence about human characteristics has been produced by each of these approaches? Most research by psychologists into the role of heredity has concentrated on the influence of heredity and environment on scores in intelligence tests. This is partly the result of a historical accident. Soon after the turn of the century psychologists had developed an adequate test of intelligence, but there is still no comparable measure of personality. Moreover, an older generation of psychologists believed that intelligence was a central factor in personality. By knowing the intelligence of an individual, they held, it was possible to know many other things about him—his honesty, his leadership ability, his values. Today's psychologists are much less certain that a high IQ automatically makes an individual trustworthy, loyal, obedient, God fearing, and kind; thus studies of intelligence seem to have less bearing on personality structure than they once had. And although psychologists would like to know more about hereditary influences on personality characteristics, this is an area in which they are least knowledgeable. Research is, however, increasing, in number and in quality of studies, as may be seen in McClearn's (1964) and McClearn's and Meredith's (1966) recent reviews of the literature. We know much of what we need to know and soon will know more.

Intra-Pair Resemblances between Identical and Fraternal Twins

About 100 years ago Galton realized the importance of twin studies in the investigation of hereditary influences on behavior. It was not known at that time that there were two kinds of twin, identical (MZ) and fraternal (DZ), so in reading Galton we can discern his bafflement at finding that members of some sets of twins (those we would now call MZ) looked and acted almost exactly alike, whereas members of other twin pairs (probably DZ) showed no more resemblance than any pair of siblings. Once it became known that there were two varieties of twin, and once techniques were developed by means of which MZs and DZs could be differentiated reliably (see Sutton, Clark, and Schull, 1955; and Nichols, 1965, for discussions of recent developments in diagnostic techniques), the comparison of MZ and DZ pairs became an important approach in the study of heredity. (See Vandenberg, 1966b, for a comprehensive review of twin research.)

Whether identical or fraternal, twin pairs share a common environment. Identical twins also are alike genetically, whereas fraternals share no more genetic similarity than any other pair of siblings. Therefore, if greater resemblance is found within pairs of identicals than within pairs of fraternals, it generally is assumed that the trait under investigation is determined to a significant degree by heredity. This assumption has been challenged. It can be argued that greater resemblances between identicals than fraternals may be a consequence of a more similar environment shared by the identicals. This issue finally has been dealt with by Scarr (1968). She studied pairs of MZ twins believed by the parents to be MZ; MZ twins believed by the parents to be DZ; DZ twins believed by the parents to be DZ; and DZ twins believed by the parents to be MZ. If MZ twins resemble one another more than DZs because of greater genetic similarity, they should show this resemblance whether the parents believe they are MZ or DZ. If environmental similarity is the key factor, and if MZs have greater intra-pair resemblances than DZs because they are reared in a more similar environment, pairs believed to be identical by the parents should resemble one another more closely, regardless of actual zygosity. Scarr's data suggest that, although parental belief concerning zygosity does influence similarities, actual zygosity is more important; that is, MZ twins, whether treated by their parents as MZ or DZ, resembled one another more than did DZ twins, even when DZ pairs were believed to be MZ. Thus her data indicate that greater resemblances between MZ as compared with DZ pairs cannot be attributed, to any large extent, to differences between identicals and fraternals in the degree of environmental similarity within pairs.

Another approach to the problem of determining whether the greater resemblance of MZ than DZ twins results from more similar parental treatment of MZ pairs would be to establish the degree of MZ and DZ resemblance on subtle as opposed to culturally obvious psychological traits. The term subtle is used here to denote traits about which few of us know our ability, and for which we seldom receive training in the schools or at home. For example, we generally do not know our short-term memory span, our ability to perceive and recall stimuli shown us for very short time intervals, or our relative learning ability under conditions of massed versus distributed practice. Despite the fact that these capacities are centrally involved in learning and memory, we have no formal training in these areas. On the other hand, parents often expend considerable efforts to train their offspring in such culturally obvious areas as mathematics and language (especially in vocabulary). If the greater degree of resemblance of MZ as compared with DZ twins is of the same magnitude for subtle, untrained traits as for culturally important and obvious traits, it would appear that differences in the treatment and training of MZs or DZs are not the cause of the observedly greater intra-pair similarity of MZ pairs.

As noted in Table 2-1, identicals (MZs) show a much stronger intra-pair resemblance in tested intelligence than do fraternals (DZs). This repeatedly obtained finding shows that heredity plays a considerable role in producing individual differences in tested intelligence. However, most studies of MZ-DZ pair differences make use of such tests as the Stanford-Binet or one of Wechsler's tests, and these tests are a conglomeration of items measuring many different intellectual domains. Probably of more theoretical and also more practical value are MZ-DZ comparisons making use of tests in which the different factors that make up intelligence are measured. A number of these "Primary Mental Ability" tests have been used by various investigators in tests of MZ and DZ twins, in order to determine the degree to which each distinct ability resulted from hereditary influences. The results of four separate studies are shown in Table 2-3.

These studies indicate that *some* intellectual abilities, and especially spatial ability—the ability to visualize objects in three-dimensional space —appear to be determined largely by heredity, while other abilities, such as reasoning ability and memory, are influenced little, if at all, by hereditary factors. Certain questions can be raised regarding these results. For example, the low amount of hereditary influence shown in the memory test may be a result of the kind of task presented the persons

TABLE 2-3 Ratio of DZ to MZ Within-Pair Differences for the Six Scores of the Chicago Primary Mental Abilities Test

Name of Score	Blewett 1953	Thurstone et al. 1955	Vandenberg 1962	Vandenberg 1966a
Verbal	3.13 *	2.81 *	2.65 *	1.74 *
Space	2.04 *	4.19 *	1.77 *	3.51 *
Number	1.07	1.52	2.58 *	2.26 *
Reasoning	2.78 *	1.35	1.40	1.10
Word fluency	2.78 *	2.47 *	2.57 *	2.24 *
Memory	not used	1.62 *	1.26	not used
Number				
DZ pairs	26	53	37	36
MZ pairs	26	45	45	76

* Hereditability differences between MZ and DZ pairs are statistically significant (from Vandenberg, 1967a).

tested—there seem to be at least two distinct kinds of memory, short term and long term (and there may be more)—or of the low reliability of the PMA test. However, the results strongly suggest that certain abilities are far more environmentally determined than others. Therefore, at a practical level, one might expect far more success at training children in reasoning or in memory than in training them in spatial ability.

On the Mental and Motor Scales of the Bayley Infant Behavior Profile, Freedman and Keller (1963) compared sets of identical and fraternal twins within the first year of life, when the effects of differential treatment between types of twin could be expected to be minimal, if not nonexistent (especially since a number of twin pairs were misdiagnosed with regard to zygosity). The differences in scores, shown in Figure 2-2, were found to be significantly smaller between identical twins than between fraternal twins. This closer resemblance at such an early age supports the notion that hereditary influences produce variations in scores in these tests.

Using the same MZ-DZ comparison techniques, Gardner has begun a still-continuing investigation of cognitive styles (1965). This study

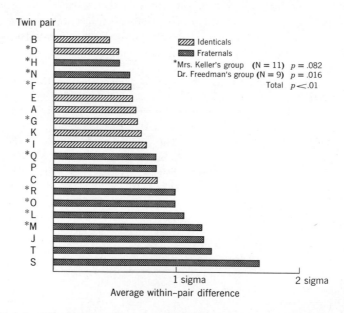

FIGURE 2-2   The Bayley Mental and Motor Scales averaged to form a single distribution. Average within-pair differences in the first year, based on 8 to 12 monthly administrations (Freedman & Keller, 1963, p. 197).

is intended to determine the contributions of heredity and of environment in the ways in which persons organize their thought processes. Gardner (1966) has already established that the ability to block out overlearned old habits in a new learning situation is determined in large part by heredity. Other valuable data concerning complex intellectual processes undoubtedly will be obtained from this continued investigation.

Just as MZ and DZ intra-pair resemblances can be compared on different intellectual or motor factors, they can be compared on different dimensions of personality. Gottesman (1963) studied 34 pairs each of MZ and DZ high-school-age twins in Minnesota and, later (1965), a larger number of MZ and DZ twin pairs in the Boston area. The results of the two studies differed somewhat but, as in other studies (see Vandenberg, 1967b), it appears that introversion-extroversion—the tendency to approach or withdraw from environmental stimulation—contains a very strong hereditary component. Psychopathic deviancy, a measure of tendencies toward antisocial behavior, seems second most strongly influenced by heredity. This may be because it is at least in part a result of emotionality and activity levels, and these have significant hereditary components (Scarr, 1966). Freedman's and Keller's (1963) research on infant MZ and DZ twins also supports the position that approach-withdrawal tendencies, measured in this case by *social orientation* and *fear of strangers,* has a hereditary base. Koch's (1966) data also support this position, since the study indicates that MZ twins are more often equal in dominance than are DZ twins. It may be that a strong hereditary component in approach-withdrawal tendencies is the reason individual differences in this area are highly stable over time, as shown in longitudinal studies (Tuddenham, 1959; Schaefer and Bayley, 1963).

Comparisons of MZ and DZ twins not only tell us that motor, mental, and personality characteristics result, in part from hereditary factors, but also tell us the degree to which particular characteristics are (as are spatial ability and introversion-extroversion) or are not (as reasoning and a number of personality traits appear not to be) inherited.

Separated Identical Twin Studies

Genetically, identical twins are exactly alike. By separating two individuals identical in heredity and raising them in quite disparate environments, thus holding heredity constant while varying the environment, it becomes possible to discern the relative influences of each.

The group of twins discussed most intensively were those studied by Newman, Freeman, and Holzinger (1937). These men investigated

50 sets of fraternal twins, a like number of sets of identical twins raised together, and 19 sets of identical twins raised apart from one another. The 19 pairs of identical twins raised separately are of present concern. Some rather startling resemblances were discovered among them. For example, consider these findings about Ed and Fred.

The most interesting feature of this story is the remarkable parallelism in the lives of these twins in spite of the fact that they lived without knowledge of each other's existence for twenty-five years. They were both reared as only children by childless foster-parents, both being led to understand that they were own children. Though they lived a thousand miles apart, they had about the same educational experience, and both found employment as repair men in branches of the same great telephone company. They were married in the same year and each had a baby son. Each owned a fox terrier dog named Trixie. According to their statements, both of them from early boyhood on were obsessed with the idea that they had a brother who died and often stated this to their playmates.

The story of their discovery of each other's existence is almost stranger than fiction. When Ed was twenty-two he was accosted by a jovial fellow who had just come from a distant city to work at Ed's department. "Hello, Fred! How's tricks?" he inquired. Ed explained that he was not Fred and denied that he knew the newcomer, but the latter was hard to convince, declaring that Ed was trying to cover up his identity. Soon afterward another man accosted him as "Fred" and stated that if he was not Fred Blank he was exactly like a fellow of that name with whom he had recently worked in a distant city. Ed was by this time rather disturbed about the matter and told his parents about it. Reluctantly, the parents were forced to admit that Ed was an adopted son and that he was one of a pair of twins; the other of them had been adopted by a couple who lived in their home town but with whom they were not acquainted. They also revealed the fact that when the twins were small boys they had attended school together for a short time and that the other children often noticed their close resemblance. It occurs to us that this early association of the twins may have led to the above-mentioned mutual feeling about a brother who had died.

Needless to say, Ed lost no time in getting in touch with Fred. The latter was out of work at the time and came to visit Ed. It was during this time that we succeeded in inducing them to come to Chicago to see the Fair and, incidentally, to be examined. Their visit with us was made even more interesting to them and to us by reason of a confusion of dates which resulted in their coming to us at the same time as a pair of young women twins, Ethel and Esther, whose story comes next in this series. The two pairs of twins became great friends and were much impressed by similarity in the circumstances that led to their discovery that they were twins. The visits to the Fair were made together, each young man taking one of the young women. When they walked about, people were startled to see one couple walking ahead and a duplicate couple following behind. Everywhere they went they attracted attention and enjoyed the sensation they created. On one occasion they attended a side show featuring a pair of Siamese twins and, according to their statement, stole the show, attracting more attention than the exhibits (pp. 147–148).

The 19 pairs of separated identical twins were studied at maturity. Members of each pair showed a close resemblance in physical size and in other phases of growth. They resembled one another closely in IQ and less closely in personality. Perhaps the degree to which heredity determines development diminishes from size to IQ to personality. Or perhaps the correlations were highest on concrete physical growth because here is where the best, most exact, and most reliable measuring instruments are available. Devices for measuring intelligence are less precise and reliable than devices used to check physical dimensions. The reliability of measures for personality is low even at the present time and was certainly a good deal lower at the time of the Newman et al. study in the 1930's. Actually, the reliability of most tests was so low in the 1930's that it was surprising to find any resemblance at all between twins.

Since the measures of intelligence were most central to the matters that concerned psychologists at the time, these tests have been the most widely discussed. Woodworth (1941) offered both IQ and environmental data for the 19 sets of twins studied by Newman and his associates, and for three other sets as well. As he noted:

> Taken without regard to sign, the average IQ difference between separated identicals is 7.6 points. Correction for chance errors of observation would bring this difference down to 6 points net, a figure to be compared with the estimated net difference of 3 points between identicals reared together, and of 15 points or more between children paired at random from the same community. It is probable, then, that environment did make these separated twins differ in tested intelligence, though not to any such extent as obtains among the children of a community (Woodworth, 1941, p. 357).

The correlation obtained between identical twins reared in *separate* environments was +.767. This was a more substantial relation than was obtained between fraternal twins raised in the *same* environment. Although Newman, Freeman, and Holzinger considered their data to support an environmentalist view, heredity seemed to have played an important part in determining the level of intelligence. A more recent study of variations in intelligence among a comparable sample of identical twins who were raised separately (Burt & Howard, 1956) has turned up similar results. In this case it seems clear that some variability can be attributed to environmental circumstances, even though the heredity factor is quite strong.

One other intensive study of a single pair of identical twins (Burks, 1942) supplies considerable information about the interests and personalities of the twins, as well as the more customary measurements of intelligence and physical size. The twins were girls, who had been separated before they were two weeks old. At the age of 12, personality ratings showed them to be quite similar to one another, despite a variability in certain areas of adjustment, which was produced by familial and environmental influences. The girls differed markedly in Strong Interest Test scores. At 18 they seemed even more similar to each other than at 12 and their interest profiles showed a distinct increase in comparability. Moreover, Rorschach tests at 18 indicated a high degree of likeness; the patterns of response were more alike than might have been anticipated even from previous studies of identical twins who had been reared together. The greater likeness at 18 suggested that as one grew older, hence freer from parental dominance, innate predispositions became more apparent. This study, one of the few to have measured separately raised identical twins with adequate devices for assessing personality, suggested that the extent to which individuals displayed *certain* personality traits was in large part the consequence of genetic inheritance.

Enrichment.   Studies of identical twins who have been separated also have bearing on one controversial area of the subject of heredity and environment: the question of how "enrichment" affects intelligence-test scores and, presumably, intelligence. This dispute has centered around the value of the kindergarten experience in developing children's general abilities and around the variation in closeness and richness of mothering in the determination of children's level of intellectual performance.

The latest phase of enrichment to be explored is that of very early enrichment. This is the area of enrichment to which the study of identical twins is most relevant, although so far most of the experimental work has been conducted with laboratory rats. Hebb (1949, pp. 298–299) reported that rats from an ordinary strain of laboratory species who were reared as home "pets" performed in significantly superior manner on a learning task to rats from the same strain who were reared in a normal laboratory environment. Other well-controlled experiments have extended these findings. In a representative study of this sort conducted by Forgus (1956), infant rats were exposed to visual forms from the time they first opened their eyes at the age of 16 days until they reached 41 days of age. A second group of rats was exposed to these same forms during the interval from 41 to 66 days of age. In both cases control groups of littermates were reared without the visual experience. Tests of both enriched and both control groups showed that the two enriched groups learned more rapidly than the control groups, and that the group that had been enriched early learned more rapidly than the late-enrichment group. Several similar studies (Cooper & Zubek, 1958; Gibson & Walk, 1956; and Luchins & Forgus, 1955) concurred in this finding. These indicate that deprivation retards later learning, whereas early enrichment increases the rate of learning.

Studies in the early enrichment of lower organisms contain implications for problems of human development. This has been suggested by Hunt (1961), McCandless (1961, pp. 261–262), Smith and Stone (1962, pp. 6–7), and Thompson (1959, p. 33). Perhaps, for example, the enrichment or deprivation of problem-solving experience to which a human is exposed before the age of two or three may be related to later ability.

If early enrichment or deprivation bears on the intellectual ability of humans, then identical twins who are exposed to a common early environment and share the stimulation it offers should resemble each other more closely on IQ tests than identical twins who have not shared a common environment for any length of time. Johnson (1963) tested this proposition using data from 23 pairs of separated identical twins reported in the literature. Vandenberg and Johnson (1968) obtained data on 14 more pairs of twins tested on conventional intelligence tests, making a total of 37 pairs. These data, bearing on the relation between age of separation and similarity in IQ, are presented in Table 2-4.

Pairs of twins in the early (before one year) separation group differ by an average of 5.50 IQ points; in the late (one year or later) separation group by 9.59 points. The mean within-pair difference for the entire 37 pairs is 7.64 points.

Thus the similarity in IQ between identical twins, significantly, is *inversely* related to the time spent in the same environment. Since the two groups did not differ significantly in the age at which they were tested, in duration of separation, or in degree of environmental difference, it is hard to explain why the twins in the early separation groups were more similar. The fact that twins who spend more time in a common environment are more dissimilar in IQ appears to run counter to the animal research literature on environment and deprivation discussed above.

TABLE 2-4   Age at Separation, Source of Data, and Differences in IQ for 37 Pairs of MZ Twins from Various Studies*

Age	Source	Difference	Age	Source	Difference
1 day	(S & T)	4			
1 day	(J-N)	6	1 yr.	(J-N)	9
9 days	(B)	1	1 yr.	(J-N)	14
½ mo.	(M)	4	1 yr.	(NFH)	19
3 wk.	(J-N)	1	1 yr.	(NFH)	5
3 wk.	(J-N)	1	1 yr.	(NFH)	1
1 mo.	(S)	4	14 mo.	(NFH)	4
1 mo.	(G & N)	3	18 mo.	(NFH)	12
1 mo.	(NFH)	1	18 mo.	(NFH)	12
1 mo.	(NFH)	6	18 mo.	(NFH)	24
1 mo.	(NFH)	1	18 mo.	(NFH)	7
6 wk.	(J-N)	11	2 yr.	(NFH)	10
2 mo.	(NFH)	2	2½ yr.	(NFH)	2
3 mo.	(NFH)	15	3 yr.	(NFH)	8
3 mo.	(G & B)	19			
5 mo.	(NFH)	17	3½ yr.	(J-N)	8
6 mo.	(NFH)	1	3½ yr.	(J-N)	6
7 mo.	(J-N)	4	5¾ yr.	(J-N)	13
9 mo.	(J-N)	6	6 yr.	(NFH)	9
10 mo.	(J-N)	3			

* The following abbreviations are used for sources:

J-N =	Juel-Nielsen (1964)	S & T =	Stephens & Thompson (1943)
B =	Burks (1942)	G & N =	Gardner & Newman (1940)
M =	Muller (1925)	G & B =	Gates & Brash (1941)
S =	Saudek (1934)	NFH =	Newman, Freeman, & Holzinger (1937)

Adopted-Child Studies

Something about the influence of heredity and environment may also be learned by investigating the intelligence of a number of adopted children, of their true parents, and of their foster parents.   Inferences may be drawn about the role played by heredity (true parent) and by environment (foster parent) in shaping the child's ability level from correlations between true parent and child ability and between foster parent and child ability.   Yet for several reasons the results of this kind of investigation are not as clear-cut as those of the studies of identical twins.   Even when children are raised by their true parents, the correlation of parent-child IQ is only about +.50. Moreover, as a result of the placement policies of adoption agencies, foster parents are somewhat similar to the true parents in ability and in appearance.

The most widely cited studies on adopted children were done years ago. They were conducted by Burks (1928), Leahy (1935), Skodak (1939), and Skeels (1936). Burks's and Leahy's studies argued for the hereditarian point of view. The opposite position was taken by Skodak and Skeels.

Together, Skodak and Skeels (1945, 1949) followed up 154 children, their true mothers, and foster parents after having independently studied the true mothers and the children some years earlier. They found that according to test results the true mothers were retarded in mental ability, whereas the foster parents were above average. Examining 100 of these children longitudinally, they discovered that they did not resemble their true mothers in test scores, but instead resembled the foster parents in tests given over a period of years. At various test ages their mean IQs ranged from 104 to 118 (Skodak & Skeels, 1949). These means were more than 20 points higher than the true-mother mean. Although mean scores resembled the foster parents by the age of eight, the correlation between the IQ of a given child and the ability of its true mother, as estimated from her level of education, ranged from +.33 to +.38 (see Goodenough, 1940), whereas correlations with the ability of its foster parents, estimated from their educational level, were only +.16 to +.19. How can this be explained? These children, separated from their true mothers soon after birth, obtained mean IQs higher than their mothers', yet, by middle childhood, resembled them almost as closely, in a correlational sense, as children raised by their own mothers. This may be seen in Figure 2-3. Quite likely the IQs obtained from the true mothers were not truly representative of ability. Many of them were tested shortly after having given birth, a rather inopportune time to test any woman—and especially a woman who had given birth to an illegitimate child in Iowa in the 1930's!

As a group, therefore, the adopted-child studies again point to the importance of heredity as a producer of individual differences.

Evidence from Selective Breeding

Selective breeding is the breeding of organisms for the presence or absence of some particular trait. If the breeding is successful, the trait must necessarily have some hereditary base. The speed at which selective breeding progresses indicates, in part, the importance of heredity in determining how much of the trait is present in any organism.

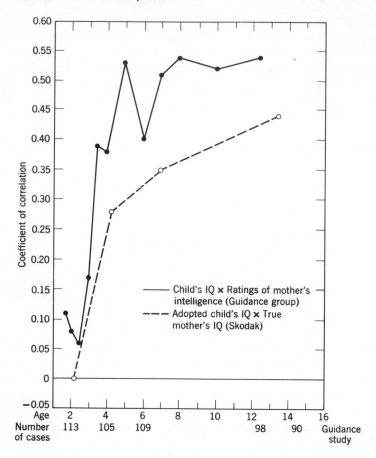

FIGURE 2-3 The correlation, at different ages, between true mother-off-spring ability for children reared by biological parents (guidance groups) and for children reared by adoptive parents (Skodak's group) (from Honzik, 1957).

Galton's study persuaded him that humans should engage in selective breeding. The able person should seek an equally able mate in order to improve the human race. This process of selective breeding Galton called *eugenics*. Although eugenics societies still exist, human beings have not taken Galton's ideas very seriously. They continue to fall in love without giving the slightest consideration to what the eugenicist might think of their choice. Yet even if people turned about and suddenly adhered to Galton's formula, problems would remain. What should be the goal of the breeders—vigor, beauty, intelligence? Often these are not found in the same individual, as the well-known story about George Bernard Shaw, the playwright, and Ellen Terry, the beautiful actress, illustrates. Miss Terry suggested to Shaw that they could produce a true *wunderkind* with her beauty and his brains. Shaw rejected the proposal, replying things might turn out the other way around; the child might inherit *his* beauty and *her* brains. The difficulty in any sort of selective breeding is thus the matter of choosing the objective of the process.

The few situations in which humans have bred selectively are indeed odd, since only eccentric people could and would indulge in such experiments. Frederick the Great is said to have married off a large number of his tallest guards to a group of strapping peasant girls and provided them with villages in which to live so as to ensure future rulers of Prussia a ready source of tall soldiers for honor-guard usage. Hitler attempted to breed "Aryan Supermen." The most interesting example of selective breeding among humans stemmed from the ideas of an American religious sect. John Noyes (see Holbrook, 1957) believed that the violent, antisocial emotions, such as jealousy and anger, resulted primarily from the existence of the *nuclear* family—the family composed of father, mother, and children formed into a tightly knit unit. Doing away with this family, Noyes held, also does away with possessiveness and hence with greed, jealousy, and anger. In its place he advocated a utopian scheme as part of a religion he called *Perfectionism.*

At Oneida, New York, Noyes and his followers maintained themselves for years in a communistic community. They practiced what outsiders called "free love" but what they themselves considered "multiple marriage." Although sexual behavior was, in a sense, free, Noyes and other leaders of the Oneida community decided who could have children, how many they could have, and who would be the partner of a particular individual in conceiving a child. Noyes desired only the brightest, most capable adults to reproduce. Long before Galton he practiced eugenics, though he called it *stirpiculture.*

The community flourished long enough for two generations, in some cases, to be bred selectively. Then federal prosecution of Mormon polygamy in the 1880's spilled over into Oneida, forcing the end of the experiment, the only one in which humans were bred for general physical and intellectual excellence. Although there have been assertions (Noyes, 1937) that children of the community have demonstrated high levels of ability, only an empirical study of the group's descendants can truly assess the success of the venture.

Among lower organisms it is easier to observe the results of selective breeding. Physical size and structure, ability, and emotionality are

among the variations between organisms that can be genetically determined. By selecting and breeding dogs for smallness, as well as for
other characteristics, one obtains the Chihuahua, whereas for largeness,
one obtains the Great Dane. Moreover, dogs of different breeds vary in
temperament and in ability almost as widely as they do in size. Since
the ancestry of pedigreed dogs is known for generations, the researcher
has purer strains at his disposal than he can obtain among humans.

Scott (1958, pp. 117–125) has reported studies conducted by Fuller
and himself which disclose the effect on temperament of hereditary differences produced by selective breeding. In several of these studies,
they compared cocker spaniels with *basenjis* (African barkless dogs).
Basenjis proved considerably shier and more fearful than cockers, even
when they were reared by cocker mothers. As a result of breeding
cockers to basenjis, the hybrid progeny were as shy as fullblooded
basenjis, suggesting that shyness was a dominant genetic trait in dogs.
Breeds of dogs, which differ in parental stock and in the traits for which
they are bred, also differ widely in other respects. Figure 2-4, for example, illustrates another hereditary trait of cockers. It may well be
that humans, too, possess behaviors once bred into the species as a result
of selection but now of no utility, or, as in the case of quick and strong
aggressive responses in the face of frustration, of presently dubious survival value—at least for the species as a whole.

By shifting from dogs to rats, we move from the domain generally
inhabited by the animal fancier to the domain of the animal scientist.
Many rats have been bred by investigators to study the influence of
genetic inheritance on a variety of animal characteristics. The most
famous rat-breeding experiment was conducted by Tryon (1940). Krech
and Crutchfield (1958) have succinctly summarized Tryon's work.

> Tryon started with a "parental" generation of 142 male and female
> rats. Each animal was run for 19 trials through a 17-unit maze. The
> brightest animals made a total of approximately 14 errors in learning the
> maze, the dullest, about 174. The bright females were then mated with
> the bright males, the dull females with the dull males—the other ani-
> males being discarded. Then the offspring of these matings were tested
> on the same maze. On the basis of their performance, the brightest
> rats within each of the bright litters were mated, and the dullest within
> each of the dullest litters were mated. This testing and selective breed-
> ing procedure was followed for 18 generations. The results are sum-
> marized in the distribution curves of [Figure 2-5] showing the errors
> made by the parental group, the third generation (F_2), the seventh gen-
> eration (F_6) and the ninth generation (F_8). With successive generations
> the two strains of rats pull apart, until by the F_8 generations the dullest

FIGURE 2-4 Setting birds for the net. Above, having found the birds, the spaniel was trained to drop flat on the ground while men came up behind him and threw a net over both bird and dog. (Drawn after Blome, *The Gentleman's Recreation*, London, 1688.) Below, this tendency to crouch still survives in many modern cocker spaniels, which will drop flat at a threatening gesture (adapted from Scott, 1958, p. 121).

FIGURE 2-5   Error scores made by animals of successive generations.   On the vertical axis is indicated the per cent of the total group of rats of any one generation making the number of errors indicated on the horizontal axis (Krech & Crutchfield, 1958, p. 572).

of the bright rats are about as bright or brighter than the brightest of the dulls (p. 572).

The Tryon experiment is itself of considerable significance and has led to further work in the biochemical aspects of brightness and dullness (see Chapter 6, pp. 194–195).   Conceivably, this might be a key to the treatment of certain kinds of mental defect.

If, in eight generations, one can produce differences so great that strains of organisms do not overlap in a trait such as brightness or emotionality, then genetic factors are indeed powerful in establishing individual differences. The many studies in selective breeding, although dealing for the most part with lower organisms, strongly support the notion that human beings do not enter the world as a *tabula rasa*—a blank tablet. Instead they are born with certain abilities and propensities that are further accentuated by the environment. In fact, it might be said that any characteristic that has a structural base, such as activity level, tendency toward schizophrenia, emotionality, or intelligence, is inheritable.

A Special Problem Presented by the Results of Studies of Heredity

All the studies described here demonstrate that heredity rather strongly influences certain dimensions of intelligence, as measured by the most frequently used intelligence tests, and important domains of cognitive style and of personality.

It sometimes is assumed—although it should not be—that an acceptance of the belief that certain of our intellectual and personality characteristics have strong hereditary components also implies an acceptance of the belief that racial differences in IQ are hereditarily determined. The question of whether Negroes and whites are equal in intelligence is a complicated one. The controversy between Garrett (e.g., see Garrett, 1961), who believes in innate (hereditary) racial differences in intelligence, and Klineberg (1935; 1954), who does not, has continued for decades. Shuey (1966), in her review of the literature on racial differences in intelligence, concluded that a genetic intellectual difference exists separating whites and Negroes. The evidence that Shuey presents is sufficiently compelling that Dreger (1967), who takes the position that races are equal in ability, reviews her book favorably. The basic problem in studies of Negro-white intelligence is whether one can assume that the environments of the two groups are equal; there is ample evidence (e.g., the fraternal-twin-versus-sibling data presented in this chapter and the cross-generational studies and studies of socially isolated groups discussed in Chapter 6) that the nature of the environment greatly influences tested intelligence. Dreger and Miller (1960) comment on the many problems involved in actually matching Negroes and whites, even on such objectively defined variables such as place of residence, parental education, and years of education. Even in studies where these variables supposedly are controlled, subtle yet potent influences are not controlled. For example, Deutsch and Brown (1964) compared lower-class Negro, lower-class white, middle-class Negro. and middle-class white children on measures of intelligence and achievement.

As is almost always the case, middle-class youngsters performed more adequately than those from lower-class groups; and within economic groups whites performed more adequately than Negroes. Deutsch and Brown were aware, perhaps as a result of having encountered Mischel's (1961) research in this area, that father absence from the home has a number of deleterious consequences on behavior and on intellectual performance. They controlled for frequency of father absence in the four groups. Not surprisingly, lower-class children were reared in father-absent homes more often than middle-class children, and, within each social class, Negroes were reared in father-absent homes more often than whites. When father absence was controlled among the four groups, differences in intelligence and achievement were markedly reduced. Since the studies that claim to demonstrate racial differences in ability have not controlled for such important sociopsychological factors as father absence, they cannot be accepted as having demonstrated what they claim. Studies like that of Deutsch and Brown, as well as data such as those presented in Chapter 8, suggest that programs such as Operation Head Start might gain at least as much from employing male teachers as from attempting to enrich the environment. Changing the affective-emotional environment in positive ways may well be more important than intellectual enrichment in producing positive change in intellectual performance.

The evidence that Shuey reviews is thus of little or no value in determining whether racial differences in intelligence exist, since sociopsychological factors such as father absence are uncontrolled, even when racial groups are matched on income and education. Cross-cultural data (Gay & Cole, 1967) obtained from white Americans and from westernized and tribal Africans suggests that African Negroes are superior to American whites on tasks that are important to them and with which they have had experience, but that are not of importance and are not experienced by Americans, and that the reverse is equally true. Finally, it should be mentioned that whites, as compared with nonwhites, appear to be more likely to carry genes, such as the recessive gene causing phenylketonuria, that produce a severe amount of mental defect (Johnson, 1967). The data on racial differences in ability generally are uninterpretable because key variables are uncontrolled. When interpretable, they generally support racial equality or, in single gene effects, support the notion of white *inferiority,* perhaps as a result of a longer period of relaxation of natural selection (see Post, 1962) among the white group. Acceptance of the influence of heredity on intelligence and personality does not imply a belief in race differences in ability.

SUMMARY AND CONCLUSIONS

In many ways humans resemble lower organisms; in many ways humans resemble one another. These basic resemblances result from the hereditary process. These effects of biological inheritance, although of great significance, are often overlooked, since they are universal. Besides similarities, heredity produces individual differences in such matters as size, intelligence, and temperament. The role of heredity is more apparent in shaping these differences than in determining similarities. People who differ genetically in some way, as in intelligence, are also treated differently; thus environmental forces magnify the original hereditary distinctions. Some aspects of intelligence and personality appear to have a substantial hereditary component (e.g., spatial ability, approach-withdrawal) while other aspects of the same general domains of individual difference do not. Further, even when aspects of the self result largely from heredity, for example, physical size and appearance, how we view these qualities and respond to them results from environmental influences.

The study of genetic similarities helps to develop a point of view about how far human character can be modified. The human is a medium-sized omnivorous animal. He lacks specialized weapons of offense or defense, but possesses native curiosity, hands free for exploring and manipulating the environment and for carrying weapons, moderately high aggressiveness, and communicative skills that make cooperation possible. It is doubtful whether a tendency to respond bred in by thousands of years of natural selection—for example, a quick and aggressive response to threats from the environment—can be eliminated unless natural selection takes a new course. Veblen (1911) maintained that such a new course began at the time of the industrial revolution. Actually, there is hope for humanity, since built-in responses are susceptible to some modification as the social environment shifts.

It may seem pessimistic to hold that much of the variation between human beings in physique, intelligence, and some aspects of personality results from genetic factors. Yet, for various reasons, this is not a pessimistic view. First, if this view is correct, humans are what they are and no environment, however deprived, can wipe out those aspects of human beings that are most endearing: the forming of close attachments, the need for one another, curiosity, and the sense of wonder. Second, although heredity imposes limits on individual achievement, one cannot tell whether the limit has been reached for any individual unless that individual has been exposed to the best possible social and intellectual environment. Each child and each adult differs from all others. Unless opportunities for expression are made available, potential abilities cannot be judged. However, one should not be surprised to find that some individuals gain more than others from any single environmental opportunity.

Through the study of individual differences in general, and genetically determined individual differences in particular, people become aware of the vast range of these distinctions. We humans are even more different from each other than we seem and in more ways than was once realized. Although these differences at times impede communication between individuals and make the human being a baffling subject for scientific study, they do add richness to human interaction.

One specific result of the study of individual difference is apparent in child psychology. As we shall see in later chapters, child psychology was once "formula happy"—if you do *this* to the child, you will get *that* result. This approach to child rearing, however, has never proved effective because humans vary so much from one another in their reactions to any treatment. Through increased awareness of the fact that individual differences exist, that they are of great magnitude, and that, to a fair degree, they are hereditary in nature, child psychology has progressed beyond oversimplified approaches to child-rearing practices and philosophies. This is the most important way that the study of individual differences has influenced child development.

REFERENCES

Blewett, D. B.   An experimental study of the inheritance of intelligence. *Journal of Mental Science*, 1954, **100**, 922–933.

Burks, B. S.   The relative influence of nature and nurture on mental development: A comparative study of foster parent-foster child resemblance. *Yearbook of the National Society for the Study of Education*, 1928, **27** (I), 219–316.

Burks, B. S.   A study of identical twins reared apart under differing types of family relationships. In Q. McNemar & M. A. Merrill (Eds.), *Studies of personality*. New York: McGraw-Hill, 1942.

Burt, C., & Howard, M.   A multiple factorial theory of inheritance and its application to intelligence. *British Journal of Statistical Psychology*, 1956, **9**, 95–131.

Butler, R. A.   Discrimination learning by rhesus monkeys to visual-exploration motivation. *Journal of Comparative and Physiological Psychology*, 1953, **46**, 95–98.

Butler, R. A.   Curiosity in monkeys. *Scientific American*, 1954, **190**, 7–75.

Cooper, R. M., & Zubek, J. P.   Effects of enriched and restricted early environments on the learning ability of bright and dull rats. *Canadian Journal of Psychology*, 1958, **12**, 159, 164.

Darwin, C. R. *The variation of animals and plants under domestication.* New York: Appleton, 1890.

Deutsch, M., & Brown, B. Social influences in Negro-White intelligence differences. *Journal of Social Issues*, 1964, **10**, 24–35.

Dreger, R. M. Review of *The testing of Negro intelligence* by Audrey M. Shuey. *Contemporary Psychology*, 1967, **12**, 49–51.

Dreger, R. M., & Miller, K. S. Comparative psychological studies of Negroes and Whites in the United States. *Psychological Bulletin*, 1960, **57**, 361–402.

Erlenmeyer-Kimling, L., & Jarvik, L. F. Genetics and intelligence: A review. *Science*, 1963, **142**, 1477–1479.

Forgus, R. H. Advantage of early over late perceptual experience in improving form discrimination. *Canadian Journal of Psychology*, 1956, **10**, 147–155.

Freedman, D. G., & Keller, B. Inheritance of behavior in infants. *Science*, 1963, **140**, 196–198.

Galton, F. *English men of science: Their nature and nurture.* London: MacMillan, 1874.

Galton, F. *Hereditary genius.* London: Clay and Sons, 1869.

Galton, F. *Inquiries into human faculty and its development.* New York: MacMillan, 1883.

Gardner, I. C., & Newman, H. H. Mental and physical traits of identical twins reared apart, Case XX. *Journal of Heredity*, 1940, **31**, 119–126.

Gardner, R. W. Genetics and personality theory. In S. G. Vandenberg (Ed.), *Methods and goals in human behavior genetics.* New York: Academic, 1965. Pp. 223–229.

Gardner, R. W. *The Menninger Foundation study of twins and their parents.* Topeka, Kan.: Menninger Foundation, 1966.

Garrett, H. E. The equalitarian dogma. *Mankind Quarterly*, 1961, **1**, 253–257.

Gates, N., & Brash, H. An investigation of the physical and mental characteristics of a pair of like twins reared apart from infancy. *Annals of Eugenics*, 1941, **11**, 89–101.

Gay, F., & Cole, M. *The new mathematics and an old culture.* New York: Holt, Rinehart and Winston, 1967.

Gibson, E. J., & Walk, R. D. The effect of prolonged exposure to visually presented patterns on learning to discriminate them. *Journal of Comparative and Physiological Psychology*, 1956, **49**, 239–242.

Goodenough, F. L. The Kuhlman-Binet tests for children of preschool age: A critical study and evaluation. *Institute of Child Welfare Monographs Series*, No. 2, 1928.

Goodenough, F. L. New evidence on environmental influence on intelligence. *Yearbook of the National Society for the Study of Education*, 1940, **39**, (I), 367–384.

Goodenough, F. L., & Anderson, J. E. *Experimental child study.* New York: Century, 1931.

Gottesman, I. I. Heritability of personality: A demonstration. *Psychological Monographs,* 1963, **77,** No. 9.

Gottesman, I. I. Personality and natural selection. In S. G. Vandenberg (Ed.), *Methods and goals in human behavior genetics.* New York: Academic, 1965. Pp. 63–74.

Harlow, H. Learning motivated by a manipulative drive. *Journal of Experimental Psychology,* 1950, **40,** 228–234.

Hebb, D. O. *The organization of behavior.* New York: Wiley, 1949.

Holbrook, S. H. *Dreamers of the American dream.* Garden City, N. Y.: Doubleday, 1957.

Honzik, M. P. Developmental studies of parent-child resemblance in intelligence. *Child Development,* 1957, **28,** 215–228.

Hunt, J. McV. *Intelligence and experience.* New York: Ronald, 1961.

Johnson, D. M. Application of the standard score IQ to social statistics. *Journal of Social Psychology,* 1948, **27,** 217–227.

Johnson, R. C. Similarity in IQ of separated identical twins as related to length of time spent in the same environment. *Child Development,* 1963, **34,** 745–749.

Johnson, R. C. Demographic characteristics of institutionalized phenylketonurics. Boulder, Colo.: Western Interstate Commission on Higher Education, 1967.

Juel-Nielsen, N. Individual and environment. A psychiatric-psychological investigation of monozygotic twins reared apart. *Acta Psychiatrica Scandinavia,* 1964 (Supplement 40), **183,** 152–292.

Klineberg, O. *Negro intelligence and selective migration.* New York: Columbia University Press, 1935.

Klineberg, O. *Social psychology.* (Rev. ed.) New York: Holt, 1954.

Koch, H. *Twins and twin relations.* Chicago: University of Chicago Press, 1966.

Krech, D., & Crutchfield, R. S. *Elements of psychology.* New York: Knopf, 1958.

La Barre, W. *The human animal.* Chicago: University of Chicago Press, 1954. Pp. 86–87.

Leahy, A. M. Nature-nurture and intelligence. *Genetic Psychology Monographs,* 1935, **17,** 236–308.

Loehlin, J. C., & Vandenberg, S. G. Genetic and environmental components in the covariation of cognitive abilities: An additive model. Report 14, Louisville Twin Study, Louisville, Ky., 1966.

Luchins, A. S., & Forgus, R. H. The effect of differential post-weaning environments on the rigidity of an animal's behavior. *Journal of Genetic Psychology,* 1955, **86,** 51–58.

McCandless, B. R. *Children and adolescents: Behavior and development.* New York: Holt, Rinehart & Winston, 1961.

McClearn, G. E.   Genetics and behavior development.   In M. L. Hoffman & L. W. Hoffman (Eds.), *Review of child development research.* (Vol. 1) New York: Russell Sage Foundation, 1964, pp. 433–480.

McClearn, G. E., & Meredith, W.   Behavior genetics.   *Annual Review of Psychology,* 1966, **17,** 515–550.

Mischel, W.   Father-absence and delay of gratification.   *Journal of Abnormal and Social Psychology,* 1961, **63,** 116–124.

Muller, H. J.   Mental traits and heredity.   *Journal of Heredity,* 1925, **16,** 433–448.

Muller, H. J.   The crushing of genetics in the U.S.S.R.   *Bulletin of the Atomic Scientists,* 1948, **12,** 369–371.

Newman, H. H., Freeman, F. N., & Holzinger, K. J.   *Twins: A study of heredity and environment.*   Chicago: University of Chicago Press, 1937.

Nichols, R. C.   *The National Merit twin study.*   In S. G. Vandenberg (Ed.), *Methods and goals in human behavior genetics.*   New York: Academic, 1965.   Pp. 231–243.

Noyes, P. B.   *My father's house: An Oneida boyhood.*   New York: Farrar & Rinehart, 1937.

Post, R. H.   Population differences in red and green color vision deficiency: A review and a query on selection relaxation.   *Eugenics Quarterly,* 1962, **9,** 131–146.

Saudek, R.   A British pair of identical twins reared apart.   *Character and Personality,* 1934, **3,** 17–39.

Scarr, S.   Genetic factors in activity motivation.   *Child Development,* 1966, **37,** 663–673.

Scarr, S.   Environmental bias in twin studies.   In S. G. Vandenberg (Ed.), *Progress in human genetics.*   Baltimore, Md.: Johns Hopkins Press, 1968, pp. 205–213.

Schaefer, E. S., & Bayley, N.   Maternal behavior, child behavior, and their intercorrelations from infancy through adolescence.   *Monographs of the Society for Research in Child Development,* 1963, **28** (3, Whole No. 87).

Scott, J. P.   *Animal behavior.*   Chicago: University of Chicago Press, 1958.

Shuey, A. M.   *The testing of Negro intelligence.*   New York: Social Science Press, 1966.

Skeels, H. M.   Mental development of children in foster homes.   *Journal of Genetic Psychology,* 1936, **49,** 91–106.

Skodak, M.   Children in foster homes: A study of mental development.   *University of Iowa Study in Child Welfare,* 1939, **16,** No. 1.

Skodak, M., & Skeels, H. M.   A follow-up study of children in adoptive homes.   *Journal of Genetic Psychology,* 1945, **66,** 21–58.

Skodak, M., & Skeels, H. M.   A final follow-up study of one hundred adopted children.   *Journal of Genetic Psychology,* 1949, **75,** 85–125.

Smith, H. T., & Stone, L. J.   Developmental psychology.   *Annual Review of Psychology,* 1961, **12,** 1–26.

Stephens, F. E., & Thompson, R. B.   The case of Millan and George.   *Journal of Heredity,* 1943, **34,** 108–114.

Sutton, H. E., Clark, P. J., & Schull, W. J.   The use of multiallele genetic characters in the diagnosis of twin zygosity. *American Journal of Human Genetics,* 1955, **7**, 180–188.

Terman, L. M., & Merrill, M. A.   *Measuring intelligence.*   Boston: Houghton Mifflin, 1937.

Thompson, G. G.   Developmental psychology.   *Annual Review of Psychology,* 1959, **10**, 1–42.

Thurstone, L. L.   *The Primary Mental Abilities Tests.*   Chicago: Science Research Associates, 1941.

Thurstone, T. G., Thurstone, L. L., & Strandskov, H. H.   A psychological study of twins.   Report No. 4 from the Psychometric Laboratory, University of North Carolina, Chapel Hill, N. C., 1955.

Tryon, R. C.   Genetic differences in maze learning in rats.   *Yearbook of the National Society for the Study of Education,* 1940, **39** (1), 111–119.

Tuddenham, R. D.   The constancy of personality ratings over two decades. *Genetic Psychology Monographs,* 1959, **60**, 3–29.

Vandenberg, S. G.   The hereditary abilities study.   *Eugenics Quarterly,* 1956, **3**, 94–96.

Vandenberg, S. G.   The hereditary abilities study: Hereditary components in a psychological test battery. *American Journal of Human Genetics.* 1962, **14**, 22–237.

Vandenberg, S. G.   The nature and nurture of intelligence.   Report No. 20, Louisville Twin Study, University of Louisville, Louisville, Ky., 1966.   (a)

Vandenberg, S. G.   Contributions of twin research to psychology. *Psychological Bulletin,* 1966, **66**, 327–352.   (b)

Vandenberg, S. G.   Genetic factors in poverty, a psychologist's point of view. Report No. 27, Louisville Twin Study, University of Louisville, Louisville, Ky., 1967(a).

Vandenberg, S. G.   Heredity factors in normal personality traits (as measured by inventories).   In *Recent advances in biological psychiatry.* (Vol. 9) New York: Plenum, 1967.   Pp. 65–104.   (b)

Vandenberg, S. G., & Johnson, R. C.   Further evidence on the relation between age of separation and similarity in IQ among pairs of separated identical twins.   In S. G. Vandenberg (Ed.), *Progress in behavior genetics.*   Baltimore: Johns Hopkins Press, 1968, pp. 215–219.

Veblen, T.   *The theory of the leisure class.*   New York: MacMillan, 1911.

Watson, J. B.   *Psychology from the standpoint of a behaviorist.*   Philadelphia: Lippincott, 1919.

Woodworth, R. S.   *Heredity and environment.*   New York: Social Science Research Council, 1941.

Zirkle, C.   *Death of a science in Russia.*   Philadelphia: University of Pennsylvania Press, 1949.

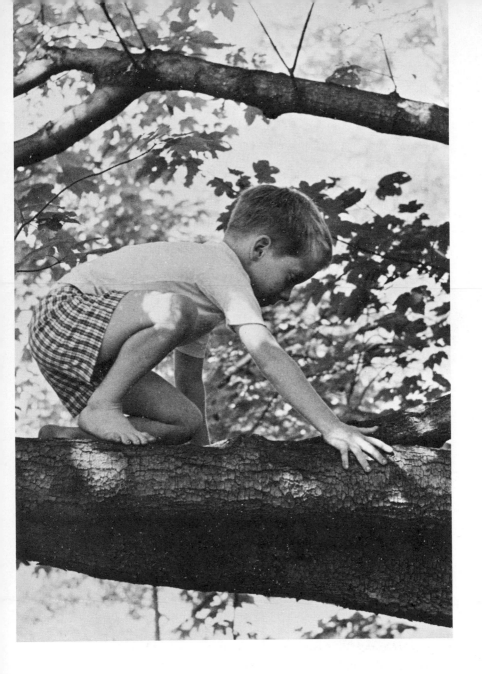

3

Growth and Maturation

Anything that lives grows. Among the higher species, growth proceeds along specific lines producing physical changes in the organism. At the same time, changes in behavior occur, which are believed to be direct consequences of growth. These behaviors, attributable principally or entirely to structural development, are called *maturational*. Many such behaviors occur in orderly fashion in young organisms, often appearing for the first time during the prenatal period. Their sequence of development is similar among widely divergent species. By their origins they illustrate the substantial role played by biological inheritance in the development of behavior.

PRENATAL GROWTH AND BEHAVIOR

After the egg is fertilized, it receives nurture from surrounding tissues and starts to grow. The mass of the cell increases more rapidly than its surface area, thus limiting the size of any cell while permitting sufficient nourishment to penetrate its walls. Perhaps because of the pressure of the bulkier mass on the cell's surface, the cell divides. This division continues as cells grow and split, until a ball-like cluster of cells emerges.

Up to this point in development, all cells are presumably the same and interchangeable. Now the cells begin to separate into layers according to their position in the cluster. The outer layer—*ectoderm*—becomes, for the most part, the sense organs and nervous system of the growing new organism. The middle layer—*mesoderm*—is the primary source of the skeleton and muscles, and the inner layer—*endoderm*—leads to the viscera and glands of later development.

Once these three layers have formed, specialized development overtakes the new organism. Development advances faster in the head than in the tail region of the embryo and in the central areas before the peripheral areas. These courses of development are called *cephalocaudal* —from head to tail—and *proximodistal*—from central to peripheral. In the embryo, and later in the newborn infant, many of the early behaviors are massive in approach because of this uneven nature of growth, whereas later movement becomes more specific. The young child, owing to less adequate distal development, uses his whole body in reaching and grasping, employing many distinct muscle groups. As he ages and as distal development improves, he is eventually able to use his fingers alone; this is a change from mass to specific movement.

Many behaviors become apparent before birth. These include a large number of reflexes, such as breathing, swimming, or sucking, as well as behaviors like flexing the leg, which occur as a direct response to stimulation. As a result, the infant is born with a large repertoire of un-

82

learned behaviors in addition to some that may have been acquired through learning.

PRENATAL DEVELOPMENT AND INDIVIDUAL DIFFERENCES

The newborn infant is born with certain characteristics and capacities. It is difficult to determine whether these characteristics and capacities are a result of hereditary or of prenatal influences. For example, the form of mental deficiency called Down's syndrome (mongolism) results from several different kinds of chromosomal abnormality. The most frequent kind of Down's syndrome, trisomy 21, which is caused by the presence of an extra chromosome 21, is also closely associated with maternal age; that is, older mothers produce most cases of trisomy 21. This fact led researchers to believe for a long time that maternal aging produced an inadequate intrauterine environment that in turn caused Down's syndrome. In this case a genetically caused defect was incorrectly believed to result from an adverse prenatal environment. In the opposite direction, studies of maternal nutrition during pregnancy, such as those carried out by Pasamanick and his associates (discussed below), suggest that many instances of mild mental retardation believed to show polygenic type of familial inheritance actually may be a result of maternal malnutrition and inadequate prenatal care across generations. Thus errors in the attribution of causes occur in both directions: defects in the newborn are sometimes believed to be caused by prenatal conditions when they actually result from genetic factors, and are sometimes believed to be caused by genetic factors when they actually result from prenatal influences.

Our present state of knowledge suggests most strongly that inadequate maternal nutrition and inadequate prenatal care produce many kinds of defect in offspring. Improvement of maternal nutrition (and care) seems certain to markedly reduce certain varieties of problem behavior.

The most thorough study so far of the connection between maternal health and problem behavior was undertaken by Pasamanick and his associates. In one study, the subjects were 363 white and 108 Negro children who had been referred to a division of special services in the Baltimore Department of Education because of behavioral disturbances (Pasamanick, Rogers, & Lilienfeld, 1956). Their disorders were described as hyperactivity, confusion, and disorganization. During their pregnancies, the mothers of these children had had a higher proportion of complications than mothers of a corresponding group of white and Negro control children. The pregnancy complications most closely associated with behavioral disorders were maternal *toxemia,* a pathological condition resulting from poison in the blood, and maternal hypertension. It seemed likely that these complications produced *anoxia,* a shortage of oxygen supply for the tissues, and that this, in turn, gave rise to brain injury.   As Kawi & Pasamanick (1959) noted, there was within the uterus a continuum of maldevelopment "with a lethal component consisting of abortions, still births, and neonatal deaths, and a sublethal component consisting of cerebral palsy, epilepsy, mental deficiency, and behavior disorders in children."

Since inadequate maternal diet and care is more frequent in lower economic groups, and is particularly frequent among Negroes (as noted in the Pasamanick studies), many social class and racial differences in the frequency of problem behavior probably can be traced back to this prenatal period.

Maternal attitudes toward pregnancy may produce biochemical changes that are transmitted to the offspring (Sontag, 1958; Montagu, 1962).   However, if we can generalize from animal studies, the effect of maternal stress on prenatal and postnatal behavior probably is variable, with genetic differences determining both the amount of effect and the direction of that effect (Weir & DeFries, 1964; DeFries, Weir, & Hegmann, 1967).

POSTNATAL MATURATIONAL GROWTH

Since many prenatal behaviors develop at a time and in a sequence that do not vary from child to child, occurring as the result of the growth of the embryo, we may naturally wonder about the development of postnatal behaviors.   Are these, too, the result of growth?

Developmental Norms

Sequences of postnatal development common to all members of a species are readily observable.   If any of these sequences is orderly, it may possibly stem from physiological maturation.   Table 3-1 contains four sets of norms for stages of development, each obtained from a different sample of children.   Figure 3-1 illustrates one of these sets. As both Table 3-1 and Figure 3-1 indicate, postnatal development is essentially cephalocaudal and proximodistal, thus suggesting that prenatal growth trends continue into the postnatal period.   Reisen and Kinder (1952) believe that an increasingly large number of muscle groups is engaged in each successive behavior and that the pattern progresses from simple to more complex responses.   Perhaps it is this passage from sim-

TABLE 3-1   Four Sets of Developmental Norms

Test Items	Mean Age in Months (to Nearest Full Month)			
	Shirley (1933)	Bayley (1935)	Aldrich & Norval (1946)	Frankenberg & Dodds * (1965, 1967)
Fetal position	0			
Chin up (can raise chin when prone)	1			0–1†
Head erect		2		2
Chest up (can raise chest when prone)	2			3
Head control when sitting			3	3
Head erect and steady		3		3
Sits with support	4	4		
Sits alone	7	6	6	6
Crawls	9	9	7	7
Creeps	10			
Walks with help	11	12	10	
Stands alone	14	13	11	11
Walks alone	15	13	12	11

* It should be noted that the Frankenberg & Dodds norms are excellent ones, based on testing 1036 children between ages two weeks and 6.3 years. The sample is representative of the population (not middle-class biased, in terms of family status of the subjects, as sometimes is the case with norms). Along with the mean or average age at which an item is passed, one has data in the age at which 25 per cent, 75 per cent, and 90 per cent of the children pass the item. Items themselves are divided into four areas—gross motor, fine motor-adaptive, language and personal-social—so that a developmental profile can be constructed.
† 90 per cent pass item by one month.

plicity to complexity rather than gradients of inner growth that accounts for the apparent continuation of prenatal growth sequences. Either way, the order of development seems similar to all four studies cited in the table; the sequences of behavioral change are lawful and predictable even though the mean ages at which any behavior occurs vary somewhat among the four sets of norms.

As may be seen in Table 3-1, certain behaviors of infants of six months or more seem to occur earlier now than they did in the 1930's, perhaps

FIGURE 3-1 The motor sequence (Shirley, 1933, frontispiece).

as a result of better nutrition. Indeed, the whole course of physical maturation seems to have been speeded up considerably (Tanner, 1968), so that it is not surprising that behaviors that are more a result of growth and maturation than of experience now occur earlier.

One final point. It recently has been claimed that children who skip the crawling stage will show later impairment; for example, in reading ability. Experimental tests of this proposition (e.g., Robbins, 1966, 1967) suggest that this position is of dubious validity. Since many of the exercises required by therapists who suscribe to this position require many hours of close parent-child contact, this contact may produce (independently of crawling exercises, etc.) those gains that are claimed to occur, if and when they occur at all.

LEARNING AND MATURATION

Psychologists have often asked whether certain human behaviors are learned or maturational. In a sense this is another version of the question regarding heredity and environment. Maturation is hereditary; it is an orderly sequence of events determined by changing physical structure, which in turn is governed by heredity. Learning, on the other hand, results from environmental stimulation. If the behaviors of a young child, whether physical, emotional, or social, are largely the result of maturation, the role of parents is largely to let children grow by themselves, since development and change come from within rather than from without. Under these circumstances, whatever adults do to children, good or bad, will not change children drastically. If, however, early behaviors are learned, what children are taught, how they are taught, and when they are taught are of prime significance. We return to the question posed at the outset of Chapter 2: How mutable is the human organism?

If humans actually vary because of changes in the environment, the study of learning and maturation may shed some light on the extent to which they do. For example, one of two similar groups of subjects is exposed to environmental stimulation, while this stimulation is withheld from the other group. The two groups should differ in behavior if learning is a product of such stimulation and if learning really influences the development of that behavior. On the other hand, if innate maturational mechanisms occasion the behavior, the environmental difference between the two groups should be of no consequence. In another situation the experimental group may be stimulated excessively while the control group is limited to the ordinary amount of environmental stimulation. Both situations may use identical twins; this is called the *co-twin* method.

From studies of this kind, it becomes possible to establish roughly the relative influences of hereditary, maturational factors on the one hand, and of learning, which is dependent on the environment, on the other.

Experiments in Nature

The first area of maturation studied by psychologists was that of physical maturation. One repeatedly hears the assertion, "We are teaching Johnny to walk." Is this true, or will the child learn without training—in fact, without having much opportunity to attempt to perfect his walking? Since withholding the opportunity to walk from a group of children merely to test an idea would hardly be ethical, researchers turn to "experiments in nature" in the hope of finding the information they desire. Among various cultures for example, there are many that restrict —sometimes very severely—the movement of a child. The practice of *swaddling*—that is, wrapping and binding an infant in long, narrow bands of cloth—was and is an accepted cultural practice in the Near East, the Balkans, Poland, and Russia.

> In the great Russian peasant population, and to a varying degree in all the regions and classes which shared and continue to share the common cultural heritage of the great central plains of Russia, the item of child care called swaddling was developed to an extreme. While the custom of bandaging newborn infants is widespread, the ancient Russian extreme insists that the baby be swaddled up to the neck, tightly enough to make a handy "log of wood" out of the whole bundle, and that swaddling be continued for nine months, for the greater part of the day and throughout the night (Erikson, 1950, p. 344).
>
> When asked why babies must be swaddled, simple Russians have answered with astonishment: What other way was there to carry a baby and to keep him warm through a Russian winter? And besides, how could one otherwise keep him from scratching and harming himself, and of scaring himself with the sight of his own hands? Now it is probably true that a swaddled baby, especially when just unswaddled, has not sufficient mastery over his own movements to keep from scratching and hitting himself. The further assumption that *therefore* he has to be swaddled again is a favorite trick of cultural rationalization. It makes a particular pattern of infant-restraint culturally self-supporting. You must swaddle the infant to protect him against himself; this causes violent vasomotor needs in him; he must remain emotionally swaddled in order not to fall victim to wild emotion. This, in turn, helps to establish a basic, a preverbal, indoctrination, according to which people, for their own good, must be rigidly restrained, while being offered, now and then, ways of discharging compressed emotion. Economically and politically seen, swaddling, then, is part of a system of stubborn institu-

tions which support and prolong the Russian combination of serfdom and "soul" (pp. 346–347).

More important to the present discussion than the Russian "soul" is something much simpler—the effect of deprivation of motor experience on the rate of motor development. Danziger and Frankl, as reported in Orlansky (1949), ventured into Albania to test swaddled children and compare their development with that of Viennese infants. This is what they found:

> Until they are one year old, the Albanian children are bound securely to a wooden cradle customarily placed in the darkest corner of the room, often with a cloth thrown over their heads so that no light is visible. These children displayed poor muscular coordination, but once given an opportunity to practice, their performance improved rapidly so that it was clear no permanent retardation had been effected. Their social behavior, as measured by response to the experimenters in a series of standardized tests, was equal or superior to the norms for Viennese children of the same age. Identical observations could undoubtedly be made on the children of many primitive peoples who, tied securely to cradleboards during their first year of life, may experience comparatively little bodily contact or fondling by the mother (Orlansky, 1949, p. 16).

Most American Indian tribes believe—or once believed—that infants should be reared on some type of cradleboard. A cradleboard usually consists of a straight board for a back. The child, covered with skins or blankets, is bound to the board so that, as the Indians believe, its posture will be good.

In southern Alaska some Indians still have heads that slope upward as a result of having spent their infancy in cradleboards with their soft, growing heads pressed against a slanted top. According to their tribe, this was the proper shape for a human head.

In studying various groups of Hopi Indians, Dennis and Dennis (1940) noted that in most villages infants were placed on a cradleboard shortly after birth and remained on it almost continuously for the first three months of their lives. Then they spent less time on the board but were attached to it at least for some periods until reaching about 14 months of age. Compared with other Hopi infants reared in the same general fashion but without cradleboards, these children showed no difference in the age of walking.

Co-Twin Studies

In another study by Dennis and Dennis (Dennis, 1935, 1938, and 1941), a pair of fraternal female twins was raised under restricted opportunities to practice motor or social responses. These conditions prevailed from the thirty-sixth day to the fourteenth month in the lives of the twins. Writing years later to summarize their research, the Dennises gave the following description of the environmental background.

Throughout the experiment the twins lived in our home but they were confined to the nursery. This was a second-floor room, so situated that from the infants' position only sky and tree tops were visible through the windows. The room itself contained only the subjects' cribs, a bureau, a table, two chairs, and a screen near the door. No picture or decoration of any sort was permitted in the nursery. The door of the room was kept closed, and we entered the room only to care for the subjects, to observe them, and to experiment with them. . . .

The subjects were placed in individual cribs, of the trade name "Kiddie Koop." The cribs were placed side by side with a screen equal in height to the cribs between the two, so that the twins could see each other only when taken from their beds. During the first nine months the subjects were taken from the cribs only for feeding and bathing or when removal from the cribs was demanded for the purposes of experimentation.

With the exception of a few occasions during the latter part of the experiment the sole care of the twins was supplied by the experimenters. This means that we bathed and fed the infants, changed the diapers and bed clothing, and cleaned the room. The infants seldom saw other people, and when they did it was with our knowledge and supervision. Visitors were required to adhere to the same practices which we imposed upon ourselves. . . .

With a few exceptions, we never encouraged or discouraged any act of the twins. The exceptions to this rule, and to other such general rules, occurred in the last month of the investigation, when the experimental conditions were partially suspended. . . .

We not only avoided reward and punishment but we avoided acts which might have provided examples for imitation. With certain exceptions to be noted later our behavior in the nursery was limited to changing diapers, bathing, feeding, etc. We carefully refrained from baby talk and from babbling, as we wanted to know whether such vocalizations would occur without example. Likewise, we never performed for the twins such acts as patting their hands or playing with their toes.

Thus far we have spoken only of the conditions which remained relatively constant until the last few weeks of the experiment. We turn now to more stringent restrictions in the environment of the subjects which, in the main, were applied only for the first half-year. The conditions to be described were designed to provide answers to specific questions and were abandoned when the answers were obtained.

We wished to determine whether or not the infants would smile upon hearing the voice of the adult, if speech were not associated with the care and attention which the adult supplied. For this reason, until the twins were 26 weeks of age, we never announced our entry into the nursery and never spoke to the subjects. We were not totally silent, for we occasionally commented to each other while in the nursery, but we were careful not to make comments while we were feeding or otherwise caring for the twins. Our speech when we were outside the nursery could be heard by the infants, but it had no more relation to their behavior than did traffic noises or other common sounds (Dennis & Dennis, 1951, pp. 106–109).

From this description, it is clear that the twins were raised in an environment as cold and as unstimulating as the Dennises could make it. Yet it was the Dennises and not the children who found the routine trying, so trying that they ended it before they had planned in order to respond in a normal way to the infants. Figure 3-2 illustrates the age at which certain behaviors appeared in each of the twins as compared with a normally raised sample of children also studied by the Dennises. In the figure the symbol ○ represents one of the twins and the symbol △ the other. The vertical bar represents the mean; the horizontal bar indicates the normal range. Although somewhat retarded in motor skills but less retarded in social responses, the twins' sequences of development seemed normal and their retardation slight. It should be noted, however, that the twin symbolized by △ suffered from moderate brain injury during birth and that some, if not all, of her slowness can be attributed to this.

Another method of testing whether walking is inherent or taught is to compare the performances of a set of identical twins in which one twin T is trained and the other C is not. In the first experiment to use this approach (Gesell & Thompson, 1929) the experimental twin T was trained to climb stairs while the control twin C was given no such training. Once T had learned to climb stairs both twins were tested on stair-climbing ability. In several studies of essentially maturational phenomena, it was found that C, merely by growing older and becoming more developed—as well as receiving normal environmental stimulation—was immediately the equal of T as soon as confronted by a test of behavior—in this case, stair climbing. Other studies of the same sort, such as McGraw's study of Johnny and Jimmy, discussed below, found C's ability inferior but "ready" for learning. Since C was now older than T was when trained, C could be trained to the same proficiency as T in far fewer sessions.

To move to another example, let us consider the McGraw (1940) study of bladder training. One twin, Hugh Putney, was initiated to the toilet at the age of 30 days and spent a large portion of his waking hours on it

Age in Weeks

	Cases	1	7	13	19	25	31	37	43	49	55	61	67	73

1. Fixate near object — 21
2. Start at sound — 15
3. Follow moving object — 17
4. Hand to mouth — 15
5. Head follows object — 13
6. Tears — 12
7. Smile at person — 20
8. Head up, supine — 11
9. Fixate distant object — 15
10. Vocalize vowel — 16
11. Grasp objects — 16
12. Chest up, prone — 9
13. Visual blink — 12
14. Vocalize to person — 11
15. Laugh — 24
16. Balance head — 9
17. Vocalize syllable — 13
18. Cry at sound — 17
19. Turn toward sound — 19
20. Nursing inhibited — 12
21. Object to mouth — 19
22. Watch own hand — 18
23. Play with own hands — 13
24. Stare at stranger — 15
25. Sit when propped — 13
26. Chest up, supine — 10
27. Vocalize two syllables — 13
28. Cry at stranger — 11
29. Crow — 10
30. Visually directed reaching — 26
31. Pull to sitting — 12
32. Grasp own foot — 14
33. Drop or throw object — 12
34. Supine to prone — 9
35. Cry at loss of toy — 10
36. Duplicated syllable — 11
37. Toes to mouth — 13
38. Grasp person's face — 13
39. Sit alone — 22
40. Pat, beat, or strike — 14
41. Roll several feet — 13
42. Rise to sitting — 10
43. Pull to kneeling — 10
44. Stand holding furniture — 11
45. Creep — 24
46. Walk holding furniture — 19
47. Pull to standing — 25
48. Walk when led — 14
49. Stand alone — 10
50. Few steps alone — 25

FIGURE 3-2   (Dennis & Dennis, 1951, p. 112.)

until the study ended, when he was 800 days old. For his twin, Hilton, bladder training was begun at 700 days. Figure 3-3 shows the respective patterns of their success. Since hereditary differences in the development of bladder control presumably remain constant, any gain on Hugh's part may be attributed to training and to the learning resulting from it. Indeed, other children may vary in the age at which maturation has reached the point that permits bladder control, but this study suggests that training prior to the age of maturational readiness has little value.

Several similar studies all have led to the same conclusion. So far as *phylogenetic* skills are concerned—those abilities, such as walking or toilet performance, that are common to all humans—early training consumes valuable time and does not often achieve more than a transitory improvement in skills. However, if one is willing to invest the enormous amount of time and effort required, one might find, as evidence suggests, that early training of motor behaviors results in increased expertness in such behaviors in later life. An earlier McGraw study of maturation (1935; both the book and a film entitled *Growth: A Study of Johnny and Jimmy* are available) supports this view. In this study twin T was trained in various motor skills from the age of 21 days to 22 months. The training was extremely extensive and may be seen in the book or film. The control twin received no special training, except for regular tests of motor ability, which might, in themselves, have constituted some train-

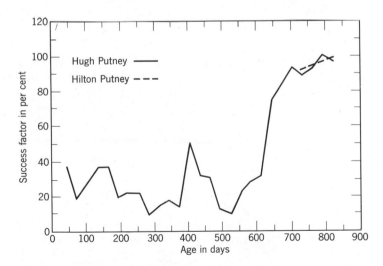

FIGURE 3-3 Achievement curves showing the percentages of successful responses to the toilet situation for twins whose training for bladder control was started at different times (McGraw, 1940, p. 586).

ing. As a result of his training the experimental twin advanced greatly in some ways; for example, he was an accomplished roller skater before he was two. His greatest superiority turned up in *ontogenetic* skills— that is, individual or uncommon skills—whereas he showed little superiority in phylogenetic skills such as walking. Among skills like climbing, which are probably phylogenetic but only slightly exercised in normal child development, the experimental twin also disclosed a considerable degree of superiority. The value of this experiment is decreased, however, by the fact that although these twins at first seemed identical, they were actually fraternal. Yet the great differences between them seem unlikely to result from genetic distinction. Of even greater interest is the knowledge that twin T, in tests conducted years after the differential training had ceased (McGraw, 1939), retained his motor advantages over twin C.

Mickey Mantle, the baseball player, is said by sportswriters to have been trained by his father in catching, throwing, and batting from the moment he could first respond. The McGraw study suggests that if someone wants badly enough to produce an expert and is prepared to spend the necessary amount of time, this is the right course to pursue. In the case of ontogenetic skills, the evidence points clearly to the efficacy of early training.

The co-twin approach is an excellent experimental procedure that has told us much of what we need to know regarding the effects of maturation on the development of skills. Although it has many advantages (see Vandenberg, 1966), it has not been used often in the last two decades. In recent years, however, both Fowler (1965) and Naeslund (1956) have used the co-twin approach on the very important problem of determining the most effective time and way of teaching children to read. Hopefully, this procedure may again become popular.

Readiness

Ontogenetic skills apparently can be acquired through training, as we have seen. Phylogenetic skills, in contrast, turn up in their own good time as a result of growth; neither training nor deprivation, within wide limits, has marked effect on their development. This suggests that an age of readiness exists for the appearance of many behaviors and that before this age these behaviors can be learned only with difficulty, if at all.

Readiness is discussed most frequently in relation to such academic skills as reading. The idea of reading readiness is of some utility; reading depends, for example, on the ability to discriminate symbols. This facility may be maturational. Nevertheless, some children learn to read much earlier than the age at which they are considered ready; according to Gates (1937) and others, this age is six and one-half years.[1]

If reading readiness is a common maturational skill, the variation in the age at which it is reached is far wider than in other areas of maturational development. It would thus seem that a number of unique factors contribute to the ability to read, only some of which contain maturational elements. One way to test this speculation, a way probably never tried to date, would be to obtain a large sample of children and subject different random subsamples of them to instruction in reading beginning at various ages, such as five, six, and seven. It would then become possible to measure the mean amount gained by each subsample during several intervals of time—six months, one year, two years. Insofar as ontogenetic skills bear on the process, the groups may be expected to gain about the same, whereas to the degree that phylogenetic skills are involved, the older group may be expected to benefit the most from such training. Those who believe that phylogenetic skills dominate in reading must suspect that the oldest group, quite apart from its advanced mental age, would benefit most from instruction in reading.

Let us consider some other research that seems to support the position that maturation may not be of as great importance in reading as the reading-readiness concept would imply. The length of time that a child will concentrate on a specific task is called the child's *attention span*. Attention span increases systematically with age. Van Alstyne (1932), for example, obtained mean attention spans of seven minutes for two-year-olds, 8.9 minutes for three-year-olds, 12.4 for four-year-olds, and 13.6 for five-year-olds. This increase might be assumed to be maturational. Perhaps it is. Highly relevant, however, are the findings of Moyer and Gilmer (1955), who used one simple toy, a red plastic automobile, and six carefully designed, relatively intricate toys as stimuli in a study of attention span. Some of their results appear in Table 3-2.

Two things may be noted. First, there is no age progression in length of attention span among the complex toys. Second, all of the spans are very high compared with those of many previous studies of this sort, of which many are reviewed by Moyer and Gilmer, or as compared with the attention span evoked by the toy automobile. Attention span is governed primarily by the type of stimulus—in this case, the type of toy—not by age. The results make it clear that the cliché about young children having too short an attention span to tackle a specific task is so

---

[1] For a discussion of children who learned to read at considerably earlier ages, see Fowler (1962).

TABLE 3-2   Mean Attention Span for Toys, in Minutes

Toy	Mean Attention Span by Age						
	1½	2	3	4	5	6	7
Red automobile			3.1	4.9	5.4		
Complex toy No. 1*	24.3	26.5	21.2	22.7	18.5		
Complex toy No. 2		34.0	32.9	32.4	28.9		
Complex toy No. 3			30.3	33.0	30.7		
Complex toy No. 4			15.6	22.2	26.7	31.9	
Complex toy No. 5				29.0	29.4	33.0	
Complex toy No. 6				39.2	35.0	39.7	28.5

* Each complex toy was not presented at each age level because they were designed to arouse interest within a limited age range.

much nonsense. If the task can be made challenging and interesting enough, even very young children have extremely long attention spans.

How does attention span apply to reading? It applies both directly and indirectly. In a direct sense teaching a child to read requires continued attention; indirectly, attention span is similar to reading readiness, for it purportedly shows a progression of age produced by maturation. Like attention span, reading readiness seems conditioned more by the amount of interest stimulated by the reading materials than by any development of phylogenetic skills. That is, reading readiness is more a matter of stimulation than maturation.

Now that Fowler (1965) and Moore (1966) have demonstrated that average children can learn to read by age three or four, the maturational point of view regarding reading readiness appears clearly incorrect. Presumably, in conventional methods of teaching reading, six and a half may be the cutoff point; but conventional methods of teaching reading are analogous to the red auto in Table 3-2; they do not appear to make use of potential that is present. We see no particular reason why three-year-olds should learn to read, but they can, if proper teaching procedures and materials are used—maturational concepts to the contrary.

Although evidence supports the tremendous importance of maturation in the development of simple motor behaviors such as walking, it seems evident that the concept of maturation has been extended too far when carried into more complex areas such as attention span or reading. Saying that a child has an "inadequate maturational level" (as shown by a limited attention span or by seeming inability to learn how to read) often is used by a teacher as an explanation for that child's limited gains. The explanation can be only partial, at best. Proper stimulus materials markedly increase attention span; innovative teaching techniques, such as those developed by Moore, dramatically increase rate of gain in reading ability.

Extreme Deprivation of Stimulation

Within a rather wide range, the deprivation of experience may result in nothing more than a temporary slowing down of the development of phylogenetic behaviors. Although moderate deprivation has no appreciable effect on the development of motor behaviors, severe deprivation has a profound influence. Moreover, there may be a *critical period* for the learning of certain common developmental skills. During this period any exposure to learning, even if brief, brings out behavior at a normal pace. Any exposure before this period has only a small, transient impact. But a lack of exposure, that is, a deprivation, until the period has passed, results in permanent injury, leaving a lasting inferiority.

In the first study pertaining to this area, von Senden (1932) examined medical reports written about people who were born nearly blind as a result of congenital cataracts. These individuals were often able to distinguish light from darkness but could not differentiate forms. Since some patients who have cataracts removed do achieve approximately normal vision (von Senden, 1932; London, 1960), these people presumably should have been capable of making adequate visual discriminations after undergoing appropriate surgery. Yet interestingly and surprisingly, when their cataracts were removed, some of them remained unable to make certain types of visual distinction. They could tell that the visual field was varied, but could not identify objects or describe their shapes from visual cues. When allowed to feel the objects, they were able to identify them immediately. Colors were perceived and named accurately as soon as color names were learned; color mazes were learned quickly. Nevertheless, it took many trials for an individual to learn even so simple a difference as that between a square and a triangle. After learning, if required to make this discrimination in a new setting or under new conditions of illumination, the individual was again unable to differentiate. Despite an apparently adequate, although perhaps somewhat abnormal, visual mechanism (see Riesen, 1960), many who were studied remained unable to distinguish between different persons on a purely visual basis even after years of visual experience. Furthermore, some of them could not learn to discriminate between objects on the basis of their shapes, despite seemingly normal vision. Others learned, but very slowly. Von Senden's findings suggested strongly that many aspects of vision were permanently impaired by lack of visual experience during a critical period ending somewhere above the age of four.

These data were based on individual patients, one physician reporting on a single patient. Such accounts do not constitute the best scientific data. Besides, these patients had learned to cope with the world through other sensory means, such as touch, so that the motivation to make full use of their newly acquired vision might not have been great. However, other studies of humans who have not had early visual experience also support the critical period view. Dennis (1934), although finding the data to be equivocal, reached many of the same conclusions as von Senden. London (1960), reporting on recent cataract patients in the U.S.S.R. whose cases were followed with more adequate scientific controls, fully supports von Senden. From all this, it seems likely that even innate behaviors cannot be at all adequate in later development unless they undergo at least some exercise during a critical period. In the same vein, a commonly held (but, so far as we are aware, never experimentally tested) belief of ophthalmologists and optometrists is that if crossed eyes are corrected before about age eight, the child will develop adequate binocular vision. If corrected after this time, a cosmetic effect will result, but each eye will be used in a monocular fashion, so that binocular cues to depth will not be of use to the individual.

MATURATION RELATED TO SOCIAL AND EMOTIONAL BEHAVIOR

So far, this chapter has dwelt entirely on the maturation of motor behaviors. More interesting and less well settled, however, is the influence of maturation on social and emotional behavior. One may well ask: to what extent are social and emotional responses maturational in character? How does deprivation affect these responses? Are there critical periods for learning them?

In an early and thorough investigation of emotion conducted by Darwin (1881; present reprint edition, 1955), the noted scientist presented several main arguments. If human emotional expressions evoked by a certain kind of stimulus were shared by animals lower than humans, he maintained, then evolutionary linkage to these lower orders would be proved. Second, if all humans, irrespective of age or culture, responded in the same way when expressing a given emotion, one would have to concede that specific emotional expressions arose as a result of natural selection and were inherited and innate in the human.

The following quotation from Darwin's writings pertains to the first hypothesis.

. . . Young chimpanzees make a kind of barking noise, when pleased by the return of any one to whom they are attached. When this noise, which the keepers call a laugh, is uttered, the lips are protruded; but so they are under various other emotions. Nevertheless I could perceive that when they were pleased the form of the lips differed a little from that assumed when they were angered. If a young chimpanzee be tickled—and the armpits are particularly sensitive to tickling, as in the case of our children,—a more decided chuckling or laughing sound is uttered; though the laughter is sometimes noiseless. The corners of the mouth are then drawn backwards; and this sometimes causes the lower eyelids to be slightly wrinkled. But this wrinkling, which is so characteristic of our own laughter, is more plainly seen in some other monkeys. The teeth in the upper jaw in the chimpanzee are not exposed when they utter their laughing noise, in which respect they differ from us (Darwin, 1955, p. 131).

In another quotation, Darwin deals with both hypotheses:

. . . That the chief expressive actions, exhibited by man and by the lower animals, are now innate or inherited,—that is, have not been learnt by the individual,—is admitted by everyone. So little has learning or imitation to do with several of them that they are from the earliest days and throughout life quite beyond our control; for instance the relaxation of the arteries of the skin in blushing, and the increased action of the heart in anger. We may see children, only two or three years old, and even those born blind, blushing from shame; and the naked scalp of a very young infant reddens from passion. Infants scream from pain directly after birth, and all their features then assume the same form as during subsequent years. These facts alone suffice to show that many of our most important expressions have not been learnt; but it is remarkable that some, which are certainly innate, require practice in the individual, before they are performed in a full and perfect manner; for instance, weeping and laughing. The inheritance of most of our expressive actions explains the fact that those born blind display them, as I hear from Rev. R. H. Blair, equally well with those gifted with sight. We can thus also understand the fact that the young and the old of widely different races, both with man and animals, express the same state of mind by the same movements (Darwin, 1955, pp. 350–351).

Darwin concluded that specific emotional expressions in response to particular emotional stimuli showed so great a degree of commonness that they had to be innate, inherited, and unlearned. On the other hand, certain emotions required practice before they could appear in their fullest form. Darwin was referring here to changes occurring with age which seemed likely to be the result of maturation rather than learning.

With its emphasis on innate characteristics, Darwinism was one of the forces that brought forth, in psychology, an environmentalist reaction led by John B. Watson (1919). Watson and others who shared his point of view believed that little human behavior was innate or unlearned; to the contrary, they held that a vast majority of behavior was learned. These "behaviorists" did much to make psychology a science by causing it to concern itself with observable, measurable behavior. Let us note that it was against such presumably innate characteristics as *instinctive motives,* rather than against phenomena now called maturational, that Watson's main criticism was directed.

The first experimental study of emotions by Watson and Morgan (1917) was undertaken to test the hypothesis that a large number of human emotions, such as fear of snakes or darkness, were innate to the species. By studying infants during the first months of life, they concluded that three basic, innate emotions were discernible. These emotions were fear, rage, and love. Fear, they maintained, was aroused chiefly by loss of support and by loud noises; it was *not* occasioned by experiences previously thought to be innately productive of fear, such as exposure to snakes or darkness. Rage emerged from restriction of movement, and love was the response to fondling and stroking.

This investigation inspired other psychologists to study the emotional development of infants. Some of these found reason to question parts of the Watson and Morgan conclusions. For example, Sherman (1927), in studying the responses of infants less than 12 days of age, noted that judges were unable to agree on the character of specific infant reactions *unless they saw the stimulus that preceded the response.* This suggests that adults read into the responses of the young infant the emotion that they themselves would feel if stimulated in the same way. As Watson and Morgan knew the stimulus preceding the response of their subjects, their observations were contaminated by this knowledge. They, too, may have read into the infant's responses the way that they would have felt under the same circumstances.

Another study to refute a portion of the Watson and Morgan findings was Dennis's (1940). This showed that infants habituated to restricted movement as a result of being reared on a cradleboard did not manifest any signs of anger because of the restrictions on their movements. Thus, it is possible that learning might have been involved in the responses of rage observed by Watson and Morgan, or else that the responses were provoked by "rough handling" rather than by restriction itself.

Other studies indicate, however, that specific forms of emotional responses to particular stimuli are unlearned. Again we turn to the fraternal twins raised by the Dennises. These twins were restricted in physical movement and also in exposure to the emotional responses of others. The Dennises, for example, did not smile at them. Having had no experience at seeing others smile, did the twins nevertheless respond with smiles?

> We wished also to know whether positive responses toward us would develop if we refrained from smiling at the twins and from petting, cuddling, and fondling them. In order to determine the answer to this question we avoided these expressions during the first 26 weeks. Withholding of demonstration of affections of this sort was not an easy task to impose upon ourselves, particularly as the subjects themselves were very expressive. From the 15th week onward they almost invariably greeted us with a smile and a vocalization. After this fact was thoroughly established, we decided in Week 27 to return their smile of greeting, and to speak to them as we approached (Dennis & Dennis, 1951, p. 109).

Clearly, smiling is a response to pleasurable events or experiences and is not the result of exposure to the smiling of others. As shown in Figure 3-2, even without social stimulation or opportunity for imitation, emotional responses such as smiling still occur at a normal time.

Similarly, a blind and deaf girl, who obviously had no opportunity to see others express emotions (Goodenough, 1932), displayed essentially the same responses to various forms of stimulation as children not subjected to such environmental deprivation. A more thorough and complex recent study and literature review of the emotional expressions of blind infants (Freedman, 1964) is in essential support of Goodenough. However, the *frequency* of emotional responsiveness such as smiling appears to depend on reinforcement from the environment (Brackbill, 1958; Freedman, 1964). Therefore, to the degree that reinforcement through visual experiences plays a role, we may expect blind infants and children to show a diminishing frequency of smiling behavior as compared with children who can see. As in most other maturational phenomena, experience facilitates and increases the frequency with which the behavior occurs.

Another study by Goodenough (1931) returns us to the problem of judges' ability to agree on the nature of infant responses. In her study, judges viewed pictures of a 10-month-old infant accompanied by captions describing various emotional states—dissatisfaction, astonishment, anger, pleasure, fear. The judges showed substantial agreement with the descriptions, indicating that the emotional expressions of a child of 10 months can be categorized with a fair amount of success. This, of course, counters Sherman's findings and supports Watson's and Morgan's position.

One further study pulls together the apparently contradictory findings into a unified whole. This is the frequently cited study by Bridges (1932), who observed for periods up to four months groups of children ranging in age from birth to slightly over two years. As shown in Figure 3-4, during the interval shortly after birth the only differentiation that could be made was between quietude and excitement. By six months a number of emotions might be distinguished from one another, whereas by two years even more emotional patterns might be reliably noted. The contradictory findings of Watson, Sherman, and Goodenough become understandable since each studied infants of markedly different ages.

The Bridges study suggests that Darwin was right. What is observed as a response associated with a specific emotion, such as blushing with shame, appears to be innate, that is, a result of maturation. In other words, emotional behaviors appear in a rather stable sequence, very much like motor behaviors. However, the frequency and intensity of emotional expression is largely learned. The feeling or emotion evoked by a stimulus has an element that is learned, and this phase of emotional development will be explored in later chapters. But once an emotion is felt the physical demonstration of the feeling seems largely *un*learned and indeed, as in the case of blushing, almost entirely beyond conscious control.

Critical Periods

Several students of emotions have suggested that the response of love depends on having received love during infancy, especially in the last half of the first year of life (see, for example, Ribble, 1943; Bowlby, 1952). Perhaps there is also a critical period in social and emotional development. In Chapter 9 we shall consider at length studies relating to the deprivation in infancy of love and other forms of stimulation. Those who believe that deprivation of contact with a single mother symbol during infancy causes a lasting emotional deficit, especially in the area of being able to give love, are often called the *maternal deprivation school*. Although this school is open to many criticisms, certain experiments support its view. However, not many of these are easily conducted among humans. Researchers are therefore obliged to search for analogous findings in the animal kingdom.

The ability of dogs (Melzack & Scott, 1957) and chimpanzees (Nissen, Chow, & Semmes, 1951) to adapt to pain stimuli requires early exposure to pain. Later exposure apparently produces little or no learning. A dog lacking early experience of pain will do such things as

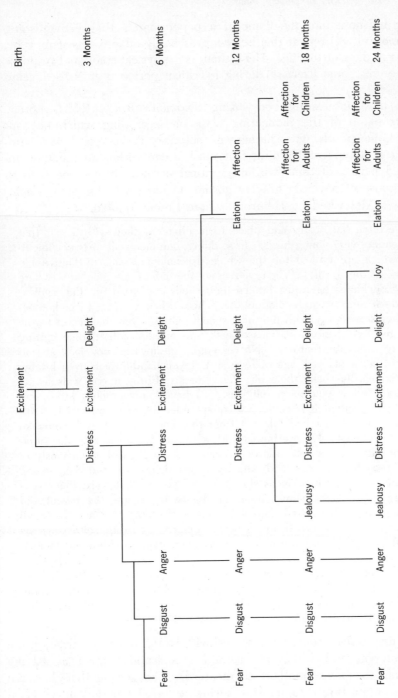

FIGURE 3-4 The approximate ages of differentiation of the various emotions during the first two years (from Bridges, 1932, p. 340. Copyright 1932 by the Society for Research in Child Development; published with permission).

103

putting his nose into the flame of a paper match, thus extinguishing the flame; he will repeat this behavior, as badly adaptive as it may be, over many days of testing. Here, then, is a physical-emotional response that requires some exercise during a critical period if it is to develop at all.

In a most interesting book, *King Solomon's Ring* (1952), Lorenz presents much of the pioneering work on *imprinting* which he conducted concurrently with Tinbergen (see also Tinbergen, 1953). Imprinting is a type of learning that must occur within an innately determined period of time—within a critical period. It may be seen in the response of a young graylag gosling to objects in its environment, which was described by Heinroth, whom Lorenz quoted.

> I have often had to try and place an incubator gosling with a pair that was leading very young birds. In so doing, one meets all sorts of difficulties, which are typical for the whole psychological and instinctive behavior of our birds. When you open the lid of an incubator where young ducklings have just broken their shells and dried off, they will at first duck and sit quite motionless. Then, when you try to pick them up, they scoot away with lightning speed. Quite often they jump to the floor and hide beneath various objects, and one has a hard time getting hold of the tiny creatures. Not so young goslings. They look at you without betraying any sign of fear; and, if you handle them even briefly, you can hardly shake them off. They peep pitifully if you walk away, and soon follow you about religiously. I have known such a little creature to be content if it could just squat under the chair on which I sat, a few hours after I had taken it from the incubator! If you then take such a gosling to a goose family with young of the same age, the situation usually develops as follows. Goose and gander look suspiciously at the approaching person, and both try to get themselves and their young into the water as quickly as they can. If you walk toward them very rapidly, so that the young have no chance to escape, the parents, of course, put up a spirited defense. This is the time to place the small orphan among the brood and leave in a hurry. In the excitement, the parents at first regard the newcomer as their own, and show an inclination to defend it as soon they see and hear it in human hands. But the worst is yet to come. It doesn't even occur to the young gosling to treat the two old birds as geese. It runs away, peeping loudly, and, if a human being happens to pass by, it follows him: it simply looks upon humans as its parents (Lorenz, 1957, pp. 103–104).

The first object to enter the gosling's world during a fixed, quite short interval and which fits certain specifications, such as having movement, becomes "mother" to the bird. The gosling that does not have the opportunity to imprint during its critical period never identifies itself with a mother. It is unable to attach itself to a mother symbol and engage in the behavior of "following" which Heinroth described.

The length of time during which imprinting may occur varies for different species. Among jackdaws, the period for imprinting lasts up to 20 days of age (Lorenz, 1957, p. 106), whereas for certain types of ducks, it is successful only between 11 and 18 hours after hatching.

Imprinting appears to become less rigid, time-bound, and irreversible as the order of mammals ascends. Yet certain patterns of imprinting are evident in higher mammals; bottle-reared lambs, for example, identify with humans, not with sheep (Scott, 1958, p. 179). Even so, it is perhaps unsound to generalize too widely from the experiences of other species to humans because even such closely related species as the goose, duck, and jackdaw differ considerably from one another in length of critical periods and in the irreversibility of imprinting. Among humans, imprinting certainly seems possible but has never been shown to occur. Showing interesting parallels in the patterns of socialization of canine and human infants, Scott (1963) subscribes to the view of a critical period in human maturation during which something closely akin to imprinting presumably takes place.

Moreover, the work of Harlow (1958) on various types of mothering of monkeys and their aftereffects also bears on any discussion of this sort. Harlow reared young monkeys with artificial substitute (*surrogate*) mothers. His artificial mothers fell into two major groups, as may be seen from his description of them and from Figure 3-5.

> . . . In devising this surrogate mother we were dependent neither upon the capriciousness of evolutionary processes nor upon mutations produced by chance radioactive fallout. Instead, we designed the mother surrogate in terms of modern human-engineering principles. . . . We produced a perfectly proportioned, streamlined body stripped of unnecessary bulges and appendages. Redundancy in the surrogate mother's system was avoided by reducing the number of breasts from two to one and placing this unibreast in any upper-thoracic, sagittal position, thus maximizing the natural and known perceptual-motor capabilities of the infant operator. The surrogate was made from a block of wood, covered with sponge rubber, and sheathed in tan cotton terry cloth. A light bulb behind her radiated heat. The result was a mother, soft, warm, and tender, a mother with infinite patience, a mother available twenty-four hours a day, a mother that never scolded her infant and never struck or bit her baby in anger. Furthermore, we designed a mother-machine with maximal maintenance efficiency since failure of any system or function could be resolved by the simple substitution of black boxes and new component parts. It is our opinion that we engineered a very

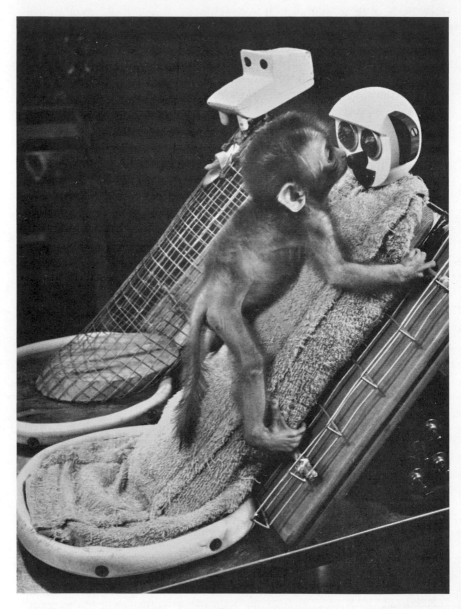

FIGURE 3-5   Cloth and wire mother surrogates were used to test the affection of infant monkeys.   The infants spent most of their time clinging to the soft cloth "mother" (foreground), even when nursing bottles were attached to the wire mother (background) (from Harlow, Scientific American, 1959, 200, p. 69; photograph by Gordon Coster).

superior monkey mother, although this position is not held universally by the monkey fathers.

Before beginning our initial experiment we also designed and constructed a second mother surrogate, a surrogate in which we deliberately built less than the maximal capability for contact comfort. This surrogate mother . . . is made of wire-mesh, a substance entirely adequate to provide postural support and nursing capability, and she is warmed by radiant heat. Her body differs in no essential way from that of the cloth mother surrogate other than in the quality of the contact comfort which we can supply . . . (Harlow, 1958, pp. 675–676).

A feeding bottle was attached to one of the mothers of each pair of monkeys. Even when fed by the wire-mesh mother, the young monkey spent a majority of its time clinging to the terry-cloth mother (see Figure 3-5). This suggests that body contact, not the primary reward of food when hungry, is the dominant factor that produces the young mammal's affection for its mother; terry-cloth mothers were good mothers, always there, never rejecting. The young monkey was not harmed by being reared by a terry-cloth mother; it was, in fact, more secure and emotionally stable than infant monkeys reared by their biological mothers (Harlow, 1958). *However,* monkeys reared by artificial mothers have been generally unable to mate (Harlow & Harlow, 1961).

The majority of cloth-mothered animals are sexually mature. Yet none of the males has achieved any semblance of normal sex behavior, even though they show sexual excitement during mating opportunities. The females have been slightly more responsive, no doubt because their role is relatively passive compared with the male's, although success has been achieved only with three and only after numerous exposures to selected breeding males. . . .

At the present time, we have very limited data on the effect of early mothering experience on the child's maternal affectional pattern, but we have discovered enough to present some fairly suggestive findings. As already stated, through the use of patient measures, one cage-raised and three cloth-mothered females were successfully bred. All are now raising their babies in a playpen situation. . . .

The first mother paid no attention whatsoever to her baby after it was born but, instead, would sit in her cage staring vacantly into space. She gave no evidence of protective maternal responses either when her infant was threatened or when the experimenter took the baby away several times a day for artificial feeding. As soon as the baby could locomote, it struggled desperately to establish a normal contactual relationship with its mother. It would climb on its mother's back only to be brushed away by the mother as if she were brushing off flies. When the baby persisted, the mother would crush the baby's face or body down on the floor of the cage with her hand or foot while either looking at the infant or staring blankly into open space . . . (Harlow & Harlow, 1961, pp. 54–55).

The other three mothers, themselves reared without a real monkey mother, were also quite inadequate as mothers with regard to their first offspring. However, when mated again, they were completely normal in their responses to second offspring. Deficiencies were reversible, as a result of experience in raising the first offspring (Seay, Alexander, & Harlow, 1964). These data, as well as a comparison of the offspring of normal monkey mothers that have had one, as opposed to more than one offspring (Mitchell, Ruppenthal, Raymond & Harlow, 1966), suggest that human firstborns are not unique in having more than their share of problems.

Festinger (1961) has suggested "that rats and people come to love things for which they have suffered." Perhaps punishment as well as reward is a necessary part of the mother-child relationship; hence, the young mammal that does not receive both during early immaturity— and conceivably within a specific critical period—may not make a normal social adjustment as an adult. In support of this statement, Rosenblum and Harlow (1963) found that surrogate mothers that were punishing as well as always loving and accessible evoked more affection from offspring than nonpunishing mothers of the same sort. The source of love and of punishment need not be the mother, however. Young monkeys reared with artificial mothers, who otherwise would be abnormal, are completely normal if allowed contact with agemates (Harlow, 1963). Like the work of students of imprinting, the work of Harlow is merely suggestive with respect to human infancy. It may, however, provide the key to understanding the crucial elements of early socialization, the timing of the development of emotional responses, and the consequences of inadequate rearing among humans, in terms of when stimulation should be applied or the type of stimulation to be used. In short, it may supply the clue to handling the critical period in the social and emotional development of children.

SUMMARY

Several human motor behaviors seem to result largely from genetically determined patterns of growth rather than from learning. Because of this, the sequence in which the behaviors occur does not differ appreciably between individuals. Neither special stimulation nor deprivation of experience, within fairly wide limits, appears to influence the development of those behaviors that are phylogenetic or common to all members of the species. However, special training of ontogenetic skills seems to benefit performance. Phylogenetic behaviors, although not affected by moderate deprivation, require at least some exercise during a critical period if permanent or near-permanent deficiencies are to be avoided.

The motor accompaniments of many emotional states seem to be unlearned and innate, yet require the individual to have reached a certain level of maturation before they can appear. Certain social and emotional responses *may* also require exercise during critical periods if they are to be present in the individual's repertoire of behaviors.

Least influential in the child's motor development, of only moderate importance in the development of emotional expression, but probably of prime importance in the development of social responsiveness, is the role of the parent.

REFERENCES

Aldrich, C. A., & Norval, M. A. A developmental graph for the first year. *Journal of Pediatrics*, 1946, 29, 304–308.

Bayley, N. The development of motor abilities during the first three years. *Monographs of the Society for Research in Child Development*, 1935, 1, 1, 3.

Bowlby, J. *Maternal care and mental health.* Geneva: World Health Organization, 1952.

Brackbill, Y. Extinction of the smiling response in infants as a function of reinforcement schedule. *Child Development*, 1958, 29, 115–124.

Bridges, K. H. B. Emotional development in early infancy. *Child Development*, 1932, 3, 324–341.

Darwin, C. R. *The expression of the emotions in man and animals.* New York: Philosophical Library, 1955.

DeFries, J. C., Weir, M. W., & Hegmann, J. P. Differential effects of prenatal maternal stress on offspring behavior in mice as a function of genotype and type of stress. *Journal of Comparative and Physiological Psychology*, 1967, 63, 332–334.

Dennis, W. Congenital cataract and unlearned behavior. *Journal of Genetic Psychology*, 1934, 44, 340–351.

Dennis, W. The effect of restricted practice upon the reaching, sitting and standing of two infants. *Journal of Genetic Psychology*, 1935, 47, 17–32.

Dennis, W. Infant development under conditions of restricted practice and of minimal social stimulation: A preliminary report. *Journal of Genetic Psychology*, 1938, 53, 149–157.

Dennis, W. Infant reactions to restraint. *Transactions of the New York Academy of Science,* 1940, Series II, **2,** 202–217.

Dennis, W. Infant development under conditions of restricted practice and of minimal social stimulation. *Genetic Psychology Monographs,* 1941, **23,** 143–189.

Dennis, W., & Dennis, M. G. Development under controlled conditions. In W. Dennis (Ed.), *Readings in child psychology.* New York: Prentice-Hall, 1951.

Dennis, W., & Dennis, M. G. The effect of cradling practice upon the onset of walking in Hopi children. *Journal of Genetic Psychology,* 1940, **56,** 77–86.

Erikson, E. H. *Childhood and society.* New York: Norton, 1950.

Festinger, L. The psychological effects of insufficient rewards. *American Psychologist,* 1961, **61,** 1–11.

Fowler, W. A study of process and method in three-year-old twins and triplets learning to read. *Genetic Psychology Monographs,* 1965, **72,** 3–90.

Fowler, W. Cognitive learning in infancy and early childhood. *Psychological Bulletin,* 1962, **59,** 116–152.

Frankenberg, W. K., & Dodds, J. B. (with J. F. Carland, E. G. Gloster, S. C. Hess, & S. R. Meachman). *Denver Developmental Screening Test.* Denver, Colo.: University of Colorado Medical Center, 1965.

Frankenberg, W. K., & Dodds, J. B. The Denver Developmental Screening Test. *Journal of Pediatrics,* 1967, **71,** 181–191.

Freedman, D. G. Smiling in blind babies and the issue of innate vs. acquired. *Journal of Child Psychology and Psychiatry,* 1964, **5,** 171–184.

Gates, A. I. The necessary mental age for beginning reading. *Elementary School Journal,* 1937, **37,** 497–508.

Gesell, A., & Thompson, H. Learning and growth in identical infant twins. *Genetic Psychology Monographs,* 1929, **6,** 1–124.

Goodenough, F. L. The expression of emotions in infancy. *Child Development,* 1931, **2,** 96–101.

Goodenough, F. L. Expressions of the emotions in a blind-deaf child. *Journal of Abnormal and Social Psychology,* 1932, **27,** 328–333.

Harlow, H. F. Effects of early experiences on personal-social, sexual, and maternal behavior. Paper read to the Society for Research in Child Development, Berkeley, California, April 11, 1963.

Harlow, H. F. The nature of love. *American Psychologist,* 1958, **13,** 673–685.

Harlow, H. F. Love in infant monkeys. *Scientific American,* 1959, **200,** 68–74.

Harlow, H. F., & Harlow, M. K. A study of animal affection. *Natural History,* 1961, **70,** 48–55.

Harlow, H. F., & Harlow, M. K. Effects de la privation precose de contacts sociaux chez les primates. *Revue de Medecine Psychosomatique,* 1966, **8,** 11–24.

Kawi, A. A., & Pasamanick, B.   Prenatal and paranatal factors in the development of childhood reading disorders.   *Monographs of the Society for Research in Child Development*, 1959, **24**, No. 4.

London, I. D.   A Russian report on the postoperative newly seeing.   *American Journal of Psychology*, 1960, **73**, 478–482.

Lorenz, K.   *King Solomon's ring: New light on animal ways.*   New York: Crowell, 1952.

Lorenz, K.   Companionship in bird life.   In C. H. Schiller (Ed.), *Instinctive behavior.*   New York: International Universities Press, 1957.

McGraw, M. B.   *Growth: a study of Johnny and Jimmy.*   New York: Appleton, 1935.

McGraw, M. B.   Later development of children specially trained during infancy. Johnny and Jimmy at school age.   *Child Development*, 1939, **10**, 1–19.

McGraw, M. B.   Neural maturation as exemplified in achievement of bladder control.   *Journal of Pediatrics*, 1940, **16**, 580–590.

Melzack, R., & Scott, T. H.   The effects of early experience on the response to pain.   *Journal of Comparative and Physiological Psychology*, 1957, **50**, 151–161.

Mitchell, G. D., Ruppenthal, G. C., Raymond, E. J., & Harlow, H. F.   Long term effects of multiparous and primiparous monkey mother rearing, *Child Development*, 1966, **37**, 781–791.

Montagu, M. F. A.   *Prenatal influence.*   Springfield, Illinois: Thomas, 1962.

Moore, O. K.   Autotelic responsive environments and exceptional children.   In O. J. Harvey (Ed.), *Experience, structure and adaptability,* New York: Springer, 1966. Pp. 169–216.

Moyer, K. E., & Gilmer, B. von H.   Attention spans of children for experimentally designed toys.   *Journal of Genetic Psychology*, 1955, **87**, 187–201.

Naeslund, J.   *Metodiken vid den forsta lasundervisningen.*   Stockholm: Norstedts, 1956.

Nissen, H. W., Chow, K. L., & Semmes, J.   Effects of restricted opportunity for tactual, kinesthetic and manipulative experience in the behavior of a chimpanzee.   *American Journal of Psychology*, 1951, **64**, 485–507.

Orlansky, H.   Infant care and personality.   *Psychological Bulletin*, 1949, **46**, 1–48.

Pasamanick, B., Rogers, M., & Lilienfeld, A.   Pregnancy experience and the development of behavior disorder in children.   *American Journal of Psychiatry*, 1956, **112**, 613–617.

Ribble, M. A.   *The right of infants.*   New York: Columbia University Press, 1943.

Riesen, A. H.   Effects of stimulus deprivation on the development and atrophy of the visual sensory system.   *American Journal of Orthopsychiatry*, 1960, **30**, 23–36.

Riesen, A. H., & Kinder, E. F.   *Postural development of infant chimpanzees:*

A *comparative and normative study based on the Gesell Behavioral Examination.* New Haven, Conn.: Yale University Press, 1952.

Robbins, M. P.   A study of the validity of Delacato's theory of neurological organization, *Exceptional Children,* 1966, **32,** 517–523.

Robbins, M. P.   Test of the Doman-Delacato rationale with retarded readers. *Journal of the American Medical Association,* 1967, **202,** 389–393.

Rosenblum, L. A., & Harlow, H. F.   Approach-avoidance conflict in the mother-surrogate situation. *Psychological Reports,* 1963, **12,** 83–85.

Scott, J. P.   *Animal behavior.* Chicago: University of Chicago Press, 1958.

Scott, J. P.   The process of primary socialization in canine and human infants. *Monographs of the Society for Research in Child Development,* 1963, **28,** No. 1.

Seay, B., Alexander, B. K., & Harlow, H. F.   Maternal behavior of socially deprived Rhesus monkeys. *Journal of Abnormal and Social Psychology,* 1964, **69,** 345–354.

Sherman, M.   The differentiation of emotional responses in infants: I. Judgments of emotional responses from motion picture views and from actual observation. *Journal of Comparative Psychology,* 1927, **7,** 265–284.

Shirley, M. M.   *The first two years of life.* (Vol. 2). Minneapolis: University of Minnesota Press, 1933.

Sontag, L. W.   Maternal anxiety during pregnancy and fetal behavior.   In *Physical and behavioral growth.*   Columbus, Ohio: Ross Medical Co., 1958.

Tanner, J. M.   Earlier maturation in man. *Scientific American,* 1968, **218,** 21–27.

Tinbergen, N.   *Social behavior in animals.* New York: Wiley, 1953.

Van Alstyne, D.   *Play behavior and choice of play materials of preschool children.* Chicago: University of Chicago Press, 1932.

Vandenberg, S. G.   Contributions of twin research to psychology. *Psychological Bulletin,* 1966, **66,** 327–352.

Von Senden, M.   Space and sight: The perception of space and shape in the congenitally blind before and after operation.   (Translated by P. Heath) New York: Free Press of Glencoe, 1960.   (Original German edition, Leipzig: Barth, 1932)

Watson, J. B.   *Psychology from the standpoint of a behaviorist.* Philadelphia: Lippincott, 1919.

Watson, J. B., & Morgan, J. J. B.   Emotional reactions and psychological experimentation. *American Journal of Psychology,* 1917, **28,** 163–174.

Weir, M. W., & DeFries, J. C.   Prenatal maternal influence on behavior in mice: Evidence of a genetic basis. *Journal of Comparative and Physiological Psychology,* 1964, **58,** 412–417.

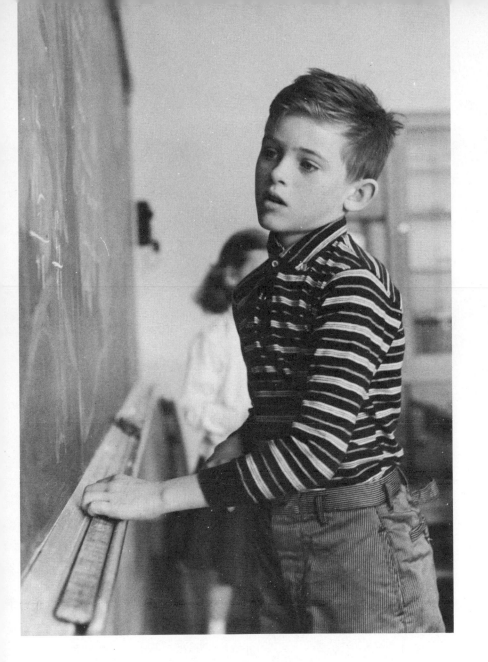

4

Learning and Motivation

Although some human behaviors appear to have larger unlearned than learned components, most human behavior is learned. The behaviors we learn come about through a pattern of reacting to stimuli and to the reward accompanying such reaction; the response may either be initiated by the human organism itself or copied from the responses of some other organism. Either way, the human differs in this respect from lower orders of the plant and animal worlds, which inherit their major patterns of response, even though these behaviors may be inspired by specific conditions in the environment. Learning, of course, takes many forms, which gradually become more complex from childhood to adulthood or from simple to more intricate organisms. In this chapter we shall explore these various forms and then the forces that motivate learning.

LEARNING

Essentially, there are two kinds of learning—simple and complex. Setting aside for the present the latter category, let us consider the two techniques through which simple learning occurs. Simple learning is either *respondent* or *operant*. Respondent learning is the classical method of conditioning often called *Pavlovian* after the Russian physiologist I. P. Pavlov (1927). In this type of learning the organism remains relatively passive as it learns; all that is required of it is to respond. Operant learning, on the other hand, engages the active participation of the organism seeking to learn. It is a trial-and-error process, sometimes called *instrumental* learning, in which the organism acts and in so doing generates results.

Both forms of simple learning blend together at times, so that in some cases it may be difficult to say whether a given behavior is learned in an operant or respondent way. However, the two forms generally can be distinguished from one another.

Operant and respondent learning may have differing degrees of importance as age changes. In general, young humans (below age three) seem likely to learn most rapidly in respondent learning situations. On the other hand, Turner and Solomon (1962) have demonstrated that older humans learn more efficiently, at least with regard to some kinds of stimuli, when operant learning techniques are used.

Respondent Learning

Pavlov had already won a Nobel Prize for his work on gastric secretions by the time he turned his attention to his now famous experiments on conditioned reflexes. Noting that the dogs he used in his experiments salivated before food entered their mouths, he saw that the mere presence of food or even the sound of the keeper's footsteps was enough to bring on salivation. Pavlov was so taken by this phenomenon that he dedicated the latter part of his life to pursuing it and its implications.

An organism instinctively responds to a stimulus in some concrete manner. The dog salivates, for example, on the presentation of food. This salivation is assumed to be innate and not learned. The dog is exposed to the sound of a bell and is then given food in the form of meat powder. After several repetitions of this pattern, the dog salivates at the sound of the bell even before the food arrives. The meat powder is called the *unconditioned stimulus* and the salivation it engenders, the unconditioned response or *unconditioned reflex*. The bell is the *conditioned stimulus* and the salivation occasioned by its sound, in the absence of the meat powder, is the conditioned response or *conditioned reflex*.

Besides the conditioned stimulus itself, other stimuli resembling it also produce the same effect. Thus, if an organism is conditioned to respond to a medium tone of bell, it will also react to a high or a low tone, although to a lesser degree. This phenomenon is known as *stimulus generalization* because it extends the power of the stimulus to other objects and events. The spread of effect from the positive stimulus to all stimuli like it was believed by Pavlov to be a powerful influence in learning. As we shall see when we consider complex learning later in the chapter, stimulus generalization contributes significantly to the concepts human organisms form.

The conditioned reflex diminishes and eventually ceases if the conditioned stimulus is presented repeatedly without the accompanying unconditioned stimulus. The conditioned reflex is then said to have been *extinguished*. Yet, curiously enough, this cessation may not be final. An environmental change can revive the reflex. Even a small change in the surroundings, such as slamming a door, is sometimes enough to reawaken an extinguished response for a time.

Several well-known examples of conditioning in humans illustrate the process. The first is the case of "Little Albert" who was conditioned by Watson and Rayner (1920). As remarked in Chapter 3, Watson believed that the young child was innately afraid of sudden, loud noises. In an experiment that demonstrated the fear of sudden loud noises, Watson and Morgan (1917) also found that infants showed no fear of darkness, snakes, or other stimuli which to that time had been thought to be innately or instinctively productive of fear. Watson therefore concluded that all fears, except for those involving sudden loud noises or loss of support, were learned—and further, were learned through conditioning. His experiment with Rayner around a nine-month-old boy, "Little Albert," demonstrated the conditioning of the fear response.

The infant was presented with a white rat. He was not afraid of it. Thereafter, whenever the rat was presented to the boy, a steel bar was struck, producing a sudden loud noise. Following relatively few conditioning trials, Little Albert responded to the rat with reactions of fear. In addition, he was also afraid of a fur coat, a rabbit, a Santa Claus mask, and a wad of absorbent cotton. Rather wide stimulus generalization had occurred, apparently among soft, white, hairy substances.

The Watson and Rayner study of "Little Albert" may well have influenced the plot of Aldous Huxley's *Brave New World* (1932). In this imaginary society of the future, ability is determined by the amount of oxygen allowed to enter the bloodstream of a fetus, which is grown in an artificial uterus. Each intelligence group is so adapted as to be best able to perform a given level of job. Problems of overproduction are solved by conditioning individuals to consume, whereas such nonconsumptive behaviors as enjoying books or nature are extinguished. This conditioning process is described in the following passage from the book and illustrated in Figure 4-1.

Turned, the babies at once fell silent, then began to crawl towards those clusters of sleek colours, those shapes so gay and brilliant on the white pages. As they approached, the sun came out of a momentary eclipse behind a cloud. The roses flamed up as though with a sudden passion from within, a new and profound significance seemed to suffuse the shining pages of the books. From the ranks of the crawling babies came little squeals of excitement, gurgles and twitterings of pleasure.

The Director rubbed his hands. "Excellent!" he said. "It might almost have been done on purpose."

The swiftest crawlers were already at their goal. Small hands reached out uncertainly, touched, grasped, unpetaling the transfigured roses, crumpling the illuminated pages of the books. The Director waited until all were happily busy. Then, "Watch carefully," he said. And, lifting his hand, he gave the signal.

The Head Nurse, who was standing by a switchboard at the other end of the room, pressed down a little lever.

There was a violent explosion. Shriller and even shriller, a siren shrieked. Alarm bells maddeningly sounded.

The children started, screamed, their faces were distorted with terror.

"And now," the Director shouted (for the noise was deafening), "now we proceed to rub in the lesson with a mild electric shock."

He waved his hand again, and the Head Nurse pressed a second lever.

FIGURE 4-1   Conditioning in *Brave New World.*

The screaming of the babies suddenly changed its tone. There was something desperate, almost insane, about the sharp spasmodic yelps to which they now gave utterance. Their little bodies twitched and stiffened; their limbs moved jerkily as if to the tug of unseen wires.

"We can electrify that whole strip of floor," bawled the Director in explanation. "But that's enough," he signalled to the nurse.

The explosions ceased, the bells stopped ringing, the shriek of the siren died down from tone to tone into silence. The stiffly twitching bodies relaxed, and what had become the sob and yelp of infant maniacs broadened out once more into a normal howl of ordinary terror.

"Offer them the flowers and the books again."

The nurses obeyed; but at the approach of the roses, at the mere sight of those gaily-coloured images of pussy and cock-a-doodle-doo and baa-baa black sheep, the infants shrank away in horror; the volume of their howling suddenly increased.

"Observe," said the Director triumphantly, "observe."

Books and loud noises, flowers and electric shocks—already in the infant mind these couples were compromisingly linked; and after two hundred repetitions of the same or a similar lesson would be wedded indissolubly. What man has joined, nature is powerless to put asunder.

"They'll grow up with what the psychologists used to call an instinctive hatred of books and flowers. Reflexes unalterably conditioned. They'll be safe from books and botany all their lives." The Director turned to his nurses. "Take them away again" (Huxley, 1932, pp. 21–22).

Despite the potentially negative use, described above, classical conditioning has many practical applications with infants and young children. For example, conditioning involving sound often has been used in testing infants for deafness when they still are so young that other procedures are not feasible (Glorig, 1965). Classical conditioning procedures have been used most effectively for decades in such areas as toilet training (Mowrer & Mowrer, 1938) and, as discussed in Chapter 16, have now been used in the treatment of many other types of problem behavior. In the Mowrer and Mowrer treatment of bed wetting, the child sleeps on a pad. The pad is electrically wired, so that the voiding of the bladder causes a circuit to be completed, which rings a bell. The bell, in this case, is the unconditioned stimulus, and the unconditioned response is waking. Since bladder tension is paired with the bell, it becomes the conditioned stimulus, evoking the conditioned response of waking. So now the child wakes up and *then* wets the bed. The conditioning procedure described above must be combined with the building in of a set of operant behaviors leading to a trip to the bathroom, resulting in an effective treatment of bed wetting.

It seems clear that much infant learning is respondent learning; learning procedures that are basically respondent have been shown to influence behavior such as sucking (Lipsitt, Kaye, & Bosack, 1966) and responding to olfactory (Engel, Lipsitt, & Kaye, 1963) and kinesthetic (Kaye, 1965) stimuli in the first few days of life. Later, though still in infancy, the frequency of vocalization (Rheingold, Gewirtz, & Ross, 1959), of smiling (Brackbill, 1958), and of crying (Etzel & Gewirtz, 1967) have been modified through the use of respondent learning procedures.

These procedures typically involve positive reinforcement or reward of the behaviors that the experimenter wishes to increase and/or non-reinforcement (neither reward nor punishment) of behaviors that the experimenter wishes to decrease in frequency.

Much learning is respondent, in adults as well as in infants. Simple enough in principle, it may be used to account for most, if not all, human learning. Watson (1919) thought so, and the Soviets continue to think so (see Razran, 1961). Russian acceptance of classical conditioning as the only form of learning, although quite foreign to American way of thinking, has, as Brackbill (1960) has noted, produced research of both practical and theoretical importance. However, most American psychologists, unlike their Soviet colleagues, believe also in a second way of learning—the operant way.

Operant Learning

One of the foremost early students of learning was E. L. Thorndike. Concentrating his investigations on lower organisms rather than on humans, he placed his subjects in mazes and puzzle boxes where they were neither required to show sudden understanding of a problem at hand nor called on to solve it. Instead they had to learn a set of motor responses that had essentially no pattern, that is, no right-left-right-left turns. Thorndike (1913) noted, not surprisingly, that much like illiterates learning to find their way about a strange city without assistance, his organisms decreased their errors of entering blind alleys only slowly. Correspondingly, the amount of time they required to get from the start of the maze to the goal decreased slowly. From this, Thorndike concluded that learning in lower organisms was slow and lacked insight. He further believed that human learning was also of this trial-and-error sort.

Consider the acquisition of the ability to ride a bicycle. Complex operant or trial-and-error behaviors, as Skinner (1958, 1960) has shown, can be learned by organisms. Such learning occurs most rapidly when the "method of approximations" is used in the training process and the learner tries to approximate or imitate the behavior of others. There is no magic way of learning to ride a bicycle; learning must take place by a simple, trial-and-error procedure. The beginner falls frequently, whenever he leans too far to one side to retain his balance at the speed at which he is then moving. But as he is highly impelled to ride, even crude approximations of bicycle-riding behavior bring him gratification; to be able to move even a few feet without falling is at first rewarding, indeed, a victory. Behaviors that lead to this victory tend to be repeated as a result of *positive reinforcement*. Meanwhile, the behaviors that precede falling begin to diminish in frequency. As the rewarding behaviors gradually increase, the child ultimately reaches the point at which he rides off alone, tipsy, insecure, and not really inspiring confidence in either himself or anyone watching. Eventually, of course, he makes it.

There is nothing intrinsically different between a child learning to ride a bicycle and a rat learning to run a maze. For both, learning is a slow, gradual, trial-and-error process in which rewarded responses are retained while those that do not bring reward are eliminated. Most likely, a substantial proportion of learning in infancy and childhood, such as the acquisition of motor skills or of speech, consists largely of simple operant activity, common to all organisms. As discussed in Chapter 16, many forms of psychotherapy now make use of these simple, operant procedures, usually to good effect. Though respondent and operant learning may decrease in relative significance for the human with increasing age, they always are important forms of learning that may be used to change or modify behavior.

Learning Sets

It is a mark of progress to pass from the simple to the complex. But such transitions are not always easily made. Often they require some extra effort or some intermediate step. In learning, many believe that one connecting link is an understanding of *learning sets,* a concept that was developed by Harlow (1949) in the course of his experiments with monkeys. Learning sets, in substance, are groups of habits employed by organisms in the process of learning. Subjects in experiments on learning sets are presented with a series of problems. Each of these problems has its own stimuli, which are entirely different from those of the remaining problems, yet each must be solved by application of the same learning habits. If the organism learns the habits rather than the simple, operant solution to a particular problem, it can then apply them to any succeeding problem. The organism has learned to learn; it can extend its responses to other situations, transfer its habits of problem solving from one problem to the next. The organism has thus developed a *learning set,* by which it can cope with even unusual situations. Indeed, the learning set leads directly, as we shall soon see, to the formation of concepts, one of the principal forms of complex learning.

There are wide differences in the speed at which various species establish learning sets. Although it may take 100 or more trials for a monkey to acquire a learning set (Harlow, 1949), very young humans (Koch & Meyer, 1959) or severely retarded humans of below 50 IQ (Fehmi, 1960) develop them quite rapidly, often in fewer than 10 series of problems. As a rule primates are markedly superior to nonprimates in this form of learning, even when previous learning has been controlled. Moreover, there are great differences even among members of a primate order in the development of learning sets. That humans surpass other primates and primates surpass nonprimates suggests a distinct superiority among primates—and especially humans—in the transfer of old learning to new problems. It is this ability to transfer that contributes substantially to the formation of concepts.

Concept Formation

In simple learning adults are not always superior to young children, nor do humans invariably surpass other organisms. But in complex learning, to which we now shift attention, wide chasms separate all these groups. Except in rare instances, the human excels all others in the various forms of complex learning—concept formation, thinking, and creativity.

It is quite possible that from coping with problems that develop in a learning situation, a subject may evolve a concept for solving them all. Yet this is not necessarily so. The subject might actually solve each problem independently without ever becoming aware of a common principle or concept applicable to the entire series. Concept formation requires an organism to develop an understanding, which can be measured by the organism's behavior, that certain objects, events, or characteristics of a stimulus have a common element. On the basis of this element the organism then classifies the phenomena. The actual source of the concept lies in respondent or operant learning. It is the transfer—or generalization—of what is learned to other situations sharing common elements that constitutes the formation of a concept.

Humans generalize more adequately than other organisms. In large measure they succeed more widely than others in transferring learning because they have the facility of language. *Transposition,* in learning, involves learning to make a relational choice. In the example below, transposition means learning to choose the higher of two tones, no matter to what particular pair of tones the subject is exposed. Subjects are exposed to two musical tones, *do* and *re,* and are rewarded for choosing *re.* Once they learn to choose *re,* they are exposed to succeeding pairs such as *re-mi, mi-fa, fa-sol,* and so on. Lower organisms will choose the higher of the two tones only when it is one step removed from the learned tone. Beyond this point they tend to choose the stimulus most similar to the one rewarded in the original training session. For example, they would choose *mi* in a *mi-fa* choice situation. However, human children able to use words to describe the learning principle involved seem capable of transposing and generalizing responses to new stimuli no matter how far removed these may be from the original learning stimuli (Alberts & Ehrenfreund, 1951; Kuenne, 1946). Problems of transposition, such as establishing the conditions under which it will occur, are among the most intriguing that psychology has to offer (see Hebert & Krantz, 1965), partly because transposition is an area in which humans and nonhumans, or verbal as opposed to nonverbal humans, differ greatly in the way that they respond to a task.

Discrimination learning occurs whenever an organism learns to choose one stimulus rather than other stimuli because he is rewarded for making the particular choice. *Discrimination reversal,* or *cue reversal,* is another type of task that appears to produce substantial differences between children who can as opposed to those who cannot use verbal mediators in dealing with a learning task. The typical discrimination-reversal task goes something like this: The child is presented with a red circle and a white square, with the position of the two objects varying randomly between trials. He is rewarded for choosing the red circle. Then, after the habit has been learned thoroughly (i.e., the subject has chosen the red circle on 14 out of 15 successive trials), the ground rules are changed; the white square now is rewarded. Young children generally find this second task, overcoming a learned preference for the red circle and responding to the white square, more difficult than an entirely new task, while older children learn the new set of reward contingencies associated with the circle and square very rapidly (Kendler, Kendler, & Wells, 1960). Results in discrimination reversal are similar to those in transposition, in which children may have the verbal terms needed but will not transpose in tests of far transposition unless they not only know, but also *use* verbal cues in learning (Kuenne, 1946; Cole, Dent, Eguchi, Fujii, & Johnson, 1964). In the same sense, children may have the necessary verbal labels in a discrimination reversal situation, yet discrimination reversal is a most difficult task unless the labels are *both* available and used in learning (Kendler, Kendler, & Wells, 1960). These areas of research suggest that the use of verbal mediators produces a rather abrupt change in the manner in which learning takes place, and in the generalization of this learning to comparable new learning tasks.

The learning of both concrete and abstract concepts seems to gain from language. Words provide additional, constant cues for the distinguishing of different "concrete" objects. Spoons, for example, vary in size and shape; nevertheless, they have enough common elements to fall into a single perceptual grouping. Despite their variations, they are identical in name, which facilitates development of the concept of "spoon." The mere presence of a name imposes limits on the concept more simply and perhaps more accurately for the young child than would a variety of stimuli lacking a name. Language simplifies the formation of concepts and also reduces the differences between individuals in the content of their concepts.

Language also enables the adequate development of "abstract" concepts that are independent of specific concrete physical stimuli or physical reference. Since specific objects cannot serve as cues in these cases, learning tends to be slower than for concrete concepts. Those concepts with few or misleading—sometimes both—verbal designations are generally considered abstract and are learned slowly and often erroneously (Johnson, 1962b; Voeks, 1954). This may be seen in the study of animism, the belief that certain important objects in the environment are living, or that they have some conscious purpose. Whether children (see Piaget, 1930) or college students (see Dennis, 1953), subjects have an inadequate concept of life, of what is alive. They attribute animacy to many nonliving things, such as the sun, the ocean, and a lighted match. The inadequacy of the concept appears to result from the sparseness and at times misleading nature of the verbal terms used to define life. The attribute of life most commonly mentioned is movement. But this is actually a characteristic shared by the animate and the inanimate, such as the railroad engine, the automobile, or the sun; hence an accurate demarcation between living and nonliving, and therefore an adequate concept of life, is difficult to obtain as long as movement remains life's chief criterion. Probably because of this, children have more difficulty in determining whether moving objects are alive than they do in determining whether things that do not move are alive (Laurendeau & Pinard, 1962).

Concept formation, then, rests on the bases of generalizing and transferring learning across stimuli, processes that are common to man and lower organisms. Man's supremacy over other organisms stems from the ability to organize in a wide variety of ways, through the use of symbols, a greater amount of experience, only some of which is sensory. Although not unique to humans, concept formation is an area of learning in which human capacity far exceeds that of other organisms.

Thinking

The leading theories on children's thinking come from the European psychological tradition and are intimately tied to theories of concept formation. Best represented in American circles by Werner (1957), they have also been given attention in several critiques published in the United States (Fowler, 1962; Johnson, 1962b). These theories maintain that the thought processes of children differ in quality from those of adults.

The best known and most comprehensive of these theories was developed by the Swiss psychologist Jean Piaget (see Flavell, 1963, for a most comprehensive summary and evaluation of Piaget's research). In his view, a child passes through three stages of mental activity en route to maturity. First, there is a *sensorimotor* stage in which action is governed by sensations; simple learning occurs, but the child does not think. Next, the child moves into a phase of egocentricity; by *egocentricity* Piaget means neither selfishness nor self-centeredness, but more likely the inability to put oneself in the place of another. The major portion of this period, also termed *concrete operational*, lasts from the age of seven or eight to the age of 11 or 12; during it, the child is concerned with concrete ideas. In this stage the formation of concepts is felt to involve "operational groupings concerning subjects that can be manipulated or known through the senses" (Piaget, 1952, p. 123). Finally, the child advances to the stage of abstract concepts; "from 11–12 years and during adolescence, formal thought is projected and its groupings characterize the completion of reflective thought" (p. 123). By "reflective thought" Piaget refers to the ability to form adequate abstract concepts.

Piaget's theory might well be included in the chapter on growth and maturation; it is in many ways a maturational theory, in the sense that a child progresses through a set of stages of intellectual development in an orderly and invariant fashion. Environment does enter in, since experiences help the child to move from one stage of development to another.

Piaget's research has touched on many areas, but all of his investigations have had as a central aim the discovery of the nature of intelligence —its function, structure, and content—as well as the means by which it changes with age and experience. To Piaget, a biologist, the purpose of intelligence is to enable an organism to make adaptations of the environment that increase the probability of survival. Behavior is the action taken by the organism to establish and maintain states of equilibrium with the environment (Piaget, 1960). The organism attains this equilibrium by adaptation to the environment through *assimilation,* the influence of the organism on environment, and *accommodation,* the influence of the environment on the organism. Thus, by actively manipulating the environment (assimilation), and, somewhat more passively, being acted on by the environment (accommodation), a child comes, over time, to have an accurate understanding of reality. Piaget's position to this point is environmentalistic. However, his sequence of development through sensorimotor, concrete operational, and formal operational (abstract) thought must be invariant and maturational.

Every new experience is understood by a child on the basis of all relevant previous experiences. A given new experience is often misperceived because the child's inadequate understanding of the event is based on his previously held incorrect interpretations of reality. Yet each new experience brings him new information, and this new information finally leads to a modification of his understanding of the world. If the child is presented with an experience he cannot understand, he will transform it into something that he can understand. He himself is changed by the new experience, however, so that he may arrive at a more adequate understanding of the experience as a result of the experience itself. An example of this kind of development is seen in Piaget's work on the development in children of the *concept of conservation of substance*.

The concept of conservation is a general rule that the shape of an object can be changed, but, so long as nothing is added to or taken away from the object, its substance remains the same. For example, if two clay balls are of equal size, and one of them is made into a sausage shape, there is still the same amount of clay in both. An experimenter and a child agree that the two balls are of the same size; the experimenter then changes the shape of one of them and asks the child whether there is as much clay in the sausage as in the ball. The child has attained the concept of conservation if he says yes, and can explain why it is so (nothing added, nothing taken away, just changed shape).

A young child has a tendency to believe that things that change in shape change in quantity as well. Often, of course, this is true; a half-gone ice cream cone has changed in shape *and* quantity, and it is difficult for a young child to separate these effects. Given sufficient experience, however, he may come to see that changes in shape need not necessarily indicate changes in quantity. Testing a child on a number of conservation tasks in the manner described above frequently causes him to move rapidly toward an understanding of conservation of substance (Randall, 1967). Apparently the mere fact that he is required to make judgments of this sort produces sufficient dissonance, or, to use Piaget's term, "disequilibrium," that he is forced to re-evaluate his beliefs. Further, if the child himself makes the transformation, a sufficiently greater disequilibrium leads him to more frequently manifest conservation of substance (Johnson & Developmental Seminar, 1967). Finally, if a child manipulates the stimuli (e.g., makes the clay ball into a sausage) and, further, manipulates the stimuli in two directions (from a ball into a sausage; from a sausage into a ball), conservation responses are markedly increased over those shown in child-manipulated, one-way transformations, so that even four-year-olds frequently show a grasp of conservation of substance (Simmons & Johnson, 1968), though conservation is relatively rare even in five-year-olds when conventional procedures (experimenter manipulates stimuli, one-way transformations) are used. The increasingly obvious dissonance between previously held beliefs and experience appears to account for the obtained increase in conservation responses.

Piaget's work holds up remarkably well in some ways. For example, despite the fact that children are suggestible (in the sense that if they are asked whether two clay objects are the same they will probably say yes; if, instead, they are asked whether the two objects are different they are also likely to agree), in this instance it makes little difference how the question is phrased, as long as it is in simple and unambiguous language. If they have attained a grasp of conservation they will say that the ball and the sausage are the same; if they have not, they will say the two are different (Pratoomraj & Johnson, 1966).

Despite his concern for experience, Piaget states in nearly all of his writings that changes in the nature of the thought process occur at given ages without consideration for differences in experiences that might confirm or disconfirm previously held beliefs. He says, in effect (though he does not always mean to), that thought processes change with advances in age by sudden (saltatory) jumps. Thus any given five-year-old would differ qualitatively from any given 12-year-old in the way he thinks.

Piagetan theory really does not rest on the idea that given changes in capacity occur at given ages, but rather on the proposition that these changes are sequential, with absolute rate of change through the sequence resulting from experience. Piaget has confused the issue by emphasizing age of change in both his early and his recent work. But the real task of the psychologist is not to investigate further the age at which certain abilities come into existence, but to determine the kinds of child-environment interaction that cause the change to occur. An even greater problem is to evaluate fully the main thrust of Piaget's theorizing—that qualitative differences exist between the thought processes of young children and older ones.

Opposed to the Piagetan view that children's thinking differs in quality from that of adults is the position, expressed less often, that children think in the same way as adults, only on the basis of less adequate information. Presumably, abstract concepts should be formed only after about 12 years of age. However, research on children shows clearly that such concepts are formed rather early, but with inaccurate or insufficient content. The three-year-old has a concept of life; adults just happen to believe that the *content of his concept* is wrong if he attributes life to a racing locomotive. But to be wrong in terms of concept content is far different from being incapable of dealing with the concept at all.

Examination of intelligence tests shows that items do not appear to change appreciably in character from middle childhood on to adulthood.

The correlations between a given individual's test scores across time—for example, the correlations between IQ at age 11 and at age 18 for a group of subjects—are quite high (Honzik, McFarlane & Allen, 1948), and factor analyses reveal that the same basic factors (e.g., numerical ability, spatial ability, word fluency) make up tested intelligence in childhood, adolescence, and young adulthood (Thurstone & Thurstone, 1941). While it is true that intelligence tests do not measure all domains of thought and cognition, the results described above suggest that although a gradual accretion of knowledge occurs in the interval between age seven and adulthood, no qualitative changes in the nature of intelligence occur during this time interval. Further, studies interpreted as supporting Piaget's developmental stages in cognition show no more than a gradual increase to occur with age in ability to deal with various presumably abstract problems (e.g., see Elkind, 1961).

So much for the way behavior and knowledge are acquired. Through these various techniques organisms learn the things they need to know in order to survive. Indeed, learning is crucial to survival. But how does the necessity to survive make organisms learn? How do forces in the environment and in the organisms themselves activate the many techniques of learning? They do so by stimulating the organism, by supplying it with motivation to learn, and by reinforcing or not reinforcing the things that are learned. Because learning and motivation are almost two fitting pieces of the same jigsaw puzzle, the rest of this chapter deals with the second piece, motivation—including the effects of reinforcement and nonreinforcement on learning and behavior.

MOTIVATION

Motivation is the force or condition within the organism that impels it to act or respond. Presumably organisms are motivated by physiological needs, such as hunger or thirst. These needs generate drives, that is, tendencies to behave in a manner likely to reduce the needs. Indeed, there is widespread belief that behaviors will be learned only if they can reduce an organism's needs or tensions.

The primary needs of an organism are biological—hunger, thirst, and, to a lesser degree, sex. In a society of plenty, such as American civilization, it is not often likely for drives engendered by primary needs to produce behavior among children or adults. Rather *secondary* drives, derived from primary drives, are considered to be more significant. The infant's affection for its mother comes from her feeding it; she reduces its primary drive of hunger. Not only is the feeding rewarding to the infant, but so is the mother, because she is always associated with reduction of the hunger. She becomes rewarding in her own right, if only on a secondary basis; this secondary reward, or *reinforcement,* is taken to be the basis for human socialization. The infant now needs the mother as well as the food and expands this need to encompass human beings in general. Although plausible, this explanation of the relationship between mother and child may not be correct. In Chapter 3, it will be recalled, Harlow's data (1958) regarding monkeys indicated that the development of infantile affection had nothing to do with feeding.

Perhaps, then, the mainspring for human motivation, and especially the motivation of the very young human, lies in other needs not tied to immediate biological necessity. Because of their value for survival, these other needs have become, through natural selection, part of the human condition. In their specific forms, they have been described as constituting curiosity and manipulative drives, which quite likely fit under the heading of *arousal* (see Hebb, 1955).

Arousal refers to the capacity of various sensory stimuli to excite the organism. It covers both primary and secondary drives, since all drives and all stimuli have the power to arouse. Actually, stimulation by the environment serves two purposes. The first of these, which is rather obvious, is to provide the organism with *cues* or hints on how to respond. The second, far less apparent, is highly significant: it is to *arouse* the organism and keep it actively engaged in dealing with the environment. This second function of stimulation may very well explain why primates seek stimulation for its own sake. Be that as it may, the amount of cueing supplied by a stimulus depends on when the organism is aroused. Figure 4-2 illustrates a cue-arousal curve, showing the quantity of cueing at various levels of arousal.

The validity of this curve is demonstrable. The organism that is overaroused because it is subjected to a large number of highly relevant stimuli receives very little cueing or information from the stimuli and is thus often wrong in its responses. In extreme cases, this may bring on panic. More typically, several studies (e.g., Birch, 1945; Johnson & Thomson, 1962) disclose that both high and low motivation are less effective in producing learning than moderate amounts. In fact, there appears to be a point of diminishing return beyond which any increase in the amount of motivation results in a deterioration rather than an enhancement of learning. This point occurs at different places in different age groups and also varies among individuals within any given age bracket. Results of experiments in motivation indeed indicate the necessity for parent and teacher to show as much concern over learning situations in which motivation is very high as those in which motivation is very low.

In one study that appears to measure the effect of high arousal on

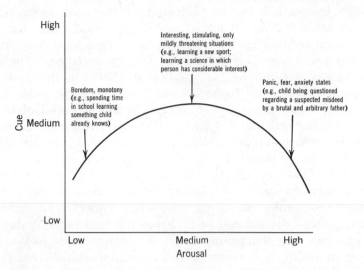

Interesting, stimulating, only
mildly threatening situations
(e.g., learning a new sport;
learning a science in which
person has considerable interest)

Boredom, monotony
(e.g., spending time
in school learning
something child
already knows)

Panic, fear, anxiety states
(e.g., child being questioned
regarding a suspected misdeed
by a brutal and arbitrary father)

High

Medium

Low

Cue

Low   Medium   High
            Arousal

FIGURE 4-2 The amount of behavioral cues offered by a given stimulus at different levels of arousal.

children, Leitch and Escalona (1949) produced overstimulation in infants by presenting them with a succession of toys—all enjoyable, but too many and for too long. Behavior deteriorated rapidly. Although the children were highly alert or aroused, their behavior began to resemble that of an earlier stage of development; in other words, the children regressed. In fact, the case, observed rather frequently, of the child who has too many toys, too many experiences, too much contact with an excessively directive mother, and who becomes "difficult" might be explained as an instance of overarousal.

At the opposite extreme, monotony develops (see McBain, 1961). In this condition so few stimuli are present in the environment that the organism does not respond accurately to those at hand. The most striking example of this among children is found in the institutional care of infants. Institutionalization during infancy is said by many to inflict permanent psychic damage on those involved. But as we shall see in Chapter 9, this is a dubious view; the effects that are found tend to be temporary. Generally they consist of an apparent mental retardation, frequent tics, and peculiarities in affect. According to Casler (1961) lack of variation in the environment is a major factor in the generation of these deviant behaviors. Some of them, such as head banging, may stem from the child's own efforts to increase the environmental stimulation.

Although human behavior is motivated by the necessity to reduce tensions or arousal when biological needs grow too strong, far more behavior is engendered by the necessity to increase tension or arousal when the environment fails to provide enough variation. The most obvious thing about children, said Anderson (1948), is that they seek stimulation. There seems to be a need for maintaining arousal, and for increasing it when it falls too low. The optimal level of tension or arousal for any individual is likely to increase with maturation; this level lies somewhere in the middle, as Figure 4-2 shows, for that is where stimuli supply the most cues to guide behavior.

Rosenzweig (1945) found that if younger children were permitted to choose between easy and difficult—in this case, insoluble—tasks, they would, as a rule, choose the easy one. Older children, on the other hand, chose the difficult one. From this and other studies like it, one can conclude that young children, although they seek a wide variety of stimulation, are more easily overaroused than older children. Yet individual differences at any single level of maturation are probably influenced by inherited differences in emotional instability, emotionality, learned tolerance of frustration, capacity to reduce tensions, and a number of other variables.

Seeking stimulation, or being curious, certainly is almost synonymous with seeking arousal. We see, in this area, that less anxious (McReynolds, 1958; Penny, 1965) and more mentally healthy people (Howard, 1961; Sidle, Acker, & McReynolds, 1963) seek stimulation and apparently have a higher level of optimal arousal than more anxious, sick people. Degree of arousal seeking may be a major dimension of mental health.

The motivation to behave and to learn, then, may come from primary and secondary needs. The goal of the behavior may be the reduction of tensions produced by these needs. However, in primates, and particularly in young humans, such tension-*producing* behavior as curiosity or manipulation seems so marked that it may be sounder scientifically to accept the probable need to increase arousal and generate tension as well as to reduce both.

Reward, Punishment, and Nonreinforcement

The concept of arousal helps to account for the influence of three possible outcomes of any act on the probability of the act's recurring in the future. These possibilities are positive reinforcement—*reward;* negative reinforcement—*punishment;* and *nonreinforcement*—neither reward nor punishment. Thorndike (1913) in his "Law of Effect" stated that reward stamped in a behavior and punishment stamped it out. If things were this simple, life would also be simple, since most problem behaviors would vanish. The child who is a behavior problem has undergone considerable punishment through rejection by those around him, yet remains a problem. If punishment worked, then prisons—at least harsh prisons—should be 100 per cent effective. The matter of reward and punishment, and especially punishment, is much more complicated than might be expected from the original law of effect. Moreover, questions regarding the influence of reward, punishment, and nonreinforcement are, of course, closely related to the very practical subject of disciplining children.

Reward. Before we can consider the influence of reward or positive reinforcement on learning, we must decide what constitutes reinforcement. All behaviors that lead to the reduction of primary and secondary drives must be regarded as positively reinforcing. Any behavior that decreases the probability of overarousal or underarousal may also be included in this category. Since pain, for example, is usually overarousing, behaviors that lead to its avoidance are positively reinforcing. Even the painful consequences of behavior *can* be positively reinforcing. When they are, they increase the tendency for the behavior to recur. The head banging of institutionalized infants noted earlier may be viewed as positively reinforcing merely because it increases arousal. The daydreams and fantasies commonly reported by individuals in monotonous industrial, school, or prison situations are rewarding in the same sense.

There seems little doubt that positive reinforcement following a response increases the probability of the response's recurring. Thus, if a behavior is rewarded but does not increase in frequency, the positive value of the reinforcement may very well be open to question. On the other hand, if an act is rewarded every time it occurs—that is, if there is 100 per cent reinforcement—the organism ultimately ceases to perform it (Hovland, 1936; Calvin, Clifford, Clifford, Bolden, & Harvey, 1956). Although this process has been interpreted in various ways, it may merely indicate that 100 per cent reinforcement becomes monotonous. In other words, it decreases arousal, and the negative reinforcement associated with this decrease overtakes the positive reinforcement resulting from the reduction of specific needs.

Although full reinforcement may bring about the halting of a rewarded behavior, a program of reinforcement composed of smaller proportions of reward proves quite effective in impelling a behavior to recur. Skinner (1938, 1960) experimented with reinforcing organisms both at fixed intervals and at fixed ratios. In the first instance, he supplied reinforcement only once per time interval—once every five minutes in his original studies. In the other, he conferred a reward for every so many occurrences of behavior, such as one reward for every tenth appearance. He found that behaviors are learned best under 100 per cent positive reinforcement. However, once learned, they are maintained best (show most resistance to extinction; recur most frequently), when there is far less than full reinforcement.

Anyone working with children does not need to be too concerned about reinforcing a child excessively. Even those behaviors that adults most desire to inculcate are usually not rewarded at anywhere near the 100 per cent level, since children often perform them even when adults are not at hand. And often, when present, the parent or teacher may be too busy with other things to provide reinforcement. Moreover, it is as important to make certain that the same behavior is not rewarded on some occasions and punished on others as it is natural and good from the standpoint of learning neither to reward desirable behaviors nor to punish undesirable ones all the time.

Behavior, then, is likely to recur when rewarded. That intermittent reward is more effective than constant reinforcement suggests that other factors, perhaps related to arousal, may be significant aspects of the reinforcement, quite apart from its specific capacities to reduce needs and drives.

Punishment. The effects of punishment seem to be more varied than those of reward. If it is severe enough, punishment effectively reduces the frequency of a behavior's occurrence. In research with animals, Masserman (1943) exposed cats to severe punishment. A single, very painful exposure was often sufficient to bring about a permanent cessation of the behavior that led to the punishment. Bettelheim (1943), in describing his own experiences in a Nazi concentration camp, reported an analogous situation among humans. The harsh punishment of the concentration camp, along with other features of camp life, successfully broke the will of the inmates and made them innocuous. However, in such situations far more is changed than the behavior that originally occasioned the punishment. Severe punishment is capable of producing catatonic types of psychotic-like behavior, responses of extreme rage often directed toward the self, and a number of other bizarre symptoms, in addition to extinguishing more commonly accepted behaviors.

Azrin and Holz (1961), varying the intensity of punishment, have demonstrated that punishment may serve as a cue that increases the punished behavior (at the lowest level of punishment); may cause the behavior to cease temporarily; may cause a permanent but partial cessation; or may cause a permanent and complete end of the punished behavior, as the severity of punishment increases. But, as noted, severe punishment seems likely to have undesirable side effects, especially with humans.

Even relatively mild punishment produces a temporary decline in the frequency of a behavior's appearance. Skinner (1938) first demonstrated this phenomenon in an experiment with rats. Rewarded by food, the animals had learned to press a lever. Then the reward was withdrawn. Some rats were never punished; merely no longer rewarded. Some were punished by having their paws slapped during the first 10 extinction tests. For a while, the lever-pressing responses of the punished rat stopped. However, by the time the responses of the unpunished rat were extinguished, the punished rat had made as many lever-pressing responses as the unpunished; responses are not eliminated, they merely are postponed. Not long after this study, Estes (1944) discovered that punishment continued for a sufficient time did produce some decrease in the frequency of a response, but that Skinner was essentially right in his belief that the main function of punishment was to delay, not to extinguish or do away with the occurrence of undesired behavior.

During the temporary period of inhibition following punishment, the organism is more variable in behavior. Thus the chance of accidentally hitting upon the desired response and being rewarded for it increases. For example, Lovaas, Schaeffer, and Simmons (1965) punished rather severely "schizoid" or "autistic" (self-directed) types of children *until* they sought contact with an adult. Then punishment (shock) ceased, and they were rewarded in other ways as well. Learning of a valuable characteristic, that of being aware of and attracted to other humans came as a result of punishment that disrupted well-learned but maladaptive modes of behavior. Clearly, punishment is helpful in producing changes in behavior. It is effective among humans for another reason as well. Humans tend to "internalize" punishment; they accept it as valid and punish themselves when performing the response that has led to punishment in the past. The toddler who has been punished for turning on the TV set at full volume may be seen to slap himself when approaching the console. He has become self-punishing.

On a less overt level, the same self-punishment occurs in the individual who feels guilt. Anthropologists distinguish between societies based on guilt and those based on shame, as we shall observe in Chapter 7. Guilt involves the development of a form of anxiety after performance of an act that is not approved or sometimes after considering the commission of an act that is "bad." Shame, on the other hand, is merely a sense of inferiority at being caught. The individual who experiences guilt engages in self-punishment, whereas the person who feels only shame does not. Margaret Mead has suggested that the development of guilt depends on the individual's having loving, concerned, nurturing parents whose disciplinary techniques are based on love (1943, pp. 127–130). If the withdrawal of love is to be punishing, parental love must first be present. But once this withdrawal occurs and has been associated with deviant behavior, the child begins to link anxiety with the consideration or commission of such behaviors and to punish himself. Since the child now carries his own punishment around with him, the extinction of previously punished behaviors becomes relatively permanent. MacKinnon (1938) found that college students who had cheated in an experimental test of honesty had usually been physically punished as children, whereas those who did not cheat had been psychologically punished. Similarly, Glueck and Glueck (1950) noted that delinquents had been raised by parents who had used a high amount of physical punishment, whereas carefully matched nondelinquents had been raised by parents whose disciplinary techniques were based on love. These data corroborate Mead's ideas and show that the effects of psychological punishment are relatively lasting in their influence on human behavior. Physical punishment, to the contrary, seems to produce more often the psychological state of shame and to have the same temporary impact on behavior as observed by Skinner in his experiments.

More recently, Hoffman and Saltzstein (1967) have found that physical versus psychological punishment by parents did not produce major differences in children's behaviors, but rather that "unqualified power assertion" on the part of the parents ("I'm the boss, I don't explain, you just do what I say") produces observable defects in the character of the offspring.

Unless extremely severe or traumatic, the punishment of a response may not decrease the organism's tendency to perform it again. Sometimes, as we have seen, it is effective in achieving a temporary reduction in the frequency of a behavior. This reduction may be relatively permanent, of course, if the individual internalizes the punishment. Yet even these patterns are not inevitable. For example, in a study of parent practices and resultant child behavior, Sears, Maccoby, and Levin (1957) noted:

> The unhappy effects of punishment have run like a dismal thread through our findings. Mothers who punished aggressive behavior severely had more aggressive children than mothers who punished lightly.

Mothers who punished toilet accidents severely ended up with bedwetting children. Mothers who punished dependency to get rid of it had more dependent children than mothers who did not punish. Harsh physical punishment was associated with high childhood aggressiveness and with the development of feeding problems. Our evaluation of punishment is that it is ineffectual over the long term as a technique for eliminating the kind of behavior toward which it is directed (Sears et al., p. 484).

Apparently the forms of punishment to which their findings allude were most often physical in character.

A specific form of punishment found to be extremely disruptive is the random reward and punishment of the same behavior. In his conditioning experiments, Pavlov observed that requiring a dog to make a distinction between an ellipse and a circle, a task apparently beyond a dog's sensory capacities, produced a breakdown in behavior. In some of his animals this breakdown took the form of aggressive behavior in which the animal would indiscriminately bite himself, his harness, or the researcher. Other dogs would exhibit withdrawn behavior, and still others, stereotyped, compulsive behaviors.

Dogs subjected to this experience generally lost the ability to make simple discriminations that had previously been learned easily. On the basis of this discovery, Pavlov developed a theory of neurosis and spent his final decades working on it (Pavlov, 1941). In the United States, Maier (1939) obtained the same results. Requiring organisms that had learned simple discriminations to make finer and finer ones, he rewarded the correct response and punished the other. The process of discriminating became so arduous that the organisms responded by chance. Since they had one chance in two of being right, they were rewarded half the time and punished the rest of the time for responses that, to them, seemed identical. Behaviors became extremely stereotyped and remained so even after discriminations were again made simple.

No doubt the effects of such random or seemingly random reward and punishment, in which the organism cannot distinguish between the rewarded and the punished response, are as detrimental to humans as they are to lower organisms. The analogy to Pavlov's dogs is probably the unfortunate child whose arbitrary parent rules with an iron whim—who punishes a behavior on one occasion and rewards it on another.

Sears, Maccoby, and Levin (1957) indicated that punishment does not eliminate the behavior toward which the punishment is directed. Others who have studied authoritarianism (e.g., Adorno, Frenkel-Brunswik, Levinson, & Sanford, 1950; Block, 1955) and creativity (e.g.,

MacKinnon, 1962) have suggested that an overly controlling parent reduces a child's curiosity, creative bent, and problem-solving ability. In many cases, the punished child is timider and less counteractive toward adults—although generally more aggressive toward peers. Thus he may be easier for parents to deal with and control even further. Punishment also helps to establish conflicts of approach and avoidance. Although punishment does not reduce motivation, the fear of it throws the organism into conflict; it still desires the goal at which the punished behavior is aimed, yet is afraid of pursuing it. Conflict of this sort, of course, disrupts behavior.

It should be noted that Solomon (1964), an astute student of punishment and its effectiveness, believes punishment to be very effective in changing behavior. Other reviews by Baumrind (1966) (see a discussion of Baumrind's conclusions in Chapter 10) and Marshall (1965) suggest that most forms of punishment are not as damaging as indicated in the earlier literature and that, under some circumstances, punishment is effective in producing the desired behavioral changes.

Even after considering these reviews, however, we still must conclude, from the evidence we have discussed above, that punishment has only limited utility in extinguishing a punished act that has been relatively well learned, and is far more likely than either reward or nonreinforcement to produce unexpected and often undesirable side effects.

Nonreinforcement. "A response can be permanently weakened only by a sufficient number of unreinforced elicitations . . ." (Estes, 1944). If it is neither rewarded nor punished, it is not reinforced. Western culture, which is evaluative as a rule, judges acts as good or bad and believes accordingly that they should be rewarded or punished. Other cultures are different. Their members merely note whether an act occurs, without taking the extra step of judging it. Perhaps because of this distinction, Westerners scarcely consider nonreinforcement as a possibility, whereas some other cultures make it a major mode of social control. Among Eskimos, for example, even the most permissive parent in American society would be considered quite punitive by their standards. Eskimo children have far wider latitude than American children in making decisions. Errors in judgment or in behavior are not punished. Neither are "bad" behaviors. They just are not reinforced. They appear to fall into a vacuum since they are ignored and no response is made to them (however, this ignoring of a behavior or an action may well constitute a punishment in the mind of a child seeking approval). As both Skinner and Estes point out, the way to extinguish a behavior permanently is neither to punish nor reward it. Sometimes this is a slow technique. One of the authors spent considerable time among Eskimos, who generally frown on any punishment of children, and believes that at ages two to six, or thereabouts, Eskimo children are quite troublesome. But nonreinforcement, though slow, is effective, and by about age nine Eskimo children appear remarkably well adjusted *and* well behaved.

Nonreinforcement is thus more efficient than punishment, if one has the necessary patience and is dealing with behaviors for which a lesser speed of learning to inhibit responses is not dangerous to the learner or to others.

Nonreinforcement seems a difficult technique for persons to use in Western culture. Even if a parent attempts to use it to control behavior, the whole Western culture opposes him. Yet both the effectiveness and some of the difficulties of nonreinforcement may be seen in Chapter 16 in Williams' (1959) succinct description of the elimination of tantrums in a toddler.

One area of psychology in which the effectiveness of the nonreinforcement technique is demonstrated is "play therapy." In play therapy, a form of nondirective therapy described by Axline (1947), in which disturbed children spend their time at play, the child is permitted to engage in all behaviors—except hitting the therapist, although sometimes even this is permitted. Toys that call forth aggression predominate—water to throw about and flood the room, life-size dolls to punch, dolls that can be dismembered without permanent damage, and toys of a similar sort. The child, assumed to have a great deal of hostility but to be incapable of handling its expression, is placed in a setting where aggression is not only permitted but, in fact, is deliberately provoked. Since all children who are "behavior problems" have been punished in the past, this child, fearing a trap, is usually nonaggressive for a time. Gradually he becomes more aggressive. Upon discovering that aggression is no longer punished the child grows rapidly in aggressiveness, hostility, and destructiveness, both inside and outside the therapeutic situation. Although this increase is vexing to parents and others who have to deal with the child, he gradually becomes more manageable and very frequently better adjusted as therapy progresses, despite the unlikelihood of the outside environment changing markedly.

The reduction in problem behavior appears to occur for several reasons. The therapist interacts with the child and presumably provides him with insight and understanding. The child exhausts the vast store of hostility brought into therapy and at the same time learns to express anger in less explosive ways. Finally, the aggressive response is extinguished through nonreinforcement.

Reward, Punishment, Nonreinforcement, and the Problem of What Is Learned

Organisms do learn. The question remains, what do they learn? Do they learn to express behaviors that are rewarded, to inhibit behaviors that are not rewarded, or both? The earliest position regarding the effect of reinforcement on learning was that of Pavlov, who believed that organisms learned to respond to the stimulus that had previously led to reward. Spence (1937) resolved many contradictions among research findings (especially in the area of transposition) by suggesting that the learning process involves both increasing the organism's tendency to make rewarded behaviors and decreasing the tendency to perform behaviors that are not rewarded. Harlow and Hicks (see Harlow, 1959) later claimed that organisms, in learning, for the most part do not learn what to do; rather, they learn what not to do. Recent evidence suggests that organisms, whether pigeons (Terrace, 1963, 1964) or human children (Cole, Dent, Eguchi, Fujii, & Johnson, 1964), learn far more from being rewarded for correct responses than for being punished (or nonreinforced) for making incorrect responses. The old folklore saying that we learn best by mistakes does not appear to be true. The best procedure, so far as learning an act is concerned (and probably more so in training dull than bright children), is to structure the learning event so that chances of failure are reduced to a minimum and success probability is maximized so that it can be rewarded. However, errorless learning has been shown to limit the range of generalization of learning (Terrace, 1964; Gollin & Savoy, 1968). The utility of punishment and nonreinforcement may be greater in situations requiring the generalization of what is learned than in situations when such generalization is not required. Perhaps the relatively slight importance of learning what not to do, as compared with what to do, in many learning situations, accounts for the fact that the effects of punishment are less strong and less predictable than those of reward.

SUMMARY

Simple learning may be either respondent or operant. Humans and lower organisms do not differ appreciably in the way they approach learning problems of this kind, nor do they show substantial differences in rates of learning. It is with the introduction of learning sets that wide distinctions may be noted across species, with humans showing considerable superiority. The learning set is a bridge to complex learning and in particular to concept formation at which humans excel. Humans are best at concept formation because of their wider experience, greater ability to transfer training, and language skills. Thinking is another form of complex learning that is considered unique to humans. The most comprehensive theory concerning the development of the thought process is that of Piaget, who believes that qualitative differences in thinking occur with age. Piaget to the contrary, we believe that evidence suggests that children probably think much the same way as do adults, although children's thought processes are handicapped chiefly by their smaller stores of information.

All these aspects of behavior, from simple respondent learning to complex problem solving, are part of the learning functions of humans. After years of concentrating on those phases of learning common to all organisms and the motivations for learning, researchers are finally acquiring information about the phases that are uniquely human. Although much remains to be learned, psychology has begun to develop considerable understanding of the forces that motivate higher levels of human functioning.

The learning of a response presumably depends on the reduction of a need and its related drive. Whereas nonprimates more often tend to act in order to reduce tension or arousal, primates need to maintain arousal. For this reason the latter engage in many learning experiences that are difficult to explain in terms of reducing the tensions produced by the more conventional primary biological needs or the secondary needs stemming from them.

A behavior may be either rewarded, punished, or nonreinforced. In most cases reward causes behavior to increase. Punishment *sometimes* decreases the frequency of a response, but also has a number of side effects. Nonreinforcement seems most effective in reducing the probability of response but is not likely to be widely used in Western society.

REFERENCES

Adorno, T. W., Frenkel-Brunswik, E., Levinson, D. J., & Sanford, R. W. *The authoritarian personality.* New York: Harper, 1950.

Alberts, E., & Ehrenfreund, D. Transposition in children as a function of age. *Journal of Experimental Psychology,* 1951, **41**, 30–38.

Anderson, J. E. Personality organization in children. *American Psychologist,* 1948, **3**, 409–416.

Axline, V. *Play therapy: The inner dynamics of childhood.* Boston: Houghton Mifflin, 1947.

Azrin, N. H., & Holz, W. C. Punishment during fixed internal reinforcement. *Journal for the Experimental Analysis of Behavior,* 1961, **4**, 343–347.

Baumrind, D.   Effects of authoritative control on child behavior.   *Child Development,* 1966, **37,** 887–907.

Bettelheim, B.   Individual and mass behavior in extreme situations.   *Journal of Abnormal and Social Psychology,* 1943, **38,** 417–452.

Birch, H. G.   The role of motivational factors in insightful problem solving.   *Journal of Comparative Psychology,* 1945, **43,** 259–278.

Block, J.   Personality characteristics associated with fathers' attitudes toward child rearing.   *Child Development,* 1955, **26,** 41–48.

Brackbill, Y.   Extinction of the smiling response in infants as a function of reinforcement schedule.   *Child Development,* 1958, **29,** 115–124.

Brackbill, Y.   Experimental research with children in the Soviet Union.   *American Psychologist,* 1960, **15,** 226–233.

Bronfenbrenner, U.   The role of age, sex, class, and culture in studies of moral development.   *Religious Education, Research Supplement,* 1962, **57,** S3–S17.

Bruner, J. S., Oliver, R., & Greenfield, P., et al., *Studies in cognitive growth.* New York: Wiley, 1966.

Calvin, A. D., Clifford, L. T., Clifford, B., Bolden, L., & Harvey, J.   Experimental validation of conditioned inhibition.   *Psychological Reports,* 1955, **2,** 51–56.

Casler, L.   Maternal deprivation: A critical review of the literature.   *Monographs of the Society for Research in Child Development,* 1961, **26,** Serial No. 80, No. 2.

Cole, R. E., Dent, H. E., Eguchi, P. E., Fujii, K. K., & Johnson, R. C.   Transposition with minimal errors during training trials.   *Journal of Experimental Child Psychology,* 1964, **1,** 355–359.

Dennis, W.   Animistic thinking among college and university students.   *Science Monthly,* 1953, **76,** 247–250.

Engel, T., Lipsitt, L. P., & Kaye, H.   Olfactory responses and adaptation in the human neonate.   *Journal of Comparative and Physiological Psychology.* 1963, **56,** 73–77.

Elkind, D.   Quantity concepts in junior and senior high school students.   *Child Development,* 1961, **32,** 551–560.

Estes, W. K.   An experimental study of punishment.   *Psychological Monographs,* 1944, **57,** No. 263.

Etzel, B. C. & Gewirtz, J. L.   Experimental modification of caretaker-maintained operant crying in two infants (Tyrannotearus infantus), 6 and 20 weeks.   *Journal of Experimental Child Psychology,* 1967, **5,** 303–317.

Fehmi, L. G.   The formation of learning sets in severely retarded brain injured and familial children.   Paper presented at the Spartan Psychological Association, San Jose, Calif., 1960.

Flavell, J. H.   *The developmental psychology of Jean Piaget.*   Princeton, N. J.: Van Nostrand, 1963.

Fowler, W.   Cognitive learning in infancy and early childhood.   *Psychological Bulletin,* 1962, **59,** 116–152.

Glorig, A. *Audiometry: Principles and practices.* Baltimore: Williams & Wilkins, 1965.

Glueck, S., & Glueck, E. *Unraveling juvenile delinquency.* New York: Commonwealth Fund, 1950.

Gollin, E. S., & Savoy, P. Fading procedures and conditional discrimination in children. *Journal of Experimental Analysis of Behavior,* 1968, **11,** 443–451.

Harlow, H. F. The formation of learning sets. *Psychological Review,* 1949, **56,** 51–56.

Harlow, H. F. The nature of love. *American Psychologist,* 1958, **13,** 673–685.

Harlow, H. F. Discrimination learning theory: Uniprocess vs. duoprocess. *Psychological Review,* 1959, **64,** 104–109.

Hebb, D. O. Drives and the C.N.S. (conceptual nervous system). *Psychological Review,* 1955, **62,** 243–253.

Hebert, J. A., & Krantz, D. L. Transposition: A re-evaluation. *Psychological Bulletin,* 1965, **63,** 244–257.

Hoffman, M. L., & Saltzstein, H. D. Parent discipline and the child's moral development. *Journal of Personality and Social Psychology,* 1967, **5,** 45–57.

Honzik, M. P., McFarlane, J. W., & Allen, L. The stability of mental test performance between two and eighteen years. *Journal of Experimental Education,* 1948, **17,** 309–324.

Hovland, C. I. "Inhibition of reinforcement" and phenomena of experimental extinction. *Proceedings of the National Academy of Science* (Washington, D. C.), 1936, **22,** 430–433.

Howard, K. I. A test of stimulus seeking behavior. *Perceptual and Motor Skills,* 1961, **13,** 416.

Huxley, A. L. *Brave new world.* Garden City, N. Y.: Doubleday, Doran, 1932.

Johnson, R. C. A study of children's moral judgments. *Child Development,* 1962, **33,** 327–354. (a)

Johnson, R. C. Linguistic structure as a variable in concept formation and concept content. *Psychological Bulletin,* 1962, **59,** 468–476. (b)

Johnson, R. C., & Developmental Seminar. Manipulation of test stimuli social class, and the attainment of conservation. Paper presented at the meetings of the Society for Research in Child Development, New York, New York, March 30, 1967.

Johnson, R. C., & Thomson, C. W. Incidental and intentional learning under three conditions of motivation. *American Journal of Psychology,* 1962, **75,** 284–288.

Kaye, H. The conditioned Babkin reflex in human new borns. *Psychonomic Science,* 1965, **2,** 287–288.

Kendler, H. H., Kendler, T. S., & Wells, D. Reversal and non-reversal shifts in nursery school children. *Journal of Comparative and Physiological Psychology,* 1960, **53,** 83–87.

Koch, M. B., & Meyer, D. R.   A relationship of age to learning set formation in the preschool child.   *Journal of Comparative and Physiological Psychology*, 1959, **52**, 387–389.

Kuenne, M. R.   Experimental investigation of the relation of language to transposition behavior in young children.   *Journal of Experimental Psychology*, 1946, **36**, 471–490.

Laurendeau, M., & Pinard, A.   *Causal thinking in the child.*   New York: International Universities Press, 1962.

Leitch, M., & Escalona, S.   The reactions of infants to stress.   *Psychoanalytic Study of the Child.*   **5,** New York: International Universities Press, 1949.

Lipsitt, L. P., Kaye, H., & Bosack, T. N.   Enhancement of neonatal sucking through reinforcement.   *Journal of Experimental Child Psychology*, 1966, **4**, 193–168.

Lovaas, O. I., Schaeffer, B., & Simmons, J. Q.   Building social behavior in autistic children by use of electric shock.   *Journal of Experimental Research in Personality*, 1965, **1**, 99–109.

McBain, W. N.   Noise, the "arousal hypothesis," and monotonous work.   *Journal of Applied Psychology*, 1961, **45**, 309–317.

MacKinnon, D. W.   Violation of prohibitions.   In H. A. Murray (Ed.), *Explorations in personality.*   New York: Oxford University Press, 1938, pp. 491–501.

MacKinnon, D. W. The nature and nurture of creative talent.   *American Psychologist*, 1962, **17**, 484–495.

McReynolds, P.   Exploratory behavior as related to anxiety in psychiatric patients.   *Psychological Reports*, 1958, **4**, 321–322.

Maier, N. R. F.   *Studies of abnormal behavior in the rat: The neurotic pattern and an analysis of the situation which produces it.*   New York: Harper, 1939.

Marshall, H. H.   The effect of punishment on children: A review of the literature and a suggested hypothesis.   *Journal of Genetic Psychology*, 1965, **106**, 23–33.

Masserman, J. H.   *Behavior and neurosis.*   Chicago: University of Chicago Press, 1943.

Mead, M.   *And keep your powder dry.*   New York: Morrow, 1943.

Mowrer, O. H., & Mowrer, W. M.   Enuresis—A method for its study and treatment.   *American Journal of Orthopsychiatry*, 1938, **8**, 436–459.

Pavlov, I. P.   *Conditioned reflexes* (translated by G. V. Anrep).   London: Oxford University Press, 1927.

Pavlov, I. P.   *Conditioned reflexes and psychiatry* (translated by W. H. Gantt).   New York: International Publishers, 1941.

Penny, R. K.   Reactive curiosity and manifest anxiety in children.   *Child Development*, 1965, **36**, 697–702.

Piaget, J.   *The child's conception of the world.*   New York: Harcourt, Brace, 1930.

Piaget, J. *The origins of intelligence in children.* New York: International Universities Press, 1952.

Piaget, J. How children form mathematical concepts. *Scientific American,* 1953, **189,** 74–79.

Piaget, J. *Psychology of intelligence.* Totowa, N. J.: Littlefield, Adams, 1960. (Originally published in translation in 1947.)

Pratoomraj, S., & Johnson, R. C. Kinds of questions and types of conservation tasks as related to children's conservation responses. *Child Development,* 1966, **37,** 343–353.

Randall, D. L. *Examination of the hereditary assumptions underlying Piaget's theory of the development of intellectual structure.* Unpublished doctoral dissertation, University of Colorado, 1967.

Razran, G. The observable unconscious and the inferable conscious in current Soviet psychophysiology: Interoceptive conditioning, semantic conditioning, and the orienting reflex. *Psychological Review,* 1961, **68,** 81–147.

Rheingold, H. L., Gewirtz, J. L., & Ross, H. W. Social conditioning of vocalizations in the infant. *Journal of Comparative and Physiological Psychology,* 1959, **52,** 68–73.

Rosenzweig, S. Further comparative data on repetition-choice after success and failure as related to frustration tolerance. *Journal of Genetic Psychology,* 1945, **66,** 75–81.

Sears, R. R., Maccoby, E., & Levin, H. *Patterns of child rearing.* Evanston, Ill.: Row, Peterson, 1957.

Sidle, A., Acker, M., & McReynolds, P. "Stimulus-seeking" behavior in schizophrenics and nonschizophrenics. *Perceptual and Motor Skills,* 1963, **17,** 811–816.

Simmons, C., & Johnson, R. C. Conditions influencing the learning transfer of conservation of substance. Unpublished manuscript, University of Colorado, 1968.

Skinner, B. F. *The behavior of organisms.* New York: Appleton-Century-Crofts, 1938.

Skinner, B. F. Are theories of learning necessary? *Psychological Review,* 1950, **57,** 193–216.

Skinner, B. F. Reinforcement today. *American Psychologist,* 1958, **13,** 94–99.

Skinner, B. F. Pigeons in a pelican. *American Psychologist,* 1960, **15,** 28–37.

Solomon, R. L. Punishment. *American Psychologist,* 1964, **19,** 239–253.

Spelt, D. K. The conditioning of the human fetus in utero. *Journal of Experimental Psychology,* 1948, **38,** 338–346.

Spence, K. W. The differential response in animals to stimuli varying within a single dimension. *Psychological Review,* 1937, **44,** 430–444.

Terrace, H. S. Discrimination learning with and without errors. *Journal of the Experimental Analysis of Behavior,* 1963, **6,** 1–27.

Terrace, H. S. Wavelength generalization after discrimination learning with and without errors. *Science,* 1964, **144,** 78–80.

Thorndike, E. L. *Educational psychology.* New York: Teachers College, 1913.

Thurstone, L. L., & Thurstone, T. G. *The Primary Mental Abilities Tests.* Chicago: Science Research Associates, 1941.

Turner, L. H., & Solomon, R. L. Human traumatic avoidance learning: Theory and experiments on the operant respondent distinction and failures to learn. *Psychological Monographs,* 1962, **76** (40, Whole No. 559).

Voeks, V. Sources of apparent animism in students. *Science Monthly,* 1954, **79,** 406–407.

Watson, J. B. *Psychology from the standpoint of a behaviorist.* Philadelphia: Lippincott, 1919.

Watson, J. B., & Morgan, J. J. B. Emotional reactions and psychological experimentation. *American Journal of Psychology,* 1917, **28,** 163–174.

Watson, J. B., & Rayner, R. Conditioned emotional reactions. *Journal of Experimental Psychology,* 1920, **3,** 1–14.

Werner, H. *Comparative psychology of mental development.* (Rev. ed.) New York: International Universities Press, 1957.

Williams, C. D. The elimination of tantrum behavior by extinction procedures. *Journal of Abnormal and Social Psychology,* 1959, **59,** 229.

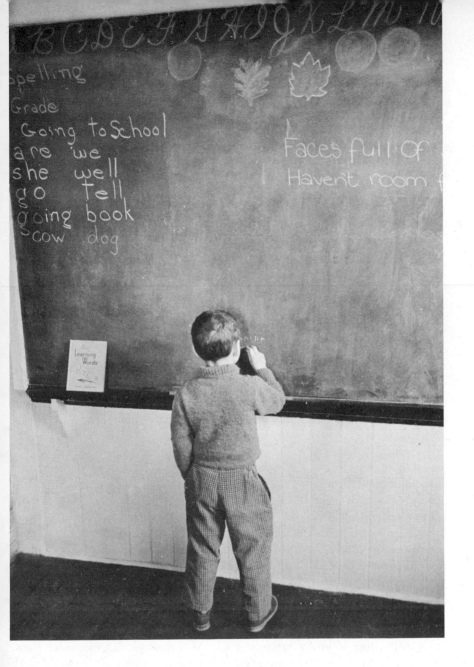

5

Language

The tools of communication are of two kinds. All organisms use signs and signals, but symbols are unique to humans. Symbolic communication, or language, is so closely related to learning that any attempt to separate them, even for purposes of discussion, is doomed to failure because of the tightness of their bond. Equally allied, as we shall see eventually, are language and memory. Since human achievement rests on both learning and memory, language, their common kin, is the central force in man's dominance over his environment.

Animals make a variety of sounds; in fact, a sound count published by Yerkes and Learned (1925) renders it possible to determine the relative frequency of different sounds uttered by chimpanzees. These utterances are specific and occur only in a single context. One cry may signify "food," another, "danger," but none is used in a new sense. Nor are two sounds combined to form a third sound distinct from the original two. These vocalizations refer to immediate situations, to the present danger and not to the danger of five minutes ago or to the danger yet to be discerned. Thus only objects or events that have been sensed can give rise to utterances. These sounds and other sign or signal types of communication in lower organisms are often compelling, for the animal exposed to a stimulus *must* respond to it. An exception to this statement may occur in the communication of porpoises, which are believed by some researchers to communicate symbolically.

In contrast, human symbolic behavior is highly varied. Humans are capable of emitting many sounds, each of which can be used in any combination with a large number of other sounds. Any single sound or group of sounds may have several meanings that are based on mutual agreement rather than on some innate response mechanism. Human speech can deal with the abstract or nonphysical and with the past and future as effectively as the present. It can also handle objects out of visual range as well as those sensed at the moment of vocalization. Sign-signal behavior appears to be oriented toward the communication of feeling or affect; symbolic communication contains a lesser proportion of affect and generally conveys more information. Although highly informative, human communication is not compelling in the same way that communication of lower organisms is. An extended discussion of these points may be found in Lorenz's (1952) and Tinbergen's (1953) work on animal communication.

Language permits the communication of information from one generation to the next. Since the wisdom as well as the errors of the past are thus available to the present generation without the necessity of having to learn by direct imitation, a fuller mastery of the environment is possible. Moreover, symbolic behavior through its intricacies enables in-

146

dividuals to understand one another better. With this understanding comes an increased prospect for cooperation and for the development of feelings. It is language that separates humans most clearly from all other organisms. In this chapter we shall first consider the normal development of language in childhood, then individual differences in language development, and, finally, the impact of language on thought, learning, and memory.

THE COURSE OF LANGUAGE DEVELOPMENT

Sounds

The first sound uttered by a child is its cry at birth. Most of its vocalizing of the next few months falls under the heading of crying. Early crying consists of vowel sounds, Lewis (1959) has pointed out, especially a-a-a-a as in *fat*. Some of the sounds of the English language are difficult, if not impossible, to make before one has teeth, since several of them depend on the action of the tongue against the teeth. Other sounds are difficult for other reasons. But soon after birth the change from vowel cries to consonant-vowel combinations commences. Some sounds involving oral movements like those occurring in sucking—for example, *ba-ba*—come to be associated with comfort whereas others—for example, *na-na* with a nasal *a*—are linked to states of discomfort (Lewis, 1959). Consonants then increase in proportion to vowels (Irwin & Chen, 1946). Within a few months after birth, the child makes a wide assortment of sounds and by about a year of age is capable of uttering most of the different sounds used in the various languages of mankind (Irwin, 1947a, 1947b, 1948a).

Theories abound as to how humans progress from babbling to speaking meaningful words. Primates are noisy creatures as a rule, but it seems probable that the association of sounds with comfort, as in a mother's conversation when changing, feeding, and bathing an infant, causes sounds to become somewhat rewarding in themselves. The child receives pleasure through his own production of sounds. Sound making is thus reinforced and increases in frequency. In somewhat different ways both Mowrer (1950) and Miller and Dollard (1941) emphasize the emotive quality of early sound making. It is very pleasant for a parent to lie abed in the morning, soon after the sun comes up, and listen to a baby babbling in his crib. Although part of the pleasure comes from not having to get up, some of it comes from sharing the apparent joy of the infant as he works through his storehouse of sounds. It is this joy that is considered the first step in meaningful communication.

The English language does not contain all the sounds made by humans in communication. The French rolling *r*, the German umlauts, the Zulu or Bushman tongue-clicks, and some of the sounds the Swede must make to pronounce the name *Skjellbjörn* are foreign to the English-speaking adult. Yet infants in any culture can make them all, although those not found in English disappear quite rapidly in American and other English-speaking children. When an infant or young child in the English-speaking orbit utters foreign sounds, his parents more often look baffled and do not reinforce the sound-making behavior. The parents do, however, directly reinforce the sounds germane to English by parental attention and also by making the sounds themselves. This provides the sounds with an indirect or secondary rewarding quality. Through reward of sounds found in a language and nonreinforcement of others alien to it, infants begin to utter more often those sounds to be used later by them in forming words.

The emotive and affective aspects of sound making appear first in infants' awareness; the value of speech as a means to convey more specific information comes later. Although the two components of speech are associated with one another, the affective feeling component may remain relatively distinct from the informational cognitive component even into adulthood. Some support for this position may be found in the investigation of *aphasia,* a disorder in communication resulting from some forms of brain injury. If the speech capacity of the aphasic is impaired, as is often the case, the ability to express emotions (e.g., to swear) usually remains intact, even when the capacity to communicate information is totally or at least partially lost.

Intonation. As we shall discuss later, the investigation of the factors involved in the young (e.g., two-year-old) child's ability to form sentences is vigorously being pursued. One aspect of saying a sentence is changing the pitch of sounds as the speaker progresses from beginning to end. English-speaking peoples typically begin sentences at a rather high pitch, and lower them at the end. Scandinavians, on the other hand, generally reverse the procedure. No matter what means we use, changes in tone, like characteristic pauses, serve to break up a continued discourse into smaller, more easily digested elements. To learn intonation, then, is to learn one aspect of sentence construction. This particular aspect of sentence construction appears to be learned in the babbling stage— the child frequently makes a long succession of babbling sounds, none of which have meaning to the adult listener, yet which in intonation have a sentence-like sound to them. This is particularly noteworthy because when children finally begin to use real words in sentences, these sentences are usually of two words, far less complex in terms of number of sounds than the babbling "sentences" that have preceded them by about a year. It appears that this aspect (intonation) of what it takes to make a sentence in a given language is learned earlier than the constituent elements of sentences (words) and earlier than the ordering of words within sentences.

Use of Words

Some sounds occur more frequently than others in infant vocalization, and it is to these that adults attach meaning. Since infants in all cultures often make the same sounds, the basic infant vocabulary of all languages is common, even though cultures differ in the association of specific sounds with specific meanings. In English-speaking homes, the child utters the sound *ma-ma* and the meaning *mother* is attached to it. But in other cultures *ama* is mother, and in still others, *da-da*. In some languages *ama* means grandmother; elsewhere it is nurse. To Americans *baba* signifies baby but to many Slavic peoples it means grandmother. And so on. Adults grasp at the sounds uttered frequently by children in babbling and invest them with meanings according to the cultures in which they live. This process hastens the learning of language, for the child now makes sounds denoted as words and reinforced as words.

From reiterated infant sounds, therefore, come the first words. Often they are recognized by the parents as words having specific meaning but not necessarily the same meaning they have for the child. A boy of six months said "da-da" on his father's return from work each day. Although this gratified the father, it later developed that the response was a rather low-level, conditioned reaction to a situation in which the father was present. The da-da was associated with him but did not mean father to the child. Much later, the child, upon acquiring an understanding that words denote physical things, began "naming behavior" in which he spent considerable time in naming everything in sight, looking to his parents for confirmation, and thus developed speech. Now he dropped the da-da altogether and referred to both parents as "ma-ma" for several months.

Although the young child may be capable of emitting sounds without knowing their denotations, it is more common for him to become aware first of a word's meaning and then to attempt to approximate its sound in order to convey that meaning. Humans of all ages, of course, understand the meaning of words they do not articulate. The young child has an awareness of many word meanings even though he cannot yet emit them. Through the constant association of word with stimulus in a wide variety of settings, he recognizes that the sound combinations that man calls words have meaning. This is where speech begins.

Parents are well known for their understanding of their children's utterances. Although they doubtless find meanings even where none is intended, they also understand the approximations employed by one- and two-year-olds that are incomprehensible to strangers. One little boy living in a wet climate, for example, said "Ne-Ne-Lah-Lah." This is a relatively difficult sound pattern to decipher. So far as the boy was concerned, it appears that what the child meant was "Roni's (his sister's) umbrella." Actually, the syllables had a number of meanings. They could mean "It is raining," "Roni has her umbrella," "I want her umbrella," or "Here comes Roni with her umbrella," depending on the inflection of the sounds. From such slender roots, consisting of primitive sound groups that only in a very limited sense approximate the words they are intended to signify, yet that *have meaning for both speaker and listener,* stems symbolic communication.

Infants utter words such as da-da even before it is likely that they attribute sense to them or even know that words have meaning. Quite possibly infants may have their own meanings for words that adults cannot apprehend. Yet symbolic communication requires agreement in meaning between speaker and listener. Symbolic communication is a two-way affair; it cannot occur in a vacuum, nor can it take place unless the listener understands the speaker's utterances. Because understanding is essential, it is hard to ascertain when the first word appears in infant speech.

Available data suggest that a child's first word is uttered at about one year of age (McCarthy, 1946). Averages, however, are not always reliable. Gifted children are advanced in speech (Terman, 1925), whereas retarded children are slow in developing it. In fact, retarded children are infantile in speech, using fewer consonants and more vowels than normal children of the same age (Irwin, 1942). Nevertheless, although early speech is a reasonably good indication of general precocity, delayed speech is not, of itself, a portent of later deficiency. Some children are slow in developing speech merely because they have received little reinforcement and others because their mothers are so solicitous that their demands are met without having to speak. Some, of course, are behind in speech development owing to sensory or intellectual weaknesses, whereas others are retarded for no discernible reason at all.

Once a child has begun to speak, there are two ways to determine the number of words in his vocabulary. The first is to spend enough time with a child to hear every word he knows. Leopold (1937–1949) kept an accurate diary of the speech development of his daughter from the eighth week to the seventh year of her life. Although word counting was quite incidental to his major purpose, this diary is an excellent example of the approach in which *all* words the child says become part of a vocabulary score. The more common method for studying language growth is to select a sample of words and then present a child with pictures or other stimuli capable of leading him to say the word if he knows it. From the child's responses to this sample of words, his total vocabularly can be estimated. Figure 5-1 presents data presented by Lenneberg (1966) in a study of vocabularly growth.

Although these figures indicate the rapid increase in verbal compre-

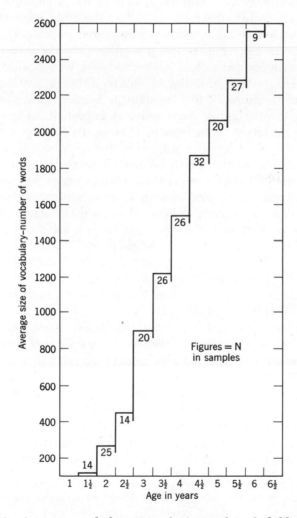

FIGURE 5-1   Average vocabulary size of 10 samples of children at various ages.   (Data from Smith, as presented by Lenneberg, 1966.)

hension, especially between two-and-a-half and three years, they do not say anything by themselves about the range of individual differences. Among the 25 children Shirley (1933) studied from birth to two years of age, the number of words spoken in the presence of examiners just prior to their second birthdays varied from six to 126. This was a tremendous range for a normal population.

Construction of Sentences

Granted that a young child (e.g., age 15 to 18 months) knows the meaning of a number of words, how does the child learn to put these words into understandable, syntactically correct sentences? Syntax, in English, consists largely of ordering words. "No say mama" is not an unusual construction for a child just turned two, who means that "Mama says no." The correct ordering of words within a sentence so as to follow the conventions of the language is learned rather early by the child. This is so whether word order is important, as in English, or relatively unimportant, as in Russian (Slobin, 1966).

Further, the child must learn, from the way words are used in sentences, what class the words belong to, so that they can be transformed and used in contexts other than those in which they were learned. Clearly, the young child just learning to make sentences does not know the formal names of various word classes, such as "nouns" and "verbs," but once he understands syntax so that he can use word position and connective terms as clues, he can begin to make adequate transformations. Berko (1958) developed a test using stimuli such as those shown in Figure 5-2. The general approach of using nonsense words within a sentence such as "The mog wibbled the gomp," has been used by other researchers as well (e.g., Bellugi, 1965).

Children show early skill in learning inflections. For example, children usually call the two creatures in Figure 5-2 wug/z, not wug/s. Adults usually do not notice that they pronounce plural nouns ending in "s" either with a "z," as in wug/z or dog/z, or with an "s" as in cat/s or bik/s (another of Berko's figures), and many foreign-born speakers of English never learn this distinction. Yet children know it early.

Berko tested out other propositions of this same sort, using possessive endings of nouns, the simple past tense, and so on, and tested children from preschool through grade 3. As Brown and Fraser (1964) note,

The productivity of the regular inflections of children seems to be greater than it is for adults. Both kinds of subjects were shown a picture of a man swinging something about his head and told: "This is a man who knows how to gling. He glings every day. Today he

This is a wug.

Now there is another one.
There are two of them.
There are two _____ .

FIGURE 5-2   Illustration of Berko's method for eliciting inflections.

glings. Yesterday he _____." Adults hang suspended between *gling, glang, glung,* and even *glought* but children promptly say *glinged.* Berko also tested to see whether children who generalize the regular inflection would correctly imitate irregular forms or would assimilate them to the rules. She showed a picture and said, for instance, "Here is a goose and here are two geese. There are two _____." Most of her subjects said *gooses* and performed similarly with other irregular forms. These observations suggest that rules of great generality may survive and override a number of counter instances (Brown & Fraser, 1964, pp. 46–47).

In Berko's study of syntax, nonsense syllables were placed in sentences in such a way that they were identifiable as various parts of speech. For example:

Where *wug* was to be identified as a transitive verb, the investigator said: "This is a little girl who wants to wug something." As the intransitive verb the same sentence was used with the omission of *something.* With *wug* as a mass noun the little girl would be "thinking about some wug." *Wug* became an adjective by having the girl think of "something wuggy" and an adverb by having her think of "doing something wuggily." Children in the first, second, and third grades all went on to make up sentences using their new words, but they did not always use them correctly. They did better as they got older and better at all ages with the count noun, adjective, transitive and intransitive verbs than with the mass nouns and adverbs. For the purposes of the present argument the important result is that children showed an ability, increasing with age, to construct grammatically correct sentences using new words (Brown & Fraser, 1964, p. 48).

At an early age (e.g., four to five) most children know the proper transformational rules of English, as in changing from singular to plural. They know how to handle tenses, although, as noted above, the general rule (e.g., add "ed" for past tense—"want" to "wanted"; "went" to "wented") overrides the specific rule, for a time, perhaps as a result of far greater experience with the general than the specific rule (Palermo & Eberhart, 1968). And they know how to handle different parts of speech, as shown in Berko's experiment.

Such things as knowledge of word meaning, intonation, word order, transformational rules, even if combined together, do not, in their totality, comprise the art of making sentences; they are merely elements that may be required before sentence construction occurs. Yet all of these, plus other aspects of sentence making, must form a gestalt or whole before the art of sentence construction is fully learned.

Young (two- to three-year-old) children's sentences are by no means complete sentences, when compared with those of adults. Table 5-1 shows the sentences spoken by Adam, a 28½-month-old boy, in which he used the words "Mum," "Dad," "Here," and "There." Few of these sentences would have been spoken by adults. It seems unlikely that direct imitation (resulting from reinforcement of imitative efforts) of adult speech can explain the character of early sentence making, as is claimed, for example, by Skinner (1957, p. 31). The idea that children imitate adults, and thus learn to combine words into sentences, also appears invalid; young children make less adequate sentences when directly imitating adults than when making their own sentences (Ervin, 1964, p. 171).

It may be true, as Chomsky (1959) claims, that grammatical speech is a built-in human propensity. Even if built-in, it requires exercise to come into being. Until Weir's (1962) research, during which she tape-recorded her young son's speech while he was lying in his crib, no one knew how much conscious, conscientious effort went into learning words and sentences. Weir's little boy would lie in the crib, going through monologues of this sort:

"Fiss"
"Fiss"
"Fiss"
"No Fiss! Fiss"
"No Fiss! Fiss"
"Fish"
"Fish"
"Fish"

TABLE 5-1   Total Contexts of Four Words in the Record of Adam

Total Contexts of "Mum"

Here it is, Mum.	(The) pan, Mum.	Apple, Mum.
Here, Mum.	I want apple, Mum.	Again, Mum?
Here (the) coffee pot	I want blanket, Mum.	Out, Mum?
broken, Mum.	I want blanket now,	Salad, Mum?
More sugar, Mum.	Mum.	See, Mum?*
There it is, Mum.	I want juice, Mum.	Coffee, Mum?
What's that, Mum?	Mum, I want some,	Turn, Mum?
Mum, (where is the	Mum.	No, you see, Mum?
cards)?	Popeye, Mum?	No help, Mum.
Mum, (where's the	I wanta do, Mum.	Won't help, Mum.
rags)?	I wanta help, Mum.	Coffee, Mum.
Want coffee, Mum.*	I found, Mum.	Hi, Mum.*
Want apple, Mum.	I do, Mum.	O.K., Mum.
Want blanket, Mum.	I don't, Mum.	Here, Mum.
Want more juice, Mum.	I get it, Mum.	Over here, Mum.
I want blanket, Mum.	(Gonna) dump, Mum.	Enough, Mum.
I want (it), Mum.	Fall down, Mum.	Silver spoons, Mum.
I want paper away,	Fall, Mum.	
Mum.	An apple, Mum.	

Total Contexts of "Dad"

See paper, Dad.	See, Dad?*	Work, Dad?
Want coffee, Dad.*	Dad, want coffee?	Hi, Dad.*
I want cream, Dad.	Some more, Dad?	

Total Contexts of "Here"

Here (a car).	Here more bricks.	Here (we go).
Here all gone.	Here more blocks.	See the bolt here, see?
Here (block).	Here more firetruck.	That block here.
Here brick.	Here more toys.	That one here.
Here chairs.	Here more truck.†	That one right here.
Here coffee is.	Here Mum.†	I put bucket here.
Here comes Daddy.	Here Mummy.	Come here.
Here flowers.	Here my bricks.	Do here.
Here goes.†	Here not a house.	Leave that block here.
Here is.†	Here stars.	Put it here.
Here it goes.†	Here (the) coffee pot	Here not a house.
Here it is.†	broken, Mum.	Right here.†
Here it is, Mum.†	Here the card.	Over here.
Here's it here.	Here the cards.	Over here, Mum.
Here light.	Here the cheese.	Now here.
Here (mail) more paper.	Here the paper.	
Here more.		

Total Contexts of "There"

There goes.†	There more block.	I wanta put (it) right
There (he) goes.	There more truck.	there . . . (under) the
There is.†	There more nails.	couch.
There it goes.†	There Mum.†	Me see (in there).
There it is.†	There my house.	Blanket in there.
There it is, Mum.†	There my nails.	In there.
There kitty.	There Noah.	Right there.†

*Identifies contexts common to "Mum" and "Dad."
†Identifies contexts common to "Here" and "There."
(From Brown & Fraser, 1964, p. 55.)

Word making and sentence making are, in a way, innately determined human propensities, since we humans are unique in this respect; yet these activities also require practice. The use of words and sentences is so rewarding, in the sense that one can make his needs and ideas known to and responded to by others, that this general reinforcing quality of speech itself appears to be a much stronger motivational force than specific parental rewards for such things as imitation of adult sentences. Learning to speak sentences probably requires more than learning the rules of sentence construction; it also requires, probably before any specific rule learning, awareness on the part of the child that communication pays off in terms of obtaining desired ends. Once provided with speech models, but in a process different from direct imitation and reward for direct imitation, the child—still really an infant—expends a great deal of time on drilling himself in speech in order to gain these desired ends. Despite high motivation toward learning to speak, the child has certain handicaps that interfere with learning; adequate speech models may not be available; a short memory span limits learning and performances. But within these limits, Weir's data suggest that the child's learning of a first language is motivated by the same kinds of force that any of us, as adults, would feel if thrown into a group whose language we did not understand. To understand and to be understood leads to rewards; we would work hard, if need be, to get these rewards. Weir's data suggest that children learn in much the same way as do adults, for highly similar reasons. Their lack of prior knowledge may slow down learning in situations when prior learning could facilitate the new learning, but may cause learning to be more rapid in situations when prior learning would produce negative transfer of training, as often is the case in learning a second language.

Short-Term Memory and Sentence Construction. Young children face one special problem in learning to make sentences. Even if they have highly adequate models, they have a very short memory span. The adult says to the child, "There's a funny little brown doggie playing in the grass." This is too much for the child to handle, and if responding, he might say "Funny doggie play grass." Many students of children's speech call this type of sentence "telegraphic speech." It certainly is common among young children. Adults can retain and use about seven units of information at a time (Miller, 1956); at age two, when sentence construction begins, two units is about average; three units is superior. Being able to hold only a few things in the mind at any one time probably leads to the telegraphic sentences that children emit. The child copes with this problem in several ways. First of all, he does do away with unimportant (so far as conveying meaning) aspects of the sentence, as in the example above. Secondly, he may "chunk" or put together separate elements of meaning, so that they are held in memory as though they were a single unit. "Itsa" may be a convenient chunking or combining of the words "it is a" into a single unit, so far as memory is concerned. Through such tactics as telegraphic speech and chunking, the child attempts to produce meaningful, hopefully correct sentences even though he is severely handicapped in short-term memory span.

Children's defects in short-term memory lead to interesting questions regarding the effects of language structure, within a given culture, on the child's language development. Yngve (1960) hypothesized that (at least to the speaker) languages are right-branching; that is, that the first word determines, to a degree, what the second word could be, and so on, through the sentence (for example, with a first word of "A," we could say "cat" but could not properly say "cats").

For us, left-branching structures are difficult and sound ill-constructed (see McNeill, 1966, for examples of left-branchingness developed in rocketry). In English, for the most part a right-branching language, we need only to keep a few words ahead of ourselves in our thoughts. We do not need to know how a sentence is going to end before we begin it, since, so long as syntax is correct, each new word involves many different choices, as shown in Figure 5-3.

Left-branching languages do exist, although they are in the minority. Japanese, most American Indian languages, and Turkish are examples of

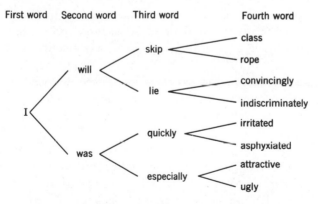

FIGURE 5-3 Some of the possible alternatives of sentence construction of a right-branching sentence starting with "I."

largely left-branching languages. In these languages the speaker must know the end of a sentence before he can construct the beginning of the sentence correctly. Rather than moving from beginning to end, as in English and other right-branching languages, he must construct each of the preceding portions of the sentence to fit the end word or phrase. Clearly, left-branching sentences demand a great deal more from memory than do right-branching sentences, and are difficult even for adults to handle—especially if they have been raised in a right-branching language group, but even if they have been raised in a left-branching language group (Forster, 1966). Imagine the problems of a two-year-old attempting to learn sentence construction of a left-to-right-branching sentence. The limits of short-term memory are such that sentence construction would present a tremendous problem and be learned very late, as compared with the same kind of learning in a right-to-left-branching system. Comparisons of how children from these two kinds of language system learn to make sentences could tell us much about the relative role of each of a number of aspects of language (e.g., syntax, inflection) and of the forces influencing sentence construction (e.g., short-term memory). German youngsters would be especially interesting to study in this respect. Most German sentences, like those in English, are right-branching; however, certain types of sentence [1] make German more left-branching than other existing European languages, for example: (1) dependent and relative clauses in which the main verb of the clause is the last element of the clause (the boy, who to the store went); (2) compound tenses in which the participle or the infinitive is the last element of the sentence (the boy has to the store gone); and (3) the so-called separable-prefix verbs in which the prefix is the last element of the sentence in the present and simple past tenses (no English equivalent). In these structures the final element or elements (in the case of compound verbs) must be retained in the temporary or short-term memory until the rest of the structure has been produced.

There are many problems to be solved by the child if he is to construct sentences in right-branching languages, such as English. Children learning left-branching have still more problems, and should differ markedly in the rate of language development, being retarded in at least some aspects of sentence construction unless parents provide a "baby syntax" similar to our "baby talk." But somehow we all manage to do it. Maybe we are innately grammarians, as Chomsky and Lenneberg have suggested.

[1] Mrs. Linda Klank provided these examples.

INDIVIDUAL DIFFERENCES IN LANGUAGE DEVELOPMENT

The high amount of variability among children in rates of language development has impelled psychologists to trace the sources of these individual differences. To a degree language skills depend on maturation. Language requires a highly accurate control of tongue and lip movements; like most motor behaviors, this control is largely maturational in its development.

Sex Differences

One would naturally expect girls to excel boys in language skills because females mature more rapidly than males. Most of the earlier studies of sex differences in language development show female superiority in vocabulary, articulation, length of sentences, complexity, and grammatical correctness up through the age of about 10 (see McCarthy, 1946, pp. 551–555). As to sheer number of words spoken, girls again lead (Jersild & Ritzman, 1938). Reasonable as it may seem to attribute this feminine superiority to maturational factors, this may not be the case. Most early students of sex differences in language development were women. It now has been shown that the sex of the tester, as well as the sex of the child tested, influences scores on tests of language development (Cowan, Weber, Hoddinott, & Klein, 1967). Girls respond best to female testers, boys to male testers; therefore many of the reported differences favoring girls in early language development may result from the fact that most of the testers were female.

Family Size and Structure

Family Size. The average three-year-old uses a vocabulary of nearly 1000 words as compared to the average adult who uses at least 20,000. Clearly, the more a child associates with adults, the more words he is exposed to and may learn. The only child is superior in nearly all forms of verbal ability to children with siblings; twins are more retarded than children with siblings (Davis, 1937); and triplets have less verbal facility than twins (Howard, 1934). The Dionne quintuplets were markedly slow in language development (Blatz, 1937). How could the five girls learn to speak at a normal rate when a great deal of their time was spent with one another? There is not much that a toddler can learn from four other, equally naive toddlers. Doubtless the amount of contact a child has with conversation of adult complexity is directly related to the rate of language growth.

Deprived Children. Studies over the years of neglected children (Büh-ler, 1931; Pringle & Bossio, 1958) and of institutionalized children (Skeels, Updegraff, Wellman, & Williams, 1937; Haggerty, 1959) concur that the lack of adult contact and speech reinforcement occasions con-siderable retardation of speech among children thus deprived. These four studies found among the children they tested a greater backward-ness in language than in any other area of development. To the ex-tent that communication is limited, all other aspects of development are handicapped. Nevertheless, the effect of severe language retarda-tion can be transitory. Tutoring and enrichment of the environment are capable of producing marked, rapid, and permanent language gains in previously retarded youngsters (Dawe, 1942; Luria & Yudo-vich, 1959; Skeels et al., 1938).

The Bilingual Child. Great numbers of Americans in the past grew up knowing the language of their immigrant parents as well as Eng-lish. Now again as the nation's isolation dissolves in a shrinking, con-temporary world, a growing proportion of young Americans are learn-ing two languages. Working in Hawaii, Smith (1939) observed that bilingual children were distinctly retarded in speech development. The deficiency was so pronounced that at school-entrance age the bilingual child was about equal in language skills to a *haole* (how-lee = Caucasian) monoglot three years old. Smith noted that both bilingualism and pidgin English might be involved in this retardation. The bilingual children were probably not exposed to standard English to any marked degree, but instead learned pidgin, the *lingua franca* of the Pacific. This tongue of 600 to 700 words that could be easily learned by all evolved from an admixture of many races and languages.

Except for a few individual cases, the Smith study did not compare true bilinguals. It compared people who spoke English with others who spoke a peculiar and impoverished English dialect as well as an archaic Oriental language. Small wonder that these Hawaiian "bilin-guals" were retarded. It was not bilingualism per se that seemed likely to have caused their deficiency, but rather the poverty of the languages they used.

At the other extreme is the upper-class European tradition of ordering the environment in a manner that produces bilingual, trilingual, or even polylingual children. Although empirical data are largely lacking, the learning of several languages, when each of them is used at high level by adults in the environment, appears to have no harmful effects. In Leopold's four-volume description (1937–1949) of his daughter's lan-guage development, he told of how she was brought up as a bilingual in German and English. His account was an argument for the assertion that learning two languages need not retard language development.

Several factors enter into the successful rearing of a bilingual child who is fully competent in both tongues. The languages themselves must be bona fide languages, not simple dialects. Each language should be learned from a different source [(Smith, 1939); for example, each parent might communicate with the child in only one of the two languages], since it seems important for the child to become aware, as soon as possible, that the two languages are distinct from one another. Having separate speakers for each tongue is one way of handling this problem. Using the languages at different times or in different contexts might also serve this purpose. Finally, to produce a truly bilingual child, it would seem imperative to maintain situations in which each of the languages must be used. Most bilingual children have bilingual parents; if the parents respond to one language more than the other, the child will gradually cease using the less established one in the interest of communicating with as little effort as necessary. This is another argument for the position taken above, that knowledge of words and of sentence construction is *intrinsically* rewarding, and does not depend entirely on such things as parental reward of correct language behavior.

Recent Changes

As we have seen, it was believed years ago that in language skills children with many adult and few child associations excelled those with few adult and many child associations, and children from lower-economic backgrounds lagged behind children from upper-economic homes. This is no longer entirely so. Signs of decrease in the differences in some of these areas are evident. Templin (1957) noted that children in her study of language development were generally more talkative and used a more mature level and organization of speech than children studied 25 years earlier. Sex differences seemed substantially diminished, and although socioeconomic differences continued to be significant, they had apparently decreased in magnitude.

Television may be a very important factor in this change. It produces a general improvement in the language skill of young children at the same time that it narrows the variations between children exposed to different environmental circumstances. Two of the most intensive studies of television's impact on the child (Himmelweit, Oppenheim, & Vince, 1958; Schramm, Lyle, & Parker, 1961) agree that television increases the information—and presumably, the vocabulary—of all children, but that children of lesser ability and from lower-economic backgrounds receive more benefit for a longer time.

Take two hypothetical situations. Child A, five years old, comes from a lower-economic group. Because of the pressures on them, his parents spend little time with the child, so they seldom serve as models and as reinforcers. Their vocabulary is relatively impoverished, so they are less adequate than others as models. Child A spends much time with siblings aged two, three, and six, who have a combined vocabulary of about 2500 words. The family purchases a television set and Child A spends 25 hours a week in front of it. The average vocabulary to which he is now exposed is probably well above 15,000 words since even comic strips and comic books have vocabularies of over 10,000 words (Thorndike, 1941). The television set is more stimulating for language development, so far as providing a model, than the pre-TV environment. Of course, it cannot completely overcome environmental handicaps, since it does not reinforce the child's vocalizations; as Rheingold et al. (1959) have noted, reinforcement of verbal behavior seems likely to determine its quantity—and quality.

Child B, also five years old, is the only child of a nonworking mother and a father who is a member of the medical profession. Both parents are college graduates. Each has a speaking vocabulary of approximately 30,000 words. They spend a good deal of time talking to the child and they read stories aloud to him every night before bedtime. The child has much exposure to adults, including visitors, grandparents, and neighbors as well as parents. Introduction of a television set into this child's life sharply reduces the amount of verbal stimulation he receives during every hour spent viewing.

Although television does narrow the differences in the way of life between families of separate regions and classes, it has not been able to eliminate individual differences between children in areas so influenced by environment as language because of its inability to provide the necessary reinforcement.

Language in the Disadvantaged Child [2]

Social-class differences in children's language have long been recognized. In McCarthy's (1930) study, consistent differences were found in favor of upper-social-class children in terms of general language

[2] For a review of social-class differences in language development, see C. Cazden, Subcultural differences in child language: An inter-disciplinary review. *Merrill-Palmer Quarterly,* 1966, **12**, 185–219.

maturity. Similar findings were obtained by Templin (1957) in a replication of the McCarthy study. Again, lower-class children performed less well on nearly all of the language measures used, including accuracy of articulation, speech sound discrimination, vocabulary, and amount of verbalization. These social-class differences apparently emerge, or are apparent, by the end of the second year of life (Irwin, 1948b, c).

A number of factors have been described to account for social-class differences in language development. Less verbal interaction between parent and child occurs in the lower-class as compared with the middle-class home. Lower-class parents do not encourage verbalization and they do not stimulate the child linguistically by reading to him, discussing events with him, or reasoning with him. Further, the parents themselves are handicapped linguistically, and thus provide poor speech models for the child. In a study of maternal language in four social-class levels (Hess & Shipman, 1965), taped samples of the mothers' language were analyzed on a number of different measures. The total amount of verbal output was found to be greater for the middle-class as compared with the lower-class mothers. With respect to quality of the language used, middle-class mothers were more likely to use abstract words and they used more complex sentences.

Martin Deutsch (1963) has argued that a lower-class child is handicapped by a general restriction in the variety of stimulation to which he is exposed. This is true in language as well as in other areas (M. Deutsch, 1964). Further, the "signal-to-noise ratio" may be very low in a crowded lower-class home. Although there is a great deal of language (television, yelling, etc.), the young child has difficulty sorting out of this "noise" meaningful language, which, indeed, is seldom directed specifically to him. Moreover, John and Goldstein (1964) maintain that language development is retarded if it is learned only through receptive exposure (hearing). Corrective feedback in which the parent expands the child's utterance and corrects word usage is extremely important. Thus when the child says, "Johnny eat," the parent responds, "Yes, Johnny is eating his lunch." This provides the child with additional information regarding sentence structure, verb form, and vocabulary.

In an analysis of social-class differences in language usage, Bernstein (1961) has identified two styles of communication: *restricted* and *elaborated*. Working-class speech is characterized by a restricted style that is stereotyped and condensed; it is lacking in precision and composed of clichés that are readily understood by the listener. Elaborated style, employed by the better-educated middle class, is more specific, precise, individualized, and flexible. Bernstein's approach views language as part of larger social behavior in terms of organizing and structuring experience. The lower-class child exposed to limited and restricted language usage is handicapped in his ability to deal with his environment at an abstract and conceptual level.

The lower-class child has been found to be handicapped in auditory discrimination of speech sounds, which is related to reading ability (C. Deutsch, 1964). The important role played by language in concept formation, problem solving, and in communication of ideas is apparent. It is not surprising, therefore, to find the lower-class child retarded in the various skills required for school success. This strongly suggests that a remedial program for the disadvantaged child must place great emphasis on the language area.

The structured language approach developed by Bereiter and Englemann (1966) is designed to facilitate in the disadvantaged child the acquisition of knowledge concerning pronunciation, sentence structure, and vocabulary. The learning of polar opposites, prepositions, connectives, and classes or categories of objects is stressed. While the social-emotional aspects of language are important, the disadvantaged child is most deficient in the use of language as a cognitive tool—a tool required for logical thinking.

In summary, the early concern with describing social-class differences in language development has given way to attempts to identify the reasons for such differences. In turn, remedial programs have been developed, based upon a careful analysis of the significant aspects of language required for conceptual thinking.

Stuttering

Certain findings regarding the basis of stuttering have wide implications for the whole area of problem behavior. Although other speech problems, such as the substitution of sounds, tend to vanish speedily as a function of age, stuttering is rather persistent. As such, it has evoked wide interest; various theories have attempted to account for the phenomenon. A pleasant and chivalrous explanation of stuttering is the "dirty word" theory. This view explains stuttering by saying that children learn profane and obscene words among their playmates. They come home and in talking begin to say these words. They catch themselves in time and block their speech, so that instead of saying, "Pass the damn sugar," they say, "Pass the d-d-d-d sugar." Stammering and stuttering emerge from these dirty words, and the child becomes a stutterer. Since six to eight times as many boys stutter as do girls, this theory rests on the assumption that boys swear among their mates six to eight times as often as girls. This may be chivalry but it is hardly scientific.

A second, older theory involves cerebral dominance. For the right-handed individual, the left cerebral hemisphere dominates the control of motor responses; the reverse holds true for left-handed persons. The theory of cerebral dominance got its start from the observable fact that there is a connection between handedness—and especially "changed handedness"—and stuttering. The left-handed child, forced into becoming right-handed upon entering school, stutters more often than would be expected to occur by chance alone. This observation gave rise to the theory that exercising the right hand had made the cerebral hemispheres equal in dominance, so that neither had control, whereupon stuttering resulted. However, this explanation accounted neither for sex differences in stuttering nor for the fact that few stutterers stuttered equally in all situations. If a physiological mechanism is of prime significance, it is difficult to understand why most stutterers stutter with adults but not with animals, or babies, or when alone. More likely the adults who change children's handedness may also manipulate children in other ways, with the direct manipulation of speech producing the stuttering.

This "manipulation of speech" leads to a third explanation of stuttering, which is now most widely accepted. Johnson (1944) noted wide differences between groups in the incidence of stuttering. American Indians, despite an emphasis on excellence in speaking, had no stutterers—and, in fact, have no word in their languages to denote stuttering. Indians assume that all children will speak well if one merely waits. Johnson began to suspect that parent attitudes, more than child articulation, caused stuttering. Intensive study demonstrated that this was indeed the case; that stuttering developed after diagnosis. This fact formed the basis of Johnson's semantic or *diagnosogenic* theory of stuttering (Johnson, 1946).

All human beings have nonfluencies in their speech—that is, stammering and stuttering. This is primary stuttering. Young children have more of it than adults. Within any age and either sex the individual variations in the proportions of nonfluency are considerable. Although a few children are so pronouncedly nonfluent that almost any parent would diagnose them as stutterers, the nonfluency of most children lies in a range that may or may not cause parents to show concern over their speech development. If a parent is concerned when a child blocks on a word or stutters and responds frequently with such comments as, "Start over again and talk more slowly" or "You'd better be careful and talk slowly—you're beginning to stutter," the child becomes anxious and thus has more nonfluencies. Some things are done best, however, when humans are not conscious of them. Speech is one of these. As a child's speech deteriorates, the parent is increasingly inclined to diagnose him as a stutterer. It is this diagnosis by parents, or teachers, or others, plus the child's acceptance of it that makes him a stutterer. He is now a secondary stutterer. Once an individual accepts this status and becomes aware of his nonfluencies, his stuttering worsens and he takes to using "tic-like" behaviors in the vain hope of reducing it. A considerable body of findings (e.g., see Johnson, 1955, 1959) supports this theory of stuttering.

Here is a clear case of the effect on behavior of the assignment and acceptance of a social role. Perhaps less fluent than most other children, very likely as a result of biological causes, the child is given the role of stutterer, accepts the role, and becomes a *secondary* stutterer rather than remaining a primary stutterer with a larger proportion of nonfluencies than usual. The point of all this is that if humans can make stutterers by diagnosis, perhaps they can produce other problem behaviors such as delinquency or illiteracy with the same techniques. The experience of Lecky (1945) with intellectually competent young people who could not learn to read further supports the position that many problems are caused by diagnosis, as soon as the person diagnosed accepts the diagnosis.

THE IMPACT OF LANGUAGE ON THOUGHT, LEARNING, AND MEMORY

Language and Thought

Many of the early psychologists conceived of thought as a stream of mental images. To understand the thought process, they believed, one had to look inward, to *introspect*, to discern this flow of images. The "Würzburg school" of psychologists (see Humphrey, 1951, pp. 30–131) demonstrated, however, that thought could occur without any conscious awareness of imagery. As a result, the Würzburgers and descendants of the imagery school of thought, led by Titchener, emphasized the relation of muscle tensions and other kinesthetic-proprioceptive responses to thought. This idea, that thought is primarily a set of motor behaviors, was brought to fruition by Watson (1914), who believed that human thought was nothing but subvocal speech. It was at this point that language reached its peak as an explanatory device: to many psychologists of this era language was not merely associated with thought, it *was* thought.

This view is not without support. Young children do speak without the intent of communicating to others and appear to be overtly verbalizing their thoughts, just as adults may covertly verbalize them. This observable phenomenon is the basis of Piaget's (1926) notion of children's egocentric speech—speech not based on the idea of social communication. Even as adults, people "think out loud," talking to themselves especially when confronted with complicated problems. Further, lip, tongue, and laryngeal movement increases among individuals as they silently solve problems of an increasing challenge (Jacobson, 1932). Yet despite this supporting evidence, the notion that language and thought are synonymous is generally rejected. It seems more likely that the movement of lip, tongue, and larynx accompanying thought are incidental consequences having no more significance than the snapping of fingers or the scratching of the head has when attempting to recollect a forgotten event. Several studies, beginning with Thorson's (1925), suggest that the motor accompaniments of thought are a nervous discharge rather than necessary substrata of thought. Although not synonymous with thought, language seems to be intimately related to learning and memory, as we shall discover in the remainder of this chapter.

Language and Learning

The relation of language to learning was mentioned in Chapter 4. There we said that language benefited learning by allowing a higher degree of—and more rapid—vicarious trial and error than occurred in other species. Language facilitates the formation of concrete concepts, providing a common name—for example, spoon—to link together a class of objects with a variety of physical characteristics despite their external variations. Because verbal terms are available, they govern the dimensions along which categories form and set the limits for the generalizing of stimuli. This leads to concept formation. Moreover, language enables the formation of abstract concepts as well.

Language not only facilitates learning. In many (e.g., Ervin, 1960; Kuenne, 1946) but not all (e.g., Kendler, Kendler, & Wells, 1960) studies, it also produces a more adequate transfer. Here are two examples of the effect of language on learning. The first is from the autobiography of Helen Keller, deaf and blind from infancy; at the age of seven her beloved teacher, Annie Sullivan, returned her to the world by making her aware of symbolic communication. Miss Keller describes her awakening to an awareness of language in her book, *The Story of My Life.*

. . . The morning after my teacher came she led me into her room and gave me a doll. The little blind children at the Perkins Institution had sent it and Laura Bridgman had dressed it; but I did not know this until afterward. When I had played with it a little while, Miss Sullivan slowly spelled into my hand the word "d-o-l-l." I was at once interested in this finger play and tried to imitate it. When I finally succeeded in making the letters correctly I was flushed with childish pleasure and pride. Running downstairs to my mother I held up my hand and made the letters for doll. I did not know that I was spelling a word or even that words existed; I was simply making my fingers go in monkey-like imitation. In the days that followed I learned to spell in this uncomprehending way a great many words, among them *pin, hat, cup* and a few verbs like *sit, stand* and *walk*. But my teacher had been with me several weeks before I understood that everything has a name.

One day, while I was playing with my new doll, Miss Sullivan put my big rag doll into my lap also, spelled "d-o-l-l" applied to both. Earlier in the day we had had a tussle over the words "m-u-g" and "w-a-t-e-r." Miss Sullivan had tried to impress it upon me that "m-u-g" is *mug* and that "w-a-t-e-r" is *water*, but I persisted in confounding the two. In despair she had dropped the subject for the time, only to renew it at the first opportunity. I became impatient at her repeated attempts and, seizing the new doll, I dashed it upon the floor. I was keenly delighted when I felt the fragments of the broken doll at my feet. Neither sorrow nor regret followed my passionate outburst. I had not loved the doll. In the still, dark world in which I lived there was no strong sentiment or tenderness. I felt my teacher sweep the fragments to one side of the hearth, and I had a sense of satisfaction that the cause of my discomfort was removed. She brought me my hat, and I knew I was going out into the warm sunshine. This thought, if a wordless sensation may be called a thought, made me skip with pleasure.

We walked down the path to the well-house, attracted by the fragrance of the honeysuckle with which it was covered. Some one was drawing water and my teacher placed my hand under the spout. As the cool stream gushed over one hand she spelled into the other the word *water*, first slowly, then rapidly. I stood still, my whole attention fixed upon the motions of her fingers. Suddenly I felt a misty consciousness as of something forgotten—a thrill of returning thought; and somehow the mystery of language was revealed to me. I knew then that "w-a-t-e-r" meant the wonderful cool something that was flowing over my hand. That living word awakened my soul, gave it light, hope, joy, set it free! There were barriers still, it is true, but barriers that could in time be swept away.

I left the well-house eager to learn. Everything had a name, and each name gave birth to a new thought. As we returned to the house every object which I touched seemed to quiver with life. That was because I saw everything with the strange, new sight that had come to me. On entering the door I remembered the doll I had broken. I felt my way to the hearth and picked up the pieces. I tried vainly to put them together. Then my eyes filled with tears; for I realized what I had done, and for the first time I felt repentance and sorrow.

I learned a great many new words that day. I do not remember what they all were; but I do know that *mother, father, sister, teacher* were among them—words that were to make the world blossom for me, "like Aaron's rod, with flowers." It would have been difficult to find a happier child than I was as I lay in my crib at the close of that eventful day and lived over the joys it had brought me, and for the first time longed for a new day to come (Keller, 1917, pp. 22–24).

This is not only a testimonial to the role of language in learning, it is also a moving example of insightful learning.

The other illustration of the effect of language on learning is drawn from a study by Luria and Yudovich (1959) of a pair of twins who were retarded in speech development. Although both were defective in speech, one twin was more deficient than the other. The two were separated for a large part of their waking hours and the more retarded twin (Twin A) was given training in language development. Following this training, both twins were exposed to various test situations. This is a description of one of these tests:

Both children are asked to play out several examples of a game which involves attaching conditional meanings to objects. They are told that the pencil is "mama"; the vase, "a tree"; the spoon, "a wolf," etc. The game, which comprises subject matter covering corresponding things, is played out with the aid of the objects.

The differences between the twins are here very substantial.

Twin A deciphers the meaning of the gesture game at once, during manipulation of objects; decoding does not present any difficulties to him and he immediately describes the whole game verbally; "The engine drives along, the mother wolf runs, the little wolf goes up the tree, mama comes out of the house, sits on the engine, takes the boy," etc.

When asked to make up a game independently with the same objects, he does this easily; some of the conditional meanings are retained, others created anew. "Mama caught a hare, the wolf ran to look for the hare, the engine drove along, the hare was in the house with mama, it jumped through the window straight on to the fir-tree. . . ."

The same operation was performed altogether differently by Twin B who had not undergone speech training.

He could not decode the stories related by gestures immediately but was only able to do this in parts and then only in reply to questions put to him.   When asked to repeat the game, he repeated it without any changes, as it had been shown to him by gestures, and when asked to give new meanings to the objects he refused (Luria & Yudovich, 1959, pp. 104–105).

Clearly, from these examples and from the studies cited in the previous chapter, language facility has a distinct influence on learning and knowledge.

Language and Memory

Although lower organisms and human infants are not capable of symbolic communication, they certainly are capable of remembering. Memory, as both Watson (1914, 1930) and Guthrie (1952) have held from different theoretical positions, may be at least partly motor.   In a simple situation suggested by Tomkins (1961), a motor activity recalls events associated with the activity's original use.   An individual is instructed to write his name in letters one inch high at the rate of one letter every five seconds.   Not only does his signature look like that of many years ago, but also a flood of associations frequently accompanies the motor act.   Similarly, visceral tensions, muscular states, and the like do at times evoke the behaviors tied to them in the past, so that in a sense they constitute a memory system.

Eidetic Imagery.   More important, with regard to memory not dependent on symbolic skills, is eidetic imagery (EI).   Eidetic imagery, first investigated by German psychologists, especially Jaensch (1930), is essentially synonymous with what is popularly called "photographic memory."   EI consists of being able to evoke an extremely clear image or picture of an absent object or event.   Upon being tested for ability to recall, the eidetic individual is sometimes 100 per cent accurate, because the visual image evoked has such clarity that every detail of the picture is available to him during the test.   Eidetic imagery is not remarkably common at any age, but it seems to decline appreciably in incidence after about the age of nine.   The most detailed review of the subject may be found in Klüver (1933).   Actually, eidetic imagery has fallen from grace and has not been a live topic for research for many years, perhaps because Jaensch was an apologist for the Nazis.

However, while conducting psychological tests in the public schools, one of the authors of this book came across a boy who, in the course of testing, displayed eidetic talents.   The child had been referred for testing because of his difficulty at learning to read.   Nevertheless, further testing showed him to be a genuine *eidetiker*.   Inspired by this experience, the researcher undertook a larger-scale investigation of EI (Zelhart & Johnson, 1959). This study employed nonsense shapes like those shown in Figure 5-4; such shapes have been used with adult populations (Vanderplas & Garvin, 1959) to determine their associative value, that is, the extent to which individuals are reminded of something by sight of the shape.

In the study, the associative values of 48 nonsense shapes were first determined among a sample of third-grade children. These shapes were then classified into the 16 lowest, 16 medium, and 16 highest in associative value for the sample group of children and were presented in individual tests to other third-graders who had not been part of the original group. The shapes, cut from masonite, were placed on a checkerboard of 16 squares, one to a square. Following a 30-second exposure, the board was swept clean and the child was told to restore the shapes to their proper places. It was assumed that any eidetics among the third-graders would be able to put back the shapes into the proper squares with a high degree of accuracy, that they would do as well with shapes in the center squares as in the peripheral ones, and

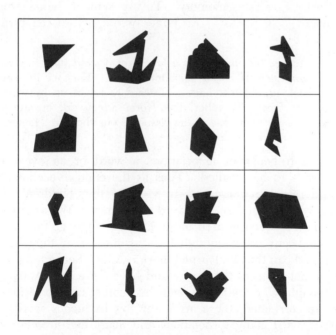

FIGURE 5-4   Nonsense shapes of differing association values (McBain & Johnson, 1963, p. 98; from Vanderplas & Garvin, 1959).

that they would do equally well on the three classes of shape, even though these differed in associative value.

The results were generally disappointing. Children performed the task poorly, despite the fact that they generally enjoyed it. There was one exception. Eight children who were remedial readers—actually nonreaders—did significantly better than the others and showed a high degree of accuracy in recall. These findings suggest that eidetic imagery is rare, but that it does exist. High eidetic talent may be related in some way to difficulty in dealing with the symbolic system of reading and writing.

Using an approach similar to that of Zelhart and Johnson, but using meaningful objects rather than nonsense shapes, Hayden (1967) found only two cases of eidetic imagery among more than 100 children tested. These two eidetic children were inadequate readers, as was found in the previous study. Further, Doob's (1964, 1966) work in Africa suggests that eidetic talent is in some way negatively associated with reading experience. In most cases, rural and/or illiterate Africans showed a higher degree of eidetic imagery than town and/or literate Africans.

Words and Memory. Although memory exists without language, language evidently facilitates memory. To use William James's term, language provides "fish hooks." As James wrote before the turn of the century,

> In mental terms, *the more facts a fact is associated with in the mind, the better possession of it our memory retains.* Each of its associates becomes a hook to which it hangs, a means to fish it up by when sunk beneath the surface. Together, they form a network of attachments by which it is woven into the entire tissue of our thought (James, 1892, p. 294).

The more fish hooks or associations a word or an event has, the more likely it is to be recalled. Thus as the child's vocabulary grows, learning and retention increase. In view of this, children's textbooks are written with a concern for word frequency. Words are selected from those most frequently used in the English language for two reasons. First, if they occur often enough it is assumed that they have many associations and can thus be learned more readily. Second, once learned, they will be met often in the future and have a greater positive transfer value. Although word frequency and the number of associations evoked by words are correlated, there are many low-frequency words, such as *zoo* or *circus*, with many associations and many high-frequency words, like *the, when,* or *where,* that awaken few associations. Johnson, Frincke, and Martin (1961) have suggested that the choice of words for textbooks might better be based on a large number of associations rather than on word frequency per se, as is now done.

Words vary in the number of associations they evoke. Developmental differences exist as well. As children gain in vocabulary, more "fish hooks" come into existence. Further, the kind of "fish hooks," that is, the kind of associative net, changes with age. In word-association tests, the subject is presented with a stimulus word such as "table" and then responds with the first word he thinks of when he hears "table." Adults most frequently respond with "chair." Children show far less agreement in their associations than do adults, and also differ from adults in the class of associations that they make. For example, at grade 4 or 6, a child presented with the word "robin" would be more likely than would an adult to say "bird"—a superordinate class to which robins belong—while the adult would be more likely than the child to say "worm," a contrast or opposite association (Palermo, 1965). Both number and kind of associations change with age. Part of the variance in rates of learning and in memory between age groups may be due, basically, to differences in association. Thus, although language is not thought, as was once believed, it is closely linked with both learning and memory.

SUMMARY

Humans are a noisy bunch. Infants make many sounds and make them often. From their sound-making activity emerges language. Sound making becomes emotionally rewarding to the infant, thus increasing the amount of vocalization. Parents selectively reward or reinforce the sounds that are like those of words, thus causing the frequency of certain sounds to increase even more. Certain sounds come to have mutual meaning for the infant and the parent; at this point sound making has become symbolic communication.

Vocabulary growth is slow for a time, and then shows rapid increase at about age three to four. The child learns, beginning at about age two, to construct sentences. These sentences become longer and more grammatically correct as age and abilities associated with age, such as short-term memory, increase. The child learns the ground rules of communication. By about age four, errors in word usage result from the failure of the English language to follow the rules very closely.

Wide individual differences in communicative skills, especially vocabulary, have been shown to exist between children. The sex of the child, his family's size, his parents' occupational and educational levels, the number of languages spoken in the home, and parental attitudes toward their children's speech are among the factors associated with individual differences. Since IQ, on most intelligence tests, depends largely on language ability, children from lower occupational groups and large families may be unfairly handicapped on such tests. Some presumed handicaps to adequate language development, such as bilingualism, may have been greatly exaggerated in their influence. Apparently increasing homogeneity of the environment is decreasing the individual differences between children in rate of language development.

Although it was once held that the entire thought process was merely subvocal speech, this view is not supported by the majority of research findings. Language does seem to alter and enhance learning and to strengthen memory. All said and done, language is the uniquely human characteristic that sets humanity apart from all other organisms.

REFERENCES

Bellugi, U. The development of interrogative structures in children's speech. In K. Riegel (Ed.), *The development of language functions.* Ann Arbor, Michigan: University of Michigan Center for Human Growth and Development, 1965. Pp. 103–137.

Bereiter, C., & Englemann, S. *Teaching disadvantaged children in the preschool.* Englewood Cliffs, N. J.: Prentice-Hall, 1966.

Berko, J. The child's learning of English morphology. *Word,* 1958, **14,** 150–177.

Bernstein, B. Language and social class. *British Journal of Sociology,* 1961, **11,** 271–276.

Blatz, W. E., et al. *Collected studies on the Dionne quintuplets.* Toronto: University of Toronto Press, 1937.

Brown, R., & Fraser, C. The acquisition of syntax. In U. Bellugi & R. Brown (Eds.), The acquisition of language. *Monographs of the Society for Research in Child Development,* 1964, **29,** Serial No. 92, No. 1, 43–79.

Bühler, C. *Kindheit and Jugend.* (3rd ed.) Leipzig: Hirzel, 1931.

Chomsky, N. Review of B. F. Skinner, *Verbal Behavior.* *Language,* 1959, **35,** 26–58.

Cowan, P. A., Weber, J., Hoddinott, B. A., & Klein, T. Mean length of a spoken response as a function of stimulus, experimenter, and subject. *Child Development,* 1967, **38,** 191–203.

Davis, E. A. The development of linguistic skill in twins, singletons with siblings, and only children from age five to ten years. Minneapolis: University of Minnesota Press, *Institute of Child Welfare Series,* No. 14, 1937.

Dawe, H. C. A study of the effect of an educational program upon language development and related mental functions in young children. *Journal of Experimental Education,* 1942, **2,** 200–209.

Deutsch, C. Auditory discrimination and learning: Social factors. *Merrill-Palmer Quarterly*, 1964, **10**, 277–296.

Deutsch, M. The disadvantaged child and the learning process. In A. H. Passow (Ed.), *Education in depressed areas*. New York: Bureau of Publication, Teachers College, 1963. Pp. 163–179.

Deutsch, M. Facilitating development in the pre-school child: Social and psychological perspectives. *Merrill-Palmer Quarterly*, 1964, **10**, 249–263.

Doob, L. W. Eidetic images among the Ibo. *Ethnology*, 1964, **3**, 357–363.

Doob, L. W. Eidetic imagery: A cross cultural Will-o'-the-Wisp? *Journal of Psychology*, 1966, **63**, 13–34.

Ervin, S. M. Training and a logical operation by children. *Child Development*, 1960, **31**, 555–563.

Ervin, S. M. Imitation and structural change in children's language. In E. H. Lenneberg (Ed.), *New directions in the study of language*. Cambridge, Mass.: M.I.T. Press, 1964. Pp. 163–189.

Forster, K. I. Left to right processes in the construction of sentences. *Journal of Verbal Learning and Verbal Behavior*, 1966, **5**, 285–291.

Guthrie, E. R. *The psychology of learning.* (Rev. ed.) New York: Harper, 1952.

Haggerty, A. D. The effects of long term hospitalization or institutionalization upon the language development of children. *Journal of Genetic Psychology*, 1959, **94**, 205–209.

Hayden, S. P. *Eidetic imagery.* Unpublished master's thesis, University of Colorado, 1967.

Hess, R., & Shipman, V. Early experience and socialization of cognitive modes in children. *Child Development*, 1965, **36**, 869–886.

Himmelweit, H. T., Oppenheim, A. N., & Vince, P. *Television and the child*. London: Oxford University Press, 1958.

Howard, R. *A developmental study of triplets.* Unpublished doctoral dissertation, University of Minnesota, 1934.

Humphrey, G. *Thinking.* London: Methuen, 1951.

Irwin, O. C. The developmental status of speech sounds of ten feeble-minded children. *Child Development*, 1942, **13**, 29–39.

Irwin, O. C. Infant speech: Consonantal sounds according to place of articulation. *Journal of Speech and Hearing Disorders*, 1947, **12**, 391–401. (a)

Irwin, O. C. Infant speech: Consonantal sounds according to manner of articulation. *Journal of Speech and Hearing Disorders*, 1947, **12**, 402–404. (b)

Irwin, O. C. Infant speech: Development of vowel sounds. *Journal of Speech and Hearing Disorders*, 1948, **13**, 31–34. (a)

Irwin, O. C. Infant speech: The effect of family occupational status and of age on use of speech sounds. *Journal of Speech and Hearing Disorders*, 1948, **13**, 224–226. (b)

Irwin, O. C.   Infant speech: The effect of family occupational status and of age on sound frequency.   *Journal of Speech and Hearing Disorders,* 1948, **13,** 320–323.   (c)

Irwin, O. C., & Chen, H. P.   Infant speech: Vowel and consonant frequency. *Journal of Speech and Hearing Disorders,* 1946, **II,** 123–125.

Jacobson, E.   Electrophysiology of mental activities.   *American Journal of Psychology,* 1932, **44,** 677–694.

Jaensch, E. R.   *Eidetic imagery.*   New York: Harcourt, Brace, 1930.

James, W.   *Psychology: briefer course.*   New York: Holt, 1892.

Jersild, A. T., & Ritzman, R.   Aspects of language development: The growth of loquacity and vocabulary.   *Child Development,* 1938, **9,** 243–259.

John, V., & Goldstein, L.   The social context of language acquisition.   *Merrill-Palmer Quarterly,* 1964, **10,** 265–275.

Johnson, R. C., Frincke, G., & Martin, L.   Meaningfulness, frequency, and affective character of words as related to visual duration threshold. *Canadian Journal of Psychology,* 1961, **15,** 199–204.

Johnson, W.   The Indians have no word for it: I. Stuttering in children. *Quarterly Journal of Speech,* 1944, **30,** 330–337.

Johnson, W.   *People in quandaries: The semantics of personal adjustment.* New York: Harper, 1946.

Johnson, W. (Ed.)   *Stuttering in children and adults: Thirty years of research at the University of Iowa.*   Minneapolis: University of Minnesota Press, 1955.

Johnson, W., et al.   *The onset of stuttering: Research findings and implications.*   Minneapolis: University of Minn. Press, 1959.

Keller, H.   *The story of my life.*   New York: Doubleday, Page, 1917.

Kendler, T. S., Kendler, H. H., & Wells, D.   Reversal and non-reversal shifts in nursery school children.   *Journal of Comparative and Physiological Psychology,* 1960, **53,** 83–88.

Klüver, H.   Eidetic images.   In C. Murchison (Ed.), *A handbook of child psychology.*   (Rev. ed.)   Worcester, Mass.: Clark University Press, 1933.

Kuenne, M. R.   Experimental investigation of the relation of language to transposition behavior in young children.   *Journal of Experimental Psychology,* 1946, **36,** 479–489.

Lecky, P.   *Self consistency, a theory of personality.*   New York: Long Island Press, 1945.

Lenneberg, E. H.   The natural history of language.   In F. Smith & G. A. Miller (Eds.), *The genesis of language.*   Cambridge, Mass.: M.I.T. Press, 1966.   Pp. 219–252.

Leopold, W. F.   *Speech development of a bilingual child,* Vols. I–IV, Evanston, Ill.: Northwestern University Press, 1937–1949.

Lewis, M. M.   *How children learn to speak.*   New York: Basic Books, 1959.

Lorenz, K.   *King Solomon's Ring.*   New York: Crowell, 1952.

Luria, A. R., & Yudovich, F.   *Speech and the development of mental processes in the child.*   London: Staples, 1959.

McCarthy, D. *The language development of the preschool child.* Institute of Child Welfare Monographs Series, 4. Minneapolis: University of Minn. Press, 1930.

McCarthy, D. Language development in children. In L. Carmichael (Ed.), *Manual of child psychology.* (2nd ed.) New York: Wiley, 1946. Pp. 492–630.

McNeill, D. Speaking of space. *Science,* 1966, **152,** 875–880.

Miller, G. A. The magic number seven, plus or minus two: Some limits on our capacity for processing information. *Psychological Review,* 1956, **63,** 81–97.

Miller, N. E., & Dollard, J. *Social learning and imitation.* New Haven: Yale University Press, 1941.

Mowrer, O. H. *Learning theory and personality dynamics.* New York: Ronald, 1950. Pp. 688–726.

Palermo, D. S. Word associations as related to children's verbal habits. In K. Riegel (Ed.), *The development of language functions.* Ann Arbor, Michigan: University of Michigan Center for Human Growth and Development, 1965. Pp. 53–64.

Palermo, D. S., & Eberhardt, V. L. On the learning of morphological rules: An experimental analogy. *Journal of Verbal Learning and Verbal Behavior,* 1968, **7,** 337–344.

Piaget, J. *The language and thought of the child.* New York: Harcourt, Brace, 1926.

Pringle, M. L., & Bossio, V. A study of deprived children. II. Language development and reading attainment. *Vita Humana,* 1958, **I,** 142–170.

Rheingold, H. L., Gewirtz, J. L., & Ross, H. W. Social conditioning of vocalizations in the infant. *Journal of Comparative and Physiological Psychology,* 1959, **52,** 68–73.

Schramm, W. L., Lyle, J., & Parker, E. B. *Television in the lives of our children.* Stanford, Calif.: Stanford University Press, 1961.

Shirley, M. M. *The first two years of life: A study of twenty-five babies,* Vols. I and II. Minneapolis: University of Minnesota Press, *Institute of Child Welfare Monographs Series,* No. 7, 1933.

Skeels, H. M., Updegraff, R., Wellman, B. L. & Williams, H. M. A study of environmental stimulation: An orphanage preschool project. *University of Iowa Study in Child Welfare,* 1938, **15,** No. 4.

Skinner, B. F. *Verbal behavior.* New York: Appleton-Century-Crofts, 1957.

Slobin, D. I. Acquisition of Russian as a native language. In F. Smith & G. A. Miller (Eds.), *The genesis of language.* Cambridge, Mass.: M.I.T. Press, 1966. Pp. 129–148.

Smith, M. E. An investigation of the development of the sentence and the extent of vocabulary in young children. *University of Iowa Study in Child Welfare,* 1926, **3,** No. 5.

Smith, M. E. Some light on the problem of bilingualism as found from a study of the progress in mastery of English among preschool children of non-American ancestry in Hawaii. *Genetic Psychology Monographs,* 1939, **21,** 121–284.

Templin, M. C.   *Certain language skills in children: Their development and interrelationships.*   Minneapolis: University of Minnesota Press, 1957.

Terman, L. M., et al.   *Genetic studies of genius: Vol. I.   Mental and physical traits of a thousand gifted children.*   Stanford, Calif.: Stanford University Press, 1925.

Thorndike, E. L.   Words and the comics.   *Journal of Experimental Education,* 1941, **17,** 110–113.

Thorson, A. M.   The relation of tongue movements to internal speech.   *Journal of Experimental Psychology,* 1925, **8,** 1–32.

Tinbergen, N.   *Social behavior in animals.*   New York: Wiley, 1953.

Tomkins, S. S.   Address presented at the Spartan Psychological Association Meetings, San Jose, Calif., 1961.

Vanderplas, J. M., & Garvin, E. A.   The association value of random shapes.   *Journal of Experimental Psychology,* 1959, **57,** 147–154.

Watson, J. B.   *Behavior: An introduction to comparative psychology.*   New York: Holt, 1914.

Watson, J. B.   *Behaviorism.*   (Rev. ed.)   New York: Norton, 1930.

Weir, R. H.   *Language in the crib.*   The Hague: Mouton, 1962.

Yerkes, R. M., & Learned, B.   *Chimpanzee intelligence and its vocal expression.*   Baltimore: Williams & Wilkins, 1925.

Yngve, V. H.   A model and a hypothesis for language structure.   *Proceedings of the American Philosophical Society,* 1960, **104,** 444–466.

Zelhart, P., & Johnson, R. C.   An investigation of eidetic imagery.   Paper presented to the Spartan Psychological Association, San Jose, California, 1959.

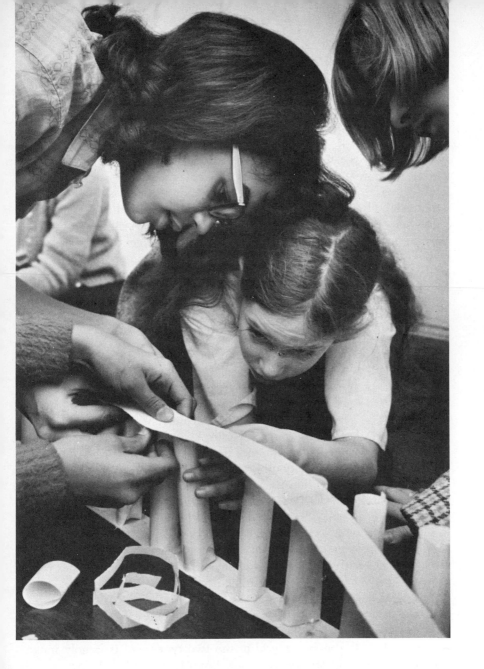

6

Intelligence

Certainly one of the most basic factors in human development is intelligence. Although intelligence is intimately related to both learning and language, psychologists are still of two minds as to whether it is a single trait of the individual or the sum of many abilities to cope with all sorts of situations. This chapter deals with intelligence from various vantage points. It begins with a review of various definitions of intelligence and ideas about its nature, then considers the growth of intellectual ability, the constancy of that ability, and the relation of individual differences in intelligence, as it is ordinarily measured, to learning capacities and social skills. Specific intelligence tests are noted here only as they pertain to the topics under examination. A more comprehensive discussion of them has been reserved for Chapter 14, which treats individual appraisal.

DEFINITIONS

In the first useful intelligence test (see Binet & Simon, 1916), Binet maintained that intelligence consisted of comprehension, invention, direction, and censorship. This definition contains several interesting elements. One interesting aspect of Binet's definition is its inclusion of direction; this is really a measure of purposiveness and perseverance rather than ability. Also, Binet includes censorship, that is, self-censorship; this is an aspect of intelligence not included in any other definition, yet is clearly one of considerable significance.

In designating invention as a mark of intellectual ability, Binet foreshadowed Guilford (1950, 1959), who emphasized creativity in his definition of intelligence. Because of this position, Guilford has expressed dissatisfaction with conventional intelligence tests, developing in his own research tests of divergent thinking that he believes allow the prediction of creativity more than conventional intelligence tests, which measure "convergent" thinking for the most part.

Another who attacked such conventional tests was Cattell (1957), who held that there were two types of intelligence, which he labeled *fluid* and *crystallized*. Fluid intelligence solves novel or "culture-free" problems; it is the more general of the two types and is largely innate. Any decline in fluid ability from, say, brain injury will influence a wide variety of intelligence-test scores. Crystallized intelligence, on the other hand, is seen in acquired, complex, familiar cultural activities and skills —for example, reading or mathematics; it is composed of quite specific factors, such as verbal fluency and mechanical ability, and is dependent largely on environmental forces. For the most part, conventional intelligence tests measure crystallized intelligence while neglecting the fluid

180

kind of ability most closely allied with the creative talent stressed by Guilford. Studies of the nature of crystallized and fluid intelligence are discussed later in this chapter.

A distinction similar to Cattell's had been made earlier by Hebb (1949, pp. 294–303). In Hebb's view, intelligence tests tapped far more than they should, namely, those aspects of intelligence influenced substantially by forces in the environment. Even if one does not agree completely with Hebb and Cattell on the role of environment in conventional intelligence-test scores, he must concede that such tests leave much to be desired as instruments for measuring high levels of intellectual ability, such as skills in solving problems and creativity.

How one defines intelligence determines and is determined by the the kind of behavior he wishes to tap by intelligence tests and also his satisfaction with the testing apparatuses available. Porteus (1941, 1959, 1965) waged a long and lonely fight to emphasize planfulness, the capacity to use a long-term perspective, as a measure of ability. Another view (Goddard, 1946) defined intelligence as the amount of experience available for the solution of immediate problems and the anticipation of future ones. Addressing a seminar, John E. Anderson, long the director of the Institute of Child Welfare at the University of Minnesota, once said he believed that intelligence could be defined as the ability to maintain a high level of response under stress. This definition may be synonymous with another based on the maintenance of an optimal level of arousal in the face of variations in the environment. Finally, the one definition of intelligence that has had the most influence on intelligence-test construction, although it may not be the most adequate definition, was Terman's (1916), which said that intelligence was the individual's capacity to think abstractly and use abstract symbols.

Since Terman and his associates produced all of the more widely accepted revisions of the Binet test, which have received extensive use both as a test and as a criterion for other tests, Terman's definition has had a marked impact on test construction and on theories about the nature of intelligence. Perhaps most conventional intelligence tests measure too much verbal but too little performance ability, too much crystallized but too little fluid intelligence, and too much abstract material slanted to the middle class. This essentially results from the pervasive influence of Terman's belief that intelligence consists of the talent to deal with abstract symbols, which is another way of saying verbal skill. One thing that may be said on behalf of Terman's definition is· that the sort of facility he wished to measure was apparently the kind of intelligence most closely correlated with success in formal academic undertakings. Although Terman's definition did not lead to the construction of a test that could measure with accuracy such personal characteristics as perseverance, planfulness, and creativity, it did give rise to a device apparently well suited to its most frequent task, that of predicting success in academic endeavors.

Nature of Intelligence

Quite special in their approach to the nature of intelligence are the factor analysts. Factor analysis is a technique for determining the number of basically unrelated capacities that by their total impact produce individual differences in some observable characteristic. For example, athletic ability seems to depend on three unrelated factors—weight, intelligence, and reaction time. The relation of each of these to athletic success differs with the sport concerned. Weight would be expected to count in success as a football tackle but would be negatively related to prowess at ping pong. However, a major part of the variance between individuals in any type of athletic competition could be explained if measures of each of these three factors were available for every competitor.

The scientist seeking to measure the factors that constitute intelligence is in a much more difficult position. No simple, directly observable criterion exists for intelligence as for athletic success. In fact, if Cattell, Hebb, and others are correct in their analysis, there appears to be more than one kind of intelligence. In the view of Spearman (1904), there seems to be a *g* or general factor present in all forms of intellectual behavior. His conclusions were based on students' examination scores in such things as classics and mathematics, on rated capacities—that is, on cleverness and common sense—and on responses in laboratory tasks such as weight discrimination. As he put it: "All branches of intellectual activity have in common one fundamental function." Yet promptly after this statement Spearman noted that the "one fundamental function" might actually consist of a group of functions. His data, discussed in both his 1904 and 1927 studies, suggested, in addition to the *g* factor, the presence of specific or *s* factors whose importance varied from subject area to subject area, with *s* factors being of least significance in the study of the classics and of highest significance in musical accomplishment.

The findings of other factor analysts who have studied intelligence have depended largely on the tests used to measure intelligence. The Binet test, a conglomeration of diverse test items with an emphasis on verbal skills, implies that intelligence is composed of a *g* factor plus certain *s* factors, especially *v* or verbal ability (McNemar, 1942). The Wechsler Intelligence Scale for Children (WISC) measures both verbal and performance capacity and consists of fewer and more disparate test items. Probably because of this difference in structure, a different set of factors emerges, with g having much less significance (Digman, 1962).

Since the results of factorial studies are conditioned, to a considerable extent, by the instruments used to acquire the raw data, current views may be outmoded by the emergence of a new and radically different test of ability. At the time of this writing, the long-term trend seems to depart clearly from the emphasis on g toward a belief that intelligence comprises a large number of distinct factors, facets, or dimensions (Guilford, 1956; Humphreys, 1962; Thurstone, 1946). What Thurstone (1946) called the "primary mental abilities" are: S (space), N (number), V (verbal comprehension), W (word fluency), and M (memory), in addition to induction, deduction, flexibility, and speed of closure. Others have posited a different number of factors, perhaps containing the same elements designated by different names. Indeed, the great number of rather specific factors discovered since Spearman's time leads to a far different notion of intelligence than might be obtained from a thorough-going acceptance of his g.

Factor analytic studies of young children, and of retarded individuals (Meyers, Dingman, Orpet, Sitkei, & Watts, 1964) show essentially the same factors to be present from mental age two to six, though their emergence is not as full at two as it is at six. Other studies suggest that the number and type of factors found from middle childhood on through to adulthood are remarkably similar. These data also suggest that the organization of intellectual factors is relatively constant across the developmental span, but that the factors become more distinct and independent with increasing age.

In the same line of factor analytic approach, the constituent elements of crystallized and fluid intelligence have been determined by Horn and Cattell (Horn & Cattell, 1966a, 1966b, 1967). Although the same types of ability (e.g., perceiving relations, educing correlates) seem to be involved in both types of intelligence, differences (1) in amount of pretraining involved in fluid versus crystallized tasks (Horn & Cattell, 1966b); (2) in age trends in ability (Horn & Cattell, 1966a, 1967); (3) in the importance of visualization skills (Horn, 1968), with fluid intelligence being closely associated with imagery [this last finding bodes ill for the social sciences, including psychology, since social scientists are notoriously deficient in visual imagery (Roe, 1951)], all indicate that these two types of intelligence are clearly distinct from one another.

Those who believe that intelligence is composed of many separate and unrelated specific factors should also believe that most individuals are good at *something* and can be greatly benefited vocationally if the area in which they manifest high ability is exploited. On the other hand, those who consider intelligence as consisting largely of a g factor would expect individuals to show a good deal of consistency in their level of functioning in many widely diverse areas of behavior. They would look for "common level traits"—that is, the individual who is academically able should also score high in such other areas as social and mechanical intelligence. Since there seems to be evidence for believing in at least a moderate amount of similarity in performance across a wide array of intellectual domains [e.g., the high-level performance of individual members of Terman's (1925; Terman & Oden, 1947, 1959) gifted group in diverse areas of behavior] the authors of this book are inclined to believe that a fairly strong g factor is present. Nevertheless, the variability in performance of different types of activity is certainly great enough to suggest that highly specific factors also exist. The whole of vocational and academic counseling rests on the premise that any individual has areas of relative strength and relative weakness; that is, that there are specific factors present. Intelligence, as usually measured, seems to consist of a moderately strong g factor and a number of specific factors. There seems also to be another g factor, usually not adequately measured at present, that taps fluid intelligence.

THE CURVE OF INTELLECTUAL GROWTH

Although the nonparent may not recognize it, a one-year-old child has gained tremendously in ability as compared to his capacity at birth. In any year of infancy or early childhood the changes in symbolic and problem-solving skills are profound. Yet we do not expect any marked gain in native wit to occur between the ages of 20 and 21. Casual observation leads to the belief that there are unequal increments in mental growth during various stages of development. This belief is reinforced by the postulation of several possible curves of mental growth.

Many intelligence tests are designed to show that the average person gains one year in mental age for each year of chronological age, usually up through the age of 15. In the 1937 Stanford-Binet test, this curve of mental growth—actually a straight-line function—is a built-in feature. Tests of this kind are constructed to display an equal gain in mentality for each year of gain in chronological age. In the Stanford-Binet, this holds through 15. At that point the growth curve breaks down because no items can be presented beyond 15 to indicate a significant increase with age in percentage of subjects able to pass them. From the structure of the test, therefore, it need not follow that any intellectual growth will

take place beyond this age.   This particular growth curve is represented
by curve A in Figure 6-1.

Thurstone and Ackerson (1929) established, statistically, an absolute
zero of intelligence shortly before birth, a point where there is no
variation in ability between individuals.   By equating mental growth
units at various ages, they obtained curve B in Figure 6-1.   From this
curve, it may be seen that growth is slow at first, but then positively
accelerates for about the first 10 years of life.   After 10 it slows
down and is negatively accelerated by 11.   According to Thurstone and
Ackerson growth continues at least through 18.

Using data from the Berkeley Growth Study, from studies by Owens
(1953), and from Terman's work on intellectual growth during maturity,
Bayley (1955) developed curve C.   This curve shows intellectual growth
to continue at least to age 50.   Terman and Oden (1959) indicate this
to be true for gifted individuals.   Owens (1953) shows it applics to a
bright, but not remarkably talented, sample of subjects.   And Bradway,
Thompson, and Cravens (1958) demonstrate that essentially the same
growth curve exists for a random sample of the population.

The final type of mental growth curve is suggested by the work of
Gesell (1928) and to an even greater degree by data provided by Goodenough (1954, p. 479).   This kind of curve, represented by curve D,
implies a far higher proportion of mental growth occurring very early
in life than do any of the other curves.   Consider the newborn infant,

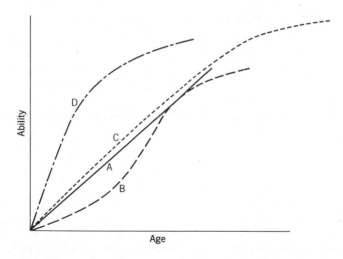

FIGURE 6-1   Hypothetical curves of intellectual growth (see the text for
a description of the basis of these curves).

his conceptual skills, and his ability to cope with his environment. Now consider an average adult in the same way. At what point in development does the individual come halfway from the almost "absolute zero" intelligence of the newborn child to the capacities of the adult? Goodenough posed this general question to experts in the field of developmental psychology. The mean age of their responses was three. A fair amount of experience with young children tempts one to agree with Goodenough's view and to believe that curve D most accurately represents mental growth. Yet there is little empirical evidence to support this position, perhaps because researchers do not often attempt to measure ability below the age of two, and even when they do attempt it, they are handicapped by the general inadequacy of infant measures.

Individual Differences

The curves of mental growth contained in Figure 6-1 represent various hypotheses on general patterns of intellectual development. In charting the intellectual growth of any single individual, it becomes necessary to switch to his actual intelligence-test scores. For the Stanford-Binet test, the mental growth curve should resemble curve A in Figure 6-1, as the test is designed to show this type of development. However, the variations from this curve are numerous in individual cases, even when using the Stanford-Binet test. Figure 6-2 illustrates this variability.

The figure shows two kinds of variation. First, the differences in ability become increasingly apparent with age. Cases 5M and 13M differ enormously in ability, and since 13M is not too capable, his growth is slow as compared with more intelligent individuals. This should not surprise anyone who believes that individuals vary in ability. Second, there is the irregularity found in the growth curves of specific individuals. For instance, Honzik, McFarlane, and Allen (1948) analyzed the data from the Berkeley Growth Study, from which Bayley also acquired her information, and found that many of the 252 individuals studied longitudinally from shortly after birth through the age of 18 varied widely in intelligence-test scores. Take the extreme case presented in Figure 6-3. Although few young people vary as greatly as this boy, several studies (Honzik et al., 1948; Sontag, Baker, & Nelson, 1958) demonstrate that the *average* amount of deviation from the highest to the lowest scores among children followed from early childhood to early adulthood is at least 15 points. Thus there could be

FIGURE 6-2   Individual curves of intelligence (16 D units) for five boys, one month to 25 years, Berkeley Growth Study (Bayley, 1955, p. 815).

a change in intellectual rank from being fiftieth among 100 to being one of the lowest 25 or the highest 25 in test score.

Table 6-1, adapted from Honzik et al. (1948), shows the amount of variation in individual test scores over a period of time. The table contains correlations between test scores of individuals at different ages. If individual scores remained constant, if each individual maintained the same position in the group from the first to the final test, the correlations would all be +1.00. Were there no connection between an individual's score on one test and his score on any other test, the correlations would all be .00. As Table 6-1 indicates, the IQ at age 18 can be predicted from very early test scores no better than

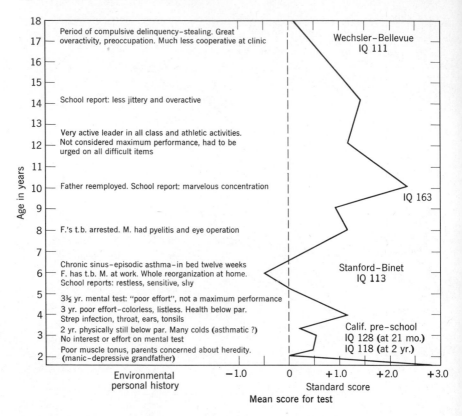

FIGURE 6-3 Variation over time in one subject's intelligence-test scores (Honzik et al., 1948, p. 320).

by chance, as, for example, by coin flipping: heads he is bright, tails he is dull. Indeed, test scores at two are not very good at predicting scores achieved at five or six. On the other hand, it is possible to predict more accurately over a period of time at a later age, say from 14 to 18. This greater reliability of prediction at later ages may signify that ability becomes more stable at later ages, or it simply may be an artifact of the test.

The data in the table disclose that intelligence-test scores vary much more than is commonly supposed. This may be explained in a number of ways. First, the variation may stem from the changing amounts of intellectual enrichment in the child's environment at various times. Differences in enrichment may indeed contribute to the variance, yet even those who most believe that intelligence test scores are influenced by

TABLE 6-1   Correlations* between Test Scores Obtained at Different Ages

Age	5	7	10	14	18
2	.32	.46	.22	.07	.07
5		.73	.75	.61	.56
7			.77	.73	.71
10				.85	.70
14					.73

* The tests from which these correlations are derived are the California Pre-School Schedule through age five, the Stanford-Binet (Form L) from seven through 14, and the Wechsler-Bellevue at age 18. (Data from Honzik et al., 1948.)

such enrichment probably would not hold that it produces so much variation. Second, Anderson (1939) argued that intelligence tests tapped quite different abilities at different ages and therefore should not be expected to yield identical scores, even if the actual level of ability remained constant. Early tests, for example, contain several sensorimotor items and the Binet tests place greater emphasis on vocabulary and memory as age increases. Because there is far more overlap in the areas tested among 14- to 18-year-olds than among two- to six-year-olds, this would explain the increase in test reliability with age. In dealing with the same question, Bayley (1955) reached different conclusions. Her explanation of the variation in IQ over a period of time was that the component elements of intelligence changed with age: "The very fact that the scores of mental growth in individual children tend to exhibit gradual shifts in relative status supports the theory that a changing organization of factors is in process." Is change in intelligence-test score due, then, largely to the changing character of the items in the tests, as Anderson contended, or to the changing character of intelligence, as Bayley said? Pinneau (1961), in analyzing the Berkeley longitudinal data, noted some of both. Part of the variation in test scores results from the characteristics of the test, he concluded, and part from actual changes in intelligence with age.

Honzik et al. (1948) imputed individual deviations in test scores to persisting social and emotional factors. Their findings showed that these factors, when more than mere day-to-day fluctuations in feeling, bore a substantial relation to test-score variation.

Bayley and Schaeffer (1964), again working with the Berkeley data, found that the emotional atmosphere of the home had considerable influence on IQ level in boys, with loving and warm mothering being associated with high ability and maternal hostility being associated with low ability. Girls appear far more influenced by parental ability level. The influence of home atmosphere also is shown in the Fels studies (Baldwin, Kalhorn, & Breese, 1945), which demonstrated that children reared in warm, democratic homes gained eight points in mean IQ over a three-year interval, whereas the mean IQ of children from rejecting, indulgent, and less emotionally gratifying homes either fell or remained constant. Personality factors that appear to be mediated by the home environment also play a considerable role. The children within the Fels sample who showed the most gain in IQ also were more independent, competitive, and "self-initiating" in activities (Sontag, Baker, & Nelson, 1958) and showed higher need for achievement (Kagan, Sontag, Baker, & Nelson, 1958). Far more boys than girls show gains in ability, possibly because independence and achievement are more often valued and rewarded for boys than for girls. It may be that parents, regardless of their own ability and educational level, generally reinforce these traits in boys, but that only parents of relatively high ability and educational attainment reward independence and high achievement motivation in girls. If so, this might explain Bayley's and Schaeffer's finding, noted above, that IQ gain in girls, but not in boys, is most adequately predicted by parental ability, while IQ gain in boys, but not in girls, is predictable from maternal characteristics regarding the use of positive reinforcement that are only minimally related to parental ability and educational level.

Although all these explanations of variation in tested intelligence have some merit, the one regarding social and emotional influences, advanced by Honzik et al. (1948) and supported in various ways by Bayley and Schaeffer and by the Fels studies, apparently accounts for the largest proportion of the IQ changes found in longitudinal studies. Certain hypotheses may be derived from it. If this explanation is correct, changes in tested intelligence should occur in direct proportion to improvements in adjustment resulting from psychotherapy. Furthermore, class differences in tested ability may be narrowed by matching children in adjustment across class lines, since children from various social classes generally differ in adjustment, with those from lower economic groups manifesting a larger number of social and emotional problems.

Generational and Subcultural Differences

The differences in intellectual growth discussed so far have concerned children of the same generation, all reared within the mainstream of

American culture. There are also differences between generations as well as between members of the dominant culture and those who belong to divergent subcultures, such as Southern mountaineers or partially assimilated Mexican-Americans.

Nearly a hundred years ago, Galton was worried. He felt that human ability would decline because the least able members of the population produced the most children. This worry, supported by a fair amount of data (e.g., Maxwell, 1954), persists to the present day. Maxwell has shown that duller individuals have more children; the correlation between IQ and number of children is approximately −.30.

However, Higgins, Reed, and Reed (1962) demonstrate that in following up the siblings of individuals of varying intellectual ability, there is a higher and higher proportion of childless siblings as one moves down in the ability scale. In other words, a dull individual may have many children, if he has any at all, but his brothers and sisters are less likely to have any children. Once this correction is made, there is a slight positive correlation between IQ and family size. Since people of low ability have a remarkably high death rate (Baller, Charles, & Miller, 1967)—particularly as a result of accidents that might have been avoided with a bit of forethought—the positive correlation between parental IQ and number of offspring who in turn reproduce would undoubtedly be larger if one looked only at those offspring who themselves managed to survive to childbearing age. Galton need not have worried; natural selection, both in terms of individual survival and in terms of mating and having offspring still seems to be at work, and still favors the more able.

Average level of ability, as measured by conventional intelligence tests, is rising as time moves onward (Tuddenham, 1948; Wheeler, 1942), judging from tests of succeeding generations. While some of this gain may be a result of natural selection, it seems almost certain that the most likely explanation for the majority of the gains is that many intelligence tests, assumed to be relatively "culture free," are heavily influenced by educational and cultural factors. American culture has grown so much richer and the term of formal education has been so greatly extended over the last several generations that these forces have raised performance levels.

Once it was thought that intelligence-test scores were essentially free of cultural influences. Were this so, differences in opportunity would have little, if any, role in producing individual differences in tested ability. Operating on this assumption, many early students of mental retardation (e.g., Goddard, 1912) tested individuals living under extreme deprivation and concluded these people were mentally defective. It is quite true, of course, that brighter people tend to flee deprived environments and settle in more adequate ones (Maxwell, 1954). Because of this selective migration, with the duller members of each generation remaining behind, it is not surprising to find the stay-at-homes quite dull after several generations. Nevertheless, much of the dullness reported in the early studies appears to result from environmental considerations. This is borne out by intergenerational studies (e.g., Wheeler, 1942) and also by studies of the change in intelligence-test scores among children of different ages within the same generation, such as the one conducted by Sherman and Key (1932).

This latter study, later described in more detail by Sherman in his book, *Hollow Folk* (1933), dealt with the intelligence testing of children in a Southern country town and a number of mountain hollows. These hollows decreased in civilization the further one went into the mountains. In the most acculturated of these hollows, the local school was in session about seven months a year; the most isolated hollow had no school at all. Moving up through the hollows, one found the mean IQ of the children decreasing. This could be accounted for either by selective migration or by the influence of environment on test scores. Within each hollow, and especially the more remote ones, the average IQ decreased from very near average at six to a positively defective level by 14 to 16. If the scores of these children resulted from selective migration across generations, the six-year-olds should have been as retarded as the 16-year-olds. The vast difference in scores of children separated by only a 10-year span, during which few of them would be able to migrate of their own accord, strongly suggests that these hollows had something in common with the major American culture, in which the Stanford-Binet test was standardized: the mountain six-year-olds had been exposed to the information needed to respond correctly to test items at the six-year level, but by adolescence the content was so foreign to the experience of these young people as to make the test no longer a fair measure of their ability.

Sherman's study, and others like it, show that groups not exposed to the common American culture are so handicapped that the mental growth curve flattens appreciably with advancing years, resulting in a mounting inferiority in score as the child ages. [For a highly graphic account of the changing life in these hills one can turn to Jesse Stuart's *God's Oddling* (1960). An American novelist reared in Appalachia, Stuart gives a vivid autobiographical report of his youth and manhood, and of the cultural and educational changes in the mountain country over the past generations.]

Yet this decline in tested ability among the culturally undernourished is not indicative of deficiencies in real ability. During World War II many young mountaineers learned to read and write to fifth-grade level within five weeks at the Navy's school for illiterates at Bainbridge, Maryland. They then underwent conventional training for recruits, received their orders, found their way across the continent, and joined their ship in California. Although most of them had never been more than a few miles from home, and never had seen electric lights, flush toilets, or shower baths, much less the ocean and warships, prior to their military service, they adapted well. Within a few months they were indistinguishable from fellow seamen. Ironically, if conventional intelligence tests had been administered to them upon first leaving their mountain haunts, their mean scores would almost certainly have fallen well within the mentally defective range.

Clearly the amount of education to which an individual is exposed and the closeness of his culture to the dominant American culture have a pronounced influence on intelligence-test scores. May this not also be true of variations with the prime cultural setting? If mountaineers are grossly handicapped because of educational and cultural shortcomings, and consequently score low on intelligence tests, perhaps the differences in IQ found between socioeconomic groups may similarly be attributed to this same cause. This thesis has been advanced most vigorously by Allison Davis (1948). Davis said that the higher mean IQ on tests of middle-class children than of lower-class children was caused by the bias of intelligence tests in favor of the former and certain class differences in motivation, not by any real differences in ability. If class differences produce biases in test construction, it should be possible to build a test that is unbiased or "culture free," which would not discriminate among social classes. Various individuals have attempted this. Davis and Eells (1953) constructed the Davis-Eells Games Test, an entirely new test. Haggard (1954) revised a conventional intelligence test in an effort to make it culture free. He also attempted to control class differences in motivation by using such techniques as offering concrete rewards, which are supposedly necessary to get the best performances from lower-class youngsters, for improvement in test scores.

Notwithstanding, there is a good deal of evidence that so-called culture-free tests do not erase class differences; these differences are as prominent on culture-free tests as on conventional intelligence tests (Angelino & Shedd, 1955; Knief & Stroud, 1959). Moreover, Haggard's endeavor to reduce class differences in ability through varying such factors as motivation was largely unsuccessful; several of his efforts actually increased these differences. Since American society is open and its members rise or fall in occupational level on the basis of ability, differences between occupational groups, as long as all are exposed to the mainstream of American culture, are not surprising, no matter which tests are used or which motivational techniques are tried.

Studies such as those described above underscore the differential amount of reliance that can be placed on high as opposed to low IQ scores. There is only one way—being bright—to get a high score on the IQ tests. There are many possible reasons for low scores—being genuinely dull, being severely culturally deprived, having undiagnosed sensory defects, being unmotivated, suffering from emotional disturbance, or any combination of these. It is for this reason that greater faith can be placed on the validity of high than of low IQ scores.

From all this it would seem that cultural and educational factors affect conventional intelligence-test scores more than was once assumed, yet their influence is not very great among individuals of the same generation raised in the same cultural milieu.

THE CONSTANCY OF ABILITY

Although an individual's IQ does vary over the long run, the cause of the variance is not yet clear. Some of this may be due to test construction, some to the fact that intelligence tests are not entirely culture free, and some to long-term variations in the emotional healthfulness of the environments of those being tested. But how much can be attributed to a deliberate manipulation of the intellectual richness of the environment? This is the major question and its wide implications have yet to be satisfactorily resolved.

If a rich early environment produces lasting changes in ability, these changes must have some physiological base. Among lower organisms this has been shown to be so. Rats reared in an enriched environment differ in brain chemistry from rats not exposed to the same conditions (Krech, Rosenzweig, & Bennett, 1960). In addition, enrichment produces an increase in brain weight (Rosenzweig, Krech, Bennett, & Diamond, 1962). And as noted in an earlier chapter, enrichment or deprivation by the environment influences the later learning capacities of lower organisms, quite possibly because of the effects of these factors on brain structure and function.

Presumably these findings should apply across species. If enrichment occasions lasting physiological and behavioral change in lower organisms, it should have the same impact on humans. Yet, paradoxically, the evidence suggests something else. Analyses of data pertaining to separated identical twins (Johnson, 1963; Vandenberg & Johnson, 1968), the slight and ephemeral effects of special nursery-school training (see

Chapter 12), and the inability of Honzik et al. (1948) to find a discernible consistent relation between amount of environmental enrichment and IQ variation, as well as many other studies, all run counter to the hypothesis.

At least two explanations are possible for the differing results of research on humans and subhumans. To begin with, laboratory rats reared in cages are far more severely deprived than even the most deprived humans. Thus, by starting from a far lower base, the effects of enrichment may be much more apparent for subhumans. Put another way, the influence of enrichment among humans within the normal range of environmental variation may not be enough to produce an appreciable change in IQ. The nursery-school studies noted above were studies of middle-class children, for the most part. Since these children had been exposed to the "built-in curriculum" of the middle-class home, it is not surprising that gains were relatively slight. As noted in Chapter 12, it may well be that starting from a lower base —that is, from a more deprived environment—the beneficial effects of environmental stimulation may become more sizable and more apparent. Skeel's (1966) follow-up study of the later careers of individuals reared under conditions of deprivation (orphanage) or of relative stimulation (lovingly cared for by older retardants) appears to support the position that performance can be changed by enrichment, so long as one is dealing with truly deprived youngsters.

The second explanation maintains that bright and dull organisms differ more pronouncedly in learning ability when learning is *massed,* that is, when learning events follow one another in rapid succession, than when learning is *distributed,* when there is a longer interval of time between them. This applies alike to rats (Jennings, 1960; McGaugh, 1961; McGaugh, Westbrook, & Burt, 1961) and children (Madsen, 1963; Dent & Johnson, 1964; Shapiro, 1964). Among rats, changes in the internal or external environment of the organisms effect a greater impact on massed than on distributed learning (Breen & McGaugh, 1961; McGaugh, 1961; McGaugh, Westbrook, & Thomson, 1962). Thus massed learning appears to be far more susceptible to various hereditary and environmental forces. Perhaps humans, like rats, are greatly benefited by enrichment, but this has not been evident to researchers because they have tried to measure the influence of enrichment on tasks that are *not* highly responsive to such influence. Or it may be that enrichment has more impact if one moves away from the study of IQ change to investigate the influences of environment on proficiency at tasks that involve massed learning techniques, such as maze learning or the verbal learning of paired associates.

Data gathered to date imply that although IQ is far from constant, little of the variation results from enrichment or deprivation, except when deprivation is extreme. Yet recent research on animals suggests that a large amount of influence may have escaped detection through use of the wrong measuring devices.

Intelligence and Creativity

Creativity might well be discussed as an area of problem solving, yet might also be considered an aspect of intelligence. Relatively high formal intelligence, as measured by intelligence tests, seems to be a necessary but not in itself sufficient cause for creativity to be manifested, while the form of intelligence that might be termed fluid and divergent seems a central element to creativity. Creativity has been described by Drevdahl as follows.

> Creativity is the capacity of persons to produce compositions, products, or ideas of any sort which are essentially new or novel, and previously unknown to the producer. It can be imaginative activity, or thought synthesis, where the product is not a mere summation. It may involve the forming of new patterns and combinations of information derived from past experience, and the transplanting of old relationships to new situations and may involve the generation of new correlates. It must be purposeful or goal directed, not mere idle fantasy—although it need not have immediate practical application or be a perfect and complete product. It may take the form of an artistic, literary or scientific production or may be of a procedural or methodological nature (Drevdahl, 1956, p. 22).

Originality and creativity are probably present in all individuals—adults and children—but clearly in quite different degrees (Wilson, Guilford, & Christensen, 1953). The measures used most frequently to test creativity are those developed by Guilford and his colleagues.

The basic components of creativity, Guilford (1950) maintained, are a sensitivity to problems, an ability to produce many novel ideas or solutions, a flexible approach to solving problems, and the capacity to analyze and synthesize a complex collection of ideas. The tests he and his colleagues devised (see Wilson, Guilford, and Christensen, 1953) were aimed at measuring these qualities. On these tests, adult subjects are asked to do such things as describe how the United States might have developed if there had been no Mississippi-Missouri river system or think up a title for a movie scenario presented to them. Their responses can be rated on the basis of quantity and quality, since most studies show the two to be closely related, and then compared with criteria of creativity in real life. Responses to the Barron-Welsh Art

Scale (Barron & Welsh, 1952) or the Welsh Figure Preference Test (Welsh, 1959) predict creativity in real life among both adults and children fairly well (MacKinnon, 1962). Creative individuals prefer nonrepresentative art and complex and asymmetrical figures to representative art or the simple and symmetrical figures. They also produce a very high proportion of unusual word associations (MacKinnon, 1962); hence tests of such associations also may help to judge creativity.

In following up these findings, Houston and Mednick (1963) discovered creative adults to be far less tolerant of the banal or the commonplace. And Jacobsen and Asher (1963) have remarkably predicted creativity in real life from the way individuals reacted to a perceptual task. The task in question consisted of a series of 21 pictures during which the silhouette of a dog gradually changed into one of a cat. The more flexible subjects caught the change early in the series; these individuals generally proved the most creative in the actual life task which, in this experiment, was to design a desk. Thus these various tests in their different forms were able to measure the presence in an individual of the basic components of creativity.

Presumably these components relate to a manner of intellectual functioning, but they are at least somewhat independent of intelligence as it usually is measured through IQ. In most creative endeavors, a minimal IQ (somewhere around IQ 115–120) may exist below which an individual cannot function. However, above this level, IQ has little significance (MacKinnon, 1962). If one compares, for example, the 150 least creative and productive males with the 150 most creative and productive from Terman's study of gifted children (Terman, 1954) there is little difference in IQ between the two groups. Other studies (Drevdahl, 1956; MacKinnon, 1962; Torrance, 1960) contain similar findings. Among individuals selected to form an above-average group in terms of creativity, the specific performance of any one of them on a conventional intelligence test is no indication of creativity. Creativity may involve divergent thinking—described by Guilford as "thinking different, new, or unusual directions"—fluid but not crystallized intelligence. Formal IQ, on the other hand, may depend on memory and on convergent thinking—an awareness of the recognized best or conventional answer (Guilford, 1959).

Writers who value creativity and sometimes appear to downgrade the kinds of ability measured by formal intelligence tests (e.g., Getzels & Jackson, 1962; Wallach & Kogan, 1965) may well be correcting past errors of psychology, since creativity generally has been undervalued. Yet creativity must be coupled with at least a minimal and probably a considerable amount of intelligence in IQ terms, or else it is so idiosyncratic that it cannot be evaluated or made use of; after all, schizo-phrenia, the most serious mental disorder of our time, also has as a symp-tom extremely divergent thinking—sometimes interesting, it is true, but certainly maladaptive.

Besides intellectual traits such as fluency of ideas and flexibility, certain personality characteristics differentiate the creative from the noncreative individual.   There are those who say that creative persons are less anxious (Reid, King, & Wickwire, 1959), less defensive, and more willing to concede faults (MacKinnon, 1962).   They are by no means problem-free, but have sufficient ego strength that they can cope adequately with their problems (Cattell & Drevdahl, 1955; Barron, 1963).   Creative individuals tend to be radical, unconventional, and sensitive to the feelings of others (Drevdahl, 1956).   On tests of masculinity versus femininity they score more toward the feminine end of the scale (MacKinnon, 1962).   This does not signify any sexual aberration, but merely indicates a higher number of cultural interests.   Creative persons are also independent and self-sufficient, not overly concerned with main-taining close ties with social groups or with receiving the approval of others (MacKinnon, 1962).   The data cited above indicate that creative people are highly aware of, yet unconcerned with, the evaluations of others—a combination of traits that suggests a realistically high level of self-esteem.

Since highly creative individuals share all these traits that are believed to be shaped by environment, creative individuals should also have common elements in their backgrounds.   Abundant evidence shows they tend to have close ties with parents.   McCurdy (1957) demonstrated that historic geniuses had very little contact with their peers, but had intensive, generally warm relations with parents and siblings.   Both Greenacre (1958) and MacKinnon (1962) also found this to be true. The family of a genius is a tightly knit unit, often estranged from its neighbors because of different values or cultural aspirations, and the creative individual himself is often alienated from his mates during childhood (MacKinnon, 1962; Torrance, 1960).   The family, therefore, has a more profound influence on him than on most of his peers, since the peers, the neighborhood, and probably the school have less opportunity to induce behavioral change.

Possessed of the necessary formal intelligence (IQ), the creative individual benefits most by growing up in a home that is hospitable and sympathetic to creative interests.   In such a home there is marital harmony.   This intimate, closely knit family relationship is marked by warmth and by mild discipline of a psychological turn rather than severe and physical discipline.   The child is presented with a clear set of parental standards but is given much freedom of expression, which he is encouraged to exercise (MacKinnon, 1962). Parental democracy also stimulates creativity and imaginativeness among children (Baldwin, 1949). The emphasis is on achievement and independent action, with parents establishing conditions that allow the child to meet these expectations. Moreover, Terman's (1954) comparison of creative as opposed to noncreative gifted children showed that the noncreative came from homes having more stress, more conflict, and less interest in achievement than the homes of the creative subjects among his sample.

These data indeed suggest that parents have a great deal of influence in developing the ability of their children to cope creatively with tasks requiring the solution of problems. If a parent wishes his child to be creative, to be a productive artist, scientist, or innovator, his parental behavior must follow directions that are fairly well marked. Yet it is possible that many parents are unwilling to accept these conditions for having a creative, self-directed child (since this kind of child will question any parental claim to omniscience) despite their lip service to the idea that creativity is good.

It sometimes is suggested that all young children are creative, and that it is the school situation that destroys creativity. Torrance (1962) demonstrated that both teachers and peers show some disapproval of highly creative children, believing them to have "silly" or "wild" ideas. Teachers, as usual, take the rap quite willingly. Yet of all the forces that most of us encounter, teachers may well be the group that do most to promote creativity. Most people who get through college can remember at least a few teachers who did more than anyone else did to encourage their creativity and originality, even in opposition to parents and to school boards.

It seems more likely that pervasive cultural influences, rather than specific teacher behaviors, are the chief forces producing the sometimes observed diminution of creativity that accompanies getting older. For example, as cited in various portions of this book, girls are expected to be dependent, unambitious, and unoriginal. Although there are creative women (see Helson, 1967, for a description of creative women), they are few in number, probably because of sex differences in pressures toward conformity. If the general tone of the culture does so much that is negative for girls, it is likely that it has the chief role in producing a similar but less deleterious effect in males.

INTELLIGENCE DIFFERENCES AND BEHAVIOR

If intelligence tests have validity, knowledge of an individual's IQ should enable a prediction of his behavior to the extent that behavior depends on intellectual capacity. Through conventional laboratory measures of learning, such as mirror drawing or maze learning, IQ has been shown to be only minimally related to performance (Woodrow, 1946). On the other hand, as we have already seen, conventional measures of ability do not enable a highly accurate prediction of creativity, except that there may be a floor below which an individual can engage in little creative endeavor. It is in the tasks falling between these two extremes that intelligence tests can most adequately predict performance. Conventional academic tasks—reading, writing, arithmetic, and other studies of the type—fit this specification and performance of them can be predicted with a reasonable degree of accuracy from individual intelligence-test scores. Scholastic achievement is what the Binet test sought to forecast, and in this area the Binet and other tests like it prove most effective. Children with high IQs generally perform well in the school setting (Anderson, Hughes, & Dixon, 1957; Terman, 1925), whereas children of low IQs do poorly from the beginning and become progressively more retarded in scholastic achievement with age (Johnson, 1950). These findings demonstrate the validity of the IQ test: it fulfills its major purpose of predicting success in school, even though it is not as adequate at predicting learning in tasks that are either less or more demanding intellectually (e.g., maze learning or creativity) as those encountered in the academic setting.

Individuals do vary in ability. Figure 6-4 is a graphic illustration of individual IQ scores. The score corresponding to a particular point on the curve depends, in part, on the test administered. One test administered to all children of the same age in a large school might yield IQs ranging from 50 to 150, whereas a second test might range

FIGURE 6-4   The curve of intelligence (McBain & Johnson, 1962, p. 151).

in scores from 60 to 140. A child scoring 60 on the second test achieves the lowest score, whereas a 60 on the first test would be a low score, but not the lowest. Table 6-2, taken from Pintner, Dragositz, and Kushner (1944, p. 135), presents the percentile breakdown of individuals of varying IQs on the Stanford-Binet test or any other test having approximately the same mean and standard deviation.

As a rule, researchers concern themselves with the two extremes when considering the influence of IQ on behavior and adjustment. The general comparison of these extremes in a diversity of situations seems best to indicate the validity of intelligence tests. Let us, therefore, pay some attention to each of these extremes.

High Intellectual Ability

Once it was believed that highly intelligent young people were physically weak, of questionable moral character, rejected by their agemates, antisocial, prone to psychotic or neurotic disturbances, and likely to become mentally defective in later years. Although unsupported by acceptable evidence, these notions were widely held. Possibly the reason for this acceptance is that it is only fair to have "compensatory traits." It would be manifestly unfair for one individual to have everything—brains and brawn, and beauty, too. If this latter idea were buttressed by empirical evidence, the gifted would certainly suffer.

Shortly after World War I, Terman and his associates undertook their extensive study of gifted children in order to test currently prevalent ideas on the exceptional. Starting in 1921, Terman gathered data on more than 1000 children with IQs of over 140, except for a few cases in which a sibling of an exceptional child, whose IQ fell between 135 and 140, was included. Thus the children in Terman's sample constituted the top 1 per cent of the population as judged by tested ability. These youngsters differed completely from popular belief. They were physically superior, highly acceptable socially, of good character, and in excellent health—a superior group *generally;* most superior in intellectual pursuits, but superior in other ways as well.

This group was followed from 1921, when its mean age was 10, to 1956 and a mean age of 45 (Terman et al., 1925; Burks, Jensen, & Terman, 1930; Terman & Oden, 1947, 1959). Almost all performed well in academic pursuits. Most entered college and received bachelor degrees. Many went on to obtain graduate degrees. Those who did not achieve as well as might have been expected from their IQ scores seemed handicapped by little emphasis on scholarly accomplishment and many tensions at home. These particular individuals, however,

TABLE 6-2   Percentile Values of Various IQ Scores

The Child Whose IQ Is:	Is Equalled or Excelled by
160	1 out of 10,000
156	3 out of 10,000
152	8 out of 10,000
148	2 out of 1,000
144	4 out of 1,000
140	7 out of 1,000

The Child Whose IQ Is:	Equals or Exceeds	The Child Whose IQ Is:	Equals or Exceeds
136	99 per cent	99	48 per cent
135	98	98	45
134	98	97	43
133	98	96	40
132	97	95	38
131	97	94	36
130	97	93	34
129	96	92	31
128	96	91	29
127	95	90	27
126	94	89	25
125	94	88	23
124	93	87	21
123	92	86	20
122	91	85	18
121	90	84	16
120	89	83	15
119	88	82	14
118	86	81	12
117	85	80	11
116	84	79	10
115	82	78	9
114	80	77	8
113	79	76	8
112	77	75	6
111	75	74	6
110	73	73	5
109	71	72	4
108	69	71	4
107	66	70	3
106	64	69	3
105	62	68	3
104	60	67	2
103	57	66	2
102	55	65	2
101	52	64	1
100	50	63	1
		62	1

gained considerably over their young adult days. At last check (1959), many of them seemed finally to have overcome the adverse effects of their childhood environment and to have begun at last to achieve. Far from "burning out" or becoming mentally defective, the entire group seemed to grow progressively more superior in accomplishment as well as in tested ability at least through the age of 45. During these 35 years, the group had a low death rate, low divorce rate, low crime rate, and a low rate of psychological disturbance. The findings about this group indeed demonstrated the falsity of many beliefs about the gifted.

However, the optimal level of IQ in relation to adjustment is believed to lie between 125 and 155 (Hollingworth, 1942). In her book, *Children Above 180 IQ*, Hollingworth described a number of children far above this level. These youngsters were prolific achievers to judge from a summary of the scholastic accomplishment of one of her subjects whose IQ was 187:

> In addition to his regular school work E, by the time he was 8 years old, had covered the following special work in language and mathematics, either with a tutor or with his mother:
>
> Mathematics: Algebra as far as equations; geometry.
>
> Latin: Partial knowledge of the four declensions (he has been taught by the direct, informal method, and reads easy Latin).
>
> Greek: Worked out the alphabet for himself from an astronomical chart, between the ages of 5 and 6 years.
>
> French: Equal to about two years in the ordinary school.
>
> German: Ordinary conversation.
>
> Spanish: Attended class with his mother—reads and understands.
>
> Italian: Reading knowledge and simple conversation.
>
> Portuguese: Asked his mother to take this course at the Columbia Summer School because he could not be registered himself.
>
> Hebrew: A beginning.
>
> Anglo-Saxon: A beginning.
>
> Astronomy: He has worked out all the constellations from MacCready, and displays a very great interest in this subject.
>
> One evening this winter he noticed a new planet near the Twins. He said it was Saturn but his mother thought it was Mars. E went home, worked the position out from the chart and found it to be Saturn.
>
> Miscellaneous: He has a great interest in nature, wherever found. . . .
>
> His writing is not equal to his other accomplishments. He is very slow at it and for this reason dictates most of his "home work" to a stenographer.
>
> History is his chief and absorbing interest among school subjects (Hollingworth, 1942, p. 140).

Although high achievers, the young people studied by Hollingworth were not well-adjusted members of the age group to which they belonged. They were neither antisocial nor actively maladjusted; rather they were largely asocial, uninterested in their agemates and their activities, and apparently living in a different world from their classmates, teachers, and sometimes their parents. They did not interact easily with agemates; in fact, children of this high a level of ability might benefit from isolation from peers.

Perhaps the most interesting personal account of childhood experiences of a genius, not merely genius in IQ terms, but a genius in the sense of changing the world around him, is that of Norbert Wiener. His two books, *Ex-Prodigy* (1953), dealing with his childhood and college years, and *I Am a Mathematician* (1956), dealing with his professional career, describe the joys and sorrows of being of such high ability that an entirely normal childhood is impossible. As is frequently the case with highly intelligent and highly creative individuals, Wiener's family ties were close. His father played the largest role in his education, and his books provide an interesting example of the emotional ambivalence that often results from this close yet demanding father-son relationship that is a highly frequent aspect of the boyhood of genius. Wiener's description of some aspects of his first year in college provides an interesting picture of the problems involved in living in two worlds, that of a child and that of an adult, at the same time.

> With my high school days over, my father had decided to send me to Tufts College rather than to risk the strain of the Harvard entrance examinations and the inordinate publicity which could have been caused by sending an eleven-year-old boy to Harvard. . . .
>
> I began to get acquainted with the children of the neighborhood. In my early reading I had learned something about hypnotism and decided to try it out myself. I succeeded in nothing, except in offending and terrifying the parents of my playmates. I played a good deal with children of my own age, but without any great community of interest. I found the clerk at the corner drugstore an interesting young medical student, who was prepared to discuss my scientific reading with me and who seemed to be acquainted with the whole of the writings of Herbert Spencer. I have since found Herbert Spencer to be one of the most colossal bores of the nineteenth century, but at that time I held him in esteem. . . .
>
> I had not yet reached the proper stage of social maturity for my English courses. Moreover, the mere mechanics of writing were a serious hurdle to take. My mechanical clumsiness in writing tended to make me omit any word that I could eliminate, and to force me into a great crabbedness of style.

I was already beyond the normal freshman work in mathematics. There was no course which exactly fitted my requirements, so Professor Ransom took me on in a reading course on the Theory of Equations. . . .

The course was really over my head, particularly in the parts concerning Galois' theory, but with a great deal of help from Professor Ransom I was able to get through. I had started my mathematics at the hard end. Never again at Tufts did I have a mathematics course that demanded so much of me. . . .

I had several . . . extracurricular adventures in physics and engineering, more especially in the study of electricity. I shared electrical experiments with a Medford neighbor. We used to generate electricity by turning a hand-run dynamo for the making of colloidal gold and colloidal silver. Whether we actually made these substances I cannot remember, but we thought we did. We also made attempts to realize in practice two physical ideas of mine. One of them was an electromagnetic coherer for radio messages different from the electrostatic coherer of Branly. It depended on the effect of a magnetic field independently of its direction, in compressing a mass of iron filings and powdered carbon, and thus in changing its resistance. There were times when we thought we had obtained a positive effect, but we were not certain whether it was due to this magnetic cohesion or to something quite different. Nevertheless, the idea was sound and if the day of all such devices had not passed with the invention of the vacuum tube, I should be interested to undertake these experiments over again from the beginning.

The other piece of apparatus we tried out was an electrostatic transformer. It depended on the fact that the energy or charge of a condenser is carried as a dielectric strain. The trick was to charge a rotating glass disk or series of disks through electrodes arranged in parallel and to discharge them through electrodes arranged in series. It differed from the electromagnetic transformer in acting on direct currents, and also in the fact that it was essential to the apparatus that the disks should be revolved. We broke an indefinite number of panes of glass in trying to make the machine, and we never quite got it to work. Unbeknown to us, the idea was already in the literature and had been there for a long time. In fact, I have seen a very similar piece of apparatus within the last two years in the laboratories of the School of Engineering of the University of Mexico. It functioned very well. Two successive stages of this machine multiplied the potential by several thousand (Wiener, 1964, pp. 102–106).

The adjustment of the gifted depends, to a large extent, on the criterion used for giftedness. With Terman's criterion of a 140 IQ, adjustment is indeed superior. With the criterion of Hollingworth (1942) or of McCurdy (1957), adjustment most likely could not be considered optimal. In any case, with respect to intellectual performance, *achievement* is high.

The Mentally Deficient

At the other end of the intelligence curve are those individuals who are regarded as mentally deficient. It is not entirely fair, as is often done, to designate individuals below IQ 70 as "mentally defective." An IQ score alone is not enough to justify this diagnosis. Social competence is a better standard of measurement. If an individual with an IQ of 50 makes his own way in the world without supervision and manages to keep employed, out of trouble, and even marry and successfully raise a family, it would be very unfair to label him defective. The most recent set of diagnostic criteria for mental deficiency or mental retardation includes criteria involving both measured intelligence and socially adaptive behavior (Heber, 1959).

The earliest studies of social competence, some of them undertaken long before the introduction of intelligence tests, were actually investigations of families that displayed social incompetence for several generations. The best known of these probably is Goddard's (1912) study of the "good" and the "bad" Kallikaks, in which one family line generally evinced social competence and the other social incompetence, presumably because of the inheritance of these characteristics.

Because of these studies and their findings, it once was believed that all mental defects, except for clear instances of anomalies of development, were hereditary. Nowadays it seems apparent that although some defective individuals may inherit general low ability, a large number of persons are called defective because of brain injury, biochemical factors such as phenylketonuria (the incomplete oxidation of certain amino acids), deprived backgrounds, or a number of other reasons. There are many sources for a low IQ, and individuals of the same low level of ability differ substantially from one another, depending on the specific etiology (cause) of their low scores. Some of these persons will show considerable social competence and will benefit greatly from training, whereas others will not. In other words, only *some* individuals with low IQs are mentally defective within the customary definition.

Most individuals with low IQs would seem to do poorly in school. A low intelligence-test score was once thought to be an almost certain indication of social and scholastic incompetence. This is not the case. During the depths of the Depression, Baller (1936) studied 206 individuals, most of whom were in their middle twenties, whose IQs fell below 70 and who, in grade school, had attended "opportunity classes" for extremely slow learners. Of these 206, 33 had completed elementary school, three had finished high school, and one had entered college.   Despite the challenging economic conditions of the time, 84 per cent were partially or wholly self-supporting.   Only 8 per cent were confined in institutions.   Following up Baller's subjects in the late 1940's and early 1950's, Charles (1953, 1957) found 80 per cent of them to be employed and self-supporting.   Their mean age at the time he began studying them was 42.   Their types of home and percentage of home ownership closely resembled the general population's.   Those who had married did not have "herds of children" as is sometimes the case with persons of low ability; the average number of children was actually a little under the national norms.   The children on the whole fell into the range of low-average ability.

The most recent follow-up of this group of individuals (Baller, Charles, & Miller, 1967) plus two control groups, one dull but not retarded and one normal, demonstrates that while the group diagnosed as defective made few highly positive contributions to their community, they generally became normal, noncriminal, self-supporting people.   The most startling difference among the three ability groups was death rate, with the mentally defective group having a remarkably high rate. Of the three groups, the retarded individuals gained most in IQ over the approximately 40 years since they had been in school, moving from an average IQ of 60 to an average of 80.   It may be that, with age, retarded individuals are more likely to encounter learning situations under conditions of distributed practice from which they can benefit, and, as a result, more and more closely approximate normal functioning.

These data are not isolated.   Other studies have supplied similar results.   Kennedy (1948) also demonstrated that most individuals who were below IQ 70 while in school did reasonably well on the job once they got out of school.   Muench (1944), like Baller, Charles, and Miller, showed that many who scored in the defective range in childhood and early adolescence scored within the normal range as adults.

The Binet test seems to be a good forecaster of school success so long as no special intervention is introduced to the learning situation. However, if the learning situation is structured so that conditions of practice are controlled (Shapiro, 1964), the correct response is made highly salient (Cole, Dent, Eguchi, Fujii, & Johnson, 1964), and correct responses, when made, are immediately positively reinforced, then even children quite low in ability can learn relatively adequately.   We believe that bright children can learn under almost any condition, but that dull children's learning experiences must be very carefully structured if learning is to occur at a proper rate.

Since little is done to make the learning of retarded and dull children more comparable to that of normal and bright children, they generally suffer through the school years. After this period of frustration and low esteem during school years, many persons of low ability (in terms of IQ) come into their own when finally employed. More important, they not only perform well on the job, but also often do relatively well as adults on intelligence tests. This may be explained in various ways. First, the low-ability individual has "regression toward the mean" operating on his side. If he scores low on his first test, he has nowhere to go but up on his second one. Second, many individuals with a low tested IQ may score low because of emotional problems (Honzik et al., 1948) or because of a deprived environment. Age and independence from parents may cure both these ills. Third, as noted above, they may encounter learning situations under optimal learning conditions.

Since the diagnosis of mental deficiency depends largely on social competence, many persons with low IQs are not mentally defective as children but are merely academically inept—and even fewer can be legitimately termed mentally defective as adults. While the gifted stay gifted, the retarded or defective frequently do not remain retarded.

SUMMARY

There are many definitions of intelligence. Different definitions accent such distinctive aspects of intelligence as comprehension, direction, invention or creativity, censorship, availability of past experience, ability to operate at a high level under stress, and ability to use abstract symbols. Terman emphasized the capacity to deal with abstract problems and to use abstract symbols. Since he devised the most widely used intelligence test and shaped the format of most others, his definition appears to have been most influential. As a result, conventional intelligence tests, as usually interpreted, provide an adequate measure of abstract symbolic skills, but are far from satisfactory at checking the kind of *fluid* intelligence involved in creativity or the abilities central to other definitions of intelligence. Factorial studies differ in their conclusions at least partly because different tests, or even the same test at different age levels, seem to measure other aspects of intelligence. The evidence suggests strongly that intelligence consists of a g factor of moderate strength plus a number of specific factors.

Various theories try to account for the shape of the curve of intellectual growth. It seems reasonable to believe that the average growth curve accelerates sharply during infancy and early childhood, slows down after this point, but continues to rise at least into middle maturity. Individual growth curves of persons reared in typical American environments show much irregularity. Differences in the kinds of material tapped by intelligence tests at various ages and differences in the emotional well-being or intellectual stimulation of those being tested might be responsible for this variation. A comparison of generations discloses that the present generation demonstrates greater intellectual growth than its forebears, as measured by scores on conventional group intelligence tests. The mental growth curves of individuals raised outside the mainstream of American culture indicate a deceleration that apparently results from the intellectual impoverishment of their environment.

Individual differences in intelligence-test scores do not relate substantially to most laboratory measures of learning, nor do they always predict creative capacities. Intelligence-test scores, however, do permit prediction of academic success with a fairly high amount of accuracy. Individuals who score high on such tests, when compared to the general population, are not only superior in accomplishment, but also are better physical specimens and seem better able to withstand psychic stresses. Individuals found in the ranks of the genius category as children maintain their superiority at least through the mid-forties. Individuals on the low end of the intelligence curve do poorly in school but perform better on the job. In many cases they also test within the normal range of intelligence as adults.

Although measures of intelligence are far from perfect, thus preventing an understanding of the nature of intelligence and of intellectual growth from being complete, psychologists have come a long way toward achieving accuracy in predicting performance in a highly complex area of behavior.

REFERENCES

Anderson, I. H., Hughes, B. O., & Dixon, W. R.   The rate of reading development and its relation to age of learning to read, sex, and intelligence. *Journal of Educational Research,* 1957, **50,** 481–494.

Anderson, J. E.   The limitations of infant and preschool test in the measurement of intelligence.   *Journal of Psychology,* 1939, **8,** 351–379.

Angelino, H., & Shedd, C. L.   An initial report of a validation study of the Davis-Eells tests of general intelligence or problem solving ability. *Journal of Psychology,* 1955, **40,** 35–38.

Baldwin, A. L.   The effect of home environment on nursery school behavior. *Child Development,* 1949, **20,** 49–62.

Baldwin, A. L., Kalhorn, J., & Breese, F. H.   Patterns of parent behavior. *Psychological Monographs,* 1945, **58,** No. 268.

Baller, W. R.   A study of the present social status of a group of adults, who, when they were in the elementary schools, were classified as mentally deficient. *Genetic Psychology Monographs,* 1936, **18**, No. 3.

Baller, W. R., Charles, D. C., & Miller, E. L.   Mid-life attainment of the mentally retarded: a longitudinal study. *Genetic Psychology Monographs,* 1967, **75**, 235–329.

Barron, F.   The needs for order and disorder as motives in creative act activity. In C. W. Taylor & F. Barron (Eds.), *Scientific creativity.* New York: Wiley, 1963.

Barron, F., & Welsh, G. S.   Artistic perception as a possible factor in personality style: Its measurement by a figure preference test. *Journal of Psychology,* 1952, **33**, 199–203.

Bayley, N.   On the growth of intelligence. *American Psychologist,* 1955, **10**, 805–818.

Bayley, N., & Schaeffer, E. S.   Correlates of maternal and child behaviors with the development of mental abilities: Data from the Berkeley growth study. *Monographs of the Society for Research in Child Development,* 1964, **29**, No. 6, Serial No. 97.

Binet, A., & Simon, T.   *The development of intelligence in children.* (Translated by E. S. Kite) Vineland, N. J.: Vineland Training School, 1916.

Bradway, K. P., Thompson, C. W., & Cravens, R. B. Preschools IQs after twenty-five years. *Journal of Educational Psychology,* 1958, **49**, 278–281.

Breen, R. A., & McGaugh, J. L.   Facilitation of maze learning with posttrial injections of picrotoxin. *Journal of Comparative and Physiological Psychology,* 1961, **54**, 498–501.

Burks, B. S., Jensen, D. W., & Terman, L. M.   *Genetic studies of genius: III. The promise of youth: Follow up studies of a thousand gifted children.* Stanford, Calif.: Stanford University Press, 1930.

Cattell, R. B.   *Personality and motivation structure and measurement.* New York: Harcourt, Brace & World, 1957.

Cattell, R. B., & Drevdahl, J. E.   A comparison of the personality profile of eminent researchers with that of eminent teachers and administrators and that of the general population. *British Journal of Psychology,* 1955, **46**, 248–261.

Charles, D. C.   Ability and accomplishment of persons earlier judged mentally deficient. *Genetic Psychology Monographs,* 1953, **47**, 3–271.

Charles, D. C.   Adult adjustment of some deficient American children. *American Journal of Mental Deficiency,* 1957, **62**, 300–304.

Cole, R. E., Dent, H. E., Eguchi, P. E., Fujii, K. K., & Johnson, R. C. Transposition with minimal errors during training trials. *Journal of Experimental Child Psychology,* 1964, **1**, 355–359.

Davis, A.   *Social class influences upon learning.* Cambridge, Mass.: Harvard University Press, 1948.

Davis, A., & Eells, K.   *Davis-Eells Games: Davis-Eells test of general intelligence or problem solving ability.* Yonkers, N. Y.: World Book, 1953.

Dent, H. E., & Johnson, R. C.   The effects of massed vs. distributed practice in the learning of organic and familial defectives. *American Journal of Mental Deficiency,* 1964, **68,** 533–536.

Digman, J. M. A factor analysis of WISC IQ test scores. Unpublished manuscript, University of Hawaii, 1962.

Drevdahl, J. E. Factors of importance for creativity. *Journal of Clinical Psychology,* 1956, **12,** 21–26.

Gesell, A. *Infancy and human growth.* New York: Macmillan, 1928.

Getzels, J. W., & Jackson, W. *Creativity and Intelligence.* New York: Wiley, 1962.

Goddard, H. H. *The Kallikak family.* New York: Macmillan, 1912.

Goddard, H. H. What is intelligence? *Journal of Social Psychology,* 1946, **24,** 51–69.

Goodenough, F. L. The measurement of mental growth in childhood. In L. Carmichael (Ed.), *Manual of child psychology.* (2nd ed.) New York: Wiley, 1954. Pp. 459–491.

Greenacre, P. The family romance of the artist. *Psychoanalytic Study of the Child,* 1958, **13,** 9–43.

Guilford, J. P. Creativity. *American Psychologist,* 1950, **5,** 444–454.

Guilford, J. P. The structure of intelligence. *Psychological Bulletin,* 1956, **53,** 267–293.

Guilford, J. P. Three faces of intellect. *American Psychologist,* 1959, **14,** 469–479.

Haggard, E. A. Social status and intelligence: An experimental study of certain cultural determinants of measured intelligence. *Genetic Psychology Monographs,* 1954, **49,** 141–186.

Hebb, D. O. *The organization of behavior.* New York: Wiley, 1949.

Heber, R. A manual on terminology and classification in mental retardation. *Monograph Supplement to the American Journal of Mental Deficiency,* 1959, **64,** No. 2.

Helson, R. Personality characteristics and developmental history of creative women. *Genetic Psychology Monographs,* 1967, **76,** 205–256.

Higgins, J. V., Reed, E. W., & Reed, S. C. Intelligence and family size: A paradox resolved. *Eugenics Quarterly,* 1962, **9,** 84–90.

Hollingworth, L. S. *Children above 180 IQ.* Yonkers, N. Y.: World Book, 1942.

Honzik, M. P., McFarlane, J. W., & Allen, L. The stability of mental test performance between two and eighteen years. *Journal of Experimental Education,* 1948, **17,** 309–324.

Horn, J. L. Organization of abilities and the development of intelligence. *Psychological Review,* 1968, **75,** 242–259.

Horn, J. L., & Cattell, R. B. Age differences in primary mental ability factors. *Journal of Gerontology,* 1966, **21,** 210–220. (a)

Horn, J. L., & Cattell, R. B. Refinement and test of the theory of fluid and crystallized intelligence. *Journal of Educational Psychology,* 1966, **57,** 253–270. (b)

Horn, J. L., & Cattell, R. B.   Age differences in fluid and crystallized intelligence. *Acta Psychologica*, 1967, **26**, 1–23.

Houston, J. P., & Mednick, S. A.   Creativity and the need for novelty. *Journal of Abnormal and Social Psychology*, 1963, **66**, 137–141.

Humphreys, L. G.   The organization of human abilities. *American Psychologist*, 1962, **17**, 475–483.

Jacobsen, T. L., & Asher, J. J.   Validity of the concept constancy measure of creative problem solving. *Journal of Genetic Psychology*, 1963, **68**, 9–20.

Jennings, R. D.   Strain differences in the effects of distribution of practice on maze learning.   Unpublished master's thesis, San Jose State College, 1960.

Johnson, G. O.   A study of the social position of mentally handicapped children in the regular grades. *American Journal of Mental Deficiency*, 1950, **55**, 60–89.

Johnson, R. C.   Similarity in IQ of separated identical twins as related to length of time spent in the same environment. *Child Development*, 1963, **34**, 745–749.

Kagan, J., Sontag, L. W., Baker, C. T., & Nelson, V. L.   Personality and IQ change. *Journal of Abnormal and Social Psychology*, 1958, **56**, 261–266.

Kennedy, R. J. R.   *The social adjustment of morons in a Connecticut city.* Hartford, Conn.: Mansfield-Southberry Training Schools, 1948.

Knief, L. M., & Stroud, J. B.   Intercorrelations among various intelligence, achievement, and social class scores. *Journal of Educational Psychology*, 1959, **50**, 117–120.

Krech, D., Rosenzweig, M. R., & Bennett, E. L.   Effects of environmental complexity and training on brain chemistry. *Journal of Comparative and Physiological Psychology*, 1960, **53**, 509–519.

MacKinnon, D. W.   The nature and nurture of creative talent. *American Psychologist*, 1962, **17**, 484–495.

McBain, W. M., & Johnson, R. C.   *The science of ourselves.* New York: Harper & Row, 1962.

McCurdy, H. G.   The childhood pattern of genius. *Journal of the Elisha Mitchell Scientific Society*, 1957, **73**, 448–462.   Also in R. A. King (Ed.), *Readings for an introduction to psychology.* New York: McGraw-Hill, 1961.   Pp. 269–278.

McGaugh, J. L.   Facilitative and disruptive effects of strychnine sulphate on maze learning. *Psychological Reports*, 1961, **8**, 99–104.

McGaugh, J. L., Westbrook, W. H., & Burt, G.   Strain differences in the facilitative effects of 5-7-diphenyl-1-3-diazadamantan-6-OL (1757I.S.) on maze learning. *Journal of Comparative and Physiological Psychology*, 1961, **54**, 502–505.

McGaugh, J. L., Westbrook, W. H., & Thomson, C. L.   Facilitation of maze learning with posttrial injections of 5-7-diphenyl-l-3-diazadamantan-6-OL (1757I.S.). *Journal of Comparative and Physiological Psychology*, 1962, **55**, 710–713.

McNemar, Q.   *The revision of the Stanford-Binet Scale: An analysis of the standardization data.*   Boston: Houghton Mifflin, 1942.

Madsen, M. C. Distribution of practice and level of intelligence. *Psychological Reports*, 1963, **13**, 39–42.

Maxwell, J. Intelligence, fertility, and the future. *Eugenics Quarterly*, 1954, **1**, 244–247.

Meyers, C. E., Dingman, H. F., Orpet, R. E., Sitkei, E. G., & Watts, C. A. Four ability factor hypotheses at three preliterate levels in normal and retarded children. *Monographs of the Society of Research in Child Development*, 1964, **29**, No. 5, Serial No. 96.

Muench, G. A. A follow-up of mental defectives after eighteen years. *Journal of Abnormal and Social Psychology*, 1944, **39**, 407–418.

Owens, W. A. Age and mental abilities: A longitudinal study. *Genetic Psychology Monographs*, 1953, **48**, 3–54.

Pinneau, S. R. *Changes in intelligence quotient—infancy to maturity.* Boston: Houghton Mifflin, 1961.

Pintner, R., Dragositz, A., & Kushner, R. Supplementary guide for the Revised Stanford-Binet Scale (Form L). *Applied Psychology Monographs*, 1944, No. 3.

Porteus, S. D. *The practice of clinical psychology.* New York: American Book, 1941.

Porteus, S. D. *The maze test and clinical psychology.* Palo Alto, Calif.: Pacific Books, 1959.

Porteus, S. D. *Porteus Maze Tests: Fifty years' application.* Palo Alto, Calif.: Pacific Books, 1965.

Reid, J. B., King, F. J., & Wickwire, P. Cognitive and other personality characteristics of creative children. *Psychological Reports*, 1959, **5**, 729–737.

Roe, A. A study of imagery in research scientists. *Journal of Personality*, 1951, **19**, 459–470.

Rosenzweig, M. R., Krech, D., Bennett, E. L., & Diamond, M. C. Effects of environmental complexity and training on brain chemistry and anatomy: A replication and extension. *Journal of Comparative and Physiological Psychology*, 1962, **55**, 429–437.

Sherman, M. *Hollow folk.* New York: Crowell, 1933.

Sherman, M., & Key, C. B. The intelligence of isolated mountain children. *Child Development*, 1932, **3**, 279–290.

Shapiro, G. M. The effects of massed and distributed practice on the learning ability of bright, average, and dull children, matched in mental age. Unpublished master's thesis, University of Hawaii, 1964.

Skeels, H. M. Adult status of children with contrasting early life experiences. *Monographs of the Society for Research in Child Development*, 1966, **31**, No. 3, Serial No. 105.

Sontag, L. W., Baker, C. T., & Nelson, V. L. Mental growth and personality development: A longitudinal study. *Monographs of the Society for Research in Child Development*, 1958, **23**, No. 2. Whole No. 68.

Spearman, C. "General intelligence," objectively determined and measured. *American Journal of Psychology*, 1904, **15**, 201–292.

Spearman, C. *The abilities of man.* London: MacMillan, 1927.

Stuart, J. *God's oddling.* New York: McGraw-Hill, 1960.

Terman, L. M.   *The measurement of intelligence: An explanation of and a complete guide for the Stanford Revision and Extension of the Binet-Simon Intelligence Scale.*   Boston: Houghton Mifflin, 1916.

Terman, L. M.   The discovery and encouragement of exceptional talent. *American Psychologist,* 1954, **9,** 221–230.

Terman, L. M., et al.   *Genetic studies of genius: I. Mental and physical traits of a thousand gifted children.*   Stanford, Calif.: Stanford University Press, 1925.

Terman, L. M., & Oden, M. H.   *Genetic studies of genius: IV. The gifted child grows up.*   Stanford, Calif.: Stanford University Press, 1947.

Terman, L. M., & Oden, M. H.   *The gifted group at mid-life: Thirty-five years' follow-up of the superior child.*   Stanford, Calif.: Stanford University Press, 1959.

Thurstone, L. L.   Theories of intelligence. *Science Monthly,* 1946, **62,** 101–112.

Thurstone, L. L., & Ackerson, L.   The mental growth curve for the Binet tests. *Journal of Educational Psychology,* 1929, **20,** 569–583.

Torrance, E. P.   Explorations in creative thinking. *Education,* 1960, **81,** 216–220.

Torrance, E. P.   *Guiding creative talent.*   Englewood, N. J.: Prentice-Hall, 1962.

Tuddenham, R. D.   Soldiers in World Wars I and II. *American Psychologist,* 1948, **3,** 54–56.

Vandenberg, S. G., & Johnson, R. C.   Further evidence in the relation between age of separation and similarity in IQ among pairs of separated identical twins.   In S. G. Vandenberg (Ed.), *Progress in human genetics.*   Baltimore: Johns Hopkins, 1968.

Wallach, M. A., & Kogan, N.   *Modes of thinking in young children.*   New York: Holt, Rinehart & Winston, 1965.

Wiener, N.   *Ex-prodigy,* Cambridge, Mass.: M.I.T. Press, 1964 (originally published in 1953).

Wiener, N.   *I am a mathematician.*   Cambridge, Mass.: M.I.T. Press, 1964 (originally published in 1956).

Welsh, G. S.   *Welsh Figure Preference Test: Preliminary manual.*   Palo Alto, Calif.: Consulting Psychologists Press, 1959.

Wheeler, L. R.   A comparative study of the intelligence of East Tennessee mountain children. *Journal of Educational Psychology,* 1942, **33,** 321–334.

Wilson, R. C., Guilford, J. P., & Christensen, P. R.   The measurement of individual differences in originality. *Psychological Bulletin,* 1953, **50,** 362–370.

Woodrow, H.   The ability to learn. *Psychological Review,* 1946, **53,** 147–158.

SECTION III
THE FAMILY
AND ITS INFLUENCE
ON DEVELOPMENT

This section, composed of the next four chapters, concerns the child in his family setting. Such forces as heredity and maturation impose limits on the influence that parents and other social groups may bring to bear. At the present time this subject of the influence of family on the behavior and personality of the child is a matter of lively interest among researchers, and much effort is being expended in its investigation.

Chapter 7 considers the anthropological, sociological, and historical forces that have made the family in America what it is today and that determine, in part, the way in which the family influences development. Chapter 8 examines various aspects of the family and of the child's place within it. Such matters as "onliness," sibling position, physical or mental defects of siblings, maternal employment, and divorce are discussed.

Chapter 9 covers the interaction of the child with parents during infancy. Among the topics explored are Freudian concepts; the relation of early parent practices, such as toilet training and weaning, to personality and behavior; and the effects of maternal deprivation. Chapter 10, the final chapter of the section, pertains to parental influences during the period of childhood following infancy. It includes such matters as the impact of parent personality, parent attitudes, and parent behavior on child personality and behavior.

All told, the cultural, psychological, and social forces in the family situation, together with the personalities, attitudes, and behaviors of each parent and other members of the family, affect the child. Born with certain characteristics that form the core of his uniqueness, the child finds this uniqueness increased by these many influences. Their interplay within the family renders accurate prediction of the effect of any single force on any single child difficult. As this section indicates, however, child psychology is developing predictive skills, notwithstanding the complexity of the problem.

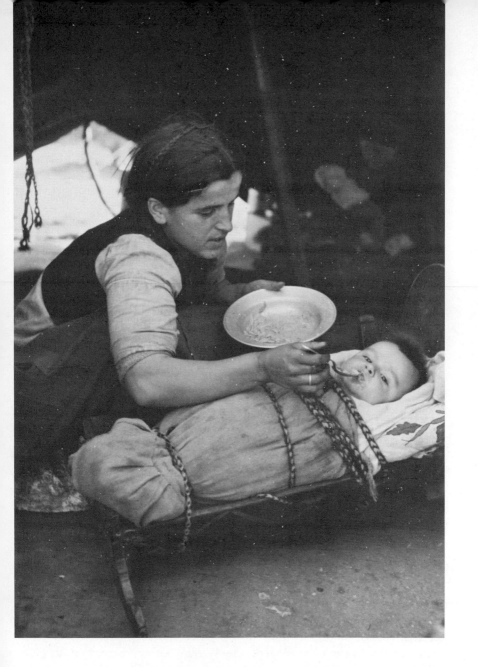

7

The Influence of Culture
on Child-Rearing Practices

Individuals who share a set of values, beliefs, practices, and information, and who pass these views from one generation to the next, constitute a culture. Americans are part of Western culture, a broad grouping of individuals in North America, Europe, the British Commonwealth, and other areas of the earth. Western culture, an amalgam of Judeo-Christian, Greco-Roman, and other influences, differs from other cultures in the "world view" it builds into people. Although philosophers since Hume have argued that it is improper to talk of "cause" and "effect," Westerners at a very early age accept the ideas that present conditions have their roots in the past, that the future can be predicted from the present, and that the future, moreover, can be changed. Yet the implied notion that there is lawfulness and predictability in the world, based on orderly cause and effect, is far from universally held. Further, the idea that we determine the nature of the future by our own actions is very much of a minority opinion, viewed crossculturally.

Other ideas common to the West also are not accepted by all cultures. Such value judgments as that life in this world is "good," that progress is possible and desirable, that individuality should be developed to as high a degree as it can, or that the individual human is of considerable worth are not necessarily shared by others. Nor are the values prized by others always acceptable to the West. We cannot imagine many Americans believing that the goal of existence is to lead such a good life that once dead reincarnation is no longer necessary and instead one again becomes nothing. Few within Western culture take the position that if an individual develops a skill more than others do, he is disturbing the equilibrium of the group and thus making supernatural beings unhappy. Americans do not believe that the old way is necessarily the best way. Instead they welcome change for its own sake.

Beliefs shape patterns of child rearing in various subtle ways. But since all within a culture are subjected to the same influences, these factors and their effect of making people similar to one another in basic approach are often overlooked. Frequently it is necessary to be thrown suddenly into another culture to recognize the essential oneness underlying the apparent diversity of the West. Although part of the same Western culture, Americans have produced within it their own adaptation of it, the *American* culture. This chapter begins with an examination of various cultural considerations that bear on the social environment of the child. This will be followed by discussion of the forces, both past and present, that have produced current child-rearing practices, and by an attempt to show the impact of these forces on various groups in their approaches to child rearing.

218

DIMENSIONS OF CULTURE

Cultures can be variously divided into distinct groups, but all such dichotomies have a certain inherent falsity. Things seldom are "either-or." More likely they are blends of various sorts, shading toward one or the other of the types that form the dichotomy. Such is the case with the dimensions of culture to be discussed. Cultures probably do not differ from one another in kind, but rather in the degree to which certain characteristics are present.

Child-Rearing Practices of Primary versus Secondary Groups

This distinction is mentioned first for several reasons. First, having formed an important aspect of sociological theory since the 1860's, it has a certain historical priority. More important, considerable evidence suggests that the development of the *self concept*—an individual's attitudes and beliefs about himself—is an extremely significant phenomenon. The concept of self comes largely from a person's ideas about his social roles; and the type, consistency, and clarity of the roles played seem to depend on whether he grows up in a primary- or a secondary-group society. *Primary groups* are characterized by intimate, face-to-face contact, by the mutual social support of the individuals who belong, and by the group's ability to proscribe, constrain, or order a considerable proportion of the behavior of its individual members. Family and peers, two such primary groups, have considerable influence in American society. Such groups as the typical urban community or neighborhood, or a trade union or professional association are *secondary groups*. These are not characterized by close or continual contact or by a concern in any but a limited segment of a member's behavior. They do not offer any great deal of support, nor generally can they exert any great degree of pressure, except perhaps within rigidly limited areas, toward conformity to group standards of behavior. Historically, according to many social theorists (Durkheim, 1947; Tonnies, 1940; Becker, 1948), societies composed solely of primary groups reigned supreme. In a primitive culture or even in a contemporary rural one, all individuals know one another. Although not much happens, everyone knows everything that does happen. These social groups are primary groups; little conflict of value systems occurs among them, since everyone holds much the same values. A high proportion of behaviors are "public" behaviors, known to all members of the group and judged by them in terms of propriety.

One of the authors of this book recalls, for example, coming home in a newly acquired 1939 Buick phaeton to the rural community in which he grew up. Everyone in the community asked him, at first encounter, how much he paid for it. They told him that going to college must have made him foolish—that no one in northern Minnesota should buy a convertible. Had they been reprimanded, "None of your business," they would have been surprised as well as hurt. In their opinion it *was* their business to pass judgment on the behavior of members of the group, just as it was to take up a collection and have a building bee if someone's house or barn burned down, or to do the farm chores for a neighbor with a broken leg. It is their business to help members of the group. This combination of inquisitiveness and psychological support found in a primary-group society makes the majority of people escape as soon as possible and then remember the society with nostalgia for the rest of their lives.

A city, on the other hand, is largely a secondary-group society. The individual is exposed to a wide variety of groups, most of which are not characterized by intimate, face-to-face contact across a broad range of behavioral settings. Multiple group membership is the rule. Since urban groupings, such as trade unions, church organizations, P.T.A.s, and fraternal organizations, differ in composition and often in values and goals, an individual can easily encounter conflict between two antagonistic social roles. Further, the roles prescribed by any one group generally do not deal with wide varieties of behavior, but only with that narrow range of public behaviors of concern to the group. Because no universal consensus exists regarding the "goodness" or "badness" of a given behavior, all values are relative, and none is held as strongly as in a primary-group society (Durkheim, 1915).

Some segments of American culture are still dominated by primary-group associations. This is true of isolated farm groups, members of pietist religious sects (see Francis, 1955; also Kaplan & Plaut, 1956), and probably the very rich. An ever-increasing proportion of Americans, however, lives in urban areas. U. S. Census figures show that well over three-fourths of the population now, as opposed to one-half in 1890, are city dwellers or suburbanites. This majority does not often have such ties as those of religious zealots or of the very rich and thus is not as subject to the influence of primary codes.

Children reared in these two types of environment are subjected to discernibly different forms of parental training. The parent within that part of society still composed largely of primary groups takes a stand toward behavior based on the one traditional set of values to which he has been exposed. There is only one acceptable way for him to respond to any given situation; his whole group agrees on the matter.   Once he *knows* what is right, it becomes his duty to teach this to his children and to extirpate any tendencies they may disclose to respond in other manners.   Social roles are clearly defined and strengthened by the views of the group.   If the child learns to play his allotted share of roles correctly so that they do not conflict with the group and so that he fulfills its expectations, the parent's task is essentially complete.   If none of the few available roles seems desirable to the child, he must be induced to make do with them. The function of the parent is to hammer home "self-evident, universally held truths" and to defend the group against the youngster's tendency toward change.   Small wonder that parents in primary-group societies are believed to be highly conservative (Spencer, 1912; Durkheim, 1951) and authoritarian (Jaensch, 1938).

The child-rearing practices of a secondary-group society vary to an ever-increasing degree from those of a primary-group environment.   An urban culture is dynamic and rapidly changing.   Traditional behaviors are of little utility in preparing a child for adulthood, since the adulthood of any child will differ greatly from that of his parents.   As a result the parent is quite uncertain as to what to teach the child (Riesman, 1953; Boehm, 1957).   Despite the desire to rear children with values consonant with their own, parents often must grant their children autonomy in a number of decision-making areas quite early in the developmental process.   This is because the differences in experiences are so great between generations.   Moreover, because the parent is less certain that he knows the correct course of action, he delegates authority to other groups.   The peer group and the schools take over and thus influence the development of conscience, as shall be discussed presently.   The American urban child as opposed to the Swiss, Boehm (1957) has shown, is far more autonomous and far less guilt ridden, presumably because of this weakened parental and increased peer influence.

Owing to economic changes accompanying the development of an industrial, urban, secondary-group society, the parent is warmer and more permissive.   Equalitarian treatment of the child follows both from the viewing of the child primarily as a love object and from the parent's own lack of certainty as to what the child should be like. The child is exposed to many differing social groups with diverse values; none of these groups has a high degree of dominance in its influence.   No group, not even the family, can keep a constant check on the child in all areas of activity as in a less complex social setting. The child, as a result, knows many sets of conflicting values and probably accepts none of them wholeheartedly until he must select from them as well as from diverse social roles those that he finds best. Then he must adapt them to form a self-consistent set of roles, often referred to as the major component of the *self concept.*

The historical changes in child-rearing practices apparent in American culture may result largely from the continuing shift from a relatively uniform, rural, agrarian society to a variegated, urban, industrial one.

Child-Rearing Techniques in Cultures of Want and of Plenty

Urbanization requires the development of technology and the division of labor. These, in turn, are necessary for a materially rich culture. The American culture is presumably the richest the world has yet known. Certain aspects of child rearing within it appear to relate to economic circumstances.

Because of advanced scientific technology, the death rate among children is very low. A grandmother stressed the significance of this fact, with respect to child rearing. In discussing the changes that occurred in the 80 years she could remember, she commented on one quite noticeable development, the greater amount of love that parents lavish nowadays on children. "Back in the old days," she said, "parents couldn't get involved with younger children as greatly. They were afraid that deep love would lead only to deep sorrow, for so many children died before reaching maturity." Although other factors undoubtedly enter into this increased parental involvement and love, mortality figures indicate that a parent at the turn of the century could not *assume* that his children would live to maturity.

Advanced technical achievements appear likely to have contributed in other ways to increased parental love and involvement. Children of a few generations ago were viewed primarily as economic assets. The farmer with a crop of growing boys knew that if he could only hold on for a few more years, he would have plenty of help. Moreover, this help would be of the very best sort, since wages would not be required nor would there be any complaints about a 12-hour day, seven-day work week. No longer can children be viewed in this fashion. There are fewer and fewer things a child is useful for, even on the farm. It is easier, cheaper, quicker, and more efficient to buy a new hay baler or harvesting machine than to breed a crop of farm hands. Since another function of children is that of receiving and giving love, this role has come to the fore, no longer overshadowed by economic necessity. Children are to be loved.

Not only are children loved more, but they are also loved as children far longer. The closer a culture is to a subsistence economy, the shorter the period of childhood, one writer has suggested (Landis, 1945). Hunting or fishing cultures, nearly always only a few days away from starvation, have the shortest childhoods, whereas agrarian cultures are intermediate, and industrial societies are longest in the period they term childhood.

A century ago, the grandfather of one of the authors sailed from a fishing village on the island of Gotland in Sweden at the age of 10 and was a ship's officer on a windjammer at 17. He had stayed home longer than his two brothers, since he was the youngest—the "baby" of the family. How the world has changed in less than 100 years! Most segments of Western culture are now sufficiently affluent that children are no longer needed on the labor market. Besides, most occupations demand a relatively high degree of formal training. The young person must now remain dependent on the family for a considerable period of time after having reached physical maturity in order to receive this training. Although the influence of the family on children's values may not be as it once was at any time during the early years, the family does have many more years in which to shape the child.

Continuous versus Discontinuous Cultures

Anthropologists such as Ruth Benedict make a distinction between continuous and discontinuous cultures. In a continuous culture, the child begins learning adult roles as soon as he begins to understand the world about him, as the following examples indicate.

. . . The gravity of a Cheyenne Indian family ceremoniously making a feast out of the little boy's first snowbird is at the furthest remove from our behavior. At birth the little boy was presented with a toy bow, and from the time he could run about serviceable bows suited to his stature were specially made for him by the man of the family. Animals and birds were taught him in a graded series beginning with those most easily taken, and as he brought in his first of each species his family duly made a feast of it, accepting his contribution as gravely as the buffalo his father brought. When he finally killed a buffalo, it was only the last step of his childhood conditioning, not a new adult role with which his childhood experience had been at variance.

The Canadian Ojibwa show clearly what results can be achieved. This tribe gains its livelihood by winter trapping and the small family of father, mother and children live during the long winter alone on their great frozen hunting grounds. The boy accompanies his father and brings in his catch to his sister as his father does to his mother; the girl prepares the meat and skins for him just as his mother does for her husband. By the time the boy is 12, he may have set his own line of traps on a hunting territory of his own and return to his parent's house only once in several months—still bringing the meat and skins to his sister. The young child is taught consistently that it has only itself to rely upon in life, and this is as true in the dealings it will have with the supernatural as in the business of getting a livelihood . . . (Benedict, 1949, pp. 300–301).

A discontinuous culture, on the other hand, does not prepare the young child for adulthood through a continuous inculcation of social roles. Discontinuous cultures teach children roles that are in opposition to those they will assume later. For example, the mainstream of American culture (see Haimowitz, 1960, p. 2), like the American Indian subculture, places high value on courage. The Indians, who desire this attribute more than any other, are continuous in their training for it. A bold act, such as that of a two-year-old boy physically attacking his father, is applauded. The prevailing American culture, on the contrary, is truly discontinuous; it expects the individual to be submissive while young and then magically to become dominant at maturity.

American society is clearly discontinuous—not only in failing to provide training for certain adult functions, but also in establishing childhood roles that are antagonistic to the roles demanded by adulthood. It may not be as discontinuous, however, as is believed by many anthropologists. Nor is it certain that discontinuity is undesirable. Perhaps in a complex, rapidly changing, secondary-group society, a certain facility in taking new roles is necessary. Conceivably the ease in making these shifts and adjustments comes from the discontinuity of roles and from the conflicts among those roles faced and mastered during the growing-up process.

Guilt versus Shame Cultures

A traditional aim of a parent in urban industrial culture is to produce a child with what used to be called a well-developed conscience but is now more often termed a strong superego—in any case, a child who feels guilt following wrongdoing. Guilt comes from within. If cultural conditioning has been successful, many humans are self-regulating organisms who punish themselves without being caught. This is an explicitly stated goal in Western culture. It is not common to all cultures. Anthropologists say that the very notion of guilt is lacking in some cultures, and that social controls are based on shame. Shame results from an act being found out by others; as long as one is not caught, any action is acceptable.

It should be noted that there is no one-to-one relation between primary versus secondary groups and the guilt-shame dichotomy. Many primary groups use shame as a means of control, but others base social controls on guilt. Some secondary-group societies emphasize guilt; others shame.

Many clinical psychologists believe that Americans have succeeded only too well at building in the guilt response. The basis of neurotic symptoms, they hold, frequently lies in the patient's strong, often unjustified, feelings of guilt. A certain type of training is necessary to produce a child who feels guilt. A child must be reared in such a fashion that its parents are primarily responsible for the inculcation of values—not other groups of individuals, such as peers, hired caretakers, or the community at large. The parents must be convinced that they are correct and must be willing to reject the child, and even risk rejection by the child, when the child's behavior deviates. A withholding of love, rather than physical punishment, must be the chief means of discipline (Mead, 1943).

Let us suppose that a child is found to be engaging in childhood sex play in a culture in which sex play is prohibited. Guilt-oriented parents might admonish the child in this way: "We love you so much and now you have disobeyed us and done something *bad*. We feel so hurt we don't want you to be near us for a while. How can parents love a child who does things like that? You go to your room and think about how *bad* you are and when you're ready, come out and say that you're sorry and won't ever do that again." The response of a shame-oriented parent would follow a different form. Physical punishment would be likely to occur and be followed by statements of this kind: "No little child is supposed to do this. If someone saw you he would tell others and everyone would laugh at you or be disgusted with you. Then wouldn't you feel like a fool? You must remember that you would have to hang your head in shame if you were caught."

Shame, as a technique for controlling behavior, is probably quite effective when used by a primary-group society, since most behaviors are public. Many primary-group societies do use shame as a major technique. For an urban industrial culture shame does not appear to be an effective technique, since it is so simple to maintain anonymity. Few group ties are strong enough to cause concern about the opinion of the group. Even if one belonged to groups before which one would feel shame, one would first have to be caught and then forced to remain in the group that would be aware of the misdeed. Persons in urban societies are less likely to be caught, and if caught, can probably join another group that either does not know of the shameful deed or else does not care. Here guilt has the greater influence. Although irrational and excessive guilt may dispose one toward neurosis, members of a mass society may need at least a moderate sense of guilt to maintain the society.

It is believed, however, that urbanites are moving away from a guilt toward a shame orientation (Riesman, 1953). This may result, in part, from the influence of psychoanalysis, as has recently been claimed (LaPiere, 1959). Other forces probably have contributed far more greatly to this shift. American culture is changing at so rapid a rate that parents are unsure of their own values, and as a result, abandon much of their function to other groups such as the school and the peers. The peers, unlike the usual parent, use shame as a major disciplinary technique. Parents also do a less adequate job of building a sense of guilt since, as already noted, children are more precious these days. Hence the parent is unwilling to withhold love for fear that it may lead to his own rejection by the child. Lessened parental influence, differing to some degree in type from that of a generation ago, appears to have resulted in a shift away from guilt and toward shame as a means of social control.

Persons such as LaPiere, concerned with "the subversion of the American character" as a result of the impact of the Freudian ethic, might view this secular change negatively, whereas the more frequently observed variety of clinical psychologist might view the same change with pleasure because, if the predominant clinical position is correct, this shift might be expected to result in a lowered proportion of neurosis and "withdrawn" behavior problems.

The basic proposition underlying the clinical position is that Freud was right, that adjustment is on a normal curve, as shown in Figure 7-1, with sociopaths and/or psychopaths (people unconcerned with and uninfluenced behaviorally by the disapproval of others) on one end of the normal curve, "normal" persons in the middle, and neurotic, that is, overly guilty, persons on the other extreme of the curve. Mowrer (1960, 1961, 1967), on the other hand, believes that the neurotic is disturbed because of real guilt, over real misdeeds, and that the curve of adjustment is that shown in Figure 7-2, with the normal person being the most adequately socialized, the neurotic being intermediate, and the psychopath or sociopath least well socialized.

The majority of empirical research supports Mowrer's point of view (e.g., see Peterson, 1967), despite the fact that it is a somewhat unpopular position. However, Mowrer does not distinguish in his writings between two separate domains of conscience: resistance to temptation

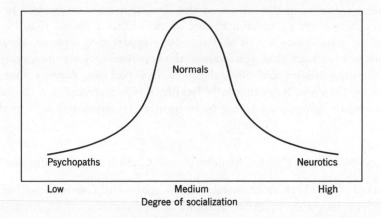

FIGURE 7-1   The usual clinical position concerning adjustment.

and guilt following yielding; further, he shows little concern regarding resistance and a great deal of concern with regard to guilt following yielding.   Recent research (Johnson, Ackerman, Frank, & Fionda, 1968) indicates that although prevailing clinical theories associate excessive guilt with mental health problems, there may be no real relationship. However, there is a strong relationship between high resistance to temptation and mental health.   These data suggest that both sides of the

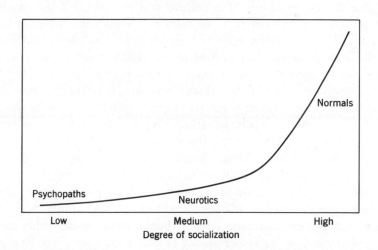

FIGURE 7-2   Mowrer's view of the adjustment of continuum (from Peterson, 1967).

argument concerning the effects of the Freudian ethic on mental health in America are wrong, since amounts of guilt and/or shame may be unrelated to mental health.   The data still support the view of Mowrer, LaPiere, and others that the commonly accepted popular position derived from psychiatry and clinical psychology (act out; express your impulse life; then you'll be mentally healthy) is incorrect, since the tendency to *resist* temptation tends to be positively associated with mental health.

Cultural Norms in Family Structure and Conscience Development

Mischel (1961) demonstrated that a male child reared without a father was less able to delay a small immediate reward in favor of a larger delayed reward.   Seigman (1966) showed that even within a highly select group (medical students), those whose fathers had been absent while they were ages one to five were more psychopathic and criminal in their behavior than those whose fathers were not absent during this time period.   These data suggest that cultural differences in family structure, resulting in differential amounts of father-son contact, should have highly important effects on conscience development and in other forms of behavior as well (see Deutsch & Brown, 1964). This proposition was put to the test by Bacon, Child, and Barry (1963). Their crosscultural study shows quite clearly that the less the opportunity in a culture for a son to get to know, love, and identify with his father, the higher the crime rate of that culture will be.   While father absence versus presence may have little or nothing to do with the amount of guilt a member of a given culture feels after he has committed a misdeed, it seems a strong determinant of whether a male member of that culture (males comprise the majority of offenders against society) will resist the temptation to violate cultural norms.   Therefore it seems clear, both within and between cultures, that certain culturally or subculturally determined aspects of family structure have a marked influence on behavior.   These data, both intracultural and crosscultural, appear to be relevant to the questions of why Negroes are now at the low end of the economic scale and of what particular ameliorative steps might have the most influence.   Growing up in a matriarchal, frequently father-absent subculture provides real handicaps in willingness and ability to achieve that perhaps can be overcome only if the culture provides other means of male identification for father-absent boys, for example, "Big Brothers," or more male elementary-school teachers.

Culture, Childhood Determinism, and the Freudian Variables

The Freudian variables (discussed in Chapter 9 as they apply to the American experience), having to do chiefly with such aspects of parent practices as toilet training and weaning, often have been studied by anthropologists in an attempt to determine a modal personality structure of a given culture, a structure that presumably results from certain childhood experiences. For example, the Japanese are said to be concerned with ritual, tidiness, and orderliness (Benedict, 1946; Gorer, 1943), and this concern is said to be a *consequence* of extremely early and rigid toilet training. This general position may be questioned from two points. First, are Japanese overly compulsive and overcontrolled? One of the authors has heard an honored, elderly, and dignified Japanese scientist describe to a group of American and Japanese colleagues how he became so drunk at Maxim's of Paris that he could not walk, faked a heart attack, and was taken back to his hotel in an ambulance. This account, and a general Japanese permissiveness toward drunkenness, do not suggest an overly compulsive, rigid, or ritualistic approach to the world and suggests that certain stereotypes concerning the Japanese are incorrect. Second, even if we grant, for the moment, that Japanese are ritualistic and compulsive, could these behaviors be attributed to early toilet training, as Benedict and Gorer suggest? Both Benedict and Gorer assume that toilet training in Japan is early and harsh. Unfortunately, for their position, actual studies of Japanese toilet-training practices (Sikkema, 1949; Lanham, 1956; Norbeck & Norbeck, 1956) show Japanese to be no more early or rigid in training than are Americans. It may be that Japanese as a group are more ritualistic and compulsive than Americans (though there are no data demonstrating this) but even if they are, there appears to be no link between the supposed personality traits and toilet training. Anthropological data often can be questioned. Margaret Mead's (1935) gentle Arapesh tribe, within which both males and females were "maternal" in their interests in gardening and in child rearing, and which was portrayed by Mead as a culture in which both male and female adult roles were kindly, nurturant, and "feminine," also was a group whose male members were among the most feared warriors and headhunters in New Guinea (Fortune, 1939). Kindly, motherly, cannibalistic headhunters! There appear to be contradictions in the description, just as there are contradictions in describing the tradition-oriented (yet highly adaptable), rigid and orderly (while condoning thoroughgoing intoxication and the complete chaos of Tokyo traffic) Japanese. As will be seen in Chapter 9, the Freudian variables do not hold up well within a culture as an explanation of adult behavior. These variables seem better able to predict behavior across cultures (e.g., see Whiting & Child, 1953), since the range of differences between cultures is greater than the range of differences in parental treatment within one culture, but even crossculturally seem to be only partial and inadequate.

Crosscultural Variation in Parent Practices

The investigation of the Freudian variables as elements of parental treatment of children that determine the modal personality of members of a given culture appears to have produced a minimal payoff in terms of reliable information. There are other aspects of parenthood that do seem to influence personality development. As in our own culture (see Chapter 9), it is the more global aspects of parenthood that seem to be important. Such things as maternal warmth, emotional stability, the degree to which parents feel responsible for children, and the means by which children are trained to fulfill cultural norms regarding responsibility and aggression appear to be the significant determinants of the nature of the mother-child relationship, which, in turn, has profound influence on the behavior and personality of the child (Triandis & Lambert, 1961).

THE CHILD IN AMERICA

So much for cultural factors. Historical influences also appear to be significant in modes of child rearing. Some of these influences, such as the Protestant Ethic, operate in Europe as well as America. The effects of other influences, such as that of the frontier, are uniquely America's own.

The Frontier and American Child-Rearing Practices

The settler of the Atlantic seaboard was a transplanted European, generally an Englishman, still tied to Old World behavior patterns. Clad in homespun, he bowed to the squire and deacons, and still "knew his betters." Entering the Allegheny Mountains, he fought it out with the Indians. A generation later, clothed in the skins of wild animals, swinging strings of scalps, and refusing to admit any man to be their equal, much less their better, some of his descendants emerged on the western side of the Alleghenies. The frontiersmen were called, with considerable justice, "White Indians" by those who remained on the seaboard. They moved on to master the continent.

The frontier did much to shape American attitudes toward the world. Since the pervasive attitudes of a culture shape its child-rearing practices, the experience of the frontier necessarily contributed markedly to the differences in child rearing between the American and the European branches of Western culture.[1] Frederick Jackson Turner in his classic study, *The Frontier in American History* (1921), described some of the changes in American attitudes and character wrought by the frontier. The frontiersman was optimistic: the promised land was always just over the next hill. Today may be bad but tomorrow will be better. Even now, in Alaska, as the season closes and winter nears, one frequently hears the statement, "Well, I didn't make it this year, but next year—well, watch me go." This hopeful attitude, resulting from the fluidity of social position on the frontier, may have much to do with high levels of aspiration for oneself and one's children. The hope and belief, so widespread in America, that one's children can and should surpass oneself in accomplishment may well stem from this basically optimistic world view of the frontier.

Most European visitors to America such as the Trollopes, the mother in the 1830's and the son 30 years later (see F. Trollope, 1832, and A. Trollope, 1862), have remarked on the wilfulness, independence, and general orneriness of American children. This general feeling persists to the present time and probably has a certain basis in fact; it is attested to by anyone who has spent much time in Europe. Equalitarian treatment of children—equalitarian by European standards—was and is at least partially the result of the frontier experience.

The frontiersman, as a member of a relatively anarchistic hunting society, may have desired independence in his children in order to improve their chances of survival. Further, he apparently believed, with a fervor not understandable today, in the idea of equality in social relations. The frontiersman also may have been exposed sufficiently to American Indian child-rearing practices to have received social reinforcement for his beliefs from them; the Indians valued a fairly high degree of self-assertion on the part of children, especially male children, because they believed this to be indicative of later strength and determination. Whatever the relative influences of specific underlying causes may have been, American experience has resulted in the American parent granting to the child a greater degree of freedom and equality than is granted by his European counterpart at any given period of time. As the content of the American experience has changed, it is not surprising that different modes of child

[1] Like the American branch of Western culture, the Australian branch underwent the same experiences and, similarly, differed from the Europeans.

rearing have appeared, as was evidenced in shifts associated with the decline of the Protestant Ethic and the rise of the Social Ethic.

Protestant Ethic, Social Ethic, Self-Reliance, and Child-Rearing Practices

Max Weber (1930) introduced the term *Protestant Ethic* to denote a set of ideas about man's relation to the natural and supernatural which gained prominence during the period of the Reformation. This new "world view" emphasized the development of the individual. The individual, within this framework, was without a mediator in his church and had to find salvation for himself. Self-reliance was emphasized as opposed to reliance on the social group. Further, the Protestant Ethic contained within itself the doctrine of "stewardship," the belief that God had made us the stewards or caretakers of His material world. The amount of possessions a person had was a good predictor of whether he would fall among the sheep or the goats, the elect or the damned. Thus hard work, self-sacrifice, and thrift, leading to the acquisition of funds, indirectly served as a measure of an individual's probability of being saved. Within the Protestant Ethic man became steward not only of his possessions, but of his time; God granted humans only a brief time to serve Him and this was not to be wasted on frivolous activities. The Protestant Ethic, in pure form, has as an ideal a pleasureless, hard-driven, and independent individual, ultimately responsible for his own affairs in both this and the next world.

It has been argued that the Protestant Ethic is being replaced in contemporary American society by the Social Ethic, an ethic that emphasizes adjustment to and dependence on others at the cost of independence and self-reliance; an ethic in which "other-direction," a concern for group approval, takes precedence over "inner-direction," the satisfaction of one's own standards and values (Riesman, 1953; LaPiere, 1959; Whyte, 1956). Adherents of this position believe that we have:

> . . . On the one hand, "the man of enterprise" of The Protestant Ethic, self-confident that through reason, integrity, industry, initiative, and faith in God he can bring into being the perfect social order, and, on the other hand, the delicate, womb-yearning individual of The Freudian Ethic, lacking self-reliance, at odds with "pathological society" from birth to death, chafing under its restraints, socially irresponsible, needing to be constantly nourished with love and pampered through such consideration as condones his offenses, delinquencies, and crimes, no matter what his age or status (Wescott, 1960).

This is an extreme view (not held, by the way, by Wescott). The changing structure of society forces people in some ways, as in decreased reliance on the support of primary groups, to be *more* independent. Yet it seems likely that dependency relations are increasing within the family at one extreme and toward the federal government at the other. This results from the weakening of extrafamilial primary group ties that used to sustain individuals.

With regard to child rearing, it has been demonstrated that child-training practices differ between hunting and fishing as opposed to agricultural societies (Barry, Child, & Bacon, 1959). Achievement and independence are more highly prized by hunters and fishers than by agriculturalists, whereas the reverse holds true for obedience and responsibility. The aims of child rearing differ according to the manner in which food is acquired. It may be that forces equally strong as those differentiating hunting and fishing from agricultural societies produce differences in child-rearing patterns in entrepreneurial, industrial societies, in contrast to bureaucratic, welfare-state societies. The independence, inner-directedness, and self-reliance that were the goals of the Protestant Ethic might have been a result of an adaptation to the industrial revolution, whereas the supposedly increasing emphasis on other-direction and reliance on, and conformity to, larger social groups may be a necessary adjustment to the new and growing welfare-state bureaucracy.[2]

This explanation of the shift from Protestant Ethic to Social Ethic finds considerable support in contemporary psychological research. In a most interesting and important book entitled *The Changing American Parent*, Miller and Swanson (1958) differentiate between entrepreneurial and bureaucratic parents.

We discuss the distinction between entrepreneurial and bureaucratic attitudes later in this chapter. Here, however, let us point out that results of studies of occupational types, bureaucrat and entrepreneur, show considerable agreement in finding entreprenuers to be more closely tied to the values of the Protestant Ethic. As a consequence, their goal is to produce independent children. To do so, they are more inclined to reject the child's impulse life—his responding to impulses rather than to reason—and to allow less variability in role playing than are bureaucrats. The bureaucrat, probably because his life is less demanding and his world more secure, is more optimistic. He appears to emphasize adjust-

[2] We should note that the words *welfare state* and *bureaucracy* have acquired negative connotations. We do not intend to use the words in either a positive or a negative sense, but merely to describe an existing phenomenon.

ment—the Social Ethic—rather than independence. The child is given wider areas of freedom, since mistakes, when made, do not bear as dire consequences. The bureaucrat generally is more permissive.

In the view of William H. Whyte (1956), the independent entrepreneur has abdicated in favor of the "organization man." Although the Protestant Ethic, and the parent attitudes and behaviors that went along with it, might have been admirably suited to an earlier economic era, the milder, more socially oriented Social Ethic has supplanted it, and parents have adapted their demands on children to newer circumstances. For better or worse, change has occurred in the basic orientation of Americans toward the world, and with it, changes in child-rearing practices. As the proportion of bureaucrats continues to increase in the future, present trends should become even more pronounced.

Is the Child Basically Good or Bad?

Until the middle of the 1950's it was often assumed that before the advent of psychology parents had led a relatively untroubled life in which each generation was reared in the same fashion as the one before. The father was a bearded, stern but fair judge, and the mother a subordinate, warm, loving, motherly, house-bound woman. Research has since shown that even that era of comparative calm was rocked with such controversies as those having to do with the morality of bottle feeding and with "breaking the will of the child" (Sunley, 1955). The golden age was less golden than had been believed.

One historical analysis of child rearing in America demonstrated that religious orientation prompted certain assumptions about the nature of children. The major orthodox Christian point of view is that man is depraved. Adherents of the Calvinistic point of view, for example, believed the newborn to be damned as a result of Original Sin, and to be full of "the Old Adam." From this point of view, the young child was both evil and rebellious. The child's will had to be broken so that he would submit to parents and to God's will. This Calvinistic tradition was very strong in America in the 1800's, leading to episodes like the following:

> . . . One mother, writing in the Mother's Magazine in 1834, described how her sixteen-month-old girl refused to say "dear mama" upon the father's order. She was led into a room alone, where she screamed wildly for ten minutes; then she was commanded again, and again refused. She was then whipped, and asked again. This kept up for four hours until the child finally obeyed. Parents commonly reported that after one such trial the child became permanently submissive. But not all par-

ents resorted to beatings to gain this end.   One mother spoke of "constant though gentle drilling," which consisted partly of refusing to give the child an object just out of its reach, however much it cried.   Another mother taught submission and self-denial at one and the same time by taking objects away from the child.   Strictness in diet and daily routine was apparently frequently an accompaniment to obedience training. However, many mothers seemed to find it hard to follow out such prescriptions, and the Mother's Magazine carried many exhortations to mothers to do their duty toward their child (Sunley, 1955, p. 160).

This point of view was not without opposition, even in the 1700's. Jean Jacques Rousseau taught that natural man—man before he was socialized—was good, and that society produced evil.   Rousseau's ideas about child rearing are described in his book *Émile*.   They consist in part of advocating that the child be let alone so that natural goodness can become manifest, and in part of hardening the child, through vigorous exercise, for a difficult and harsh world.   A third point of view, held most fully and defended most ably by Froebel (1898), also was present in this early era.   This maintained that the child was like an unfolding flower and needed love and nurture.

Benjamin Franklin, first in so many things, was one of the first to espouse the "tender loving care" point of view.   In 1770 he wrote his friend Polly Henson, advising her how to care for her son (his godson). He said:

> . . . Pray let him have everything he likes, I think it of great consequence while the features of the face are forming; it gives them a pleasant air, and, that being once become natural and fixed by habit the face is everafter the handsomer for it; and on that much of a person's good fortune may depend.   Had I been crossed as much in my infant likings and inclinations as you know I have been of late years, I should have been—I was going to say—not near so handsome, but as the vanity of that expression would offend other folks' vanity, I change it, out of regard for them and say a good deal more homely (Franklin, 1770, cited in Van Doren, 1952, p. 411).

It is this last set of beliefs that appears to have gained ascendancy, but only after a long and bitter struggle.

Sunley (1955) suggested that the view of the child as evil had prevailed for a long time, and still has some adherents.   This attitude has decreased in strength, as shown in analyses of the changes in the child-rearing practices advocated over the years by the U. S. Children's Bureau pamphlet, *Infant Care* (see Wolfenstein, 1951).   One of these analyses compared the attitudes about the nature of children that served as bases for practices recommended in the 1914 edition with the attitudes reflected in the 1942–1945 editions of this guide. It concluded that, in 1914:

> . . . The infant appeared to be endowed with strong and dangerous impulses. These were notably autoerotic, masturbatory and thumb-sucking. This child is described as "rebelling fiercely" if these impulses are interfered with. The impulses "easily grow beyond control" and are harmful in the extreme: "children are sometimes wrecked for life." The baby may achieve the dangerous pleasures to which his nature disposes him by his own movements or may be seduced into them by being given pacifiers to suck or having his genitals stroked by the nurse. The mother must be ceaselessly vigilant; she must wage a relentless battle against the child's sinful nature. She is told that masturbation "must be eradicated . . . treatment consists of mechanical restraints." The child should have his feet tied to opposite sides of the crib so that he cannot rub his thighs together; his nightgown sleeves should be pinned to the bed so that he cannot touch himself. Similarly for thumb-sucking "the sleeve may be pinned or sewed down over the fingers of the offending hand for several days and nights," or a patent cuff may be used which holds the elbow stiff. The mother's zeal against thumb-sucking is assumed to be so great that she is reminded to allow the child to have his hands free some of the time so that he may develop legitimate manual skills; "but with the approach of sleeping time the hand must be covered . . ." (Wolfenstein, 1951, p. 16).

In the 1942–1945 editions of *Infant Care,* it was noted that:

> . . . the baby has been transformed into almost complete harmlessness. The intense and concentrated impulses of the past have disappeared. Drives toward erotic pleasure (and also toward domination, which was stressed in the 1929–1938 editions) have become weak and incidental. Instead we find impulses of more diffuse and moderate character. The baby is interested in exploring his world. If he happens to put his thumb in his mouth, or to touch his genitals, these are merely incidents, and unimportant ones at that, in his over-all exploratory progress. The erogenous zones do not have the focal attraction which they did in 1914, and the baby easily passes beyond them to other areas of presumably equal interest. "The baby will not spend much time handling his genitals if he has other interesting things to do." . . . Everything amuses him, nothing is excessively exciting.
>
> The mother in this recent period is told how to regard autoerotic incidents: "Babies want to handle and investigate everything that they can see and reach. When a baby discovers his genital organs he will play with them. . . . A wise mother will not be concerned about this." . . . Similarly with thumb-sucking: "A baby explores everything within his reach. He looks at a new object, feels it, squeezes it, and almost always

puts it in his mouth." Thus again that that was formerly a "fierce" pleasure has become an unimportant incident in the exploration of the world. . . . "As he grows older other interests will take the place of sucking" . . . (Wolfenstein, 1951, p. 17).

One might question whether dirty diapers and thigh rubbing are as much fun as the early editions of *Infant Care* implied. Early assumptions that the infant finds "fierce pleasure" in his world and that this pleasure is "bad" was questioned and rejected. We are becoming warmer and more lenient, largely as a result of the shifts occurring in the culture. Some of these shifts are material, such as greater wealth and higher technical level, but others have to do with the changing view of man— the increasing conviction that humans are not, by their nature, depraved.

Influence of "Experts" on Child-Rearing Practices

Evidence indicates that there have been two "revolutions" during the twentieth century in the definition of parental roles and practices. These definitions have been made by experts and accepted by individuals in the mass media of communication, who advise parents. Actually parents have not shifted in behavior as much as might have been expected from the written media, but the experts have influenced parental practices, with the amounts of any particular influence differing among social classes at various times.

Table 7-1 contains data on child-rearing topics discussed and methods advocated in three women's magazines from 1890 through 1948, providing a view of the changes and continuities over the period (Stendler, 1950, pp. 122–134). Although the ladies' magazines are not the most accurate reflection of reality, their writers have concerned themselves with reader problems and expert opinion. The reader problems have been resolved according to the expert opinion then prevalent, thus disseminating these opinions to the reading public. Table 7-1A shows that parent problems do not vary greatly over the years. Opinions on how to deal with children and their problems, however, change materially, especially with regard to the care of infants, as is indicated in Table 7-1B. Clearly, the women's magazines have shifted the ground rules for being "a good parent."

Watsonianism. From Table 7-1 it is apparent that tight scheduling of infant feeding was beginning to be advocated by 1900. The trends toward early weaning and toilet training, toward rigid scheduling, toward a rejection of play, rocking, fondling, and other forms of bodily contact between parent and child, and toward a prohibition of such devices as

TABLE 7-1

A. Percentage of Topics Dealing with Various Aspects of Child Training as They Appeared in Three Women's Magazines Analyzed in 10-Year Intervals

Aspect of Child Training	1890	1900	1910	1920	1930	1940	1948
Physical development	38%	19%	24%	30%	49%	22%	27%
Specific behavior problems	11	20	13	22	15	18	10
Infant disciplines	11	10	17	8	12	15	12
Character and/or personality development	35	31	39	3	24	23	21
Development stages	1	3	7	1	5	10	9
Sex education	0	6	0	1	1	4	0
Place of father	0	4	3	1	5	0	2
Miscellaneous	3	4	10	31	3	6	17
Total topics	63	95	75	82	65	76	80
Total articles	53	78	62	65	49	59	66

B. Percentage of Methods Recommended for Two Aspects of Child Training as They Appeared in Three Women's Magazines Analyzed in 10-Year Intervals

Method Recommended	1890	1900	1910	1920	1930	1940	1948
Guiding character or personality development:							
Discipline	18%	14%	34%	34%	38%	28%	2%
Provide a good home influence	61	53	30	12	14	5	3
Ignore undesirable behavior	12	5	9	0	12	18	4
Look for cause and plan accordingly	0	0	0	1	14	48	84
Invoke divine aid	15	20	15	0	0	0	0
Feed properly	0	0	0	50	0	0	0
Miscellaneous	4	8	12	3	21	2	8
Infant disciplines:							
Tightly schedule	0	22	77	100	75	33	0
Loosely schedule	100	78	23	0	0	0	0
Self-regulate, "mother"	0	0	0	0	25	66	100

pacifiers that gave the child passive pleasure increased in force.   This often is called Watsonianism, since John B. Watson culminated these trends in his book, *Psychological Care of Infant and Child,* published in 1928.   From the data in Table 7-1 and the aforementioned analysis of *Infant Care,* it seems clear that Watson was merely riding the tide and did not himself produce the trends.   Yet his book did add weight to the idea of how child rearing should be conducted.   Here are some of the typical passages from it.

> The behaviorists believe that there is nothing from within to develop. If you start with a healthy body, the right number of fingers and toes, eyes, and the few elementary movements that are present at birth, you do not need anything else in the way of raw material to make a man, be that man a genius, a cultured gentleman, a rowdy or a thug (p. 41).
>
> There is a sensible way of treating children.   Treat them as though they were young adults.   Dress them, bathe them with care and circumspection.   Let your behavior always be objective and kindly firm.   Never hug and kiss them, never let them sit in your lap.   If you must, kiss them once on the forehead when they say good night.   Shake hands with them in the morning.   Give them a pat on the head if they have made an extraordinarily good job of a difficult task.   Try it out.   In a week's time you will find how easy it is to be perfectly objective with your child and at the same time kindly.   You will be utterly ashamed of the mawkish, sentimental way you have been handling it (pp. 81–82).

The aims of this system of child rearing are described by Watson as follows.

> We have tried to sketch in the foregoing chapters a child as free as possible of sensitivities to people and one who, almost from birth, is relatively independent of the family situation. . . .   Above all, we have tried to create a problem-solving child.   We believe that a problem-solving technique (which can be trained) plus boundless absorption in activity (which can also be trained) are behavioristic factors which have worked in many civilizations of the past and which, so far as we can judge, will work equally well in most types of civilizations that are likely to confront us in the future (pp. 186–187).

Watson positively valued independence, a lack of concern for others, a controlled impulse life, and an active, manipulative, striving posture toward the world.   He wished to rear children in a way consonant with the Protestant Ethic, not the Social Ethic.   Watsonianism, most fashionable in the entrepreneurial 1920's, may have begun losing its influence partially as a result of the accelerated growth of bureaucracy in the 1930's.

There are other reasons why Watsonianism was not destined for a long life. Its child-rearing technique appeared to be full of stress to parents. One still finds, occasionally, a Watsonian mother rearing her infant on a rigid, four-hour schedule. Three hours and 55 minutes since the last feeding, the baby is howling as it has been for 15 minutes, and has turned red with rage. The mother's eye is on her wristwatch. The remaining five minutes seem like hours. The psychic wear-and-tear alone of such aspects of Watsonianism seemed sufficient to turn parents away from this philosophy of child rearing. Many mothers of the era say that they reared the first child a la Watson; the later ones in terms of what seemed to be the most expedient procedure. Besides, as has been noted, the role of children is more and more that of being a love object. It is difficult to express this love when every kiss leads to future neurosis, and even such relatively innocuous activities as bouncing the baby on one's knee may produce sexual feelings in the young child and lead to later sexual abnormality.

Certain ideas ran counter to Watsonianism and helped its decline. Although Watson apparently accepted the reality and significance of the Oedipus complex, and for this reason advocated a "distant" relation with the child in order to reduce the Oedipal conflict, other interpreters of Freud used the same theory to defend the gratification of the child's impulse life. More important in bringing about the eventual decline of Watsonianism was the idea of *homeostasis,* or *internal equilibrium,* originated by Claud Bernard in the 1860's and developed by Walter B. Cannon in the early 1920's, culminating in his book *The Wisdom of the Body* (1932). Cannon's thesis, in brief, was that the body adapted to environmental stresses and among other adaptive mechanisms often "told" the individual through cravings what the body needed. The tendency of pregnant women in some parts of the world to eat earth as the result of an "irresistible urge" really occurred because the women suffered mineral deficiencies that could be reduced through the eating of certain kinds of earth. Cannon's theory, buttressed with facts, suggested that if individuals craved something, the craving might be the result of actual physiological needs. Clara Davis (1931) operating from this same general point of view, allowed infants to self-select their diets. They chose the nourishment they desired from a rather wide variety of foods. Although any infant might go on short "food jags" during which he ate only one type of food, each infant over a long time interval chose a perfectly balanced diet. This fact showed that Cannon's theory was correct and also countered Watson's view that children almost necessarily liked what was bad for them.

People began to think that if infants thrived on self-selected diets, they also might thrive on self-regulated schedules, and also might "need," in a physical sense, the contact and cuddling they seemed to enjoy, despite Watson's belief that these behaviors led to later maladjustment.   Their demands were probably because they needed the gratification, not because of perversity.

"Tender Loving Care."   The first complete reversal of the Watsonian trend was by Margaret A. Ribble in her book *The Rights of Infants* (1943).[3]   From the earlier position that fondling, hugging, kissing, rocking, and other forms of body contact between parent and child was *bad*, she demurred, maintaining that these activities were all important, and that the child denied them was deprived as significantly as one denied nourishment or sunshine.   She held that the complex of treatments often lumped together as "tender loving care" was necessary for the physical, intellectual, and emotional growth and well-being of any child.   Research data (Harlow, 1958) suggest that she might be basically correct regarding the need for body contact, even though certain of her hypotheses have been shown to be incorrect (Hopper & Pinneau, 1957; Pinneau, 1951).

Support for Ribble's position came fast.   A new, "easier," warmer approach gained ascendancy.   Yet there have been suggestions that the field is being reversed again—that society is moving back to the tough approach (Wolfenstein, 1951).   It seems doubtful, however, that parent practices will swing back completely to Watsonianism.   If they should, they will be bucking a strong current of forces, such as increasing bureaucracy and greater involvement with children, which dispose parents toward increased mildness.[4]

There is not much probability that expert opinion will intensify future changes in child-rearing practices.   Naive acceptance of expert opinion has dwindled.   The higher level of general education and the several rapid about-faces in advocated techniques have made the public wary about experts.   Parents wonder whether the experts really know what they are talking about.   Besides, the experts themselves are less likely to be certain of having *the* formula for perfect child rearing as they grow aware of the wide range of innate individual differences in temperament and ability among humans.   Watson and his followers explicitly rejected the notion of innate individual differences, and the "tender lov-

[3] Other prominent adherents of this orientation were Spitz (1945) and Bowlby (1952).
[4] No observable increases in parental toughness can be discerned in the four-year interval between the first and second editions of this book.

ing care" school has largely ignored them. If individual differences are great, then no single method of rearing can be expected to work for all. Nevertheless, as shown in Chapter 10, there are ways to increase the probability of rearing children with the virtues prized most highly by parents and the defects they find least offensive.

Class Variations in Child-Rearing Practices

Social class has continued to attract the interest of child psychologists. This variable, drawn from sociology, has had considerable significance in child-psychology research because of the wide belief that parental practices vary among classes, which results in discernible differences in the personality and behavior of children in these classes. Education, occupation, area of residence, and income play major roles in the definition of social class. To the extent that children are reared differently by parents who vary in these respects and who respond in diverse ways to social institutions, class differences may be expected to produce variance in their upbringing.

Researchers once found that social classes differed substantially, but races only slightly, in child-rearing practices. The middle class showed greater harshness and an earlier and more general curbing of the child's impulse life than the lower class (Davis & Havighurst, 1946). These observations may have been entirely correct in describing the child-rearing patterns of the 1940's. But apparently what was true of the 1940's no longer applies. A study conducted, for example, in the Boston area in the early 1950's (Maccoby & Gibbs, 1954) obtained results markedly opposed to the Davis-Havighurst study. Although both studies found the middle class to have higher educational and occupational aspirations for its children, the Maccoby-Gibbs study noted that the middle, not the lower, class was more tolerant of aggression, sex play, and other expressions of impulse life. It was less demanding in toilet and cleanliness training, and it used less severe punishment. This reversal is probably due in part to the later researchers' inclusion in their lower-class sample of individuals who by other criteria of social class would perhaps fall in the lower-middle class. The shift in the opinion of experts, whose influence is likely to be greater among the middle class as a result of wider exposure to the mass media, may also have been a contributing factor. In addition, the reversal may have been prompted by other forces.

Still more recent and more psychologically important data (Miller & Swanson, 1958; Klatskin, 1952) lead to the conclusion that differences in classes decreased appreciably in the postwar years.

As of 1957, there are suggestions that the cultural gap may be narrowing.   Spock has joined the Bible on the working-class shelf. . . .
Apparently "love" and "limits" are both watchwords for the coming
generation of parents.   As Mrs. Johnson, down in the flats, puts away
the hairbrush and decides to have a talk with her unruly youngster "like
the book says," Mrs. Thomas, on the hill, is dutifully striving to overcome her guilt at the thought of giving John the punishment she now
admits he deserves (Bronfenbrenner, 1958, p. 423).

The differences in world view that once existed among classes must
have had some basis in sociological, anthropological, and historical influences.   Doubtless the differences in child rearing and in child personality have dwindled substantially as a result of the increased homogeneity of the culture.   One distinction often noted—the willingness of
the middle, but not the lower, class to delay gratification—has been
attributed to the uncertainty of lower-class life (Davis, 1946). It also
may be accounted for by the fact that father absence reduces the ability
to delay gratification (Mischel, 1961), and father absence is more frequent in lower-class families (Deutsch & Brown, 1964).   This uncertainty
led individuals to seize gratifications immediately; otherwise the opportunity would very likely vanish.   As members of lower economic groups
acquired the greater security of relatively low but certain income, resulting from union protection on the job, unemployment compensation, and
other features of a welfare state, their lives were likely to become more
predictable.   Hence they became more willing to postpone reward and
develop long-range goals.   Accompanying this kind of change comes
what the sociologists call "upward mobility."   There is an increased interest in education as a means of self-improvement, and a greater acceptance of the Protestant Ethic at the very time that it appears to be losing
its appeal for the middle class.

A final force narrowing the differences between the classes is the mass
media of communication.   Middle-class patterns of democracy, consultation, and arbitration; of paternal involvement in household chores and
child care; of parental permissiveness; and of delayed gratification, long-
range planning, and high aspirations for children—all these are grist for
the mills of producers of television family series.   Exposure to any set of
values should have some effect on exposed individuals.   Although television and other mass media may present a distorted image of middle-
class life, their picture is an intimate one that allows social learning to
occur.

Though class differences in life experiences and in finances and housing have diminished, some value differences persist.   Kohn (1963)
suggests that working-class parents are more traditionally oriented and

middle-class parents more positively oriented toward social change; and that for these reasons working-class parents have the goal of teaching children to conform to parental values, while middle-class parents continue to be interested in producing children more capable of self-determination of values and self-direction of behavior.

Class differences that persist in the area of maternal behavior more often are associated with maternal coerciveness (with lower-class mothers being more restrictive and severe) than with affection or nurturance (Waters & Crandall, 1964). It would seem that mothers love their children as much across social classes, and have roughly the same goals for them, but that there are class differences in the procedures used in attempting to help the children reach these goals.

Some social-class differences may be expected to persist. Both Negro and Mexican families, each group differing in its own way from the Anglo-American model, are concentrated in the lower economic levels. Thus, because of differences in ethnic composition and associated differences in family structure, some class differences (though directly associated with ethnicity) can be expected to persist.

Entrepreneur versus Bureaucrat. As previously noted, beyond the more conventional social-class differences considerable variation exists between entrepreneurial and bureaucratic individuals in the upper occupational brackets, probably as a result of conflicting social demands. The entrepreneur, an independent individual, accepts the Protestant Ethic and feelings of guilt as a means of controlling behavior more than does the more socially minded bureaucrat. This difference is less discernible than the one concerning classes. Yet entrepreneurs and bureaucrats are faced with different sets of social pressures; this occasions a variance between them in their attitudes toward the world. Because they view the world differently, they raise their children differently; and the children have to adjust to the world as perceived by their parents.

According to Miller and Swanson (1958), the basic difference between the two groups appears in the area of risk taking, and their differentiation should be made in these terms. Such representative entrepreneurial occupations as physician or clinical psychologist in private practice, small businessman, door-to-door salesman on straight commission, or contract fruit picker, though differing widely in status and required skills, have in common the fact that they require the older ethic of self-reliance and independence. Income depends on hard work, individual initiative, and a fair degree of risk taking. In bureaucratic occupations, on the contrary, job security is high and risk taking minimal. A "womb-to-tomb" security is available to anyone who accepts the system and represses the once necessary trait of independence. Adjustment to the group and its norms becomes an important aspect of employment. Small wonder that bureaucrats and entrepreneurs differ in their attitudes toward the world, in what they believe their children should be like, and in how they go about obtaining the kind of behavior they seek from their children.

Entrepreneurs, as a group, believe the world to be harsher than do bureaucrats. They believe that children should be trained early to cope with this hostile environment. At least so far as early parent practices are concerned, the entrepreneur is more severe. Toilet training, weaning, and the completion of many other developmental tasks are demanded earlier of children by entrepreneurs than by bureaucrats (Miller & Swanson, 1958). As compared with bureaucrats, entrepreneurs are more authoritarian and lean toward a more rigid delineation of sex roles and a more traditionalistic orientation to family life (Johnson, Johnson, & Martin, 1961). These differences may result in part from the higher educational achievements of bureaucrats than of entrepreneurs of comparable social-class level.

Perhaps many conflicts regarding child-rearing practices, such as the question of the school being overly concerned with adjustment at the expense of achievement, have their roots in the entrepreneurial-bureaucratic antithesis. The bureaucratic orientation of educators, for example, may be at odds with the entrepreneurial orientation of school boards dominated by businessmen. The differences between these groups are substantial and, unlike some of the previously discussed social-class differences, may retain their significance for some time.

Race, Religion, Region

It is sometimes claimed (e.g., Davis & Havighurst, 1946) that race differences in child-rearing practices are slight, once racial groups are equated on social class. This may be so, with regard to such things as age of weaning and toilet training. However, differences in family structure may produce marked differences in child behavior. As noted in Chapter 2 the absence of a male figure in the home appears to produce a number of deleterious effects: reducing achievement and ability to delay gratification; increasing psychopathic tendencies. The Negro family is much more frequently characterized by father absence than is the white family (Deutsch & Brown, 1964; Frazier, 1966). This difference in family structure might be expected to have considerable social consequence regarding the behavior of the offspring—especially the male offspring. Ethnic differences in family structure may also differentially influence the offspring of Latin-American as opposed to Anglo-American families. Latin-American fathers (including many of the Latins in the United States) play a more patriarchal role than is common among the Anglos. The Latin father has, as an ideal, a highly dominant but somewhat distant role (e.g., see Lewis, 1959, 1964). Even when equated in social class, a father-absent Negro boy, frequently involved in gangs to learn the masculine role, has a problem very different from that of a Mexican-American boy, who usually has an adequate opportunity to learn the masculine role at home but joins gangs more often in an attempt to gain freedom from paternal dominance in order to exercise his masculine role.

The effects of religious orientation on patterns of child rearing often have to do with such "unworldly" groups as the Hutterites (Kaplan & Plaut, 1956) and the Amish (Francis, 1955). Nunn (1964) discussed parents who attempt to control their children through a "coalition with God"—for example, "If you do what I told you not to do, then God will be angry." This approach to controlling children appears to be a maladaptive one, usually used by incompetent and ineffectual parents, and probably has deleterious influences on the children. Type of religious affiliation has a strong influence on the frequency with which this approach to child training is used. Democracy and mother-father equality in sharing of authority seems also to be associated with religion; Catholic children believe that authority is *not* shared in their homes more frequently than do children from other religious groups (Hess & Torney, 1962).

Another comparison of religiocultural groups is found in Kluckhohn's and Strodtbeck's *Variations in Value Orientations* (1961), which compares, among other things the child-rearing practices of Spanish Americans, Texans, Mormons (Latter Day Saints), Zuni, and Navajo (also see Hollenberg, 1952; and Vogt & Roberts, 1956, for other publications involving the study of certain of these groups). Despite the fact that these five groups live close together in an area of the American Southwest, they have very different views of their relations to the environment (e.g., does man attempt to master the physical environment, does he accept it fatalistically, or does he attempt to place himself in harmony with it?) and as a result vary in the values transmitted to offspring and in the manner in which these values are transmitted.

Even within America, race, religion, and regional subcultural differences produce some of the diversity in attitudes toward child rearing, and the goals of child training.

CONCLUSION

Benjamin Lee Whorf (1956), whose studies of language have played a significant role in contemporary psychology, concluded from a study of Indo-European tongues that the differences among them are very minor—so minor, in fact, that he lumped them all together as "Standard Average European." This may be small consolation to a student learning a language. Yet German, Classic Greek, French, Latin, and Latvian resemble one another so closely that the differences among them are slight in comparison with the distinction between all of them and non-Indo-European languages. The same might be said about variability within the Western culture. Although Westerners differ from each other, they nevertheless have been subjected to sufficiently similar experiences to show a strong resemblance. Since experiences within American society disclose a common quality even greater than that of its ties with Western culture, variability among Americans is reduced still further.

To draw another analogy from language, Americans speak a number of dialects. The differences among Down East Yankee, "Brooklynese," the dialects of the Midwest and Far West, and the drawl of the Southerner are easily discerned, but all Americans can understand each other without strain. So, too, with differences in child-rearing patterns. Differences certainly exist, but within a larger pattern of homogeneity.

This common bond in the socialization process is strong enough to produce an "American type," an individual different from all others yet patently similar to fellow Americans in basic orientation. Since all individuals are exposed to the various influences described in this chapter, if in somewhat varying degrees, the differences between parents in child-rearing practices and between children in personality and behavior are markedly narrowed. It is within this cultural homogeneity that the specific life situation of an individual child produces a unique person.

REFERENCES

Bacon, M. K., Child, I. L., & Barry, H. A cross cultural study of correlates of crime. *Journal of Abnormal and Social Psychology,* 1963, **66,** 291–300.

Barry, H., Child, I. L., & Bacon, M. K. Relation of child training to subsistency economy. *American Anthropologist,* 1959, **61,** 51–63.

Becker, H., & Meyers, R. C. Sacred and secular aspects of human socialization. *Sociometry,* 1948, **5,** Nos. 4 and 5.

Benedict R.   *The chrysanthemum and the sword: Patterns of Japanese culture.* Boston: Houghton Mifflin, 1946.

Benedict, R.   Continuities and discontinuities in cultural conditioning.   In P. Mullahy (Ed.), *A study of interpersonal relations.* New York: Hermitage, 1949. Pp. 297–308.

Boehm, L.   The development of independence: A comparative study.   *Child Development,* 1957, **28,** 85–92.

Bowlby, J.   *Maternal care and mental health.*   Geneva: World Health Organization, 1952.

Bronfenbrenner, U.   Socialization and social class through time and space. In E. E. Maccoby, T. M. Newcomb, and E. L. Hartley (Eds.), *Readings in social psychology.* (3rd ed.)   New York: Holt, 1958.   Pp. 400–425.

Cannon, W. B.   *The wisdom of the body.*   New York: Norton, 1932.

Davis, A.   The motivation of the underprivileged worker.   In W. F. Whyte (Ed.), *Industry and society.*   New York: McGraw-Hill, 1946.   Pp. 84–106.

Davis, A., & Havighurst, R. J.   Social class and color differences in child rearing.   *American Sociological Review,* 1946, **11,** 698–710.

Davis, C. M.   Self-selection of diets: An experiment with infants.   *The Trained Nurse and Hospital Review,* 1931, **86,** 629–634.

Deutsch, M., & Brown, B.   Social influence in Negro-white intelligence differences.   *Journal of Social Issues,* 1964, **10,** 24–35.

Durkheim, E.   *The elementary forms of religious life.*   (Translated by J. W. Swain)   New York: Macmillan, 1915.

Durkheim, E.   The division of labor in society.   (Translated by G. Simpson) Glencoe, Ill.: Free Press, 1947 (originally published in 1902).

Durkheim, E.   *Suicide.*   (Translated by J. A. Spaulding and G. Simpson) Glencoe, Ill.: Free Press, 1951 (originally published in 1897).

Fortune, R. F.   Arapesh warfare.   *American Anthropologist,* 1939, **41,** p. 28.

Francis, E. K.   *In search of Utopia.*   Glencoe, Ill.: Free Press, 1955.

Frazier, E. F.   *The Negro family in the United States.*   (Revised and abridged edition)   Chicago: University of Chicago Press, 1966.

Froebel, F.   *Mother play.*   (Translated by H. R. Eliot and S. E. Blow)   New York: Appleton, 1898.

Gorer, G.   Themes in Japanese culture.   *Transactions of the New York Academy of Sciences,* Series II, 1943, **5,** 106–124.

Haimowitz, M. L.   What price virtue.   In M. L. Haimowitz and N. R. Haimowitz (Eds.), *Human development: Selected readings.*   New York: Crowell, 1960.

Harlow, H.   The nature of love.   *American Psychologist,* 1958, **13,** 673–685.

Hess, R. D., & Torney, J. V.   Religion, age, and sex in children's perceptions of family authority.   *Child Development,* 1962, **33,** 781–789.

Hollenberg, E.   Child training among the Zeepi.   Unpublished doctoral dissertation, Harvard University, 1952.

Hopper, H. E., & Pinneau, S. R.   Frequency of regurgitation as related to the amount of stimulation received from the mother. *Child Development,* 1957, **28**, 229–235.

Jaensch, E. R. *Der Gegentypus.* Leipzig: Barth, 1938.

Johnson, R. C., Ackerman, J. M., Frank, H., & Fionda, A. J. Resistance to temptation, guilt following yielding, and psychopathology. *Journal of Consulting and Clinical Psychology,* 1968, **32**, 169–175.

Johnson, R. C., Johnson, C. M., & Martin, L. Authoritarianism, occupation, and sex role differentiation of children. *Child Development,* 1961, **32**, 271–276.

Kaplan, B., & Plaut, T. *Personality in a communal society: An analysis of the mental health of the Hutterites.* Lawrence, Kan.: University of Kansas, 1956.

Klatskin, E. H. Shifts in child care practices in three social classes under an infant care program of flexible methodology. *American Journal of Orthopsychiatry,* 1952, **22**, 52–61.

Kluckhohn, F. R., & Strodtbeck, F. L. *Variations in value orientations.* Evanston, Ill.: Row, Peterson, 1961.

Kohn, M. L. Social class and parent-child relationships: An interpretation. *American Journal of Sociology,* 1963, **68**, 471–480.

Landis, P. H. *Adolescence and youth.* New York: McGraw-Hill, 1945.

Lanham, B. B. Aspects of child care in Japan: Preliminary report. In D. G. Haring (Ed.), *Personal character and cultural milieu. A book of readings.* (3rd ed.) Syracuse, N. Y.: Syracuse University Press, 1956.

LaPiere, R. *The Freudian ethic: An analysis of the subversion of American character.* New York: Duell, Sloan & Pearce.

Lewis, O. *Five families.* New York: Basic Books, 1959.

Lewis, O. *Pedro Martinez.* New York: Random House, 1964.

Maccoby, E. E., & Gibbs, P. K. Methods of child rearing in two social classes. In W. E. Martin and C. B. Stendler (Eds.), *Readings in child development.* New York: Harcourt, Brace, 1954.

Mead, M. *Sex and temperament in three primitive societies.* New York: Morrow, 1935.

Mead, M. *And keep your powder dry.* New York: Morrow, 1943.

Miller, D. R., & Swanson, G. D. *The changing American parent.* New York: Wiley, 1958.

Mischel, W. Father-absence and delay of gratification. *Journal of Abnormal and Social Psychology,* 1961, **63**, 116–124.

Mowrer, O. H. Psychotherapy and the problem of guilt, confession, and expiation. In W. Dennis (Ed.), *Current trends in psychology, X.* Pittsburgh: University of Pittsburgh Press, 1960.

Mowrer, O. H. *The crisis in psychiatry and religion.* Princeton, N. J.: Van Nostrand, 1961.

Mowrer, O. H. (Ed.) *Morality and mental health.* Chicago: Rand McNally, 1967.

Norbeck, E., & Norbeck, M. Child training in a Japanese fishing community.

In D. G. Haring (Ed.), *Personal character and cultural milieu. A book of readings.* (3rd ed.) Syracuse, N. Y.: Syracuse University Press, 1956.

Nunn, C. Z.   Child control through a "Coalition with God." *Child Development,* 1964, **35,** 417–432.

Peterson, D. R.   The insecure child: Over-socialized or undersocialized.   In O. H. Mowrer (Ed.), *Morality and mental health.*   Chicago: Rand McNally, 1967.

Pinneau, S. R.   A critique on the articles by Margaret Ribble.   *Child Development,* 1951, **21,** 203–228.

Riesman, D. (with N. Glazer & R. Denny).   The lonely crowd: A study of the changing American character.   New Haven: Yale University Press, 1953.

Ribble, M. A.   *The rights of infants.*   New York: Columbia University Press, 1943.

Seigman, A. W.   Father absence during early childhood and antisocial behavior.   *Journal of Abnormal Psychology,* 1966, **7,** 71–74.

Sikkema, M.   Observations on Japanese early child training.   In D. G. Haring (Ed.), *Personal character and cultural milieu.* (2nd ed.)   Syracuse, N. Y.: Syracuse University Press, 1949.

Spencer, H.   *The study of sociology.*   New York: Appleton, 1912.

Spitz, R.   Hospitalism.   In O. Fenichel et al. (Eds.), *The psychoanalytic study of the child.* (Vol. 1)   New York: International Universities Press, 1945.

Stendler, C. B.   Sixty years of child training practices.   *Journal of Pediatrics,* 1950, **36,** 122–134.

Sunley, R.   Early nineteenth century American literature on child rearing.   In M. Mead and M. Wolfenstein (Eds.), *Childhood in contemporary cultures.*   Chicago: University of Chicago Press, 1955.   Pp. 150–167.

Tonnies, F.   *Fundamental concepts of sociology: Gemeinschaft and Gesellschaft.*   (Translated by C. P. Loomis)   New York: American Book, 1940.

Triandis, L. M., & Lambert, W. W.   Pancultural factor analysis of reported socialization practices.   *Journal of Abnormal and Social Psychology,* 1961, **62,** 631–639.

Trollope, A.   *North America.*   New York: Harper, 1862.

Trollope, F.   *Domestic manners of the Americans.*   New York: Knopf, 1949 (originally published in 1832).

Turner, F. J.   *The frontier in American history.*   New York: Holt, 1921.

Van Doren, C.   *Benjamin Franklin.*   New York: Viking, 1952.

Vogt, E. Z., & Roberts, J. M.   A study of values.   *Scientific American,* 1956, **195,** 25–31.

Waters, E., & Crandall, V. J.   Social class and observed maternal behavior from 1940 to 1960.   *Child Development,* 1964, **35,** 1021–1032.

Watson, J. B.   *Psychological care of infant and child.*   New York: Norton, 1928.

Weber, M. *The Protestant Ethic and the spirit of capitalism.* (Translated by Talcott Parsons) London: Allen and Unwin, 1930.

Westcott, R. H. Man of enterprise: Whither bound? A review of LaPiere's "the Freudian ethic. . . ." *Contemporary Psychology,* 1960, **5**, 258–259.

Whiting, J. W. M., & Child, I. L. *Child training and personality: A cross cultural study.* New Haven: Yale University Press, 1953.

Whorf, B. L. *Language, thought and reality.* Cambridge, Mass.: Technology Press, 1956.

Whyte, W. H. *The organization man.* New York: Simon and Schuster, 1956.

Wolfenstein, M. The emergence of fun morality. *Journal of Social Issues,* 1951, **7**, 15–25.

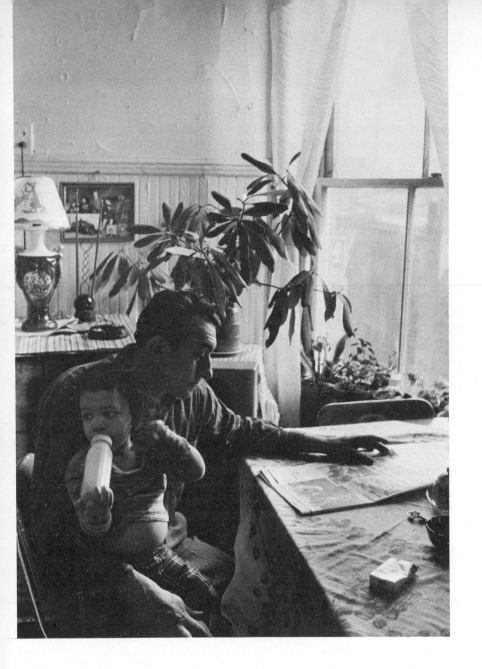

8

Psychosocial Aspects of
the Family Setting

What a child learns in the home is conditioned by a number of diverse influences. Such things as order of birth, position of siblings, family size, marital relations of parents, the presence of a handicapped child, whether the mother works, and whether the family belongs to a minority group all affect the social learning experiences of the child in his home. These factors might be called, as Sears (1950) designated them, "sociological variables." How much, if any, psychological bearing they have can be judged only through examining the research in existence, sparse as this may be in several of these areas. In some instances, little more than reports of clinical impressions are available; in others, the research undertaking has not been designed adequately enough, having neglected many controls. Thus, the precise *psychological* import of these *sociological* variables remains to be uncovered through research. Even so, there is sufficient evidence of some psychological content in these factors to warrant their close examination in order to understand the psychosocial nature of the family environment.

Later in this book we shall encounter some of the major psychological forces prevalent in the home, such as democracy and acceptance. As they affect the child these forces may outweigh the sociological variables to be considered here, even though the latter may well diminish the significance of the psychological influences. Often omitted in a psychological treatment of childhood, the sociological variables so contaminate and interact with the psychological that the result of their interaction, the child's behavior, is the product of both. The exact impact of each set of variables, however, is not easy to assess. For example, we might believe that democracy in the home is a pervasive influence on the child's behavior, yet it would be misleading to ignore the presence of one or more of the sociological variables. How does divorce, to cite one of them, affect parental use of democratic policy?

Psychology has been relatively unconcerned with the sociological variables. Ex post facto study based on retrospective reports has been the main source for investigating such matters as the effects of divorce on the child. Although some other procedure may pose greater difficulty, the pursuit of it may be worthwhile, if only because of the greater conclusiveness of the results likely to be obtained. As we shall see presently, the Koch investigation, which dealt with sibling position, exemplifies both the complexity of a well-designed study and the richness of findings yielded by a well-planned empirical exercise.

FAMILY COMPOSITION

Early in this century an unusual amount of time and effort was invested in discovering the effects of order of birth and ordinal position in the family—that is, family composition—on personality.   Nearly every phase of behavior of any psychological import was studied in relation to the order in which the child was born.   Many publications contained studies on the ties between birth order and "(a) genius and feeble-mindedness, (b) suggestibility and aggressiveness, (c) dominance-feeling and sensitivity to pain, (d) sociability and ascendancy, (e) religious attitudes and political attitudes, (f) emotionality and stability, (g) neurotic make-up and psychotic trend, (h) happiness and jealousy, (i) school failure and fame" (Krout, 1939, pp. 5–6).   In a handbook on child psychology, Murchison (1931) devoted an entire chapter to the "Order of Birth in Relation to the Development of the Child," mentioning 78 references.

Onliness

Before discussing birth order and sibling position, let us view the narrower topic of "onliness."   Largely refuted by research findings, statements regarding the effect on personality of being an only child provide a lesson for child psychologists.   Students of child psychology know that statements unsupported by research, even if made by so-called experts, are to be taken with caution.   Scientific thinking differs from nonscientific thinking, as we saw in Chapter 1, in that ideas, hypotheses, or theories are abandoned whenever research proves them wrong.   One can be truly critical of statements in the area of scientific endeavor only when aware of the research findings.   In child psychology, the literature on onliness illustrates the point.

"Being an only child," said G. Stanley-Hall, "is a disease in itself." In an early book on child guidance, the Blantons (1927) asserted: "The only child is greatly handicapped.   He cannot be expected to go through life with the same capacity for adjustment that the child reared in the family with other children has" (p. 175).   And a book concerned with abnormal psychology (Maslow & Mittleman, 1951) maintained: "The only child is likely to be overprotected, and he is never dethroned by any later children.   His parents may spoil him, make him dominating, egotistical, and, at the same time, essentially weak in his character structure.   In that case he tends to be deeply hurt when he is not the center of interest and attention" (p. 147). All three statements were made in textbooks written by reputable practitioners of psychology.

But what does research show on the bearing of onliness on development and personality?   Several studies have compared only with *non-only* college students on standard behavior and adjustment tests as well as on achievement (Fenton, 1928; Campbell, 1933; Dyer, 1945), whereas other studies have employed teacher ratings of elementary school children (Fenton, 1928; Guilford & Worcester, 1930). In general, the findings have indicated no essential differences between only and other children. One researcher (Campbell, 1933) felt that his results suggested a more pronounced effect of onliness among girls than among boys. He attributed this to the fact that boys are given more freedom than are girls. This enables boys more than girls to associate with other children outside the home, which compensates for the absence of siblings at home.

Consistently in language development, as noted in Chapter 5, only children advance more rapidly than children with siblings (Davis, 1931). The superiority of only children in language facility is significant because it leads to the real psychological importance of onliness—the effect on the child of the undeniably greater contact he enjoys with his parents. What are the results of a comparatively intensive parent-child relationship? How does a greater amount of interaction with adults affect development and personality as compared with interaction with children of one's own age?

As we have seen, a child with adults as his primary speech models is advanced in language development. There are also indications that relative isolation from peers, including siblings, contributes to intellectual achievement and scientific eminence (Faris, 1940; McCurdy, 1957; West, 1960). Two related explanations support this hypothesis. One holds that an individual who finds great satisfaction in his social relationships has little motivation to partake of the intense effort required for high achievement. The other point of view, which is more attuned with this discussion, emphasizes the influence of close contact with interested adults who stimulate the child in intellectual spheres. Combined with isolation from children of one's own age, this influence encourages a rich fantasy life, independence, and originality.

As to the effects of onliness on personality, the research is inconclusive, and with good reason. Undoubtedly the significant factor is the quality of the relationship between child and parent. The adjustment, personality, child-rearing attitudes, and behavior of the parent need investigation before we can make assumptions about the impact of onliness on a child. When research lumps together all only children and investigates various aspects of personality, small wonder that the findings show few differences between only and nononly children. Important as onliness may be in directing attention to the crucial importance of the parent-child relationship, the fact of wide differences among parents of only children suggests that onliness is phenotypical. Too often, as mentioned in Chapter 1, research in child psychology has investigated phenotypes with inconclusive results. It has failed to account for really important psychological characteristics and for wide differences among children and parents within any single group, differences which cancel each other out when subjects are bunched together for research purposes.

Birth Order and Sibling Position

For both birth order and sibling position the literature and findings are as contradictory as they are voluminous. This results, of course, from the importance of a child's "psychological position" in the family, which may bear no relation whatsoever to his order of birth.

> The question whether the child feels accepted and loved; his emotional relation with his parents; the competition or support which brothers and sisters bring to him; and the specific pressures or areas of freedom and stimulus that come along with one position in the family or another are probably more important than the objective fact of ordinal position (Murphy, Murphy, & Newcomb, 1937, p. 363).

No one would argue that the child's psychological environment is not significant, or that siblings are an unimportant part of this environment. Siblings, interacting with each other, create an ever-changing psychological environment in the family. Jealousies and hostilities, favoritism, the extent to which the child meets the unconscious needs of the parent—all these arise early in the family situation and may have intense emotional bearing on the child's personality and development.

It may be useful to note what Adler (1928) had to say on this subject.

> The oldest child feels dethroned by the coming of his brother and wants to restore his place by fighting. Unless he can overcome in the struggle for supremacy in his universe he is apt to become depressed, peevish, more or less hopeless, and will show his hopelessness later in life if confronted by problems. He is very likely to be conservative, to understand power and to agree with it. If he is strong enough he becomes a fighting child.
>
> As for the second child he is never alone, but is always confronted by the older child. This constant picture before him of an older and bigger child begets in him a sense of rivalry. If successful, he is an excellent type, but if defeated, for instance, if he is not able to compete successfully with the older child in word and in play, he loses hope, becomes depressed and has a bad time of it.
>
> The third child has to fight for a place in the sun, but he has no successor. This gives him a great sense of power, and if he is capable he often overcomes the older children in the family by his sense of impor-

tance. If he is not capable, he perhaps hides behind the fact of being spoiled, and becomes lazy, escaping from tasks, wasting time and making excuses.

First-born and early-born children have been found to be inferior in size and weight to children born later. First-borns also show higher percentages of premature births and stillbirths. Findings regarding intelligence are contradictory but generally there seems to be no connection between order of birth and intelligence. Some evidence shows, as Table 8-1 indicates, that gifted children and American men of science come disproportionately from first-borns.

Although first-borns are sometimes thought to be handicapped in emotional adjustment, conclusive research is lacking. One early study found that first-borns were more likely than children born later to be given ratings of undesirable traits by their teachers (Goodenough & Leahy, 1927). It cited the comparative inexperience of parents in the case of first-borns, the imposition of tasks on the eldest child, and the difficulty of changing from only child to *non*only child as possible explanations for its findings. Another study (Sears, 1951) noted less doll-play aggression among older than among younger siblings. This would indicate that, at least in the family setting, the older sibling experiences fewer frustrations than the younger sibling. The older sibling has fewer

TABLE 8-1   Percentages of Gifted Children and of American Men of Science in Each Birth Order for Each Size of Family

Size of Family	Birth Order			
	First	Second	Third	Fourth
2	56.1*	43.9		
	(57.4)†	(42.6)		
3	36.9	31.9	31.2	
	(44.0)	(31.2)	(24.8)	
4	33.0	26.8	15.4	24.7
	(36.1)	(22.4)	(21.8)	(19.7)

*Terman, L. M., et al. *Genetic studies of genius, Vol. 1: The mental and physical traits of a thousand gifted children.* Stanford, Calif.: Stanford Univer. Press, 1925.
†Cattell, J. McK. *American men of science.* (4th ed.) Garrison, N. Y.: Science Press, 1927.

more powerful frustrating agents in his environment.   Moreover, in the doll play there was stronger identification with the mother among older brothers than among their younger siblings.

While a majority of the studies of birth-order effects have been concerned with either the young child or the college student, a study (Douvan & Adelson, 1966) involving interviews with 3050 adolescents produced a number of interesting findings.   First-borns of both sexes exhibited strong drive and ambition; they were achievement oriented. Two areas distinguished middle children from other birth-order positions: they tended to be downward mobile with regard to aspirations, a fact that was associated with faulty development of the processes of internalization and behavior controls.   While the oldest child showed close identification with parents, the youngest was more closely identified with the peer group.   He relied less on the family for social interaction. This difference may reflect changes in parental needs and concerns.   The youngest child is given greater freedom of social interaction because the parents do not need to form the close emotional attachment with him that they had with the first child.   Moreover, by the time the youngest child reaches adolescence, the parents may be faced with various occupational and physiological concerns that reduce their involvement with any one child in the family.

The Koch Study.   The extensive study by Helen Koch (1956a, b, c, d, and e; 1960) deserves special mention.   It is one of the few relatively recent investigations of sibling influence on a child's psychological development.   Its rarity and extensiveness both stress the great complexity of this zone of research, especially if a study is to be designed adequately, employing most of the necessary controls.   This study covered 360 five- and six-year-old children from two-child, urban, native-born, white, intact families (Koch, 1956e, 1960).   Investigated as independent variables were the sex of the child under study, the sex of the sibling, ordinal position, and three spacings between siblings—less than two years, two to four years, and four to six years.   Each of 24 subgroups contained 15 children.   Through analysis of the ratings assigned by teachers for a variety of traits, the impact of these variables on the characteristics of child behavior was discerned.   The following are samples of Koch's findings.

1. In language development (Koch, 1956a), first-born children consistently spoke more articulately than second-born.   The greater the gap in age between siblings, the better the articulation tended to be.   In addition, there were indications that stuttering might be related to the sex of the sibling and the difference in age between the two children; the

amount of stuttering was thought to stem from how much jealousy and conflict there was as a result of the sibling's sex and difference in age. Similarly, the degree to which the child was frustrated by its sibling as well as the extent to which the child was allowed to express these frustrations was felt to have some bearing on the amount of stuttering.

2. Identification with a sex role was studied through ratings of sissiness in boys and tomboyishness in girls (Koch, 1956b). Boys with a slightly older sister were rated as relatively sissified. This characteristic tended to decrease as the age differential between siblings widened. In parallel manner, girls with older brothers were considered more tomboyish than girls with sisters. Such findings provided evidence for the psychological impact of having a sibling.

3. In intellectual development, children with male siblings scored higher than those with female siblings on both verbal subtests and total scores of the Primary Mental Abilities Test (Koch, 1954). Possibly the broader experience of boys, a result of a higher level of activity, might have had some relevance. The greater competitiveness and aggressiveness associated with boys may create a more stimulating environment for the sibling.

4. Both ordinal position and spacing of siblings influenced range of interest. The wider the spacing, or age difference, the greater was the number of interests held by the child under study. Indeed, second-borns were noted to have more numerous interests than first-borns. Again, familiarity with an older sibling's preoccupations and association with his companions proved important influences on the later-born child.

5. Even when the gap in age was minimal, first-born children seemed better planners than second-born. To Koch this implied a greater responsibility as the lot of the first-born as well as a necessity to plan carefully in order to maintain his superior position.

In her findings, Koch proceeded beyond mere description to offer valuable clues and insights concerning the motivations for various traits and behaviors of children (Koch, 1956c). Her analysis of ratings of several emotional factors pointed to the existence of greater stimulation or strain when siblings belonged to opposite sexes than when they were of the same sex (Koch, 1956d). Perhaps this may be explained by sex rivalry, parental preference for one sex over the other, or other subtle factors in the family and sibling relationship.

Largely the data indicated that as spacing between siblings increased the tendency grew for each to go his own way. It might be said that the narrower the spacing, the more easily various emotional characteristics of the child could be imputed to sibling interaction, whereas the wider the gap, the greater were the influences of the child's interaction with his parents (Koch, 1956d).

Several studies have modified some of Koch's findings. While Koch's results indicate that male siblings enhance the IQ scores of their siblings, Cicirelli (1967) found that children in three-child families who have brothers only score lower on IQ and reading achievement measures. This suggests that in such families boys turn the sibling's attention to nonintellectual types of activity, including sports. Cicirelli also found that children with a like-sex sibling close in age scored higher on measures of creativity and reading and arithmetic achievement than children with like-sex sibling separated in age or with an opposite-sex sibling. In a difficult-to-interpret finding Brittain (1966) showed that adolescent girls with an older sister were more peer oriented while girls with a younger brother were higher in parent conformity.

In a further analysis of the Koch data, Brim (1958) advanced several hypotheses from role interaction theory. Through interaction with others an individual learns something of the characteristics of other roles. Thus a boy learns a great deal about a girl's role (her behavior, attitudes) through daily contact with a female sibling. Moreover, this interaction results in a certain amount of assimilation of roles, the incorporation of aspects of another's behavior into one's own behavior repertoire. Related to this is the fact that an individual is more likely to adopt characteristics of a more powerful person than a less powerful one. The Koch findings reported above substantiated these hypotheses. Thus a girl with a male sibling was rated higher in masculine traits than a girl with a female sibling, thus showing the result of cross-sex interaction. Similarly, boys with sisters were rated as more feminine than boys with brothers. These findings were especially marked for the younger child, supporting the prediction that the more powerful figure (in this case, more powerful because of age) is more influential. An interesting secondary finding of the Brim analysis indicated that girls were rated more feminine than boys were masculine. This may be interpreted in the light of our discussion of sex-role identification in Chapter 10. In the process of learning the sex-appropriate role, the girl continues to identify with the mother while the boy must shift from an early identification with mother to an identification with father somewhere around the age of five or six years.

The Koch findings illustrate the enormous complexity of both the research on sibling influence and the influence itself. While parents play the major role in influencing the child in a variety of areas (sex-role learning, attitudes, interests), the part played by siblings cannot be ignored. Sex and age of siblings, perceived parental favoritism toward a sibling, and the general interaction and relationship among siblings are important factors to be considered in understanding and interpreting an individual's behavior.

Studies of Maternal Behavior.   Three studies in particular have probed the crucial area of maternal attitude.   In the first of these Dean (1947) asked 20 mothers of pairs of children of the same sex to compare their youngsters with regard to a number of traits.   The mothers reported their older child to be more fearful, dependent, worrisome, and anxious, whereas they described their younger one as more physically aggressive, negativistic, stubborn, affectionate, happy, and good-natured.   Whether these children actually possessed the characteristics is less important than the fact that the differences in how the mothers perceived their first as compared with their second child were consistent.   If expectations as to the behavior of first and second children are uniform, they could well exert an influence on the outcome.

In the second study, Lasko (1954) compared the behavior of mothers toward first and second children.   Mothers of 46 pairs of children were rated on the Fels Parent Behavior Rating Scales, based on interviews with the women and observations of mother and child interaction in the home.   Because the families considered in this project had been participants in a longitudinal investigation lasting a number of years, ratings of the mother's behavior toward her two children at the same chronological age could be matched.   In general, the mothers were less warm emotionally and were more restrictive and coercive toward their first child than toward their second.   Moreover, they tended to baby and protect the second child more than the first.   Analyzing the shifts in parent behavior as the two children grew older, Lasko concluded that the most important trend for the first child was a lessening of parent-child interaction.   There seemed to be no parallel change for the second child.   The first child was subjected to much verbal stimulation and attempts to speed up its development during the first two years of life, whereas no such regimen was imposed on the second child.   There was also a tendency for disciplinary frictions to be exacerbated in dealing with the oldest child.   As women had more children, they seemed to develop warmth combined with a sense of strictness.

In an interesting experimental study Hilton (1967) attempted to identify differences in maternal behavior toward first- and later-born children in such aspects as interference and inconsistency.   Each child was given a series of puzzles to complete, with the mother instructed to remain unobtrusive while observing him.   After five minutes the testing was interrupted and the mother was given either a success or failure induction; the child's performance was either complimented and praised or it was noted that he did not measure up to his age level. Subsequently the mother was observed interacting with her child for a five-minute period. First with regard to child behavior, first-borns, as compared with later-borns, were significantly more dependent. They were more likely to run to their mothers during the intermission period and to ask for help and reassurance. The mothers of the first-borns were more likely to interfere with and direct the child's behavior. They were more extreme and more inconsistent in their emotional responsiveness to the child. These mothers showed a significant decrease in their supportiveness following the "failure" comments by the examiner, whereas the mothers of the later-borns showed little change. It is clear from the results of this study that there is a higher level of interaction and greater emotional involvement between a mother and her first-born as compared with later-born children. The inconsistency and intemperateness of the mother's behavior may well serve to produce dependency in the first-born child.

That the differences in maternal attitudes and behavior pointed out by Lasko and Hilton could produce differences in the personalities of children is indeed plausible. The reduction in babying and protectiveness, the decreased contact with the mother, less parental solicitude, and the less child-centered home experienced by the first child could well influence his perception of the extent to which he is accepted by his parents. The first child, upon the birth of a sibling, must adjust to a change in the quality of his interaction and relationship with parents. The second child, on the other hand, enjoys a greater stability of parental policies. From all these considerations, we can see how position in the family may very well explain differences in personality and behavior among children.

Recent Research on Birth-Order Effects. As a result of Schachter's (1959) observation that birth order is a determinant of social affiliation, a number of brief studies have examined the relation between birth order and numerous other variables. The most consistent finding is that first-borns are over-represented in the college population (Altus, 1965). Interestingly enough, the rate of college attendance decreases regularly with each later birth-order position (Warren, 1966).

Although research results are not clear-cut, there is some evidence that, under stress, first-born women indicate a stronger need for companionship or social affiliation than later-borns. This suggests that first-born females are more vulnerable to stress; they require social support in order to cope with it. First-born females also show a higher need for social approval than later-borns (Moran, 1967). In addition, first-borns have been found to be more susceptible to social pressures (Arrowood & Amoroso, 1965); are more suggestible than later-borns in social situations; are more apprehensive in surroundings that arouse anxiety (Staples & Walters, 1961); exhibit higher need for achievement (Sampson & Hancock, 1967); and are more easily influenced (Carrigan & Julian, 1966) than later-borns.   As compared with later-borns, first-borns tend to possess stronger and more demanding superegos (Palmer, 1966).   They identify with and internalize parental prohibitions and parental patterns of authority and discipline.   That first-borns may be more self-disciplined and inner-directed may account for their higher intellectual achievement.

The recent research concerning birth-order effects has not defined carefully all of the relevant variables.   For example, first-borns must be differentiated from only children.   Attention has not been paid to the fact that later-born status interacts with family size, age of parents, and pre- and postnatal health of the mother.   Despite some of these methodological shortcomings, recent findings are provocative.   Continued research in this area should lead to a fuller understanding of general family interaction and dynamics.   It may well be that some birth-order effects are of long-term significance while others are transitory.   Moreover, sibling position in the family may affect some attitude and personality dimensions while others are determined by such variables as the general psychological atmosphere of the home.

FAMILY SIZE

Like family composition, the size of the family is a sociological variable. This is an area scarcely touched by psychologists because of the problems of designing properly controlled studies of the effect of family size on personality and development.   However, sociologists have dealt at length with the changing trends over the years in size of American families.

The Small Family

Bossard (Bossard & Sanger, 1952) has contrasted the large and small family with respect to impact on the child.   In the small family, most issues such as family size, spacing of children, and the main objectives of education and child rearing are matters of general agreement. Parenthood is intensive rather than extensive.   For the child the implications are many.   Considerable emphasis is placed on individual development.   Because of the parents' tremendous investment, emotional and otherwise, in each of the few children, the child is under relentless pressure to measure up to family expectations.   His development and achievements are weighed against others in his neighborhood and social class. The primary disciplinarian is the mother, with little discipline issuing from siblings. In view of the identification of intimate relations with only a few people, mostly adults, the child's resentments, said Bossard, tend to be directed toward the same person or persons. The small family group enables a greater degree of democratic participation by all the children, something not possible in larger families.

In summary, the small family rests upon the ideas of planning, individualization, democratic cooperation, social isolation and intensive pressures. The small family system is a quality system, chiefly at the middle class level. Its driving force is one of ambition, in an open class system; its social justification, if one may thus speak of it, is that it represents an adjustment to a rapidly changing society, with its train of attendant insecurities (Bossard & Sanger, 1952, p. 6).

The Large Family

Large families are different. They take many crises in stride, partly because so many of them, large and small, occur. In a large family one has to learn to make adjustments to all sorts of changes—changes in status, in responsibilities, in role. Emphasis on the group rather than on the individual is encouraged. Often economic necessity makes cooperation mandatory. Moreover, one's own actions and behavior inevitably depend on the conduct and attitudes of others. Because a large number of persons reside within a limited space, a greater degree of administration, organization, and authoritarian control is needed (Bossard & Sanger, 1952). This suggests that the authoritarian control exercised several generations back may have stemmed from the larger family size of that day. Although this authority usually rests with the dominant member of the family—one of the parents or an older sibling—it is often wielded by the siblings toward one another. Furthermore, there is less intimate contact in a large family between the parent and any individual child. Overprotectiveness, overindulgence, and intrusiveness seldom occur. And by the very nature of the family's size, problems of internal stress and strain are manifold.

Conditions in large families have been described in a book by Bossard and Boll (1956) covering a study of 100 families with at least six children. The data were obtained from interviews and questionnaires in which at least one member of each family responded. In evaluating the findings we must bear in mind the limitations and disadvantages of the interview and case-study techniques as these were explained in Chapter 1. Although several aspects of the Bossard and Boll study were beyond the pale of psychological significance, many of its points are worthy of consideration.

Through necessity, sibling sacrifice was often inevitable. Where death befell one of the parents, the burden of caring for the rest of the family descended generally on the older children.

> My sister was the oldest of a large family. After my father's death and my mother's remarriage, the entire responsibility of the large house became hers. Instead of going to dances, parties, and playing basketball, as her friends were doing, she was at home, keeping house, doing the laundry, and watching over her younger brothers and sisters. When mother went to the hospital, she and I were left in charge altogether. The baby cried routinely every night, but still we got up and saw that the family had breakfast and were ready for school. Often my sister would miss school (Bossard & Boll, 1956, p. 121).

The responsibilities assigned to the older children were mentioned frequently.

> "From the time that I was five," writes the oldest of eight, "I can remember taking care of the children. I used to lie on my mother's bed and push my little brother back and forth in his carriage until he fell asleep. Mother kept on having babies. Many problems beset us. By the time I was in the third grade, I was always helping mother while the others played with the neighboring children. This made me old beyond my years, serious, and quite responsible for all that went on in the household. . . . Each Saturday, my mother went into the city six miles away for the groceries and stayed for the day. In the evening she and dad visited friends and came home at about midnight. From age fifteen to nineteen, I found myself responsible for seeing that the housework was finished, cooking lunch and dinner for the children, and caring for the newest baby. At night, I bathed six children, washed their heads, and tucked them into bed. Saturday nights continued like this until I rebelled. I wanted to have time for dates like other girls had" (Bossard & Boll, 1956, pp. 159–160).

Discipline was often administered by siblings. Many of the responses received during the study considered this to be perhaps more satisfactory and effective than parental discipline. For one thing, children might understand each other and each other's problems better than parents do. Besides, the respondents felt that children were often better judges than parents of what constituted misbehavior. Finally, sibling discipline might be more effective because ostracism or disapproval by one's brothers and sisters might be more meaningful than a parental spanking.

Most of the respondents believed that a large family produced a sense of security in the individual. Support by siblings and cooperation helped to foster this belief. It would be interesting to see what carefully controlled research that compared large and small families might turn up here.

Bossard and Boll (1955, 1956) also discussed the various roles played by the members of a large family. To them specialization of role, specifically personality role, was characteristic of life in the large family unit. The following eight personality types were described.

1. The *responsible* type. This was most often the oldest child, especially the older or oldest daughter because of her responsibility in rearing the young children.

2. The *popular, sociable, well-liked* type. Frequently this was the second-born, or the one following the responsible sibling in order of birth.

3. The *socially ambitious* type, or "social butterfly." Most of these were usually third, fourth, or fifth in order of birth.

4. The *studious* type. This child withdrew from sibling activities to find satisfaction in books.

5. The *self-centered isolate*. This was the child affected by the pairing off of other siblings or the child who staged a general rebellion because of a rebellion against one of the parents.

6. The *irresponsible* type. This child withdrew from family life and family responsibility.

7. The *physically ill* child. In some cases, this child suffered from chronic illness, in others, he seemed hypochondriacal.

8. The *spoiled* sibling. Often this was the youngest child.

Since each child strives for recognition in the large family, as Bossard and Boll have emphasized, he adopts a specialized role for this purpose. Quite naturally, the older children pre-empt a number of these roles, leaving the younger ones to scramble for those that are left.

The reduced parent-child contact and the greater frustration encountered by children are two aspects of the large family that have been used to explain several differences found between children from large as compared with small families. Rosen (1964) found greater similarity in value orientation relative to achievement between mother and son in small- and medium-sized families than in large families. This suggests that value and attitude internalization is enhanced by an intensive amount of parent-child interaction. In large families, interaction among siblings reduces and dilutes the amount of contact each child experiences with the parents.

Dependency behavior among nursery school children (Waldrop &

Bell, 1964) and alcoholism among adults (Smart, 1963) have been found to be related to family size. General deprivation in childhood and frustration of dependency needs may account for these findings. In the former study a measure of family density, in terms of family size and spacing, was also related to dependency. It appears that lack of maternal availability increases the dependency strivings of the young boy.

The effect of family size on behavior and values in adolescence was revealed in the extensive interviews with adolescents mentioned earlier in connection with birth-order effects (Douvan & Adelson, 1966).

> Children from small families have a higher activity level and seem to be more poised and self-confident with adults. They date earlier, and report a larger number of leisure activities and memberships in organized social groups. As a group, these children show most of the qualities we have seen earlier in our studies of the upward-aspiring. They show a longer time perspective; they are more preoccupied with educational plans; they refer to personal achievement more frequently in daydreams and in thinking about the most wonderful thing that could happen to them. They are more often upwardly mobile, and the boys, at least, use achievement criteria in judging future jobs more often than do boys from large families. Fundamentally, children from small families tend to be active, energetic, and future-oriented (Douvan & Adelson, 1966, p. 273).

Adolescents from small families were more strongly identified with parents. They reported a close relationship with parents that involved shared leisure time and reliance on parental advice. By contrast, the responses of adolescents from large families indicated a marked separation between parental interests and their own. Perhaps because of this, the adolescent from a large family is more peer-oriented than family-oriented. Related to this is his ambivalence toward parental authority, which indicates a mixture of dependency and resentment. Boys show more difference than girls between large and small families in internalization and attitudes toward authority. The adolescent from a small family does not rely too heavily on family authority; rather, his identification with parents leads to well-developed and autonomous internal controls. Undoubtedly many of these differences result in part from the greater strictness and authoritarian control of the large family.

Certainly these data pertaining to the size of the family suggest interesting and fruitful hypotheses about whether size is actually a psychological as well as a sociological variable. Nevertheless, on the basis of available evidence, we must side with Bonney (1942) who held that family size neither explained nor described adequately the personality of any particular child.

MARITAL RELATIONS OF PARENTS

Based on the conclusions of clinical studies that marital conflict and divorce affect the adjustment of children, many writers have attributed a number of child behaviors to domestic discord. Delinquency, stealing, truancy, lying, disciplinary difficulties, jealousy, hyperactivity, problems of speech, reading problems, poor social adjustment, and homosexuality are all said to result from marital strife. This list is far from inclusive. Yet not much adequately designed research is at hand to help in sorting out the effects of a variety of factors and in identifying true cause-and-effect relationships. It may seem "obvious," for example, that divorce in an adolescent's background is *the* cause of current poor social adjustment. When quizzed, in fact, an adolescent will recall a vast number of traumatic feelings associated with the divorce (Landis, 1960). However, one cannot be sure from after-the-fact recollections what the experience was like at the time of occurrence. A child's past can never be fully reconstructed, as was noted in Chapter 1. Motivated by all kinds of conscious and unconscious needs and feelings, a person may falsify in retrospect the memory of circumstances and events. Besides, it is impossible to single out one particular event as *the* source of all future behavior. Finally, the independent variable, in this case marital conflict or divorce, has not been systematically controlled: there is no control group matched with an experimental group on a number of variables, with only the factor of divorce or strife differentiating the two. With these limitations in mind, let us review the meager literature in existence on research into the effects of marital adjustment on the child.

Marital Adjustment and the Child

Several investigations have resulted in negative findings. One of these (Burchinal, Hawkes, & Gardner, 1957) analyzed the relation of parental scores on a marital adjustment inventory to scores of fifth graders on the Rogers Test of Personality Adjustment. Only in one of 10 cases did the correlations seem significant, and the magnitude of this significance was so small that no support was found for the expected connection between marital adjustment and the personality adjustment scores of children. However, the measures of both types of adjustment were so unreliable that it is difficult to tell whether any relation, even if one existed, could have been detected from these test results.

Another study (Stroup, 1956) found no relationship between the mother's marital adjustment and the child's score on a standard personality test. Medinnus (1963a, b) observed a slight bond between interparent agreement on three measures of attitude and the adjustment and popularity of the child in first grade. However, Leton (1958) noted a greater discrepancy between attitude scores of parents of poorly adjusted children than between parents of well-adjusted children. In Medinnus's study interparent agreement was found to be fairly specific, with little general consistency among the various measures. Because of this inconsistency, a researcher could hardly expect to discover a relationship between parental disagreement on a specific matter or in a specific area and so ambiguous a measure of child behavior as general adjustment. More fruitful results are likely to emerge from an examination of the effects of particular areas of disagreement between parents on particular aspects of child behavior.

A number of studies have sought to identify the marital factors in the home that have contributed to the behavior of the young child in school (Hattwick, 1936; Baruch, 1937). Children from "happy, calm" homes tend to be less negative than youngsters from the opposite type of home (Hattwick, 1936). The latter showed more signs of emotional disturbance, such as jealousy, fear, grumbling, nervousness and sulking, and tenseness. Baruch and Wilcox (1944) named the following five main tensions in the home as influencing poor adjustment among preschool children: tension over sex satisfaction, tension over lack of consideration, tension over insufficient expression of affection, tension over inability to talk things through, and tension over ascendance-submission relations. The first three were interpreted as indicating a lack of security in the marriage relationship. The fifth reflected on the child's feelings of adequacy. No doubt both parent security and adequacy exert important psychological influences on the adjustment and personality growth of the young child. But the primary significance of marital adjustment seems to be its reflection of a more basic adaptation of the two people involved in the relationship.

Divorce

That divorce hampers child adjustment cannot be denied. However, its precise effects are not easy to determine because most of the data come from clinical case studies. How much of a child's maladjustment may be charged to the divorce as such, or how much results from the long period of conflict, tension, and discord leading to divorce is hard to say. Then, too, how much may be attributed to the poor personality adjustments of the partners in the particular marriage?

Whatever the case, many child behaviors stem from parental divorce, as several research studies have indicated.

As a group, adolescents from broken homes showed less psychosomatic illness, less delinquent behavior, and better adjustment to parents than those from unhappy, unbroken homes (Nye, 1957). This would suggest that in some cases separation and disruption of the home is desirable. Perhaps this might follow from the additional finding that the adjustments of parents individually and to their spouses were superior in broken homes than in the unhappy homes that remained intact.

To Landis (1960) the grouping together for research purposes all children of divorce and treating them as if they were a homogeneous group with respect to the effects of divorce seemed unsound. He found differences between adolescents who remembered their homes as happy before they had learned of the divorce, and those who considered their homes as unhappy and full of conflict. The former were especially likely to feel that their first knowledge of the divorce was a traumatic experience; they had been caught by surprise and had been unable to accept the fact. Asked to state how they believed the divorce had affected their feelings of security and personal happiness, they replied that they had experienced little change in these areas. Those who, on the other hand, had conceived of their homes as unhappy said they felt greater security and happiness after the divorce. The children from homes regarded as happy reported greater difficulty in adjusting to their peers as the children of divorced parents. We must remember, however, that all these responses bear the disadvantages of any retrospective account.

Landis divided the respondents into three groups according to age at the time of divorce—5 to 8 years, 9 to 12, and 13 to 16. Fewer among the younger children said they felt a loss of security and were less happy because of the divorce. Memory may play tricks here, or the finding may suggest that divorce is less damaging to a young child's security than to the security of an older child. Landis thought there were certain potentially traumatic situations awaiting the child of divorcing parents.

First, there is the necessity to adjust to the knowledge that divorce will probably take place; (2) there is the necessity to adjust to the fact of divorce; (3) there is the possibility that in the predivorce or postdivorce years one or both parents may "use" the child as a weapon against the other, with traumatic effects upon the child; (4) there is the necessity for a redefining of relationships with parents; (5) the new status of being the child of divorced parents may necessitate new adjustments with the peer group; (6) some trauma may result for children who recognize the implications of their parents' failure in marriage; and (7) there may be problems of adjustment for the child if the parents remarry (Landis, 1960, p. 7).

To gather data on the effects of divorce, Goode (1956, p. 317) interviewed 425 divorcées. That these mothers did worry about the possible impact of their divorces on their children was evident from comments made throughout the interviews. Table 8-2 reports the replies to a question on this matter.

The women were questioned as to the extent to which they believed that the divorce experience had been a traumatic one for them. A link clearly related the severity of this trauma to the women's reports of how "hard to handle" were the children. The greater the trauma, the higher was the proportion of mothers who stated that their children at some time had been difficult to manage. Although half the women considered the children no harder to handle after the father's visits, 25 per cent of them believed that the child became more of a problem in management following these occasions. It would seem clear that the whole matter of custody and visiting privileges might well prove a source of anxiety for the child.

TABLE 8-2   Replies of Divorcées Regarding Impact of Divorce on Their Children

Question: Now that the divorce is all over, would you try to tell me, in your own words, how you felt about the divorce and the children. What went through your mind when you thought of the possible effects of the divorce upon him/her/them?

Coded Answers	Per Cent of Respondents Giving Answer* ($N = 425$)
Better for them; I was right	31
Worried about lack of parent; clear ambivalence with no explanation (child needs father, but not this one)	27
No effect, child too young, didn't worry	10
Didn't worry then, but negative items appeared later	3
Worried about possible effects of remarriage on child	2
Worried about social stigma for child	6
Religious difficulties: child in Catholic school; child might be rejected by congregation	1
Finances (other than education): support, clothes, etc.	8
Bad for child (answer not elaborated)	9
Miscellaneous, never thought of it, not sure	6

*Some respondents gave more than one answer.

Subtle Factors. In Western culture parents feel a responsibility to the child, not only for his physical welfare but also for his emotional welfare. Since divorce threatens the child's emotional stability, the parent contemplating such action often experiences strong feelings of guilt. These feelings may also arise from resenting the child who renders the divorce situation more difficult. To compensate for them, the parent may attempt to be overprotective of the child and to show excessive concern for its welfare. Yet, just as divorce may foster feelings of guilt in the parent, it may arouse similar sentiments in the child. To the youngster's mind, the separation may seem punishment for his own past "naughtiness" or for unconscious, hostile feelings toward his parent. More obvious, however, are the occasions when the child overhears parental controversy in which such statements as the following may be hurled at one another: "If it weren't for Jimmy we wouldn't have had all this trouble; I would have divorced you long ago." It is not too challenging to discern how the child may feel himself the cause of this discord, nor how he may view the subsequent divorce and loss of one parent as punishment (Despert, 1953).

Parents themselves in a predivorce situation are not sure of the course to be followed; their uncertainty and anxiety are communicated readily to the children. The tension and vague threat of change are hard for the child to cope with psychologically. Although the statement "the emotional stability of the child is dependent upon the emotional stability of the parent" lacks confirmation through research, it is quite evident that an unstable home environment, for whatever cause, may have harmful implications for the child's psychological adjustment.

Following divorce, moving often becomes necessary. This adds to the adjustment problems facing the child, especially if he is of school age. Furthermore, arrangements for substitute care for him may be required if the mother returns to employment outside the home.

In a later chapter we shall discuss the process of identification whereby the child patterns his behavior after that of the parent of his own sex. This process is impaired in many ways when there is only one parent present in the home. In approximately 90 per cent of divorce cases the mother receives custody of the child. This certainly affects a boy's identification with a father figure, and a gap in learning certain aspects of future adult roles may well occur when there is one parent lacking in the home. The phrase "I am marrying again because Johnny needs a father" may be another way of expressing the need for a male figure with whom a young boy can identify. Additional complications may aggravate the divorce situation when the mother deliberately endeavors to subvert the child's loyalties to the father by derogatory comments.

Recent research literature indicates clearly that paternal absence during childhood has the effect of feminizing the young boy, creating difficulties in his peer relationships, and producing initially blunted aggressiveness and greater maternal dependency. At adolescence the boy who lacks a male identification figure evidences problems in several areas (Douvan & Adelson, 1966). He has difficulty adjusting to the masculine sex role and in accepting authority, and he is deficient in the internalization of standards. The exaggerated masculinity of adolescent boys from divorced homes suggests their insecurity in this area. This insecurity is reflected also in their inability to accept and identify with any adult models. Exaggerated independence in these boys very likely involves a denial mechanism. In their interviews with adolescents, Douvan and Adelson found that those from divorced homes reported strict maternal control. While boys appeared to rebel against this authoritarianism, girls seemed to acquiesce to it. However, girls from divorced homes did not show the strength of identification with their mothers as those from intact homes. There was a psychological distance between these girls and their mothers; the girls developed strong and mature peer friendships and they sought other adult models. In general, boys suffer far more than girls from the effects of divorce. This is probably because of girls' greater resiliency and adaptability and the harmful effects of loss and devaluation of the like-sex model for the boy.

In the family, in general, the parents tend to serve as buffers or neutralizers in their mutual influences on the child. This is familiar in fiction and folk literature where the mother often is pictured as the intercessor between father and son, attempting to temper the severity of the father's punishment. When there is but a single parent in the home, the child's relation with that parent is unmitigated by the presence of another. Any conflicts and antagonisms already in existence may become accentuated.

Thus, even though research has yet to separate the effects of divorce from those of the marital strife that might have preceded it, factors present in the divorce situation are known to exert harmful influences on the child's psychological adjustment. Tensions, instabilities, lack of proper figures for identification, hostilities, guilt feelings—all these come to the fore when divorce occurs. To understand and identify the precise impact of divorce on any child one needs to know how much love and understanding will continue after the action and how much real concern and affection exists for the youngster. In other words, does the child perceive the divorce as punishment and rejection or has the situation been approached with maturity and insight so that the child's love for and confidence in the parents are not shaken?

HANDICAPPED CHILD IN THE FAMILY

Much has been written about the handicapped child, but the material is predominantly clinical in character. Few carefully designed research studies can be found, understandably. It is not easy to impose the controls necessary for effective research on investigations into the influence of a handicapped child on siblings. Left largely with clinical reports, therefore, one must beware of the pitfalls of acquiring information through these channels. Undoubtedly a host of considerations colors the parent's account. Certainly the extent of his own emotional involvement and his own needs and motivations, as noted in Chapter 1, affect his report. In addition, as we have already seen, caution must be exercised in seeking to attribute effects to specific causes. For example, many parents have ascribed marital discord to the presence in the family of a retarded child. However, one careful study (Farber, 1959) found a similarity between marital integration *before* the arrival of the handicapped child and marital integration some years after. Moreover, it may be easier for a parent to blame the presence of a handicapped child for sibling maladjustments than to impute these to disruptive factors within the parent-child relationship and within the family structure. Another very important consideration is that the presence of a handicapped child affects parent attitudes and outlook just as the reverse is true (Bell, 1964). The mutual impact of parent and child is discussed at the beginning of Chapter 9. While a number of pathogenic factors have been found to characterize parents of deviant children, the cause-and-effect relationship here is by no means clear. For example, although mothers of stutterers show signs of rejection (Kinstler, 1961), it is impossible to identify such rejection as causing the stuttering since the mother's attitude toward the child was not assessed prior to the onset of the stuttering.

Although a few studies supply direct evidence of the influence on siblings of a handicapped child in the family, most of the literature has dealt with the impact on parents and the whole family unit. Any upset such as mental illness, depression, or unemployment that affects the family structure or parental personality and adjustment may be said to concern the personalities, adjustments, and attitudes of that family's children. For this reason, we shall consider briefly some of the repercussions of the presence of a handicapped child.

Nonclinical Impact

Before examining the clinical aspects of having a handicapped child in the family, let us consider some of the other problems. First comes the obvious additional financial burden that specialized medical attention imposes. For both diagnosis and treatment, parents of a handicapped child often spend a considerable amount of money. Such outlays may directly affect the siblings and work more subtly through the worries and tensions they produce in the parents.

Family activity and the pattern of living may be curtailed, which may influence the siblings in a number of ways. Frequently parents of a mentally retarded child mention a gradual social isolation. Neighbors and the community do not understand mental retardation. They do not know its causes, or what can be expected from such a child, or how to handle the youngster. This ignorance leads to unfounded fears and apprehensions. One parent would not permit his child to play with a neighbor's mentally retarded youngster because of a fear that his child might be led "into all sorts of perversions." The isolations and withdrawals that occur certainly affect the social adjustment of the siblings. Adolescents often hesitate to invite friends into the home because of their feelings of shame and embarrassment over the appearance and behavior of the retarded child.

The extra toll levied on the parents of a retarded or handicapped child by the necessity to provide physical care and to plan for the youngster, together with the responsibility they assume, may easily produce an undue amount of anxiety and tension. The very nature of the child's limitations places more demands on a parent than would a normal child—and it is no secret that the demands of even the normal child often exhaust the parent! Any such increase in tension and anxiety in the household is likely to have profound influences on the siblings.

The possible theological conflicts (Murray, 1959) confronting the parent of a handicapped child could perhaps affect his outlook and philosophy of life. Although such problems may be resolved either with bitterness and disillusionment or with acceptance and constructive effort, the normal siblings cannot escape unscathed.

Clinical Findings

Parents of handicapped children vary considerably in the adequacy of their own personality adjustments on which the birth of such a child may impose a great strain. Many aspects and decisions stemming from the presence of a handicapped child in the family prove threatening to the parent and are capable of arousing anxiety within him. The question of whether to place the child in an institution, for example, may stir unconscious feelings in the parent; these may be repressed feelings of wishing to be rid of the child or feelings of rejection that he cannot resolve. Then, too, since the child is his own biological offspring, the parent may regard any injury, impairment, or disability in the child as an injury to himself. More important, perhaps, the parent may view the birth of a handicapped child as a reflection of his own inadequacy and incompetence. The parent may find it difficult to adjust to "this blow to the psychological self."

Often the presence of a handicapped child arouses a tremendous amount of guilt in the parent. He may interpret the birth of such a child as a punishment for real or imagined sins. Or perhaps the feeling of ambivalence, or often rejection, toward the handicapped child may generate strong sentiments of guilt. This can have unfortunate consequences of overconcern and of overprotection of the child. Such overprotection may result in neglect of the siblings as well as an intrusive behavior by the parent in the relationship between the handicapped child and his siblings.

While some parents respond to a congenitally handicapped child by creating psychological distance between themselves and the child, the more common response is intrusiveness and overprotection (Bell, 1964). This has been found to be true for mothers of children exhibiting cerebral palsy, mongoloidism, congenital heart defects, and blindness. Intrusiveness, characterized by domination, excessive vigilance, and restriction, may be the mother's reaction to actual or perceived limitations in the child's ability to cope with the environment.

All in all, self-blame is sometimes the outcome of guilt feelings. One mother, for example, expressed excessive concern that her handicapped child might fall into the family swimming pool. It developed from therapeutic consultation that her concern arose from a time when she deliberately tried to push the child into the water. The satisfactory solution of these various types of problems hinges upon the parent's own adjustment to himself and to life. How he succeeds or fails may indeed affect the personality growth of the siblings. Some parents, of course, use the handicapped child as a psychological scapegoat for their own shortcomings and inadequacies. Those who do are prevented from dealing realistically with their own problems.

A parent's disappointment at the birth of a handicapped child may have far-reaching implications for the siblings. Some children have reported increased parental pressure to achieve in academic and non-academic pursuits—for example, athletics—to compensate for the non-achievement of the handicapped sibling. One study (Zuk, 1959), in fact, found mothers more willing to accept a young mentally retarded child than an older one. This might be taken to mean that dissatisfaction with the nonperformance and nonachievement of the child increases over the years.

What, then, do research studies have to say about all this? What do they find about the effects on families of the presence of a retarded child? In a study of the adjustment of parents and siblings of institutionalized and noninstitutionalized retarded children (Caldwell & Guze, 1960), which combined psychiatric interviews with several objective measures, including a family attitude scale and a children's anxiety scale, few differences were generally found between the two groups of siblings. Yet the study showed that although most siblings of the institutionalized mentally retarded thought institutionalization worked best, most of the siblings of the retarded who were not institutionalized felt that home care was preferable. Perhaps the demands of a handicapped child in the household produce a sense of responsibility and a certain amount of resourcefulness among the siblings. That such a situation may also result in increased sensitivity to the needs, misfortunes, and problems of others is a matter for speculation.

Farber's large-scale, well-designed study (Farber, 1959), which covered 240 families with a severely mentally retarded child, was based on interviews with both husband and wife and on results of a variety of measures. The study sought to check the effects on family integration of such a handicapped child in the home. These were the results obtained from two of the indices, an index of marital integration and another of sibling role tension: in general it was noted that the marital integration of parents of mentally retarded boys at home was lower than that of mentally retarded girls similarly at home. One possible explanation for this is the usually more disruptive effect of the boy; another is the thwarting of greater parental expectation for the boy than for the girl. Although the sex of the retarded child did not affect the integration of its siblings, a high degree of dependence on the part of the deficient youngster did do so adversely. The pressures on the mother of caring for the retarded child and the added responsibilities falling to the siblings had relevance here. Supporting this interpretation was a finding that the younger the retarded child was the more he influenced the adjustment of his siblings. Since the retarded child often assumes the role of the youngest child (even though there may be younger siblings), the effects of a handicapped child appear to be greater on the youngest children in the family. Girls appear to be affected more than boys by the presence of a retarded sibling. This may result in part from their greater responsibility in caring for the child.

In an excellent summary of research on the handicapped child, Jordan (1962) has suggested that research on the significance of handicapped children in other cultures would be enlightening. Different cultures view children and childhood in various ways. Some cultures, such as our own, value and place great emphasis on independence. Thus the inability of the handicapped child to achieve independence may be particularly stressful to parents in our society. Several subgroups in our society show strong family cohesiveness. Might a handicapped child be less disruptive to family unity in these groups? Because of the group arrangement for child care in Israeli kibbutzim, it would seem that siblings would be less affected by a handicapped child. Also, some societies might accept institutionalization more readily than others.

There is evidence that a handicapped child in the family may affect the siblings in various ways. This seems to be fairly well established even though research in this area has been sparse. To recapitulate, a handicapped child in the family affects parental personality and adjustment. It also causes financial strain, curtailment of family activity, possible social isolation and withdrawal, anxiety, and tension in the parents, and an increase of expectations and pressures among normal siblings.

MATERNAL EMPLOYMENT

Since World War II, when women entered the labor force on an unprecedented scale, there has been increasing interest shown in the influence of a working mother on child adjustment. In fact, a large number of wartime and postwar juvenile problems have been charged to the absence of the mother from the home. But here, as with other family situations discussed in this chapter, early claims regarding the harmful consequences of maternal employment have not been confirmed by subsequent research.

The traditional view of the family pictures the mother, as the helpmate of the male breadwinner, standing in the doorway eagerly awaiting the children's return from school; but this is no longer an accurate portrayal of reality. In March 1966, there were 9.9 million working mothers with children under 18 (Waldman, 1967). These working mothers constituted 37 per cent of the total number of women in the labor force and 36 per cent of all mothers in the population. The thriving economy of the 1960's and federal legislation outlawing sex discrimination in employment practices have helped to account for the tremendous increase in the number of working wives in recent years. Of the 1 million persons added to the civilian labor force in the year ending in March 1966, 63 per cent were women, either married, divorced, separated, or widowed. Approximately the same percentage of wives of employed versus nonemployed males were working; this suggests that the husband's lack of employment is not the principal reason for the wife seeking work outside the home. March 1966 employment statistics indicate that, among families with children under three years of age, 23 per cent of the mothers were in the labor force. For mothers with children between three and five years of age, the proportion was 32 per cent, and 47 per cent of mothers with children six to 17 years of age were employed.

As Nye and Hoffman (1963) have pointed out, "Few, if any, single changes in family life have as profoundly affected so many families in so few years as the movement of mothers into paid employment" (p. 3). As we shall see from the largely inconclusive research mentioned below, maternal employment has a greater impact on the family structure than on specific aspects of the children's psychological adjustment; perhaps it is for this reason that so much attention has focused on this variable. By tradition, "the mother's place is in the home," and she seeks outside work only if the family economic situation demands it. The position taken by a particular group of psychologists, that the child's eventual personality adjustment depends upon a close relationship with his mother during his early years, has lent support to this point of view. This position stresses that unless there is a "continuous mother figure" present, harmful consequences are likely to ensue.

Traditional family ideology defines the male as the provider for the family welfare and the dominant member with regard to decisions affecting the family. While it is difficult to say whether maternal employment has led to a more equalitarian conception of the family structure, or whether this conception has made maternal employment more acceptable, the fact remains that family organization has altered considerably in the past three decades. Limitation of family size and labor-saving devices resulting from technological advances have contributed to this change.

Research Findings

Discussion of the research concerning the effects of maternal employment is divided into three main areas: effect on the children, the husband-wife relationship, and the adjustment of the mother.

Effect on the Children. Early research investigations that compared children of working mothers with those of nonworking mothers ignored important variables that cut across this division. Some of these variables include age and sex of child, social class, full-time versus part-time maternal employment, provisions for substitute care, the consistency between mother and substitute in attitudes and behavior, the personality and personality needs of the particular child, the motivations for maternal employment, and the mother's attitude toward working and toward child care. Only if the fact of maternal employment were more pertinent to the well-being of the children than these other factors would one expect to find significant distinctions between the children of working and nonworking mothers.

While Douvan and Adelson (1966) found little relation between maternal employment and the adolescent boy's activities and psychological characteristics, several effects were noted for the adolescent girl. Daughters of working women are more likely to share in home responsibilities; they participate in fewer leisure activities. As compared with daughters of nonworking women, those whose mothers work admire and respect their mothers more. They enjoy a close relationship with their mothers and identify with them. In addition, maternal employment affects the daughter's conception of the female role. In Hartley's study (1960) more daughters of nonworking mothers said "housewife" when asked what they expected to do when they grew up, whereas more daughters of working mothers mentioned various professional aspirations. Also, more daughters of working mothers said they would continue to work after marriage.

Although Douvan and Adelson found maternal employment (part- or full-time) affected adolescent girls in a positive fashion in several areas, the social class variable was an important consideration. As compared with middle-class girls whose mothers frequently choose employment for achievement reasons, working-class adolescent girls spend less time with their families and yet exhibit greater emotional dependency on them. This may be because their need for security within the family has not been met.

The variables of age and sex of child may interact in determining the effects of maternal employment. In early childhood, a boy may be adversely affected, showing dependency (Hoffman, 1961; Siegel, Stolz, Hitchcock, & Adamson, 1959), withdrawal (Rouman, 1956), and maladjustment (Hand, 1957). These findings may reflect an inadequate male model in families in which the mother is employed; or, as in our discussion of divorce, they may suggest that a young boy is more negatively affected than a girl by any deviation in the family structure that reduces his feelings of security.

Often listed as causes of delinquency are neglect and lack of supervision by the working mothers. Yet some investigations have failed to set up controls for the socioeconomic status of the family. Because both the employment status of the mother and juvenile delinquency are moderately related to the economic level of the home, the variable of socioeconomic status clearly must be controlled before valid comparisons can be made. In a study of 500 delinquent boys matched with an equal number of nondelinquents for age, ethnic and racial derivation, and general intelligence, the Gluecks (1957) observed no difference in the proportions of delinquents and nondelinquents whose mothers were regularly employed. However, a larger number of delinquents than nondelinquents had mothers who worked irregularly. Still, it does not follow that irregularity of employment is the cause of delinquency; the irregular worker may be the kind of mother who works to escape house-hold tasks and maternal obligations. In other words, both the sporadic employment of the mother and the child's delinquency may be products of a more basic emotional maladjustment of the parents. In a further analysis of several studies yielding conflicting results concerning the effect of maternal employment on juvenile delinquency, Hoffman (1963) concluded that the two are positively related only in the middle class. While reasons for this are only speculative at this point, one factor may be that middle-class delinquency differs from lower-class delinquency in terms of its causes and its nature.

Hoffman (1961) found that the mother's attitude toward employment affected her relation with her children. Mothers holding positive at-titudes toward work employ less severe discipline and less power-as-sertive techniques. They feel more sympathy, more affection, and less hostility in their interaction with their children.

Husband-Wife Relationship. It seems clear that the mother's em-ployment outside the home alters the traditional structure of the family, including such aspects of the husband-wife relationship as participation in household tasks, decision making, and power and dominance roles. Indeed, when the responses of children of working mothers were com-pared with those of nonworking mothers regarding parental perform-ance of various household tasks, the former group reported that their mothers participate less and fathers participate more in all areas (Hoff-man, 1960). Related to this is the fact that working mothers make fewer decisions about routine household matters while the fathers make more. However, with regard to general family decisions, especially in the economic area, the working wife plays a more powerful role than the nonworking one (Nye, 1963).

Although most studies show more quarreling and more marital conflict in families where the wife is employed, a number of other variables such as social class, reasons for the employment, and the husband's attitude toward his wife's employment, are important here. Powell (1961) found no difference in reported marital adjustment between working and non-working mothers if the oldest child was of elementary or preschool age. However, if the oldest child was an adolescent, the working mothers reported a poorer adjustment. Further analysis of the data suggested that fathers of adolescents participated less in househould tasks than fathers of younger children. This could account in part for the poorer marital adjustment of these mothers.

Adjustment of the Mother. A number of aspects of maternal adjustment in relation to employment have been examined. These include emotional adjustment, satisfaction or dissatisfaction with employment and with the maternal role, physical health, and community and recreational participation.

Most studies agree in showing a more favorable attitude toward children on the part of working mothers as compared with those not employed outside the home. Nye (1963), for example, found that nonemployed mothers were more likely to say that "children make me nervous." From the finding that "adjustment to children" improved the longer the mother worked, Nye concluded that although her employed status at first produced some conflict, these contentions began to disappear as the mother became reconciled to her new role in the family structure.

As compared with nonemployed mothers, employed ones express more satisfaction with their daily work and with the community in general. In addition, employed mothers express more positive self-attitudes, including higher self-esteem. Moreover, they report fewer physical symptoms, suggesting that their health is not impaired by the demands of home and employment.

In summary, maternal employment has not been found to exert marked effects on the behavior and adjustment of the children involved. It is the quality, not the quantity, of interaction between mother and child that is of psychological significance. In individual cases where the mother's employment seems to have adverse effects, it is likely that other disruptive factors in the home are responsible. The American family structure is changing markedly. It will continue to do so. Perhaps a more equalitarian approach is no less favorable to the mental health of children than the traditional one.

MINORITY GROUP MEMBERSHIP

Finally, there is the impact on the child of membership in a minority group. Although the country abounds with racial, religious, and political minorities, the present discussion deals largely with the Negro minority group; to a large extent what is said about Negroes applies equally to other minority groups.   The Negro group is distinguishable from other minorities for several reasons.   To cite two of the most obvious, Negroes are more readily identifiable by the color of their skin and they constitute the country's largest minority.

Awareness and Identification

At what age do racial awareness and accurate racial identification develop?   The typical procedure for finding this out involves individual interviews with young children in which they are presented with dolls or drawings that include white and colored figures.   The children are asked questions to elicit information concerning racial identification and racial preference.   This is the set used by Clark and Clark (1947, p. 169):

1. Give me the doll that you like best.
2. Give me the doll that is a nice doll.
3. Give me the doll that looks bad.
4. Give me the doll that is a nice color.
5. Give me the doll that looks like a white child.
6. Give me the doll that looks like a colored child.
7. Give me the doll that looks like a Negro child.
8. Give me the doll that looks like you.

Table 8-3 (from data by Clark & Clark, 1947) lists the results obtained from 253 Negro children divided according to age levels.   It is evident that in general there was an increase with age in the percentage of children who identified themselves accurately with the colored doll. There was also a marked tendency for the children to show a preference for the white doll.   This tendency decreased with age, although most children at each level preferred the white to the colored doll.

That the extent or severity of discrimination affects the Negro child's rejection of his own race was shown in a study comparing race awareness and race attitudes of northern and southern preschoolers (Morland, 1966).   As compared with northern Negroes, those from the South indicated a greater preference for whites, and indeed both groups showed a preference for whites over their own racial group.

In attempts to identify various aspects of the self concept, investigators have posed the question "What are you?" to young children. As children increase in age, they shift from describing themselves by their own names or with reference to individuals in their specific environment to the use of ethnic designations (Hartley, Rosenbaum, &

TABLE 8-3   Choices of Subjects at Each Age Level

	Age 3	Age 4	Age 5	Age 6	Age 7
Request 1 (play with)					
colored doll	42	24	26	29	40
white doll	55	76	74	71	60
Request 2 (nice doll)					
colored doll	36	24	28	46	44
white doll	58	76	72	53	52
Request 3 (looks bad)					
colored doll	68	52	78	63	43
white doll	19	24	11	15	17
Request 4 (nice color)					
colored doll	39	28	20	43	48
white doll	58	72	78	56	48
Request 5 (for white)					
colored doll	13	14	7	3	0
white doll	77	86	94	97	100
Request 6 (for colored)					
colored doll	77	83	94	96	100
white doll	13	17	7	4	0
Request 7 (for Negro)					
colored doll	55	59	61	78	85
white doll	29	35	30	17	7
Request 8 (for you)					
colored doll	36	66	48	68	87
white doll	61	31	52	32	13

Schwartz, 1948). This vividly illustrates the increasingly important role played by ethnic membership in one's feelings and attitudes about oneself.

Accurate racial identification, of course, does not necessarily imply full awareness of racial prejudice and of the significance of racial membership. Yet several investigators have reported great emotionality among some of the Negro children asked to make a racial self-identification. That racial awareness itself has certain psychological implications is borne out by its earlier occurrence among Negro children than white children (Horowitz, 1939). Actually, psychological factors such as the effect of minority group membership on parents produce this earlier awareness in Negro youngsters.

Studying racial awareness in four-year-olds, Goodman (1952) discovered strong evidence for its presence among these children. The recognition of racial differences exceeded their capacity to express their feelings about them. One of the children interpreted the significance of membership in a minority group in these succinct terms: "The people that are white, they can go up. The people that are brown, they have to go down" (Goodman, 1952, p. 28). This is cut from the same cloth as the statement by a Negro adult: "You live in a city all your life, but you're never home. Maybe that's what it means to be a Negro" (Karon, 1958, p. 1). Goodman further noted a strong inclination for Negro children to refuse to identify, or to resent identification, with their own group.

> [Dianne] is a dark brown child, even darker than her mother, and she likes whiteness to a rather extreme degree. There are only a few colored children in her nursery school. She is conspicuous among the assorted whites, and conscious of the fact. She went home one day and asked her mother "am I colored?" The affirmative answer was followed by the explanation that "some people are black and some are white." Dianne, like most of our four-year-olds, was most concerned about herself. "I don't *want* to be colored," she declared. Back at nursery school again one day, Carol (w) took a good look at Dianne and asked her if she were colored. "Yes, I am. Don't touch me! Don't sit near me!" And Dianne sat away by herself looking unhappily at her arms. Then there were days when she vigorously lathered her arms and face with soap. After one of these efforts, she said triumphantly to Peter: "This morning I scrubbed and scrubbed and it came almost white." But she knew it had not really done so . . . (Goodman, 1952, pp. 37–38).

There is a kind of desperation in Tony's cry of "Brown—brown—brown!!" as he throws down the picture about which we have been talking, and talking too long for his piece of mind. The matter is becoming more and more personal and personally threatening. He and others must have felt like Barbara, who was obviously unhappy. She did not enjoy being asked to tell which doll or picture looked most like herself, and her parents. And finally she said so, with intensity and exasperation: "Don't ask too many questions!—*I can't stand it*" (p. 42).

Tony A. admits that his parents look like the pictured Negro couple, but finds it necessary to add, about his father and mother, "they're *good* people." Viola likes the white doll better " 'cause it's cuter than the other one" (the brown doll to which she has given scarcely a glance). Tony R. evades self-identification, as a good many of these children do occasionally. He says that he was like neither of the baby dolls, when he was a baby. But he adds wistfully: "I was called 'Butch' when I was a baby. Is that one (white) 'Butch'?" Joan G. says of the matching boy dolls that the brown one is nicer because "the white one is too heavy." But her resolution to like brown fails her when we come to the girl dolls.

She fondles the white one, and then—briefly—the brown one.   "This one," she says, "this one I'm holding (brown)—*it just gets on my nerves*" (p. 43).

. . . "Then one night when he wasn't yet seven he did a queer thing. After he'd had his bath he put powder all over himself—he loves to do that—and he came out of the bathroom with this powder all over his face.   I said to him 'you look awful—go wipe that stuff off your face.' He looked at himself in the mirror and said: 'No, I don't mummy.   I look just like a little white boy now' " (p. 124).

Using ratings by the nursery-school teacher, Goodman unearthed evidence indicating that the personalities of the Negro children were affected by minority group membership even by the age of four.   These youngsters were rated higher in activity, emotionality, sensitiveness, competitiveness, and aggressiveness than their white schoolmates. Greater aggressiveness among Negro children also showed in other studies.   In a study by Hammer (1953), for example, the drawings of Negro children in a projective-type drawing test received higher ratings for the amount of hostility and aggression expressed.

Over half of the Negro youngsters in the Goodman study conveyed a sense of inferiority to whites through an assertion that whites were "nicer," "prettier," and "more desirable as playmates."   This kind of acceptance of white standards leads not only to a depreciation of one's own group but also to a deprecation of oneself.   "Though living in a democracy, many Negro citizens apparently learn by three years of age that skin color is important, that white is to be desired, dark to be regretted" (Landreth & Johnson, 1953).   This same feeling is shared by members of other minority groups.   At a Mexican baptismal party, the father was heard to utter the shocking imprecation, "*negro, negro; malo, malo*" (black, black; bad, bad).   This was a terrible verdict to pronounce on one's own son at his baptism and seemed to be prophetic of the later life experiences of an unusually dark child (a "Black Mexican") in a light-skinned family.   It pointed out the potentially dreadful consequences for self-acceptance in the minority group member's surrender to the majority group dictum that light is good and dark is bad.

The minority group child's early acceptance of the prevailing prejudices of the white majority is illustrated in an interesting study of fifth-grade Negro children (Epstein & Komorita, 1966).   The children were shown slides of a fictitious group labeled "Piraneans."   Both race and social class were introduced by pictures depicting Negro and white Piraneans in middle-class and working-class environments.   After viewing the slides, the children completed a seven-item social distance scale designed to elicit their attitudes toward the fictitious group. The items ranged from "would you want to marry these people when you grow up?" to "would you want these people to visit your country?". Results indicated that the children manifested greater social distance toward the Negro than toward the white Piraneans. The social class variable was not related to social distance. This suggests that the Negro child perceives his skin color, rather than his typically lower socioeconomic status, to be the basis for the white person's hostility and prejudice. The reverse was found to be the case, however, when white children were tested using a similar technique. Social distance toward the Negro was related to his inferior social status rather than to skin color.

That knowledge of the relative status of Negro and white is developed early is dramatically illustrated in the book *Children of Crisis* (Coles, 1967), which examines the reactions of Negro and white children in the South to school desegregation. Though initially unable or unwilling to verbalize their attitudes and feelings, the children revealed through drawings their profound understanding of the social context of race relations. Johnnie, a seven-year-old Negro child, described his drawing (Fig. 8-1) of a white and Negro boy as follows:

> Freddie wishes he were up top, like Billy, but he isn't, because there's not room for both of them up there, at least not now there isn't. They're not talking, they're just there. Freddie would be afraid to be on top. He wouldn't know what to do. He's used to where he is, just like Billy is. . . . When they talk it's real hard, because they are far from one another, so they have to shout (Coles, 1967, pp. 67–68).

Figures 8-2 through 8-4 are done by white children. In spite of an otherwise generally careful attention to detail, these children drew their Negro classmates in a very sketchy manner and often, as in Figures 8-2 and 8-4, assigned them to special sections of the picture. In Figure 8-4 the sunny, "white" side of the street, with its grass and trees and large, sturdy buildings, is very much in contrast with the "Negro" side. This boy carefully drew a red traffic light, which he said never turned green, as a reminder that the road was "a big highway, and you're not supposed to cross over" (p. 70).

Problems Encountered Later

Although much psychological theory relating to the development of personality has stressed the critical nature of the early years, it would be misleading to overlook forces that impinge on the individual during

FIGURE 8-1　Johnnie draws a Negro friend and a white classmate.

FIGURE 8-2　Ruby in school, by Jimmy at age 7.

FIGURE 8-3 Ruby, by Jimmy at age 6.

FIGURE 8-4 Allen draws the difference between Negro and white.
Drawings are from Coles (1967).

his growing-up years as well. In fact, particularly with reference to the Negro in the South, Davis (1943) suggested that the full impact of belonging to a minority group was not felt until the individual sought a job; at that time he became fully aware of the educational, social, and economic barriers in his path. Frustration, disillusion, and cynicism followed.

The responses of 150 preadolescent Negroes concerning their feelings and impulses when placed in unfortunate situations illustrated some of the emotional difficulties of Negro children because of their race (Goff, 1950). Disparagement, rude treatment, direct ridicule, and physical ill-treatment were some of the things they suffered.

"One day the teacher told us she wouldn't take us on no trips because it would be a disgrace to be seen on the street with a bunch of monkeys and laughing hyenas. She said, 'What would my friends say?' "

"I went to get on the street-car and a white man jerked me off, and let a white woman on and then he got on."

"One day I was swinging in the park, and a white girl stuck out her tongue at me and wouldn't use the swing when I got through using it. She waited for a white girl to get through."

"I was riding my bicycle and got a flat. I took it in the station to get it fixed. The man wouldn't let me have no air, and he said he couldn't fix things for colored people" (Goff, 1950, pp. 154–155).

Material from the interviews indicated that ridicule alone had a marked effect on development of personality. There seemed to be a sex difference in reaction to the kinds of treatment related in the responses. More resentment was found among boys, whereas girls were more likely to express feelings of inferiority.

The discrepancies between the impulses of the Negro youngsters in response to mistreatment by whites and what actually occurred dramatically demonstrate the psychological impact of such mistreatment. Although a desire to fight or to argue was reported in 57 per cent of the instances, withdrawal followed 82 per cent of the time. No wonder that frustration and ill-concealed hostility are psychological earmarks in the personalities of many minority group members.

Some of the problems faced by the Negro child in the process of school desegregation are described in a moving account written by a high-school teacher in Clinton, Tennessee (Anderson, 1966). In the book entitled *The children of the South,* Mrs. Anderson comments on the long-term effects resulting from the atmosphere of tension and violence. This is not surprising in view of the persecution to which the Negro children were subjected.

The Negro children had eggs smashed on their books, ink smeared on their clothes in the lockers, knives flourished in their presence, nails tossed in their faces, and spikes left on their seats. Obscene words were constantly whispered in their ears (Anderson, 1966, p. 62).

Some of the Negro children, though persisting in the face of almost insurmountable handicaps, felt at times that the price was far too great. Like any individual, the Negro child needs acceptance and approval in addition to the basic need for safety and physical well-being that the white child takes for granted.

A teacher can rebuke students who mistreat a Negro child openly. If a fight breaks out, you can go into the corridor and separate the children and stop the fight. But the more subtle harassment is not so easily detected or stopped. You can see the effects it has on the children; you watch them struggle to adjust to this order, and you try to change it. You see how difficult the change is going to be for everybody and how long it is going to take, so that in a sense the Negro child of today is giving up some part of his childhood to bring about a social change.

The struggle produces in the Negro child an anxiety, a deep fear which seems to be ever present. It is revealed in such questions as:

"Will I be able to play ball with white boys?"

"Will there be a place for me when the class goes on an overnight field trip? Where will I eat and sleep?"

"Will there be someone who will walk down the aisle with me on graduation night?"

"What would happen if I sat down at the table with white students?"

It is a kind of apprehension that makes the child wonder who he is and why. For, above all else, a child desires to be accepted by those around him. The Negro boy or girl worries about being accepted in the white school by the other students and by those in authority. He comes in frightened and insecure, concerned not only for his physical safety— will he be treated kindly?—but by something else which goes very deep: his need to be wanted and loved. And he knows, as do all children, who cares about his well-being and who does not (Anderson, 1966, pp. 67–68).

The full significance of membership in the Negro minority, of course, cannot be discussed apart from factors of social class. A spate of circumstances has relegated most Negroes to the lower socioeconomic group. Thus, they are members not only of the lower *caste* but also of the lower *class*. In this country lower-class families are characterized by two things: material deprivation and low standards of conduct (Dai, 1956). Broken homes, dominance of maternal authority, residence in impoverished and deteriorating neighborhoods, parent-child friction and antagonism accompanied by harsh and severe parental treatment, encouragement of delinquency by the environment—all these are the lot of Negro lower-class, lower-caste membership.

In a study of 25 Negroes through psychoanalytic interviews, Rorschach tests, and Thematic Apperception Tests, Kardiner and Ovesey (1951) maintained that the direct effects of discrimination were low self-esteem and anger. Low self-esteem might be manifested in unrealistically high aspirations, or in apathy, in living for the moment, in hedonism, or in criminal behavior. Denial of aggression and of hostility together with the anxiety-provoking feeling of being angry lead the Negro adult to contradictory behavior; he is good humored, affable, irritable, fearful, submissive, capable of explosive outbursts, and generally constricted in his emotional life. In the opinion of Kardiner and Ovesey, the failure of the Negro subjects to use their potential intelligence might be attributable to inner conflicts that rendered them incapable of focusing their attention.

Similar findings were reported by Karon (1958), who compared the personality characteristics of southern Negroes with those of northern whites and Negroes. Eleven characteristics differentiated the southern Negro from the latter two groups. Six of these were related to aggression, either with its denial or with the suppression of anger. The southern Negro was characterized also by "weakened affect," which may be interpreted as a "deadening of one's emotions" through the stifling of one's anger and hostility and through inability to express feelings of aggression and to solve frustrations.

Much variation exists among individuals in their reactions to membership in a minority group. This variation may be ascribed to psychological factors in the home. How does the parent respond to the situation: positively and constructively, or negatively and self-defeatingly? More important, to what extent is the child accepted by the parents? How far does the child, in consequence, develop feelings of self-worth, self-esteem, and self-acceptance? It has been noted that Negro children who are most self-accepting also tend to disclose more positive attitudes toward other Negro and white children (Trent, 1953). Unquestionably, the greater the child's sense of adequacy and security, the less need he has for counteraggression, and the less stinging, as a rule, the detrimental blows of prejudice and intolerance will be.

SUMMARY

In this chapter we have examined the psychological consequences of six sociological variables: family composition, family size, marital adjustment and divorce, handicapped child in the family, maternal employment, and minority group membership. Conclusions are difficult to draw because of the problems of conducting adequate research. Although most researchers would agree that these variables are of potential significance to the personality development of the child, they would have to concede that the precise influence remains to be clearly established.

Unfortunately, research follows the easiest course. Consider maternal employment. The research suggests that the quality of the interaction between mother and child is more pertinent to the child's behavior and adjustment than whether the mother is employed outside the home. But it is much easier to ascertain the employment status of the mother than to evaluate the psychological relation between mother and child. So it goes for the other variables considered in this chapter. Yet since the psychological factors in the home stem from a variety of circumstances, it would be unwise to ignore the possible influence on the parents and, in turn, on the child, of the variables discussed in these pages.

REFERENCES

Adler, A.   Characteristics of the first, second, third child.   *Children,* 1928, **3**, 14 and 52.   Quoted in H. E. Jones, Order of birth in relation to the development of the child, in C. Murchison (Ed.), *A handbook of child psychology.*   Worcester, Mass.: Clark University Press, 1931.   Pp. 204–241.

Altus, W.   Birth order and academic primogeniture.   *Journal of Personality and Social Psychology,* 1965, **2**, 872–876.

Anderson, M.   *The children of the South.*   New York: Farrar, Straus & Giroux, 1966.

Arrowood, A., & Amoroso, D.   Social comparison and ordinal position.   *Journal of Personality and Social Psychology,* 1965, **2**, 101–104.

Baruch, D. W.   A study of reported tension in interparental relationship as co-existent with behavior adjustment in young children.   *Journal of Experimental Education,* 1937, **6**, 187–204.

Baruch, D. W., & Wilcox, J. A.   A study of sex differences in preschool children's adjustment co-existent with interparental tensions.   *Journal of Genetic Psychology,* 1944, **64**, 281–303.

Bell, R. Q.   The effect on the family of a limitation in coping ability in the child: A research approach and a finding.   *Merrill-Palmer Quarterly,* 1964, **10**, 129–142.

Blanton, S., & Blanton, M. G.   *Child guidance.*   New York: Century, 1927.

Bonney, M. E.   A study of the relation of intelligence, family size, and sex differences with mutual friendships in the primary grades. *Child Development*, 1942, **13**, 79–100.

Bossard, J. H. S., & Boll, E. S. Personality roles in the large family. *Child Development*, 1955, **26**, 71–78.

Bossard, J. H. S., & Boll, E. S. *The large family system.* Philadelphia: University of Pennsylvania Press, 1956.

Bossard, J. H. S., & Sanger, W. P. The large family system—a research report. *American Sociological Review*, 1952, **17**, 3–9.

Brim, O. G., Jr. Family structure and sex role learning by children: A further analysis of Helen Koch's data. *Sociometry*, 1958, **21**, 1–16.

Brittain, C. Age and sex of siblings and conformity toward parents versus peers in adolescence. *Child Development*, 1966, **37**, 709–714.

Burchinal, L. G., Hawkes, G. R., & Gardner, B. Marriage adjustment, personality characteristics of parents and the personality adjustment of their children. *Marriage and Family Living*, 1957, **19**, 366–373.

Caldwell, B. M., & Guze, S. B. A study of the adjustment of parents and siblings of institutionalized and non-institutionalized retarded children. *American Journal of Mental Deficiency*, 1960, **64**, 845–861.

Campbell, A. A. Personality adjustment of only and intermediate children. *Journal of Genetic Psychology*, 1933, **43**, 197–205.

Carrigan, W., & Julian, J. Sex and birth-order differences in conformity as a function of need affiliation arousal. *Journal of Personality and Social Psychology*, 1966, **3**, 479–483.

Cattell, J. McK. *American men of science.* (4th ed.) Garrison, N. Y.: Science Press, 1927.

Cicirelli, V. Sibling constellation, creativity, I.Q., and academic achievement. *Child Development*, 1967, **38**, 481–490.

Clark, K. B., & Clark, M. P. Racial identification and preference in Negro children. In T. M. Newcomb & E. I. Hartley (Eds.), *Readings in social psychology.* New York: Holt, 1947. Pp. 169–178.

Coles, R. *Children of crisis.* Boston: Little, Brown, 1967.

Dai, B. Some problems of personality development among Negro children. In C. Kluckhohn & H. A. Murray (Eds.), *Personality in nature, society, and culture.* New York: Knopf, 1956. Pp. 545–566.

Davis, A. Racial status and personality development. *Science Monthly*, 1943, **57**, 354–362.

Davis, E. A. The mental and linguistic superiority of only girls. *Child Development*, 1931, **8**, 139–143.

Dean, D. A. The relation of ordinal position to personality in young children. Master's thesis, State University of Iowa, 1947.

Despert, J. L. *Children of divorce.* Garden City, N. Y.: Country Life Press, 1953.

Douvan, E., & Adelson, J. *The adolescent experience.* New York: Wiley, 1966.

Dyer, D. T.   Are only children different?   *Journal of Educational Psychology,* 1945, **36**, 297–302.

Epstein, R., & Komorita, S.   Prejudice among Negro children as related to parental ethnocentrism and punitiveness.   *Journal of Personality and Social Psychology,* 1966, **4**, 643–647.

Farber, B.   Effects of a severely mentally retarded child on family integration. *Monographs of the Society for Research in Child Development,* 1959, **24**, No. 2 (Serial No. 71).

Faris, R. E. L.   Sociological causes of genius.   *American Sociological Review,* 1940, **5**, 689–699.

Fenton, N.   The only child.   *Journal of Genetic Psychology,* 1928, **35**, 546–556.

Glueck, S., & Glueck, E.   Working mothers and delinquency.   *Mental Hygiene,* 1957, **41**, 327–352.

Goff, R. M.   Problems and emotional difficulties of Negro children due to race.   *Journal of Negro Education,* 1950, **19**, 152–158.

Goode, W. J.   *After divorce.*   Glencoe, Ill.: Free Press, 1956.

Goodenough, F. L., & Leahy, A. M.   The effect of certain family relationships upon the development of personality.   *Journal of Genetic Psychology,* 1927, **34**, 45–71.

Goodman, M. E.   *Race awareness in young children.*   Cambridge, Mass.: Addison-Wesley, 1952.

Guilford, R. B., & Worcester, D. A.   A comparative study of the only and non-only child.   *Journal of Genetic Psychology,* 1930, **38**, 411–426.

Hammer, E. F.   Frustration-aggression hypothesis extended to socio-racial areas: comparison of Negro and white children's H-T-P's.   *Psychiatry Quarterly,* 1953, **27**, 596–607.

Hand, H.   Working mothers and maladjusted children.   *Journal of Educational Sociology,* 1957, **30**, 245–246.

Hartley, E. L, Rosenbaum, M., & Schwartz, S.   Children's use of ethnic frames of reference: An exploratory study of children's conceptualization of multiple ethnic membership.   *Journal of Psychology,* 1948, **26**, 367–386.

Hartley, R. E.   Children's concepts of male and female roles.   *Merrill-Palmer Quarterly,* 1960, **6**, 83–91.

Hattwick, B. W.   Interrelations between the preschool child's behavior and certain factors in the home.   *Child Development,* 1936, **7**, 200–226.

Hilton, I.   Differences in the behavior of mothers toward first- and later-born children.   *Journal of Personality and Social Psychology,* 1967, **7**, 282–290.

Hoffman, L. W.   Parental power relations and the division of household tasks. *Marriage and Family Living,* 1960, **22**, 27–35.

Hoffman, L. W.   Mother's enjoyment of work and effects on the child.   *Child Development,* 1961, **32**, 187–197.

Hoffman, L. W.   Effects on children: Summary and discussion.   In F. I. Nye and L. W. Hoffman (Eds.), *The employed mother in America.*   Chicago: Rand McNally, 1963.   Pp. 190–212.

Horowitz, R. E. Racial aspects of self-identification in nursery school children. *Journal of Psychology,* 1939, **7**, 91–99.

Jordan, T. Research on the handicapped child and the family. *Merrill-Palmer Quarterly,* 1962, **8**, 243–260.

Kardiner, A., & Ovesey, L. *The mark of oppression.* New York: Norton, 1951.

Karon, B. P. *The Negro personality.* New York: Springer, 1958.

Kinstler, D. Covert and overt maternal rejection in stuttering. *Journal of Speech and Hearing Disorders,* 1961, **26**, 145–155.

Koch, H. L. The relation of "Primary Mental Abilities" in five- and six-year-olds to sex of child and characteristics of his sibling. *Child Development,* 1954, **25**, 209–223.

Koch, H. L. Sibling influence on children's speech. *Journal of Speech and Hearing Disorders,* 1956, **21**, 322–328. (a)

Koch, H. L. Sissiness and tomboyishness in relation to sibling characteristics. *Journal of Genetic Psychology,* 1956, **88**, 231–244. (b)

Koch, H. L. Children's work attitudes and sibling characteristics. *Child Development,* 1956, **27**, 289–310. (c)

Koch, H. L. Some emotional attitudes of the young child in relation to characteristics of his sibling. *Child Development,* 1956, **27**, 393–426. (d)

Koch, H. L. Attitudes of young children toward their peers as related to certain characteristics of their siblings. *Psychological Monographs: General and Applied,* 1956, **70**, No. 19 (Whole No. 323). (e)

Koch, H. L. The relation of certain formal attributes of siblings to attitudes held toward each other and toward their parents. *Monographs of the Society for Research in Child Development,* 1960, **25**, No. 4.

Krout, M. H. Typical behavior patterns in twenty-six ordinal positions. *Journal of Genetic Psychology,* 1939, **55**, 3–30.

Landis, J. T. The trauma of children when parents divorce. *Marriage and Family Living,* 1960, **22**, 7–13.

Landreth, C., & Johnson, B. C. Young children's responses to a picture and inset test designed to reveal reactions to persons of different skin color. *Child Development,* 1953, **24**, 63–79.

Lasko, J. K. Parent behavior toward first and second children. *Genetic Psychology Monographs,* 1954, **49**, 97–137.

Leton, D. A. A study of the validity of parent attitude measurement. *Child Development,* 1958, **29**, 515–520.

Maslow, A. H., & Mittleman, B. *Principles of abnormal psychology.* (Rev. ed.) New York: Harper, 1951.

McCurdy, H. G. The childhood pattern of genius. *Journal of the Elisha Mitchell Scientific Society,* 1957, **73**, 448–462.

Medinnus, G. R. The relation between inter-parent agreement and several child measures. *Journal of Genetic Psychology,* 1963, **102**, 139–144. (a)

Medinnus, G. R. The consistency of inter-parent agreement on several measures. *Journal of Genetic Psychology,* 1963, **102**, 145–150. (b)

Moran, G.   Ordinal position and approval motivation.   *Journal of Consulting Psychology,* 1967, **31,** 319–320.

Morland, J.   A comparison of race awareness in northern and southern children.   *American Journal of Orthopsychiatry,* 1966, **36,** 22–31.

Murchison, C. (Ed.).   *A handbook of child psychology.*   Worcester, Mass.: Clark University Press, 1931.

Murphy, G., Murphy, L. B., & Newcomb, T. M.   *Experimental social psychology.*   (Rev. ed.)   New York: Harper, 1937.

Murray, Mrs. Max A.   Needs of parents of mentally retarded children.   *American Journal of Mental Deficiency,* 1959, **63,** 1078–1088.

Nye, F. I.   Child adjustment in broken and in unhappy unbroken homes.   *Marriage and Family Living,* 1957, **19,** 356–361.

Nye, F. I.   Marital interaction.   In F. I. Nye and L. W. Hoffman (Eds.), *The employed mother in America.*   Chicago: Rand McNally, 1963.   Pp. 263–281.

Nye, F. I., & Hoffman, L. (Eds.).   *The employed mother in America.*   Chicago: Rand McNally, 1963.

Palmer, R.   Birth order and identification.   *Journal of Consulting Psychology,* 1966, **30,** 129–135.

Powell, K. S.   Maternal employment in relation to family life.   *Marriage and Family Living,* 1961, **23,** 350–355.

Rosen, B.   Family structure and value transmission.   *Merrill-Palmer Quarterly,* 1964, **10,** 59–76.

Rouman, J.   School children's problems as related to parental factors.   *Journal of Educational Research,* 1956, **50,** 105–112.

Sampson, E., & Hancock, F. T.   An examination of the relationship between ordinal position, personality, and conformity.   *Journal of Personality and Social Psychology,* 1967, **5,** 398–407.

Schachter, S.   *The psychology of affiliation.*   Stanford: Stanford University Press, 1959.

Sears, P. S.   Doll play aggression in normal young children.   Influence of sex, age, sibling status, father's absence.   *Psychological Monographs: General and Applied,* 1951, **65,** No. 6 (Whole No. 323).

Sears, R. R.   Ordinal position in the family as a psychological variable.   *American Sociological Review,* 1950, **15,** 397–401.

Siegel, A. E., Stolz, L. M., Hitchcock, E., & Adamson, J.   Dependence and independence in the children of working mothers.   *Child Development,* 1959, **30,** 533–546.

Smart, R.   Alcoholism, birth order, and family size.   *Journal of Abnormal and Social Psychology,* 1963, **66,** 17–23.

Staples, F. R., & Walters, R. H.   Anxiety, birth order, and susceptibility to social influence.   *Journal of Abnormal and Social Psychology,* 1961, **62,** 716–719.

Stroup, A. L.   Marital adjustment of the mother and the personality of the child.   *Marriage and Family Living,* 1956, **18,** 109–113.

Terman, L. M., et al. *Genetic studies of genius:* Vol. I. *The mental and physical traits of a thousand gifted children.* Stanford: Stanford University Press, 1925.

Trent, R. Analysis of expressed self-acceptance among Negro children. Unpublished doctoral dissertation, Teachers College, Columbia University, 1953.

Waldman, E. Marital and family characteristics of workers, March 1966. *Monthly Labor Review,* 1967, **90,** 29–36.

Waldrop, M. F., & Bell, R. Relation of preschool dependency behavior to family size and density. *Child Development,* 1964, **35,** 1187–1195.

Warren, J. R. Birth order and social behavior. *Psychological Bulletin,* 1966, **65,** 38–49.

West, S. Sibling configurations of scientists. *American Journal of Sociology,* 1960, **66,** 268–274.

Zuk, G. H. The religious factor and the role of guilt in parental acceptance of the retarded child. *American Journal of Mental Deficiency,* 1959, **64,** 139–147.

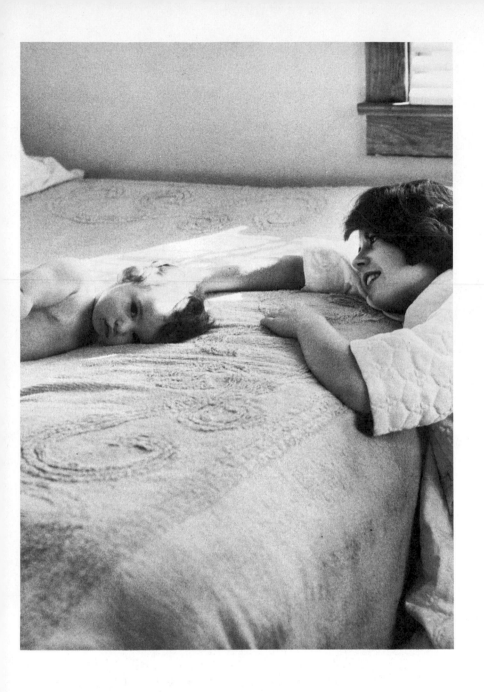

9

Family Influences in Infancy

Both sociologists and anthropologists have paid great attention to the family. Sociologists have dwelt at length on the functions served by the family in modern industrial society. Anthropologists have contrasted the role of the family in various cultures that differ widely in complexity and in their goals for socialization. Despite the vast differences in child-rearing practices from one culture to another, the family in most societies appears to serve three principal functions. First, it must be responsible for the physical care of the child, at least in infancy. Second, the parents must educate or train the child in certain areas that are essential to an adequate adjustment to the particular culture. Third, the family must accept the responsibility for the psychological and emotional welfare of the child. Although the first two functions have long been recognized, the third has been stressed only recently as a result of the growing body of psychological theory and research concerning the importance of the very early years and their influence on adult personality and adjustment.

The total physical helplessness of the human infant is immediately apparent. Although the newborn babe is capable of making a number of responses and enacting a number of behaviors, he is completely dependent on other human beings for his physical survival. Some of his responses actually elicit behaviors from the persons in his immediate environment; thus, from the very beginning, the infant plays some part in the continuing interaction between himself and other individuals. Most of this interaction, however, is initiated by others for the purpose of meeting the infant's physical needs. Whether this early environmental pattern of physical care affects the infant's psychological development will be considered presently.

It is the second main function of the family, the training and education of the child for adjustment to the culture, which has received the most attention from psychologists interested in the socialization process. This function can be broken down into two broad categories. The first is the training in the methods whereby the child gratifies his physical needs such as feeding and excreting. He is also trained in the development of such skills as self-help in dressing and tidiness, which seem to be important in Western culture. The second category is the inculcation of various attitudes and values that, although varying greatly among subcultures within the culture, deal with uniform aspects of socialization. The attitudes toward siblings, adults, and other persons in authority, and toward such social institutions as school and law-enforcement agencies all fall into place here. The child is also made aware of various cultural prohibitions, ranging all the way from sanctions against biting another individual to the taboos associated with incest. Since cultural values filter down to the child from the parent who colors the transmission with his own particular sense of them, the values held by one child may indeed vary in some respect from those possessed by any other child.

The third function of the family, responsibility for the child's psychological and emotional welfare, emphasizes the importance of the early psychological relation between parent and child. Although few psychologists would contend that the early years have no psychological significance, two related controversial issues are explored in this chapter. The first grows out of the notion that the child is most susceptible to psychological influences in the environment during the first year or two of life. The second concerns the extent to which very early experiences exert long-range influences on the child's personality.

MUTUAL INFLUENCE OF PARENT AND CHILD

Research into parent-child relations has by tradition viewed the parent as the independent variable and the child as the dependent one. In this light all of the child's characteristics, his behavior, his personality, and his adjustment, are seen as the direct product of various parental characteristics, namely, parental behavior, personality, and attitudes. Table 9-1A depicts this one-way relationship. Yet there are those who believe that, although parents exert a tremendous influence on a number of aspects of the child's development, the parent is affected reciprocally by various child characteristics that develop quite apart from parental actions. This results in the two-way, circular interaction represented by Table 9-1B. Under this process come the several listed characteristics, which vary from child to child and

TABLE 9-1 Two Conceptions of Parent-Child System

A. All of child's characteristics attributed to parental treatment and handling

Parental characteristics ⟶ Child characteristics

B. Parent and child characteristics mutually interacting

Parental characteristics ⟷ Child characteristics:
physical appearance
health
sex of child
alertness
activity level

---

which appear so early in life that it would be misleading to attribute them to parental handling.

That there are marked differences among infants at birth has been documented in recent research dealing with the infancy period. In one study (Birns, 1965), infants from two to five days of age were presented with various stimuli including a loud and soft tone, a cold disk applied to the thigh, and a pacifier inserted in the baby's mouth. Ratings were made of the intensity of the infant's response to these stimuli. The major finding of the study was that there were consistent individual differences in response intensity. Further, the infants were consistent from one day to the next in their responsiveness; each responded in a way characteristic for him. Other studies have furnished additional evidence for the uniqueness and individuality of response capacity in early infancy. This is true for autonomic functions such as cardiac and respiratory rate and for the stability versus the lability of their responsiveness (Lipton & Steinschneider, 1964). Using fixation time, behavioral measures, and cardiac and respiratory rate as measures of attention, Kagan and Lewis (1965) noted early sex differences, with girls displaying more mature and more stable fixation patterns in the first year of life. Although the extent to which some of these early individual differences in physiological and behavioral functioning are related to later behavior is not clear, it is apparent that the environment acts upon an organism that possesses certain initial characteristics. Development is a function of the continuous interaction between innate and environmental factors.

In the course of research in which he analyzed the interaction between mother and infant, Yarrow (1963) became greatly impressed by the variability in a mother's behavior depending upon the characteristics of the infant. The following case example illustrates this point. The two infants, Jack and George, were placed in a foster home at the same time.

> The one infant, Jack, was, from early infancy, a passive baby, with a low activity level and a generally low level of responsiveness to environmental stimuli. He usually accepted environmental frustrations without overt protest. He tended to wait quietly if he was not fed immediately when hungry. Even at three months, much of his day was spent in sleeping. He was not much interested in food, ate without much zest. By three months, he could be encouraged to respond socially with a smile or a mild increase in activity, but only after very strong stimulation. At five months he still showed no initiative in social interaction. He did not reach out toward people or make approach responses. He enjoyed his thumb, and when awake spent much of his time in a state of passive contentment, sucking his fingers or thumb.

In marked contrast to Jack, George was a vigorously active infant. He ate with great zest and sucked on the bottle with exceptional vigor. By three months, he was showing much initiative in attempting to handle and master his environment. He actively went after objects, expressed his needs directly, was very forceful in demanding what he wanted, and persisted in his demands until he was satisfied. By six months, he was showing a high degree of persistence in problem situations. George was highly responsive to social stimulation and took the initiative in seeking social response from others.

On only one dimension of the maternal rating scale—routine physical care—was the home environment comparable for these two infants. To some extent, there may have been differences even in this aspect of the environment, inasmuch as George's greater forcefulness in making his needs known probably resulted in more immediate response. On most other dimensions, the environment was markedly different for these two infants. George received a great deal of physical stimulation, not only from the foster mother, but from all members of the foster family. He was very much a part of this family; they related to him as a family member. He was held and played with a great deal by the foster mother, the foster father, and all the children.

On all aspects of physical contact, social stimulation, and relatedness to the family, Jack's environment was markedly different. He spent much of his time lying on the floor of the playpen. The playpen was in an isolated corner of the dining room, outside of the main stream of family traffic. The life of the family tended to flow on past him. He demanded very little and received very little stimulation. This pattern of isolation and stimulus-deprivation started very early. Even at seven weeks, the foster mother referred to him as "the other one," and talked about him as the "poor little thing." By three months, the foster mother came around to verbalizing basic feelings of rejection toward this infant. Her evaluations of him were consistently negative. It seemed as if he possessed no characteristics which were seen as desirable. He slept too much; he was not interested in anything. The one positive was that he had a nice smile—*when* he smiled. Whereas she spontaneously made many projections about George's future development, there was little investment in Jack's future. With regard to the quality of physical contact, the foster mother reported how the members of the family fought for the privilege of holding George for his feedings because they enjoyed his "cuddly" qualities. On the other hand, they were all reluctant to take care of Jack for his feedings because of his restlessness and apparent discomfort in being held. As a result, his bottle was often propped (Yarrow, 1963, pp. 109–110).

Yarrow and Goodwin (1965) have commented on the possible disturbances that may be produced by an incompatibility between mother and child in characteristics such as activity level if this incompatibility remains relatively stable over lengthy periods of time (Thomas, Chess, Birch, Hertzig, & Korn, 1964). While it is, of course, impossible to match natural mother and infant on some of these characteristics, attention might be given to this matter when placing infants for adoption or foster-homes. Schaffer and Emerson (1964) have used the term "mutual adaptation" to describe the interaction between mother and infant in the area of emotional attachment. The emotional needs or emotional responsiveness of the infant interact with the mother's ability to respond to these needs.

Psychological Environment at Birth

Although the principal concern of this chapter is the influences in infancy that affect personality development in later life, there are not many long-range studies capable of pinpointing them. Therefore, let us consider the broader area of the environmental differences that are potentially significant in this regard.

Among 38 of 46 couples, LeMasters (1957) found "extensive" or "severe" crises in adjusting to their first child. Most of them found the transition to parenthood hard to take. In another study (Sears, Maccoby, & Levin, 1957), a number of factors were seen to affect the mother's attitude toward pregnancy. Table 9-2 (Sears et al., p. 32) lists the attitudes of mothers covered in this investigation when they discovered they were with child.

By and large, the fewer the children the mother had, the more pleased she was to learn she was pregnant. Thus 64 per cent of the mothers were judged "delighted" to find themselves pregnant if the child was their first, but only 34 per cent of those who already had children fitted

TABLE 9-2   How Mother Felt When She Discovered She Was Pregnant

1. Delighted; very happy; had been waiting and hoping for this	50%
2. Pleased, but no evidence of enthusiasm (includes: "This was a planned baby," said matter-of-factly)	18
3. Pleased generally; some reservations	6
4. Mixed feelings; advantages and disadvantages weighed about equally	9
5. Generally displeased, although some bright spots seen	9
6. Displeased; no reservations	7
7. Not ascertained	1
Total	100%

this description. In addition, the favorable response to the news increased as the age gap between the expected child and the next older one widened. To some extent the mother's attitude was affected by the sex of the children already in the family. That mothers tended to be more pleased with their condition if their family consisted entirely of girls than if it was composed of only boys or of boys and girls may be interpreted in diverse ways. Either parents are more eager to have at least one boy than at least one girl, or they are more willing to take on the responsibility of another child if they have only girls, assuming that girls are easier to raise in the early years; having only boys, a mother may quickly become discouraged from inviting further burdens. Age did not seem to be an important factor affecting the mother's attitude toward her pregnancy.

Clearly the psychological atmospheres into which children are born vary greatly. A child may have been anticipated with some eagerness, with numerous favorable parental attitudes accompanying the birth. Or a pregnancy may have been unwanted, in which case the newborn infant is considered an unbearable burden. The harmful long-range impact of these early negative attitudes on eventual personality and adjustment has been pursued in clinical case studies, but regrettably these undertakings have lacked control groups. And since clinical reports are not the most reliable source of data for scientific endeavor, one must be careful in attributing long-term influences to experiences in early life, though differences in attitudes among parents with respect to a newborn infant must indeed exist.

Is there a kind of communion between mother and infant so that the child is able to perceive various emotional states of the mother and respond to them (Escalona, 1945)? Sullivan (1940) maintained there was, and gave to this emotional linkage the term *empathy*. Disturbances in the mother are often reflected in feeding upsets in the infant. At birth the child was seen as possessing innate tendencies that permitted him to "sense" disturbances in his relationship with his mother (Ribble, 1944). Since most of the literature regarding such emotional linkage has been based on clinical observation, there is little research to illuminate the situation. It becomes necessary to examine developmental characteristics of the newborn and infant as established through observational research. In the opinion of William James the world to the newborn was a "blooming, buzzing confusion." The newborn's perceptual and intellectual faculties are only immaturely developed. He can neither focus on nor follow a moving object until four weeks of age, and he does not smile in response to the human face until three months. The infant cannot distinguish between strange and familiar faces until he is 24 weeks old. And only at the age of four does the child begin to understand the meaning of sarcasm. From these various considerations it is difficult to conceive of the infant as able to interpret and fathom the significance of nuances or subtleties in its mother's feelings, moods, and motives. True, the infant responds with crying and restlessness to bodily tensions induced by unmet biological needs. But it is probably unscientific to regard this behavior as the infant's response to insensitivity on the part of its mother.

EFFECTS OF EARLY EXPERIENCE ON LATER BEHAVIOR

In one form or another the rest of this chapter pertains to the relationship between experiences in infancy and early childhood and subsequent behavior. For example, consider this passage:

"That's not the point," replied Mrs. Overmeyer. "Did you see The Snake Pit?"

"Yes."

"Lady in the Dark? Spellbound? All those other psychological things?"

"Yes."

"In every single one of those pictures, people go nuts because of something their parents did to them when they were kids."

"But what has that to do with you?" I asked, "You and George would never treat a child unkindly or cruelly."

"You don't get the idea at all," answered Mrs. Overmeyer. "In those movies the parents weren't unkind or cruel. They were perfect bricks to their children. And yet they did some mild little thing—something so unimportant they didn't notice it—and twenty years later the kids end up in the laughing academy. Remember Lady in the Dark? Remember what knocked the heroine off her trolley? When she was a little girl, her mother was all dressed up to go to a party. The girl wanted to kiss the mother good night, but the mother wouldn't let her because she was afraid the girl would muss her hair. The next thing you know, the girl's got a neurosis as big as the Ritz."

Mrs. Overmeyer poured herself another brandy and continued. "Who knows what goes on in their goddam subconsciouses? Anything can be traumatic, and it's always the parents' fault. It doesn't matter what you do for a kid—you buy him toys and candy and clothes; you send him to camps, take him to shows, bring him on trips; you never say a hard word to him—and then one day you happen accidentally to scowl at him and —wham!—he thinks he's Napoleon."

She sighed mightily. "How do you cope with something like that? Take our daughter Linda—a mean little bastard if you ever saw one. A good clout in the chops is what she needs. But how can we risk it? We're scared even to raise our voices to her. How do we know what would happen? We yell at her today and ten years later she's exposing herself on streetcars" (Shulman, 1959, pp. 91–92).

One of the hazards arising from the emphasis on the long-term effects of early childhood experiences, a point so prevalent in recent and current psychological research among children, is depicted stunningly in this excerpt from a popular work of fiction. Modern parents are confronted by the problem in their handling of the child. "Common sense," a term grossly misapplied in parent-child relations, and child-rearing practices and attitudes learned from their own parents conflict with the idea that each and every childhood experience leaves an indelible mark on the child. Current points of view, however, argue against this notion. Since research here, as in many other phases of parent-child associations, is both sparse and inconclusive, how one regards the contribution of early experience to subsequent behavior depends inevitably on one's view of the infant and the young child.

Conceptions of Infancy and Early Childhood

Oversimplified, inaccurate, and unjust as it may be to separate points of view and writers into two camps, suppose we do so for purposes of discussion. On the one hand there is the *clinical* point of view, probably traceable back to Freud but given impetus more recently by Ribble. This view holds that infantile experiences are of primary importance because of the early age at which they occur and the impressionability of the infant at this time. The other point of view is the *developmental;* from it, the infant is seen as having tremendous capacity for adjustment, flexibility, and modifiability.

First, let us consider the Ribble position (Ribble, 1943, 1944). Her main thesis is the importance of mothering for the infant. This arises from her conception of the infant as inadequately developed at birth. Because of an immature nervous system, Ribble believed, the infant is dependent on maternal stimulation for the development of proper physiological functioning.

All good science begins by defining its terms, so that it is essential to make clear first of all just what we mean by mothering. It is really a continuance of the closeness of the prenatal state, and the more clearly it imitates certain of the conditions before birth the more successful it is in the first weeks. The newborn baby still needs to be carried about at regular intervals until he can move and coordinate his own body.

This helps to strengthen his sense of equilibrium and to give him reassurance. Contact takes the place of equilibrium and to give him a feeling of security. Also he must have frequent periods of actual contact with the mother because the warmth and the holding give him reassurance. Contact takes the place of the physical connection before birth when the child was like an organ of the mother's body. In addition, mothering includes the whole gamut of small acts by means of which an emotionally healthy mother consistently shows her love for her child, thus instinctively stimulating his psychic development. Obviously, feeding, bathing, and all the details of physical care come in, but in addition to these duties, which can easily become routine and perfunctory, we mean all of the small evidences of tender feeling—fondling, caressing, rocking, and singing or speaking to the baby. These activities have a deep significance (Ribble, 1943, p. 9).

From physiological functioning Ribble moved to psychological functioning. Lacking consistent mothering, she held, the infant feels tense, insecure, and frustrated. The infant's development of personality depends on this early relationship with one consistent mother figure.

It is difficult to draw a clear line between the infant's physical and psychological needs, for the very act of making him more comfortable physically, if done by a kindly hand, may at the same time stimulate his sense of aliveness and his consciousness of personal contacts. Certainly we know now that the capacity for mature emotional relationships in adult life is a direct outgrowth of the parental care, more specifically the mothering, which an infant receives. It is the first relationship of life which activates the feelings of the baby and primes his dormant nervous system into full functional activity, giving to each individual personality its original slant. Social impulses are part of our primary equipment; emotional hunger is an urge as definite and compelling as the need for food. When we deny an infant fulfillment of these needs, we stifle his emotional and social life (Ribble, 1943, p. 13).

Ribble believed that deprivation of mothering not only definitely produces permanent psychological ill effects but also can bring on physical deterioration. Consistent mothering, on the other hand, facilitates speech development, intellectual development, and emotional development. Danger lurks in thwarting the infant's needs or desires. "The human infant in the first year of life should not have to meet frustration or privation, for these factors immediately cause exaggerated tension and stimulate latent defense activities" (Ribble, 1943, p. 72).

According to Ribble, then, the infant is characterized by immaturity and incompleteness, dependent on consistent maternal administrations for physiological and psychological welfare. The early relationship with the mother sets the pattern for all future emotional involvements. Thus any disturbance, even in the early months of life, has far-reaching implications for the child's development of personality.

The developmental view is represented most clearly by Anderson (1948). As the developmentalists see the infant, it is an active energy system that seeks stimulation, is able to withstand a variety of stresses and strains, and has a great capacity for self-repair and readjustment. Both as infant and young child, the youngster reacts to a large number of stimuli each day, of which only a few are retained in memory to affect later behavior. When trauma occurs it does not result from a single instance but from the repetition and reiteration of events in the child's life. This keeps the events alive to achieve their traumatic effect. Thus, sexual assault may have a long-range traumatic significance for the child only if his parents react to it in a highly emotional manner and continue to talk about it.

In this view the child is a persistent and consistent personality system that maintains its integrity and resists "deformation, stress, and trauma." Out of his environment the infant selects those stimuli or events that are congruent with his personality structure. He is not subject, willy-nilly, to all of the influences surrounding him, nor does he respond passively to the many stimuli in his environment. Instead, he is at least somewhat selective and reacts to the stimuli in a manner determined by his goals and attitudes toward himself. To Anderson, the child is a tough, resilient organism, capable of adapting to different environments and environmental pressures, and of responding actively to the world around him.

Evaluation of these two views is difficult. To begin with, research in the area is really not definitive. Once more, the controls required for clear-cut results are almost impossible to impose. For example, Anderson took the position that in order to have traumatic consequences for a child an event had to be repeated or reiterated in the child's experience. Quite obviously, it is not very easy to control a child's subsequent experiences so that the long-term impact of single traumatic events can be tested.

Yet somewhat stronger evidence seems to support the developmental rather than the clinical position. The following case report typifies the kind of data used to justify Ribble's "clinical" conception of the child.

> A man suffered from a phobia of being grasped from behind, the disturbance appearing early in childhood and persisting to his fifty-fifth year. When walking on the street he was under a compulsion to look back over his shoulder at intervals to see if he was closely followed. In

social gatherings he arranged to have his chair against the wall. It was impossible for him to enter crowded places or to attend the theater.

In his fifty-fifth year he returned to the town in which he had spent his childhood. After inspecting his old home, he went to the corner grocery and found that his old boyhood friend was still behind the counter. He introduced himself and they began to reminisce. Finally the grocerman said this, "I want to tell you something that occurred when you were a boy. You used to go by this store on errands, and when you passed you often took a handful of peanuts from the stand in front. One day I saw you coming and hid behind a barrel. Just as you put your hand in the pile of peanuts, I jumped out and grabbed you from behind. You screamed and fell fainting on the sidewalk."

The episode was remembered and the phobia, after a period of readjustment, disappeared (Bagby, 1922, p. 17).

The issue is not whether experiences and relationships in childhood are important in shaping future attitudes and personalities. Rather, it revolves around the susceptibility of the infant to effects of single specific events and the extent to which these events in the long run are powerful determinants of personality. The balance hangs on how one approaches the subject and regards the emotional and mental nature of the infant.

A common weakness of the clinical view is its interpretation of the child's feelings in terms of adult attitudes, feelings, and responses. Thus, holding the infant tightly is said to give him feelings of security. It may do so for the adult, but can we validly project such feelings into the infant? Stevenson (1957) stressed the fact that experiences have one meaning for the infant and the child and another for the adult; this results from differences in memories, in the meaningfulness of the contexts of events, and in the nature of thought processes. "If you take a toy away from a child, he will probably cry, but if you tell him the mortgage has been foreclosed he will probably go on playing with the toy. We have no proof that within the world as he sees it, a stress is any harder to bear in infancy than in adulthood" (Stevenson, 1957, p. 158). Anderson similarly discussed the fallacy of interpreting children's feelings on the basis of adult behaviors.

At a recent panel discussion another error was made. A participant talking on jealousy described the situation of the jealous child as like that in which a husband tells his wife that he is bringing a new wife into the home, expatiates on her desirability and asks his wife to assist in preparing for the new wife's coming. While this analogy has obvious dramatic qualities, it is far from a good description of child behavior. There is little evidence that marked jealousy on the arrival of a new

In an extensive analysis of data obtained in the California Guidance Study described in Chapter 1, Heinstein (1963) examined the relation between early nursing experience and subsequent behavioral adjustment. In addition to length of breast and bottle feeding, ratings were made of three psychological variables: warmth of the mother, nervous stability of the mother, and marital adjustment of the parents. The results indicated that "there were no apparent over-all advantages in behavioral adjustment associated with either breast or formula feeding as such" (p. 33). Fewer behavior problems were noted in those children whose mothers were rated as warm rather than cold in their interactions with them. For boys, the combination of length of nursing, and warmth of mother was particularly important. Those who experienced a long period of nursing by a cold mother were the most maladjusted group. Breast feeding by a cold mother was most conducive to problem behavior in girls. In both of these instances the mother's behavior appears to contradict her feelings with regard to the maternal role. The conflict between a cold attitude and behavior reflecting nurturance (breast feeding and long nursing periods) seems to produce harmful effects in the child. This strongly suggests that the adoption of approved maternal behavior cannot nullify a negative attitude toward the child or toward the maternal role.

Heinstein concluded that early feeding experience may be important only when considered in the context of the psychological relation between mother and child. Further, the sex of the child must be taken into account when examining the effect on the child of infant feeding practices.

Schedule versus Self-demand Feeding. Over the years there have been many variations in expert advice on this topic. Thus it seems fruitless to examine in detail the research that has endeavored to relate this aspect of early infant care to factors of maternal or child personality. In the Pattern Study an inverse relationship was noted between a mother's confidence in her ability to employ correct child-rearing procedures and the fidelity with which she followed her pediatrician's advice; the less confident the mother, the more she was likely to accept her doctor's recommendation of feeding techniques. This finding suggested once more that although a mother's methods of child rearing might be related to other aspects of her general attitudes and personality, her procedures might not reflect her feelings toward the child or toward child rearing itself.

A study by Durrett (1959) will serve to illustrate the inconclusive relationships typically obtained between measures of early infant scheduling and child behavior. Based on home interviews, a group of mothers of preschoolers were rated on a scale concerning feeding schedules, ranging from a strict schedule to complete self-regulation. The children were scored on the extent of verbal and physical aggression displayed in a doll play session. No significant relations were found between the mother and child variables, although according to the frustration-aggression hypothesis (see Chapter 15), one would expect more aggressive behavior in those children who had experienced a stricter, and therefore presumably more frustrating, feeding schedule.

Sucking and Thumb Sucking.   Psychoanalytic theory contends that if an infant lacks sufficient oral gratification through his sucking to obtain food, he will indulge in sucking behavior unrelated to the feeding process.   Learning theory, on the other hand, maintains that the greater the reinforcement received by the infant from sucking, the stronger his sucking drive will be.   Each of these theories thus predicts different consequences for the infant's early sucking experience.   Psychoanalytic theory would hold that an infant who is cup fed from birth or whose breast- or bottle-feeding experience is brief would exhibit more "nonnutritional" sucking than an infant who received much oral gratification through sucking.   If it could be shown that sucking the thumb were caused by lack of oral gratification, a mother could be advised with some assurance as to the appropriate method for preventing this behavior. The controversy is indeed an interesting one.

Although here, too, the research findings are contradictory, we must conclude that there is a variety of reasons for prolonged thumb sucking, some of which bear absolutely no relation to gratification or deprivation in early sucking.   For example, Simsarian (1947) observed five thumb suckers among a group of 26 children who had been breast fed on self-demand schedules and who had been permitted to nurse as long as they wished.   In another study, Traisman and Traisman (1958), who interviewed mothers of more than 2000 infants and children, noted little difference in the occurrence of thumb sucking between children fed by bottle and those partially or completely fed by breast.   They also found only slight differences of types of psychological problem between those who did and those who did not suck their thumbs.

As a clinical matter, thumb sucking is taken as one sign of maladjustment or personality disturbance in a child.   The seriousness of thumb sucking would depend, of course, on the frequency and extent of the behavior and the age of the child.   In a three- or four-year-old such conduct would not be considered unusual in the face of a new, strange, or challenging situation.   In an elementary-school child it may, however, require prompt investigation by a person trained in psychology.

Even if one does not adhere strictly to psychoanalytic explanations of behavior, sucking the thumb may be regarded as regression, in the broad psychological sense of the term; the child reverts to an earlier form of behavior, which assured gratification. In an older child, therefore, thumb sucking is sometimes interpreted as indicating strong feelings of insecurity.

Not much is known through definitive medical research about the effects of such behavior on the teeth. Current thinking generally holds that prolonged thumb sucking after the child's permanent teeth have appeared may very well affect the bite, especially where there is some tendency toward irregularity. Prior to this time, there is not much likelihood that sucking of the thumb would harm the dental structures. Nor is there any knowledge to speak of about the thumbs themselves becoming deformed through such activity!

Weaning. In the Pattern Study both the age at which weaning occurred and the severity of the process, that is, the amount of pressure exerted on the infant, were linked to a rating of the child's emotional upset during the procedure. Although nearly twice as many youngsters were rated as having shown some upset when weaning was initiated after 11 months of age as when it was started before five months, the children weaned in the intervening period showed the fewest emotional reactions. Then, too, the less severe the procedure was, the fewer the emotional upsets. What was learned about the relation of age of weaning to the emotional reaction to it contradicted the idea implied in psychoanalytic theory that the longer the infant remained breast or bottle fed, the more emotionally healthful this would be. The Sewell and Mussen study detected no connection between the personality adjustment ratings of its five- and six-year-olds and the age at which they were weaned or the character of the weaning process, whether sharp or gradual.

More than one writer (Fries, 1941; Escalona, 1945) has stressed the importance of feeding as a particularly sensitive indicator of both the child's relationship with its mother and its general adjustment. However true this may be, the point of concern here is the difference between short- and long-range effects of various maternal practices. Conceivably the mother's behavior toward her infant with respect to feeding may influence the infant's responses during the infancy period. But there is little support for the view that her conduct in this one aspect of child rearing exerts long-range impacts on the child's personality. To anticipate the beginning of the next chapter, there may be shifts in maternal behavior and attitudes toward child rearing over a period of time.   Although a mother may employ a rigid, insensitive approach toward the young infant, she may revise her methods and attitudes as a result of both the child's changing developmental characteristics and capabilities and of her own learning about child care.

Another consideration is the interrelationships among the various practices a mother employs.   One study (Klatskin, Jackson, & Wilkin, 1956) explored the tie between the flexibility of the mother's practices in feeding, sleeping, toilet training, and socialization, and evidences of disturbance in the child.   Among its findings appeared a tendency for the relation between maternal flexibility and problem behavior in the child to be a discrete one; specific deviation from optimal handling by the mother led to problems in the child only in the one particular area.   Thus, extreme rigidity in toilet training might lead to disturbances in toilet habits but leave unaffected the child's sleeping and eating behaviors.   Second, the study uncovered no link between the mother's behavior in areas of feeding and socialization in the child's first year and his behavior then or in the year which followed.

In a study by Sewell, Mussen, and Harris (1955) mothers of a group of five- and six-year-olds were interviewed to try to ascertain the relationships among child-rearing practices during infancy and the years immediately following.   Obtaining information on 38 items bearing on infant care, child-training procedures, and the handling of disciplinary problems, the study generally showed low and insignificant correlations.   Apparently a mother's attitude in one area of child training was germane to that area alone and did not affect her behavior in others.   Inconsistency *as to the favorableness of the practice* was the rule.

What, then, are the effects of feeding practices on the child?   First, regarding the significance of the mother's decision to breast or bottle feed, a host of factors, some without much psychological relevance, influence it.   Several studies even propose that breast feeding may have some sexual implications for the mother, which may be more important than her attitude toward the infant in deciding whether to breast feed.   Second, no permanent effects of weaning activities on the child have been noted, although there is some evidence for a curvilinear relationship between age of weaning and emotional upset.   Third, despite support for both deprivation and reinforcement of sucking as causes for thumb sucking, actually several causes exist.   Finally, a child-rearing technique may exert immediate or short-range influence on child behavior but have no long-term significance; and the links among the various child-training practices employed by a mother are slight, so that it would seem hardly likely for one specific practice to have a general bearing on the child's development of personality.

Toilet Training

Every culture regulates toilet behavior. Cultures vary widely, however, in how much control and restrictiveness they impose. Present-day American society is relatively strict in this phase of child training. It is likely that the urban, crowded conditions of American life, which create an almost fanatical consciousness of germs and dirt, contribute to this strictness. Be that as it may, mothers express great amounts of concern over the toilet habits of their young children, frequently mentioning the development of bladder and bowel control as a "problem" area.

Notwithstanding Freud's heavy emphasis on the crucial importance of toilet training to the child's subsequent development of personality, research offers little corroborating evidence for a relationship between the two. In an ingenious study designed to test the relation predicted by Freudian theory between early maternal toilet training practices and the anal personality type characterized by obstinacy, orderliness, and parsimony, Hetherington and Brackbill (1963) found stronger evidence for identification theory than for psychoanalytic theory. Significant correlations were found between boys and their fathers and between girls and their mothers in these three personality traits, suggesting that identification with like-sex parent is an important determinant of the child's personality characteristics. Inconclusive relations were obtained between ratings of age and severity of toilet training and the child's personality ratings. Abundant clinical reports, however, indicate the harmful consequences of overly severe toilet training. Examining case histories of children referred to a child-guidance clinic, for example, Huschka (1942) observed that in more than half of the children bladder and bowel training was started prematurely. The list of child behaviors seen to derive from coercive toilet training includes negativism, aggressiveness, fearfulness, compulsiveness, rigid behavior, rage, guilt, excessive cleanliness, and defiance. But as we shall presently see, the relationship between toilet training and behavior or personality is by no means simple. More influential than the mother's practices are her own personality and the factors prompting her behavior. Moreover, the greater permissiveness of child-rearing practices in America suggests that coercive toilet-training procedures are much less common today than formerly. The practices of most mothers in this respect, therefore, fall within the normal range and do not contribute to aberration.

Although there are some similarities between weaning and toilet training, the differences are more significant. In both procedures built-in reflexes help the child to perform these behaviors. The basic mechanisms involved exist and operate efficiently at birth. Toilet training differs from feeding behavior, however, by requiring the child to control the built-in reflexes and prevent their operation except at certain approved times and places.

At first the child has no desire to control the process of elimination. To develop control he must learn to recognize signs that indicate the imminent relaxation of the anal sphincter muscles. Besides inhibiting action, voluntary control also involves the ability to "let go." Such a relatively complicated process requires much learning. If anxiety, resulting from punishment, is introduced into the situation, learning becomes more difficult and the process prolonged. Take the analogy of the impatient husband who attempts to teach a hopeful but unsure wife to drive a car. Punishment takes the form of disapproval, which causes the wife to give up in despair. In both cases, toilet training and learning to drive, pressure and its resulting frustration so complicate and retard the learning process that negative attitudes may affect the whole "teacher-learner" relationship, whether between husband and wife or mother and child.

When does toilet training customarily begin? It should not begin before the child is ready to undertake the necessary learning. Because some amount of physiological maturation is probably required and children mature at different rates, it becomes impossible to state a precise age at which toilet training should be initiated. In the Pattern Study 87 per cent of the mothers started bowel training before the child was 20 months old. Eleven months represented the average age. In 80 per cent of the cases the training was completed by the time the child reached 24 months of age, the average age of completion being 18 months. The data showed that the later the training was undertaken, the quicker it succeeded.

A wide variety of reasons prompt a mother to undertake toilet training at a particular age, but the Pattern Study noted that maternal anxiety about the sexual sphere was an important element in her decision to begin training early and complete it as rapidly as possible. And this anxiety may indeed influence the restrictiveness with which she regards manifestations of sexuality in the child.

Severity of Training. From descriptions by mothers of their practices, ratings were made of the severity of toilet training. More important than the percentages listed in Table 9-3 (Sears, Maccoby, & Levin, 1957, p. 119) are the details of each of the five rating categories. As might be expected, the severity of the training was an influential factor in causing emotional upset in the child. But severity alone was not the full story. The attitudes of the mother also bore on the amount of upset. Severe toilet-training procedures became far more emotionally disturbing if accompanied by maternal coldness and undemonstrativeness than if presented in an atmosphere of maternal warmth that made the child feel emotionally secure. Thus the entire emotional context within which day-to-day child-rearing methods occur must be evaluated to ascertain the effect of child-care techniques on child development.

Many writers have said that coercive and insensitive toilet training damages the parent-child relationship, perhaps with long-range consequences. If so, this assertion is entirely speculative. No doubt, coercive techniques are unwise for several reasons, yet other considerations are worth restatement. That no over-all favorableness or unfavorableness characterizes child-rearing methods implies that although a mother may use ill-advised techniques in toilet training, some of her other procedures may be perfectly acceptable. Moreover, the basic attitudes of the mother may be more significant for the child's development than any single child-rearing practice.

Taken together, these points suggest the need to assess the pervasiveness of a mother's attitudes toward her child before trying to pre-

TABLE 9-3   Severity of Toilet Training

1. Not at all severe. Child more or less trained himself. Not his fault when he has accidents; they are considered natural. No punishment or scolding.	10%
2. Slight pressure. Mild disapproval for some late accidents. Mother makes some efforts to show child where, when, and how to go to toilet.	42
3. Moderate pressure. Scolding for some late deviations; fairly frequent toileting.	29
4. Fairly severe training. Child scolded fairly often; mother clearly shows disapproval. Child may be left on toilet for fairly lengthy periods.	16
5. Very severe training. Child punished severely for deviations; mother angry and emotional over them.	2
Not ascertained	1
Total	100%

dict their bearing on his future personality. Then there is the possibility that maternal attitudes may change in time. A mother may pressure her child into early toilet control and may not seem to accept him until he has achieved it, but once he has attained this goal, she may grow relaxed and accepting in her relationship with him.

To summarize, various explanations may account for the failure of the Freudian variables—feeding, weaning, and toilet training—to yield many clues to the personality development of the child. First, the range of practice for mothers in Western culture is limited, with few mothers at either extreme. Part of this situation may be charged to the widespread expert advice available and the general trend toward permissive child rearing. Second, the fact that a mother's child-training methods are often shaped by pediatric counsel or by current fads rather than by her own attitudes and personality makes them less pertinent psychologically than might otherwise be the case. Finally, since there is little connection among a mother's various child-rearing techniques, the general quality of the relationship between parents and child is more predictive of future personality than are the clearly observable effects of specific, short-term practices.

Other Infant Care Variables

Caldwell (1962, 1964) has noted that the tremendous concern with feeding and elimination practices has left a large number of psychological variables unexplored. For example, little attention has been paid to early intellectual and verbal stimulation or to early autonomy given the child in terms of physical activity and exploration. Was the child pressured to perform some of the early developmental tasks such as walking and talking? How early did the parents begin to read to the child? Was infant care consistent from one area to another? Was the infant cared for primarily by a single mother figure or was the caretaking shared by several individuals? In this section three studies are examined, each focusing on a somewhat different set of variables.

In the Yarrow study (Yarrow, 1963; Yarrow and Goodwin, 1965) mentioned earlier in this chapter the main maternal care categories were:

(1) the amount and varieties of stimulation provided by the mother; (2) the activities of the mother primarily concerned with need gratification and tension reduction in the infant; (3) the conditions under which stimulation and need gratification are provided, broadly conceived as learning conditions; and (4) the underlying feelings and attitudes of the mother toward the infant (Yarrow & Goodwin, 1965, p. 475).

The relation between these maternal behaviors and a number of infant personality and developmental characteristics at six months of age were examined. The learning conditions were significantly correlated with the measure of IQ and moderately related to the infant's exploratory and manipulative behavior. Strong relations were found between the infant's ability to handle stress and the maternal affectional variables. While no longitudinal data are available showing the long-term stability of these early infant ratings, it is clear that Yarrow has identified important interactions between mother and infant characteristics during the infancy period.

Schaefer and Bayley (1963) have analyzed the longitudinal data collected in the Berkeley Growth Study in order to identify the effects of maternal behavior on the child's social and emotional development. Since data bearing on the relation between mother and child behavior in later childhood and adolescence are dealt with in the next chapter, the present discussion is confined to their study of the early age period. The infants were tested periodically during their first three years. Extensive written observations were made of the interactions of the mother with the examiners, the child, and any other persons present. Later, behavior ratings scales were developed and the written records were evaluated on each of the 32 scales. A factor analysis of these scales revealed two main factors (Schaefer, 1959): love versus hostility and autonomy versus control. These broad dimensions are discussed in greater detail in the next chapter. Following each of the 12 testing sessions between the ages of 10 to 36 months the infants were rated on these seven-point rating scales:

Degree of strangeness: shy—unreserved

Speed of movements: slow—rapid

Amount of positive behavior: negative behavior—positive behavior

Emotional tone: unhappy—happy

Activity: inactive—vigorous

Responsiveness to persons: slight—marked

Irritability (or tendency to be sensitive to and react to stimulation): excitable—calm

Figure 9-1 illustrates the kinds of relationship that were established between maternal behaviors and child characteristics. In general, the love-hostility dimension showed strong correlations with happy, calm, and positive behaviors of both sons and daughters. Stronger correlations were found between mothers and sons than between mothers and daugh-

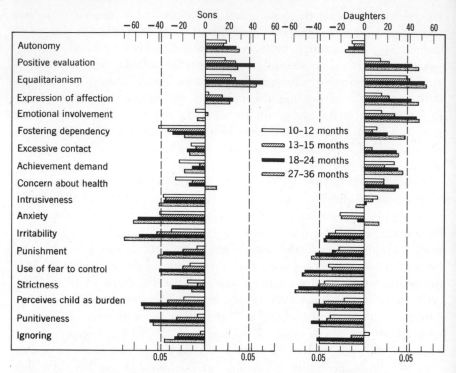

FIGURE 9-1   Correlations between maternal behavior (0–3 years) and children's happiness at four age levels (10–36 months) (Bayley, 1965, p. 205).

ters, suggesting that boys are more deeply influenced than girls by the interaction between them and their mothers.

While investigating infant behavior and personality development, Brody (1956) and her associates studied the conduct of mothers during a four-hour period in which they performed their normal functions of caring for the infant's needs. Their study had a great methodological advantage over the investigations dealing with feeding and toilet training. It actually observed the mothers caring for their infants, whereas the information acquired in the other studies came from retrospective verbal reports by the mothers.

The Brody team concentrated on 32 infants, four males and four females at each of four levels of age, 4, 12, 20, and 28 weeks. The mothers brought their children to a central location where rooms were expressly equipped with the supplies needed to care for infants. Although the ostensible purpose was to observe infant patterns of behavior, two researchers kept detailed records of each mother's behavior in relation to her child. They particularly attended to six maternal activities: feeding, cleaning, moving, touching, offering objects, and speaking. In each of these areas they rated behavior on a five-degree scale in terms of the sensitivity with which the mother responded to the needs or wishes of her infant. Three indices, each describing a particular quality of maternal behavior, were computed for each of the six activities. The first, *frequency,* measured the absolute amount of a mother's sensitivity in the specific activity. The second, *mean,* measured the average amount of her sensitivity. The third, *standard deviation,* measured the consistency of the sensitivity.

Judged by these measures, the mothers fell into four main groups or types.

> The mothers of group A were conspicuous for their ability to accommodate to the needs of their infants. By virtue of the kind of physical and emotional support they provided and the steadiness of their interest in and communicativeness toward their infants, they gave them freedom to move about, to vocalize, feed, rest or play with a minimum of interference. More regularly and with more ease than all the other mothers they recognized and tried to relieve passing discomforts in the infants. The mothers themselves were not without tension, but most of the time that tension appeared to heighten their intimacy with the infants.

> The mothers of group B were conspicuous for their conscious willingness to accommodate to their infants. At first glance some of their behavior resembled that of the A mothers, but on the whole they were more tense, less communicative and less steadily attentive. At times they tried more actively to stimulate their infants and at other times they were mildly distant or insensitive to the infants' immediate needs. The quality of satisfaction with the infant and of enjoyment of their mothering tasks, outstanding in the A mothers, was much less evident, although B mothers were generally positive toward their infants.

> The mothers of Group C were conspicuous for their lack of spontaneity and their intentions to be efficient above all else. Physically and socially they were detached from their infants. Some reduced their attention to the carrying out of a minimum of essential details of infant care, and showed a low degree of interest in any activity with the infant of a nonphysical nature.

> The mothers in group D were conspicuously active but also erratic in their attentiveness, efficiency and sensitivity. They quite sedulously governed their infants' actions by stimulating, restricting or instructing them, apparently hardly aware of the possible effects of their behavior on the infants' condition (pp. 265–266).

Thus, group A mothers were sensitive, consistent, and attentive. Group B mothers, as a rule, closely followed the group A pattern but fell short of the mark on each index; they were less sensitive, less consistent, and somewhat overactive or overattentive.   Group C mothers were insufficiently sensitive, moderately inconsistent, but adequately attentive, whereas the mothers in group D were hypersensitive, very inconsistent, and hyperactive.

Besides probing aspects of maternal behavior, the study sought to relate the behavior and activity patterns of the infants to it.   Few differences were found, generally speaking, among the four groups of infants either in level of activity or on scores obtained on Gesell Development Schedules.   Although some correlation appeared between maternal behavior and the developmental status of the infant, Brody concluded that the relationship might not be causal.   Innate differences among infants might easily have influenced the behaviors of the mothers.

Brody's study demonstrated, of course, that differences did exist among mothers in their behavior toward the infant.   If these differences are based on or are related to fundamental characteristics of attitude and personality in the mother which persist over the years, they may actually affect the child's development in ways as yet unknown.

Maternal Deprivation

This is a subject that has aroused much current interest and much controversy.[2]   Essentially, maternal deprivation is a circumstance in which an infant or young child does not have a relationship with his mother because of his separation from her.   If its importance were to be judged by the number of infants suffering from maternal deprivation, the issue would be relegated to oblivion.   However, both the issue itself and the findings on the effects of such deprivation on the child are relevant to many basic aspects of child development and the mother-child relationship.

Although few psychologists would argue against the useful and necessary functions performed by the mother in the infant's early years, the issue of maternal deprivation revolves about the long-range, debilitative repercussions on the infant separated from his mother.   Granted that every infant may need tender loving care, will deprivation of it scar him permanently?

The appearance of Ribble's *The Rights of Infants* in 1943, together

[2] For comprehensive reviews of the subject, see: Casler, L., Maternal deprivation: A critical review of the literature, *Monographs of the Society for Research in Child Development*, 1961, **26**, No. 2; and Yarrow, L. J., Maternal deprivation: toward an empirical and conceptual re-evaluation, *Psychological Bulletin*, 1961, **58**, 459–490.

with an essay by the same author (1944) heralded a new conception of the mother-infant relationship. As was evident in the excerpts from Ribble's book quoted earlier in the chapter, she conceived of the infant as incomplete and immature physiologically at birth and totally dependent on the mother's ministrations for survival.

When the umbilical cord is cut at birth, the child, as we have said, is far from being a complete and independent individual. The infant is peculiarly helpless, and it is not until after the faculties of speech and locomotion have developed that he can cope with any separation from the mother without danger. Mother and child after birth are psychologically still a unit, and close relationship is as important for early mental development as was the more primitive connection with the fetus for physiological development. As we have seen in the study of marasmus, interference with this natural relationship means that the infant starves for mothering, and as a result the vital activities, first of alimentation, then of breathing and circulation, get out of order, and we find the small body functioning much as it did before birth (Ribble, 1943, p. 12).

Having observed 600 infants, Ribble (1944) concluded that tension was seen to disappear when the infant was in physical contact with the mother, whereas separation produced anxiety. Ribble imputed a wide variety of infant reactions to inadequate mothering: negativism, refusal to suck, hypertension, vomiting, wild screaming, a stuporous sleep, diarrhea, and finally, marasmus.[3]

Much interest was stimulated by Ribble's contentions. Her position was strengthened in a series of articles by Spitz (1945; Spitz & Wolf, 1946) which described the deleterious effects of institutionalization on infants separated from their mothers. A sharp drop in developmental quotient, a high mortality rate, and the appearance of disturbed behavior occurred in a group of foundling-home infants in the final third of their first year (Spitz, 1945). These phenomena were ascribed to the absence of a mother-child relationship; in the foundling home the ratio of nurses to infants was one to eight. Spitz asserted that impairment of the mother-child relation for more than a three-month interval during the first year of life inflicted irreparable damage on the infant.

The terms used to describe infant reaction to the loss of maternal love and maternal stimulation are *hospitalism* and *anaclitic depression*. The principal symptoms of these syndromes are weepiness, withdrawal and lack of contact with the environment, refusal to act, and stupor. Take this case reported by Spitz:

[3] A disease, characterized by apathy and deterioration, said to be caused by an infant's separation from its mother.

White female.   Intelligent, friendly child who smiles easily and ecstatically at the approaching observer.   No notable event in the course of the first 7 months.   At this time a change occurred in the child.   The observers got the feeling that the child was apprehensive.   A week or two later the change was accentuated.   The temper of the child had become unequal.   She still was mostly friendly to the observer, but as often as not broke out crying when the observer approached closer.   After another two weeks she could no longer be approached.   No amount of persuasion helped.   Whenever approached she sat up and wailed.   Two weeks later, she would lie on her face, indifferent to the outside world, not interested in the other children living in the same room.   Only strong stimulation could get her out of her apathy.   She would then sit up and stare at the observer wide-eyed, a tragic expression on her face, silent.   She would not accept toys, in fact she withdrew from them into the farthest corner of her bed.   If the approach was pressed she would break into tears.   This went on until the child was 9 months old (Spitz & Wolf, 1946, p. 315).

Sharp criticism by Pinneau (1950, 1955) of the efforts of Ribble and Spitz induces one to question many of the effects of maternal deprivation which they postulated.   To cite one example of this criticism, Pinneau pointed out that the drop in development quotient described by Spitz occurred before, not after, the infants were separated completely from their mothers; thus it could not possibly be charged to this circumstance.

It is not within the scope of this book to examine at length all the studies that have confirmed or invalidated the Ribble-Spitz belief.   Yet certain lines of evidence of several key ideas help to clarify some of the basic matters at issue, of which the four main ones are consequences of institutionalization, the need for a single mother figure, deprivation of stimulation, and the contrast between long-range and short-range effects.

Institutionalization.   Unfortunately, many of the investigations into the impact of institutionalization are weak methodologically.   A number of important variables have not been controlled.   Some of those that must be considered are the age at which separation occurs, the nature of the mother-child relation prior to separation, the reason for the separation, and the quality and atmosphere of the institution.   Individual characteristics of the child must be considered also.   Schaffer (1966) has shown that inactive infants are affected more adversely than active ones by a deprivation experience.   The reduced vulnerability of active infants is due to their ability to maintain a state of alertness and to avoid perceptual monotony by initiating contact with new environmental stimuli.

If a separation occurs after the infant's first six months of life, any ill effects upon the child may result from the separation itself and the breaking of an affectional relationship rather than from the subsequent deprivation of a mother. Thus, a distinction must be made between separation and deprivation. To which of these are the ill effects being specifically attributed? Besides, if the child is separated at the mother's own instigation, the possibility must not be overlooked that the later harmful effects may stem from the mother's earlier rejection and neglect, and not from the actual separation and consequent deprivation.

Although the ratio of adults to children is low in most institutions, the percentage can vary widely, as can the amount and quality of care. In a study comparing maternal care between institutionalized and home-reared infants, Rheingold (1960) found that the latter group received 4.5 times more "caretaking," although differences between the two groups varied depending on the specific caretaking activity. For example, the home infants were shown affection 18 times more frequently than the institutionalized infants.

In addition to the sheer number of children assigned to each adult for care, one must also assess the quality of the care. Is affection shown by the nurse or attendant? How much stimulation do the infants receive from the caretakers? How much consistency exists in the handling of the infants? Then there are the physical characteristics of the surroundings. Are they drab and colorless? Are the infants deprived of visual and aural stimulation as well as the social and emotional stimulation of an adult? Nor can the length of institutionalization nor the ages at which it occurs be ignored in investigating the consequences.

In sum, the effects of institutionalization may result as much from a lack of emotional involvement in relations with other persons as from an insufficient amount of sensory stimulation. Having conducted research among lower organisms, Scott (1962) argued that "the speed of formation of a social board is dependent upon the degree of emotional arousal, irrespective of that arousal" (p. 951). The emotional chill that often pervades the general psychological atmosphere of institutions as well as the relationship between caretaker and child may hinder the development of normal social, affectional ties.

Single Mother Figure. Various kinds of "multiple mothering" would certainly argue against Ribble's belief in the need for an infant to enjoy a relationship with a single mother figure. As Margaret Mead (1935) has reported, the extended family is the prevailing pattern in many South Seas cultures. The responsibilities of child rearing are shared by many members of the community. Brothers, sisters, and other members of the larger family may assume several of the maternal functions. Yet no effects on personality adjustment and development comparable to those noted by Ribble and Spitz have been attributed to this type of child care.

In the communal nurseries established in many Israeli settlements today the children are cared for by more than one significant adult. Although the child spends most of his day in the nursery he often sees his parents for several hours each evening as well as on weekends. This is an example of what might be called "intermittent mothering." The *metapelet,* the trained caretaker of the children, performs most of the traditional functions of motherhood related to routine care and training of the child. Accounts of the daily contacts between the children and their natural mothers indicate a warm, permissive, and affectionate relationship. Perhaps such a separation of care and training from the "affectional" functions of the maternal role might reduce some of the ambivalent feelings of parents and children characteristic of traditional parent-child relationships.

Compared with Israeli children raised in their own homes, these children reared in the settlements, or kibbutzim, show few differences in personality and intellectual development. Either this sort of multiple mothering does not exert any deleterious influence on the development of personality or experiences occurring after early childhood nullify any potentially harmful effects. Possibly both are true.

One study (Rabin, 1958) found that 10-year-old boys reared in the kibbutzim showed less intense feelings of sibling rivalry than boys reared in another fashion. Although the topic at hand is maternal deprivation, this finding suggests that some of an individual's most intense, destructive emotional feelings emanate from the traditional family arrangement of Western culture. Sibling jealousies, parent-child hostilities, and other long-lasting conditions of like kind may emerge from this scheme. Support for this point comes from a fascinating report (Freud & Burlingame, 1943) on the nurseries provided for the children evacuated from war-gutted London. At one point artificial families were created in which four children were assigned to one nurse, or mother substitute, investing the relationship with some continuity and stability. Out of this arrangement flowered violent attachments, possessiveness, and anxiety resulting from fear of loss of the mother figure, and jealousies resembling sibling rivalry. There were also positive consequences in evidence. Thus the small family group, somewhat isolated, heavy on contact between its members, which symbolizes the family arrangement in Western society, may exert both negative and positive influence on the child's development of personality.

Stimulus Deprivation.   Few controlled experiments pertaining to lack of sensory stimulation have been conducted among children. Several have used adults as subjects, and even more have involved lower organisms. A kinesthetic need or drive in infancy has been postulated by Kulka, Fry, and Goldstein (1960). It is a need for incoming stimulation through a variety of modalities related to the senses: light, touch, pressure, and temperature. The infant obtains gratification of this kinesthetic need when an adult cuddles him, rocks him, or supplies similar soothing services. Severe early deprivation of this need may lead to apathy and inactivity, or rocking, banging of the head, and other rhythmic movements by the infant that may represent an attempt to satisfy this yearning for stimulation. Could it be that the infant often stops crying when rocked because his need for such stimulation is fulfilled?

Although research concerning the importance of early sensory stimulation in animals is not conclusive, it is clear that the quality, the intensity, and the timing (age at which stimulation is provided) of such stimulation can affect later behaviors, such as activity level and emotionality. An interesting study (Korner & Grobstein, 1966) with newborn infants showed that crying stopped when they were picked up and put to the shoulder, and that the infants then showed signs of alertness and visual scanning of the environment. These investigators concluded that tactile stimulation may activate visual behavior, thus providing the infant with more opportunities to explore the environment and to become acquainted with it. This conclusion was supported in a study by White and Castle (1964), which indicated that extra handling of newborn institutionalized infants increased their visual interest in the environment later.

In a typical experiment involving adults (Goldberger & Holt, 1958), volunteer college students were placed in isolation in a specially designed chamber that admitted only a minimum amount of stimulation, whether visual, aural, or tactile. During an eight-hour period or less in the chamber, these students manifested anxiety, decreases in complex reasoning, and hallucinations. They reported disturbances in their awareness of time, unpleasant emotional feelings, and a sense of intellectual disorganization. Clearly, a certain level of sensory stimulation appears to be necessary for adequate intellectual performance. This notion is supported by the isolation included in the brainwashing of American prisoners by the Chinese communists, which has apparently resulted in a variety of psychological repercussions.

Long-Range versus Short-Range Effects. Most of a series of papers by Goldfarb (1943a, b, c; 1945a, b; 1947; 1949) on the harmful long-range effects of early institutionalization dealt with a set of 15 children who entered an institution at about four-and-a-half months of age and remained there a little more than three years before placement in foster homes. These children were compared with a control group reared wholly in foster homes. When tested, they ranged from 10 to 14 years of age. Subjected to a number of personality and intelligence measures, the group that had experienced institutionalization showed itself to be inferior to the control children in many respects. Its members were apathetic, passive, fearful, apprehensive, less persistent, withdrawn, retarded in social maturity, and inferior in intelligence, language, vocabulary, and concept formation. Goldfarb concluded that the poorer adjustment of this group was caused by its early privation during institutionalization.

Although Goldfarb's studies have been criticized for their methodology, the possibility of some inferiority in language and on intelligence tests, insofar as the latter depend on language ability, seems reasonable. As observed in the chapter on language, the superiority of only children in this area stems from their extensive contact with adults. Whether the limited association of Goldfarb's institutionalized group with adults during the first three years of life could exert so long-range an effect on language development remains a matter of speculation. There is little in the literature to substantiate this view.

Two other studies take an opposite position. They suggest that any deleterious effects institutionalization may produce in children do not persist. Dennis and Najarian (1957) examined the development of infants and children in a Beirut, Lebanon, foundling home. At the institution a ratio of one to 10 prevailed between the caretaking staff and the children. Swaddling was employed until the infants reached about four months of age. Except for feeding and bathing the infant had very little contact with adults and was seldom taken out of his crib. From one to three years, the children spent most of the day in play groups of about 20 youngsters, with play equipment quite limited. At four kindergarten was provided.

Through tests administered to infants between two and 12 months of age and children between four-and-a-half and six years old, as well as to comparable control groups of noninstitutionalized Lebanese children, the investigators found the experimental infants markedly inferior to the control infants in the two- to 12-month range. However, among the four-and-a-half- to six-year-olds the institutionalized children were only slightly retarded in abilities measured. For the infants, the Cattell Infant Scale was used; for the children, the Goodenough Draw-A-Man Test, the Knox Cube Test, and the Porteus Maze Test were employed.

These investigators attribute the early retardation to lack of learning opportunities resulting from environmental restriction. But such privation did not seem to have lasting effects. It may be that the child gains from his peers the minimal amount of stimulation required for adequate development once he is able to behave actively toward his environment.

In a later study Sayegh and Dennis (1965) again found the institutionalized infants to be markedly retarded in early development. In order to test their earlier hypothesis that the retardation resulted from the insufficiency of learning opportunities provided the infants, a small group of infants was given an hour of supplementary experiences each day for a period of 15 days. The infants were placed in upright positions; their interest in objects was stimulated; and they were encouraged to develop skill in object manipulation. As compared with the controls, these experimental-group infants showed significant gains on the developmental test administered after the enrichment experience. These findings suggest that lack of appropriate stimulation retards early development, but this retardation can be remedied by providing enrichment experiences.

Experimental modification of the social environment of a group of institutionalized infants was tried by Rheingold (1956). For the typical institutional "multiple mothering" type of care, she substituted care by a single mother figure for a term of eight weeks, five days a week, seven-and-a-half hours per day. Each control and experimental group consisted of eight infants about six months old. Before the experiment, at weekly intervals during it, and for four weeks thereafter, a battery of tests, including a test of social responsiveness, tests of postural development and of cube manipulation, and the Cattell Infant Intelligence Scale, was administered to the infants. Because the experimental group of infants became more socially responsive than the control group, Rheingold concluded that the social behavior of infants could be modified by changes in their environment. Contrary to predictions, however, the experimental group did not perform significantly higher on the postural, cube, or Cattell tests.

A year later, 14 of the original 16 children were subjected to a similar set of tests (Rheingold & Bayley, 1959). Apart from the fact that more members of the experimental group engaged in vocal expression during the social tests, there were no statistically significant differences between the two groups. Although attentive mothering produced some differences in behavior during infancy, the differences did not endure, except perhaps in the area of verbal performance. One can only guess as to the effects of a longer period of "single mothering," in view of the failure of this study to show long-range consequences of a brief period during which social surroundings were modified.

Several writers have mentioned that taking a child away from its mother is most harmful in the second half of its first year; during the first six months of life the infant has not developed sufficiently in intellect to differentiate between strange and familiar faces or to be aware of changes of environment. In an extensive longitudinal study of the development of emotional attachment in infants, Schaffer and Emerson (1964) found that a phase of indiscriminate attachment is followed by a period of specific attachment in the third quarter of the first year. Fear of strangers was correlated with the onset of attachment behavior, suggesting that both are part of a developmental trend in emotional, intellectual, and perceptual behavior. Maternal deprivation after the first six months may be a matter of *separation* after an emotional bond has been established and as a result, harmful effects of perhaps long duration may appear in the emotional area.

SUMMARY

There are differences in the psychological environments into which infants are born. That such differences may not have long-range effects is because of the possibility that early parental attitudes toward the child may change in time, or because of the subsequent experiences of the child. From birth the various characteristics of the infant affect the mother's attitude toward him, so that from the very beginning the infant plays a part in creating his psychological environment. There is mutual interaction between parent and child.

The position one takes on the long-range effects of early experiences is determined in part by one's conception of the infant. Is he a passive recipient of environmental stimulation, impressionable, irreversibly affected by early events? Or does he react actively toward his environment, thus showing himself capable of resisting the long-term effects of traumatic experiences? Are single events crucial or is the repetitive pattern of events most influential?

Since Freudian theory emphasizes the importance of feeding and toilet training in affecting the child's development of personality, maternal practices in these areas were surveyed. The literature suggests that no long-range effects on the child's personality have resulted from the wide variation in maternal behavior in these two areas of early socialization. Since much maternal concern in the early years revolves about feeding and toilet training, these are important areas at the time, but their effects are of short-run significance for the child.

Maternal deprivation was examined at some length because of the light it casts on important elements in the early mother-child relation. Sensory deprivation seems to explain many of the harmful consequences of maternal deprivation. Attention from the mother is important because it provides the infant with a variety of stimuli.

REFERENCES

Adams, A. B. Choice of infant feeding technique as a function of maternal personality. *Journal of Consulting Psychology,* 1959, **23,** 143–146.

Anderson, J. E. Personality organization in children. *American Psychologist,* 1948, **3,** 409–416.

Bagby, E. The etiology of phobias. *Journal of Abnormal and Social Psychology,* 1922, **17,** 16–18.

Bayley, N. Research in child development: A longitudinal perspective. *Merrill-Palmer Quarterly,* 1965, **11,** 183–208.

Birns, B. Individual differences in human neonates' response to stimulation. *Child Development,* 1965, **30,** 249–256.

Brody, S. *Patterns of mothering: Maternal influences during infancy.* New York: International Universities Press, 1956.

Caldwell, B. M. Assessment of infant personality. *Merrill-Palmer Quarterly,* 1962, **8,** 71–81.

Caldwell, B. M. The effects of infant care. In M. L. Hoffman & L. W. Hoffman (Eds.), *Review of child development research.* Vol. I. New York: Russell Sage Foundation, 1964.

Dennis, W., & Najarian, P. Infant development under environmental handicap. *Psychological Monographs: General and Applied,* 1957, **71,** No. 7.

Durrett, M. Relationship of early infant regulation and later behavior in play interviews. *Child Development,* 1959, **30,** 211–216.

Escalona, S. K. Feeding disturbances in very young children. *American Journal of Orthopsychiatry,* 1945, **15,** 76–80.

Freud, A., & Burlingame, D. T. *War and children.* New York: Willard, 1943.

Fries, M. E. Mental hygiene in pregnancy, delivery, and the puerperium. *Mental Hygiene,* 1941, **25,** 221–236.

Goldberger, L., & Holt, R. R. Experimental interferences with reality contact (perceptual isolation): Method and group results. *Journal of Nervous and Mental Diseases,* 1958, **127,** 99–112.

Goldfarb, W. The effects of early institutional care on adolescent personality (graphic Rorschach data). *Child Development,* 1943, **14,** 213–223. (a)

Goldfarb, W. The effects of early institutional care on adolescent personality. *Journal of Experimental Education,* 1943, **12,** 106–129. (b)

Goldfarb, W. Infant rearing and problem behavior. *American Journal of Orthopsychiatry,* 1943, **13,** 249–265. (c)

Goldfarb, W. Effects of psychological deprivation in infancy and subsequent stimulation. *American Journal of Psychiatry,* 1945, **102,** 18–33. (a)

Goldfarb, W. Psychological privation in infancy and subsequent adjustment. *American Journal of Orthopsychiatry,* 1945, **15,** 247–255. (b)

Goldfarb, W. Variations in adolescent adjustment of institutionally-reared children. *American Journal of Orthopsychiatry,* 1947, **17,** 449–457.

Goldfarb, W. Rorschach test differences between family-reared, institution-reared, and schizophrenic children. *American Journal of Orthopsychiatry,* 1949, **19**, 624–633.

Heinstein, M. Behavioral correlates of breast-bottle regimes under varying parent-infant relationships. *Monographs of the Society for Research in Child Development,* 1963, **28**, No. 4.

Hetherington, E., & Brackbill, Y. Etiology and covariation of obstinacy, orderliness, and parsimony in young children. *Child Development,* 1963, **34**, 919–943.

Huschka, M. The child's response to coercive bowel training. *Psychosomatic Medicine,* 1942, **4**, 301–308.

Kagan, J., & Lewis, M. Studies of attention in the human infant. *Merrill-Palmer Quarterly,* 1965, **11**, 95–127.

Klatskin, E. H., Jackson, E. B., & Wilkin, L. C. The influence of degree of flexibility in maternal child care practices on early child behavior. *American Journal of Orthopsychiatry,* 1956, **26**, 79–93.

Korner, A., & Grobstein, R. Visual alertness as related to soothing in neonates: Implications for maternal stimulation and early deprivation. *Child Development,* 1966, **37**, 867–876.

Kral, V. A. Psychiatric observations under severe chronic stress. *American Journal of Psychiatry,* 1951, **108**, 185–192.

Kulka, A., Fry, C., & Goldstein, F. J. Kinesthetic needs in infancy. *American Journal of Orthopsychiatry,* 1960, **30**, 562–571.

LeMasters, E. E. Parenthood as crisis. *Marriage and Family Living,* 1957, **19**, 352–355.

Levy, D. M. *Maternal overprotection.* New York: Columbia University Press, 1943.

Lipton, E., & Steinschneider, A. Studies on the psychophysiology of infancy. *Merrill-Palmer Quarterly,* 1964, **10**, 103–117.

Mead, M. *Sex and temperament in three primitive societies.* New York: Mentor, 1935.

Peterson, C. H., & Spano, F. L. Breast feeding, maternal rejection, and child personality. *Character and Personality,* 1941, **10**, 62–66.

Pinneau, S. A critique on the articles by Margaret Ribble. *Child Development,* 1950, **21**, 203–228.

Pinneau, S. The infantile disorders of hospitalism and anaclitic depression. *Psychological Bulletin,* 1955, **52**, 429–452.

Rabin, A. I. Some psychosexual differences between kibbutz and nonkibbutz Israeli boys. *Journal of Projective Techniques,* 1958, **22**, 328–332.

Rheingold, H. L. The modification of social responsiveness in institutional babies. *Monographs of the Society for Research in Child Development,* 1956, **21**, No. 2.

Rheingold, H. L. The measurement of maternal care. *Child Development,* 1960, **31**, 565–575.

Rheingold, H. L., & Bayley, N. The later effects of an experimental modification of mothering. *Child Development,* 1959, **31**, 363–372.

Ribble, M. *The rights of infants.* New York: Columbia University Press, 1943.

Ribble, M. Infantile experience in relation to personality development. In J. McV. Hunt (Ed.), *Personality and behavior disorders.* New York: Ronald, 1944. Pp. 621–651.

Sayegh, Y., & Dennis, W. The effect of supplementary experiences upon the behavioral development of infants in institutions. *Child Development,* 1965, **36,** 81–90.

Schaefer, E. A circumplex model for maternal behavior. *Journal of Abnormal and Social Psychology,* 1959, **59,** 226–235.

Schaefer, E., & Bayley, N. Maternal behavior, child behavior, and their intercorrelations from infancy through adolescence. *Monographs of the Society for Research in Child Development,* 1963, **28,** No. 3.

Schaffer, H. Activity level as a constitutional determinant of infantile reaction to deprivation. *Child Development,* 1966, **37,** 595–602.

Schaffer, H., & Emerson, P. The development of social attachments in infancy. *Monographs of the Society for Research in Child Development,* 1964, **29,** No. 3.

Scott, J. P. Critical periods in behavioral development. *Science,* 1962, **138,** 949–958.

Sears, R. R., Maccoby, E. E., & Levin, H. *Patterns of childrearing.* Evanston, Ill.: Row, Peterson, 1957.

Sewell, W. H., & Mussen, P. H. The effect of feeding, weaning, and scheduling procedures on childhood adjustment and the formation of oral symptoms. *Child Development,* 1952, **23,** 185–191.

Sewell, W. H., Mussen, P. H., & Harris, C. W. Relationship among child training practices. *American Sociological Review,* 1955, **20,** 137–148.

Shulman, M. *Sleep till noon.* New York: Bantam Books, 1959.

Simsarian, F. P. Case histories of five thumbsucking children breast fed on unscheduled regimes, without limitation of nursing time. *Child Development,* 1947, **18,** 180–184.

Spitz, R. A. Hospitalism: An inquiry into the genesis of psychiatric conditions in early childhood. *Psychoanalytic Study of the Child,* 1945, **1,** 53–74; 1946, **2,** 113–117.

Spitz, R. A., & Wolf, K. Anaclitic depression. *Psychoanalytic Study of the Child,* 1946, **2,** 313–342.

Stevenson, I. Is the human personality more plastic in infancy and childhood? *American Journal of Psychiatry,* 1957, **114,** 152–161.

Sullivan, H. S. Conceptions of modern psychiatry. *Psychiatry,* 1940, **3,** 1–117.

Thomas, A., Chess, S., Birch, H., Hertzig, M., & Korn, S. *Behavioral individuality in early childhood.* New York: Universities Press, 1964.

Traisman, A. S., & Traisman, H. S. Thumb- and finger-sucking: A study of 2650 infants and children. *Journal of Pediatrics,* 1958, **53,** 566–572.

White, B., & Castle, P.   Visual exploratory behavior following postnatal handling of human infants.   *Perceptual and Motor Skills*, 1964, **18**, 497–502.

Yarrow, L.   Research in dimensions of early maternal care.   *Merrill-Palmer Quarterly*, 1963, **9**, 101–114.

Yarrow, L., & Goodwin, M.   Some conceptual issues in the study of mother-infant interaction.   *American Journal of Orthopsychiatry*, 1965, **35**, 473–481.

10

Family Influences on the Growing Child

The adult fills a variety of roles—father or mother, husband or wife, son or daughter, brother or sister, teacher, colleague, friend. For each of these roles, certain sets of behavior seem particularly appropriate. Thus the behaviors that characterize or typify any individual permit him to fulfill one role more suitably and more adequately than another. Similarly, an individual's personality fits him better for one role than for some other. To paraphrase Abraham Lincoln, all people can play some of these roles, some people can play all of these roles, but all people cannot play all of these roles with equal facility. How successfully any individual fills any one of them depends on the sum total of his characteristics and the requirements of the particular role.

Take parenthood. Western culture prescribes general requirements for the role of parent. The father must provide food, clothing, and shelter for his children—that is, economic support. He is also responsible for the children's behavior in public. Increasingly it is thought that the role of father includes emotional and psychological support for the children, too. What are some of the specific behaviors demanded of the modern, urban father beyond his occupational pursuits? He may accompany his son to the weekly cub scout meeting, mend a broken bat, punish his daughter for misbehavior, change the baby's diapers while the mother is shopping, attend a meeting of the P.T.A. to hear another daughter recite some verse, watch a two-year-old try to catch a bird, rush a child to the doctor to set a broken arm, arbitrate a battle between siblings, teach a four-year-old the proper form for cartwheels, or drive the baby-sitter home at two o'clock in the morning. This is merely a smattering of the behaviors performed by the typical father.

What of the mother? Society dictates that she provide physical care for the children—feed them, keep them healthy and, if possible, clean. She must comfort and console them when necessary and in general nurture them and provide emotional support. Long extolled by novelist and bard, the role of mother has been made almost impossible of fulfillment by the ordinary woman. Her feelings of inadequacy are matched only by her undying efforts. What, then, are some of the day-to-day behaviors demanded of her? A mother's typical day might begin—or end—with waking to give her infant a two o'clock feeding. Later she may urge a son to the breakfast table to spoonfeed him cereal or hurry him off to school, clean up spilled orange juice, diaper and bathe the baby, wipe a daughter's running nose, tend to another child's chicken pox, listen to a five-year-old's account of his day, drive another daughter to a music lesson, enjoy the two-year-old's
342

mimicry of his mother's household activities, or soothe a seven-year-old's broken heart because her best friend pushed her into the mud.

The young child depends totally on these parents who must be capable of meeting his needs. As the child grows older, the dependency on the parent lessens, so that father and mother must be able to relinquish some of the earlier control. Different behaviors and attitudes are required at different times; this is the price of parenthood. To say that some adults find the parental role more satisfying than others is to belabor the obvious. But how acceptable a woman finds the maternal role may indeed influence how adequately she performs it. As an individual, a parent possesses many psychological needs, most of which must be met if he is to be moderately well adjusted. However, if the demands of the parental role conflict or are incompatible with the needs of the parent as an individual, difficulties almost invariably ensue.

THE NATURE OF PARENT-CHILD RELATIONS

Although all human relationships are unique, those existing between parents and child possess certain characteristics that explain the tremendous and permanent impact of one upon the other. The intimacy and intensity of contact and the everyday interaction and interchange exist in an emotionally charged atmosphere. A child serves as a mirror to the parent, who sees reflected there his own childhood, his own unresolved and frequently long-term conflicts, and his own needs and aspirations.

The mutual interplay of psychological needs among family members creates a dynamic system such that a breakdown of any member affects the entire system. Clinical reports suggest that the family member who seeks psychological treatment often may be the one least in need of it. This indicates that the psychological disturbance of that individual reflects a more basic disturbance in the family system. Further, family-therapy case studies show that when the psychological symptoms are relieved for one family member, they frequently reappear, though perhaps in different form, in another member.

The phenomenon of child abuse illustrates vividly the emotional intensity of parent-child interaction. Recent professional and public concern with the "battered child syndrome" has revealed the startling extent of its occurrence. A 1962 study by the American Humane Society found 662 cases of child abuse reported in newspapers—and many, of course, are not reported. Most of the victims were under four years of age; most of the parents were young. The legal aspects of child abuse are multiple, with 47 states adopting statutes similar to the model law proposed by the United States Children's Bureau (Paulsen, 1966). But whatever the legal solutions to the problem may be, the psychological implications are indisputable. Frustrated and disturbed parents, unable to cope with the psychological, economic, and social problems facing them, discharge their hostility onto the young child, who may be a partial cause of the hostility. More important, however, the young child is a part of an ailing family system. Although child abuse is hardly new, its extent may represent in part modern society's failure to create the kinds of conditions that are conducive to the mental health of the individual, and that permit him to function successfully within the family system—at once a demanding and rewarding interpersonal network.

HOW THE PARENT BECOMES AS HE IS

Does parenthood require a certain kind of person? Perhaps to some extent it does. Parenthood involves a number of demands and behaviors: sacrifice, relating emotionally to a child, intense emotional rewards and perhaps disappointments, willingness to let a child be a child—all these and more.

At the human level there is little evidence for the existence of a "parental instinct" or even a "maternal instinct." Although there is a connection between hormonal secretion and lactation, for example, this in no way implies that maternal behavior and the various activities and functions it involves are a direct outgrowth of hormonal activity. A mother cannot rely on innate, "built-in" mechanisms to guide her maternal behavior. How, then, does she become the kind of mother she is? To what sources may we attribute her maternal behavior and attitudes? As noted in the previous chapter, current fads and fashions in child rearing and her individual personality structure influence her behavior as a parent. There is also *generational continuity*, the relationship between parent and offspring in the way in which each, in due turn, fills the parental role. An individual's own parents are probably the only persons he observes intimately in the parental role. Like it or not, they serve as the models for his own behavior as a parent, in addition to wielding an enormous influence on his personality development and adult character.

Several studies have looked into the similarity between parent and offspring in their handling of the parental role and into the influence of a person's own childhood and early attitudes toward parents on his own performance as a parent. In a study of four groups of parents—accepting, rejecting, dominating, and submissive—Symonds (1939) observed that the accepting type grew up in homes marked by good adjustment and acceptance. Dominating parents were dominated by their parents, whereas submissive parents enjoyed much freedom in their own childhood. A parent behaved just like his own parents and established a similar relation with his children; he repeated his early experiences in the home. More specifically, Symonds held, parents adopted an attitude toward their children that resembled the attitude taken toward them by the parent of the same sex.

Radke (1946) noted a tendency for parents to use disciplinary techniques similar to those remembered from their own childhood. And in Bronson, Kalten, and Livson's study (1959), mothers were inclined to exercise strong authority in their homes if they remembered their own mothers as having done so. A similar pattern was found among fathers; they emulated their paternal parent, but rather in the area of affectional relationship than of authority. Why in one area and not in others is a matter for speculation. Methodologically, both studies involved an individual's memory of his parents' practices and behaviors. Although an individual's perception and memory of parental treatment in childhood may have significance for his own behavior as a parent, it would be useful to have actual information of what happened years ago.

Attempting to trace the transmission of authority in the home from one generation to the next, Ingersoll (1948) defined the patterns in terms of leading or controlling the family activities. Four main patterns were discerned: *matricentric*—a pattern of authority in which the mother had the greater control; *patricentric*—the father exercised the greater control; *balanced*—fairly equal husband-wife control; and *intermediate*—lying midway between balance and control by either husband or wife. The parental backgrounds of second-generation couples were *homogamous* or *heterogamous*. In the former, husband and wife were reared in homes having the same prevailing pattern of authority, whether matricentric, patricentric, or balanced. In the heterogamous situation, husband and wife came from homes of opposing authority patterns. Among homogamous marriages, the patterns of parental authority tended to be reproduced. In heterogamous marriages, the patterns were modified to form a balanced compromise. Nevertheless, in all cases, the Ingersoll study found that there were exceptions to the dominant trends.

In a study of the backgrounds of a group of normal children, Harris (1959) noted that what had happened to the mothers "as children was happening to their own children; what happened to their parents was happening to them as parents" (p. 39). Four factors influenced this continuity. The first was the degree to which the mothers were aware of it: "Joan is just like I was at that age—flighty and unconcerned." The second was the degree to which they wished to see repeated the experiences of their own youth: "I want our children to enjoy the kind of summer outings which I loved as a child." The third was the degree to which the mothers were involved in the continuity of their childhood, wishing to assume similar roles of dependence or independence as adults, and the fourth was concern with their own unfulfilled childhood expectations: "I want to be a better mother to my children than my mother was to me."

The kind of continuity experienced by a mother with her own childhood affected the adjustment she made to the maternal role. Too rigid an adherence to the past or too much conflict with it created problems of dependability and understanding between a mother and her children. Three types of mothers were discerned: traditional mothers, rebellious mothers, and dependent mothers. The traditional mother was satisfied with her own mother's child-rearing tactics and attitudes, and used them as a reference point in raising her own family. The rebellious mother sought to be less controlling than her own mother, with whom she was dissatisfied because of excessive control, strictness, and interference. The children of such mothers tended to rebel against any rule interfering with their quest for pleasure. Indeed, there was some evidence that these mothers were endeavoring to work out their rebellious feelings against their own parent through their children. The third type, the dependent mother, was dissatisfied with her own mother because she thought she had not been accorded proper attention, love, or interest. Children of such mothers seemed to search for interpersonal warmth.

Not all the factors of continuity may operate at the conscious level, nor do they necessarily work directly on the child. Moreover, how a woman regards her husband may, in subtle ways, affect her children's attitude toward him. Thus, although parental behavior may not be inherited in a biological sense through the genes, it may be transmitted through the mechanisms of personality. Observations of mothers of problem children seen in clinics substantiate the notion that the "sins of the fathers are visited on the sons."

THREE PRINCIPAL PARENT VARIABLES

More important than how individuals model their behavior after perceptions of their parents' behavior is the influence parents exert on the adjustment and personality of their children, which determines the kind of adults and, in turn, the kind of parents they will be. A mother spanks her five-year-old son if he flaunts her command to obey instantly when an order is given.   Her choice of disciplinary tactic may be related to her belief or attitude that physical punishment is necessary when children do not submit readily to parental authority. This belief may emanate from her authoritarian personality structure, a vestige from her parents.   It is one of three main parent variables— parent behavior, parent attitudes, and parent personality.   Although it may seem obvious that the three variables are closely related—that is, a parent behaves toward his child in accord with his attitudes toward child rearing, which are an aspect of his personality structure relatively little research has been undertaken to find the nature of their relationships.   Several studies (Zunich, 1962; Brody, 1965) attempting to relate maternal attitude scores to actual maternal behavior with the child have met with little success, although some significant trends were observed. For example, Brody found that mothers scoring high in authoritarianism were more restrictive toward their children than mothers scoring low on this dimension.   Although this is what we would expect, assuming a relation between parent attitudes and parent behavior, the problems involved in assessing parent attitudes make research in this area extremely difficult.

Parent Personality

If personality is the sum of an individual's character traits, attitudes, and values, the personality of a parent may be expected to influence the personality development of his child.   Although not much is known about the precise operation of this influence, we can get some idea of how the parent's personality affects the atmosphere and emotional tone of the home and the child's development by categorizing parental personality as either healthy or neurotic.   In addition, there are many other aspects of personality that psychologists have described.

Behrens (1954) assessed the adjustment of a small group of children and related their ratings to the feeding, weaning, and toilet-training practices of their mothers.   Also, she rated each mother as a "total mother person," which signified the woman's character structure as reflected in how she fulfilled the maternal role.   Behrens found little consistency among the three child-rearing practices and no tie between ratings of children's behavior and their mothers' procedures.   There was, however, a close relation between child adjustment and "total mother person" ratings.   Apparently what a mother *is* bears more on child adjustment than what she *does*.   Actually, the Behrens study noted that the majority of mothers in the particular sample functioned reasonably well in specific child-rearing tasks, even though poorly adjusted themselves.

Various studies have sought to learn whether parental attitudes and parental behavior are tied in with parent personality. One factor analytic study (Becker, Peterson, Hellmer, Shoemaker, & Quay, 1959) found no close connection between parental behavior and personality as these affected problem behavior in children. But, inspired by publication of *The Authoritarian Personality* (Adorno, Frenkel-Brunswik, Levinson, & Sanford, 1950), considerable research has been undertaken to uncover the relation between authoritarian attitudes and personality structure. In the original investigation, the research team found persons having authoritarian attitudes to be rigid, inflexible, and concrete in their thinking, conforming and conventional in their values, excessive in their respect for authority, and prejudiced or ethnocentric in their view toward others who differed from them racially or in national origin.

Zuckerman and Oltean (1959), while studying maternal attitudes and characteristics of maternal personality, observed a correlation between scores of authoritarian–control on a standard parent attitude test and scores on the California F Scale, which measures authoritarian social attitudes. Presumably both authoritarian social and child-rearing attitudes reflect a basic tendency of personality. Significantly, these investigators found a relationship between the scores of mothers on a hostility–rejection scale and three measures of personality. Mothers who tended to be hostile and rejecting as parents as a rule had a high need for achievement, a similar need for aggression, but a low need to provide nurture. The study also indicated that hostility and rejection were related to psychopathological symptoms in the mother.

Another study (Block, 1955) endeavored to describe permissive and restrictive fathers from their scores on a child-rearing attitude scale. Assessment of 20 fathers in each group characterized those with permissive attitudes as self-reliant, ascendant, and rebellious toward persons in authority, whereas the restrictive set was seen as submissive, suggestible, conforming, indecisive, ineffectual, and overcontrolled. The latter group clearly possessed traits denoting an authoritarian personality. Generally, the permissive fathers were stable but flexible, demonstrating an optimal degree of integrated personality.

Clinical research has found that parents of children referred to child clinics score in a deviant direction on personality tests as compared with parents of normal children; however, attempts to differentiate parents of children in various diagnostic categories have been unsuccessful (Wolking, Dunteman, & Bailey, 1967).

Several studies (Morris & Nicholas, 1950; Phillips, 1951; Hanvik & Byrum, 1959) have noted similarities between parents and children in the nature of personality disturbances. One can only speculate about the origin of these similarities. Are they the result of the child's modeling his behavior after his parent's? Or is the parent's behavior toward the child dictated in part by his own unresolved psychological needs, which, in turn, produce like disturbances in the child? Parents, of course, are people whose own childhoods influence their adult personalities and behavior. Perhaps they project unmet needs and unsolved childhood problems onto their own children, as the following example illustrates.

> "Tom," age six, was referred because of enuresis, and this was the behavior which concerned the mother most. The interviews finally brought out that the mother had been enuretic until she began to menstruate, that ". . . people used to kid me about it." The mother recalled in this context that as a child she had been so afraid that she would wet the bed that she refused to go to bed at night, or when she did go to bed she would lie awake for long periods of time disturbed over possible bed-wetting (Phillips, 1951, p. 189).

Perhaps the personality of the parent may be more influential than his child-rearing practices in shaping the personality development of the child. The challenge for research is to ferret out the exact mechanisms through which parental personality affects the personality of the child.

Parent Attitudes

How the adult conceives of the parental role in relation to the child influences his attitudes as a parent. Does he see the parent's primary function as one of restricting and controlling child behavior? Does he view the socialization process as essentially a taming of the young child's uncivilized nature? Or does he regard the parental role as mainly one of guidance and setting the proper example for the child to emulate? The conception of the responsibilities, functions, and obligations of a role mold the individual's attitudes in the role which, in turn, presumably engender his behavior in it. The interest of the child psychologist in parental attitudes stems, therefore, from the notion that a basic, underlying attitude influences many behaviors of parenthood that are assumed to affect the personality development of the child.

"The essence of parent-child relations, it must be emphasized, lies more in how a parent *feels* than in what a parent *does*," Symonds (1949, p. xiii) remarked. In this respect Symonds's concern lay with parental attitudes *toward the child*. Subsequent research has also been concerned with attitudes *toward child rearing*.

The assessment of parent attitude poses a number of problems (Bell, 1958), most of them arising from attempts of psychologists to find a cause-and-effect relationship between these attitudes and child behavior. The first problem results from changes in parental attitudes.   It is extremely hazardous to maintain in the assessment of parent attitudes that certain ones *cause* particular child behaviors when the measurement is made *after* the appearance of the behavior.   One cannot know the attitude of the parent *before* the onset of the behavior, whether it be schizophrenia, stuttering, delinquency, or anything else.   More important, one must be aware of the possibility of changes in parent attitudes.   For example, a large percentage of parents can readily name the age level of children that they prefer and the level that they regard least endurable.   Since one age level is more satisfying and rewarding than another, it might be assumed that the parent-child relationship is most conducive at that period to healthy personality development in the child.   The following case study illuminates the point.

Billy was born after a labor of six and a half hours which Mrs. A. experienced as being much less painful than she had anticipated from the stories she had heard from her older sisters and friends.   From the very beginning in her handling of the baby—a boy—she was not only surprisingly technically skillful and competent but she seemed particularly responsive to clues from him related to his needs and had great success in making him comfortable and happy.   For example, by the time he was four days of age she was noting that he had particular objections to being wet, was able to change his diaper competently and was exceedingly pleased that she was able to comfort him.   In the first visit of the pediatrician to the home when Billy was three weeks of age a note was made that Mrs. A.'s way of comforting him, once she picked him up and once when she patted him in his bassinet seemed to be "all he needed and not more."

During the first nine to ten months she was described by all members of the research team who saw her as a particularly warm and skillful mother and the impression of unity and understanding between her and Billy was repeatedly commented upon.   This came up not only in relation to her ability to persuade Billy to respond as she wished him to in the areas of eating, sleeping and toileting, but also in the definite but indirect and subtle ways of prohibiting things of which she did not approve. It was noted, for example, that she interrupted the thumb sucking which she did not like not by pulling his thumb out, but by enticing him to become busy with something else—i.e., playing with her or with a toy. . . .   She seemed to set limits in a way that aroused a minimum of protest from the baby.   She anticipated no difficulty and seemed to feel perfectly sure that everything would go well between them. . . .

Some time must here be given to a description of Billy who showed surprising adaptability and smoothness in many of his physiological and maturational patterns from the beginning. As a newborn he was described as well developed, moderately active and mature. There was a specificity about his way of expressing this discomfort or wishes which seemed to make comforting him quite easy (i.e., not just by his mother but by others as well). One might say he gave clues which could easily be interpreted. His parents found him attractive, entertaining and easy to live with.

Thus those first nine to ten months gave us the impression of such an untroubled, conflict-free, mutually satisfying and stimulating mother-child relationship that the period of the "crisis" which became apparent during the tenth month was impossible to overlook. The first indication of this came on the occasion of Mrs. A.'s and Billy's visit to the clinic for his regularly scheduled checkup. It was both reported by Mrs. A. and observed that Billy was more difficult to dress. He did not "co-operate" in this as he had before and it looked as if his mother's usual ways of restraining him by distraction or touch could no longer control his drive toward activity. At this time he was creeping and cruising. He walked with two hands held. When his mother tried to hold him on her lap, he tried to get down. He was reaching out and scratching at her neck or face in a now provocative way and she was scolding him with a new sharpness in her tone. She looked more harassed and tired at that visit than the pediatrician had ever seen her and said about Billy, "I really work up a sweat trying to figure out what he wants now." She reported that Billy was now so active that he seemed to want to be down on the floor, out of his crib, or chair, or the previously satisfactory laps of his elders. She spoke with much more feeling than ever before about how much she wanted a "place of our own"—and added, "big families are nice in a way, but I'm tired of crowds." Such a move seemed impossible at that time as they had just bought a car which Mr. A. had to have for his work. At that point Billy would permit no one except his mother to feed him his meals and she was both pleased and irritated by this behavior. He also was making persistent grabs for the spoon during feeding and she found this annoying.

During the next three months she indicated her irritation at certain continuing aspects of her environment which had previously seemed less important to her. She complained about her husband's doing things for his mother. There was distinct displeasure expressed for the first time at Billy's enjoyment of his paternal grandmother, and the need to say, "but she [paternal grandmother] can't *really* take care of him" and an ever increasing determination to have a place of her own as soon as possible. She talked about Billy's behavior in a different way. For example, his activity and impatience with the lap were often spoken of as though they were primarily aimed at irritating her. His wish for certain objects to play with was seen as "everything he shouldn't have he wants." She was bothered by the fact that Billy could no longer be so easily persuaded to comply with her wishes. She summarized her difficulty in saying: "I can't figure him out any more."

Under the pressure of the dissatisfaction Mrs. A. returned to work and left the part-time care of the child to her sister. This does not mean that her relationship to B. had deteriorated, that she had become a "rejecting mother." The relationship has remained close, but has lost one impressive component—the full unity of mother and child. The relationship between mother and child now bears more resemblance to her relationship with other people. She is a woman who tries gently but firmly to dominate every situation. This is apparent in her relationship with her husband, and could be studied in some detail in her relationship with interviewer and pediatrician.

Retrospectively we find from this material that her reaction to the child's growing independence might have been anticipated, but we missed an even more significant clue. When the pediatrician discussed with her the giving of solid foods and in enumerating mentioned that he might not like the taste of some of them, Mrs. A. quickly responded, "Oh, he'll like spinach; I like it." What we saw in this was the unity; what we missed was the germ of discord since what she implied was that Billy was not thought of as having a taste of his own (Coleman, Kris, & Provence, 1953, pp. 30–33).

The second problem relates to the first. It is the impact on the parent's attitudes of the feedback provided by a certain kind of child. That children at birth differ in many ways is obvious and that these differences affect the parent's attitudes toward a child must be considered. Since parental attitudes condition the child's further development of personality, the point is especially important in relation to the effect of such attitudes on the personality growth of the handicapped, the chronically ill, or the extremely sensitive child. This brings up the matter of the "vicious circle" phenomenon which has such dreadfully harmful consequences for the youngster. Two examples will suffice. That a child's intellectual capacities are below his parents' expectations may first come to parental attention when the youngster experiences some difficulty in learning to read in the first grade, or when he is placed in a reading group that the parents consider beneath his level. The child must thus face the frustrations flowing from reading difficulties as well as the equally bitter torment of parental rejection. At a time when the child most needs parental acceptance and reassurance to bolster his self-confidence and sense of security, he is met with criticism and disapproval. This change in parental attitude only serves to handicap the child further in his efforts to improve his reading. Or, to cite the other example, perhaps for deep-seated reasons rooted in his own psychological past, a parent may find himself unable to accept fully one of his children. From this nonacceptance may emerge undesirable school behavior such as attention seeking. When the teacher or other school officer expresses concern over this behavior, the nonacceptance may increase. Here again the change in parental attitude may aggravate rather than ameliorate the child's disturbance.

Third among these problems is the necessity for identifying the attitudes of the parent toward a particular child. It is well known that an individual views each of his children differently. Not only does a parent's attitudes vary according to the age of the child but also, undoubtedly, on the basis of such factors as sex, intelligence, personality, and appearance.

The fourth problem is that the emphasis is psychological literature on the crucial significance of parental attitudes for child adjustment has made parents highly sensitive and defensive about revealing their attitudes. Tapping a parent's attitudes directly is no simple task. How difficult this may be through a paper-and-pencil test may be judged from the failure of the Parent Attitude Research Instrument (PARI) to distinguish among the attitudes of various groups of mothers. For example, the PARI cannot differentiate significantly between the attitudes of parents of well-adjusted and poorly adjusted first-grade children (Medinnus, 1961), nor among the attitudes of mothers of children with speech articulation problems, delayed speech development, or lack of speech (Moll & Darley, 1960), nor among mothers of asthmatic, chronically ill, or healthy children (Margolis, 1961).

Parent attitude testing has an extensive history. The PARI scale, consisting of 23 subscales that assess a variety of attitudes, is the most recently devised vehicle. Developed at the National Institute of Mental Health (Schaefer & Bell, 1955, 1958), it contains these subscales:

Encouraging verbalization	Fostering dependency
Seclusion of the mother	Breaking the will
Martyrdom	Fear of harming the baby
Marital conflict	Strictness
Irritability	Excluding outside influences
Deification	Suppression of aggression
Rejection of the homemaking role	Equalitarianism
Approval of activity	Avoidance of communication
Inconsiderateness of the husband	Suppression of sex
Ascendance of the mother	Intrusiveness
Comradeship and sharing	Acceleration of development
Dependency of the mother	

From the various attitude tests two dominant attitudes emerge. One is the pattern of authority in the home. The other is the acceptance of the child as an individual. This is what the findings of research have to say about each of them.

Authoritarian Attitudes. To understand fully the effects of a parent's authoritarian attitudes on the personality development of a child requires a knowledge of their source. Several possibilities have been raised: the personality structure of the individual, his own upbringing and his parents' pattern of authority, his conception of both parent and child roles. Regardless of the cause, an authoritarian attitude implies an emphasis on authority and a belief in the value and efficacy of an autocratic approach to child rearing. Control is pre-eminent. The parent is dominant, the child subordinate. Insufficient respect is shown for the youngster as an individual, for his rights, his wishes, and his individuality. Hoffman (1963) found some evidence for a relation between parental authoritarian attitudes and power-assertive behavior toward the child. A parent who attempts to control his child's behavior in a direct and physical way without using explanation or reasoning may be expressing a more general attitude of authoritarianism that pervades his social relations.

From this it would seem possible to predict that authoritarian parental attitudes would lead to a child who is submissive, lacking in security and independence, and who is, therefore, less popular with his companions. In general such predictions have been borne out by research (Read, 1945; Radke, 1946; Miles, 1946). Yet Radke discovered that children from autocratic homes were rated by preschool teachers as more likely to fight and quarrel with other children, as more inconsiderate of others, and as more insensitive to praise or blame than those from democratic homes. A child from a home in which the notion of power is highly important assumes a role similar to his parents' when he finds himself in a relatively permissive nursery-school environment. His behavior leads to belligerence, inconsiderateness, and consequently, to unpopularity.

In general, children of autocratic parents are seen as emotionally unstable. This may be ascribed to a number of reasons. The difference in approach between autocratic parents and more permissive teachers leads to uncertainty and confusion for the child. Having little opportunity for choice and decision in the home, the child finds the freedom of nursery school fearsome. Harsh paternal attitudes have also been seen to relate to personality problems of shyness and withdrawal and to conduct problems of truancy and stealing among kindergarteners (Peterson, Becker, Shoemaker, Luria, & Hellmer, 1961). Such attitudes are reflected in demands for instant and unquestioning obedience, in inability to tolerate the "annoyance value" of children, and in the preference for a quiet, cautious child rather than a noisy, daring one. A relation has been found between the authoritarian attitudes of mothers and their adolescent daughters, although low correlations were obtained between the authoritarian child-rearing practices of the mother and the daughter's authoritarian attitudes (Mosher & Mosher, 1965). This suggests that although the child-rearing practices employed in the home are not unimportant, certain attitudes may be transmitted fairly directly from parent to child.

While the above discussion paints a grim picture of the negative consequences for the child of parental authoritarianism, several qualifications must be added. First, the effect of certain parental attitudes may depend upon the age and sex of the child. Assertiveness in a five-year-old girl is less socially acceptable than assertive behavior in a fifth-grade boy. Second, within a given parent, various attitudes toward child rearing interact and modify each other, so that the combination of attitudes is more important than the effect of any single attitude. For example, one study of third- through sixth-grade boys (Hoffman, Rosen, & Lippitt, 1960) found that those who rated their parents high in coerciveness (extent of parental punishment) and high in granting autonomy (freedom from adult supervision) were high in academic performance, group leadership, and active friendliness. These boys tended also to be successful in influencing peers and high in popularity. Apparently parental coerciveness produces self-assertive needs in a young boy. Facilitated by parents' granting of autonomy, these needs find successful expression in academic achievement and in interpersonal assertiveness, a trait valued by the peer culture of boys.

Parental Acceptance-Rejection Attitudes. A 40-item scale specifically designed to measure parental acceptance of children (Porter, 1954) posited four traits in the accepting parent. He is a parent who (a) "Regards his child as a person with feelings and respects the child's right and need to express these feelings"; (b) "Values the unique makeup of his child and does what he can to foster that uniqueness within the limits of healthy personal and social adjustment"; (c) "Recognizes the child's need to differentiate and separate himself from his parents to become an autonomous individual"; and (d) "Loves his child unconditionally." However, the results obtained from relating parents' scores on the Porter scale to the adjustment of children have been negative (Burchinal, Hawkes, & Gardner, 1957; Burchinal, 1958a). No significant tie has been found between the two.

Because of the emphasis in Western culture on maternal love and the affectional obligations of motherhood, strong feelings of guilt arise in a parent who, for one reason or another, cannot fully accept his child. Any attempt to assess this sensitive area on an objective, paper-and-pencil level is therefore almost doomed to failure. What is needed is a subtle, disguised, projective-type instrument that does not arouse the parent's defense system. Psychologists have long shown concern over acceptance and rejection. Yet not much research has been directed toward creating an instrument for tapping these vital parental attitudes. Medinnus and Curtis (1963) defined maternal acceptance on the basis of the discrepancy between a mother's rating of her child on a series of traits and her description of how she wanted the child to measure up on them. A significant correlation was obtained between self-acceptance scores of a group of mothers and their acceptance of their children; this finding will be discussed in Chapter 14 on "individual appraisal." Presumably the psychological adage that one can accept others only to the extent that one first accepts oneself applies to the mother-child relationship.

There is undoubtedly a wide margin of safety in parent attitudes (Ausubel, 1958, p. 362). Only when they deviate markedly from the typical do these attitudes exert harmful influences on child adjustment. In such cases, it is more likely the attitudes toward the child, relative to acceptance or rejection, rather than toward child rearing that are significant.

Parent Behavior

From what has been seen of parent behaviors in Chapter 9, it is apparent that an isolated examination of them is not likely to bear much fruit. At this point in man's knowledge more is to be learned from exploring the characteristics that describe the *general* behavioral atmosphere of the home. Table 10-1 contains some of the principal parent characteristics identified over several decades of research activity.

Two characteristics recur throughout the studies; these are acceptance versus rejection and autonomy versus control, depicted in Figure 10-1. In theory, the psychological atmosphere of a home may fall into any of the four quadrants, each of which represents one of four general combinations: acceptance-autonomy, acceptance-control, rejection-autonomy, rejection-control.

Acceptance versus Rejection. The most significant aspect of the home is the warmth of the relationship between parent and child. Both the Pattern Study (Sears, Maccoby, & Levin, 1957) and the Fels research, to be considered presently, have maintained that warmth is the most crucial and pervasive factor affecting the child.

TABLE 10-1   Major Parent-Child Dimensions

Investigators		Psychological Dimensions
Symonds (1939)	Dimensions:	Acceptance-rejection
		Dominance-submission
Baldwin, Kalhorn, & Breese (1945)	Syndromes:	Democracy in the home
		Acceptance of child
		Indulgence
Baldwin, Kalhorn, & Breese (1949)	Clusters:	Warmth
		Adjustment
		Restrictiveness
		Clarity
		Interference
Roff * (1949)	Factors:	Concern for child
		Democratic guidance
		Permissiveness
		Parent-child harmony
		Sociability-adjustment of parents
		Activeness of home
		Nonreadiness of suggestion
Lorr & Jenkins † (1953)	Factors:	Dependence-encouraging
		Democracy of child training
		Organization and effectiveness of control
Milton ‡ (1958)	Factors:	Strictness or nonpermissiveness of parent behavior
		General family interaction or adjustment
		Warmth of the mother-child relationship
		Responsible child-training orientation
		Parents' attitude toward aggressiveness and punitiveness
Schaefer (1959)	Dimensions:	Autonomy-control
		Love-hostility

*Based on the Baldwin, Kalhorn, & Breese (1945) data.
†Based on the Baldwin, Kalhorn, & Breese (1945) data and Roff's (1949) factor analysis.
‡Based on the Pattern data (Sears, Maccoby, & Levin, 1957).

Symonds' Studies.   After a careful review of the literature, Symonds (1939) concluded that the matter of acceptance or rejection was one of the two most significant considerations in the home, the other being autonomy as opposed to control. Although it left much to be desired methodologically, since its findings were based on case histories compiled by Symonds' former students, the study was fruitful enough to warrant examination. These were some of the parent behaviors that served as evidence for acceptance or rejection according to the study:

Evidence for Acceptance	*Evidence for Rejection*
Participates with child in games, sports, hobbies, takes trips together, special vacations together, pals	No interest in child
	No time for child—neglect
	Unfavorable comparison with siblings
	Verbal punishment—nagging, scolding
Parents make rearing child their main job—devoted	Failure to support child
Interested in child's plans and ambitions	Criticism or blame of child
	Physical punishment or cruelty
Gives child loving care and protection	Turned out of home or threaten to place in an institution
Interested in school progress	Does not speak well of child
Demonstrative in affection	Ridicule
Speaks well of child	Child unwanted at birth
Wanted at birth	Suspicious of child's behavior
Child encouraged to bring friends home	Too much supervision
Parents worry when child is ill	Neglect health, clothes, training, etc.
Accepted as individual rather than as child	(pp. 60–61)
Child trusted	
Parents talk over plans with child	
Parents do not expect too much of child	
Parents give wise counseling and encouragement	
(pp. 62–63)	

Symonds sought to find differences in behavior between accepted and rejected children in order to discover the causes of such differences in the marital relations of the parents and in the parents' own childhood. In general, he noted that accepted children engaged predominantly in socially acceptable behavior, whereas rejected children manifested a number of unacceptable behaviors. Specifically, the behaviors characteristic of accepted children included good-naturedness, consideration of others, cheerfulness, interest in work, friendliness, cooperativeness, and

FIGURE 10-1 Two major psychological dimensions in the home.

emotional stability. Among rejected children, on the other hand, attention-getting behavior, tendency toward delinquency, and problems in school were evident. More important, however, than descriptions of behavioral differences between accepted and rejected children is the need to understand how parental acceptance and rejection produce them.

Symonds (1949) observed that an individual's attitudes toward himself grew out of the attitudes displayed toward him by his parents during childhood. A child who was rejected developed feelings of insecurity and inferiority because it seemed to him that if he were unworthy of parental love, he was evidently worthless. A low conception of the self resulted from a low view of the child by his parents.

Such rejection brings on attempts by the child to win parental affection. These efforts may take the form of various attention-getting behaviors: refusal to eat, refusal to talk, temper tantrums, bed wetting, and whining. If these tactics prove futile, two general types of behavior often result: the child becomes hostile and aggressive or withdrawn and submissive. Symonds pointed out that whereas rejection might lead to good social adjustment outside the home and to close identification with and attachment to one's peers, it more frequently resulted in more negative consequences—feelings of insecurity, inferiority, inadequacy, worthlessness, isolation, humiliation, and anxiety. Even though a number of childhood experiences might not exert long-range influences on the child, a persistent pattern of rejection might very well prove pervasive in its effect on the child's adult personality and adjustment.

In a later study Symonds (1949) examined a number of factors, conscious as well as unconscious, contributing to the parent's rejection of the child. Among the more obvious were the economic burden imposed by the youngster, the invasion of the parents' privacy and activities, the strain of childbirth and child care on the mother, the child's failure to meet parental expectations, and parental disappointment in the sex of the child. Symonds maintained that some children are easier to accept than others; the child who is easiest to accept is the one most likely to be accepted by his parents. In this respect, the characteristics of the child definitely figure in the degree to which he receives parental acceptance.

Six elements, in particular, play an unconscious part in parental rejection, Symonds believed. First, the pattern of rejection adopted by a parent might be similar to the one experienced in his own childhood. Second, the parent might kindle in the child the hostility he felt toward his own parents. Third, one parent might show hostility toward the child as a means of injuring the other parent. Fourth, the parent might transfuse into the child the hostility he felt toward one of his own siblings. Fifth, he might implant in the child some of the feelings of hostility and rejection that he feels toward himself. Sixth, a mother—or a father, for that matter—might be so immature and narcissistic as to be unable to love another person wholeheartedly, and the resultant guilt might cause her to reject the child.

Maternal behavior toward the child on the love-hostility dimension has been found to be quite consistent over time (Schaefer & Bayley, 1963). This consistency may reflect a basic aspect of the mother's personality. Maternal hostility appears to be related to the woman's emotional maladjustment, to poor relations with her husband, and to environmental stresses and frustrations.

Fels Studies. Let us now explore parental acceptance as seen in the Fels studies (Baldwin, Kalhorn, & Breese, 1945). The Fels Research Institute has dealt largely with the scientific collection of data on the home environment. To quantify these data obtained from direct observation and interviews with mothers, the Institute devised a series of rating scales. The theory underlying the choice of areas for study and the rationale behind the assessment procedure have been described in detail by Champney (1941a, b). The Institute's directors assumed that the parent behaved consistently in certain ways toward the child from situation to situation, thus providing the child with an environment for learning from which he could develop social habits and form his personality. Figure 10-2 represents one of the 30 scales in the Fels set.

One syndrome, or cluster of variables, to emerge in the Fels studies from an examination of the interrelationships among the 30 scales was labeled "Acceptance of the Child." Scales fitting into this cluster included rapport with child, affectionateness toward child, direction of criticism (approval), effectiveness of policy, acceptance of child, child-

FELS PARENT BEHAVIOR RATING SCALE NO. 7.2

Serial Sheet No.

Acceptance of Child
(Devotion—Rejection)

1	2	3	4	5	6	7	8	9	10	Number
										Period of observation
										Ratee
										Age in
										Months at End of Period
										Child

Rate the parent's acceptance of the child into his own inner circle of loyalty and devotion. Does the parent act in such a way as to indicate that the child is considered an intimate and inseparable partner? Or does the parent act as though he resents the child's intrusion and rejects the child's bid for a place in his primary area of devotion?

Consider all evidence which in any way may impinge upon the child as acceptance-rejection, however subtle, vague, or indirect. It is not the parent's true feeling, but his <u>attitude</u>, as a functioning unit in the child's environment, which we are rating.

— Parent's behavior toward child connotes utter devotion and acceptance into his innermost self, without stint or suggestion of holding back in any phase of his life.

— Parent clearly accepts child. Includes child in family councils, trips, affection, even when it is difficult or represents considerable sacrifice.

— A "Charter member" of the family but "kept in his place". Parent accepts child in general, but excludes him from certain phases of parent's life.

— Tacit acceptance. Excludes child so frequently that to the child the rejection attitude may seem to predominate even though parent takes acceptance for granted.

— Parent's predominant tendency is to avoid, repulse, and exclude the child, but without open rejection.

— Child openly resented and rejected by parent. Never admitted to inner circle. Made to feel unwanted, ostracized.

										Score
										Tolerance
										Range
1	2	3	4	5	6	7	8	9	10	Number

Rater: Date of Rating:

Scored by: Date:
Checked by: Date:
Tabulated by: Date:

Rater's Remarks: (continue on back of sheet)

FIGURE 10-2

centeredness of the home, and nondisciplinary friction. Two other syndromes, "Democracy in the Home" and "Indulgence," also appeared. Thus a home might be classified into one of a variety of possible combinations of the three. An acceptant home might be indulgent, democratic, or both.

Generally, the studies found the acceptant home warm, granting unconditional acceptance of the child, and characterized by a relatively noncoercive policy of child rearing. Rejecting homes, on the other hand, fell into two types: nonchalant and actively rejecting. In the nonchalant home, the child was largely ignored but punished severely for infractions or disturbances. In the actively rejecting home, autocratic control required the child's constant compliance, thus reducing the chance of disturbance. Aggressiveness typified the parent's relationship with his child in both types of rejection; he was expressing his hostility toward the child.

In these studies the investigators sought to establish a link between the atmosphere in the home and the child's behavior in nursery school and later in grade school. Children were observed both in preschool and school settings, and were rated on a variety of child behaviors. In emotional traits, the actively rejected preschool children were characterized by high emotionality and low emotional control (Baldwin, 1949). They showed a certain amount of resistance to adults, but were more active physically than accepted children. Indulged children were high in both friendliness and quarrelsomeness with other children. At school age, indulged children seemed shyer and less sociable than during preschool years, whereas rejected children showed a marked increase in quarrelsomeness and a great deal of sibling hostility. Although much of the difference between the two types had disappeared by the time all of them had reached school age, the rejected children still showed themselves to be more energetic.

The Pattern Study. One of the scales used in the Pattern Study for rating extensive interviews with mothers was labeled "Mother's Rejection of the Child." From the mother's report, the investigators endeavored also to evaluate the father on his degree of acceptance or rejection of the child. Acceptance was defined as the giving of love without reservation, whereas rejection meant a withholding of love. Of the interviews assessed in this area, 220 mothers showed no rejection of the child and 101 were thought to indicate some rejection. The majority of these 101 instances, however, were closer to the acceptance end of the scale than the rejection end. As to the fathers only 47 were judged to evince some rejection.

Acceptance or rejection was seen to influence several child behaviors. First of all, children experiencing some rejection tended to show more dependent behavior than accepted youngsters. Acceptance, it would seem, promotes the wholesome development of independent behavior and of independence. The rejected child, far less secure in his relationship with his parents, needs their constant reassurance of willingness to nurture him. Thus a continuing need for dependency in a child might very well reflect a lack of dependability on the part of his parents. Second, rejected children were slightly retarded in the development of conscience. Third, how much or how little a child adopted his parents' standards and values depended in part on the warmth and acceptance they accorded him.

Because indulgence and /overprotection would seem to contain elements of both acceptance and rejection, they are pertinent to this discussion. Certainly these parental behaviors cannot be thought of as representing the extreme of acceptance. Yet their influence on the child suggests otherwise. In a classic study of maternal overprotection, in which he dwelt on 20 cases of "pure" overprotection of 19 boys and one girl, Levy (1943) pointed to four aspects of excessive maternal care in their mothers. One was *excessive contact;* "the mother is always there." Another was *infantilization;* "she still treats him like a baby." A third was *preventing independent behavior;* "she won't let him grow up" or "she won't take any risks." The fourth was *lack or excess of maternal control;* the mother may either dominate or be dominated by the child.

A number of factors in the personalities and backgrounds of the parents of these overprotected children seemed related to the overprotection. For some of the mothers there was a prolonged period of anticipation of childbearing. In other cases there were spontaneous abortions, stillbirths, and long periods of sterility. Still others experienced marital dissatisfaction and sexual incompatibility. Apparently many mothers sought to compensate for an unhappy marital relationship by establishing an intimate bond with their sons.

Incompatibility seemed to extend to social activities. The parents enjoyed little social life in common. Many of the mothers withdrew from nearly all outside social contact. Throughout the backgrounds of these overprotecting mothers ran a common thread of a lack of maternal love. The term used by Levy to describe the need in an individual that stemmed from lack of parental love involving affection, security, sympathy, and recognition was *"affect hunger."* It was as though these women attempted to satisfy their strong need for affection by maneuvering the child into an intimate affectional relationship in which he was somewhat isolated from other contacts. Yet these overprotecting mothers were, in general, responsible, stable, aggressive women who possessed strong maternal tendencies. Frequently their ambitions for education or for a career had been thwarted. The fathers of the children were seen as good providers, stable, but submissive, playing little or no authoritative role in relation to the child. They were ineffectual in counteracting the overprotective influence of the mother.

What about the children? How did they fare from overprotection? Those who, due to lack of maternal control, dominated their mothers were ill adapted to classroom discipline and reacted poorly to the authority of the teacher. However, the classroom behavior of overprotected children generally contrasted markedly with behavior at home. In achievement, they demonstrated relatively high success in language and showed special interest in reading, although they often fared poorly in arithmetic. Moreover, these children were restricted in contacts with agemates. Evidently because of the great impact of the overprotective relationship on their social life, they experienced difficulty in making friends or in having friendly relationships with peers.

Some overprotected children behaved rebelliously, aggressively, defiantly, and tyrannically toward mothers who were submissive toward them. They were disobedient, impudent, excessively demanding, and prone to temper tantrums. They were selfish and undisciplined. Others who were dominated by their mothers were, on the other hand, submissive and dependent.

Later, however, the behavior of both groups of overprotected children was better on the whole than might have been expected from their deviant early relationship with their mother. Attributable as this may be in part to the countering effect of peers and school, it may also indicate that overprotection is far less deleterious than rejection in the long run. At least the child develops a sense of self-worth when overprotected.

In the Schaefer and Bayley (1963) study, also discussed in Chapter 9, the love-hostility dimension included the following variables: Positive mother-child relationship, Equalitarianism, Expression of affection, Positive evaluation of the child, and Emotional involvement, as opposed to Ignoring, Punitiveness, Irritability, and Use of fear to control. The following scale for ignoring illustrates the manner in which the maternal behavior data were rated.

Does the mother ignore or reject her child?

1. Does she often comment on how much extra work or trouble the child is?
2. Does she tend to "leave the situation" during the examination as though she is glad the baby is in someone else's hands?
3. Would she be willing to have others assume most of the responsibility for care of the child?

4. Does the mother seem to know very little about the child?

5. Does she tend to overlook the needs of the child?

6. Does she give the impression that the child is not necessarily her principal interest?

7. Does she fail to show much beyond polite interest in the child during the examination?

(Schaefer & Bayley, 1963, p. 17)

Between the ages of 27 and 96 months the love-hostility dimension showed significant relations with ratings of boys' friendliness, cooperativeness, attentiveness, and facility. Moreover, the magnitude of these correlations increased throughout this age period, suggesting a cumulative effect of maternal love versus hostility on the behavior of boys. Again for boys, this dimension was significantly related to positive, task-oriented behaviors between the ages of 9 and 12, and at adolescence it was related to the sons' maladjustment.

Although the love versus hostility maternal ratings showed correlations with daughters' behavior, these were not so clear-cut as for boys, except during the adolescent period. At this age level maternal hostility and maladjustment were related to maladjustment in girls.

Erikson (1950) spoke of the necessity for a child to develop a sense of basic trust in his relationship with his parents; this is a requirement for development of a healthy personality. From this basic trust in parents stems a basic trust in the world, in the universe, in other people, and, most of all, in oneself. With this comes a sense of security, of self-acceptance, and it all goes back to early acceptance by parents. Much of the behavior of rejected children probably can be charged to a lack of a secure feeling and a lack of self-acceptance. Such children are hostile and aggressive, striking out at an unfriendly world. Seeking the affection and acceptance they need, they are often unsuccessful in their quest; a rejected child fails to understand others because he has never been understood himself.

Parental rejection, then, may have pervasive, long-range, harmful implications for the child's personality. Lack of parental acceptance seemed to constitute an important factor in the poor adjustment of certain first-grade children (Medinnus, 1961). Bandura and Walters (1959) maintained that the failure to satisfy the child's needs for dependency in early years contributed significantly to the development of aggressive behavior in adolescence.

Autonomy versus Control. The other important aspect of the psychological atmosphere in the home is the extent to which parents restrict the child's behavior or give him autonomy and freedom.

Symonds' Studies. Returning to Symonds' (1939) early study, these were some of the characteristics that described the behavior of dominant parents. They insisted on complete obedience. They supervised the child closely in the youngster's choice of activities. They provided too much supervision. They trained the child carefully. They expressed concern over trifles and criticized the child. Submissive parents, on the other hand, let the child have his own way. They could not control the child. They employed lax, inconsistent discipline and allowed the child to upset the home routine.

Although fathers satisfied many of their personality needs outside of the family, mothers were especially likely to fulfill their needs for dominance or submission by controlling or letting themselves be controlled by their children, Symonds noted. This finding supports the widespread notion that mothers exert a greater influence on the child than the father. The primary obligation of the mother's role is rearing the children, whereas occupational success and economic support of the family are important aspects of the father's role. Small wonder, therefore, that the mother may be more emotionally involved than the father in the end result of the child-rearing techniques used. Failure may cast a dark shadow over the mother's feelings of competence and adequacy. The father, however, can compensate for any deficiency as a parent with success in his job and the recognition it achieves. Whereas several recent investigations (Becker et al., 1959; Peterson et al., 1959) suggested that the father's attitudes and behaviors were as intimately connected as those of the mother to the development of problem behavior in the child, this finding might reflect an increased paternal participation and involvement in child rearing. It further signifies that the father's role is an important one in contemporary, urban, somewhat isolated psychologically, small-sized, child-oriented families.

Symonds found differentiation in a number of behaviors between children of dominating parents and those of submissive parents. The former were better socialized as a rule; their behavior was more acceptable, more conforming to the group. They seemed to be more interested in school work. Yet they tended to be sensitive, shy, self-conscious, seclusive, retiring, and submissive as compared with children who were given more freedom by their parents. The children of submissive parents inclined toward disobedience, irresponsibility, lack of interest in school, stubbornness, and defiance of authority. They were able, however, to express themselves effectively.

As to personality, the dominated children were more likely to be courteous, loyal, honest, polite, and dependable, albeit submissive and docile. The children of submissive parents were aggressive, disrespectful, and antagonistic, although independent and self-confident.

Fels Studies. In the Fels projects the scales fitting the syndrome "Democracy in the Home" included justification of policy, democracy of policy, noncoerciveness of suggestion, readiness of explanation, direction of criticism (approval), clarity of policy, understanding of the child, and nonrestrictiveness of regulation. Figure 10-3 contains the democracy of policy scale. From the scale's descriptive phrases it is apparent that the principal criterion of democracy is the practice of consulting the child in family decisions, giving him a voice in the policy of the home. In the autocratic or dictatorial home all decisions are made by the parents, with the child accorded little participation or choice.

Rejection often shows itself in an autocratic home, but this is not invariably the case. Some parents adopt an autocratic method because they feel this is the most desirable manner of training and rearing children. Undoubtedly the parent's personality and his conception of child nature both influence the choice of a nondemocratic approach. This choice may be a matter of expediency or of policy. Similarly, a democratic approach to child rearing may reflect an intellectual policy of the parent, who may be trying to follow the latest "expert" advice, or it may flow from a warm, accepting, understanding relation between parent and child. Thus, there is the scientific, intellectual democratic home and the warm democratic home. To the Fels researchers the latter type was the ideal home for the development of a healthy personality in the child.

The Fels group concluded that democratic parents were more likely to be better educated and more intelligent than autocratic ones. However, education was not the only element involved in producing democracy. Objectivity and emotional maturity in the parent were also involved. The parent unable to separate himself psychologically from his child could not, by the very nature of the relationship, be truly democratic.

Many child characteristics were found in the Fels studies to be linked to the presence of democracy in the home. First, as compared with other types of home atmosphere, the democratic seemed most conducive to intellectual growth. The children from such homes showed increases in IQ over a period of time (Baldwin, Kalhorn, & Breese, 1945). A democratic environment not only permitted greater freedom but also often encouraged exploration and experimentation. Restriction was at a minimum.

FELS PARENT BEHAVIOR RATING SCALE NO. 3.15

Democracy of Regulation and Enforcement Policy (Democratic–Dictatorial)

Serial Sheet No.

1	2	3	4	5	6	7	8	9	10	Number
										Period of observation
										Ratee
										Age in Months at End of Period
										Child

Rate the parent's tendency to share with the child the formulation of regulations for the child's conduct. Does the parent give the child a voice in determining what the policy shall be? Or does the parent hand down the established policy from above?

Disregard immediate issues not covered by policy (See Coerciveness of Suggestion). Rate independent of justification of policy to child, and independent of restrictiveness of regulations. Include both overt consulting with child and considering child's expressed wishes. Dictatorial policies may be wise or foolish, benevolent or selfish.

Endures much inconvenience and some risk to child's welfare in giving child large share in policy forming. Consults with child in formulating policies whenever possible.

Attempts to adjust policies to child's wishes wherever practicable. Often consults child.

Deliberately democratic in certain safe or trivial matters, but dictates when there is a sharp conflict between child's wishes and other essential requirements.

Neither democratic nor dictatorial, deliberately. Follows most practical or easiest course in most cases.

Tends to be rather dictatorial but usually gives benevolent consideration to child's desires. Seldom consults child.

Dictatorial in most matters, but accedes to child's wishes occasionally when they do not conflict with own convenience or standards.

Dictates policies without regard to child's wishes. Never consults child when setting up regulations.

										Score	Rater:	Date of Rating:
										Tolerance	Scored by:	Date:
										Range	Checked by:	Date:
1	2	3	4	5	6	7	8	9	10	Number	Tabulated by:	Date:

Rater's Remarks: (continue on back of sheet)

FIGURE 10-3

On such intellectual variables as planfulness, curiosity, and originality the democratically raised children rated high. At the nursery school these youngsters were active, aggressive, fearless, likely to be leaders, somewhat cruel, nonconformist, and disobedient (Baldwin, 1948). Although strict control in the home tended to reduce disobedience, quarrelsomeness, and negativism, it also decreased fearlessness, planfulness, tenacity, and aggressiveness. Taken together, these qualities seemed to describe a well-behaved child but one subject to constricted personality.

Perhaps autonomy is not too different from acceptance in influencing child behavior. Both recognize the individuality of the child. Democracy, of course, the environmental condition for autonomy, takes special note of children's need for activity and exploration.

It is apparent from both the Fels data and the Symonds findings that a certain type of home atmosphere may produce both "good" and "bad"—that is, desirable and undesirable—behavior in the child. Should child psychology ever reach the point at which it could accurately predict the exact behaviors to be expected from any single type of home environment, the kind of child produced would still depend on personal preference and individual value judgment. Some parents prefer a well-behaved child at the price of originality and curiosity. Others would be willing to have a child who is somewhat rebellious and nonconformist but who shows inquisitiveness and inventiveness. Child psychology cannot make these decisions. Individuals must make them on the basis of the kind of society they want.

Finally, there is the question of permissiveness. Perhaps no other word is so misunderstood, so badly abused, and so maligned. Thus it becomes difficult to formulate a clear definition of the term. Perhaps permissiveness might be considered as deriving from permit; if so, it implies that permissive parents allow their children to engage in a certain range of behaviors and make certain decisions appropriate to their capabilities. Permissiveness should not be understood to mean that a parent allows a child to do anything the child pleases; this is not permissiveness but license, a *laissez-faire* approach to child rearing. Once this distinction has been made, the situation becomes more understandable. Complete abdication of parental control and responsibility suggests indifference, neglect, and rejection of the parent role. This is *not* permissiveness.

The Pattern Study. This study considered permissiveness versus strictness and used the following scales to describe maternal child-rearing practices in this area:

1. High restrictions on play in the house and with furniture.
2. High demands for good table manners.
3. High restriction on making noise.
4. High demands for being neat and orderly.
5. Severe toilet training.
6. High standards for strict obedience.
7. Strong emphasis on doing well in school.
8. Strict and rejective response to dependency.
9. High use of physical punishment.
10. Severe punishment for aggression toward parents.
11. Low permissiveness for aggression toward parents.
12. Low permissiveness for aggression among siblings.
13. Low permissiveness for aggression to other children.
14. Low permissiveness for nudity or immodesty.
15. Low permissiveness for masturbation.
16. Low permissiveness for sex play with other children.

(Sears, Maccoby, & Levin, 1957, p. 472)

The moderate interrelation of these scales suggests a consistency in a mother's behavior with respect to strictness or permissiveness. The authors of the Pattern Study spoke of a particular trait underlying a mother's use of permissive practices. One mother seemed to be fairly consistent in her tolerance of her child's *child* behavior—that is, his aggressiveness, his noisiness, his sex impulses—whereas another tended through punitive means to try to put an end to such behavior.

The autonomy-control dimension in the Schaefer and Bayley (1963) analysis was defined in terms of the following scales: Autonomy, Strictness, Social isolation of the child, Wish to control the child, Intrusiveness, Excessive contact, and Fostering dependency. Although the correlations between this maternal behavior dimension and child behaviors were neither as significant nor as numerous as with the love-hostility dimension, some interesting relations were identified. At the 9- to 12-year level, autonomy is negatively related to a boy's ratings of friendly, cooperative, interested, and exerts effort, suggesting that a close relation with the mother contributes to certain positive behaviors in boys. An excessive amount of autonomy may well limit the degree of parental influence on the child.

At adolescence high maternal control combined with hostility is related to maladjustment in daughters, as defined by a cluster of traits including defiant, hostile, sulky, discontented, and gloomy.

In general, in the Schaefer and Bayley study the autonomy-control dimension showed less consistency over time than the love-hostility one. Several explanations appear plausible. First, the growing independence of the child requires that he be granted an increasing amount of autonomy. Second, this dimension may be less a reflection of the basic personality structure of the parent and more a product of his intellectual view of the parent role. And this view undoubtedly is modified in a variety of ways, including the individual's experience as a parent, the changing needs of the child, and changing expert opinion, as well as discussion with friends regarding problems involved in child rearing.

Present Status of Autonomy-Control Dimension. Traditionally couched in democratic-autocratic terms, this dimension has received far more attention than the love-hostility dimension. In part this is because this aspect of child rearing is easier for parents to discuss on an intellectual level, whereas parental acceptance or rejection of a child is a deeply emotional area. Another reason for study of authoritarian approaches to child rearing may be that such approaches are thought to reflect more general authoritarian attitudes, which have broad political overtones. The disproportionate attention given the autonomy-control dimension is particularly interesting in view of the Schaefer and Bayley data described above, which show much greater effect on the child of maternal acceptance or rejection.

Shifting trends in child rearing advice by experts have been discussed in Chapter 7. The rigid, autocratic Watsonian approach of the 1930's gave way to the permissiveness of the 1940's and early 1950's. Anything smacking of authoritarianism or structure was derogated as alien to our democratic way of life and to the needs of the child. Excesses became apparent, and in some cases, total self-regulation on the part of the child was advocated.

Although it is difficult to determine the predominant philosophy of child rearing in the United States today, there are many signs to indicate that the pendulum is swinging back in the direction of a firmer approach. Perhaps the most noteworthy indication of this trend is an exciting discussion by Baumrind (1966) in which, in addition to permissive and authoritarian, a third approach called "authoritative," is described:

> The authoritative parent attempts to direct the child's activities in a rational, issue-oriented manner. She encourages verbal give and take, shares with the child the reasoning behind her policy, and solicits his objections when he refuses to conform. Both autonomous self-will and disciplined conformity are valued by the authoritative parent. Therefore, she exerts firm control at points of parent-child divergence, but does not hem the child in with restrictions. She enforces her own perspective

as an adult, but recognizes the child's individual interests and special ways. The authoritative parent affirms the child's present qualities, but also sets standards for future conduct. She uses reason, power, and shaping by regime and reinforcement to achieve her objectives and does not base her decisions on group consensus or the individual child's desires (Baumrind, 1966, p. 891).

Baumrind examined eight commonly held propositions with regard to authoritarianism versus permissiveness in the light of research evidence. Several of these will be dealt with briefly.

Much has been written about the harmful effects of punishment. However, most of this concern has been with severe punishment, frequently administered in a context of a poor parent-child relationship. Mild punishment, however, may have beneficial effects:

> (a) more rapid re-establishment of affectional involvement on both sides following emotional release, (b) high resistance to similar deviation by siblings who vicariously experience punishment, (c) emulation of the aggressive parent resulting in prosocial assertive behavior, (d) lessening of guilt reactions to transgression, and (e) increased ability of the child to endure punishment in the service of a desired end (p. 896).

Further, nonaction on the part of the parent may be interpreted by the child as approval for a given act, which, coupled with whatever reinforcement the child may receive from performing that act, tends to increase the likelihood that the child may repeat the behavior. Mild punishment may, indeed, be effective if properly timed and if accompanied by explanation.

Authoritarian control, but not authoritative control, is linked with rebelliousness in children. Placing demands upon children does not provoke hostility. Parental exercise of authority in complex situations is appropriate and beneficial for the child; such authority continually exerted in simple situations seems unwise. The effect of parent control depends upon the personality characteristics of the child. Moreover, the effect of parental restrictiveness depends upon the other parent behavior variables with which it appears. Restrictiveness combined with hostility may produce passivity and dependence, whereas restrictiveness and warm involvement with the child may be beneficial. Creativity, self-assertiveness, and responsibility may be facilitated by appropriate demands, realistic standards, and an authoritative model.

Summary of Parent Behavior Dimensions. Research attempting to identify the effects on children of various parent characteristics has received increasing attention in the last decade. Because of the complexity of this area, much remains to be done before we will be able to make precise statements, based on research evidence, regarding the nature of the interrelations. Research has become increasingly sophisticated in terms of methodology, with numerous attempts to conduct carefully controlled investigations in which parents and children are observed in the laboratory in standard situations (see Bell, 1964). Several points emerge from an examination of current research in this general area.

1. No longer is it possible to speak of the effect of parents on their children. The sex of the parent and the sex of the child must be specified. For example, a complicated study of mother-child interaction (Hatfield, Ferguson, & Alpert, 1967) found that mothers reward aggressiveness in their sons but not in their daughters, while the reverse is true for dependency. In an interesting study (Rothbart & Maccoby, 1966) in which parents gave their immediate reactions to taped statements made by a four-year-old, fathers showed greater permissiveness toward girls than boys for both dependency and aggression while mothers showed greater permissiveness toward boys. Bronfenbrenner (1961) has argued that there is a risk of oversocialization in girls because they receive a combination of high affection and love-oriented discipline. Boys, receiving less affection and more physical punishment (which is less effective than love-oriented discipline in inhibiting behavior) may be undersocialized. Bronfenbrenner maintains that an optimal balance between affection and control is different for boys and girls.

2. The effect of certain parent behaviors and attitudes may depend upon the age of the child. Encouragement or acceptance of dependency, for example, may be less harmful at one age (preschool) than at another (adolescence). Schaefer and Bayley (1963) found the maternal dimension of love-hostility to be significantly correlated with sons' behavior up to the age of 12 years, but not thereafter, whereas the reverse was true of the autonomy-control dimension. In their report of longitudinal data from the Fels research, Kagan and Moss (1962) found that *early* maternal restrictiveness has a long-term effect in inhibiting behavior. Restrictiveness *later*, when the child is better able to judge the inappropriateness of this restrictiveness, is likely to generate hostility.

3. It has become apparent that it is not fruitful to attempt to establish relation between specific parent characteristics and specific child characteristics. Parent variables do not operate in isolation but in combination, so that effects upon the child can be predicted only by considering the patterning and interaction among the parent dimensions. In a study of child-care antecedents of several patterns of preschool children's behavior, Baumrind (1967) found parents of competent and mature

boys and girls to be firm, loving, demanding, and understanding. Parents of children showing disaffiliative behavior were firm, punitive, and unaffectionate. Further, parent variables that we have thought to be related may not be. Baumrind and Black (1967) found firm, demanding behavior on the part of the parent not to be associated with punitiveness or lack of warmth. Undoubtedly there are a great many combinations and permutations of parent behavior.

4. Any particular type of home atmosphere gives rise to both desirable and undesirable child characteristics. Fearless, curious, and planful as children may be from homes in which a psychological climate of democracy and autonomy prevails, they are also inclined toward cruelty, rebellion, and nonconformity. On the other hand, the well-behaved child of a home characterized by strict control may show signs of a constricted personality.

5. In the past much of parent-child research has been concerned with the development of social-emotional behaviors in the child. As mentioned in Chapter 9, increased attention is being paid currently to parental antecedents of cognitive development and cognitive abilities in children. Although some of the parent dimensions examined in this area deal with the emotional relations between parent and child, most are directly related to intellectual stimulation of the child, such as amount of time spent reading to the child (Bing, 1963), the level (quality) of the mother's communication with the child (Hess & Shipman, 1965), and parental expectations for the child (Wolf, 1964). Freeberg and Payne (1967) have constructed a questionnaire to assess parental practices that previous research has shown to influence the child's cognitive development. Six factors emerged from a factor analysis of the responses to the questionnaire of a large group of parents of preschool children: Willingness to devote time to the child, Parental guidance, Parental aspiration for achievement, Rejection versus Acceptance of the child's behavior, Provisions for the child's intellectual needs, Dependence upon external resources (toys, nursery school attendance).

6. The role of the father in affecting the child is receiving increased recognition (Nash, 1965). Although American society is considered a matricentric one, it is apparent that the father influences the children directly, and indirectly through the mother. The concept of identification, to be discussed shortly, has drawn attention to the importance of the father in affecting a boy's development. For example, the delinquent boy has been shown to hold strong feelings of paternal rejection and neglect (Medinnus, 1965b). Since in our culture the role of

the father in the family structure is less clearly defined than the maternal role, one might speculate that there are wider differences among fathers than among mothers in their parent behavior, and that the way in which the father assumes the role more clearly reflects his personality needs than the mother's behavior reflects her personality needs.

THREE FACTORS IN PARENT-CHILD RELATIONSHIPS

For an understanding of the psychology of parent-child relationships, three topics are significant. These are the child's perception of his parents, the matter of identification, and the question of discipline. We conclude this chapter with a consideration of each of these.

Perception of Parents

As we saw earlier, attempts to link parent attitudes to various child behaviors have not proved fruitful. Sufficient research is now accumulating to indicate that a more profitable approach is to elicit the child's report of his relations with his parents. Perhaps more crucial than the parents' attitudes and behaviors is the child's perception and interpretation of them. This approach is not without problems, however. First, attempts to identify cause-and-effect relations are especially tenuous. Let us say that a poorly adjusted 15-year-old perceives his parents in a very unfavorable light. It is just as likely that his present poor adjustment causes him to view all of his interpersonal relations negatively, including his relationship with his parents, as it is that his negative perception of his parents has produced his poor adjustment. Second, the young child is not a very reliable informant, not through any desire to deceive, but through inability to express himself adequately in his early years.

For example, in line with Piaget's notion (1932) that the young child felt that the harsher the punishment the "better" and more efficacious it was, one study (Radke, 1946) found that 74 per cent of preschool children interviewed mentioned spanking as the type of punishment they received, although parents said they used it rarely. In addition, 83 per cent said that spanking was the best punishment when they were naughty. Quite clearly the young child's response to the questions was not related to the actual quality or quantity of the punishment he received, but to his conception of what the most appropriate punishment was. Yet although the young child is not a very reliable informant, there is some evidence for relating a child's perception of his parents' behavior to ratings of the behavior itself by professional interviewers (Meyers, 1935; Bronson, Kalten, & Livson, 1959).

Many techniques have been employed to study children's perceptions of their parents. Directly, children have been interviewed about their parents. Indirectly, they have been asked general questions about parents, such as "What do parents do that boys and girls don't like?" Indirect methods also include drawings to obtain an idea of parental preference and pictures portraying a variety of child situations. Several standardized questionnaires are available in which items are designed to tap the child's perception of the parent on a number of dimensions. The Bronfenbrenner Parent Behavior questionnaire includes the following 15 variables (statements illustrating each variable are provided):

1. Nurturance: I can talk with her (him) about everything. Comforts me and helps me when I have troubles. Is there for me when I need her (him).
2. Affective Reward: Says nice things about me to other people. Is very affectionate with me. Praises me when I have done something good.
3. Instrumental Companionship: Teaches me things which I want to learn. Helps me with hobbies or handiwork. Helps me with schoolwork when I don't understand something.
4. Affiliative Companionship: Goes on pleasant walks and outings with me. Is happy when with me. Enjoys talking with me.
5. Prescriptive: Expects me to help around the house. Wants me to run errands. Expects me to keep my own things in order.
6. Social Isolation: Punishes me by sending me out of the room. As punishment she (he) forbids me to play with other children. As punishment she (he) sends me to bed early.
7. Expressive Rejection: Holds it before me that other children behave better than I do. Nags at me. Scolds me and yells at me.
8. Physical Punishment: Threatens to spank me. Spanks me. Slaps me.
9. Deprivation of Privileges: Punishes me by making me do extra work. When I am bad she (he) forbids me to do things I especially enjoy. Punishes me by taking my favorite things away.
10. Protectiveness: Comes with me when I go someplace for the first time to make sure that everything goes well. Worries that I can't take care of myself. Won't let me roam around because something might happen to me.
11. Power: Insists that I get permission first before I go to a movie, a carnival or some other entertainment. Wants to know exactly how I spend my money when I want to buy some little things for myself. Tells me exactly when I should come home.
12. Achievement Demands: Insists I make a special effort in anything I do. Demands that I do better than other children. Insists that I get particularly good marks in school.

13. Affective Punishment: Appears disappointed and sad when I misbehave. Makes me feel ashamed or guilty when I misbehave. Tells me, "I don't want to have any more to do with you," when I misbehave.
14. Principled Discipline: Is just when punishing me. When I must do something, she (he) explains why. Finds it difficult to punish me.
15. Indulgence: I can talk her (him) into most anything. Lets me off easy when I misbehave. Finds it difficult to punish me.

(Siegelman, 1965a, p. 165)

Another scale, the Parent-Child Relations questionnaire (Roe & Siegelman, 1963) is composed of 10 dimensions: Protective, Demanding, Rejecting, Neglect, Casual, Loving, Symbolic-love reward, Direct-object reward, Symbolic-love punishment, Direct-object punishment. Interestingly enough, factor analyses of this and the Bronfenbrenner scales have yielded factors similar to those obtained for parent behavior and attitudes.

One consistent finding of research investigating the attitudes of children toward the parent role is that children of most ages choose the mother as the preferred parent (Gardner, 1947; Harris & Tseng, 1957). Generally the mother is seen in a more favorable light than the father. She is considered friendlier, less strict, less punitive, less threatening, and more nurturing (Kagan, 1956; Kagan, Hosken, & Watson, 1961; Eisenberg, Henderson, Kuhlmann, & Hill, 1967). The father and his role, in contrast, are regarded as more powerful, more interfering, more competent, and as the major source of punishment (Emmerich, 1959, 1961; Kagan & Lemkin, 1960). Both boys and girls report their mothers as using covert, indirect methods of control more frequently than fathers (Droppleman & Schaefer, 1963). In addition, children usually ascribe "high power" to the adult role and "low power" to their own (Emmerich, 1961).

Although children ordinarily perceive their parents in positive terms, they are willing to criticize and voice dissatisfactions with them. Preschool children in the Radke (1946) study frequently mentioned punishment in this connection. The fifth and sixth graders studied by Gardner (1947) enumerated the following dissatisfactions with their fathers: scolding, general irritability, poor adjustment with the mother, and absence from home. These children's preference for their mother was based on her greater understanding, better nature, and less domineering behavior.

As children age, a trend becomes discernible of preference for the parent of the same sex. Moreover, children incline to perceive themselves as more similar to the parent of the same sex (Gray, 1959).

This will become more evident in the consideration presently of identification.

An interesting sex difference manifests itself in the perception of parents. As a rule, boys see their parents as stricter than do girls (Hawkes, Burchinal, & Gardner, 1957). Boys also seem to be more critical of their parents, especially of the father, and in general see them through their disciplinary function (Meltzer, 1943), with the father as a strong authority figure. Girls more than boys tend to perceive themselves as accepted by their parents (Ausubel, Balthazar, Rosenthal, Blackmore, Schpoont, & Welkowitz, 1954).

Although the data on differential treatment of boys and girls are inconclusive, the fact that boys more than girls believe there is disciplinary friction may account in part for the greater number of behavioral and disciplinary problems among sons than daughters. Possibly because of their higher level of activity and greater aggressiveness boys become more involved in situations requiring discipline both at home and at school. This view supports the *biosocial* explanation of human behavior, that biological differences at birth accentuated by differential environmental, or social, treatment produces substantial variation among the individuals of a society.

As to the connection between perception of parents and child behavior, Serot and Teevan (1961) observed that well-adjusted fourth-grade children were more likely to perceive their relationship with their parents as happy and "ideal" than were poorly adjusted children. Gray (1959) discovered that elementary-school children who perceived themselves as highly similar to the parent of their own sex were better adjusted than those who saw themselves less like that parent. To some extent, Gray further noted, older children who saw themselves as more distant from their parents were more socially acceptable to their peers than those who perceived themselves as closer to parents. As children approach adolescence, independence from parents evidently becomes a highly prized characteristic among peers.

Thus far, most of the studies cited have dealt with young children. In addition, investigations among college students indicate that some aspects of their personalities relate to their perceptions of their parents. One of these (Mussen & Kagan, 1958) found that male students who manifested conformist behavior during an experiment were more likely than others to perceive their parents as harsh, restrictive, punitive, and rejecting. Thus it is possible that conforming behavior as an adult may be traceable to parental demands for conformity in childhood. From the perceptions of college girls relative to the child-rearing attitudes of their mothers, Heilbrun and McKinley (1962) concluded that girls who disclosed some tendencies toward pathological personality were more likely than normal girls to see their mothers' attitudes as authoritarian, controlling, hostile, and rejecting. Within the normal range, anxious and introverted college males describe their parents as rejecting, while extroverted women students report their fathers as loving (Siegelman, 1965b). In general, there is evidence that college students who are high in self-acceptance and adjustment perceive their parents as loving and not as neglectful or rejecting (Medinnus, 1965a). Further, there is a closer relation between the students' self-acceptance and their perception of their mothers' child-rearing attitudes than of their fathers', suggesting that the mother is more important than the father in affecting the child's self-attitudes.

In a series of studies using college students, Heilbrun and his associates have examined the relationship between the individual's perception of his parents and various task-related factors, such as responsiveness to positive and negative reinforcement, achievement motivation, and response to failure conditions. Those students who perceived their parents as rejecting set lower goals for themselves, suggesting lowered self-esteem (Heilbrun & Orr, 1966); they were more readily influenced by social reinforcement (Heilbrun, Harrell, & Gillard, 1967); and they showed poorer performance in a sorting task involving concept formation (Heilbrun, Orr, & Harrell, 1966).

Identification

Even though the concept of identification has been used in many ways with a host of meanings (see Sanford, 1955), let us define it as *the process by which an individual incorporates certain aspects of someone else's behavior, attitudes, and characteristics.* The terms copying, modeling, and imitating are sometimes used synonymously with identification. However, these connote a conscious process, whereas identification may occur essentially at the unconscious level. Furthermore, these terms frequently are restricted to level of behavior, whereas identification may encompass even more. The discussion of identification in the young child primarily concerns his identification with sex role, that is, the process whereby he develops characteristics similar to those of the parent of the same sex. However, numerous other behavioral traits seem to emerge from this process. Aggressive behavior, behavior and attitudes toward others, leisure-time pursuits, and a host of other characteristics may sprout from the child's identification with another person—usually, in early years, the parent.

Why the need for such a notion as identification? Are not the principles of learning (see Chapter 4) sufficient to explain the reason for the child developing characteristics similar to those of the parent of the same sex? Parental approval should be reward enough for behaviors valued by the parent, and thus encourage their repetition. However, child behavior seems to go beyond what would be predictable from learning theory. A tremendous amount of learning occurs without any direct teaching as such. That children observe and are aware of their parents' behavior became evident to the father of a four-year-old when, after he had shouted at her, the child replied, "Don't yell at me. I'm not mommy."

The endless hours spent by a little girl playing house suggest some higher level of *patterning* or *modeling* of one's behavior after the behavior of someone else. But what is the motive for such behavior? Three main explanations have been advanced to explain the occurrence of identification. There is some research support for each of these positions.

Two types of identification have been described in psychoanalytic literature. *Anaclitic* or *developmental* identification is based on the young child's anxiety concerning the loss of love, usually from the mother, with whom a nurturant, affectionate relationship has been established. The child gains some measure of security by introjecting or incorporating the qualities of the mother. From this point of view one would predict that the warmer and more nurturant the adult figure, the stronger the identification. And, indeed, the findings of several studies have supported this. Payne and Mussen (1956) used as an operational measure of identification the actual similarity between father and son on several personality and attitude tests. A positive relation was found between identification and the boy's perception of the father as warm, helpful, and kind. Bandura and Huston (1961) found that nursery school children were much more likely to imitate a model if they had experienced a nurturant and rewarding interaction with her than if the relation had been a distant and nonrewarding one.

The second psychoanalytically based type of identification is *defensive* or *aggressive* identification. According to the theory, this occurs in the boy at the time of the resolution of the Oedipal conflict. Fearful of punishment from the father because of incestuous wishes toward the mother, the boy identifies with the father, adopting his characteristics. While it is apparent that aggressive parents frequently have aggressive children, as is the case among delinquents, there is little evidence that this has arisen from defensive identification. Based on several research investigations, Bandura and Walters (1963) have argued that children will imitate the aggressive behavior of a model if that behavior has been successful in producing social and material reward. However, if such aggressive behavior is punished, children will not imitate it.

Whiting (1960) has proposed a status-envy theory of identification. The degree of identification with another person depends on the extent to which that individual controls desired resources. The parent, for example, may give reward, either social or material; he may withhold it; or he may deprive the child of such reward as he already has. "The more a child envies the status of another with respect to the control of a given resource, the more he will covertly practice that role" (Whiting, 1960, p. 119). In an experiment designed by Bandura, Ross, and Ross (1963), children more frequently imitated a model who possessed rewarding power than one with whom they competed for these rewards. Thus it appears that children identify with the source of rewarding power, not with the competitor for the rewards, as a theory of defensive identification might suggest.

At what age does identification begin? No specific age seems identifiable, although it would appear that it could not occur until the child was able to put himself in the place of someone else, as in taking the role of the parent in play, to pretend, to "assume the role of another." Certainly by ages two to three there is evidence for the beginning of such behavior in the child.

Turning to the literature on sex-role identification, Lynn (1961) has hypothesized that marked differences exist between boys and girls in several aspects of the identification process. As he saw it, both sexes in the very early years identify with the mother. Later, however, the boy has to shift his identification to the father and to a masculine role. No such shift is required of the girl. Several factors in the boy's environment facilitate the switch, however. There are numerous pressures for the boy to behave like a "little man." Moreover, in American society, at least, the male role is more desirable for many reasons. Males enjoy positions of dominance and authority. And in so material-minded a society the occupation of the father is the major source of prestige for the family.

For the girl, of course, although she continues in her identification with her mother, she discovers that the female role is devaluated by society. She thus experiences some difficulty in identifying with the role appropriate to her sex. Moreover, her mother may feel some ambivalence about the female role because of society's downgrading of it. And there is less pressure on her to be girl-like in all behaviors than there is for boys to be manly. No punishment attaches to her wearing certain items of male apparel. Nor does tomboyishness in girls incur the stigma of sissified behavior in boys. Girls may play with boys without censure, but boys are ridiculed for playing with girls.

For these reasons, Lynn believed that with increasing age girls became less firmly tied to the female role, whereas boys who successfully make the transition from identifying with their mother to identifying with their father become more fully associated with the male role. Because of the importance in Western culture of an appropriate sex identification, Lynn equated the failure to achieve this with psychological disturbance.

There are types of parent-child relationships that encourage an appropriate sex identification. Sears (1953) noted that sons of fathers who were warm, permissive, and easygoing tended to behave in a manner appropriate to their sex. In the doll-play situation, boys who chose the maternal role came from homes in which the mother, but not the father, was high in warmth. In an earlier study, Sears (1951) observed that boys from homes lacking a father showed less fantasied aggression than boys whose fathers were living with them. Although her finding implied that the father served as the son's model for aggression, it might also indicate that a boy whose father was absent experienced fewer frustrations.

Social class influences sex identification. Rabban (1950) reported that lower-class children identified themselves with interests appropriate to their sex sooner than middle-class children. Perhaps there are stronger pressures brought at an earlier age in lower-class homes for behavior proper to the sex. Or it may be that a clearer distinction is made between the male and female roles in the lower class. Possibly there may be less tolerance of any deviation from a stereotyped norm among lower-class parents. Whatever the case, there is likely to be more difficulty of a psychological nature for the lower-class child who, for one reason or another, cannot make a suitable sex-role identification.

As to other behaviors springing from a child's identification with his parent, the Pattern Study examined the subject as it bore upon the development of inner control or conscience. Some support was found for the notion that warmth between mother and child and maternal acceptance of the youngster influence the development of conscience. The extent to which children adopt adult behavior in terms of enforcing rules broken by peers appears to be related to the strictness with which their parents enforced rules in early childhood (Maccoby, 1961). This enforcement-of-rules behavior in middle childhood is enhanced by an earlier dependency upon parents.

Girls, as we know, experience a stronger and longer-lasting identification with the mother, although both boys and girls spend more time with her than with the father. Consequently, incorporation of the mother's demands and values plays the largest part in the child's early development of conscience. It would follow from these considerations that conscience develops more strongly in girls than in boys. The Pattern Study found this to be so. Identification led to the development of conscience.

In conclusion, several types of identification have been proposed, together with various antecedent conditions to account for its occurrence. Irrespective of theory, identification clearly serves an important function in the child's life. Gratification (increased security and sense of mastery) derives from behavior that emulates that of a significant adult; and, in practicing the behavior of an adult, as in doll play, a child learns something of his future adult role and acquires some understanding of it. Although initially children identify with their parents, other adults serve as models later. Moreover, there is never a one-to-one relation between the child's behavior and that of the adult with whom he identifies and whose behavior he imitates. The child is selective and innovative, modifying the imitated behavior in various ways to produce a novel and individualistic pattern. Although specific behaviors can be imitated, it seems unlikely that more general and pervasive (and therefore more important) personality characteristics of the adult can be discerned and imitated.

Discipline

Quite likely no topic holds more interest and concern for parents than discipline. Yet relatively little research has been undertaken in this lively area. Thus ideas and theories about discipline abound, but scientific knowledge to back them up is conspicuously scarce. Why research on the subject is scant is easy to understand. The obstacles to experimental investigation are virtually insurmountable. One could hardly ask a group of mothers to administer a certain type of discipline at fixed intervals while another group employed a different kind of discipline or none at all. And even if this could be done, measurement of the effects of discipline (the independent variable) on the child's behavior and attitudes (the dependent variables) would be full of booby traps. Moreover, it is clear that the effects of discipline depend upon the emotional context in which it is administered.

In current thinking, discipline is often equated with guidance. However, discipline might be more appropriately described as the methods used by parents to ensure their child's compliance with that guidance. The socialization process of getting the child to conform to what society expects of him creates conflicts between these social demands and the child's wishes and desires. Thus discipline becomes an inevitable aspect of the parent-child relationship. That discipline may take a vast number of forms and vary widely in the frequency of its use from parent to parent is also true.

What are the functions of discipline? Most obviously, parents use disciplinary methods to obtain conformity to their demands. Discipline also provides the child with cues to behavior. For maximum effectiveness these cues should apprise the child of what constitutes approved or acceptable behavior. However, when it takes the form of punishment, discipline supplies only the cues to unacceptable behavior. This leads to a distinction between the short-term and long-range goals of discipline. Whereas the former is conformity to parental demands, the latter is the development of self-control or inner discipline. Some types of discipline are more conducive to accomplishment of the short-term objectives; others are better suited to achieving the long-range goals.

Which disciplinary techniques receive the more frequent use? Table 10-2 contains a ranking of the 10 used most often at each of three age levels. The study from which the table is drawn (Clifford, 1959, p. 69) was based on records kept by mothers over a three-week period. With the increasing age of the child, the table implies, the parent comes to rely more on verbal techniques and less on physical methods. The Pattern Study divided training techniques into positive sanctions—

TABLE 10-2   The First 10 Methods of Control by Rank and Age of the Child

3-Year-Old Group		6-Year-Old Group		9-Year-Old Group	
Method	Rank	Method	Rank	Method	Rank
Reason	1	Reason	1	Reason	1
Scold	2	Scold	2	Scold	2
Coax	3	Coax	3	Take away privilege	3
Spank	4	Threaten	4	Coax	4
Divert	5	Ignore	5	Self-esteem	5.5
Threaten	6	Isolate	6	Threaten	5.5
Ignore	7	Spank	7	Ignore	7
Remove child forcibly	8	Divert	8	Remove difficulty	8
Isolate	9	Take away privilege	9	Humor	10
Remove difficulty	10	Humor	10.5	Isolate	10
		Order	10.5	Social disapproval	10

praise and tangible reward—and negative sanctions—physical punishment, deprivation of privileges, withdrawal of love, and isolation. Generally those mothers who were above average in the group in the use of positive sanctions were also above average in ratings on warmth and affection shown to children, on satisfaction with their roles of wife and mother, and on esteem felt for their husbands. This would suggest that the use of praise and rewards reflected a mother's satisfactory adjustment to her life situation. Perhaps, then, there may be some relation between a woman's adjustment to the mother role and the reasonableness of her behavior in it.

Why is discipline used and when is it most frequent throughout the day? Clearly the most important single reason for discipline is disobedience—the child's noncompliance with parental demands. The Clifford study identified the following 11 categories as areas requiring discipline: *sibling relationships*—that is, quarreling, aggression, interference; *eating*—refusal to eat, making a mess, leaving the table during the meal; *sleep*—refusal to go to bed, noise in bed; *dressing*—refusal to get dressed, soiling clothing, changing clothes; *activities*—conflict over television, Sunday School; *school*—preparing to go to school, refusal to go to school; *health*—medication, general health protection; *inappropriate behavior*—irritability, boisterousness, destructiveness, forbidden behavior; *adult interaction*—refusing an adult request, interference with adult activity, persistent demand of adult attention; *home*—neatness of home, refusal to put things away; *social*—inappropriate social behavior, insistence on own rights, interference with activities of others.

As to frequency of discipline, Figure 10-4 represents the periods throughout the day at which discipline is most often required for each of three age levels. As the child grows older there is an apparent decrease in the frequency of situations requiring parental discipline. Perhaps this reflects a development of inner control with age; he is more aware of what is expected of him and is more able developmentally to conform to these expectations. Besides, as the child grows older, more of his time is spent interacting with others outside the home. The sheer quantity of his interaction with parents falls off. Now sanctions for inappropriate behavior spring increasingly from peers and from adults other than parents.

No discussion of discipline can ignore the effects of discipline on the child. Although discipline may achieve a behavioral goal, its accomplishment may be nullified by the emotional and attitudinal side effects it produces in the child. Several studies (Hollenberg & Sperry, 1951; Sears, 1950; Bandura & Walters, 1959; Becker, Peterson, Luria, Shoemaker, & Hellmer, 1962) have shown a positive correlation between

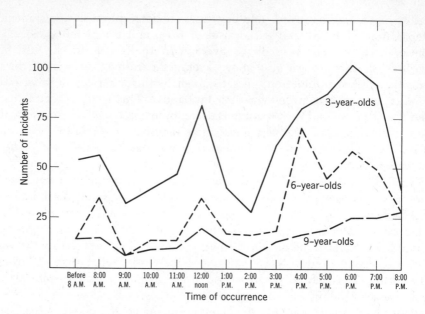

FIGURE 10-4   The frequency of discipline by the hour of occurrence and age (Clifford, 1959, p. 51).

aggressive behavior in children and severity of discipline in the home. There is little doubt that harsh, arbitrary, and inconsistent discipline arouses resentment, hostility, and anxiety in the child. Anger and crying were reported by mothers as responses to discipline (Clifford, 1959); and 63 per cent of the preschool children interviewed in the Radke (1946) study said they were sad, unhappy, and pained by punishment, whereas only 14 per cent reported feelings of penitence or resolutions for better behavior.

From strong discipline a child builds up a store of hostility that he directs toward others. This is borne out by a study conducted by Hoffman (1960). Mothers were rated according to how they coerced the child to change his entire current pattern of behavior immediately. A significant positive relation was found between a mother's use of what Hoffman called "unqualified power assertion" and the child's hostility toward others, his power assertiveness, and his resistance to the attempts of others to influence him. Thus the conforming, docile child at home may be a tiger on the outside.

Strict discipline by parents often leads to prejudiced, antidemocratic attitudes in the child (Harris, Gough, & Martin, 1950; Lyle & Levitt,

1955). This is another example of the displacement of aggression. Severe and punitive parental treatment awakens hostile and aggressive impulses in the child. Since these impulses cannot be directed toward the parent, they are leveled against others who are made into scapegoats and innocent victims. Other factors, such as the extent of prejudice in the parent and the degree to which the child identifies with the parent, are also important in the explanation of prejudicial attitudes; still, it is true that frequent use of parental discipline sensitizes the child to power relations along a strong-weak or superior-inferior dimension. In a study of social attitudes among an upper-class group of children (Epstein & Komorita, 1965), those who perceived parental punitiveness as moderate in degree showed the greatest amount of social distance toward a working-class group, as compared with those perceiving parental punitiveness as mild or severe. This finding can be explained in terms of Bronfenbrenner's notion (1961) of "optimal level of control." Parents using either lax or severe methods of control have less influence on their children than those using moderate control, in this case, in instilling class values.

The kind of discipline recalled by young adults as having been used by their parents is determined by their willingness to criticize their parents and by the favorableness of their attitudes toward them. College students who remembered their early discipline as primarily positive in nature were less critical of their parents than were those who recalled parental discipline as basically negative (Nakamura, 1959). Further, Itkin (1955) found positive correlations between the attitudes of college women toward their parents and their attitudes toward the discipline their parents had exercised. Both findings, although suffering from the weakness inherent in retrospective reports, suggest that the type of discipline employed is intimately related to a young adult's recollection of the earlier parent-child relationship as pleasant or unpleasant. These findings may also imply that rigorous, negative discipline leaves lasting emotional reactions in the child.

Let us round out this review with some general comments about discipline and child management. These are not oracular preachments to govern one's handling of children, but broad considerations that might profit a parent or a teacher to ponder.

Behavior is motivated. There is a reason, a cause for every behavior. Usually these causes are not apparent at the conscious level: the child does not know why he does the things he does. To pinch his arm and ask, "Why did you do it?" is preposterous. If he knew why, he probably would not have had to act as he did in the first place. Yet the adult must try to ascertain and understand the cause. What is the child trying to achieve? Is he trying to gain acceptance? Attention? Recognition? Affection? Meanness is not a cause but an interpretation.

Discipline is concerned too frequently with actions. Feelings are disregarded. The action or behavior may be stopped, but what happens to the feelings? These must be dealt with, too. The child needs the opportunity to express them. He will feel better if he can air his feelings and adults may learn something in the process. Since restrictions are frustrating, the child needs to give vent to his feelings. The young child usually does so; the older child learns not to, but this does him no good.

Because restrictions are frustrating, they should be kept to a minimum. The fewer there are the better. The simpler they are the better. And they should always be geared to the child's level of understanding.

Then, too, the adult might examine his own thoughts. What are his motives? Are his demands reasonable? Was the child's behavior truly not permissible, or was the adult's level of tolerance unusually low? Too great a price may be charged for conformity.

Finally, the parent-child relationship is unique; all authority, all the power, all the weight is invested in only one individual, the parent. The child must obey. For a parent to take advantage of such a relationship reflects little basic human understanding. Physical punishment is violence. It breeds a response detrimental to the individual and the society of which he is a part. Kindness, respect, and sensitivity, on the other hand, are qualities worth cultivating in a growing human being, and these may well develop out of the intimate relationship between parent and child. They flourish in a climate of mutual trust, and for mutual trust to be truly mutual, it takes the full cooperation of both parties.

SUMMARY

Parenthood involves a host of functions and duties, and imposes a variety of demands on those individuals who fill its role. Some parents are abler than others to meet these demands. Quite naturally these experience greater satisfaction in the parent role.

Many factors influence a parent's behavior, among them his own childhood experiences and the behavior and attitudes of his parents. Personality structure and current child-rearing fads also influence an individual's demeanor as a parent.

Three principal parent variables were explored, with the research relevant to the relation of each of these—parent personality, parent attitudes, and parent behavior—to the child's personality and adjustment presented.

Two main dimensions emerged from factor analytic studies of parent attitude scores and parent behavior ratings. One of them, acceptance versus rejection, assessed the parent's attitude toward the child. The other, autonomy versus control, related to parental attitudes toward child rearing.

In view of the present state of knowledge, it would seem that assessment of the broad psychological atmospheres in the home is more revealing of effects on the child than is information on specific child-rearing practices. However, the ultimate goal of parent-child research is the identification of specific aspects of the parents, the family, and the home that exert a significant psychological impact on the child.

The chapter also surveyed three factors of importance to understanding parent-child relationships: children's perceptions of their parents, identification, and discipline. The relationship between parent and child holds much in common with any relationship between two people. Mutual trust, mutual understanding, and mutual acceptance are imperative if the relationship is to be satisfying and rewarding to both.

REFERENCES

Adorno, T. W., Frenkel-Brunswik, E., Levinson, D. J., & Sanford, R. N. *The authoritarian personality.* New York: Harper, 1950.

Ausubel, D. *Theory and problems of child development.* New York: Grune & Stratton, 1958.

Ausubel, D., Balthazar, E. E., Rosenthal, I., Blackmore, L. S., Schpoont, S. H., & Welkowitz, J. Perceived parent attitudes as determinants of children's ego structure. *Child Development,* 1954, **25**, 173–183.

Baldwin, A. L. Socialization and the parent-child relationship. *Child Development,* 1948, **19**, 127–136.

Baldwin, A. L. The effect of home environment on nursery school behavior. *Child Development,* 1949, **20**, 49–61.

Baldwin, A. L., Kalhorn, J., & Breese, F. Patterns of parent behavior. *Psychological Monographs,* 1945, **58**, No. 3.

Baldwin, A. L., Kalhorn, J., & Breese, F. The appraisal of parent behavior. *Psychological Monographs,* 1949, **63**, No. 4.

Bandura, A., & Huston, A. Identification as a process of incidental learning. *Journal of Abnormal and Social Psychology,* 1961, **63**, 311–318.

Bandura, A., Ross, D., & Ross, S. A comparative test of the status envy, social power, and the secondary-reinforcement theories of identificatory learning. *Journal of Abnormal and Social Psychology,* 1963, **67**, 527–534.

Bandura, A., & Walters, R. *Adolescent aggression.* New York: Ronald, 1959.

Bandura, A., & Walters, R. *Social learning and personality development.* New York: Holt, 1963.

Baumrind, D.   Effects of authoritative parental control on child behavior. *Child Development,* 1966, **37,** 887–907.

Baumrind, D.   Child care practices anteceding three patterns of preschool behavior. *Genetic Psychology Monographs,* 1967, **75,** 43–88.

Baumrind, D., & Black, A.   Socialization practices associated with dimensions of competence in preschool boys and girls. *Child Development,* 1967, **38,** 291–327.

Becker, W. C., Peterson, D. R., Hellmer, L. A., Shoemaker, D. J., & Quay, H. C. Factors in parental behavior and personality as related to problem behavior in children. *Journal of Consulting Psychology,* 1959, **23,** 107–118.

Becker, W. C., Peterson, D. R., Luria, Z., Shoemaker, D. J., & Hellmer, L. A. Relations of factors derived from parent-interview ratings to behavior problems of five-years-olds. *Child Development,* 1962, **33,** 509–535.

Behrens, M. L.   Child rearing and the character structure of the mother. *Child Development,* 1954, **25,** 225–238.

Bell, R.   Retrospective attitude studies of parent-child relations. *Child Development,* 1958, **29,** 323–338.

Bell, R.   Structuring parent-child interaction situations for direct observation. *Child Development,* 1964, **35,** 1009–1020.

Bing, E.   Effect of childrearing practices on development of differential cognitive abilities. *Child Development,* 1963, **34,** 631–648.

Block, J.   Personality factors associated with fathers' attitudes toward childrearing. *Child Development,* 1955, **26,** 41–48.

Brody, G.   Relationship between maternal attitudes and behavior. *Journal of Personality and Social Psychology,* 1965, **2,** 317–323.

Bronfenbrenner, U.   Toward a theoretical model for the analysis of parent-child relationships in a social context. In J. C. Glidewell (Ed.), *Parental attitudes and child behavior.*   Springfield, Ill.: Thomas, 1961.

Bronson, W. C., Kalten, E. S., & Livson, N.   Patterns of authority and affection in two generations. *Journal of Abnormal and Social Psychology,* 1959, **58,** 143–152.

Burchinal, L. G.   Parents' attitudes and adjustment of children. *Journal of Genetic Psychology,* 1958, **92,** 69–79.   (a)

Burchinal, L. G.   Mothers' and fathers' differences in parental acceptance of children for controlled comparisons based on parental and family characteristics.   *Journal of Genetic Psychology,* 1958, **92,** 103–110.   (b)

Burchinal, L. G., Hawkes, G. R., & Gardner, B.   The relationship between parental acceptance and adjustment of children. *Child Development,* 1957, **28,** 65–77.

Champney, H.   The measurement of parent behavior. *Child Development,* 1941, **12,** 131–166.   (a)

Champney, H.   The variables of parent behavior. *Journal of Abnormal and Social Psychology,* 1941, **36,** 525–542.   (b)

Clifford, E.   Discipline in the home: A controlled observational study of parental practices. *Journal of Genetic Psychology,* 1959, **95,** 45–82.

Coleman, R. W., Kris, E., & Provence, S.   The study of variations of early parental attitudes. *Psychoanalytic Study of the Child,* 1953, **8**, 20–47.

Droppelman, L., & Schaefer, E.   Boys' and girls' reports of maternal and paternal behavior. *Journal of Abnormal and Social Psychology,* 1963, **67**, 648–654.

Eisenberg, J., Henderson, R., Kuhlmann, W., & Hill, J.   Six- and ten-year-olds' attribution of punitiveness and nurturance to parents and other adults. *Journal of Genetic Psychology,* 1967, **111**, 233–240.

Emmerich, W.   Young children's discrimination of parent and child roles. *Child Development,* 1959, **30**, 403–419.

Emmerich, W.   Family role concepts of children ages six to ten. *Child Development,* 1961, **32**, 609–624.

Epstein, R., & Komorita, S.   Parental discipline, stimulus characteristics of outgroups, and social distance in children. *Journal of Personality and Social Psychology,* 1965, **2**, 416–420.

Erikson, E. H.   *Childhood and society.*   New York: Norton, 1950.

Freeberg, N., & Payne, D.   Dimensions of parental practice concerned with cognitive development in the preschool child. *Journal of Genetic Psychology,* 1967, **111**, 245–261.

Gardner, L. P.   An analysis of children's attitudes toward fathers. *Journal of Genetic Psychology,* 1947, **70**, 3–28.

Gray, S.   Perceived similarity to parents and adjustment. *Child Development,* 1959, **30**, 91–107.

Hanvik, L. J., & Byrum, M.   MMPI profiles of parents of child psychiatric patients. *Journal of Clinical Psychology,* 1959, **15**, 427–431.

Harris, D. B., Gough, H. G., & Martin, W. E.   Children's ethnic attitudes. II. Relationship to parental beliefs concerning child training. *Child Development,* 1950, **21**, 169–181.

Harris, D. B., & Tseng, Seng Chu.   Children's attitudes toward peers and parents as revealed by sentence completion. *Child Development,* 1957, **28**, 401–411.

Harris, I. D.   *Normal children and mothers.*   Glencoe, Ill.: Free Press, 1959.

Hatfield, J., Ferguson, L., & Alpert, R.   Mother-child interaction and the socialization process. *Child Development,* 1967, **38**, 365–414.

Hawkes, G. R., Burchinal, L. G., & Gardner, B.   Pre-adolescents' views of some of their relations with their parents. *Child Development,* 1957, **28**, 393–399.

Heilbrun, A., Harrell, S., & Gillard, B.   Perceived childrearing attitudes of fathers and cognitive control in daughters. *Journal of Genetic Psychology,* 1967, **111**, 29–40.

Heilbrun, A., & McKinley, R.   Perception of maternal child rearing attitudes, personality of the perceiver, and incipient psychopathology. *Child Development,* 1962, **33**, 73–83.

Heilbrun, A., & Orr, H.   Perceived maternal childrearing history and subsequent motivational effects of failure. *Journal of Genetic Psychology,* 1966, **109**, 75–89.

Heilbrun, A., Orr, H., & Harrell, S.   Patterns of parental childrearing and subsequent vulnerability to cognitive disturbance. *Journal of Consulting Psychology,* 1966, **30**, 51–59.

Hess, R., & Shipman, V.   Early experience and the socialization of cognitive modes in children. *Child Development,* 1965, **36**, 869–886.

Hoffman, L., Rosen, S., & Lippitt, R.   Parental coerciveness, child autonomy, and child's role at school. *Sociometry,* 1960, **23**, 15–22.

Hoffman, M.   Power assertion by the parent and its impact on the child. *Child Development,* 1960, **31**, 129–143.

Hoffman, M.   Personality, family structure, and social class as antecedents of parental power assertion. *Child Development,* 1963, **34**, 869–884.

Hollenberg, E., & Sperry, M.   Some antecedents of aggression and effects of frustration in doll play. *Personality,* 1951, **1**, 32–43.

Ingersoll, H. L.   A study of the transmission of authority patterns in the family. *Genetic Psychology Monographs,* 1948, **38**, 225–302.

Itkin, W.   Relationships between attitudes toward parents and parents' attitudes toward children. *Journal of Genetic Psychology,* 1955, **86**, 339–352.

Kagan, J.   Children's perceptions of parents. *Journal of Abnormal and Social Psychology,* 1956, **53**, 257–259.

Kagan, J., Hosken, B., & Watson, S.   Child's symbolic conceptualization of parents. *Child Development,* 1961, **32**, 625–636.

Kagan, J., & Lemkin, J.   The child's differential perception of parental attributes. *Journal of Abnormal and Social Psychology,* 1960, **61**, 440–447.

Kagan, J., & Moss, H.   *Birth to maturity.* New York: Wiley, 1962.

Levy, D. M.   *Maternal overprotection.* New York: Columbia University Press, 1943.

Lorr, M., & Jenkins, R. L.   Three factors in parent behavior. *Journal of Consulting Psychology,* 1953, **17**, 306–308.

Lyle, W. H., & Levitt, E. E.   Punitiveness, authoritarianism, and parental discipline of grade school children. *Journal of Abnormal and Social Psychology,* 1955, **51**, 42–46.

Lynn, D. B.   Sex differences in identification development. *Sociometry,* 1961, **24**, 372–383.

Maccoby, E.   The taking of adult roles in middle childhood. *Journal of Abnormal and Social Psychology,* 1961, **63**, 493–503.

Margolis, M.   The mother-child relationship in bronchial asthma. *Journal of Abnormal and Social Psychology,* 1961, **63**, 360–367.

Medinnus, G.   The relation between several parent measures and the child's early adjustment to school. *Journal of Educational Psychology,* 1961, **52**, 153–156.

Medinnus, G.   Adolescents' self-acceptance and perceptions of their parents. *Journal of Consulting Psychology,* 1965, **29**, 150–154.   (a)

Medinnus, G. Delinquents' perceptions of their parents. *Journal of Consulting Psychology,* 1965, **29,** 592–593. (b)

Medinnus, G., & Curtis, F. J. The relation between maternal self-acceptance and child acceptance. *Journal of Consulting Psychology,* 1963, **27,** 542–544.

Meltzer, H. Sex differences in children's attitudes to parents. *Journal of Genetic Psychology,* 1943, **62,** 311–326.

Meyers, R. R. Intrafamily relationships and pupil adjustment. *Teachers College Contributions to Education,* 1935, No. 651.

Miles, K. Relationship between certain factors in the home background and the quality of leadership shown by children. Reported in J. E. Anderson. Parents' attitudes on child behavior: a report of three studies. *Child Development,* 1946, **17,** 91–97.

Milton, G. A. A factor analytic study of child-rearing behavior. *Child Development,* 1958, **29,** 381–392.

Moll, K. L., & Darley, F. L. Attitudes of mothers of articulatory-impaired and speech-retarded children. *Journal of Speech and Hearing Disorders,* 1960, **25,** 377–384.

Morris, W. W., & Nicholas, A. L. Intra-family personality configurations among children with primary behavior disorders and their parents: A Rorschach investigation. *Journal of Clinical Psychology,* 1950, **6,** 309–319.

Mosher, D., & Mosher, J. Relationships between authoritarian attitudes in delinquent girls and the authoritarian attitudes and authoritarian rearing practices of their mothers. *Psychological Reports,* 1965, **16,** 23–30.

Mussen, P. H., & Kagan, J. Group conformity and perceptions of parents. *Child Development,* 1958, **29,** 57–60.

Nakamura, C. The relationship between children's expressions of hostility and methods of discipline exercised by dominant overprotective parents. *Child Development,* 1959, **30,** 109–117.

Nash, J. The father in contemporary culture and current psychological literature. *Child Development,* 1965, **36,** 261–297.

Paulsen, M. Legal protections against child abuse. *Children,* 1966, **13,** 42–48.

Payne, D., & Mussen, P. Parent-child relations and father identification among adolescent boys. *Journal of Abnormal and Social Psychology,* 1956, **52,** 358–362.

Peterson, D. R., Becker, W. C., Hellmer, L. A., Shoemaker, D. J., & Quay, H. C. Parental attitudes and child adjustment. *Child Development,* 1959, **30,** 119–130.

Peterson, D. R., Becker, W. C., Shoemaker, D. J., Luria, Z., & Hellmer, L. A. Child behavior problems and parental attitudes. *Child Development,* 1961, **32,** 151–162.

Phillips, E. L. Parent-child similarities in personality disturbances. *Journal of Clinical Psychology,* 1951, **7,** 188–190.

Piaget, J. *The moral judgment of the child.* New York: Harcourt, Brace, 1932.

Porter, B.   Measurement of parental acceptance of children.   *Journal of Home Economics,* 1954, **46,** 176–182.

Rabban, M.   Sex-role identification in young children in two diverse social groups.   *Genetic Psychology Monographs,* 1950, **42,** 81–158.

Radke, M. J.   *The relation of parental authority to children's behavior and attitudes.*   Minneapolis: University of Minnesota Press, 1946.

Read, K. H.   Parents' expressed attitudes and children's behavior.   *Journal of Consulting Psychology,* 1945, **9,** 95–100.

Roe, A., & Siegelman, M.   A Parent-Child Relations questionnaire.   *Child Development,* 1963, **34,** 355–369.

Roff, M.   A factorial study of the Fels Parent Behavior Scales.   *Child Development,* 1949, **20,** 29–45.

Rothbart, M., & Maccoby, E.   Parents' differential reactions to sons and daughters.   *Journal of Personality and Social Psychology,* 1966, **4,** 237–243.

Sanford, N.   The dynamics of identification.   *Psychological Review,* 1955, **62,** 106–118.

Schaefer, E.   A circumplex model for maternal behavior.   *Journal of Abnormal and Social Psychology,* 1959, **59,** 226–235.

Schaefer, E., & Bayley, N.   Maternal behavior, child behavior, and their intercorrelations from infancy through adolescence.   *Monographs of the Society for Research in Child Development,* 1963, **28,** No. 3.

Schaefer, E., & Bell, R.   Parental Attitude Research Instrument (PARI). Normative data.   Unpublished manuscript.   Library, National Institutes of Health, Bethesda, Md., 1955.

Schaefer, E., & Bell, R.   Development of a Parental Attitude Research Instrument.   *Child Development,* 1958, **29,** 339–361.

Sears, P.   Doll-play aggression in normal young children: Influence of sex, age, sibling status, father's absence.   *Psychological Monographs,* 1951, **65,** No. 6.

Sears, P.   Child-rearing factors related to playing of sex-typed roles.   *American Psychologist,* 1953, **8,** 431.   (Abstract)

Sears, R. R.   Relation of fantasy aggression to interpersonal aggression.   *Child Development,* 1950, **21,** 5–6.

Sears, R. R., Maccoby, E., & Levin, H.   *Patterns of child rearing.*   Evanston, Ill.: Row, Peterson, 1957.

Serot, N., & Teevan, R.   Perception of the parent-child relationship and its relation to adjustment.   *Child Development,* 1961, **32,** 373–378.

Siegelman, M.   Evaluation of Bronfenbrenner's questionnaire for children concerning parental behavior.   *Child Development,* 1965, **36,** 163–174.   (a)

Siegelman, M.   College student personality correlates of early parent-child relationship.   *Journal of Consulting Psychology,* 1965, **29,** 558–564.   (b)

Symonds, P. M.   *The psychology of parent-child relationships.*   New York: Appleton-Century-Crofts, 1939.

Symonds, P. M. *The dynamics of parent-child relationships.* New York: Appleton-Century-Crofts, 1949.

Whiting, J. W. M. Resource mediation and learning by identification. In I. Iscoe & H. Stevenson (Eds.), *Personality development in children.* Austin: University of Texas Press, 1960. Pp. 112–126.

Wolf, R. The identification and measurement of environmental process variables related to intelligence. Unpublished doctoral dissertation, University of Chicago, 1964.

Wolking, W., Dunteman, G., & Bailey, J. Multivariate analyses of parents' MMPI's based on the psychiatric diagnoses of their children. *Journal of Consulting Psychology,* 1967, **31**, 521–524.

Zuckerman, M., & Oltean, M. Some relationships between maternal attitude factors and authoritarianism, personality needs, psychopathology, and self-acceptance. *Child Development,* 1959, **30**, 27–36.

Zunich, M. Relationship between maternal behavior and attitudes toward children. *Journal of Genetic Psychology,* 1962, **100**, 155–165.

SECTION IV
SOCIETAL
INFLUENCES ON
SOCIALIZATION

Although the family in Western culture imparts most of the society's values and beliefs and plays the largest role in molding personality and behavior, other social forces also make their impression on the child. The child's agemates, his school, and other outside influences including the community, religious experience, and exposure to the mass media all at times reinforce parental socialization. This is especially true of the school. At other times, the influence of these outside forces runs counter to that of the family. A child's peers, for example, often counter parental pressures, especially if the parents' behaviors and attitudes are deviant.

In this section, we shall consider these forces whose influence depends, to a large degree, on the adequacy of the parent-child relationship. Chapter 11 concerns the child and his agemates. Chapter 12 covers the school, and Chapter 13 is devoted to the community, the church, and the mass media. If parents are neglectful or so punitive that the child cannot have close relations with them, the influence of these social forces outside the home increases. How great an increase is determined by both the personality of the child and the behavior of the parents.

It seems reasonable to believe that the social influences forming the substance of this section are generally secondary in import to the family. Moreover, their effect is neither as deleterious as is sometimes maintained in the case of peers and the mass media nor as beneficial as is sometimes assumed in the case of school, school books, and religious instruction. More likely, these forces interacting with one another and with the family within the setting of the culture are each ambiguous in impact. Sometimes they conflict with each other, sometimes they reinforce each other. At times they dispose the child toward adaptive behavior, at other times toward maladaptive behavior.

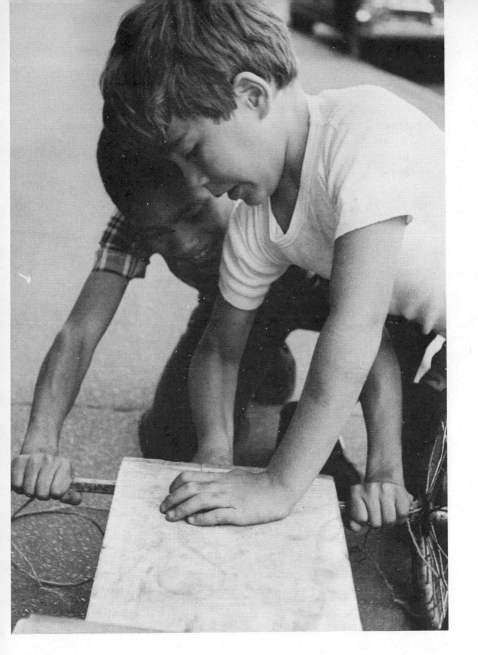

11

The Child among His Peers

The society of children is clearly a primary group. As such, it features close, face-to-face contact, the ability to regulate or constrain the behavior of its members, and psychological support for them. In most cases, other than the family, it is the only primary group to which a child belongs. Obviously this society is of great significance in shaping a child's beliefs and behaviors. Yet psychologists have not flooded this important area with research. Indeed, far more is known about parent-child relationships, however vague this knowledge may be, than about the interaction of children with other children. Nevertheless, let us look into three facets of children's groups: their change in degree of involvement and type of activity, the question of acceptance by peers, and the functions such groups serve in the socialization process.

AGE CHANGES IN PEER INVOLVEMENT

The early developmental tasks of children are primarily phenomena of a maturational kind. Such things as the development of speech and locomotion result, in large part, from physical and motor maturation. As age advances, the types of developmental tasks change, becoming essentially social in character. The socialization process increases in importance; through it, the infant, terribly egocentric in its demands and unable to suffer delay or interference, ultimately acquires concern for others and becomes able to postpone or even reject gratification at someone else's expense. How is this socialization reflected in the changing interactions of the child with his agemates, and how do these interactions contribute to the molding of the end product, the human adult?

The earliest contacts between agemates have been described by Maudry and Nekula (1939) who studied the social interactions of children under 25 months of age. Placing pairs of children matched in age in a playpen along with some toys, they found that at the earliest age level studied, six to eight months, children did not interact to any appreciable extent. Partners were treated as though they were play materials rather than individuals. Fighting over play occurred most frequently at the next level, nine to 13 months, but diminished from this point onward. At the final level studied, 19 to 25 months, children were chiefly interested in establishing social relations with one another, with the play materials being used to serve this end. More recently, Haas and Harms (1963) attempted to replicate the Maudry and Nekula study, and found that a needed first step was to develop a reliable system of observation. Their report describes the establishment of

400

reliable procedures, particularly the development of more adequate means of coding responses, for this type of study.

For many reasons, the young child does not interact too well with peers. Some of the more important ones are his rather greater distractability, his lower tolerance of frustration, his lesser ability to endure delay of gratification, and his inferior skill in communication. All these deficiencies may be related to the young child's inability to "take the role of the other." Because of a poorly developed capacity to discern the moods, motives, and feelings of others, the young child runs into the inevitable conflicts arising from social interaction. To put oneself in someone else's shoes or to empathize does much to reduce these difficulties.

Take this example. The mother is frantically attempting to cook dinner and at the same time cope with a two-year-old son with a cold who is lying on the kitchen floor, kicking his feet in the midst of a temper tantrum. The five-year-old daughter picks this moment to demand that her mother read a story, thus revealing her inability to "take the role of the other" and see the world at this juncture through the eyes of her mother. The two-year-old cannot be dealt with by arbitration; actually, as soon as he has been fed he will probably calm down anyway. But the five-year-old has come quite some way toward social maturity although this is not evident at the moment. If told, however, "I'm busy right now but I'll read you a story later; why don't you see if you can get your brother interested in something," she *may* respond maturely. The child is thus along the way to developing skills of empathy and in a few years may even be of some help to the mother in avoiding domestic crises of this sort.

From this, one can see that a pair of two-year-olds will engage in a fair amount of combat, since their personal needs generally cannot stand delay or compromise. By the time they are five, compromise and arbitration become possible, although usually these are not attempted until the efforts of either child to assert his rights have failed. While caring for a pair of five-year-olds, one of the writers kept track of the number of times they fought, made up, and reached a compromise solution to the problem engendering the conflict. In the course of the afternoon, this sequence occurred 14 times, even though both children were bright and pleasant, loved one another dearly, and both were having a "good day." Such activity is doubtless hard on the parent, but is probably of considerable value to the child since in the process he learns several things—to take the role of the other and show concern for the other's wishes, to delay gratification, to arbitrate difficulties, and to achieve compromises at his own expense in order to continue a desired activity and association.

As Barker and Wright (1955) and Anderson (1948) have emphasized, there is a tremendous amount of repetition of experience during childhood. Estimated quite conservatively, five-year-old children in free play enter into conflict with their agemates at least 20 times a day and manage to resolve most of these clashes successfully. Multiplied by 365 days, these figures yield a total of 7300 annual conflicts between children of the same age. No wonder most of us learn something of the art of diplomacy over the years!

Through growth of conceptual power and social skill, partly as a result of interaction with age equals, the child is able to increase still further his participation with his peers. This has been demonstrated by Parten's study (1929) of children's play. Because it involved one of the first uses of time sampling, the Parten project is of methodological interest besides having provided valuable information on child behavior. Over many brief intervals, Parten observed the play behaviors of children ranging in age from slightly under two to four years and 11 months and saw that she could categorize this play according to amounts of social involvement. These were her categories (see also Figure 11-1):

Unoccupied Behavior—The child apparently is not playing at all, at least not in the usual sense, but occupies himself with watching anything which happens to be of momentary interest. When there is nothing exciting taking place, he plays with his own body, gets on and off chairs, just stands around, follows the teacher, or sits in one spot glancing around the room.

Solitary Play—The child plays alone and independently with toys that are different from those used by the children within speaking distance and makes no effort to get close to or speak to the other children. His interest is centered upon his own activity, and he pursues it without reference to what others are doing.

Onlooker Behavior—The child spends most of his time watching the others play. He often talks to the playing children, asks questions, or gives suggestions, but does not enter into the play himself. He stands or sits within speaking distance of the group so that he can see and hear all that is taking place. Thus he differs from the unoccupied child, who notices anything that happens to be exciting and is not especially interested in groups of children.

Parallel Play—The child plays independently, but the activity he chooses naturally brings him among other children. He plays with toys which are like those which the children around him are using, but he plays with the toys as he sees fit and does not try to influence the activity of

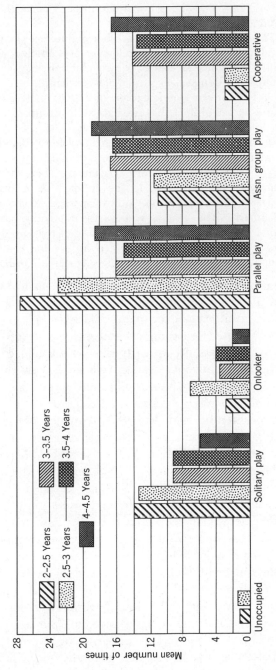

FIGURE 11-1   Mean number of times each activity was observed at different ages (Parten & Newhall, 1943, p. 517).

the children near him. Thus he plays beside rather than with the other children (cf. solitary play above).

Associative Play—The child plays with other children. There are borrowing and lending of play material; following one another with trains and wagons; mild attempts to control which children may or may not play in the groups. All engage in similar if not identical activity; there is no division of labor and no organization of activity. Each child acts as he wishes, does not subordinate his interests to the group.

Cooperative or Organized Supplementary Play—The child plays in a group that is organized for the purpose of making some material product, of striving to attain some competitive goal, of dramatizing situations of adult or group life, or of playing formal games. There is a marked sense of belonging or not belonging to the group. The control of the group situation is in the hands of one or two members, who direct the activity of the others. The goal as well as the method of attaining it necessitates a division of labor, the taking of different roles by the various group members, and the organization of activity so that the efforts of one child are supplemented by those of another (Parten & Newhall, 1943).

Though increasingly interested in his peers, as seen in the development of parallel play, the young child does not have enough imaginative, role playing, arbitrational, or compromising skill to interact to any large degree at the more complex and intimate level of cooperative play. Interest in peers occurs early, but acquisition of the necessary skills requires time and practice. Developed largely through play, these skills open the door to future play and interaction of a more highly involved kind.

As interaction proliferates with age, the frequency of specific social responses changes. The number of quarrels children enter into diminishes as age and social skills increase (Jersild & Markey, 1935). However, the duration of any single quarrel becomes greater, perhaps because the child is less distractable. The use of language to resolve conflicts grows with age, whereas screaming, crying, and general tantrum decorum declines. Competition and rivalry rise sharply between two and five and less so between five and seven (Greenberg, 1932), although Parten's data suggested that cooperation also increased during this interval. Responses of both sympathy and aggressiveness among several groups of nursery children studied by Murphy (1937) manifested an increase with age. She found, through a long series of systematic observations, that highly aggressive children were often more sympathetic to others. These various patterns suggest that some children within a particular age group are generally more inclined than others toward social interaction, irrespective of type.

In the growing child, interest in peers awakens first and is followed by increasing interaction with them. From the greater interaction come improved social skills that in turn lead to even more interaction. Children who do not seek this interaction, who prefer adult company, are probably left behind more and more in their social learning, and are more often rejected by their peers (Marshall & McCandless, 1957).

From the one-year-old, uninterested in other one-year-olds and unable to maintain friendly contact with them because of a deficiency in social skill, the child becomes a two-year-old, who is now more interested in his peers but is still incapable of compromising his own needs sufficiently to sustain friendly or cooperative relations for any length of time. By five the child has become fully involved in the world of agemates and has made great gains in acquiring social adeptness. Later on in childhood and adolescence, through a codification of rules and a genuine feeling for one another, the neighborhood band emerges as a remarkably cohesive and influential primary group that performs many functions in the socialization process.

The process by which the peer "in-group" becomes such an important force in determining behavior is described in the classic "Robber's Cave" experiment of Sherif, Harvey, White, Hood, and Sherif (1961). This study was conducted at a boy's camp. The boys spent some time together in camp before beginning the experiment proper, which allowed them time to establish friendships. Then, after friendships had developed and groups coalesced, they were divided into two groups, cutting across friendship choices whenever possible, so that friends were on opposing teams. The two groups saw very little of each other except when meeting in competition. Prior cross-group friendships ended, and members of each team expressed real bitterness toward the other team. Social ties within each group became extremely strong. Finally, when the two groups were almost at the point of battle, Sherif and his associates provided situations of real importance to the boys in which cooperation between the two groups was necessary. After cooperative experiences had occurred, rivalry and animosity decreased markedly. Having an external enemy makes for strong ties within a group; cooperating with the enemy decreases hostility toward the outsider and decreases the strength of ties within the group as well.

That acceptance by one's peers is rewarding is demonstrated in the tremendous effort made by children to establish themselves when joining a new group of peers. Since the extent to which a child is involved with and accepted by his peers varies, the influence of the society of agemates also varies from child to child. It is to the personal qualities associated with such acceptance by peers that the discussion now moves.

ACCEPTANCE BY PEERS

The measure most often used to learn the degree to which an individual is accepted by others is the sociometric method devised by Moreno (1934). The device is simple. One merely asks a group of individuals a question, of which the following are typical:

Whom would you like to have sit next to you in this classroom? (asked of sixth-grade children).

Whom would you trust to fly at your wing position? (asked of a group of fighter pilots).

Who is your best friend? (asked of kindergarten children).

How often a particular individual is chosen may be considered a measure of how much esteem he has in the group. Questions might be phrased negatively, but generally are not. The mere posing of a negative question such as "Whom would you least like to have sit next to you?" might serve to increase the overt rejection of the child, once his classmates compared notes. Therefore the actively rejected and the social isolate generally cannot be separated and studied as "types" in sociometric studies.

When choices are not limited to a specific group, the sociometric method can turn up information on the group's cohesiveness. For example, if Sunday school children were asked to name their best friends, few choices might be within the Sunday school group. Thus it would not be a very significant social group in the eyes of its members. On the other hand, if members of an informal, neighborhood group of peers were requested to name their best friends, most choices would fall within the society, for groups of peers have a great amount of cohesiveness and solidarity.

Sociometric studies also provide some indication of group morale and single out children within the group who need help to achieve a satisfactory adjustment. Figure 11-2 contains two sociograms of the same group of children. Note the change in the atmosphere of the group from October to March as the school year advanced. The number of isolates declined, the cliques disintegrated, and friendship choices increased.

A major reason for using measures of this sort is to ascertain the relative "healthiness" of a group. This healthiness is based on the satisfaction received by group members. What, then, happens to a group plagued by poor morale? If the group is a fighter squadron, it might be best to disband it and distribute its members among other groups, since their chances of physical survival would not be great if the original group remained intact. Dissolution of the group or removal of some members may also be a solution in children's groups. This applies especially to a younger child who suffers rejection or who is ignored.

Anderson (1956) said that one could not predict with any great amount of accuracy the adjustment or acceptance of a younger child, say one below the age of five. A child ignored within one group might be a highly accepted leader in another. However, this becomes less likely with increases in age. Accidental circumstances lose their importance; consistency in behavior gains; and the learning of social roles continues. The older rejected child is not likely to benefit greatly from transfer to another group, because he has developed certain roles and response tendencies that will probably persist in a new environment and lead to his rejection there. For this child, it might be preferable to teach him the skills valued by the original group, as was done by Jack (1934) and Page (1936), or to teach him mature responses, as was done by Keister and Updegraff (1937). In these areas social maturity is an important component of success.

Another rather widely employed measure of social acceptance is the "guess who" technique, first developed fully by Tryon (1939). To various classrooms of children aged 12 and 15, she put a number of questions such as, "Who always acts grown up?" By combining the "guess who" nominations with sociometric data on popularity, she discovered the traits and characteristics linked to popularity in boys and girls at the two age levels. In the eyes of the 12-year-olds, the ideal boy was aggressive, boisterous, unkempt, and, most important, skilled at games. The ideal girl, to the 12-year-olds, was friendly but demure and docile in social behavior, had quiet humor, and conformed to adult standards. At 15, the popular traits in boys did not change much from 12; the major emphasis was still on game skills. However, boisterousness and unkempt appearance were no longer positive virtues and some poise in dealing with girls became necessary. Meanwhile, the girl now had two highly acceptable new roles. First, she had to be a "girl's girl," a buoyant, rather aggressive pal of both boys and girls. The second was the role of the sophisticated and glamorous *femme fatale*. The demure conformist of 12 was now looked upon in a highly unfavororable light. Thus girls may have greater problems than boys in developing a consistent concept of the self. The role

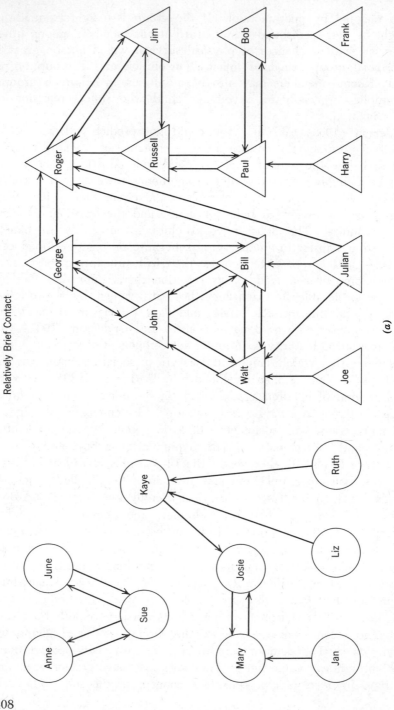

Relatively Brief Contact

(a)

FIGURE 11-2a Changes in sociometric structure as length of time in contact increases.

6 Months Later

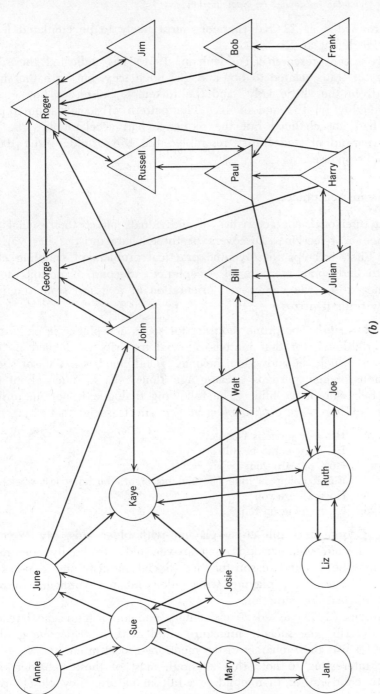

FIGURE 11-2b

(b)

409

most rewarded at 12 and therefore most likely to be emulated leads to social defeat at 15.

More recent research (Tuddenham, 1951) has indicated the same clusters of traits related to boy and girl popularity, but with the shifts away from the "little lady" and the unkempt, boisterous boy occurring roughly by the age of 10. The pattern of socialization apparently had not changed but the sequence had accelerated. The 10- to 12-year-old of midcentury resembled the 15-year-old of the 1930's in social responses.

Factors in Acceptance

Many personal characteristics of individuals affect their social acceptance or rejection. Discovery of these characteristics has various uses. First, it helps to solve the practical problem of enabling children to find some measure of acceptance. Second, it permits some inference about the values and orientation of a group from the personality traits it prizes.

Social Maturity. The prime requisite for social acceptance in childhood —and adulthood, for that matter—is social maturity as defined by the groups to which the individual belongs. Childhood is a time of sharp gradations of age, perhaps because age alone tells so much about the social behavior of a child. The following dialogue is not unfamiliar among children. Here *chronological age* affects social maturity:

George: Hi. My name is George.
Bill: Hi. My name is Bill.
George: How old are you?
Bill: Eight, going on nine (he had his eighth birthday last week). How old are you?
George: Nine, going on ten.

Both George and Bill enjoy playing with older kids, say 12-year-olds, and hold younger kids, say six-year-olds, in kindly contempt. There may be a sound reason for this. Social maturity and game skills vary with age; thus, playing with older but not younger children connotes a learning situation.

Medinnus (1962) asked 25 elementary and junior-high-school teachers to describe the socially immature child in their respective grades. Table 11-1 lists those characteristics mentioned most often.

It is interesting to note that although most of these behaviors are child to child rather than child to adult in nature, they closely parallel the factors found by Koch (1933) many years earlier to be pre-

TABLE 11-1 Characteristics of Socially Immature Children*

Grades 1–3:

Does not play with peers in a controlled manner when not directly supervised.
Wants to be "It" all the time; jealousy when playing; will not take turns.
Will not share readily.
Withdraws from the group.
Inconsiderate—pushes, shoves.
Lacks respect for others' property
Does not cooperate in group activities; does not assume his share of the responsibility.
Interrupts; talks and bothers neighbors.
Plays with children younger than himself.

Grades 4–6:

Does not play or work well with others in his group:
(a) Picks fights; consistently employs pugilistic tactics rather than attempting to "talk it out."
(b) Uncooperative in planning games.
(c) Drops out of games when decisions are made against him (e.g., being called "out" in baseball).
(d) Wants his own way.
Tattles; tendency to report very slight infractions of rules and wrong behavior which is of little actual importance; judgment of wrong behavior corresponds to the evaluation of a younger child.
Rapid changes in friendship loyalties—i.e., a sudden turn against one's seemingly best friend.
Extreme shyness with marked tendency to hang his head or cover the face when asked questions.
Does not observe common courtesies:
(a) Walks in front of people.
(b) Interrupts when others are talking.
(c) Does not use "please" and "thank you."
Lacks respect for others.
Child feels that rules are made for everyone but him; consequently, makes own rules and does not follow the rules of the group.

Grades 7–9:

Plays with children younger than his group.
Interested in the opposite sex in the manner of a much younger person (e.g., would rather play tag than do something socially with a person of the opposite sex).
Child often ignored by peers, which leads to: showing off, giggling, grimaces, pushing or poking, slapping or tripping; or to withdrawal.
Hesitancy in responding when addressed or questioned.
Has difficulty in participating in more highly organized games.
Takes no responsibility for own conduct (must be reminded to be quiet, sit down, etc.).

*From Medinnus, 1962.

dictive of unpopularity among preschool children. The following behavioral characteristics correlated negatively with popularity: the tendencies to play alone, to refuse or ignore the requests of other children,
to attack other children or offer resistance to their attacks, to escape
from undesirable situations, and to dawdle. Basically, social acceptance appears to be a reflection of social maturity.

Like chronological age, *mental age* is involved in social maturity.
The diagnosis of mental deficiency stems from social competence.
Thus a person of IQ 50 who behaved in a socially acceptable manner would not ordinarily be termed mentally defective, whereas another of IQ 100 who disclosed gross social incompetence might very
well be considered so (Doll, 1935, 1941, Heber, 1959). Then, too, as
the Terman study of genius (Terman et al., 1925) indicated, the association of popularity with high IQ (presumably indicative of social
maturity in most cases), irrespective of chronological age, can be quite
conclusively demonstrated. But this relation has an end point. In
the opinion of Hollingworth (1942), as we have seen in Chapter 6,
children above IQ 155 are neither social or antisocial. Rather, they
are asocial in their adjustment to their peers, apparently because they
operate a different conceptual frame of reference.

Sex. Social maturity is not the only factor entering into acceptance
by one's peers. One of the most potent determinants of how well
one child is accepted by another during most of childhood is the sex
of the children in question. In childhood sex cleavage in friendship
is marked (Tuddenham, 1952). This cleavage is so readily observable
that it becomes a defense, and may actually have been the basis of
Freud's idea of latency—that once a child has rejected the parent of the
opposite sex as a love object, it has also rejected all members of that sex
until reaching an adult level of sexuality. Girls initially reject boys
who, after several years of rejection, finally retaliate by rejecting girls.
By early high-school years, girls again begin to accept boys, but boys,
either because of social insensitivity or slower social maturity, continue to reject girls for several more years (Harris & Tseng, 1957).
Generally, these data show, girls are more rejecting than boys, turning away from other girls and parents as well as from boys. Because
this also implies some rejection of themselves, girls are probably less
satisfied by their roles and have lower morale, at least in Western
culture at the present time.

Body build plays a surprisingly large role in social acceptance among
boys; even at a relatively young age they assign favorable traits to
mesomorphic (athletically built) boys, and unfavorable traits, either of

a passive or aggressive character, to boys not of this body type (Staffieri, 1967). Perhaps this assignment is related to the fact that mesomorphs are reportedly more active (Walker, 1962, 1963), and young people place a high positive value on sheer activity level (Kuhlen & Lee, 1943).

Social Class. Class and caste also play a part in acceptance by peers. They begin to have considerable effect during childhood (Bonney, 1944) and increase their influence as children become more accurate judges of social class position (Hollingshead, 1949). Both class and color play large roles in acceptance partly because propinquity or closeness is an important element in determining choice of friendship. Since the chance of any two children being neighbors results in part from class and race, it is not surprising to find that the more stable choices of friendship in later childhood and adolescence depend somewhat on these two factors. This type of segregation on the basis of area of residence, does much to keep class and race differences in values (Ausubel, 1958, p. 433) and interests (Wilson, 1959) in existence. In communities in flux, as opposed to established communities, class barriers in contact play a lesser role (Udry, 1960). This may be one of the charms of such areas as California, which is the greatest "experiment in nature" of mixing races, regional groups, and social classes that has been conducted in our time.

Acceptance by peers is not all good, nor is rejection all bad. Achievement as an adult apparently depends to some extent on lack of involvement with peers (McCurdy, 1957). Yet a continuing rejection by one's peers seems to predict eventual maladjustment better than does an adult's diagnosis of "problem child" (Roff, 1961). The term *peer group* implies that one is being judged by his equals. These judges are harsh but generally accurate, perhaps because they judge less from the prejudices of society and more from individual merit than does the adult world.

CHILDREN'S GROUPS AND THE SOCIALIZATION PROCESS

Involvement with the Peer Group: Cultural and National Differences

Certain conditions must be met before a deep involvement with the peer group is likely to occur. These conditions include the amount of dependence on agemates, amount of contact with agemates, and autonomy from adult control. For example, among primitive (nonliterate) societies, greater contact with and dependence on agemates is seen in war-oriented cultures than in peaceful cultures; this is because in the former, one's agemates are likely to be fellow warriors during a lifetime military career (e.g., see the sections "Puberty" and "War and Peace-making" in Mead & Calas, 1953). Perhaps for this reason, cultures with aggressive gods (warlike cultures) place greater value on independence from parents (autonomy), and presumably encourage greater peer influence than do cultures with more benevolent and pacifistic gods (Lambert, Triandis, & Wolf, 1959). Within contemporary societies, rich, industrial cultures have less use for child labor than older, agrarian cultures, and allow young persons more time for leisure, hence more time for peer contact.

Boehm (1957) offered evidence to show that autonomy from adult control was attained a good deal earlier in the United States than in Europe (in her study, Switzerland). She believed that American parents were less secure, less sure that their way was the right way; therefore they yielded more readily than European parents to pressure from their children. In the United States also the peer group was stronger than in Europe because most Europeans permitted far less interaction between agemates (see McKenney, 1953). Through greater contact, the American society of peers acquired more clearly articulated values and extra ability both to support and coerce members of the group. Under heavier peer pressure the American child encountered weaker parental resistance as he adapted to the demands of his friends. It is indeed possible that changes in the orientation of American culture over a period of time, as well as differences between American and European cultures, may result in part from the growing socializing role of peers in this country from generation to generation and from the greater function served by the peer society in the United States than in Europe.

In Western Europe, the United States, and Canada, a young person's peer-group involvement appears generally to be viewed as an index of his rebellion against adult values. Other cultures use the peer group as an ally in the inculcation of adult-held values. This appears to be the case in the age-graded child rearing of the Israeli kibbutz (collective farm), where adult supervision guides a socialization process in which the peer group gains in significance at the expense of adult (especially parent) agents of socialization (Faigin, 1958; Spiro, 1958). In an analysis of child rearing in the U.S.S.R., Bronfenbrenner (1962) notes that, especially in the school, the peer group is the chief source of values, of rewards, and of discipline. The adult in charge of a group of children establishes the nature of the behaviors to be rewarded, and does the rewarding, but does so through the group and on the basis of group effort. Children in a given row within the classroom are jointly responsible for one another's actions, so that if a child is falling behind in learning fractions, the row leader will provide tutoring either by himself or by the math expert of the row. It is advantageous to the row that all members of this "collective" learn fractions. If the laggard is inept, he is tutored; if lazy, he is disciplined by his fellow collective members. The rows that perform best are given recognition in the form of praise and rewards (special privileges) within the classroom. In the same way, classroom competes with classroom and school with school. Members of each collective (row, classroom, school) discipline and tutor one another, and are the direct (teachers the indirect) source of reinforcement. The peer group in this case, as in that of the kibbutz, has as values such traits as responsibility and ability to delay gratification, which are more often part of the adult than the peer value system in most Western culture; thus the peer culture and adults need not be at odds in terms of values and role prescriptions. Bronfenbrenner's paper spells out procedures used to cause peer values to reflect more accurately the culture as a whole.

Involvement with the Peer Group; Individual Differences

The child who is not allowed a full opportunity to identify with parents is believed to identify more fully with peers (Ausubel, 1958). Other factors also enter into the amount of peer-group involvement. These factors have been studied in the case of boys, but not, to any extent, with girls. Absence of the father from the home produces a situation in which the boy generally has no masculine figure to serve as a model for his behavior. It seems clear that father absence produces a somewhat "feminine" boy when it occurs early (Hetherington, 1966; Lynn & Sawrey, 1959). This "feminine" boy, aware that he is not competent in the masculine role, later develops strong ties with his male peer group, and, in adolescence and early adulthood shows a somewhat uneasy overcompensatory delinquent or "sociopathic" masculinity (Siegman, 1966). Father absence leads to a greater identification with the peer culture, and this overidentification seems likely to lead to delinquent behavior in America, although, as noted above it may not lead to the same problems in some of the other groups within the Western culture. The data suggesting that early "feminization" leads to later excessive involvement with and acceptance of the peer culture by boys allows one to make certain other predictions, as yet untested. Brim (1958) reanalyzed the data in a series of studies reported by Koch (e.g., see Koch, 1956) and demonstrated that boys with older sisters, in two-child families, are more feminine in early childhood than are boys in any other age-sex combination. If the idea of later overcompensatory masculinity holds, then boys with older sisters should develop the closest ties with the male peer group in later childhood and adolescence and should show the highest degree of delinquent behavior of any of the sex-by-age comparison groups (boy-boy, girl-girl, girl-boy; older versus younger in each sex pairing) at a later age.

During childhood, the peer group of equals is remarkably cohesive. This cohesion or solidarity is voluntary. Clearly the group must provide something of value to hold its members in line. What do peers offer?

Normalizing or Leveling Influence

One of the most important contributions of the peer society is its normalizing influence. Adults differ from one another, but the astonishing fact is that they differ so little. As children they were reared with great variability. Yet as youngsters and later as adults they have not differed as much as might have been expected. So Levy's (1943) study of overprotected children, which was discussed in Chapter 10, has demonstrated. It is unlikely that any other group of children raised in their own homes and studied for any length of time was reared in as deviant a manner as this group. Nevertheless, in adulthood, these children were seen to be comparatively normal. They attributed their normality to school and, later, to the job—and to peers. No matter how deviantly an individual may be reared, he is generally exposed to essentially the same information as other individuals and has largely the same demands made of him by his peers. In return, he receives some psychological support from them.

The effect of other children on the development and adjustment of any one child is, first of all, to reduce the influence of parental idiosyncrasy in treatment. This normalizing or leveling influence, making children more similar to one another than might be expected, may prove detrimental to desirable goals. Children raised in homes free of racial prejudice, for example, learn quite quickly from their peers all the forms of bigotry to be found in the culture. Even if they also learn—perhaps more rapidly—to keep these ideas to themselves around home, certain damage has been done. They have been "normalized." A leveling process has occurred. To some moderate degree, they now hold the prejudices common to the culture.

Literature contains many illustrations of the shock of being removed from a tender and affectionate home into the rough and tumble society of peers. It seems equally clear that peers can moderate the influence of brutal, psychotic, neurotic, or otherwise deviant parents. Peer society provides a haven, at least for a time, from the unrealistic and arbitrary demands of the family. The child escapes temporarily into a world of agemates, where he undergoes basically the same experiences as all other children of his age. He becomes a member of the "gang" for better or worse—depending on what his home life was like before initiation.

Following a lecture by Bruno Bettelheim, the noted psychotherapist, a member of the audience asked: "How do parents produce a schizophrenic child?" Bettelheim replied that this could not be done unless, perhaps, the parents kept the child locked up all the time. A child attending school and playing with other children, he said, was exposed to enough of the normal world to prevent parents from making it psychotic. He concluded by saying that even the Dachau or Buchenwald concentration camp would have been unable to destroy men's wills if only the inmates, of which he himself had been one, had been let out to play with each other for a few hours in the afternoon.

In a similar vein, Harlow (1963) found that infant monkeys deprived of mothering nevertheless developed normally as long as they were allowed considerable contact with agemates during their "childhood" and "adolescence." Apparently, the influence of peers has as normalizing an effect on monkeys as on humans.

Only children appear to be deviant more often in both positive and negative directions than children with siblings. This may be because their parents' attentions, whether wholesome or harmful, are not diverted in any way. Similarly, children reared outside the world of agemates are more variable than other children, probably because they are more exclusively the products of parental pressures. Thus, although peers may teach prejudice to the unprejudiced and may divert genius, the "normalizing" effect of this society on child adjustment and behavior is generally good and ameliorative. Through it, the unjustly treated learns something of justice and the rejected finds acceptance.

Identification

To Freud (see Freud, 1935), the infant in his first groping thoughts believed that he was all powerful and that the world was merely an extension of himself. Piaget demonstrated (1954) that Freud's speculations had observable and testable validity. The child learned at about six months that he and the external world were not one. This was the point at which, in Freudian psychology, the ego or concept of self developed. Once having separated himself from the rest of the world, the child became aware of not being omnipotent, but rather of being impotent—a powerless creature in a threatening world.

Ausubel (1958) speculated that in response to this awareness of impotence, to escape the fear associated with helplessness, the child identified with his parents, the all-powerful beings of his universe, and thus vicariously regained a feeling of power and control. Some parents did not allow the child to identify himself with them; then the child remained anxious and fearful. Although Ausubel did not suggest it, the child denied this vicarious control might, as he got older, show greater concern for compulsively ordering and thus controlling his small world than might the undenied child. Gaining some measure of power and control in this way seems possible, but the cost is likely to be steep in terms of psychic well-being. If parents deny a child vicarious power, Ausubel suggested, it may be obtained through identification with one's peers. Research conducted by Lesser and Abelson (1959) provided experimental support for the notion that a child who has not identified closely with parents will be more likely to identify strongly with peers. It is probably for this reason that close parent-child ties serve to "insulate" the child from delinquency, even in high-delinquency, high-crime areas (Scarpitti, Murray, Simon, & Reckless, 1960).

Children identifying with peers should differ from others whose main identification is with parents. Such children should be lacking in inner controls, or conscience, which to a considerable degree depend for their development on the child's love relationship with his parents (Hoffman, 1962). These controls are unlikely to evolve if the parents reject the child's efforts to identify. To use Riesman's (1950) distinction, such children should be more "other directed" than "inner directed." In Freudian terminology, this type of individual should have an *externalized superego;* that is, his standards would vary with the standards of the group to which he belonged at any particular time. One might predict that children denied early identification with parents would associate more with their peers as well as adhere more rigidly to the codes of the peer culture.

Ausubel's theory fits the facts. Quite probably rejected children identify more closely with agemates, and those who make this identification very close are likely to lack inner controls and become more conforming. In everyday life one sees the gangs of juvenile delinquents composed of youths from broken homes or with no parent ties at all. Yet other, simpler explanations may account for these facts. Correct or not, Ausubel's ideas seem at present to be an interesting, if unproved, attempt to bridge the gap between psychoanalytic theory and observed differences in the degree to which children identify with parents and peers. If Ausubel's views are correct, a child would pay a price of lack of autonomy and of inner controls for identification with peers, yet would find the identification worthwhile, for without it the world would be too threatening to face with equanimity. It is an interesting sidelight that six orphaned Jewish children (Freud & Dann, 1951) who were denied any opportunity to identify with adults while forced to live in the most threatening of all environments, a Nazi concentration camp in which 30,000 Jews perished, developed peer ties that were remarkable in their strength.

Thus far, the emphasis in this discussion of identification with peers has been on the pathological, on the indications of disturbances in function. However, some degree of identification with one's agemates is a normal and useful part of child development. A major aim of child rearing in Western culture is to produce an autonomous or independent child. The child attempts to emancipate himself from parental control, while his parents gradually relinquish control in a rear-guard action to retain it. To borrow the language of Potter's *Gamesmanship* (1948), the child attempts to become one-up (dominant) with regard to parents, even when secretly desiring at times to remain one-down (submissive). The parents face the difficult task of teaching the child to be one-up by keeping him one-down until he has learned such "ploys" (maneuvers) that he bests them in the power struggle. At this point he is mature enough to be allowed to try out his ploys in the world at large: he is independent.

Identification with peers appears to be a prime force aiding in the emancipation from parents. It provides enough security for the child to risk the moderate parental rejection occasioned by each small victory in his development of independence. In the quest for emancipation, such identification forces the child to stick to the timetable used by agemates of the same sex. For example, a nine-year-old who is not allowed to go to Saturday movie matinees when other nine-year-olds are is made aware by his friends that his timetable lags. Pressing hard for this concession, he wins it after a few weeks and a number of encounters with his parents. He has thus taken one more step toward autonomy as a result of the combined coercion and support received from the peers with whom he identifies.

Learning

A vast amount of learning occurs among peers. Although this group has neither the traditional authority of the family nor the legal authority of the schools for teaching information and values, it manages to convey a substantial body of material to its members. Robert Paul Smith (1958) in his evocative, poignant book, *"Where Did You Go?" "Out." "What Did You Do?" "Nothing."*, described the learning process in this way:

I don't remember being taught how to play mumbly-peg. (I know, I know. In the books they write it "mumblety-peg," but we said, and it *was*, "mumbly-peg.") When you were a little kid, you stood around while a covey of ancients of nine or ten played mumbly-peg, shifting from foot to foot and wiping your nose on your sleeve and hitching up your knickerbockers, saying, "Lemme do it, aw come on, lemme have a turn," until one of them struck you in a soft spot and you went home to sit under the porch by yourself, or found a smaller kid to torture, or loused up your sister's rope-skipping, or made a collection of small round stones. The small round stones were not *for* anything, it was just to have a collection of small round stones.

One day you said, "Lemme have a turn, lemme have a turn," and some soft-hearted older brother, never your own, said, "Go-wan, let the kid have a turn," and there, by all that was holy, you were playing mumbly-peg . . . (Smith, 1958, pp. 4–5).

What Smith learned in a "house" he and his friends built he tells of as follows:

It was a pitiful wreck of a tarpaper hut, and in it I learned the difference between boys and girls, I learned that all fathers did that, I learned to swear, to play with myself, to sleep in the afternoon, I learned that some people were Catholics and some people were Protestants and some people were Jews, that people came from different places. I learned that other kids wondered, too, who they would have been if their fathers had not married their mothers, wondered if you could dig a hole right to the center of the earth, wondered if you could kill yourself by holding your breath. (None of us could.)

I learned that with three people assembled, it was only for the briefest interludes that all three liked each other. Mitch and I were leagued against Simon. And then Simon and I against Mitch. And then—but you remember. I didn't know then just how to handle that situation. I still don't. It is my coldly comforting feeling that nobody still does, including nations, and that's what the trouble with the world is. That's what the trouble with the world was then—when Mitch and Simon were the two and I was the one.

What else did I learn in the hut? That if two nails will not hold a board in place, three will probably not either, but the third nail will split the board. I think kids still do that. I think objects made of wood by children, left to their own devices, if such there be, will assay ten per cent wood, ninety per cent nails.

In the hut we looked and we learned. And drooled. I remember a picture of Clara Bow with one shoulder strap—and then there was Toby Wing—and look at Lily Damita—she's bending *way* over . . . (Smith, 1958, pp. 78–80).

Games and Social Learning

The chief voluntary occupation of children's groups is play. Yet children's games are among the most traditional and conservative of human institutions. It is difficult to establish the earliest historical mention of a game, but these are some of the macabre facts that have been found. *Hopscotch* seems to have originated in Greece or Crete, modeled after that most elaborate labyrinth of all, King Minos' (Spence, 1947). This mild game seems at one time to have been a method for selecting a sacrificial victim. Other games of the same original purpose abound. *London Bridge* seems very likely to be a remnant of those older times when a person chosen by this method each year was flung from the Bridge to propitiate the gods. An identical "game" with the same purpose has been described in an Icelandic source, *The Vatnsdaela Saga,* dating from the eleventh century. *Blindman's bluff,* originally "hoodman's blind," or "executioner is blind," or "Blind Harry," began as a northern European "game" in which a sacrificial "lamb" was selected at random. The game of *jacks* also seems innocuous enough, yet in its original form of knucklebones it was a fifth century B.C. device for foretelling the future (David, 1955). One throw, the "throw of Zeus," meant one could kill one's enemy and escape detection. From this bizarre form of soothsaying sprang both dice and jacks.

In her book of jump-rope rhymes, Patricia Evans (1955) wrote that rope jumping began as a form of sympathetic magic. Farmers would jump rope in the spring, believing that their small grains would grow as high as they jumped. Jump-rope rhymes are interesting in their continuity and in their geographical dispersion. Evans mentioned that the earliest rhyme she could find dated from medieval England and started with the words, "Andy pandy, sugardy candy." Coincidentally, in San Francisco in 1955, a popular rhyme began with "Amos and Andy, sugar and candy." She recorded another rhyme used in San Francisco that was almost identical to one recorded by Opie and Opie (1959) in England at approximately the same time.

Charlie Chaplin went to France	Charlie Chaplin
To teach the ladies how to dance	Went to France
First he did the rhumba,	To teach the ladies
Then he did the kicks,	How to dance.
Then he did the samba,	First the heel
Then he did the splits	And then the toe
(Opie & Opie, 1959, p. 110)	Left foot forward
	Out you go.
	(Evans, 1955, p. 8)

Spence (1947) reported that *tag* at the time of its first reference in Germany involved touching iron, a medieval safeguard from witches and other supernatural beings, in order to be safe from the *it* who was called the devil.

Since adults do not pay much attention to the games of children, it is hard to find literary reference to them. However, Virgil in Volume VII of *Aeneid* described spinning tops. Shakespeare mentioned a number of games including *hide and seek* (*Hamlet, IV, ii, 32*), *leap frog* (*Henry V, ii, 141–144*), *blindman's bluff* (*All's Well That Ends Well, IV, iii, 137–138*), *and prisoner's base* (*Cymbeline, V, iii, 19–20*).

Several books on children's games show their amazing continuity. A curious volume called *A Little Pretty Pocket Book* was published by Isaiah Thomas in 1787. (The book actually dates back to 1744 when it was written and published by John Newberry in London. Thomas pirated the book and published it in the United States.) This book describes the games and sports popular with children of that era. Of the 24 activities listed, 21 are still popular today. Two studies of games appeared at the turn of the century. One by Newell (1899) described the games of American children, and the other by Gomme, 1894, 1898) dealt with the games of English youngsters. There is a remarkable correspondence between the games contained in the two books. Moreover, most of them are still played today.

Change. Change does occur in children's games and game preferences (e.g., see Sutton-Smith & Rosenberg, 1961) but for the most part, only slowly. For example, both Newell and Gomme write of *Starlight, Moonlight,* a more complex version of hide and seek, which with the advent of traffic lights became known as *Red Light, Green Light.* Although Gomme stated her belief that traditional children's games would be forgotten with the increasing communication and urbanization of the English, these traditional games have shown an astonishing vitality. Despite modifications and changes, continuity is the rule. The Opies (1959) present an illustration of the continuity found in children's rhymes:

1725	1907
Now he acts the *Grenadier,*	Eenty, teenty, tuppenny bun,
Calling for *a Pot of Beer:*	Pitching tatties doon the lum;
Where's his Money? He's	Who's there? John Blair.
forgot:	What does he want? A bottle
Get him gone, a Drunken Sot.	of beer.
	Where's your money? I forgot.
	Go downstairs, you drunken sot.

1939	1950
A frog walked into a public house	Mickey Mouse In a public house
And asked for a pint of beer.	Drinking pints of beer.
Where's your money?	Where's your money?
In my pocket.	In my pocket.
Where's your pocket,	Where's your pocket?
I forgot it.	I forgot it.
Well, please walk out.	Please walk out.

(Opie & Opie, 1959, p. 11)

On the other hand, if something is provided to children from the adult world, children may seize on it, change it in various ways, and make it part of their oral tradition. Witness the various verses devised by English youngsters to the tune of *Davy Crockett*:

> Born on a roof top in Battersea,
> Joined the Teds when he was only three,
> Coshed a cop when he was only four
> And now he's in Dartmoor for evermore.
>   Davy, Davy Crockett,
>   King of the Teddy boys.

> Standing on the corner, swinging his chain,[1]
> Along came a policeman and took his name;
> He pulled out the razor and he slit the copper's throat,
> Now he's wiping up the blood with his Teddy boy's coat.
>   Davy, Davy Crockett,
>   King of the Teddy boys.

Once part of the oral tradition of children, a game or rhyme is transmitted across generations of children with little variation, perhaps because the older child of 11 or 12 insists that the younger child of six or seven learn it exactly. Frequently these games or rhymes are discarded aspects of the adult world. As Piaget (1932) showed, the young child is so impressed with the need for exactness that he often believes game rules are framed by God. Small wonder that child culture is conservative and allows little room for change. The question is, why are games so tradition-bound and conservative?

Perhaps games and rhymes transmit certain values of importance to the peer society. Only one person has explicitly stated this to be the case. Froebel (1898), founder of the kindergarten movement, believed

[1] Chain, i.e., bicycle chain, used as a weapon in street-gang warfare (Opie & Opie, 1958, p. 119).

that the child acquired a set of values from those inherent in the games played. For this reason he invented a series of games that he felt would teach a *better* set of values, a set involving knowledge of temporal and spatial relationships, of causality, and of human social interaction.

Information Learned. Piaget (1932) noted that game functions appeared to have vital significance for the socialization process, yet this has not been explored further by anyone else. For him, as mentioned in Chapter 4, children were morally realistic, judging acts in terms of consequences, not motives. They also showed other signs of immature moral judgment. Such immaturity, Piaget believed, resulted from adult constraints as well as from the concreteness of children's own thought processes. This was countered, however, by the child's peers who, in part, helped him to achieve maturity in moral judgment. Among peers one was judged by and judged others, exposing the basic unfairness of moral realism. As Piaget saw it, one eventually learned from contact with peers that game rules were not immutable. Rather they could be changed by mutual consent, or reciprocity. Through this knowledge an awareness of democratic processes and of fairness developed. From games, one learned arbitration.

Time spent at games is about equally divided between playing and arguing. Arguing over whether a pitched ball was a strike, over whose turn it is, over whether one has been tagged out, over whether one has been scalped by the Indians and must remain wounded for an indeterminate interval—all these are among the most common experiences of childhood. During these verbal battles, children acquire an understanding of the spirit of rules and the law, in contrast to the understanding of the letter of the law manifested by the young child. The child learns fairness and reciprocity, tact and diplomacy.

Children's games are not highly organized and are usually based on individual competition far more than on cooperative effort. If a choice is involved, most children will choose a game where the *it* role is made quite difficult and challenging (Sutton-Smith, 1955) Games youngsters like best, in contrast to those liked best by teachers and recreation leaders, are those in which a hierarchy of status on the basis of ability is manifest. Children, and in particular those children who find little chance for success at meeting adult demands, can find a position of status among their peers through skill and daring.

Most games share another characteristic, which might be referred to as "manageable fear." Although adults undertake such sport, children far more than their elders seem to relish frightening themselves as long as the fear is contained within bounds. Children's games are frequently of this sort. They create a vicarious danger that may provide the child with some of the information and strength needed to deal with real perils.

After a long lapse of interest children's games again are being investigated. One can measure age and sex differences in masculinity–femininity of game interests (Rosenberg & Sutton-Smith, 1959), and in toy preference (De Lucia, 1963), though important regional (Midwest versus East) differences exist in the masculinity–femininity of game choices between boys and girls of a given age group, and across age groups (Walker, 1964). Since a high proportion of children's time is spent in play, this increase in research interest should lead to a fuller understanding of the learning situations and values inherent in games.

Role Playing. The play activities of peers also open opportunities for role playing, and in so doing seem to fill a valuable function. The ability to play a role is apparently related to intellectual ability (Feffer & Gourevitch, 1960) and to adjustment. People differ in ability to play social roles; excessively poor role players are less adequately adjusted than individuals with some role-playing ability (Mann & Mann, 1960). Certainly the dramatic play of childhood is concerned chiefly with role playing. It provides the child with a rich variety of roles to tackle. To be a cowboy is easy. To be a railroad engineer or a parent is not much more difficult. But to be a sandbox, or something equally inanimate, may pose quite a challenge.

Most roles played offer some preparation for later roles in real life. Conceivably the play of girls with dolls, for example, provides a base for later care of real children both in attitudes toward infants and in knowledge of how to care for them. Even if a girl of four may leave her favorite "baby" out in the rain for a few days, the eight- or nine-year-old appears to have learned her maternal role quite adequately. For the boy, however, whose adult functions are not easily anticipated in play, unless he happens to become a cowboy as an adult, there is less to be gained from peer activities in this specific area, just as he probably benefits more than girls in learning arbitration, since his games are more complex and his rules more rigidly codified.

Peers as a Reality Check

A final form of learning to be discerned in the society of peers is that of growing more closely attuned to the reality about oneself. Parents may become so emotionally involved with the child that they cannot evaluate him in anything but the most favorable light. Or they may be so caught up in their own problems that they cannot evaluate him at all, or can evaluate him only negatively. Teachers seem to be moving away from comparing children with other children. But the one group that can be relied on to evaluate and to compare is the society of peers.

Seldom is it enjoyable to have reality brought home to oneself—"to see ourselves as others see us." Yet only upon becoming aware of others' opinions does one consider change. Peers are harsh but relatively unbiased judges. Any undesirable trait is quickly spotted by them and they are quite frank to deride it, thus heightening the possibility for change. The accuracy of their assessment has been indicated by a study by Roff (1961) showing that among adults who were considered behavior problems in their own childhood, one of the best auguries of adult adjustment was acceptance by peers. If a child is judged to be a problem child by adults but is accepted by his peers, his chances of making a normal adjustment are good. But if the peer society also considers him a problem his chances fall precipitously. Harsh as peer judgment and severe as its penalties may be, both seem relatively fair and accurate.

Psychologists have a vast, unexplored world to map, and the territory of peers is still largely unpenetrated. Yet it seems reasonable to believe from a brief sight of peer country that events occur to a child as a result of his interactions with other children of the same age that bear heavily on the process of growing up.

SUMMARY

Children are interested in other children early in life, yet their interactions are minimal because of their inadequate impulse control and their inability to have much feeling for the other person. With age, interaction increases, producing more quarrels and aggression as well as greater cooperation and sympathy. The degree of any child's involvement with agemates differs from age to age and also within any age group.

Children vary greatly in the degree to which they are accepted by children of the same age and to which they become involved in peer activity. Measuring devices enable the social scientist to assess the acceptance of children by their mates and to determine the personality traits associated with acceptance or rejection by peers.

By elementary school age, sex division begins to occur among children of the same age. From this time onward during childhood the influence of the peer society is principally that of agemates of the same sex.

The peer society plays a vital role in socialization. Peers have a normalizing or leveling effect. They allow the child an opportunity for identification. Peer society conveys to its members a large body of information and values. It provides a wide opportunity for the learning and playing of social roles. It makes available to the child a reality check from which he can judge his own behavior more accurately. The world of peers is largely unexplored by psychologists, but seems to be a harsh though fair one that has great significance for the socialization process.

REFERENCES

Anderson, J. E. Personality organization in children. *American Psychologist,* 1948, **3**, 409–416.

Anderson, J. E. Personal communication, 1956.

Ausubel, D. P. *Ego development and the personality disorders.* New York: Grune & Stratton, 1952.

Ausubel, D. P. *Theory and problems of child development.* New York: Grune & Stratton, 1958.

Barker, R. C., & Wright, H. F. *Midwest and its children: The psychological ecology of an American town.* New York: Row, Peterson, 1955.

Boehm, L. The development of independence: a comparative study. *Child Development,* 1957, **28**, 85–92.

Bonney, M. E. Relationships between social success, family size, socio-economic background, and intelligence among school children in grades III to V. *Sociometry,* 1944, **7**, 26–39.

Brim, O. G., Jr. Family structure and sex role learning by children: A further analysis of Helen Koch's data. *Sociometry,* 1958, **21**, 1–16.

Bronfenbrenner, U. Soviet methods of character education: Some implications for research. *American Psychologist,* 1962, **17**, 550–564.

David, F. N. Studies in the history of probability and statistics. *Biometrika,* 1955, **42**, 1–32.

De Lucia, L. A. The toy preference test: A measure of sex role identification in children. *Child Development,* 1963, **34**, 107–117.

Doll, E. A. *The Vineland social maturity scale. Manual of directions.* Vineland, N. J.: The Training School, 1935.

Doll, E. A. The essentials of an inclusive concept of mental deficiency. *American Journal of Mental Deficiency,* 1941, **46**, 214–219.

Evans, P. *Jump rope rhymes.* San Francisco: Porpoise Book Shop, 1955.

Faigin, H. Social behavior of young children in the kibbutz. *Journal of Abnormal and Social Psychology,* 1958, **56**, 117–129.

Feffer, M. H., & Gourevitch, V.   Cognitive aspects of role playing in children. *Journal of Personality*, 1960, **28**, 383–396.

Freud, A., & Dann, S.   An experiment in group upbringing. *The psychoanalytic study of the child.* Vol. 6.   New York: International Universities Press, 1951.

Freud, S.   *The ego and the id.*   London: Hogarth, 1935.

Froebel, F.   *Mother play* (Trans. by H. R. Eliot & S. E. Blow.)   New York: Appleton, 1898.

Gomme, A. B.   *Traditional games of England, Scotland, and Ireland* (Vols. 1 and 2).   London: Methuen, 1894, 1898.

Gomme, A. B.   *Old English singing games.*   New York: Dodd Merrill, 1900.

Greenberg, P. J.   Competition in children; an experimental study.   *American Journal of Psychology*, 1932, **44**, 221–248.

Haas, M. B., & Harms, I. E.   Social interaction between infants.   *Child Development*, 1963, **34**, 79–98.

Harlow, H. F.   Effects of early experiences on personal-social, sexual, and maternal behavior.   Paper read to the Society for Research in Child Development, Berkeley, Calif., April 11, 1963.

Harris, D. B., & Tseng, S. C.   Children's attitudes toward peers and parents as revealed by sentence completions.   *Child Development*, 1957, **28**, 401–411.

Heber, R.   A manual on terminology and classification in mental retardation. *Monograph Supplement to the American Journal of Mental Deficiency*, 1959, **64**, No. 2.

Hetherington, E. M.   Effects of paternal absence on sex-typed behaviors in Negro and white pre-adolescent boys.   *Journal of Personality and Social Psychology*, 1966, **4**, 87–91.

Hoffman, M. L.   The role of the parent in the child's moral growth.   *Religious Education*, 1962, **57** (Research Supplement), pp. S18–S33.

Hollingshead, A. deB.   *Elmtown's youth: The impact of social classes on youth.*   New York: Wiley, 1949.

Hollingworth, L. S.   *Children above IQ 180.*   New York: World Book, 1942.

Jack, L. M.   An experimental study of ascendant behavior in preschool children.   *University of Iowa Study in Child Welfare*, 1934, **9**, No. 3.

Jersild, A. T., and Markey, F. V.   Conflicts between preschool children.   *Child Development Monographs*, No. 21, 1935.

Keister, M. E., & Updegraff, R.   A study of children's reactions to failure and an experimental attempt to modify them.   *Child Development*, 1937, **8**, 241–248.

Koch, H. L.   Popularity in children: Some related factors and a technique for its measurement.   *Child Development*, 1933, **5**, 164–175.

Koch, H. L.   Sissiness and tomboyishness in relation to sibling characteristics. *Journal of Genetic Psychology*, 1956, **88**, 231–244.

Kuhlen, R. G., & Lee, B. J.   Personality characteristics and social acceptability in adolescence.   *Journal of Educational Psychology*, 1943, **34**, 321–340.

Lambert, W. W., Triandis, L. M., & Wolf, M. Some correlates of beliefs in the malevolence of benevolence of supernatural beings: A cross social study. *Journal of Abnormal and Social Psychology,* 1959, **58,** 162–169.

Lesser, G. S., & Abelson, R. P. Personality correlates of persuasibility in children. In I. C. Janis & C. I. Hovland et al. (Eds.), *Personality and persuasibility.* New Haven: Yale University Press, 1959. Pp. 187–206.

Levy, D. M. *Maternal overprotection.* New York: Columbia University Press, 1943.

Lynn, D., & Sawrey, W. L. The effects of father-absence on Norwegian boys and girls. *Journal of Abnormal and Social Psychology,* 1959, **59,** 258–262.

McCurdy, H. G. The childhood pattern of genius. *Journal of the Elisha Mitchell Scientific Society,* 1957, **73,** 448–462. [Also in R. A. King (Ed.), *Readings for an introduction to psychology.* New York: McGraw-Hill, 1961. Pp. 269–278.]

McKenney, R. Paris! City of children. *Holiday,* April 1953, 63–68. (Also in W. S. Martin & C. B. Stendler (Eds.), *Readings in child development.* New York: Harcourt, Brace, 1954. Pp. 199–203.)

Mann, J. H., & Mann, C. H. The relative effectiveness of role playing and task oriented group experience in producing personality and behavior change. *Journal of Social Psychology,* 1960, **51,** 313–317.

Marshall, H. R., & McCandless, B. R. Relationships between dependence on adults and social acceptance by peers. *Child Development,* 1957, **28,** 413–419.

Maudry, M., and Nekula, M. Social relations between children of the same age during the first two years of life. *Journal of Genetic Psychology,* 1939, **54,** 193–215.

Mead, M., & Calas, N. *Primitive heritage.* New York, Random House, 1953.

Medinnus, G. R. Behavioral indices of social immaturity. Unpublished manuscript, San Jose State College, San Jose, Calif., 1962.

Moreno, J. L. *Who shall survive?* Washington, D. C.: Nervous and Mental Diseases Publishing, 1934.

Murphy, B. *Social behavior and child personality.* New York: Columbia University Press, 1937.

Newell, W. *Games and songs of American children.* New York: Harper, 1899.

Opie, I., and Opie, P. *The lore and language of school children.* London: Oxford at the Clarenden Press, 1959.

Page, M. L. The modification of ascendant behavior in preschool children. *University of Iowa Study in Child Welfare,* 1936, **11,** No. 3.

Parten, M. An analysis of social participation, leadership, and other factors in pre-school play groups. Doctoral dissertation, University of Minnesota, 1929.

Parten, M. Social participation among pre-school children. *Journal of Abnormal and Social Psychology,* 1932, **27,** 243–269.

Parten, M., & Newhall, S. M. Social behavior of preschool children. In R. G.

Barker, J. S. Kounin, & H. F. Wright (Eds.), *Child behavior and development.* New York: McGraw-Hill, 1943. Pp. 509–525.

Piaget, J. *The moral judgment of the child.* New York: Harcourt, Brace, 1932.

Piaget, J. *The construction of reality in the child.* New York: Basic Books, 1954.

Potter, S. *The theory and art of gamesmanship.* New York: Holt, 1948.

Riesman, D. (with N. Glazer & R. Denny). *The lonely crowd.* New Haven: Yale University Press, 1950.

Roff, M. Childhood social interactions and young adult bad conduct. *Journal of Abnormal and Social Psychology,* 1961, **63,** 333–337.

Rosenberg, B. G., & Sutton-Smith, B. The measurement of masculinity and femininity in children. *Child Development,* 1959, **30,** 373–380.

Scarpitti, R. R., Murray, E., Simon, D., & Reckless, W. C. The "good" boy in a high delinquency area: Four years later. *American Sociological Review,* 1960, **25,** 555–558.

Sherif, M., Harvey, O. J., White, B. J., Hood, D. R., & Sherif, C. W. *Intergroup conflict and cooperation: The Robbers' Cave experiment,* Norman, Okla.: University of Oklahoma Press, 1961.

Siegman, A. W. Father absence during early childhood and anti-social behavior. *Journal of Abnormal Psychology,* 1966, **71,** 71–74.

Smith, R. P. *"Where did you go?" "Out." "What did you do?" "Nothing."* New York: Pocket Books, 1958 (first published by Norton, New York, 1957).

Spence, L. J. *Myth and ritual in dance, game, and rhyme.* London: Watts, 1947.

Spiro, M. E. *Children of the kibbutz.* Cambridge, Mass.: Harvard University Press, 1958.

Staffieri, J. R. A study of social stereotype of body image in children. *Journal of Personality and Social Psychology,* 1967, **7,** 101–104.

Sutton-Smith, B. The "it" role in children's games. *The Group,* 1955, **17,** 123–128.

Sutton-Smith, B., & Rosenberg, B. G. Sixty years of historical change in the game preferences of American children. *Journal of American Folklore,* 1961, **74,** 17–46.

Terman, L. M., et al. *Genetic studies of genius.* Vol. 1. *Mental and physical traits of a thousand gifted children.* Stanford, Calif.: Stanford University Press, 1925.

Thomas, Isaiah. *A little pretty pocketbook.* Worcester, Mass., 1787.

Tryon, C. M. Evaluation of adolescent personality by adolescents. *Monographs of the Society for Research in Child Development,* 1939, **4,** No. 4.

Tuddenham, R. D. Studies in reputation: III. Correlates of popularity among elementary school children. *Journal of Educational Psychology,* 1951, **42,** 257–276.

Tuddenham, R. D. Studies in reputation: I. Sex and grade differences in school children's evaluation of their peers.   II. The diagnosis of social adjustment.   *Psychological Monographs,* 1952, **66,** No. 333.

Udry, R. J.   The importance of social class in a suburban school.   *Journal of Educational Sociology,* 1960, **33,** 307–310.

Walker, R. N.   Body build and behavior in young children: I. Body building and nursery school teachers' ratings.   *Monographs of the Society for Research in Child Development,* 1962, **27,** No. 84.

Walker, R. N.   Body build and behavior in young children: II. Body build and parents' ratings.   *Child Development,* 1963, **34,** 1–23.

Walker, R. N.   Measuring masculinity and femininity by children's games choices.   *Child Development,* 1964, **35,** 961–969.

Wilson, A. B.   Residential segregation of social classes and aspirations of high school boys.   *American Sociological Review,* 1959, **24,** 836–845.

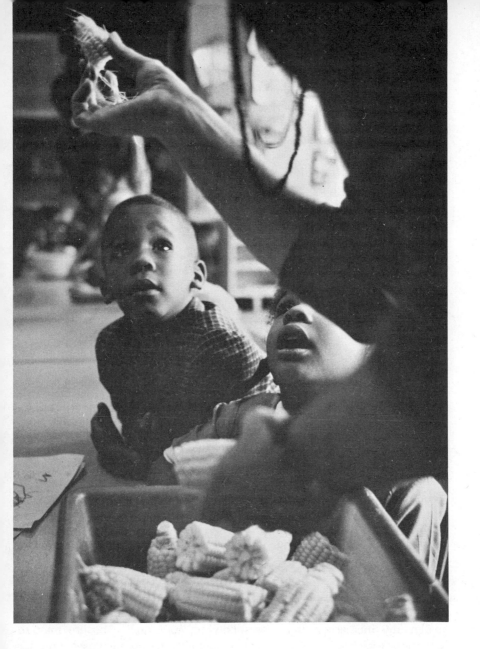

The Child in the School

The school transmits the values of the society to each succeeding generation of children, thus perpetuating the basic facets of a culture. Its significance in the child's life becomes clear from the realization that it is the setting for much of his relationship with his peers. Because of the social interaction occurring within it, the school, through its personnel, attempts to guide and facilitate the personality development of its pupils. No longer the center of community life as it was in rural America, the school continues to play an important role in the lives of young people from five to 18.

The concern of the present chapter is essentially the various aspects of school experience that influence the child's development of personality. Nursery school, the beginning of formal schooling and what it means to the child, the teacher's role in the classroom, especially her part in establishing a psychological atmosphere, the factors involved in achievement, social-class membership, and competition—all these are considered in turn. Educational methodologies and materials are better left to texts on educational practice. Besides, the teacher's fund of knowledge, her enthusiasm, and the kind of psychological and emotional relationship existing between her and her pupils are the really crucial matters that most significantly affect the child in the classroom.

NURSERY-SCHOOL EXPERIENCE

In the 1930's child psychologists spent inordinate amounts of effort endeavoring to discover the relative contributions of heredity and environment to a child's intellectual development. One aspect of this issue—or indeed, controversy—was the effect of nursery-school experience. According to one camp (see Wellman, 1932; Skeels, Updegraff, Wellman, & Williams, 1938), nursery school produced a gain in IQ; according to another (see Olson & Hughes, 1940; Goodenough & Maurer, 1940) this was not necessarily so. More likely, attendance at nursery school may increase IQ scores although it probably does not exert any long-range influence on the functioning of the intellect. Actually, any increase in IQ scores flowing from such exposure may result from a variety of nonintellective factors, such as increased familiarity with the materials and tasks contained in intelligence tests and greater adult-child rapport.

The enriched nursery-school environment may have a salutary effect on children from deprived or impoverished backgrounds, but it is doubtful whether nursery-school experience will improve the IQs of children from homes offering an adequate amount of intellectual stimulation. Yet even if one were to concede that nursery school stimulates intel-

434

lectual development, it would be difficult to identify the specific factors in the nursery-school environment that account for this.

By the 1940's, interest had shifted to the effect of nursery-school experience on the child's social and emotional adjustment. Even before that time Walsh (1931) had found a number of personality traits to be more pronounced in a group of children who had had six months of nursery-school training than in a similar group lacking such experience. The former group seemed more spontaneous in behavior and showed more independence, initiative, self-reliance, and curiosity than the control group. Other early studies noted similar differences (Hattwick, 1936; Van Alstyne & Hattwick, 1939). Later, Bonney and Nicholson (1958) saw some indications that elementary-school children who had had previous exposure to nursery school were more popular with their peers. However, this was not found to be the case in several earlier studies reviewed by them; these showed negative findings regarding the relation between preschool experience and pupil adjustment.

Notwithstanding the inconclusive nature of the research available, some comments seem to be in order. The very nature of the nursery-school situation, in which relatively large numbers of children interact under the supervision of one or two adults, would tend to encourage the development of independent behavior. In such a setting the child must learn to fend for himself. In addition, a certain amount of social learning inevitably occurs from participation in the group over a period of time. Some behaviors are discovered to be unacceptable to peers, whereas other behaviors result in pleasant, favorable responses and are thus reinforced. However, a follow-up study of a number of elementary-school children who had previously attended nursery school found consistency in behavior from nursery school through the elementary years, thus implying that peer responses alone may not suffice to remedy behavior difficulties (Van Alstyne & Hattwick, 1939). Since the source of such problems often lies in the parent-child relationship, which is a continuing one, influences outside the home cannot always counter those within it.

Nursery schools vary widely in goals and procedures. So do the behavioral results they hope to achieve in children. Certainly the quality of the school and the characteristics of the teacher determine the effects of this experience on the child. The importance of the teacher is reflected in an experimental study (Thompson, 1944) which analyzed the impact on nursery-school children of two different types of teacher-child relations. In one group the teacher was instructed to develop a warm relationship with each child and to stimulate the children's activities by providing information and assistance. In the other group contact between teacher and children remained at a minimum and the teacher participated in the children's activities only upon request. At the end of the school year the children in the first group, in contrast to those in the second, were seen to be more ascendant as well as more constructive in the face of possible failure. Moreover, they showed greater social participation and leadership. No noteworthy difference was detected between the two groups in nervous habits or IQ.

Attendance at a nursery school for at least part of the day may have some bearing on the relationship between mother and child. The time spent away from home may benefit both. The mother may enjoy temporary relief from her child-care responsibilities; the child enters a situation in which he learns to accommodate to the demands of an adult other than his parent. Like the effect of maternal employment on the child, the quality, not the quantity, of the mother-child interaction is the important thing. Quite possibly a reduction in quantity raises the level of the quality, or so it would seem from the typical report of mothers whose youngsters attend nursery school.

The nursery-school setting, through its equipment and type of supervision, is designed to reduce the amount of restrictions placed on a child and to encourage physical activity and self expression. Few homes are arranged like it either with respect to schedule or physical facilities. In consequence, frictions present in the home, such as sibling rivalries or mother-child antagonisms centering about certain areas of behavior, can be minimized or avoided in the nursery-school setting.

However, this does not mean that compulsory school attendance should be lowered to the preschool years. Early child rearing is a parental responsibility and should perhaps remain so. The value of the nursery-school experience is that it may enable the parent to gain some insight and understanding about the child-rearing process from a new perspective.

Preschool Programs for the Disadvantaged

A great surge of interest in the educational training of the preschool child is evident currently in public and professional circles. This interest has been stimulated by the fortunate confluence of two developments. First, there is a group of psychologists who have revised their thinking regarding intellectual development. Recognition has long been given to the effects of the child's early social and emotional experiences on his subsequent personality development and general adjustment. Only recently, however, have interest and research focused on the crucial importance of the early years in terms of the child's cognitive development. Second, the involvement of the federal government in the War on Poverty program has included Project Head Start, in which disadvantaged children are given preschool training during an eight-week summer period. Each of these two factors will be discussed in more detail.

Hunt (1961, 1964) has argued convincingly that certain traditional beliefs in psychology have prevented serious consideration of the value of preschool enrichment in stimulating intellectual development. These include the notion that intelligence is relatively fixed at birth and not subject to alteration by the environment. Further, the many early studies on the maturation versus environment issue concluded that development is predetermined; however, a majority of these studies dealt with simple motor skills and not with such complex abilities as intelligence. Hebb's (1949) emphasis on "primary learning" based on early perceptual experience and Harlow's (1950) principle of "learning to learn" both affirm the idea that early learning facilitates later learning and forms the foundation upon which subsequent learning is based.

Intellectual development does not proceed at a constant, linear rate. Rather, it is extremely rapid in the very early years and slows down markedly thereafter. Based on a careful review of research evidence, Bloom (1964) has estimated that half of adult intelligence is achieved by the age of four years. Moreover, Bloom has argued that environmental factors exert their greatest effect on a characteristic when it is developing most rapidly. Thus vitamin deficiency at ages 13 to 15 would have little effect on adult height, whereas such deficiency could affect terminal height if it occurred at ages 1 to 3. Similarly, environmental differences (enrichment or deprivation) in intellectual stimulation affect intellectual growth most markedly in the early years.

Since it now appears certain that the early years are extremely important in terms of intellectual stimulation, it is most appropriate that a number of large-scale studies are being conducted to determine the effects of various curricula for the disadvantaged preschool child. Among these investigators are Deutsch in New York, Gray and co-workers in Nashville, Bereiter and Engelmann in Illinois, and Nimnicht in Colorado.*

Two aspects of the federally sponsored Head Start program for disadvantaged four-year-olds merit comment. First, the importance of a low adult-child ratio has been recognized. Thus the classes are limited to 15 children under the guidance of two adults, the teacher and a

* For a discussion of some of these programs, see: R. Hess & R. Bear (Eds.), *Early education.* Chicago: Aldine, 1968.

teacher's aide. The more individualized the instruction, the more profitable it is for the child. Second, parent involvement has been made an integral part of the Head Start program. The home and the school must cooperate in preparing the child for learning. The school's efforts probably are doomed to failure unless the parent is convinced of the value of learning and is aware of ways to facilitate learning in the child.

Philosophy of Preschool Enrichment Programs

Several issues concerning the educational philosophy of these preschool programs are tremendously important in determining their effectiveness. The first and most important concern deals with the extent to which cognitive stimulation is emphasized. The second focuses on the amount of structure in a program (Medinnus & Bean, 1967).

It is clear that intellectual development is most rapid in the first four years of life. It is also well documented that the disadvantaged child does not receive the kinds of stimulation and experiences that are necessary for school readiness. It must be concluded, therefore, that any program designed for the disadvantaged child must involve an intensive amount of intellectual stimulation. The skills required for school readiness are well known. They include language (vocabulary, knowledge of sentence structure), number concepts, form discrimination, listening skills, ability to attend to and follow simple directions, and general information. These general areas might well be used as the basis for designing a curriculum for the disadvantaged preschool child.

While the amount of structure is less important than the amount of cognitive stimulation, it is unlikely that the latter can occur in a completely unstructured setting. Regularity, predictability, and consistency frequently are lacking in the lower-class home. Yet these are important characteristics of the school situation as evidenced by time schedules, classroom routine, and expected patterns of behavior. Lawfulness and predictability of behavior and of events free the child to develop his unique qualities and abilities. Further, the relation between the self and the external world can best be understood in an atmosphere characterized by dependability of the environment.

Although a structured program has been misinterpreted to mean regimentation and sternness, this is certainly not the case. Rather, certain expectations are made clear to the child, such as paying attention at reading time. As Baumrind (1966) has pointed out, there is no evidence that a structured, authoritative approach robs the child of such desirable qualities as independence, creativity, self-assertiveness and individuality. In fact, it is possible that a predictable framework facilitates the development of these behaviors and attitudes because of the security and trust it provides the child.

Weikart (1967) has noted that most preschool programs can be divided into two types. The traditional type, emphasizing social, emotional, and motor development, involves such activities as free play, arts and crafts, block play, finger painting, cutting and pasting, and singing. These are typical nursery-school activities. The second, more structured approach, as illustrated in Figure 12-1, includes activities designed to accomplish specific goals focusing on the cognitive and language areas. While insufficient data are available to determine which of these two approaches is most effective, it is clear that traditional nursery-school activities were not designed to facilitate cognitive development. Thus, as Bereiter and Engelmann (1966) point out, it is unwise to focus on these activities, which were intended for middle-class children who receive sufficient intellectual stimulation in the home. (Deutsch has succinctly termed this "the built-in curriculum of the

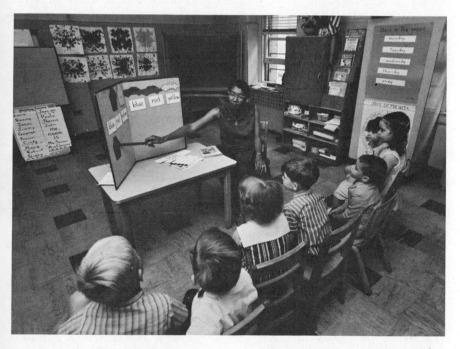

FIGURE 12-1   Preschool program of the structured type, with emphasis on the cognitive and language areas (photo by Ken Hyman).

middle-class home.") Indeed, the child's self concept and social and emotional development cannot be ignored; however, these can best be dealt with in a context of learning. The child who experiences school failure because of a lack of early stimulation will almost certainly suffer a lowered self-esteem. The only way to ensure permanent positive self-attitudes with regard to competency is to build in cognitive skills that enable the child to cope with the academic demands of school.

FORMAL SCHOOLING

The beginning of school marks the end of an era for the child, chronologically and psychologically. Before the age of five the child interacts more with parents and siblings than anyone else. They are the greatest influence on him. To be sure, he has playmates in the neighborhood but his parents are the only adults he knows intimately. They set much of the pattern of his daily life. It is their approval that is most important to him. With the beginning of school the child's world expands and becomes more complex. He spends more of his time away from home in the company of people other than his immediate family. The opinions, approval, and demands of these people now become of increasing importance. Yet he may now need his parents more than ever before—at least they wish this.

> Entrance into the conventional first grade marks a sharp break in the actual structure of the child's experience. For the first time in the case of many children, they are expected to conform to a group pattern imposed by an adult who is in charge of too many children to be constantly aware of each child as an individual. Flash cards are flashed at the group all at once. Stories are told and everybody must listen whether he will or not. Drawing paper and crayons are meted out whether you happen to feel like drawing at that moment or not. One child who found this shift quite beyond endurance remarked after his first day in school, "It's awful; all you do is mind all day long." And another day he added, "It really is awful. All you do is sit and sit and sit" (Murphy, Murphy, & Newcomb, 1937, p. 652).

School Readiness

Some children adapt to the new conditions imposed by the start of formal education, whereas others encounter difficulties. How can these differences be explained? Are they predictable before school entrance so that some ameliorative measures may be applied? What sort of preschool experiences facilitate successful adjustment in the first grade?

Although, of course, there are no final answers to these questions, data are available that permit some fairly certain conclusions.

One investigation that made use of anthropometric assessments of physique (Simon, 1959) found that students who were failing in first grade were less mature physically than a group of successful students. Thus physical maturity would seem to pertain to school readiness.

To check school readiness and adjustment to the first grade, Medinnus (1961a) subjected a small group of five-year-olds to a series of tests in the year before they started school. He also interviewed their mothers, made ratings of the psychological atmosphere of their homes, and had both parents complete a standard parent-attitude questionnaire. Upon the children's completion of the first grade, he correlated their scores on several criteria of achievement with their scores on academic skill-type tests. In addition, he related teacher ratings of general adjustment in the first grade to the scores obtained through assessment of the home psychological atmosphere. What he found was a moderate correlation of about +.50 between the children's IQ scores on a Stanford-Binet test administered before school entrance and their achievement scores at the end of the first grade. Thus, although intelligence is important in academic success in the first grade, other factors such as motivation, interest, and application also seem to have relevance. Further, Medinnus noted that the amount of information possessed by a child before entering school predicted reading achievement by the end of the first grade.

To discover how much children knew before their entrance into first grade, Medinnus confronted them with a questionnaire that modified one used by Templin (1958). These were some of its questions:

How many pennies in a nickel?
Friday, Saturday, Sunday—what day comes after Sunday?
What are the colors in the flag?
What is a helicopter?
What are clouds made of?
Whom was Red Riding Hood going to see?
What was the name of the boy who climbed the beanstalk?
What do we call a butterfly before it becomes a butterfly?
What is butter made from?
What is the brake on a car for?
In what game do you have a home run?

Among 40 five-year-olds quizzed, Medinnus found a wide range of total scores. Because of a substantial correlation between the children's mental ages and their scores, it was impossible to attribute higher performance on the information test to a richer home environment. Of course, innately more intelligent children turn up more often in the better socioeconomic homes, where parents provide a fuller, more stimulating environment than is supplied by lower-class parents. However, irrespective of socioeconomic status, the amount of time a parent spends reading to a child and the variety of experiences to which the youngster is exposed—trips, museums, zoos—serve to expand the quantity of his information.

Although IQ predicts academic success in the first grade better than any other measure, the importance of an intellectually stimulating home environment must not be underestimated. First-grade children who scored high on a standard measure of mental maturity, Milner (1951) learned, came from homes with more books available; these children were read to more often by their parents and in general experienced a more positive emotional relationship with their parents than children who scored low. Time spent reading to a child accomplishes many things. It establishes a warm, friendly relationship between parent and child, which increases the child's sense of security. The child's questions and comments inspired by the reading aid the parent's understanding of the child. And the influence of parent reading to child is certainly evident in the child's record of achievement.

From what the mothers told him in their interview, Medinnus rated their homes on a number of the Fels Parent Rating Behavior Scales. The differences in the ratings of homes of well-adjusted and poorly adjusted first graders showed a higher rating on a "dependence-encouraging factor" for those of the well-adjusted children (Medinnus, 1961b). This is borne out by Chance's (1961) study of academic achievement in the first grade. Mothers of the children who achieved above average in relation to intelligence favored later independence for them than mothers of children whose achievement on the basis of intelligence was low. Both findings seem to contradict the common notion that parents should stress early independence in their children to prepare them for school life. To Medinnus, great parental concern with the encouragement of independence perhaps reflected a basic rejection of the child. Parental clichés that children must learn to "stand on their own two feet," and "fight their own battles" may be attempts to justify an unwillingness to provide the child with emotional support, nurture, and acceptance. The teacher can teach the child to count but can never fully compensate for a lack of parental love and acceptance. Parents best prepare their children for school with affectional, accepting relationships.

Readiness Tests. A number of academic-readiness tests predict a child's capacity to master intellectual tasks and aid a teacher in identifying areas of strength and weakness in a particular child. Most of those tests at first-grade level assess reading readiness since reading is the primary preoccupation in the early elementary years. The principal element in most tests of reading readiness is the ability to discriminate word and letter forms. Comprehension and range of information are also included. Figure 12-2 illustrates the kind of item contained in a reading-readiness test.

Since the term *readiness* implies both level of maturity and prior experience, probably the best clues to academic achievement in first grade are scores of IQ tests and information tests. The former assesses mental

Test 1:

Directions: Find a letter the same as this one. Draw a line from this letter to this one. You draw it now.

Test 2:

Directions: Look at these letters. Can you find the letter that is not the same as the others? Now draw a line through it to show that it does not belong there.

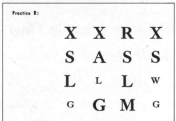

Test 3:

Directions: Put a mark on the cat. Now put a mark on the boy running.

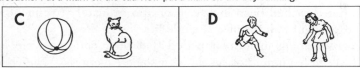

Test 4:

Directions: Look at the first large letter. Then find another which is just like it. Put a mark on it.

FIGURE 12-2 Sample items from the Lee-Clark Reading Readiness Test (Lee & Clark, 1951).

TABLE 12-1   Correlates of First-Grade Reading Achievement

	SRA Achievement Test			
	Language Perception	Verbal-Pictorial	Vocabulary	Comprehension
Stanford-Binet IQ	.51	.57	.41	.57
Gates Reading Readiness	.61	.57	.54	.64
Information test	.48	.51	.46	.42
Draw-A-Man IQ	.25	.36	.31	.22

maturity and the latter provides a measure of the range of the child's experiences.   Correlations between certain tests administered to five-year-olds and the youngsters' achievement in reading at the end of first grade are presented in Table 12-1 (Medinnus, 1961a).

School Entrance and the Child

It is only natural to expect some changes in the child as a result of exposure to the formal school situation.   Conformity to the demands of a new adult, intimate contact with a number of other children, separation from the mother for a substantial part of the day—all these must impinge on the child's behavior and his concept of the self.   Information pertinent to this point was obtained by Stendler and Young (1950, 1959) in interviews with more than 200 mothers before their children began school, after they had been in school for approximately two months, and finally, after eight months of first-grade life.

An overwhelming majority reported that their children were looking forward to the beginning of school with some eagerness.   The children's anticipations dealt with learning to read, write, and do numbers.   Although middle-class parents are more likely than lower-class parents to teach their children various intellectual skills (Stendler, 1951), six-year-olds generally know the alphabet, some nursery rhymes and songs, and counting, and can usually write their name.   Perhaps more important is the fact that parents portray the school to children as a socializing agent.   Certain kinds of behavior are required by the teacher and she has the authority to enforce them.

Most of the mothers said that behavior changed with school entrance, mainly in a positive way.   The children took more responsibility, they helped more at home, and they showed greater self-control and more independent demeanor at the table, in dressing, and in going on errands. Two kinds of difficulty encountered by the child, both arising from social relations, were mentioned by the mothers. In more than half the interviews, they spoke of aggressiveness on the part of other children or of exclusion from a group. Thus school attendance clearly involves much social learning. The child learns new behaviors, new ways of adjusting to other children, new roles to play.

No doubt some children are more successful initially at social interaction and some are more capable than others in meeting new social demands and in making the necessary social adjustments. For these reasons teachers must remain alert to children who run into difficulties in peer relations. Guidance and encouragement can be effective in aiding a child to build up self-confidence and confidence in others. If the wrong pattern is established early in the school career it may be difficult to modify.

Toward the end of the first year, a preponderant number of the mothers reported continued improvement among their children in such traits as maturity, self-control, helpfulness, responsibility, self-confidence, and getting along with playmates. Perhaps in consequence, more than half of them felt the first-grade year had been easier on them than earlier years in their relationships with their children. Most of the children themselves continued to like school and the teacher, a liking that grew for many throughout the school year.

The beginning of school, then, is a significant moment for a child. Persons other than his immediate family begin to play an important role in the socialization process. His success in this new venture and his adjustment to its demands depend intimately on the skills and attitudes he brings to the new situation. However, the child's relationship with his parents continues to exert its influence on his behavior—and so it shall continue to be.

THE TEACHER

Throughout the child's days in school, especially during his early years there, the teacher without doubt exercises the most significant psychological influence on him. The physical plant of the school, the teaching materials, the classroom schedule and routine all wane in comparison with the potential impact of the teacher on the child—on his adjustment to school, on his personality development, and on his academic achievement. Interest and encouragement shown by a teacher may determine the choice of a career or a decision about values. Second only to the role of parent in its effect on the child, the teacher role becomes costly if filled by any but the very best people. It is the teacher more than the doctor, lawyer, journalist, or entertainer who can inspire the leaders of tomorrow, the new generation, and through these children influence the world of the future.

Teacher Functions

Both teachers and parents are concerned in Western culture with the psychological and emotional welfare of the child. Both constrain behavior. Both are in a position to enforce standards of conduct. Yet the functions assigned to each differ. The teacher does not have the responsibility for the child's physical welfare outside the school setting—that is a parent function—but is charged with stimulating and guiding the child's intellectual development. Moreover, because of the nature of the school situation, the teacher is influential in determining the child's attitudes and values.

How does this influence work? Obviously the teacher's values are communicated to the pupils directly through rules, comments, commands, and discussions. But perhaps what a teacher *says* is less important than what she *does*. The teacher serves as a model for the children; they identify with her and try to emulate her. Teacher approval is sought. Teacher disapproval is avoided. Indeed, the parent may feel somewhat rejected when his first-grade child declares, "I love my teacher more than anyone else in the world," or when a second grader insists, "No, mother. My teacher wants me to do it this way and she's right." Nor is it any accident when a third grader calls the teacher "mother." She is, in fact, a mother surrogate—a mother substitute—for the young, school-aged child. The child's attitudes toward his parents may extend to the teacher or the teacher may actually take the place of an absent or neglectful parent in a child's emotional life. As late as preadolescence, *hero worship* of a teacher may still appear in a child.

However, the functions of a teacher are limited by the primary function of teaching. The teacher is not a therapist. She cannot practice individual therapy with certain children. She can, of course, create an atmosphere in the classroom that is conducive to the mental health of the pupils. In general, the teacher can alleviate or aggravate children's problems. But she can never substitute fully for a parent who is either physically absent or psychologically inadequate. Teachers function most efficiently and effectively when parents discharge their responsibility to the child. Frequently they are heard to remark that although they are aware of a particular child's emotional needs, their responsibility to the remaining 30 or 35 members of the class prevents their taking as much action toward this child as they might like. Their job is to teach certain academic skills; though responsible to an extent for the emotional and psychological well-being of their pupils, teachers can be neither psycho-therapists nor parent substitutes.

Who Become Teachers?

A host of factors determine vocational choice. Among these are per-sonality, attitudes and goals, social-class background, parental influences, and patterns of interest. Probably one or more of these differentiate the individuals in various occupations: teacher, engineer, plumber, carpenter, salesman, small businessman. Information on the backgrounds of teach-ers is slight, yet there certainly are factors favoring teaching over some other pursuit.

It has been emphasized many times that teachers come from middle-class backgrounds. Although this may be true, is it of any greater significance than personality factors that research has largely ignored? Table 12-2 contains the results of a survey of occupations of the fathers of a group of teachers (Stiles, 1957, p. 14). These figures would doubt-less vary with a shift in geographical location. However, it is apparent that notwithstanding the underrepresentation of teachers from laboring-class backgrounds in relation to the proportion of laboring-class families in the population, such teachers do constitute a fair percentage of those surveyed.

Although data on trends showing changes in the social-class back-grounds of teachers over the years are scarce, several factors suggest that present-day teachers are drawn in larger numbers from the lower class than was the case some decades back. The GI Bill, by giving financial

TABLE 12-2   Fathers' Occupations of a Sample of Detroit Teachers

Occupational Grouping	Number	Per Cent
Professional	20	10.1
Business, managerial, etc.	31	15.6
Other white collar	25	12.6
Farmer	11	5.5
Skilled labor	27	13.6
Other labor	57	28.8
Retired, unemployed, dead	27	13.6

aid to veterans of World War II who wished to attend college, made higher education available to numbers of young men who could not otherwise have afforded it. A rise in income among unskilled and skilled laborers during and since the war has enabled many a skilled worker to help his children through college. Then, too, decentralization of state colleges and universities has made these facilities accessible to more young people at lower cost. In 1962, for example, California had 70 junior and 16 state colleges. Indeed, Stiles (1957) reported that the teaching profession provided an opportunity for upward social mobility for at least 40 per cent of those who entered the field.

Numerous reasons have been advanced as the motive for choosing teaching as a profession. They include the desire for status in a respectable, middle-class pursuit, the need for security, an identification with a former teacher, a need for power and group leadership, family pressures, guaranteed superiority, and perhaps, inability to meet academic requisites of some other calling. From a survey of 150 Texas teachers (see Stiles, 1957) it was concluded that a large proportion of people entered teaching because they valued the security and predictability of behavior offered by the school system, and because doing so represented a continuance of close ties and strong identification with parent figures. Hopefully, there are teachers who are motivated to teach by the desire to make young people explore the unexplored, seek the unsought, and ponder the imponderable. Intellectual curiosity, yearning for the strange and new and novel, fearlessness in the face of unanswered questions cannot be aroused in children unless teachers themselves possess these qualities. It is not enough to be motivated to teach by a love for children. A love of their potentialities, their eagerness, their vision may be vastly more important.

Attitudes toward Child Behavior

If the teacher insists on a quiet, orderly classroom as an essential part of an efficient learning setting, anything that interferes with orderliness is of concern to her. Classroom behavior that prevents accomplishing the goal of producing academic achievement in pupils is viewed with disfavor. Certainly such achievement by the children contributes to the job satisfaction an individual finds in teaching. But are teachers overconcerned with behavior that disrupts management of the classroom and underconcerned with behavior that indicates possible maladjustment of individual personality? In a classic study of teacher attitudes toward children's behavior problems, Wickman (1928) observed appreciable differences between teachers and mental hygienists in their ratings of the seriousness of various behaviors in children. In general, the hygienists rated as most serious withdrawal, recessive behavior, and unsocial kinds of behavior. The teachers, on the other hand, regarded these particular behaviors as least serious, showing greatest concern over sex problems and behavior that transgressed authority and violated classroom rules. Wickman argued that teacher attitudes should move in the direction of those held by the mental hygienists; they should display less concern for antisocial and deviant behaviors in violation of the rules and more concern for unsocial behavior indicative of emotional or social maladjustment.

Despite the many criticisms directed against the Wickman study, a number of subsequent investigations have supported his main thesis. Moreover, recent studies indicate some shift in teacher attitudes toward the mental hygienists' point of view. Table 12-3 (Hunter, 1957, pp. 8–9) ranks the seriousness of 50 child behavior problems as seen by teachers and mental hygienists in the 1920's and by teachers in the 1950's. A more recent study (Tolor, Scarpetti, & Lane, 1967) confirms the fact that clinical psychologists are more accepting, in the sense of judging as normal, of a greater variety of child behaviors than are teachers. Greatest disagreement between teachers and psychologists occurred in the areas of regressive behavior ("carries blanket"), aggressiveness ("hits or attacks other children"), and affect expression ("shows inappropriate feeling"), with the teachers considering these as much more serious than the psychologists.

Many reasons can be expressed for the differences between teachers and hygienists in the Wickman study and for the shift in the attitudes of teachers over the years (Beilin, 1959). The principal concern of the teacher is to teach academic skills whereas the main concern of the clinician is the emotional adjustment of the child. Yet over the years, the child psychologist has communicated to teachers his concern with the personality adjustment of children. He has done so through the psychology courses that have become a part of many teacher-training programs. Besides, the mental-hygiene point of view that adjustment problems themselves impede the learning process has been widely adopted by educational psychologists. Although teachers will continue to be irked by behaviors that disrupt classroom routine—and to some extent this is a valid concern—a more thorough understanding of the place of adjustment in the learning process may lead to a true convergence of the teaching and clinical approaches to learning. Irritations caused by disruptive conduct in the classroom may interfere far less with a child's learning than emotional discomforts from within. Life during school hours can never be separated from those preceding or following them.

TABLE 12-3   Comparison of Mean Ratings * by Teachers in 1955 and by Teachers and Mental Hygienists in 1926 of the Relative Seriousness of 50 Behavior Problems

Behavior Problems	Teachers (1955) $N = 308$	Teachers (1926) $N = 511$	Mental Hygienists (1926) $N = 30$
1. Stealing	14.9	17.0	12.5
2. Destroying school materials	13.7	14.3	5.1
3. Truancy	13.6	15.6	10.3
4. Cruelty, bullying	13.5	14.8	13.5
5. Unhappy, depressed	13.4	11.5	16.2
6. Impertinence, defiance	13.4	15.0	7.1
7. Untruthfulness	13.3	15.8	10.3
8. Unreliableness	13.1	13.9	10.4
9. Disobedience	13.0	14.1	6.4
10. Heterosexual activity	12.9	17.3	9.9
11. Resentfulness	12.5	10.8	14.1
12. Impudence, rudeness	12.4	12.2	7.6
13. Lack of interest in work	12.1	12.8	9.6
14. Quarrelsomeness	12.0	11.1	8.3
15. Easily discouraged	11.9	11.5	13.4
16. Cheating	11.9	14.7	10.3
17. Carelessness in work	11.8	11.3	7.1
18. Temper tantrums	11.7	13.0	11.7
19. Unsocial, withdrawing	11.6	8.3	17.3
20. Selfishness	11.6	11.3	11.8
21. Laziness	11.6	12.2	7.2
22. Disorderliness in class	11.5	11.7	3.4
23. Obscene notes, talk	11.5	16.6	8.8
24. Suggestible	11.4	11.0	13.3
25. Domineering	11.2	10.3	13.0
26. Inattention	11.1	11.2	7.3

*Rating chart: slight consequence, 5.0; considerable difficulty, 12.0; extremely grave problem, 20.0.

Teacher Adjustment

Just as the personality of the parent may be more significant than parent attitudes and behavior in affecting the child (see Chapter 10), so it is with teachers.   After reviewing numerous studies on this point, Snyder (1947) concluded that the evidence was overwhelming that the personal adjustment of the teacher had an influence on the pupils.   Good

TABLE 12-3   *(Continued)*

Behavior Problems	Teachers (1955) N = 308	Teachers (1926) N = 511	Mental Hygienists (1926) N = 30
27. Nervousness	11.1	11.7	11.3
28. Masturbation	10.7	16.7	6.4
29. Profanity	10.5	12.3	2.9
30. Fearfulness	10.4	9.7	14.0
31. Sullenness	10.2	9.9	12.6
32. Attracting attention	10.2	8.5	8.5
33. Stubbornness	10.1	10.3	10.9
34. Over-critical of others	9.8	7.9	13.2
35. Physical cowardice	9.8	10.4	12.0
36. Thoughtlessness	9.7	8.7	6.8
37. Tardiness	9.7	10.5	5.6
38. Slovenly in appearance	9.7	10.1	7.2
39. Sensitiveness	9.6	7.0	13.1
40. Shyness	9.5	5.4	12.5
41. Suspiciousness	9.5	9.1	16.4
42. Enuresis	9.2	11.8	9.2
43. Interrupting	9.0	8.0	2.8
44. Inquisitiveness	8.8	8.0	5.3
45. Dreaminess	8.8	8.3	11.3
46. Restlessness	8.6	6.9	6.4
47. Tattling	8.1	7.5	8.8
48. Imaginative lying	8.0	8.1	7.5
49. Smoking	7.3	12.0	2.3
50. Whispering	6.3	7.5	0.8
Average	10.9	11.3	9.5

adjustment in the teacher promoted favorable adjustment in the pupils; the converse was also true. However, reviewing the same studies, Gladstone (1948) maintained there was no strong confirmatory evidence. Gladstone even proposed that certain unfulfilled needs of some teachers might result in behavior beneficial to pupils. A strong need to display affection, for example, might cause the teacher to lavish affection on some child.

To Gladstone the teacher's adjustment *to the teaching role* in the classroom was potentially most significant in affecting the children. An individual might be an inspiring, beloved teacher, yet function far less effectively in the spouse, parent, or colleague role. Indeed far more knowledge is needed on this matter than is now available. In one study that trained teachers to appreciate the mental-health point of view of children and their problems (Baruch, 1945), those teachers who showed the greatest gains in personal adjustment disclosed the greatest acceptance of child behavior. In other words, self-acceptance apparently has to precede acceptance of others.

Teacher Problems

The teacher has suffered much criticism. She is a convenient target for parents frustrated or dissatisfied by their children. But what of the view from the teacher's rostrum? Teacher complaints are many. When asked to list the mental-health hazards facing them in the classroom, teachers point out that most of their problems deal with out-of-the-classroom phenomena. Conflicting personalities among colleagues, intraschool jealousies, fear of expressing honest opinions about schools, too many interruptions, undue amounts of needless paper work, too little time for parent conferences, inadequate pay, supplies, and equipment, conflicts with administrative policy, malfunctioning of the P.T.A., lack of recognition for work well done are some of the "rewards" of selecting a teaching career (Keliher, 1950; Kvaraceus, 1951).

To understand the teacher one must understand the entire school setting. Each classroom is not an isolated unit. Each teacher must interact with other teachers as well as with administrative personnel. Good relations among the entire school staff are essential for smooth functioning of the school. Although behavior problems posed by children in the classroom are of immediate concern to the teacher and must be handled, they seem to create fewer difficulties than other aspects of the teacher role.

Teacher-Pupil Interactions

The praise, reward, disapproval, and punishment administered by the teacher inevitably affect the emotional adjustment and self concept of some, if not all, pupils. Are these forms of encouragement or discipline dispensed in equal measure to all pupils? Or are certain ones more likely to be praised or punished? Clearly, the teacher receives the most satisfaction from children who learn rapidly and who without difficulty grasp the material presented. After all, the teacher's sense of adequacy as a teacher depends in large part on how well she accomplishes her primary mission of teaching the academic skills.

A study of the pattern of teacher approval and disapproval supports this notion (DeGroat & Thompson, 1949). To a sixth-grade class a "guess who" technique of a dozen statements of teacher approval and an equal number of statements of teacher disapproval was applied. Some of these statements were: "Here is someone whose work is often pointed out as being very neat"; "Here is someone on whom the teacher calls when she wants the right answer"; "Here is someone whom the teacher often asks to do errands for her or to be monitor while she is out of the room"; "Here is someone whom the teacher often scolds for disturbing the class in some way (shooting paper wads, chewing gum, etc.)"; "Here is someone who is often suspected by the teacher when something happens while she is out of the room"; "Here is someone who is often pointed out as not doing [his] best work." By and large, relatively few children were nominated for either teacher approval or disapproval. This suggested that certain pupils enjoyed a much higher level of interaction with the teacher than others.

Several characteristics differentiated the high approval-low disapproval group from the low approval-low disapproval and high disapproval-low approval groups. Children of high approval were more intelligent; they rated higher in academic achievement and their scores on a personality-adjustment test were more favorable. Allowing for the tenuousness of cause-and-effect statements, this last point demonstrates a connection between teacher approval and pupil self-acceptance. This relationship may be viewed in various ways: those pupils who are more self-accepting elicit a favorable response in the teacher, or the teacher's good reaction to the child's behavior is conducive to an attitude of self-acceptance in the child. In any case, it seems unfortunate that teacher approval is limited to relatively few pupils—at least as perceived by the children themselves. Perhaps those who most need overt signs of teacher approval are least likely to receive them.

One investigation (Hoehn, 1954) found that teachers had more favorable contacts with children of high economic status than with those from lower economic backgrounds. Conversely, more conflict was seen between the teacher and the children of low economic status, especially among boys, than with youngsters of upper economic station. Hoehn concluded, however, that the basic factor in the contact between teacher and child was the latter's academic achievement. Quantitatively there was more contact between the teacher and low achievers but qualitatively the tie between teacher and high achievers was more favorable.

In a study by Meyer and Thompson (1956) involving both the "guess who" technique and classroom observations of teacher-pupil interaction, boys were seen to receive more teacher disapproval than girls. It is not surprising, therefore, that girls express more positive attitudes toward school than boys (Antes, Anderson, & DeVault, 1965). The demands of school routine for orderliness and quiet are alien to the active, aggressive nature of boys. And when the resulting rebellious behavior brings forth blame and disapproval from the teacher, further hostility is generated. This is hardly likely to produce an atmosphere conducive to learning.

It has been shown that interaction between teacher and pupil relates to the pupil's acceptance by others as well as to his self-acceptance. Three studies, one at the first-grade level (Medinnus, 1962), another at sixth-grade level (Gronlund, 1950), and a third at tenth-grade level (Flanders and Havumaki, 1960), have all found that pupils receiving praise from teachers and preferred by teachers were more likely to be chosen by peers in a sociometric exercise, thus indicating greater acceptance by peers. To Medinnus this suggested that at the first-grade level children so identified with the teacher that her values became theirs. Behaviors praised by the teacher acquired positive, favorable value whereas those viewed negatively by her were similarly devalued by the pupils. In like manner, the teacher is able to influence the attitudes of the pupils in a great number of areas—attitudes toward minority-group children, personal likes and dislikes in others, attitudes toward handicapped or less favorably endowed children, and the like.

CLASSROOM ATMOSPHERE

Drawn from another science, the terms *atmosphere* and *climate* denote the sociopsychological relationships existing among the group in the classroom setting. Though perhaps applied somewhat awkwardly to the classroom, the two terms accurately suggest the pervasiveness of the psychological tone present in any single schoolroom. To a large extent it is the teacher who establishes the relationships that determine the prevailing psychological atmosphere.

Types of Atmosphere

What are the principal types of relationship that create a particular atmosphere in the classroom? Many categories have been used to measure the relationship between teacher and pupils. These categories have then become indices of the over-all classroom atmosphere. They include dominating, integrating, learner-centered, teacher-centered, democratic, *laissez faire*, authoritarian, and more. In one study of the social and emotional climate of classrooms (Withall, 1949), teacher behavior fell into seven main classes, of which six fitted into the categories of learner-centered and teacher-centered. The learner-centered behaviors were of three kinds: statements supporting the learner, which reassured or commended him; statements accepting and clarifying the pupil, which helped him refine his ideas and feelings and gave him the sense of being understood; and statements or questions about the structure of problems, which provided information or raised questions about a problem in a manner that facilitated its solution. The teacher-centered behaviors were also of three kinds: directive statements, which outlined a recommended course of action for the pupil to follow; reproving or deprecatory statements, intended to deter pupils from unacceptable behavior; and self-supporting statements, designed to justify the teacher's position or actions.

Teachers who establish positive social climates in the classroom are concerned about mental-health concepts and personality dynamics. They feel responsible for the personality growth and development of their pupils as well as their academic learning. Such teachers are alert and sensitive to their pupils' anxieties, self concepts, peer-group relations, and attitudes toward school.

A further study by Withall (1952), dealing with four seventh-grade classes, showed marked differences in the atmosphere under the four teachers. Yet from day to day there was a moderate amount of consistency for any one of them. Although knowledge is rather fragmentary on the effects of different classroom atmospheres on the emotional adjustment and academic accomplishments of pupils, certain kinds of psychological relations between teacher and children are far more conducive than others to the emotional and intellectual well-being of the youngsters in a school setting.

Anderson has distinguished between dominating and socially integrating behavior. Integrating behavior was described as "flexible, dynamic, yielding, spontaneous." The individual who showed this behavior sought and found "common purposes with another; he expended energy with another, not against another." Dominating behavior, on the other hand, was "rigid, fixed, static." The dominating individual neither respected nor attempted to understand another's individuality. Energy was expended against another individual; the conflict of differences grew. Each kind of behavior tended to elicit the same kind of behavior in someone else (Anderson, 1939b). Some tie was found between integrative scores of children and chronological age, suggesting that perhaps, in a developmental sense at least, an integrating behavior was a sign of maturity (Anderson, 1937a). Although developed originally to assess the social interaction of preschool children (Anderson, 1937a, b; 1939b), the two categories of dominating and socially integrating behavior have been applied pertinently to the classroom interaction of teacher and pupils.

A group of kindergarten children were making May baskets. Terry had folded his basket on the lines which had been drawn on the material the night before by the teacher. He had pasted the flaps as he had been instructed and had the handle fastened in place. The teacher had cut out of other paper a handful of diamond-shaped pieces which she had distributed four to a child. These were to serve as decorations to be pasted horizontally on the basket. As she walked about the room she noticed Terry pasting his diamond decoration vertically.

"Oh, oh, Terry," she said. "The decorations are to be pasted on lying down and not standing up."

"But I want to paste mine this way," said Terry.

"Well, that isn't the way they are supposed to go. Here now, just paste it this way." And she turned the diamond horizontally and pasted it before Terry seemed to know what had happened. She remained while Terry at her instructions pasted two more shapes horizontally. Then she turned away, leaving Terry to paste the fourth.

At the end of the period Terry had only three decorations on his basket. When the teacher inquired about his basket, Terry, pointing to the undecorated side of his basket, said that he did not want one there.

"Oh, but every basket should have four. Here is one your color. We'll just paste it on quickly." And with Terry speechless and transfixed she pasted it on quickly.

Mary Lou had observed that at her table several handles did not stick. "I guess I don't want a handle," she remarked to the boy seated next to her. She cut up the handle of her basket and pasted the pieces as decorations all over the basket. The teacher's remark to this *fait accompli* was, "Oh, you've spoiled yours, Mary Lou; yours is all messy and doesn't have a handle" (Anderson, 1943, p. 459).

Certainly the kind of teacher behavior described in the foregoing excerpt fits Withall's teacher-centered category. Noncompliance with goals defined by the teacher is castigated. No respect is shown for either the child's wishes or his individuality.

Through observation and recording of the interaction between teacher and pupils, Anderson (1939a, b) found teachers varying in dominating and integrating classroom behavior. In contacts with individual students, two teachers had twice as many dominating as integrating relationships, whereas a third teacher had five times as many dominating associations as integrating ones. In behavior toward their whole class, the dominating

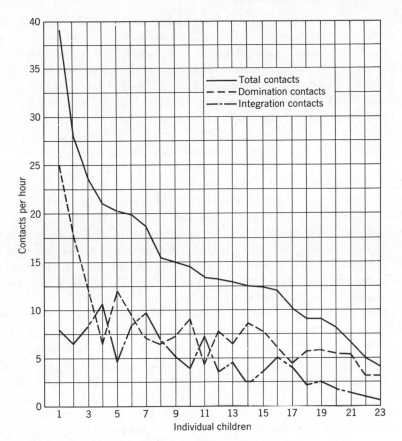

FIGURE 12-3   Mean number of contacts per hour which teacher A had with individual children enrolled in the morning session (Anderson, 1939b, p. 337).

characteristic in all three teachers outdid the integrating by a ratio of five to one. Among pupils there were wide differences in the extent and nature of their contact with the teacher, as shown in Figure 12-3.

Children's Evaluation of Teachers

When asked to name reasons for disliking school, children mention the teacher more frequently than any other factor (Tenenbaum, 1940). Unfortunately, there appears to be increasing dissatisfaction with the teacher from fourth through sixth grade, with older children rating their teacher less favorably than younger ones (Neale & Proshek, 1967). Children hold strong opinions about their teachers and the qualities they prefer in them. The qualities they single out refer as often to characteristics of the teacher as an individual as to the characteristics of her teaching ability. One study, in fact, noted that a majority of the traits used by elementary-school children to describe well-liked teachers covered personality and disposition (Leeds & Cook, 1947).

Jersild (1940) found elementary-school children mentioning these qualities as typical of the teachers they liked best: *human qualities as a person*—sympathetic, cheerful, good tempered; *physical appearance, grooming, voice*—attractive, neat, nice manner of talking; *traits as a disciplinarian or director of class*—fair, consistent, did not scold or shout; *participation in activities*—joined in or permitted games or play; *performance as a teacher*—enthusiastic, resourceful, explained well, permitted expression of opinion. The age trend in the descriptions was worth noting; high-school students more frequently picked characteristics bearing on teaching ability whereas younger children singled out interesting projects introduced by the teacher. At all ages children valued highly the teacher who showed sensitivity and understanding toward them and who was effective and enthusiastic.

Through daily contact and interaction, the personality of the teacher affects the children and is basic in setting the emotional tone of the classroom. If the emotional relation between teacher and pupil affects the latter's learning experience, the child's perception of the teacher is of vital importance, especially when the teacher is a warm, helpful individual. This is perhaps truer in elementary school, where the teacher indeed serves as a mother surrogate. An unsympathetic, ill-tempered, unfair, uninteresting teacher certainly cannot kindle children's interest in school and in the entire learning process.

SCHOOL ACHIEVEMENT

Since the primary goal of the school is the acquisition of academic skills by pupils, the extent to which this goal is attained reflects the success of the school's endeavor. It is not surprising, therefore, that great attention has been paid to academic achievement. Most research on the subject has sought to identify the factors responsible for differences in individual accomplishment. There are important reasons for this concern. Perhaps most significant is the obvious waste of human potentialities when children perform below their capacities. Furthermore, if the reason for a child's underachievement can be discovered, remedial measures may be undertaken.

Perhaps the single factor most related to academic achievement is intellectual capacity. The speed and level at which an individual acquires knowledge together with the facility to comprehend abstract concepts are key elements in learning ability. That intelligence bears on academic achievement is seen in the similarity of the tasks included in intelligence tests to those involved in school learning, at least after the early elementary school years. That is to say, the overlap helps to verify the tie. Yet other factors besides intellect influence achievement in school. This is borne out by the clustering of correlations between intelligence-test scores and scores of academic achievement at about +.55.

Much of the discussion among educators about underachievement in the first grade and in the early elementary years has centered about the question of immaturity. The term needs definition. Few attempts have been made to define or evaluate emotional immaturity. Physiological and chronological immaturity are another matter. In a study comparing the scholastic achievement of 50 overage and 50 underage pupils in grades two through six, Carter (1956) found that 87 per cent of the underaged did not measure up to the classroom performance of children of normal age. Carter further noted that chronological age had a greater affect on boys than on girls. Simon (1959) observed failing students to be less mature than successful ones on several measures of physiological configuration even when the two were matched on IQ and chronological age. Among third-grade children, Klausmeier and Check (1959) detected a connection between physical development and reading and arithmetic achievement in boys, yet not in girls. Medinnus (1961c) proposed that although chronological age might shape a child's initial adjustment to first grade, it might be less important than other factors by the end of the year. This is seen in the low correlation, +.21, between chronological age and scores of adjustment after a year of schooling. Academic achievement, however, was only one of several factors entering into the assessment of general adjustment.

Parental Factors

A variety of parental factors influence a child's achievement in every school grade. These include the emotional relationship between parent and child, the attitudes of the parent toward school and school achievement, and parental concern for and interest in the child's performance. Psychologists have sought to find the forces behind a general drive for achievement, academic as well as other kinds (see McClelland, Atkinson, Clark, & Lowell, 1953; Atkinson, 1958). One of them (Winterbottom, 1953) established a relationship between a mother's encouragement of early independence and a child's motivation to achieve. The following questionnaire, presented to 29 women whose sons fell into two groups, high and low, with respect to achievement, deals with this matter (McClelland et al., 1953, pp. 298–299).

Beside each statement there are two blanks. In the first one put a check mark if it is one of the things you want in your child by the time he is ten years old. In the second one put the approximate age by which you think your child should have learned this behavior. The sample below illustrates how to do this:

___X___   ___10___   To obey traffic signals and street lights when he is out alone

This mother has checked this as one of the things she wants in her child and she expects him to learn this by the age of 10. Lots of books have been written on how a mother should treat her child but it's surprising how little information we have on what the people on the firing-line— the mothers—actually do. We would like you to answer these questions by telling us what you find works best with your child.

_____ _____   To stand up for his own rights with other children

_____ _____   To know his way around his part of the city so that he can play where he wants without getting lost

_____ _____   To go outside to play when he wants to be noisy or boisterous

_____ _____   To be willing to try new things on his own without depending on his mother for help

_____ _____   To be active and energetic in climbing, jumping and sports

_____ _____   To show pride in his own ability to do things well

_____ _____   To take part in his parents' interests and conversations

_____ _____   To try hard things for himself without asking for help

_____ _____   To be able to eat alone without help in cutting and handling food

_____ _____   To be able to lead other children and assert himself in children's groups

_____ _____   To make his own friends among children his own age

_____ _____   To hang up his own clothes and look after his own possessions

_____ _____   To do well in school on his own

_____ _____   To be able to undress and go to bed by himself

_____ _____   To have interests and hobbies of his own. To be able to entertain himself.

Mothers of boys who achieved high, Winterbottom discovered, demanded independence of their sons earlier than mothers of low achievers. The former required twice as many skills to be mastered before the age of eight than the latter. Thus maternal stress on early independence seemed to be antecedent of high achievement. But the pattern was not so distinct. Another consideration blurred it. The mothers of boys who achieved high were more likely to demonstrate physical affection when a demand for achievement had been fulfilled. Hence it was an early encouragement of independence, coupled with a warm, affectionate mother-son relationship that produced the motivation for high achievement in the child.

Without this qualification, the Winterbottom findings would contradict the conclusion mentioned earlier in the chapter that children of parents who encourage early independence do less well in first grade than those of parents who defer demands for independence. Indeed, in the absence of an accepting relationship between parent and child, the promotion of early independence does not produce achievement. Identification is the factor of importance. As asserted in Chapter 10, a warm, accepting relationship is necessary between parent and child before the child will identify with the parent and take on his values and goals. Morrow and Wilson (1961) have provided support for this view in a study of the perceptions high-achieving and underachieving high-school boys have of their families. The former were more likely to see their family relationships in a positive light. They described their parents as approving, trusting, affectionate, relatively nonrestrictive, and encouraging—but not pressuring with respect to achievement. They said they accepted their parents' standards; in other words, they identified with them. In a similar study (Davids & Hainsworth, 1967), underachieving teenage boys perceived their mothers as high in control. Further, there was a much greater discrepancy for the underachievers than for the high achievers between the mother's report of several child-rearing attitudes and the son's perception of her attitudes. This suggests a lack of agreement and a lack of communication between the low-achieving boy and his mother.

Clinical studies of learning difficulties have commented that underachievement may signify a rebellion against parents. Despite only slight research support for this position, it seems reasonable to believe that excessive pressure for achievement unaccompanied by a satisfactory and rewarding relationship with parents may engender anxiety and resentment in the child. The anxiety may inhibit the child from working to full capacity, whereas the resentment may cause him to disappoint the parents by not meeting their expectations. Everyday observation of child behavior shows that rebellion may take a number of forms.

Rather than examining parental factors related to general school achievement, several recent areas of research have sought to delineate more precisely parental influence on specific aspects of the child's achievement.

Bing (1963) selected elementary-school children who showed marked discrepancy between verbal and mathematical ability. Through a variety of interview, questionnaire, and observational measures, maternal differences between these subgroups of children were identified. The high verbal children experienced much more verbal stimulation in the preschool years, as evidenced by such variables as amount of play time mother had with infant, verbal stimulation of infant, mother's responsiveness to child's early questions, outings with the young child, tutoring before school, and interest shown in child's good speech habits. The mothers of the high verbal children were rather controlling and pressuring, while mothers of those children high in mathematical ability were less interfering and permitted greater independence. Bing concluded that high verbal ability is fostered by intensive interaction between parent and child. High number and spatial abilities, on the other hand, develop from interaction with the physical rather than the interpersonal environment. The development of these latter abilities requires independence to investigate and explore the environment.

Using college students as subjects, Baer and Ragosta (1966) found that those males showing high verbal ability perceived their fathers as less loving and less attentive than those showing less verbal ability. They also perceived their mothers as less loving. A similar finding was obtained for elementary-school girls, in which those who scored high on reading achievement had less affectionate and less nurturant mothers than those less proficient in this academic area (Crandall, Dewey, Katkovsky, & Preston, 1964). Taken together, the findings of these two studies do not contradict those obtained by Bing. Mothers who are intrusive and pressuring insist upon a high level of interaction with the child. These mothers emphasize the achievement rather than the affectional area.

Consistently, girls have been found to excel in verbal performance and boys in mathematics. While a number of reasons have been offered to account for this, there is some evidence that sex-typing plays a part here. Hill (1967) found that fathers who had otherwise masculine expectations for their sons also expected them to do better in mathematics. This was especially true for fathers who saw mathematics as a masculine pursuit. Although in general parents who value intellectual achievement for themselves stress intellectual achievement for their children, some areas of achievement are stressed more than others. In a study of parental values for achievement in the intellectual, physical skills, artistic, and mechanical areas, parents who valued achievement in the artistic and mechanical areas tended also to value such achievement for their children (Katkovsky, Preston, & Crandall, 1964). There was a trend also for greater parental concern for their sons' achievement than for their daughters'.

Personality and Emotional Factors

Notwithstanding the emotional and adjustment problems found in children who have difficulties in learning or achieving, the drawing of cause-and-effect conclusions is dangerous. In fact, in a study of 34 children admitted for in-patient care to a psychiatric hospital, it was observed that none of them was retarded in educational achievement (Tamkin, 1960). Conceivably, emotional problems and educational disabilities may be symptoms of the same underlying disturbance. Moreover, educational difficulties may be as frequent a cause of emotional problems as the other way around.

Within the limits of these precautions, several studies exemplify attempts to uncover emotional and personality factors as causes of scholastic underachievement. Among 20 high-school boys designated as underachievers, Kimball (1953) found the following significant things in their backgrounds. There was a poor relationship between father and son, marked by an absence of strong identification with the father; there were passivity, strong needs for dependency, propensities toward aggression, and pronounced feelings of inferiority. These characteristics described a child with a low concept of self, low self-esteem, and a lack of the personal security necessary to permit a manipulation of the environment in order to achieve. Feelings of dependency and inferiority prevent an individual from realizing his potential.

Other studies (Conklin, 1940; Walsh, 1956) have implied that underachievers have a history of disturbed personal relations, especially with respect to their parents. In consequence, they feel rejection and an inability to express their hostile and negative reactions. In a longitudinal study by Haggard (1957), high achievers, in distinction to low achievers, tended to be more responsive to the socialization pressures of their parents; they accepted parental values and endeavored to live up to them and to the expectations of their elders. Yet this seemed to bring on anxiety. At the level of the third grade, and more so by the seventh, there was evidence of hostility and antagonism toward adults among high-achieving children. By the seventh grade the anxiety apparent in these youngsters impeded their originality and creativity. By and large, they were aggressive, competitive, and persistent.

It would seem that the child who is relatively free from anxiety and other emotional upsets best concentrates on academic matters. This is more likely to apply in elementary school. In high school a host of factors, some of which may not be considered to reflect sound mental health or desirable personality traits, may occasion academic achievement.

Undoubtedly past experiences of success or failure in meeting the demands of a task, together with the attitudes toward these experiences, influence both an individual's performance and the level of achievement to which he aspires. Sears (1940) has demonstrated the effect of past experiences on one's setting of goals. She experimented with two groups of fourth, fifth, and sixth graders, requiring them to select a series of goals for performance following respective successful and failing experiences. One group had successful records of achievement in reading and arithmetic, the other had been much less successful. In the experimental situation, the successful group attempted as a unit to improve performance but set realistic goals. The failing group was less consistent; some members chose goals of a very low level in the hope of attaining them, whereas others selected goals of unrealistic challenge. Both goals were dictated by a desire to avoid failure.

A word is necessary about the effect of a series of repeated failures on the child's self-esteem. Demoralization sets in. One truly cannot condone any school curriculum in which certain children cannot avoid such failure. Perhaps teachers, because of the educational attainments demanded by their positions, are unable to understand the meaning of failure to a child and the impact it has on him. Naturally, every child does not have to be protected from failure, but success, in reality, is a relative term; it is relative to the goals set by the teacher, by the parent, and by the child himself. Although a sense of success certainly comes from achievement, it may derive also from having done a job to the best of one's ability. And ability varies in a classroom as much as height, weight, and color of one's eyes.

Miscellaneous Factors

Teachers affect the achievement of their pupils by the kind of contacts they have with them. Several investigations of high-school classrooms indicate that high achievers receive more motivation than low achievers from teacher approval (Battle, 1957), and that there is a closer kinship between the values held by the teacher and by high achievers than between those of the teacher and low achievers (McDavid, 1959). That is, the teacher tends to reward with approval those students most similar to himself in certain areas and this approval inspires them to strain for higher levels of performance.

Actually, the general psychological atmosphere established by some teachers is more appropriate to learning and achievement than the atmosphere set by others. Learning occurs best when there is understanding and acceptance between teacher and pupil. For example, Christensen (1960) noted a relationship between ratings of warmth for the teacher and the achievements in vocabulary and arithmetic among pupils of 10 fifth-grade classes. Nevertheless, the level of teaching ability, a broad concept embracing a number of skills and attitudes, is the prime determinant of the quality of instruction in a classroom.

A child's attitudes also affect achievement in school. Great satisfaction with the school situation is likely to spur performance. In this regard, Malpass (1953) observed that eighth-grade children with the most positive attitudes toward the school evinced the highest achievement. Correspondingly, Briggs, Johnson, and Wirt (1962) found a close tie between susceptibility to delinquency and low achievement. In the same vein, a comparison of potential delinquents and nondelinquents in the sixth grade saw the former to be retarded in reading and arithmetic (Dinitz, Kay, & Reckless, 1957). This poorer achievement of potential delinquents was attributed to their negative attitudes toward school as well as toward other social institutions. Quite likely their resentment of the authority represented by the school reflected a general dislike of authority, an attitude stemming often from a child's relations with his parents.

Then there is socioeconomic status. The correlations between such status and achievement have been found to be consistent. Part of this result may be ascribed, as noted in Chapter 2, to differences in IQ among social classes. Moreover, the attitudes of lower-class parents toward education, the school, and educational achievement, as well as the attitudes of the typical college-educated teacher toward the values and behavior of the lower-class child cannot be ignored.

Many factors create different attitudes and motivations concerning achievement in school between children of the middle and lower classes. The press of economic problems on the lower-class family makes money earned today far more attractive than the acquisition of knowledge that may or may not prove an economic asset in the future. Additionally, the likelihood that the lower-class parent was not successful in school does not endear schooling to him. He probably believes that the years in school profited him little in terms of occupational advantage. He is not likely to urge academic achievement on his child. The middle-class parent, conversely, places great emphasis on education. He sees it as one of the few ways remaining for the maintenance and enhancement of social status. Told by a first-grade teacher that her son was intellectually "average," one middle-class mother responded, "I don't want him to be a ditchdigger. He's going to have to get a college education if he's going to support his family properly." Attitudes and values are not, however, the only factors in class differences regarding achievement. Living conditions and time and space available for study also bear heavily on the subject.

The child's relations with his peers play an important part in his adjustment to the school situation. Although a child may compensate for rejection by peers by concentrating on his schoolwork, it is more likely that such rejection leads to underachievement and withdrawal from the academic arena. In an interesting study, Ferguson and Maccoby (1966) examined the interpersonal significance of different patterns of cognitive abilities in the verbal, number, and spatial areas. Peers report highly verbal boys as showing strong dependency on the teacher. Both boys and girls high in number ability showed a high degree of social interaction with peers. High number ability in boys appears to be related to sex-appropriate behavior, as evidenced by their higher ratings by peers on masculinity and aggression. Children high in spatial ability showed sex-inappropriate behavior; the boys were rated low by peers in aggressiveness, masculinity, and mastery, while the girls were rated high in masculinity and aggressiveness. Although these findings are complex and difficult to interpret, they tend to corroborate some of the parent-child research discussed earlier. Highly verbal children experience a high level of interaction with both teacher and parents. Children high in numerical ability appear to be independent from parents and strongly involved with and accepted by their peers.

Finally, there is the matter of interest. Generally, children—and adults too—do best those things in which they are most interested, and vice versa. School achievement is no exception. Girls prefer and do best in language and literature, boys in science and history. More important than sex differences is the interest value inhering in the academic materials. Children are not all interested in the same things, happily. It behooves the teacher, the builders of curriculum, and the authors of materials for academic use to ferret out the interests of pupils and also their *potential interests* in order to meet and stimulate these effectively in the classroom. There is little excuse for history, or for literature, or for science failing to hold the interest of pupils.

SOCIAL CLASS AND THE SCHOOL

To what extent does social-class membership affect the child's school achievement and his behavior in the school setting? Is the school meeting equally well the needs of children from different social classes?

The interest in educational circles on social-class differences in attitudes and behavior grew out of a series of publications in the 1940's that focused attention on such differences (see Davis & Havighurst, 1946; Davis & Dollard, 1940; Havighurst & Taba, 1949; Hollingshead, 1949; Warner, Havighurst, & Loeb, 1944). The data cited in these studies emphasized that the school was largely a middle-class institution with a middle-class bias in personnel, curriculum materials, and advocated values for child behavior. The result was that the middle-class child was rewarded with approval and support from the school, whereas the lower-class child, because of the discrepancy between his behavior and attitudes and those approved by the school, was neglected, punished, and misunderstood.

Stimulated in part by government concern for our economically disadvantaged, which resulted in the War on Poverty program, much recent research and discussion are available on this topic. Numerous action programs are in progress. While insufficient monies are available for such programs, public concern has been aroused to some extent and the problems involved are being attacked in a variety of ways. A number of broad issues related to social class and the school are receiving attention. Each of these will be discussed briefly.

Social Class Differences in Attitudes toward the School. On the basis of a careful review of social-class differences in child-rearing practices as they historically have affected the socialization process, Bronfenbrenner (1958) concluded that the gap may be narrowing. Some differences in values remain among the classes, but there is an overlap as well as wide variations within any single social class. Kohn (1959) discovered a broadly common set of values among working-class and middle-class mothers in parental ratings of child behavior. Both groups of mothers rated happiness, honesty, consideration, obedience, dependability, manners, and self-control as traits to be desired in children in the middle elementary-school years. Although the middle-class mothers emphasized self-control and the lower-class mothers were more likely to value obedience, *the similarities between the two groups were greater than the differences.*

The poor are becoming increasingly aware of and convinced of the importance of education. It is true that lower-class people are less likely to mention higher education when asked what is necessary to "get along well in the world." But, as Cloward and Jones (1963) point out, this is probably because lower-class individuals are oriented toward a lower occupational level. The middle-class person is oriented toward the "ideal" of a professional or semiprofessional occupation, which, indeed, requires more education. However, adequate recognition is not given to the fact that in surveys more than half of the lower-class respondents mention education as important for their children, especially for boys (Cloward & Jones, 1963). The lower-class individual has thus come to understand the need for education in getting a decent job, and to realize that education enables him to cope more adequately with a complex society (Riessman, 1962)—to understand the small print in the contract for a used-car purchase; to be informed about available welfare benefits; and to be informed about such issues as the draft, income tax, and legal rights.

A sample of mothers of children enrolled in a Head Start program in Santa Clara County, California, were surveyed with regard to their expectations for the program (Medinnus, 1967). They were asked, "What would you like to have your child get out of the Head Start program?" Their responses, emphasizing academic preparation (language, number concepts) and social skills (getting along with peers, increased independence), suggest that these mothers, primarily Mexican-American, were aware of the demands of the school situation. While not so well-informed or knowledgeable as better-educated middle-class mothers, these lower-class women were not ignorant of factors making for subsequent school success. The crucial difference between the two groups is that lower-class mothers, especially those of minority background, feel unqualified and unable to give their children the kinds of experience that will prepare him academically for school. These mothers are interested and motivated, but they lack the skills. The school must make a far greater effort to involve the lower-class parent in its activities. The Head Start program has attempted to do this, and with some success.

Middle-Class Values that Prevail in the School Prevent the Lower-Class Child from Functioning Adequately in This Situation. It is true that the middle-class child enjoys a continuity between his home experiences and values and those in the school. Frequent contradictions are experienced by the lower-class child, especially with regard to such values as long-term goals, emphasis on thinking rather than doing, seriousness attached to learning, individual competition, and language as a tool. The solution is not, however, to adopt lower-class values as the norm for our school systems. Awareness of these contradictions should enable the teacher and the school in general to gain a fuller understanding of the problems faced by these children, and to develop new techniques to cope with these problems. Positive aspects of lower-class culture should be recognized and fostered.

The Poor School Achievement of the Lower-Class Child is an Inevitable Consequence of His Background. It is extremely important for the school to be aware that the lower-class child's poor achievement is frequently caused by larger social forces such as poverty, family disintegration, urban blight, and poor housing. Only when these conditions are eliminated can we expect significant improvement in school performance. As Reissman (1962) points out, a number of subtle and not-so-subtle factors operating in the school situation work to the disadvantage of the lower-class child. Teacher turnover is far greater in schools in disadvantaged neighborhoods. New and inexperienced teachers predominate in these schools. For a variety of reasons intelligence tests are inappropriate for assessing the learning potential of these children. Much of the content of schoolbooks is alien to the experiences of the lower-class child. The teacher tends to favor those children who succeed in schoolwork.

The lower-class child has not had a reinforcement history conducive to school success. He has not been reinforced or rewarded by praise and approval for the kinds of behavior (counting, reading, studying, curiosity) that make for school success. Thus he is not prepared intellectually or motivationally to cope with school-type tasks.

With adequate recognition of the deficiencies of the disadvantaged child and the reasons for them, the school, with earnestness and imagination, can develop the kinds of program that will compensate for and overcome these deficiencies. And this will require the support of society as a whole.

It is important for the school to be aware of and to understand some of the value differences between social classes. The teacher must be aware of the conditions of lower-class life and the way in which these conditions affect the child. But the child must also be respected as an individual and not dealt with as a member of one social class or another. The low relationship between a child's social-class background and various personality indices (Sewell, 1961) suggests that knowledge of social class is of little use in understanding the individual child. Insofar as social class can tell anything about a child, the information should be obtained. But more important, what is the emotional relation between the child and his parents, and between the child and his siblings? How does he get along with his peers? What is the nature of the child's concept of himself?

COMPETITION

"Children must learn early to compete and stand up for their own rights because, after all, ours is a competitive society." Is the stress on competition one of the foundations of the American philosophy of child rearing? Hopefully, it is not. Let us hope that cooperation is as much a part of the American way of life as competition.

Is competition among children a natural phenomenon or is it fostered by the culture? Both alternatives have their support. That competition and rivalry occur early in the home—by a year-and-a-half —and relatively early in the experimental situation implies an "inborn" nature to these traits. Perhaps competition is related to the urge for physical and psychological survival. Yet in some cultures little competitive behavior is evident in the older child. This would suggest that the course of competitiveness throughout the developmental span is charted largely by society's attitude toward competition. Whether it is fostered and encouraged or de-emphasized and discouraged by the particular society settles the role of competition in the social behavior of the child.

The first competition or rivalry, since it arises in the family setting, may invest this trait with an element of affection. It may represent suit for a loved one's affection and esteem. In the classroom, the teacher must be aware of the possible effects on a child of failure to compete successfully. Feelings may be involved in addition to considerations related to the failed task. The child may feel rejected by the teacher and may resent what he perceives as favoritism shown by the teacher toward those children who succeed in the competitive situation.

Several experimental studies of children's behavior and performance in controlled competitive situations indicate that competition becomes pronounced in the four- to six-year-old child (Greenberg, 1932; Leuba, 1933). Parents' handling of sibling rivalry and parental attitudes toward competition are important factors in the development of competitiveness in the child and in his position toward it. In the Greenberg study pairs of children were observed in a situation in which they were encouraged to build a block structure "prettier" and "bigger" than their companions'. The following percentages of competitive behavior were shown by the children at the various age levels:

2–3 years	0.0 per cent
3–4 years	42.6 per cent
4–5 years	69.2 per cent
5–6 years	75.4 per cent
6–7 years	86.5 per cent

These percentages may suggest that competitive behavior in children is unavoidable. This may or may not be the case. However, the concern here is with the psychological impacts of competition on the child.

The very nature of the school environment lends itself to competition. Children can readily compare their performance with others. Speed and accuracy are frequently emphasized and both of these rank pupils in an obvious manner. The child who hesitates and stumbles over words when his turn comes to read arouses the teacher's impatience and irritability; consequently, he is often followed by a child who reads with some fluency. Both teacher and children are aware of the difference between the two reading performances. It remains for the teacher to make sure that each child experiences some measure of success and competence. By its very existence competition creates differences among children with respect to success and failure.

But there may be advantages as well as disadvantages to a competitive situation. Some evidence (Stendler, Damrin, & Haines, 1951) implies that fewer negative social behaviors result from group competition than from individual competition. A competitive spirit in a group may promote a healthy interest in the activity. Feelings of personal worth and competence, of course, are less likely to be at stake than in a situation in which competition among individuals is encouraged.

It would seem most unfortunate, however, for a teacher to feel it necessary to introduce competition into the classroom in order to stimulate the children's interest in the subject matter. Reliance on such a crutch is harmful and unacceptable. The children may become more concerned with competing for the sake of competing than with learning or the content of the school work. Motivation to learn can be found in psychologically sounder methods. Indeed, the very purpose that competition is supposed to accomplish is often defeated, resulting in the opposite effect.

Third-grade Johnny was relating to his mother some of the day's events at school. "We had a race in arithmetic to see who could get done first and get the most right. I worked hard but I came in last. You know, I wish I didn't have to take arithmetic any more."

Competition may be a part of the culture. Some parents may instill it in their children. But in the school setting the teacher decides when and how much competition to prescribe for the classroom or the playground. The value of competition and of a competitive attitude must be weighed against the disadvantages with respect to the psychological effects on the individual child.

SUMMARY

The teacher's role in the classroom has been the main emphasis in this chapter. The teacher stimulates and guides the intellectual development of pupils, affects their attitudes and values, and exerts a marked influence on their emotional adjustment through the kind of psychological atmosphere established in the classroom and through differential rewards and punishments.

Many factors relate to academic achievement: intellectual ability, level of maturity, relationship with parents, emotional and personality factors, past success and failure, attitude toward school, the teacher, socioeconomic status, and patterns of interest. Because the primary function of the school is the teaching of academic skills, the extent to which a child learns these skills reflects the effectiveness of the school's endeavor and also bears heavily on the child's concept of himself.

The years spent in school are important ones. Teachers and parents must work together to make certain that for each child these years are fruitful and well used.

REFERENCES

Anderson, H. H.   An experimental study of dominative and integrative behavior in children of preschool age. *Journal of Social Psychology*, 1937, **8**, 335–345. (a)

Anderson, H. H.   Domination and integration in the social behavior of young children in an experimental play situation. *Genetic Psychology Monographs*, 1937, **19**, 341–408. (b)

Anderson, H. H.   The measurement of domination and of socially integrative behavior in teachers' contacts with children. *Child Development*, 1939, **10**, 73–89. (a)

Anderson, H. H.   Domination and social integration in the behavior of kindergarten children and teachers. *Genetic Psychology Monographs*, 1939, **21**, 287–385. (b)

Anderson, H. H.   Domination and socially integrative behavior. In R. Barker,

J. Kounin, & H. Wright (Eds.), *Child behavior and development.* New York: McGraw-Hill, 1943. Pp. 459–483.

Antes, J., Anderson, D., & DeVault, M. Elementary pupils' perceptions of the social-emotional environment of the classroom. *Psychology in the Schools,* 1965, **2**, 41–46.

Atkinson, J. W. (Ed.). *Motives in fantasy, action and society.* New York: Van Nostrand, 1958.

Baer, D., & Ragosta, T. Relationship between perceived child-rearing practices and verbal and mathematical ability. *Journal of Genetic Psychology,* 1966, **108**, 105–108.

Baruch, D. W. Procedures in training teachers to prevent and reduce mental hygiene problems. *Journal of Genetic Psychology,* 1945, **67**, 143–178.

Battle, H. Relation between personal values and scholastic achievements. *Journal of Experimental Education,* 1957, **26**, 27–41.

Baumrind, D. Effects of authoritative parental control on child behavior. *Child Development,* 1966, **37**, 887–907.

Beilin, H. Teachers' and clinicians' attitudes toward the behavior problems of children: A reappraisal. *Child Development,* 1959, **30**, 9–25.

Bereiter, C., & Engelmann, S. *Teaching disadvantaged children in the preschool.* Englewood Cliffs, N. J.: Prentice-Hall, 1966.

Bing, E. The effect of child rearing practices on development of differential cognitive abilities. *Child Development,* 1963, **34**, 631–648.

Bloom, B. *Stability and change in human characteristics.* New York: Wiley, 1964.

Bonney, M. E., & Nicholson, E. L. Comparative social adjustments of elementary school pupils with and without preschool training. *Child Development,* 1958, **29**, 125–133.

Briggs, P., Johnson, R., & Wirt, R. Achievement among delinquency-prone adolescents. *Journal of Clinical Psychology,* 1962, **18**, 305–309.

Bronfenbrenner, U. Socialization and social class through time and space. In E. E. Maccoby, T. M. Newcomb, & E. L. Hartley (Eds.), *Readings in social psychology.* New York: Holt, 1958. Pp. 400–425.

Carter, L. B. The effect of early school entrance on the scholastic achievement of elementary school children in the Austin public schools. *Journal of Educational Research,* 1956, **50**, 91–103.

Chance, J. E. Independence training and first graders' achievement. *Journal of Consulting Psychology,* 1961, **25**, 149–154.

Christensen, C. M. Relationships between pupil achievement, pupil affect-need, teacher warmth, and teacher permissiveness. *Journal of Educational Psychology,* 1960, **51**, 169–174.

Cloward, R., & Jones, J. Social class: Educational attitudes and participation. In A. H. Passow (Ed.), *Education in depressed areas.* New York: Teachers College Press, 1963. Pp. 190–216.

Conklin, A. M. Failures of highly intelligent pupils. *Teachers College Contributions to Education,* 1940, No. 792.

Crandall, V., Dewey, R., Katkovsky, W., & Preston, A.   Parents' attitudes and behaviors and grade-school children's academic achievements.   *Journal of Genetic Psychology*, 1964, **104**, 53–66.

Davids, A., & Hainsworth, P.   Maternal attitudes about family life and child rearing as avowed by mothers and perceived by their underachieving and high-achieving sons.   *Journal of Consulting Psychology*, 1967, **31**, 29–37.

Davis, A., & Dollard, J.   *Children of bondage*.   Washington, D. C.: American Council on Education, 1940.

Davis, A., & Havighurst, R.   Social class and color differences in child-rearing.   *American Sociological Review*, 1946, **II**, 698–710.

DeGroat, A. F., & Thompson, G. G.   A study of the distribution of teacher approval and disapproval among sixth-grade children.   *Journal of Experimental Education*, 1949, **18**, 57–75.

Dinitz, S., Kay, B., & Reckless, W. C.   Delinquency proneness and school achievement.   *Educational Research Bulletin*, 1957, **36**, 131–136.

Ferguson, L., & Maccoby, E.   Interpersonal correlates of differential abilities.   *Child Development*, 1966, **37**, 549–571.

Flanders, N. A., & Havumaki, S.   The effect of teacher-pupil contacts involving praise on the sociometric choices of students.   *Journal of Educational Psychology*, 1960, **51**, 65–68.

Gladstone, R.   Do maladjusted teachers cause maladjustment?   A re-review.   *Journal of Exceptional Children*, 1948, **15**, 65–70.

Goodenough, F. L., & Maurer, K. M.   The mental development of nursery-school children compared with that of non-nursery school children. *National Society for the Study of Education, 39th Yearbook*, 1940, Part II, 161–178.

Greenberg, P. J.   Competition in children: An experimental study.   *American Journal of Psychology*, 1932, **44**, 221–248.

Gronlund, N. E.   The accuracy of teachers' judgments concerning the sociometric status of sixth-grade pupils.   *Sociometry*, 1950, **13**, 197–225, 329–357.

Haggard, E. A.   Socialization, personality and achievement in gifted children.   *School Review*, 1957, **65**, 318–414.

Harlow, H.   Learning and satiation of response in intrinsically motivated complex puzzle performance by monkeys.   *Journal of Comparative and Physiological Psychology*, 1950, **43**, 289–294.

Hattwick, L. A.   The influence of nursery school attendance upon the behavior and personality of the preschool child.   *Journal of Experimental Education*, 1936, **5**, 180–190.

Havighurst, R., & Taba, H.   *Adolescent character and personality*.   New York: Wiley, 1949.

Hebb, D.   *The organization of behavior*. New York: Wiley, 1949.

Hill, J.   Similarity and accordance between parents and sons in attitudes toward mathematics.   *Child Development*, 1967, **38**, 777–791.

Hoehn, A. H. A study of social class differentiation in the classroom behavior of nineteen third-grade teachers. *Journal of Social Psychology,* 1954, **39,** 269–292.

Hollingshead, A. *Elmtown's youth: The impact of social classes on youth.* New York: Wiley, 1949.

Hunt, J. McV. *Intelligence and experience.* New York: Ronald, 1961.

Hunt, J. McV. The psychological basis for using pre-school enrichment as an antidote for cultural deprivation. *Merrill-Palmer Quarterly,* 1964, **10,** 207–248.

Hunter, E. C. Changes in teachers' attitudes toward children's behavior over the last thirty years. *Mental Hygiene,* 1957, **41,** 3–11.

Jersild, A. T. Characteristics of teachers who are "liked best" and "disliked most." *Journal of Experimental Education,* 1940, **9,** 139–151.

Katkovsky, W., Preston, A., & Crandall, V. Parents' attitudes toward their personal achievements and toward the achievement behaviors of their children. *Journal of Genetic Psychology,* 1964, **104,** 67–82.

Keliher, A. V. A day in the life of the teacher. *Mental Hygiene,* 1950, **34,** 455–464.

Kimball, B. Case studies in educational failure during adolescence. *American Journal of Orthopsychiatry,* 1953, **23,** 406–415.

Klausmeier, H. J., & Check, J. Relationships among physical, mental, achievement, and personality measures in children of low, average, and high intelligence. *American Journal of Mental Deficiency,* 1959, **63,** 647–656.

Kohn, M. L. Social class and parental values. *American Journal of Sociology,* 1959, **64,** 337–351.

Kvaraceus, W. C. Mental health hazards facing teachers. *Phi Delta Kappan,* 1951, **32,** 349–350.

Lee, M. J., & Clark, W. W. Lee-Clark Reading Readiness Test. Kindergarten and Grade I. 1951 Rev. Los Angeles: California Test Bureau, 1951.

Leeds, C. H., & Cook, W. W. The construction and differential value of a scale for determining teacher-pupil attitudes. *Journal of Experimental Education,* 1947, **16,** 149–159.

Leuba, C. An experimental study of rivalry in young children. *Journal of Comparative Psychology,* 1933, **16,** 367–378.

McClelland, D. C., Atkinson, J. W., Clark, R. A., & Lowell, E. I. *The achievement motive.* New York: Appleton-Century-Crofts, 1953.

McDavid, J., Jr. Some relationships between social reinforcement and scholastic achievement. *Journal of Consulting Psychology,* 1959, **23,** 151–154.

Malpass, L. F. Some relationships between students' perceptions of school and their achievement. *Journal of Educational Psychology,* 1953, **44,** 475–482.

Medinnus, G. R. An investigation of school readiness and first-grade adjustment. Unpublished manuscript, 1961. (a)

Medinnus, G. R.   The relation between several parent measures and the child's early adjustment to school.   *Journal of Educational Psychology,* 1961, **52,** 153–156.   (b)

Medinnus, G. R.   The development of a First-Grade Adjustment Scale. *Journal of Experimental Education,* 1961, **30,** 243–248.   (c)

Medinnus, G. R.   An examination of several correlates of sociometric status in a first grade group.   *Journal of Genetic Psychology,* 1962, **101,** 3–13.

Medinnus, G.   Evaluation of Santa Clara County Head Start.   San Jose State College.   Unpublished study, 1967.

Medinnus, G., & Bean, J.   Cognitives structured vs. collage free play. San Jose State College.   Unpublished study, 1967.

Merrill, B.   A measurement of mother-child interaction.   *Journal of Abnormal and Social Psychology,* 1946, **41,** 37–49.

Meyer, W. J., & Thompson, G. G.   Sex differences in the distribution of teacher approval and disapproval among sixth-grade children.   *Journal of Educational Psychology,* 1956, **47,** 385–396.

Milner, E.   A study of the relationship between reading readiness in grade one school children and patterns of parent-child interaction.   *Child Development,* 1951, **22,** 95–112.

Morrow, W. R., & Wilson, R. C.   Family relations of bright high-achieving and under-achieving high school boys.   *Child Development,* 1961, **32,** 501–510.

Murphy, G., Murphy, L. B., & Newcomb, T.   *Experimental social psychology.* New York: Harper, 1937.

Neale, D., & Proshek, J.   School-related attitudes of culturally disadvantaged elementary school children.   *Journal of Educational Psychology,* 1967, **58,** 238–244.

Olson, W. C., & Hughes, B. O.   Subsequent growth of children with and without nursery-school experience.   *National Society for the Study of Education, 39th Yearbook,* 1940, Part II, 237–244.

Riessman, F.   *The culturally deprived child.*   New York: Harper & Row, 1962.

Sears, P. S.   Levels of aspiration in academically successful and unsuccessful children.   *Journal of Abnormal and Social Psychology,* 1940, **35,** 498–536.

Sechrest, L.   Studies of classroom atmosphere.   *Psychology in the Schools,* 1964, **1,** 103–118.

Sewell, W.   Social class and childhood personality.   *Sociometry,* 1961, **24,** 340–356.

Simon, M. D.   Body configuration and school readiness.   *Child Development,* 1959, **30,** 493–512.

Skeels, H. M., Updegraff, R., Wellman, B. L., & Williams, H. M.   A study of environmental stimulation: An orphanage preschool project.   *University of Iowa Study in Child Welfare,* 1938, **15,** No. 4.

Snyder, W. U.   Do teachers cause maladjustment?   *Journal of Exceptional Children,* 1947, **14,** 40–46, 73–78.

Stendler, C. B.   Social class differences in parental attitudes toward school at Grade I level. *Child Development,* 1951, **22,** 36–46.

Stendler, C. B., Damrin, D., & Haines, A. C.   Studies in cooperation and competition: I. The effects of working for groups and individual rewards on the social climates of children's groups. *Journal of Genetic Psychology,* 1951, **79,** 173–197.

Stendler, C. B., & Young, N.   Impact of first grade entrance upon the socialization of the child: Changes after eight months of school. *Child Development,* 1950, **22,** 113–122.

Stendler, C. B., & Young, N.   The impact of beginning first grade upon socialization as reported by mothers. *Child Development,* 1959, **21,** 241–260.

Stiles, L. J. (Ed.).   *The teacher's role in American society.   John Dewey Society, 14th Yearbook.* New York: Harper, 1957.

Tamkin, A. S.   A survey of educational disability in emotionally disturbed children. *Journal of Educational Research,* 1960, **53,** 313–315.

Templin, M. C.   General information of kindergarten children: a comparison with the Probst study after 26 years. *Child Development,* 1958, **29,** 87–96.

Tenenbaum, S.   Uncontrolled expressions of children's attitudes toward school. *Elementary School Journal,* 1940, **40,** 670–678.

Thompson, G. G.   The social and emotional development of preschool children under two types of educational program. *Psychological Monographs: General and Applied,* 1944, **56,** No. 5.

Tolor, A., Scarpetti, W., & Lane, P.   Teachers' attitudes toward children's behavior revisited. *Journal of Educational Psychology,* 1967, **58,** 175–180.

Van Alstyne, D., & Hattwick, L. A.   A follow-up study of the behavior of nursery school children. *Child Development,* 1939, **10,** 43–72.

Walsh, A. M.   *Self-concepts of bright boys with learning difficulties.* New York: Bureau of Publication, Teachers College, Columbia University, 1956.

Walsh, M. E.   The relation of nursery school training to the development of certain personality traits. *Child Development,* 1931, **2,** 72–73.

Warner, W., Havighurst, R., & Loeb, M.   *Who shall be educated?* New York: Harper, 1944.

Weikart, D.   Preschool programs: preliminary findings. *Journal of Special Education,* 1967, **1,** 163–181.

Wellman, B. L.   The effect of preschool attendance upon the I.Q. *Journal of Experimental Education,* 1932, I, 48–69.

Wickman, E. K.   *Children's behavior and teachers' attitudes.* New York: Commonwealth Fund, 1928.

Winterbottom, M.   In D. C. McClelland, J. W. Atkinson, R. A. Clark, & E. L. Lowell, *The achievement motive.* New York: Appleton-Century-Crofts, 1953. Pp. 297–306. Also The relation of need for achievement in learning experiences in independence and mastery. In J. W.

Atkinson (Ed.), *Motives in fantasy, action and society*. New York: Van Nostrand, 1958. Pp. 453–478.

Withall, J. The development of a technique for the measurement of social-emotional climates in classrooms. *Journal of Experimental Education,* 1949, **17,** 347–361.

Withall, J. Assessment of the social-emotional climates experienced by a group of seventh graders as they moved from class to class. *Educational and Psychological Measurement,* 1952, **12,** 440–451.

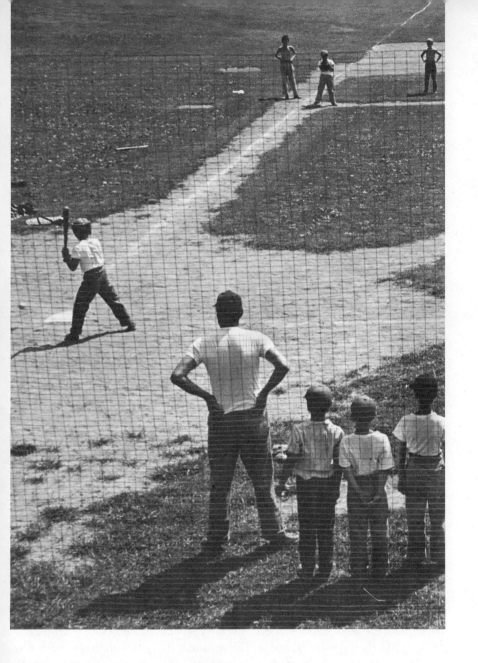

13

Other Socializing Influences

A growing child's family, his peers, and the school are not the only influences he encounters. A child grows up in a community. He is exposed to varying degrees of religious instruction. He takes cognizance of such organized groups as the Boy Scouts. He is confronted by the mass media of communication—books, comic books, movies, television. How much and in what way do these agencies of socialization affect his development?

THE COMMUNITY

The role of the community in the life of a young person depends largely on the child's parents. If they do not abdicate their responsibilities in the socialization process, the community serves more often to reinforce parental values than as a source of values themselves (Peck & Havighurst, 1960). Even if a community is a deteriorated slum fraught with delinquency and crime, the child appears to be largely shielded against its criminal influences as long as his parents provide him with a positive concept of the self through close, effective family interaction and high expectations (Reckless, Dinitz, & Murray, 1956; Scarpitti, Murray, Simon, & Reckless, 1960). It is when parents abandon their function in socializing the child that the community assumes a more central role. If the parents fail to provide values, or if they are lacking in the techniques for implanting them, the community, among other social forces, may take over by default. For children of this type of background the community has great importance.

Consider two communities. Observe the dominant values that might reinforce, replace, or rebut parental values. And note the effectiveness with which these community values are instilled and the type of reward offered for conforming to them.

The first community is a village with a population of approximately 250, located not far from a city of 10,000. The village homes are old and rambling. No major national or state highways pass through the village, and there is little local traffic. Two-year-olds can be turned loose to cross streets, since everyone drives slowly and carefully. By the age of three children have begun running about the village in small groups and at about six they begin playing around the creek, the gravel pit swimming hole, and in the forest that rings the village. The only supervision is the loose watch of the older children. There is always the hazard of drowning or of getting lost in the woods, but neither has occurred for several generations. Danger is present, though less so and possibly more predictably than in the city.

All but two of the families are Norwegian-American. All the original settlers came to the same place a few generations ago as a result of having been friends and relatives in Norway. Pressure is exerted on each generation of children to associate with one another and not with the people of the nearby countryside, who are not Norwegian and Lutheran but predominantly Polish, French-Canadian, and American-Indian Catholics. Through intragroup marriages nearly everyone is related by blood, marriage, or both to everyone else.

The population is stable. Very few new families have moved into the village, but a fair—and probably the most enterprising—portion of the children of each generation move out. The men once worked in the woods and the sawmills of the nearby city. Now the timber is gone and the men have switched to the wood-products factories of the city. These companies are paternalistic in the good sense of the term and usually have jobs available for the village's young people when they quit or graduate from high school. Net income among the families varies from about $4000 to $6000 a year, but this tends to be sufficient. Rent is below $50 a month, as a rule, and most families have a garden as well as some small livestock.

The one church is Norwegian Lutheran. The children are sent to Sunday School with great regularity and to confirmation classes for two years during adolescence. At 15 they are confirmed as full members of the church, but do not attend church again, by and large, until middle or old age. Because all members of an age group attend the same Sunday School and confirmation classes, there is an overlap between the lessons of the church and the practices among peers. Misdeeds often come to the attention of the minister who can exercise pressure, such as refusal to confirm, a terrible disgrace, to induce a change of behavior.

The legendary wildness of one of the girls during the "roaring twenties" serves the present generation as the basis for a sermon. The girl was "wild" enough as an adolescent to run around with non-Norwegian boys. Even the contemporary generation knows of this. Behavior is judged by one's elders, one's peers, and even by future generations to come.

Children in this village are reared within the typical nuclear family structure but are the responsibility of everyone in the community. Grandparents, uncles, aunts, older siblings, even godparents are so intimately involved in the rearing of a child that they will take over completely if the parents are unwilling or unable to fulfill the function. The majority of adults in the community feel free to discipline, physically or verbally, any child who misbehaves. All adults believe it to be their duty to inform the child's parents of any misdeeds committed. The child is ruled by every adult. He is also defended by every adult—defended against "mean kids," outsiders, and strangers, and, if need be, the forces of law and order.

The community is marked by the fact that a high proportion of behavior is *public* behavior. It is open, known by all, judged by all. Everyone agrees on most things; hence the children are exposed to a single, well-defined set of values. Great pressure is brought to bear to enforce conformity. Defense is communitywide if needed. This is a clear-cut illustration of a *primary group* society.

The other community is described by a boy who grew up in it.

I remember one time I hit a boy in the face with a bottle of Pepsi-Cola. I did it because I knew the older cats on 146th Street were watching me. The boy had messed with Carole. He had taken her candy from her and thrown it on the ground.

I came up to him and said, "Man, what you mess with my sister for?"

All the older guys were saying, "That's that little boy who lives on Eighth Avenue. They call him Sonny Boy. We gon see somethin' good out here now."

There was a Pepsi-Cola truck there; they were unloading some crates. They were stacking up the crates to roll them inside. The boy who had hit Carole was kind of big and acted kind of mean. He had a stick in his hand, and he said, "Yeah, I did it, so what you gon do about it?"

I looked at him for a while, and he looked big. He was holding that stick like he meant to use it, so I snatched a Pepsi-Cola bottle and hit him right in the face. He grabbed his face and started crying. He fell down, and I started to hit him again, but the man who was unloading the Pepsi-Cola bottles grabbed me. He took the bottle away from me and shook me. He asked me if I was crazy or something.

All the guys on the corner started saying. "You better leave that boy alone," and "Let go of that kid." I guess he got kind of scared. He was white, and here were all these mean-looking colored cats talking about "Let go that kid" and looking at him. They weren't asking him to let me go; they were telling him. He let me go.

Afterward, if I came by, they'd start saying, "Hey, Sonny Boy, how you doin'?" They'd ask me, "You kick anybody's ass today?" I knew that they admired me for this, and I knew that I had to keep on doing it. This was the reputation I was making, and I had to keep living up to it every day that I came out of the house. Every day, there was a greater demand on me. I couldn't beat the same little boys every day. They got bigger and bigger. I had to get more vicious as the cats got bigger. When the bigger guys started messing with you, you couldn't hit them or give them a black eye or a bloody nose. You had to get a bottle or a stick or a knife. All the other cats out there on the streets expected this of me, and they gave me encouragement.

When I was about ten years old, the Forty Thieves—part of the Buccaneers—adopted me. Danny and Butch and Kid were already in it. Johnny Wilkes was older than Butch, and Butch was older than Danny and Kid. Johnny was an old Buccaneer. He had to be. When he came out on the streets in the early forties, it must have been twice as hard as it was a few years later. Harlem became less vicious from year to year, and it was hard when I first started coming out of the house, in 1944 and 1945, and raising all kinds of hell. It was something terrible out there on the streets.

Being one of the older Buccaneers, Johnny took Butch, Danny, and Kid as his fellows. He adopted them. I guess he liked the fact that they all admired him. They adopted me because I was a thief. I don't know why or how I first started stealing. I remember it was Danny and Butch who were the first ones who took me up on the hill to the white stores and downtown. I had already started stealing in Harlem. It was before I started going to school, so it must have been about 1943. Danny used to steal money, and he used to take me to the show with him and buy me popcorn and potato chips. After a while, I stole money too. Stealing became something good. It was exciting. I don't know what made it so exciting, but I liked it. I liked stealing more than I liked fighting.

I didn't like fighting at first. But after a while, it got me a lot of praise and respect in the street. It was the fighting and the stealing that made me somebody. If I hadn't fought or stolen, I would have been just another kid in the street. I put bandages on cats, and people would ask, "Who did that?" The older cats didn't believe that a little boy had broke somebody's arm by hitting him with a pipe or had hit somebody in the face with a bottle or had hit somebody in the head with a door hinge and put that big patch on his head. They didn't believe things like this at first, but my name got around and they believed it.

I became the mascot of the Buccaneers. They adopted me, and they started teaching me things. At that time, they were just the street-corner hoodlums, the delinquents, the little teen-age gangsters of the future. They were outside of things, but they knew the people who were into things, all the older hustlers and the prostitutes, the bootleggers, the pimps, the numbers runners. They knew the professional thieves, the people who dealt the guns, the stickup artists, the people who sold reefers. I was learning how to make homemades and how to steal things and what reefers were. I was learning all the things that you needed to know in the streets. The main thing I was learning was our code.

We looked upon ourselves as the aristocracy of the community. We felt that we were the hippest people and that the other people didn't know anything. When I was in the street with these people, we all had to live for one another. We had to live in a way that we would be respected by one another. We couldn't let our friends think anything terrible of us, and we didn't want to think anything bad about our friends (Brown, 1965, pp. 268–271).

In "crimogenic" environments such as the one described by Brown, it is not surprising that delinquency rates are high; it is surprising that some families manage to maintain sufficiently close ties that a younger member grows up with an adequate feeling of self-worth and does not become delinquent, even in a situation where the criminal may seem the most successful model available.

The plush Gold Coast of Chicago's near North Side is still within walking distance of "Murder Corner," and the child who matures in either of these areas remains exposed to different experiences, values, and opportunities from those of the child raised in the other. Both of them will see another aspect of life from that seen by the rural youngster. Although the distance between rural and urban society has narrowed and differences of social class have been reduced, these continue to exercise some influence on differences between individuals.

Dr. H. was visiting with friends who had a three-year-old boy. The boy was talking about becoming a fireman. In the course of the adult conversation, Dr. H. was asked, "Well, didn't you want to be a fireman when you were a kid?" Dr. H. was a Negro, and had grown up in the heart of the New York City ghetto. He said, "Listen, when I was growing up there *weren't* any Negro firemen, and what's more, we all knew that there never would be. What I wanted to be was a pimp or else a numbers man—they were the only ones that made it good when I was growing up." It is a cruel indictment of a culture that one of its brightest members placed these realistic (for the time) limits on his ambition. But the culture, despite imperfections, had sufficient positive values that Dr. H. accepted it, at least in part, and did obtain his doctorate, just as Claude Brown did survive the street battles to become a great and moving author.

As noted in Chapter 7, the pervasiveness and intensity of parental impact on the child at any single time has decreased, even though the period of parental control and influence has grown longer. If parental influence has fallen off, what social forces have taken its place? It is doubtful that the community has increased its influence. It does not seem likely that the other agencies to be considered in this chapter have gained much influence, either. Perhaps the major legatee has been the child's peers. The older primary-group community is vanishing because of the greater physical and social mobility and the increased urbanization of the American people. The urban *secondary-group* community does not teach values or reinforce existing values as adequately, even when these are not pathological, since the value system is not backed up by the consensus of a close-knit group. Only when filling a vacuum, only when providing values in the absence of any other source, does the community achieve any real significance in shaping behavior.

Sociologists have argued that the functions of the primary-group community have been taken over, in part, by voluntary associations —interest groups such as the Boy Scouts, the Camp Fire Girls, the P.T.A., and the American Legion (see Rose, 1956). Like the community, these groups are probably only influential in molding the behavior of children when parents have neglected to do so. Young people are generally not too deeply involved in groups like the Boy Scouts and are interested in them for only a limited portion of the development cycle. Voluntary associations like the Scouts, which emphasize crafts and outdoor life, have a high rate of dropouts once puberty has been reached and interest patterns change. Yet these groups do have well-defined values and have developed excellent techniques for instilling them (see Martin & Stendler, 1959, pp. 409–412).

The sheer number of organizations to which a child may belong is great. Fox (1952), in an undoubtedly incomplete count, found 5000 voluntary groups. Although the effect of any one of these may be slight, the cumulative impact of the organizations one joins while growing up may be very heavy. These "artificial" primary groups do much to supply the sort of extrafamilial influences once provided by the primary-group type of community. The rehabilitation of urban slums like the second community described in the chapter depends, to a large extent, on the success of this new form of primary group, the voluntary association, in inculcating values as well as on the values inculcated.

THE INFLUENCE OF RELIGIOUS EXPERIENCE

Since the days of G. Stanley Hall and his disciples (Daniels, 1893; Starbuck, 1899), all of whom believed religious conversion to be an almost necessary part of adolescent experience, psychologists have shown intermittent interest in the impact of religion on development. Actually, relatively little is known of the direct influence of religion on behavior because the problem of setting up a criterion is a difficult one. How does one separate the religious from the nonreligious to determine whether the two differ in behavior and values? One criterion of a religious orientation is the individual's own statement: does he or does he not claim religious affiliation?

In interviews and tests involving hundreds of delinquents, every one of them claimed some religious tie. This surely cannot validate the hypothesis that delinquents would not be delinquent if only they had some religious experience. But a bit of probing discloses that most of these delinquents do not enter a church once a year. Their affiliation is verbal, not behavioral. Some criterion other than affiliation is necessary.

Nor will church attendance, as cited in many studies, do. Some persons attend church for nonreligious reasons—as a result of habit, of pressure, of social aspirations, or in order to acquire feelings of superiority. There are studies using test scores of religious knowledge (McDowell, 1952), but even this approach cannot uncover true religious commitment. Although Godin (1962) offered other suggestions for a criterion, the problem has not been adequately dealt with in any study of which the authors are aware. Most of the data presented here must be viewed as containing information on the relation between certain formal aspects of religion and behavior—for example, churchgoing—rather than as presenting insights into the link between degree of religious involvement and behavior.

Religious experience might be expected to change both broad social attitudes, such as belief in the brotherhood of man, and specific behaviors, such as cheating on tests. Taking the social attitudes first, the case seems to be clear that church attendance does not increase acceptance of the Bill of Rights (Stouffer, 1955). In an unpublished study conducted in San Jose, California, Walter Morgan subjected members of an upper-lower and lower-middle-class church congregation to measures of dogmatism, ethnocentrism, and fascism. He rated involvement in the church by asking subjects how frequently they attended Sunday services and the number of church-affiliated social activities they engaged in. The deeper the individual's involvement the higher was his score on each of the three measures.

Wilson (1960) found similar results in a study of religion and anti-Semitism. In another study (Kelly, Ferson, & Holtzman, 1958), subjects favorable toward religion were seen to view Negroes more negatively than did persons less religiously committed. Finally, Jones (1958) observed that adults high in authoritarianism showed higher religious training and values, and lower interest in the theoretical and esthetic areas of personal experience, than did individuals of lesser authoritarian tendencies.

If respondents are divided as to those who go to church and those who do not, or as to those high versus low in religiosity, the results discussed above generally are obtained. However, if a more finely graded measure of religiosity is obtained, a curvilinear relationship between religious involvement and prejudice appears (see Allport & Ross, 1967); those persons who are deeply involved in religion (as indicated by regular participation) and those totally uninvolved are the least prejudiced, whereas church members who attend occasionally are the most prejudiced. Allport and Ross distinguished between the extrinsically religious (who find religion useful to provide security, sociability, or status) and the intrinsically religious (who are committed to religion because it provides an internalized guide to behavior). They found that the indiscriminately proreligious (who favor religion for both intrinsic and extrinsic reasons) are more prejudiced than the extrinsically religious, who in turn are more prejudiced than intrinsically religious persons. Salisbury (1962) distinguished among three major dimensions of religion: doctrine and belief, behavior and practice, and feelings and emotions.

Since those who never attend church and those who very frequently attend seem more "moral"—in the sense of being less afraid of and discriminating toward others than are the large mass of people who fall between the two extremes—it would appear unjust to say that religious involvement *causes* prejudice. Rather, it would seem that most of those persons who are occasional church attenders differ from persons at both extremes in that they are either indiscriminately ("muddle-headedly," to use Allport's and Ross's term) or extrinsically oriented toward religion and more concerned with doctrine and belief than in behavior and practices. Religiosity per se is not associated with prejudice; however, certain of the motivational forces that cause people to be avowedly religious seem to be the same as those forces that cause people to be prejudiced.

Turning to the specific behaviors, the studies by Hartshorne and May in the late 1920's (1928, 1929) must be cited. In their first study (1928) they ascertained through a number of ingeniously designed test situations the amount of cheating done by children who attended Sunday school and by those who did not. One sampling disclosed cheating among 31 per cent and 40 per cent of the two groups, respectively. A second sampling turned up respective findings of 38 per cent and 43 per cent. Although following the direction expected, the differences were negligible. In the subsequent experiment (1929) they observed that children who attended Sunday school regularly were more helpful than others whose attendance was irregular. Once again the difference was small. And even the minor positive results of these two studies might have been produced by inadequate matching.

Middleton and Putney (1962) suggest that research concentrating on delinquency, humanitarianism, and so on, has failed to reveal differences between religious and nonreligious persons because these issues are "moral" ones, and responses are determined by the "common religion"— the general social morality—rather than by specific denominational involvement.

To all those who believe in the positive value of religious instruction this may prove disappointing. That exposure to the teachings of religion is not efficacious in combatting intolerance or dishonesty is, however, not surprising. The young person, even if regularly attending church and Sunday school, is in contact with these religious institutions for less than one-fiftieth of his waking hours. Besides, there is an abundance of evidence dating back to Hall's original study (1882) that young children have an extremely low-level and primitive conception of God and of other religious symbols such as heaven, hell, and angels. This makes it quite difficult for the young child to grasp the moral issues involved in religion and to be influenced in his behavior by the religious resolution of these questions. All these studies suffer, as we have remarked, because of the difficulty in establishing a criterion for religious involvement. But even though attending church or Sunday school does not appear to influence moral behavior, it may be that the deeper criteria of religious commitment (such as amount of intrinsic orientation) will have considerable positive influence on behavior.

MASS MEDIA OF COMMUNICATION

Just as many consider religious experience a potent positive force in shaping behavior, so they look at most of the mass media of communication as a negative influence. As we shall see, the evidence against the mass media seems about as telling as the evidence supporting religious education.

Books

The oldest of the mass media is the printed word—books, newspapers, magazines. Despite the aura of wisdom surrounding books, the children's books that are acceptable to adults are not necessarily beneficial to children, if examined at close range. In an informative study, Child,

Potter, and Levine (1946) checked the values portrayed in children's textbooks. They examined the stories presented in all third-grade readers published since 1930. Stories were broken down according to *thema*. Each theme formed a unit involving an individual confronted with a situation, behaving as a result of it, and feeling the consequences of the behavior. In the 914 stories reviewed there was a total of 3409 themes. In these themes, girls and women were depicted as being kind, sociable, inactive, unambitious, and uncreative. Boys, on the other hand, were oftener shown as being active, aggressive, and interested in achievement.

It is often proclaimed that the pre-eminence of men in all of the arts and sciences stems from the cliché belief that "it's a man's world." This is difficult to understand when one views the arts in America. Girls are rewarded at every turn for developing talent in the graphic arts and in music. Conversely, boys who display such interests are compelled to battle relentlessly against being considered effeminate. Nevertheless, there are virtually no women composers, painters, or sculptors of first rank. Even in the playing of musical instruments, perhaps a lesser accomplishment than composing, there are very few highly able woman performers. Sex distinctions in creativity may very well result from the roles that the culture attributes to girls and women in such media as children's readers.

If the analysis of the children's readers is any indication, society continually presents young women with a set of roles of being kindly, dependent, and passive, and should not be too surprised if women take these seriously. Amidst an outcry of need for scientists, the culture inadvertently may be losing a major portion of them through an influence that can, to a degree, be checked—and that, in fact, is apparently shifting rather sharply. It may not be possible to change the way that girls and women are portrayed in television, in novels, or in the other mass media, but it is possible to modify the values depicted in the books used in the public schools.

The themes of children's textbooks are unrealistic in other ways. They are inordinately Pollyanna-ish. The hero never suffers defeat. Moreover, children are rarely portrayed as aggressive and acquisitive. Adults are oftener cast in antisocial roles. The general conclusion inspired by the Child et al. study is that children's textbooks are—or were—laden with pap, sugar-coated fare of which the readers must tire.

A recent study by deCharms and Moeller (1962) resembles the Child et al. undertaking in that it, too, was based on an analysis of values expressed in children's textbooks. This study covered sample pages of readers used in the years 1800–1950. Striking changes in content occurred. The use of religious or moral sanctions diminished substantially during the century and a half, while material stressing the social ethic increasingly replaced them. Emphasis on achievement—the Protestant ethic—reached its apex about 1900 (as, incidentally, did the number of patents issued per million of persons) and has been on the decline since. Although the rise of the social ethic continued over a longer period of time than might have been expected, the conclusions reached about it in Chapter 7 seem confirmed, for the most part, by this analysis of children's reading materials (see Figure 13-1).

Comics and Comic Books

In every generation, young people have insisted on reading trash—penny dreadfuls, dime novels, big little-books, or comic books, each in their own day—at the expense of the literature approved by the school and their parents. A subcommittee of the California legislature issued a report in 1958 concluding that juvenile delinquency stemmed from children's reading of comic books. Frederic Wertham, a New York psychiatrist, presented the same view in his book *Seduction of the Innocent* (1953). In an earlier era, Healy (1915) and Healy and Bronner (1936) placed the onus of guilt on cheap novels and magazines. If this were the case, the challenges to the imagination would be great—think of how delinquency could be eliminated by censorship, blinding the multitude, or forbidding everyone to learn to read! Obviously it oversimplifies the issue to blame comic books or other mass media for the existence of juvenile delinquency. Comics are a single, minor influence in the long sweep through which a child acquires a set of beliefs, values, and behaviors. What, then, is the real role that comics play?

To begin with, comic strips and comic books, as a rule, are neither funny nor amusing. They are exciting and contain a good deal of aggression. According to Bender and Lourie (1941) they fit the needs of children striving to understand the aggression of others and their own aggressive impulses. The comics and comic books share the characteristic of having justice prevail—the hero wins, the villain is punished. The vocabulary level of the typical comic book is high, about 10,000 words (Thorndike, 1941), and may be higher than the child is exposed to in conventional school texts.

Since the pictures provide cues to the words, and since the reader is highly motivated, many children unable to learn reading skills in a conventional classroom situation may gain from exposure to comic books. Although some of them and perhaps a few comic strips may

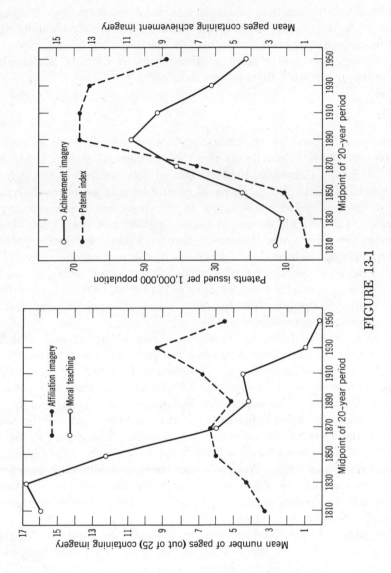

FIGURE 13-1

491

center on sadism, masochism, or other pathological tendencies, and may at times provide an explicit blueprint for a specific crime, most comics for most children seem relatively harmless and, in some ways, beneficial. The question that arises is how much, if any, censorship of comic books or any other of the mass media society should impose on the majority in order to safeguard the suggestible minority. But this, more properly, is a point of interest for sociologists, philosophers, and political scientists than for psychologists.

Movies

The moral character of movies first came under attack as a result of the peepshow "Dolorita in the Passion Dance" shown in Atlantic City in 1894 (Ramsaye, 1949). The attack intensified through the years until the late 1930's, when other problems of an economic nature plus a gradual public adaptation to movies caused a slackening of interest. Like the other mass media, movies are not closely bound to reality; in fact, movie theaters were once known as "dream palaces," which certainly indicated an awareness of the movies' unreality. They portray a wide assortment of socially disapproved behaviors and at times present a master plan for criminal conduct. On the other hand, movies provide opportunities for other forms of social learning that are socially neutral or socially desirable.

In Denver, Colorado, for example, a city of about half a million people, the movies played a central role in changing the behavior of a large number of individuals. A substantial portion of the city's inhabitants are Spanish-Americans. Often they are called "Mexicans" (a term they felt to be derogatory and inaccurate), even though some of their ancestors were living in Colorado and other parts of the Southwest at the time of the American Revolution. These people are frequently of low socioeconomic status. In the early 1950's prejudice against them ran high. Not only was there discrimination in housing and employment, but there were also numerous instances of vicious and gratuitous police brutality toward members of minority groups, especially Spanish-Americans.

The youths in this enclave were organized into loose neighborhood slum gangs. Most of them were out of school and unemployed except as agricultural laborers during the brief sugar-beet season. While idle they engaged in many delinquencies, most of them of a minor nature, and were subjected to a good deal of police investigation. Despite the justification of these investigations, they were often arbitrary and harsh.

Into this situation came a movie, *City Across the River,* based on a book by Irving Shulman, *The Amboy Dukes* (1947). The story, concerning a delinquent gang in New York City, presented a thorough description of the gang's structure and formal organization as well as of such specialized techniques as the construction of zip guns from automobile radio antennas. Every delinquent and predelinquent in Denver seems to have seen the film, many of them as many as three or four times. The most immediate consequence of the movie was the disappearance of radio antennas from automobiles at a tremendous rate. Working away in the metal and wood shops of the city's settlement houses, delinquents, including the Spanish-American youths, became skilled craftsmen and developed a real ability at constructing zip guns.

With the Amboy Dukes as a model, the Denver gangs ceased to be loosely organized neighborhood groupings. The largest gang, composed almost exclusively of Spanish-Americans, was the Heads. The Heads had six branches, one of them at the State Industrial School at Golden, Colorado. Representatives of each of the branches met frequently. The gang elected officers, created a bail fund out of its monthly dues collection, and retained its own lawyer. One of the elected officers, the Minister of War, made treaties and declared war, following the vote of the representatives. The Minister of War was also in charge of the armory.

Like most delinquent gangs (see Thrasher, 1927; Whyte, 1943) the Heads indulged as a group in a wide selection of nondelinquent behaviors: camping, dancing, team sports, and legal—as well as illegal—drag racing. The formal structure of the gang caused it to form teams and, in some cases, enter organized competition. Its illegal activities included theft of automobiles, robbing of drunks, and other offenses. Committed by individual gang members, these offenses did not reflect decisions of the Heads' executive or legislative body, as did war with other gangs. However, if a gang member were apprehended, the gang's bail fund and lawyer were at his disposal. In a city where the concept of civil liberty was taken lightly, and individuals, guilty or innocent, might be held incommunicado for days or be treated roughly, the Heads gained legal rights through money and their attorney. Inspired by the movie, techniques of crime were learned that made the behavior of these delinquents more dangerous than had been the case when they belonged to neighborhood groups. Both in terms of frequency and seriousness of offense, crimes or delinquencies against persons and property increased sharply. Yet it must be emphasized that the negative aspects of the film were the result of an already existing situation. The movie did not create delinquents; these youths had practiced delinquency long before the story was put before the cameras. Instead, it converted existing delinquents into a more skilled and dangerous group.

On the positive side, the movie produced an interest in organization and in a rough-and-ready kind of elected democracy. Many of the boys learned something of the fine art of administration and acquired executive skills. Because the gangs had power, both physical and monetary, they forced a change in the treatment of minority-group members that is still apparent; the position of minority groups in the Denver area has improved immensely since 1950. Their problems have not vanished, but they have been ameliorated. It should also be noted that there are no longer any highly organized delinquent gangs in the Denver area, despite the fact that the mass media do not appear to have changed markedly in terms of values expressed or criminal skills portrayed.

As Blumer and Hauser (1934) said many years ago, movies can make a contribution to crime and delinquency.

> Through the display of crime techniques and criminal patterns of behavior; by arousing desires for easy money and luxury, and by suggesting questionable methods for their achievement; by inducing a spirit of bravado, thoroughness, and adventurousness; by arousing intense sexual desires; and by invoking daydreaming of criminal roles, motion pictures may create attitudes and furnish techniques conducive, quite unwittingly, to delinquent or criminal behavior (Blumer & Hauser, p. 198).

Whether an individual is swayed depends on other, more basic aspects of individual personality and of the environment. A high proportion of nondelinquent Denver youngsters saw *City Across the River* and were totally unaffected by it. But these were not slum children fighting to maintain a favorable self concept in the face of harsh discrimination, economic deprivation, and a feeling of hopelessness.

Television

After years during which the public has worried about the effects of television, information needed for evaluation purposes has become available. Three extensive studies, one in England (Himmelweit, Oppenheim, and Vince, 1958), one in the United States (Schramm, Lyle, and Parker, 1961), and one in Japan (Furu, 1962), contain reliable information on the impact of television on children's personality and behavior. As with the other mass media, the chief fear expressed by the individuals concerned is that young persons become passive, anxious, or delinquent as a result of television viewing. The actual influence of television in these areas of adjustment, together with its effect on aspects of cognitive functioning that are of less public concern, may be seen from the following data.

It has been maintained that spectator activities promote passivity (e.g., Whyte, 1956). There is not much evidence for this contention as it relates to television. However, Glynn (1956), a psychotherapist, had this to say:

> Warmth, sound, constancy, availability, a steady giving without ever a demand for return, the encouragement to complete passive surrender and development—all this and active fantasy besides. Watching these [viewers], one is deeply impressed by their acting out with the television set of their unconscious longings to be infants in their mothers' lap.
>
> These, then, are traits television can so easily satisfy in adults, or foster in children: traits of passivity, receptiveness, being fed, taking in and absorbing what is offered. Activity, self-reliance, and aggression are notably absent (Glynn, 1956, p. 178).

On the other hand, the Himmelweit group (1958) observed that television viewers were more curious about the world and showed a slightly wider variety of interests than a group of nonviewers or than they themselves had shown before becoming viewers. These are the only bits of information available on the matter of passivity and television viewing and they contradict each other. However, the Himmelweit group reported data; Glynn reported an unsubstantiated personal opinion.

Much more information is at hand on the capacity of television to produce anxiety. There is no doubt that a great amount of violence is portrayed on television. The National Association of Educational Broadcasters (Purdue Opinion Panel, 1954) had a team of viewers watch all the television broadcasts visible in New York City for one week a year for four years. In the final year alone, 1954, during this one week 6868 incidents of a violent nature occurred on New York television screens. What is the general effect of this violence with respect to the production of anxiety among child viewers? The Himmelweit et al. study found one-fourth of the boys and one-third of the girls in a sample of more than 1000 young viewers aged ten to 14 to have been frightened by the events seen on television.

Violence that follows a conventional pattern with a foreseeable outcome is not frightening. Although dripping with gore, Westerns frightened only seven of the whole sample, and of these, five were below average in ability (Himmelweit et al., 1958, p. 194). It is the more complex pattern of aggression such as that shown in adult dramas which is mentioned most often as productive of fear. Particularly upsetting for children is the serious verbal expression of hostility on the part of adults (Himmelweit et al., 1958, p. 204; pp. 461–462). Children appear to be far more impressed by verbal than physical hostility, perhaps because *they* have observed their parents in verbal but not physical conflicts, and the television experience recalls the real-life conflict to them. It was also discovered that real violence, as shown in news programs, was far more capable of producing anxiety than fictional violence of the same sort.

Clearly some children are made anxious and fearful by at least some television programs. So, too, were some children of an earlier era and are some children of today by such traditional fairy tales as "Bluebeard" and by such fairy-tale figures as "Little One Eye," a girl created by the brothers Grimm with one eye, as big as a saucer, in the middle of her forehead. But, as noted in Chapter 11, children seem to like and search for situations in which they can produce "manageable" fear. Consequently, there is no reason to believe that fear itself is necessarily bad or destructive.

Violence on television is also said to cause violence and delinquency in real life. "If the proverb is true that prison is a college of crime," said one psychiatrist, "then I believe that for young disturbed adolescents, T.V. is a preparatory school for delinquency" (Banay, 1955). As we have noted, comics and movies—and if we go farther back in time, for that matter, newspapers and stage productions—have also been blamed for delinquency. One large-scale study dealing with this issue failed to discover any more aggressive, maladjusted, or delinquent behavior among television viewers than among nonviewers (Himmelweit et al., 1958, p. 215). On the other hand, a long series of studies conducted by Bandura, Walters, and their associates (e.g., see Bandura, Ross, and Ross, 1963; Bandura and Walters, 1963) suggests that exposure to aggressive models causes the person so exposed to imitate the model and to become more aggressive. These data are contradictory. Perhaps the reason that Himmelweit et al. found no increase in aggression among television viewers (despite the presence of aggressive models) while the modeling studies cited did find an increase in aggression, is that in the modeling studies testing for aggression typically took place very shortly after exposure to the aggressive model in a laboratory situation in which few constraints were placed on aggression. In comparison, aggression following television viewing might more frequently require postponement, allowing the aggressive tendency some time to dissipate. Further, aggression in the real world, as compared with the experimental laboratory, probably would encounter more often the rather strong social sanctions placed on aggression. Finally, it may be that for some children, viewing of aggression on television provides catharsis—that is, reduces real-life aggression by providing a vicarious outlet—while other children imitate what they have seen and become more aggressive. If so, one would have to establish what other child characteristics determined whether catharsis or imitation resulted, before being able to predict the effects of televised aggression on the behavior of any given child.

Now to the positive aspects of commercial television. So far as social learning is concerned, Shayon (1951) noted that television "is the shortest cut yet devised, the most accessible back door to the grown-up world. Television is never too busy to talk to our children. It never shuts them off because it has to prepare dinner. Television plays with them, shares its work with them. Television wants their attention, needs it, goes to any length to get it." As the child's back door to the adult world, television would seem likely to produce a distorted view. Surprisingly, it does not. Himmelweit and her colleagues presented the following findings. Viewers emphasized intelligence and bravery as important attributes for success in adulthood more often than did non-viewers (1958, p. 468). There were no differences between the two groups in attitudes toward school, school work, or teachers (p. 246). Television viewing raised youngsters' levels of aspiration regarding employment (p. 258), and in older children of 13 to 14 it produced quite realistic worries and fears about the problems of being grown-up (p. 250).

Television has a leveling effect on class differences in general information and vocabulary, as was seen in Chapter 5. It also promotes a general elevation in vocabulary, with younger children gaining more than older ones, dull children more than bright ones, and heavy viewers more than light viewers (Schramm et al., 1961, pp. 75–97). Viewing, for American children, does not decrease the reading of books and of most magazines but does reduce the reading of comic books and pulp magazines (Schramm et al., p. 15). Viewing does seem to decrease study time and the reading of serious books (though only slightly) in Japan (Furu, 1962), possibly because Japanese children start at a somewhat higher base; that is, they study longer hours and read serious books a greater proportion of the time than do American or English children. As Maccoby (1964) notes, television tends to decrease those activities (e.g., comic books, movies) that are functionally equivalent to television in terms of their content and in their use by children.

All told, the influence of television does not seem to be as great or as deleterious as commonly believed. There are differences between viewers and nonviewers, but they are not marked, and the existing ones do not always favor the nonviewer.

Individual Susceptibility to the Media

The adverse effects of the mass media have been exaggerated, partly because most of the studies condemning them (Blumer & Hauser, 1934; Healy, 1915; Healy & Bronner, 1936; Wertham, 1953) have not used control groups and have dealt with small and deviant samples of the entire population. Wertham could hardly be expected not to have found all delinquency to be caused by comic books when he asked delinquent youngsters such leading questions that they could reply mainly in one way. If delinquents are asked whether reading comic books caused their delinquency, most of them will respond affirmatively. For that matter, if asked whether a phase of the moon caused their delinquency, most of them would also say yes, partly to be obliging, partly to shift the blame from themselves, and partly to avoid looking deeper into their own motivations.

Adequately designed studies do not show any considerable effect of the mass media on the behavior of most children, yet *some* youngsters are greatly influenced by them. Who are these children? These are the children who are addicted to the mass media. Those addicted to comic books showed marked tendencies toward neurosis as compared with nonaddicts; they were rather small and weak and identified with omnipotent heroism such as Superman (Wolf & Fiske, 1949). In television, Himmelweit et al. found addicts to have stronger feelings of rejection and insecurity than occasional viewers (1958, pp. 390–391). In a parallel study, they noted these characteristics in ardent movie goers, implying that children who must withdraw from real situations find solace in all the media. The "findings suggest that these differences were there before television came to the home and explain why the addict views so much more than others of his age, intelligence and social background. The parallel analysis of cinema addicts showed them to be very similar kinds of children. Television meets a need which the child without television satisfies through the cinema or the radio" (Himmelweit et al., 1958, p. 390).

In a study of the same type, Bailyn (1959) confirmed the Himmelweit observations. Children subjected to considerable frustration in the home viewed television more often than children not so greatly frustrated, at least in middle- and upper-class groups (Schramm et al., 1961, pp. 130–131; Maccoby, 1954, p. 303). Not only do frustrated children have more contact with the mass media, but there is also some conflicting evidence that suggests that they may concentrate on and be better able to recall the acts of violence they have seen (Maccoby, Levin, & Selya, 1955, 1956). Even if they do more adequately recall acts of violence, frustration need not lead to imitation of an aggressive model (Kuhn, Madsen, and Becker, 1967). The viewing of aggressive behavior may teach the child something concerning the aggressive role, but children learn many roles that they do not play (Maccoby, 1959; Whiting, 1960). Whether the child, frustrated or not, imitates an aggressive model probably depends on the way parents—particularly same-sex parents, respond to frustration.

One could argue that addicts are less social, more frustrated, and more beset by problems and neurotic tendencies than the nonaddicted *because* of their addiction, were it not for the fact that the Himmelweit study covered the same children before and after the introduction of television in their locale and showed the same problems to have existed *before* the advent of television. This type of pre- and postexposure investigation allows a very different interpretation from the typical one conducted after exposure to the mass medium, which serves as a basis for attacking the mass media. In short, addiction to the mass media is a symptom rather than a cause of social disorder.

In sum, the negative effects of the mass media are fewer than is commonly believed. The mass media have some positive effects, but these are obscured by the media's major task of convincing readers and viewers that humans are overfed, undernourished, suffering from vitamin deficiencies, or, worst of all, prone to body odor.

SUMMARY

The influence of the community, voluntary associations, the church, and the mass media as agencies of socialization is secondary. If this conclusion seems to contradict the observations in Chapter 7 on the waning influence of parents on child behavior, the evidence seems to suggest that it is not the social forces discussed in this chapter that have gained ascendancy. Although the community, the voluntary associations, and the media may have acquired additional importance, the child's peers and his school have been the real beneficiaries of the parents' decline as a socializing influence.

Negative as the data may be on the influence of the social forces explored in this chapter, they are still worth knowing. Notwithstanding the array of pressures to which the child is exposed, the role of the family, though decreasing, remains primary in the socialization process. The community generally serves to reinforce parental values rather than as a source of values as long as parents meet their responsibility in child rearing. Only when parents abandon their role does community influence become more significant. As the community loses its influence through urbanization, voluntary associations fill the void, to a degree.

Religious experience does not seem to make much of an inroad on values or behavior, possibly because of the small portion of time spent by the average child in a religious setting or perhaps because researchers have not employed the proper criteria for religious commitment. Neither are the mass media, despite public outcry against them, of prime importance. However, continual influence in a fixed direction—that women should be passive and noncreative, that scientists are odd, or that violence is permissible—may ultimately bear fruit. Some young people, because of existing personal problems, show much greater interest in the mass media and appear to be more susceptible to their influence.

REFERENCES

Allport, G. W., & Ross, T. M.   Personal religious orientation and prejudice. *Journal of Personality and Social Psychology,* 1967, **5,** 432–443.

Bailyn, L.   Mass media and children: A study of exposure habits and cognitive effects. *Psychological Monographs,* 1959, **71,** 1–48.

Bandura, A., Ross, D., & Ross, S.   Imitation of film mediated aggressive models. *Journal of Abnormal and Social Psychology,* 1963, **66,** 3–11.

Bandura, A., & Walters, R. H.   *Social learning and personality development.* New York: Holt, Rinehart & Winston, 1963.

Banay, R. S.   Testimony before the Subcommittee to Investigate Juvenile Delinquency, of the Committee on the Judiciary, U. S. Senate, Eighty-fourth Congress. S. Res. 62. April 1955. Washington, D. C.: U. S. Government Printing Office, 1955.

Bender, L., & Lourie, R. S.   The effect of comic books on the ideology of children. *American Journal of Orthopsychiatry,* 1941, **11,** 540–550.

Blumer, H., & Hauser, P. M. *Movies, delinquency, and crime.* New York: Macmillan, 1934.

Brown, C. *Manchild in the Promised Land.* New York: Macmillan, 1965.

Child, I., Potter, E. H., & Levine, E. M.   Children's textbooks and personality development. *Psychological Monographs,* 1946, **60,** No. 3.

Daniels, A. D.   The new life: A study of regeneration. *American Journal of Psychology,* 1893, **6,** 61–106.

deCharms, R., & Moeller, G. H.   Values expressed in American children's readers: 1800–1950. *Journal of Abnormal and Social Psychology,* 1962, **64,** 136–142.

Fox, S. D.   Voluntary associations and social structure. Unpublished doctoral dissertation, Harvard University, 1952.

Furu, T. *Television and children's life.* Tokyo: Radio and Television Central Research Institute, Japan Broadcasting Corp., 1962.

Glynn, E. E. Television and the American character—A psychiatrist looks at television. In W. T. Elliot (Ed.), *Television's impact on American culture.* East Lansing, Mich.: Michigan State University Press, 1956.

Godin, A. (S.J.). Importance and difficulty of scientific research in religious education: The problem of the "criterion." *Religious Education Supplement,* 1962, **57,** 166–174.

Hartshorne, H., & May, M. A. *Studies in service and self control.* Vol. 1, New York: Macmillan, 1928.

Hartshorne, H., & May, M. A. *Studies in service and self control.* Vol. 2, New York: Macmillan, 1929.

Healy, W. *The individual delinquent: A textbook of diagnosis for all concerned in understanding offenders.* Boston: Little, Brown, 1915.

Healy, W., & Bronner, A. F. *New light on delinquency and its treatment.* New Haven, Conn.: Yale University Press, 1936.

Himmelweit, H. T., Oppenheim, A. N., & Vince, P. *Television and the child.* London and New York: Oxford University Press, 1958.

Jones, M. B. Religious values and authoritarian tendency. *Journal of Social Psychology,* 1958, **48,** 83–89.

Kelly, J. G., Ferson, J. E., & Holtzman, W. H. The measurement of attitudes toward the Negro in the South. *Journal of Social Psychology,* 1958, **48,** 305–517.

Kuhn, D. Z., Madsen, C. H., Jr., & Becker, W. Effects of exposure to an aggressive model and "frustration" on children's aggressive behavior. *Child Development,* 1967, **38,** 739–745.

Maccoby, E. E. Why do children watch television? *Public Opinion Quarterly,* 1954, **18,** 239–244.

Maccoby, E. E. Role taking in childhood and its consequences for social learning. *Child Development,* 1959, **30,** 239–252.

Maccoby, E. E. Effects of mass media. In M. L. Hoffman & L. W. Hoffman (Eds.), *Review of child development research, Vol. 1.* New York: Russell Sage, 1964. Pp. 323–348.

Maccoby, E. E., Levin, H., & Selya, B. V. The effect of emotional arousal on the retention of aggressive and nonaggressive movie content. (Abstract) *American Psychologist,* 1955, **10,** 359.

Maccoby, E. E., Levin, H., & Selya, B. V. The effects of emotional arousal on the retention of film content: A failure to replicate. *Journal of Abnormal and Social Psychology,* 1956, **53,** 373–374.

McDowell, J. B. *The development of the idea of God in the Catholic child.* Washington, D. C.: Catholic University of America Press, 1952.

Martin, W. E., & Stendler, C. B. *Child behavior and development.* New York: Harcourt, Brace, 1959.

Middleton, R., & Putney, A. Religion, normative values, and behavior. *Sociometry,* 1962, **25,** 141–152.

Morgan, W.   Personality correlates of involvement in religious activities.   Unpublished study, San Jose State College, San Jose, Calif., 1958.

Peck, R. F., & Havighurst, R. J.   *The psychology of character development.*   New York: Wiley, 1960.

Purdue Opinion Panel.   *Four years of New York Television.*   Urbana, Ill.: National Association of Educational Broadcasters, 1954.

Ramsaye, T.   The rise and place of the motion picture.   In W. Schramm (Ed.), *Mass communications.*   Urbana, Ill.: University of Illinois Press, 1949.

Reckless, W. C., Dinitz, S., & Murray, E.   Self concept as an insulation against delinquency.   *American Sociological Review,* 1956, **21,** 744–746.

Rose, A. M.   *Sociology: The study of human relations.*   New York: Knopf, 1956.

Salisbury, W. S.   Religiosity, regional sub-culture, and social behavior.   *Journal for the Scientific Study of Religion,* 1962, **2,** 94–101.

Scarpitti, R. R., Murray, E., Simon, D., & Reckless, W. C.   The "good" boy in a high delinquency area: Four years later.   *American Sociological Review,* 1960, **25,** 555–558.

Schramm, W., Lyle, J., & Parker, E. G.   *Television in the lives of our children.*   Stanford, Calif.: Stanford University Press, 1961.

Shayon, R. L.   *Television and our children.*   New York: Longmans, Green, 1951.

Shulman, I.   *The Amboy Dukes.*   Garden City, N. Y.: Doubleday, 1947.

Stanley-Hall, G.   The moral and religious training of children.   *Princeton Review,* 1882, **10,** 26–48.

Starbuck, E. D.   *Psychology of religion.*   New York: Scribner's, 1899.

Stouffer, S.   *Communism, conformity, and civil liberties.*   New York: 1955.

Thorndike, E. L.   Words and the comics.   *Journal of Experimental Education,* 1941, **17,** 110–113.

Thrasher, F. L.   *The gang.*   Chicago: University of Chicago Press, 1927.

Wertham, F.   *Seduction of the innocent.*   New York: Rinehart, 1953.

Whiting, J. W. M.   Resource mediation and learning by identification.   In I. Iscoe & H. W. Stevenson (Eds.), *Personality development in children.*   Austin: University of Texas Press, 1960.

Whyte, W. F.   *Street corner society.*   Chicago: University of Chicago Press, 1943.

Whyte, W. H.   *The organization man.*   New York: Simon and Schuster, 1956.

Wilson, W. C.   Extrinsic religious values and prejudice.   *Journal of Abnormal and Social Psychology,* 1960, **60,** 286–288.

Wolf, K., & Fiske, M.   The children talk about comics.   In P. F. Lazarsfeld & F. N. Stanton (Eds.), *Communications research, 1948–1940.*   New York: Harper, 1949.

SECTION V *
THE EMERGING SELF

The previous sections of this book have investigated the forces affecting the human being—his inheritance, his growth and maturation, his learning and motivation, his language, his intelligence—and his unique pattern of response to the world around him: his personality. In this section we shall take a deeper look into the child's emerging personality. The first of the section's three chapters is devoted to a study of how the individual is appraised as an infant, as a young child, and in the school years. The second chapter, concerning personality development, covers two main facets of personality change occurring with age. These are an increasingly rich and diversified but consistent response to the world and the development of a self concept based on consistent attitudes toward the self and the world. The third chapter of the section deals with the psychological problems met in the course of the developmental process. It explores their causes, diagnosis, and probability of solution, either through therapy or the individual's own inner resources.

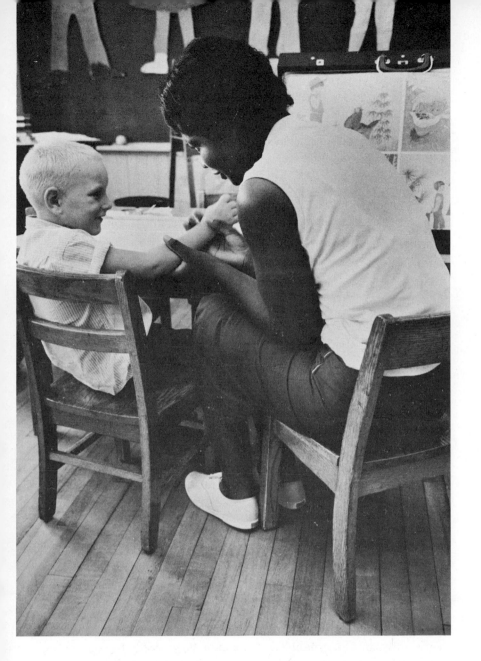

14

Individual Appraisal

Child psychologists and others concerned with the diagnosis of children's problems are often asked, "Is this child developing or progressing normally?" The question requires as accurate an answer as possible. To get at it psychologists have developed techniques for assessing the various aspects of child development. For early infancy, they have placed the accent on physical and motor development. For the period of early childhood, they have concerned themselves with intellectual functioning. And for the elementary-school years, they have shifted the attention to evaluation of the child's social, emotional, and personality adjustment. In this chapter we consider each of these areas of individual appraisal in turn, beginning with assessment of infant procedures.

INFANT ASSESSMENT

In this country, Arnold Gesell played a major role in the devising of techniques to evaluate the growth and physical development of infants. Because of his training and dedication as a man of medicine, his methods stressed the diagnosis of deviation from normality rather than an evaluation of levels of normality. In addition, Gesell's emphasis tended toward the medical rather than the psychological aspects of development. Nevertheless, from his accent on the "lawfulness of growth" evolved the notion that growth and development were predictable.

The Gesell Developmental Schedules (Gesell, 1940; Gesell and Amatruda, 1947) are concerned with four major areas of behavior: motor characteristics, adaptive behavior, language, and personal-social behavior. In examining motor behavior the primary concern is the infant's increasing control of posture in the areas of locomotion and prehension. Head control comes first, followed by sitting posture and, later, upright posture. In prehension, the infant reaches out before it is able to grasp an object accurately. Through underlying neurological development he acquires coordination that permits increasing accuracy of arm and hand movements. How these motor behaviors are executed and the ages at which they appear supply clues to the maturity level of the infant. Deviation may signify an abnormality in development.

Adaptive behaviors involve some adjustment to the environment. Their presence is detected in the child's ability to manipulate blocks by arranging them in simple structures. Tests of simple number concepts and requiring a child to copy a circle and a cross are used at a later time.

In assessing language maturity, a number of aspects are taken into

506

consideration.   One observes the child's articulation, vocabulary, use of language in communication, and comprehension.   Language development is reflected by an increase in the size of vocabulary, in the length and complexity of sentence structure, and by an increase in comprehension as revealed by the ability to respond to verbal directions and commands.

Personal-social behavior embraces such matters as feeding, dressing, toilet procedure, and play.   In all of these maturity is judged by increased self-reliance and independence.   Since environment plays a more influential part than maturation in these areas of behavior, deviations in development frequently furnish clues to the kind of psychological atmosphere in which the child is being raised.

Gesell devised the notion of a Developmental Quotient (DQ) which expresses the ratio between the child's *maturity age* and his actual age. Maturity age is based on a child's performance on a series of developmental tests, which is then compared with the norms obtained from the administration of these tests to a number of children at various age levels.   The DQ reflects the proportion of normal development attained at any given age level.   By Gesell's own admission the DQ may be useful in predicting the course of future development only if no complicating factors arise.   Since fluctuations in development are more common than not, maturity assessed at any one point in time may be more or less typical of any infant's developmental rate.   All told, the DQ adequately assesses the infant's current rate of development, taking into account its variability, complexity, and unevenness.

To Gesell, the developmental examination served not only to establish rate of development, as in the spotting of precocity and retardation, but also to diagnose neurological difficulties and other disturbances of development.   Although not much information is available on the long-term predictive ability of the Gesell Developmental Schedules, they have achieved widespread use for the evaluation of the developmental status of infants.   They have been used, for example, also as a measure for validation in a Developmental Questionnaire for infants of 40 weeks devised by Knobloch and Pasamanick (1955).

The very term *developmental diagnosis* suggests an attempt to assess level of development without considering mental growth or development as such.   Yet child psychologists have chiefly directed their energies toward perfecting instruments for measuring infant intelligence and predicting later intelligence.   The following items, along with the age in months at which they should occur, were included in one early infant mental test (Bayley, 1933a).

Age in Months	Item
(.5)	Postural adjustment when lifted
(.6)	Momentary regard of ring
(2.2)	Eyes follow pencil
(3.3)	Carries ring to mouth
(4.5)	Reaches for cube
(5.55)	Discriminates stranger
(9.3)	Fine prehension
(12.9)	Says two words

Tests administered before the age of five years have little value in predicting later ability. To begin with, a majority of the items at the earliest age levels tap the development of motor skills. As there is no relation between motor ability and abstract intelligence in adults, there is no reason to expect such a relation in infants. Furthermore, abstract ability may not be present in the infant prior to the development of language; and this ability to manipulate abstract symbols is frequently considered to be the ultimate criterion of intelligence at the adult level. As Goodenough (1949a) noted: "Attempting to measure infantile intelligence may be like trying to measure a boy's beard at the age of three" (p. 310). Anderson's comment that infant tests measure "little if at all the function which is called intelligence at later ages" (Anderson, 1939) was supported by a factor analysis of IQ scores obtained from a study in which successive tests were administered to a group of children from one month to 18 years of age (Hofstaetter, 1954). Three factors came to light. The first, called *sensorimotor alertness,* appeared prominently during the first two years. The second factor, *persistence,* reached its peak between two and four, declining and eventually vanishing in later childhood. The third factor, *abstraction and the manipulation of symbols,* began to emerge at about two and became a major consideration from four onward.

A second explanation for the low predictive value of infant tests relates to the difficulty of administering and scoring them; their reliability is uniformly low. Third, the rapid rate of development in infancy, coupled with fluctuations, increases the variability of test scores of any child from one test to the next. Fourth, motivation is well recognized as affecting test performance. However, attempts to encourage and motivate the infant are relatively fruitless. To secure his attention and cooperation alone is quite a task.

When precise scores have been obtained from infant tests and correlated with later scores, uniformly low coefficients have resulted. However, several studies (Escalona, 1950; MacRae, 1955) using somewhat broader categories of ability—mentally defective, below average, average, above average, and superior—have been more successful in predicting later ability from tests administered early. Illingworth (1960) maintained that infant assessment acquired greater predictive value through full understanding of infant development; this could be achieved by obtaining a medical-type history of the infant that included the relevant environmental factors. Because of the fluctuations in the rate of development data, a number of examinations had better predictive power than the findings of a single examination. Well-known infant intelligence scales include the California First-Year Mental Scale developed by Bayley (1933a, b), the Cattell Infant Intelligence Scale (Cattell, 1947), the Griffiths Mental Development Scale (Griffiths, 1954), and the Northwestern Intelligence Tests constructed by Gilliland (1948).

INTELLIGENCE AND SCHOOL-RELATED TESTS

Mental testing had many beginnings. However, the work of Alfred Binet in France represents the clearest and most direct forerunner of contemporary intelligence tests. In the closing decade of the nineteenth century, Binet and Simon investigated a variety of measures to differentiate bright from dull schoolchildren. These early efforts came to a head soon after the turn of the century when, in 1904, the Minister of Public Instruction in Paris appointed a commission to study the advisability of establishing special schools for children incapable of profiting from instruction in the public-school classroom. Some means of identifying such children was clearly needed. Binet and Simon were consulted, with the result that a formal scale for testing the intelligence of children was constructed. The aim of this scale was to obtain an estimate of the child's level of mental development. Although a wide variety of tasks tapping different areas of ability was included in the scale, Binet and Simon formulated a rather clear definition of intelligence: "To judge well, to comprehend well, to reason well, these are the essential activities of intelligence."

Binet Tests

The first scale, developed in 1905, consisted of 30 items arranged in order of increasing difficulty. It was revised by Binet and Simon three years later. New items were added and the method of arranging them by age level was employed, thus introducing the important notion of "mental age." Rather than denoting the number of items passed, the score now compared the child's performance with those of children of various chronological ages on whom the test items had been standardized. The following items appearing at three different age levels are drawn from the revised scale. Many of them have survived even the most recent revision of the original scale.

Three years:

Show eyes, nose, mouth
Name objects in a picture
Repeat two figures
Repeat a sentence of six syllables
Give last name

Six years:

Repeat a sentence of 16 syllables
Compare two figures from an esthetic point of view
Define, by use only, some simple objects
Execute three simultaneous commissions
Give one's age
Distinguish morning and evening

Nine years:

Give the date complete (day, month, day of the month, year)
Name the days of the week
Give definitions superior to use
Retain six memories after reading
Make change
Arrange five weights in order

(Binet & Simon, 1948)

The Binet-Simon scale made its debut in English at the Vineland Training School in New Jersey, where Goddard put it to use as a diagnostic instrument for distinguishing between intellectually normal and subnormal children and for identifying various levels of subnormality. In 1916 Terman, at Stanford University, published a revision of the Binet-Simon scales. More than merely a translation, the Stanford revision included a number of new items and, as a result of a careful and thorough standardization procedure, changed the age placement of items. Moreover, scores were now expressed in terms of a ratio between mental and chronological ages. Although Terman was not the first to conceive of such a ratio, he popularized it by presenting tables in which mental age and chronological age figures were converted into Intelligence Quotients. Terman also interpreted the meaning of IQ levels through the percentage of people receiving the various scores. The following table contains Terman's original classification.

IQ range	Classification
Below 70	Definite feeble-mindedness
70–80	Borderline deficiency
80–90	Dullness
90–110	Normal or average intelligence
110–120	Superior intelligence
120–140	Very superior intelligence
140 and above	Genius or near genius

The Stanford-Binet test continues to retain its position as the most widely used individual test of intelligence for children. In the era in which intelligence testing of children probably reached its peak, the 1940's and 1950's, the 1937 revision of the Stanford-Binet was the test used (Terman & Merrill, 1937). Although this was superseded by a 1960 revision, much of what follows applies to both.

Perhaps one of the most notable features of the Stanford-Binet is its precision of administration and of scoring. Clear instructions are provided for the examiner on the exact wording of his questions and the extent to which urging and further questioning are permissible. The scoring manual is detailed, with numerous examples supplied to assist in scoring the child's responses. Both features tend to reduce as much as possible the effects on IQ scores of such factors as differences among examiners in the administration and scoring of tests. The kind of rapport established by the examiner with the child is important, however; for this and other reasons only a trained and experienced individual is qualified to administer an intelligence test.

The nature of the Stanford-Binet test items, especially at the younger age levels, is such that they are intrinsically interesting to children. Because of this it is usually possible to hold children's attention throughout the administration of the test which lasts approximately one hour. The 1960 revision consists of six test items at each half-year age level from two to five and six tests at each year level from five to 14.

Several points of importance in evaluating any intelligence test are worth noting. First, as to test reliability, Terman and Merrill (1937) reported reliability coefficients ranging from $+.90$ to $+.98$ for the children used to set up the standardization procedure. A median coefficient of $+.91$ resulted from correlating the two forms of the 1937 revision, Forms L and M, for each of the 21 groups involved in the standardization effort. It is apparent that the Stanford-Binet is a highly reliable measuring instrument. Nevertheless, individual performances on the test may show fluctuations over a period of time. IQ scores do change upon retesting. In Terman's 1916 standardization group half of the children deviated by five IQ points or more on retesting; 16 per cent deviated by 10 points or more, 6.2 per cent by 15 points or more, and 1.85 per cent by 20 points or more. Thus caution must be exercised in interpreting the meaning of a single assessment of a child's intelligence and in making predictions on the basis of a single score. Furthermore, as noted in Chapter 6, the later the age at which a test is administered, the more closely it correlates with an IQ score obtained at the age of 18. Scores of IQ tests show a sharp increase in long-term predictive power around five or six. Before then, they should be viewed with reserve.

The next important aspect of any test is its validity. Evaluating the validity of the Stanford-Binet is far more difficult than assessing its reliability. There is no definition of intelligence on which there is general agreement. In fact, there are as many views of intelligence as there are tests to measure it. This has led to the quip that intelligence is what intelligence tests measure. Such a belief is unduly pessimistic. IQ test scores have the ability to predict such things as school achievement and later intellectual functioning. Correlations between Stanford-Binet scores and achievement in first grade imply the moderate success of IQ scores in predicting school achievement. In this sense, the Stanford-Binet possesses *predictive validity.* The Stanford-Binet also possesses what is called *construct validity;* that is, it contains items capable of measuring the kinds of abilities that Binet, and later Terman, termed as intelligence.

Finally, a number of cautions and criticisms should be noted. Although Binet attempted originally to assess a child's inborn or native capacity, an IQ is apparently only a measure of the child's *present level of functioning,* despite being moderately predictive of later functioning as well. A related point is that the Stanford-Binet assumes background experience similar to that of the children on whom the test was standardized. Many of its test materials presuppose a general familiarity with the American culture. Hence scores of children whose backgrounds depart in any degree from the American norm should be viewed with suspicion. Although IQ scores of children of recently arrived Mexican laborers in California, for example, may fall below those of typical white, middle-class, urban youngsters, such results are not really valid indications of a difference between the two groups.

The Stanford-Binet has been charged with predicting neither social nor personality adjustment, nor success in life. Such criticisms lack validity. Binet, as we have seen, designed his test originally to identify levels of academic performance. In this respect, the test continues to do an adequate job. The intelligence test was never designed to assess personality factors, musical ability, or a host of other individual qualities. There are separate tests for these things.

Another criticism of the Stanford-Binet is its preponderance of items involving verbal ability. This is thought to penalize those children whose strengths lie in other areas of functioning. Although some children, such as those from bilingual homes or afflicted with hearing deficiencies, may be handicapped by the test's verbal biases, language facility remains a major factor in academic pursuits. To predict a child's success in such endeavors, an intelligence test must measure a child's potentialities in coping with their language demands. Besides, as noted in Chapter 5, the ability to deal with and to manipulate such abstract symbols as words is distinctly human and may be man's greatest glory. Thus it is hardly inappropriate for intelligence tests to be weighted heavily in linguistic content. However, performance tests, as we shall see presently, have been developed to give a fair indication of the intellectual ability of children whose verbal facility may be limited.

One last caution. Although IQ tests and other tests differ in a number of ways, they also have many similarities. A child's performance on an IQ test, like his performance on any other test, depends, in part, on how he feels at the moment, on his mood, on his motivation, and on many similar incidental factors. An IQ result has maximal significance only if all conditions surrounding the test are optimal. It reveals no sacred, immutable truth about a child. It is only an index to one area of a child's functioning, an important area, to be sure, but one best interpreted when seen as the basis for a broad understanding of the child's behavior and personality.

Performance Tests

Although the term *performance* is something of a misnomer since performance tests require abstract abilities plus general knowledge and understanding, manipulation of objects has considerable importance in these tests. Verbal facility is a very important part of general intelligence, as has been observed, yet the evaluation of other skills uncovers valuable information regarding other areas of the child's capabilities. Studying the child's performance in the types of task usually contained in performance tests provides clinical insights into the techniques employed by the child in approaching a problem of the kind.

Appropriate for children between the ages of five and 15 is the Wechsler Intelligence Scale for Children (WISC) (Wechsler, 1949). The WISC includes both verbal and performance scales, of which the latter is probably the most widely used test of its kind at the present time. The performance scale is comprised of five subtests—picture arrangement, picture completion, block design, digit symbol, and object assembly. Figure 14-1 illustrates the administration of the WISC.

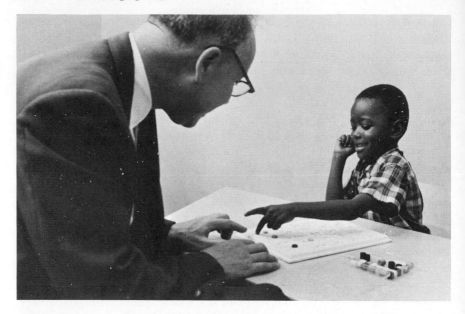

FIGURE 14-1   Administration of the WISC (by permission of The Psychological Corporation).

Because of the nature of the abilities measured by the WISC performance scale, it correlates less highly with the Stanford-Binet test than does the verbal scale. Similarly the IQs of the performance scale do not relate as well as the IQs of the verbal scale or the Stanford-Binet to school achievement. In view of the importance of verbal abilities in scholastic achievement this situation is quite understandable; even so, the lesser bearing of the performance IQs downgrades their predictive usefulness.

More recently the Wechsler Preschool and Primary Scale of Intelligence (WPPSI) (Wechsler, 1967) has been developed for the four- to six-and-a-half-year level. Although in part a downward extension of the WISC, the WPPSI is a separate scale consisting of six verbal and five performance subtests.

Another performance test, the Goodenough Draw-A-Man test (Goodenough, 1926), was one of the first such developed. The test requires the child to draw "the best man he can." In the main the scoring is based on the number of details included in the drawing. The test is relatively simple to administer and score. Although Goodenough originally obtained rather high correlations between the Draw-A-Man IQs and scores on the Stanford-Binet, Medinnus (1961a) found correlations ranging between +.26 and +.57 for a group of five-year-olds. Low correlations were also seen between Draw-A-Man IQs and subsequent first-grade achievement.   Thus, though IQ scores obtained from children's drawings may be useful for gross estimates of ability and for general screening purposes, they do not serve the end for which intelligence tests were originally developed because they do not correlate highly with academic achievement.   Samples of a child's Draw-A-Man products over a 10-month period appear in Figure 14-2.

Group Tests

Time is often a precious commodity.   There is rarely enough of it to do what one wishes.   To use time economically, tests have been developed to measure the ability of a large number of children simultaneously.   Even if some of the advantages of individually administered tests are lost, group tests function as productive screening devices to single out those children who require further testing and observation.   Indeed, a low score on a group test demands further testing because factors other than intelligence may intrude on the score. Misunderstood directions, anxiety over the test, and lack of motivation may affect a child's performance on a group test.   In the administration of an individual test, an experienced examiner endeavors to eliminate such intrusions.

Commonly one hears that group tests are never as satisfactory as individual tests.   Nevertheless, IQ scores obtained from group tests effectively predict school achievement.   The closer similarity between

FIGURE 14-2   Three Draw-A-Man samples, by the same child over a period of 10 months.

the testing situation and nature of group IQ and achievement tests than between individual IQ and achievement tests may contribute to this predictability. Besides, in the day-to-day school situation the child does not enjoy the individual attention and encouragement that are present in the individual test situation. In school, the child's achievement rests in part on his capacity to follow directions, function independently, and apply himself to the task before him.

Figure 14-3 contains items extracted from a group test, the California Short-Form Test of Mental Maturity (Sullivan, Clark, & Tiegs, 1963).

School Readiness Tests. Most kindergarten and first-grade readiness tests deal specifically with reading readiness because reading is the primary preoccupation in the early elementary years. The principal element in most tests of reading readiness is the ability to discriminate word and letter forms. Comprehension and range of information frequently are included also. While readiness to read is of major importance in assessing school readiness, other kinds of information are useful in determining whether a child is ready for school entrance or whether an additional year of maturity would be advisable. Two general tests of school readiness are described here.

As a result of their clinical work since 1950, the staff at the Gesell Institute have observed that at least 50 per cent of those children referred as school behavior problems are overplaced as to grade. This overplacement resulted from determination of school entrance by chronological age alone. The Gesell Institute Developmental Examination was devised in order to provide a more adequate basis for determining readiness for school. The examination is divided into the following seven parts:

1. *The initial interview.* Questions about age, birth date, birthday party, including favorite activity and present received; siblings—names and ages; father's occupation.
2. *Pencil and paper tests.* Writing name or letters and address; numbers 1 to 20; copying six basic forms (circle, cross, square, triangle, divided rectangle, diamond in two orientations), and two three-dimensional forms (cylinder and cube in two orientations); completing Incomplete Man figure and giving his facial expression.
3. *Right and left (adaptation of Jacobson's Right and Left tests).* Naming parts and sides of body, carrying out single and double commands, responding to a series of pictures of a pair of hands in which two fingers are touching. Response is first verbal and then motor.
4. *Form tests.* Visual One (Monroe)—matching forms; Visual Three (Monroe)—memory for designs; projection into forms.

Test 1 Opposites

Directions: In each row there is one picture that shows something which is <u>opposite</u> of the first picture. Find it and mark its number.

Test 2 Similarities

Directions: The first three pictures in each row are of things which are <u>alike</u> in some way. Decide how they are alike and then find the picture to the right of the dotted line that is most like them and mark its number.

Test 3 Analogies

Directions: In each row, the first picture is related to the second. The third picture goes with one of the four pictures to the right of the second dotted line in the same way. Find the related picture and mark its number.

Test 4 Numerical Values

Directions: Each problem tells you that a certain number of coins will add up to a certain amount of money. You are to find the correct number of coins of each kind—cents, nickels, dimes, quarters, and half-dollars.

D.	2 coins — 10 cents	
	p q r s	D

Test 5 Number Problems

Directions: Work these problems. Use scratch paper if necessary. Mark the letter of each correct answer.

E.	There are 5 birds in a tree and 3 birds on a fence. How many birds are there in both places? ᵃ 2 ᵇ 8 ᶜ 15 ᵈ 7	E

Test 6 Verbal Comprehension

Directions: Mark the number of the word that means the same or about the same as the first word.

F. blossom	¹ tree ² vine ³ flower ⁴ garden	F

Test 7 Delayed Recall

Directions: Read the following items. Mark the number of each correct answer according to the story. (Story, The Life of a Fawn, read by examiner.)

G.	The story read to you a while ago was about a ¹ fawn. ² dog. ³ bear. ⁴ wolf.	G

FIGURE 14-3 Sample items from the California Short-Form Test of Mental Maturity.

5. *Naming of animals for 60 seconds.*
6. *Concluding interview.* Reporting on what child likes to do best in general, at school indoors and outdoors and at home indoors and outdoors.
7. *Examination of teeth.* Recording of both eruption and decay or fillings.

(Ilg & Ames, 1964, p. 35)

The results of a three-year longitudinal study (Ilg, Ames, & Apell, 1965) of a group of kindergarten, first-, and second-grade children indicate that the earlier impression of approximately 50 per cent unready for their grade placement was substantially correct. A high correspondence was obtained between the developmental examination prediction score and the kindergarten teacher's rating of the children's progress throughout the year. As would be expected from previous literature dealing with sex differences in development, girls were considerably accelerated over boys in terms of school readiness.

A novel approach to answering the parents' question, "Should I keep Johnny out of school for another year?" is a readiness test designed for parents to administer to preschool children (Jordan & Massey, 1967). Readiness is assessed in seven areas: Number concepts, discrimination of form, Color naming, Symbol matching, Speaking vocabulary, Listening vocabulary, and General information. In addition the following General Readiness Checklist is included:

1. Will your child be 5 years 3 months or older when he begins kindergarten?
2. Can strangers easily understand your child's speech?

Can your child:

3. Pay attention to a short story when it is read, and answer simple questions about it?
4. Draw and color, beyond a simple scribble?
5. Tie a knot?
6. Zip a zipper?
7. Walk backward a distance of 5 or 6 feet?
8. Stand on one foot for 5 to 10 seconds?
9. Alternate feet walking down stairs?
10. Walk a straight line?
11. Fasten buttons that he can see?
12. Tell his left hand from his right?
13. Use a knife for spreading jam or butter?
14. Take care of his toilet needs by himself?
15. Set the table with the correct number of knives, forks, and spoons?
16. Be away from you 2 or 3 hours without being upset?
17. Cross a residential street safely?
18. Print his first name?
19. See a straight pin on the floor while standing up?
20. Draw or copy a plus, a box, and a ball?

(Jordan & Massey, 1967)

Games and activities for facilitating development in each of the areas are provided. Thus the parent is given specific suggestions for ways in which he may improve his child's school readiness.

Tests for Specific Learning Disabilities

While the intelligence tests described above provide a global assessment of the child's level of intellectual functioning, tests have been developed more recently to identify areas of specific disability. Most of these have arisen out of a school learning context, in which certain language and perceptual deficiencies retard the child's ability to master learning skills. For both of the tests we describe here, exercises have been developed to remediate specific deficiencies that the tests identify.

The Frostig Developmental Test of Visual Perception. This test (Frostig, Maslow, Lefever, & Whittlesey, 1964) resulted from the observation that many children with learning difficulties manifested visual or auditory perceptual disturbances. The test measures five perceptual skill areas: Eye-motor coordination, Figure-ground, Constancy of shape, Position in space, and Spatial relationships. Test items illustrating each of these subtests are shown in Figure 14-4. The Frostig Test is designed for group administration, although it should be administered individually to disturbed or handicapped children. It is appropriate for children from three through 10 years of age. Normative data provide the basis for converting raw scores into Perceptual Age scores, which yield a Perceptual Quotient when divided by the child's chronological age.

The test-retest reliability correlations for the Frostig Test appear to be satisfactory. With regard to validity, the scores are significantly related to teacher's ratings of the child's coordination and intellectual functioning. Further, significant correlations have been obtained between the visual-perceptual and reading achievement scores. Children with severe learning difficulties and neurologically handicapped children have been found to score low on the test.

Graded materials are available (Frostig & Horne, 1964) to facilitate development in the various areas identified through testing. A pilot study using these perceptual training materials with a group of kindergarten children showed that the experimental group gained significantly more than the control group.

The Illinois Test of Psycholinguistic Ability. The ITPA was designed to identify "psycholinguistic abilities and disabilities in children between the ages of two and one-half and nine" (McCarthy & Kirk, 1963, p. 1).

Test 1 Visual–Motor Coordination
Directions: This is a road. Show with your pencil how you go from one end to the other (point) without bumping. Begin right here (trace) and stop at the end, here. . .
Remember, keep your pencils on the paper. Now go ahead.

Test 2 Figure–Ground Perception
Directions: Now here is a shape like a long box. In this picture are a long box and a triangle. Take your red pencil and outline the long box only. Find the long box and outline it. Try not to lift your pencil from the paper. Now do it.

Test 3 Perceptual Constancy
Directions: This is a square (indicate). See, all the sides are just the same. This (indicate) is a long box (rectangle). On this page there are some squares and also other things like long boxes (rectangles). Now look at your books. Find all the squares you can and outline them. Do not outline anything that is not a square. . . See how many squares you can find.

Test 4 Perception of Position in Space
Directions: Look at this first row (point). These are tables. Most of the tables are right side up. But one table is upside down. Mark the one that is upside down. Now do it.

Test 5 Perception of Spatial Relationships
Directions: Now look at this picture. Draw a line on this side so that the pictures will look exactly the same.

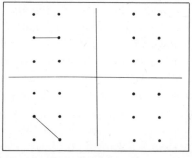

Figure 14-4   Sample items from the Frostig Developmental Test of Visual Perception.

520

The test yields scores for nine different language skills plus a total language age score.

Tests at the Representational Level. These tests assess the individual's ability to deal with linguistic symbols.

Test 1. Auditory Decoding—the ability to understand the spoken word. The words are presented in simple sentences to which the subject responds yes or no.
Examples: "Do airplanes fly?" "Do bicycles drink?"

Test 2. Visual Decoding—the ability to comprehend pictures and written words. A stimulus picture is presented, followed by four comparison pictures. The task is to select the comparison picture that is most meaningfully related to the stimulus picture.
Example: a silver knife and a jackknife

The Association Tests. These tests tap the ability to relate visual or auditory symbols in a meaningful way.

Test 3. Auditory-Vocal Association—the ability to relate spoken words is assessed through an analogies test graded for level of difficulty.
Example: Soup is hot; ice cream is _____.

Test 4. Visual-Motor Association—the ability to relate visual symbols in a meaningful way. A picture association test requires the subject to select from among four pictures the one which is most meaningfully related to the stimulus picture.
Examples: sock and shoe; hammer and nail

The Encoding Tests. These involve the ability to put ideas into words or gestures.

Test 5. Vocal Encoding. The ability to express ideas in spoken words is measured by asking the subject to describe simple objects.
Examples: ball, chalk, block

Test 6. Motor Encoding—the ability to express ideas in gestures. The subject is shown a picture of an object and asked to, "Show me what you should do with this."
Examples: drinking from a cup; strumming a guitar.

Tests at the Automatic-Sequential Level.

Test 7. Auditory-Vocal Automatic—a grammar test involving the ability to supply the correct linguistic form of a word.
Examples: Here is an apple. Here are two _____.
Father is opening the can. Now the can has been _____.

Test 8. Auditory-Vocal Sequencing—the ability to repeat a sequence of symbols is measured by a digit memory test.

Test 9. Visual-Motor Sequencing—the ability to reproduce a series of symbols is measured by requiring the subject to duplicate a sequence of pictures or geometrical designs presented by the examiner and then removed.

A number of remedial exercises have been suggested to facilitate development in the specific areas measured by the ITPA. These procedures should be useful for developing a remedial curriculum for children manifesting specific language deficiencies as well as those from culturally disadvantaged backgrounds who show general language retardation.

While some questions have been raised regarding the reliability and validity of the ITPA (Weener, Barritt, & Semmel, 1967), the test is a fruitful attempt to assess level of functioning in the language area—an area that is receiving increased attention among educators and psychologists.

Achievement Tests

The rapid increase in the testing of achievement during the 1950's stemmed partly from the self-critical, self-evaluative attitude of the nation's public schools. How effective are teaching techniques? How much have children learned from a particular course? Which areas of course content have pupils failed to assimilate? Such questions have spurred the drive to wider testing of achievement. In addition, knowledge of pupil achievement proves useful in counseling children and helps to make pertinent decisions about a child's academic strengths and weaknesses.

An indication of the importance attached to the assessment of achievement was a law passed by the California legislature in 1961 setting up a mandatory testing program throughout the state's public-school system. California school districts are now required to administer standardized achievement tests in English and mathematics as well as intelligence tests at the fifth-, eighth-, and eleventh-grade levels. The State Board of Education has certified an approved list of tests from which school districts must select those to be used. Scores must be recorded in the pupils' cumulative records.

In the early elementary years achievement tests concentrate on the child's reading ability. One test commonly used at the primary level (Metropolitan Achievement Tests, 1959) isolates and measures four aspects of reading: word knowledge, word discrimination, sentence reading, and story reading. Later, achievement tests assess a number of fairly specific skills. A test considered appropriate for junior-high-school students (Tiegs & Clark, 1957) covers three main areas: reading, arithmetic, and language, each of which is divided into the following subtests.

Reading
    Reading Vocabulary: Mathematics; Science; Social Science; General.
    Reading Comprehension: Following Directions; Reference Skills;
        Interpretations.
Arithmetic
    Arithmetic Reasoning: Meanings; Symbols, Rules, and Equations;
        Problems.
    Arithmetic Fundamentals: Addition; Subtraction; Multiplication;
        Division.
Language
    Mechanics of English: Capitalization; Punctuation; Word Usage.
    Spelling.

Sample items drawn from two achievement tests are shown in Figure 14-5.

It may seem unnecessary to speak of the validity of achievement tests. Obviously they must be valid if they measure the amount of subject matter a child has learned from a course. Yet achievement tests have been criticized because too often they measure only a child's retention of isolated facts without concern for other possible goals of the course. How much, for example, has the course stimulated the child's interest and curiosity? To what extent has the child gained a broad understanding of the principles involved? To what extent is the child able to apply the information he has learned to the solving of problems in a specific area? Since all these are reasonable educational goals, an educational achievement test, to be valid, might well assess a child's proficiency in these regions. In all fairness, it must be pointed out that authors of achievement tests have grown increasingly concerned with some of these matters. Another discernible trend is the measuring of a child's knowledge in such broad areas as natural science and social science rather than in fields of specific subject fare.

Achievement-test scores are typically interpreted on the basis of *grade norms*. The child's raw score is converted into one showing the grade level at which such a score is oftenest obtained. Despite the valid criticisms to which this method may be subjected, it has the advantage in the educational setting of denoting, at least approximately, a child's acceleration or retardation in a particular area of academic activity.

FIGURE 14-5 Items illustrating two school achievement tests.

PERSONALITY APPRAISAL

The techniques devised to access personality do not compare in effectiveness with those that appraise intellect. To begin with, personality is less clearly defined than intelligence; psychological theorists cannot agree on what constitutes personality. Furthermore, personality seems to be a subtler and more complex notion than intelligence, requiring more indirect methods of assessment (Goodenough, 1949b). Of the many appraisal techniques developed, each often assesses but one aspect of personality. Thus such measures fall short of the mark because personality is the sum of several different traits in the individual.

The methods of personality appraisal also fail to measure up to the ideal for a historical reason. Many of them grew out of a clinical need for appraising or diagnosing children referred to child guidance or child clinical centers. However, a tool useful for clinical diagnosis of the nature of a child's psychological problems may not be equally productive for appraising the personality of nonproblem children. More recent research has gone beyond the applied nature of clinical diagnosis, looking to the development of more refined and precise instruments.

Finally, personality appraisal in children presents problems not found in the appraisal of adult personality. Yet many measures developed for the adult level have been adapted for use with children. Paper-and-pencil tests, for example, are inappropriate at the younger age levels. They limit the use of self-reporting techniques. And the problems of interpretation and validation are more numerous and more difficult at the child than at the adult level.

Many attempts have been made to classify the techniques of personality assessment. For purposes of classification various aspects of the techniques have been used—the type of response required of the individual, the nature of the test materials, and the interpretation of the responses. For the present discussion the appraisal techniques are divided into four main categories: observational method, projective measures, objective tests, and parental report. Although any single technique may easily be assigned to more than one category, the present scheme has been adopted for convenience. In actual practice, several techniques supplement the information gained through each.

Observational Method

At the outset of this book, the importance of observation as a scientific method for acquiring information was heavily emphasized. Indeed, insofar as personality is revealed in behavior, the observational approach is often the only way to validate a child's score or rating on a personality test. For example, to have validity, a child's score pointing toward maladjustment on an adjustment inventory must relate to his day-to-day behavior with his associates either in the home or outside of it. Extended observation of a single child seldom is feasible, however. For this reason short-cut methods are developed. But one should never forget that an instrument is no more useful than its ability to yield information similar to that obtained by the more cumbersome approach of long-term observation of the individual.

Life Situations. Observation of the child's behavior in his day-to-day environment remains one of the most commonly used methods of personality appraisal. In fact, observation may be more productive in understanding the child's personality than complicated tests that are difficult to interpret. The child is spontaneous in his behavior, expressing himself less covertly and with fewer inhibitions than the adult. He represses little. Indeed he may reveal more in his overt behavior than in his responses to standard measures of personality assessment, which may reflect some inhibition, anxiety, and shyness.

Methods of recording observations and the kinds of behavior observed are showing increasing sophistication. Observational categories based on theory seem better at yielding information pertinent to the assessment of personality than random observations. In one study (Rafferty, Tyler, & Tyler, 1960), observational records of children's behavior were classified into six motivational categories.

> . . . recognition-status (concern with skill or competence in social, intellectual, or play activity), love and affection (concern with acceptance, warmth, liking or being liked by others), dominance (concern with direction or control of others), protection-dependence (concern with having others prevent frustration, make decisions), and independence (concern with self-mediated satisfactions including reliance on oneself) . . . (p. 693).

Based on reinforcement theory involving some of the learning principles described in Chapter 4, the behavior-modification approach frequently uses observational recording to identify reinforcement contingencies, that is, the extent to which the frequency of a response or an action is dependent or contingent upon the consequences of that response. Rewarding a certain behavior increases the likelihood that such behavior will occur again, while negative reinforcement (e.g., punishment) weakens a given response. Recent research has shown that a great variety of behaviors, including tantrums, crying, social withdrawal, and aggressive behavior, may be controlled by using reinforcement principles. One example of the way in which observation is conducted in such studies will serve to illustrate this approach. Theorizing that assertive behavior is the product of a reinforcement history in which a child has been rewarded for such behavior by parents, siblings, and peers, Patterson, Littman, and Bricker (1967) hypothesized that when a nursery-school child's aggressive-assertive behavior toward another child (e.g., hitting, pushing, grabbing toys) is followed by positive reinforcement (victim cries, relinquishes toy), the aggressor is likely to select that child again as a target for his aggression. If such aggressive behavior is followed by negative reinforcement (victim retaliates), the aggressor is likely to select another child as the target. Their procedure involved observation of the children's free play in a nursery school. Using a face-mask microphone in conjunction with a portable tape recorder, the observer dictated a detailed description of each aggressive episode. The aggressor was identified, as was the nature of the aggressive behavior. The consequences provided by the victim were described. Following each observational session the taped record was transcribed onto 3 x 5 cards, with a separate card for each episode of action and consequence. Judges independently coded all of the episodes according to the form of the aggressive attack and the victim's reaction. The categories used are shown in Table 14-1.

Frequently impressions gained through observation are quantified through the use of check lists or rating scales designed to describe the child's behavior on the basis of a limited number of traits. The following is an illustration of a check list developed to find a child's position with respect to ascendant or submissive behavior.

1. Submits to any child who takes the initiative.
2. Even submits to younger children.
3. Dominates children more mature than himself.
4. Submits to a leader only after a struggle to dominate.
5. Usually leads a small group.
6. Decides who shall participate in the group activities.
7. Is a leader in any group.
8. Directs all activity about him.
9. Neither leads nor follows; plays alone.
10. Other children make many appeals to him for information.
11. Dominates other children through his ability to talk effectively.
12. Other children appeal to him to make decisions for the group.
13. Dominates other children through their love or admiration for him.
14. Dominates other children through his wealth of ideas.
15. Definitely schemes to get others to carry out his plans.
16. Gives commands with an air of finality.
17. Helpless unless someone organizes activity for him.
18. Hesitates to initiate activity.
19. Hesitates to make suggestions to other children.

TABLE 14-1 *

Category	Example
I. Aggressor's behavior (insti-gation):	
A. Bodily attack	Ag hits V. Ag pushes V. Also includes spitting, kicking, biting, punching, jumping on, grabbing, and choking.
B. Attack with an object	Ag hits V with a book.
C. Verbal or symbolic	Ag verbally threatens V. Also includes derogations, assertive demands, or threatening gestures.
D. Infringement of property or invasion of territory	Ag takes toy from V.
II. Target's response-consequences:	
A. Passive	Ag hits V. V does not respond to Ag or V withdraws or V gives up toy.
B. Cries	Ag hits V. V cries.
C. Defensive postures	Ag hits V. V covers his head. Also includes verbal protest.
D. Telling the teacher	
E. Recover property	Ag takes truck away from V. V grabs truck back from Ag.
F. Retaliation	Ag hits V. V hits Ag back.

* From Patterson, Littman, & Bricker, 1967, p. 14.

20. Usually follows the ideas of others for activity.
21. Can take the initiative if it is absolutely necessary.
22. Usually takes the initiative.
23. Seeks the approval of the leader before he acts.
24. Does not push the issue in case of opposition.
25. Stands aside to let others participate.
26. Fights for his place as leader.
27. Opposition spurs him on to greater activity.
28. Insists that other children do as he wishes.
29. Does not defend his own rights with other children.
30. Gets willing cooperation easily.

(Stott & Ball, 1957, p. 261)

Ascendance-submission check-list data were available on 60 children over a 10-year interval from the age of two or three to over 13. Ascendant behavior increased throughout the three-year period of nursery-school attendance, with a very low frequency of interactive behavior at the age of three and under, increasing sharply up to the age of five. With the change from nursery school to kindergarten, ascendant behavior became less frequent. There were no consistent changes in the frequency of ascendant-submissive behavior after the age of five (Stott & Ball, 1957).

Observational rating scales are widely used in personality appraisal. Since the information obtained through them is purely descriptive in nature, the value of such scales is limited. Ratings of behavior do not interpret behavior in terms of its causes and the type of personality underlying it. Even so, note the following items drawn from a scale (Haggerty-Olson-Wickman Behavior Rating Schedules) designed to identify problem behavior in school children and to assess 35 physical, mental, social, and emotional characteristics (Haggerty, Olson, & Wickman, 1930).

How does he accept authority?

| Defiant | Critical of authority | Ordinarily obedient | Respectful, complies by habit | Entirely resigned, accepts all authority |

How does he react to frustrations or to unpleasant situations?

| Very sub- missive, long- suffering | Tolerant, rarely blows up | Generally self-con- trolled | Impatient | Easily irritated, hot-headed, explosive |

Is he suspicious or trustful?

| Very suspicious, distrustful | Has to be assured | Generally unsuspicious and trustful | Somewhat gullible | Accepts everything without question |

Does he act impulsively or cautiously?

| Impulsive, bolts, acts on the spur of the moment | Frequently unreflective and imprudent | Acts with reasonable care | Deliberate | Very cautious and calculating |

Miniature Life Situations. Although any interference with behavior in its natural setting introduces possible error in the accuracy of interpretation, control of a situation frequently increases the precision and significance of the data obtained. For this reason, real-life situations have been simulated in order to make appraisals of personality. The use of a miniature life situation assumes a relation between the individual's behavior in this experimental environment and his behavior outside of it. It is also argued that the child will reveal various personality characteristics by his manipulation of the materials at hand or by his solution of the problems presented.

In the Hartshorne and May (1928) study of deceit in children between the ages of eight and eleven, a variety of methods were employed. One of the measures of deception involved four athletic tests: the dynamometer test, the spirometer test, pull-ups, and standing broad jump. The children were led to believe that the tests were part of a real athletic contest in which badges were to be awarded to the winners of the four events. The directions for each test were given to the children individually and they were asked to try each procedure, the examiner taking mental note of their performance. Subsequently, the child was told to proceed alone, recording the best of several trials. The difference between the examiner's rating and the child's own was the measure of deception.

Selected general findings of the study indicated older children to be slightly more deceptive than younger ones. The sex differences were few. The more intelligent children cheated less. Children who showed symptoms of emotional instability were more likely to be deceitful than others, and children from low socioeconomic backgrounds demonstrated less honesty than those from higher levels.

Observation of Play. This technique presents the child with a wide range of play materials including toys, paints, dough, and cold cream. Freedom is permitted in their use. If he so chooses, the child may arrange, build, destroy, or smear. The rationale for this freedom is that the natural language of children is behavior and that the child will disclose his needs, attitudes, feelings, and problems through the manner in which he approaches and deals with play materials. If a completely permissive and accepting atmosphere is established, the child will have no need to conceal his feelings; the restrictions in the world of reality will not be present.

What are some of the aspects of personality revealed in a child's play? An alert observer can identify differences among children in a great many personality areas. If a child is observed playing with toys representing real-life objects, such as a doll house with dolls suggesting the family unit, one can follow the enactment of situations and events, the treatment of the various dolls, the child's emotional expressions, and his verbal behavior. When manipulating such tactile materials as clay and finger paint, the child's attitude toward middle-class strictures against dirtiness and messiness may be disclosed through the spontaneity with which he approaches these materials. Is he inhibited, anxious, relaxed, aggressive? Is he secure enough to explore the possible artistic uses of such amorphous substances or is his behavior rigid and stereotyped?

The following excerpt describes a young child's reaction to playing with dough.

> Another little girl whispered "I can't" at first, and approached the dough almost tentatively. She ran her hand in a gingerly way through the mess, and did not squeeze the dough until the experimenter had done so. However, when she did, she squeezed *very* hard, with a kind of aggressive violence which no other child showed. After more play she volunteered, however, "I don't think it's nice." Yet when the experimenter started to put away the pan, she resisted: "I'm not all finished yet." She shook her hands through the mess saying, "Gooey, gooey, gooey!" She squeezed, made balls of the dough. But at the end, after she had washed her hands, she said, "I never want to do that again . . . why did you do this to me?" Her expressive face appeared "mildly horrified and puzzled," wanting rapport at the beginning; after being released by the experimenter's example she was definitely aggressive with the paste, in contrast to the other children, and then seemed to develop a sense of guilt as she went on, apparently feeling this was naughty. Among other comments made in the context of cleaning up after the dough, she said, "My mother spanks me if I'm naughty . . . I cry so the neighbors hear . . . sometimes I scratch her and she spanks me" (Murphy, 1956, p. 124).

Sometimes situations are provided that specifically encourage the release of aggressive, destructive feelings. The intensity in the child of these tendencies, his fear or anxiety over exhibiting such behavior, and the sequence of his behavior through which some control is achieved can be observed.

There is no question that the child reveals his personality through play. Problems arise, however, in the interpretation of such behavior. For example, a child who shows little aggression in his play either may have little need for aggressive outlets or he may be restrained from expressing aggression by anxiety or fear of punishment. Therefore, data obtained from observing a child's play must be used in conjunction with information from other sources, essentially from techniques that are more objective as to scoring and interpretation. We now turn to some of these.

Projective Assessment Techniques

The idea that individuals will bring structure to ambiguous, diffuse stimuli on the basis of individual needs, feelings, and personality patterns is popular in psychology. The individual imposes on the environment his own psychological outlook, organization, and meanings. In a form-less cloud the child sees the friendly face of a man and in the shadow on the wall a vicious animal about to pounce on its prey. This idea of projection is accepted widely as an approach to the assessment of per-sonality because the individual is least willing or least able to reveal through interview or questionnaire those of his aspects that most adequately describe the uniqueness of his personality (Frank, 1939).

In the past few decades a tremendous growth has taken place in the development and use of projective techniques.[1] As a result, a great number and variety of projective instruments are now available. Taking the cue from Allport's (1961) classification, let us describe several examples of these techniques under three main headings: perceptive, apperceptive, and productive.

Perceptive Techniques. The child is confronted with ambiguous ma-terial and is asked to tell what it means to him. Either auditory or visual stimuli may be used; the latter is commoner. The most widely used instrument of this description is the Rorschach Ink Blot Test de-veloped in 1921. The test consists of a series of 10 cards, five colored and five achromatic. These are presented in sequence, and the in-dividual is instructed to describe what he sees in the ink blots. Later, the child identifies on the card the location of what he saw and the clues used in his response. In scoring the child's responses, a variety of cate-gories are employed, including the location and determinants of the re-sponse, its originality, and the time required for the individual to re-spond. From an interpretation of the record of the responses a full description of the individual's personality is constructed. The following account is a description of a nine-year-old boy referred to a child guid-ance clinic by his teacher because of his difficulties in the classroom.

> Jim's thinking is fairly well organized and there is no evidence of bi-zarreness or morbidity in his fantasies. He is able to see things as most people do and there are indications of a very early inculcation of adult standards concerning propriety, right and wrong, and how one should behave.

[1] A fuller treatment of projective techniques appropriate at the child level may be found in A. I. Rabin and M. R. Haworth (Eds.), *Projective Techniques with Chil-dren.* New York: Grune & Stratton, 1960.

Despite Jim's attempts to maintain a facade of happiness, willingness and compliance, he is rather vulnerable to emotional stimuli and is apt to react largely in terms of his feelings of the moment with immature expression of his emotions. However, when possible, Jim attempts to handle emotional impact in a superficial, behavioral way that is not essentially related to his own feelings. That is, he responds in terms of what he feels is demanded by the situation without a genuine integration of his own feelings with the realistic demands of the situation.

Jim is very concerned about handling sexual and aggressive impulses and a good deal of tension and anxiety is associated with such impulses. His great concern about aggression is reflected in Rorschach responses such as "Volcanoes," "Fire burning up the ground," and "Like they were in Africa and killed a bear." Jim is fearful of his own aggressive impulses and defends strongly against their direct expression. It appears that his fear of aggression has led to a generalized inhibition of most forms of assertiveness so that even socially acceptable strivings for attainment are inhibited. Hence, Jim's aggression is expressed primarily in indirect ways through passive resistance or passive negativism.

In part, Jim's fearfulness of aggression appears to stem from unresolved Oedipal conflicts in which castration anxiety plays a major role. While Jim would like to be able to compete aggressively against father figures, he is quite apprehensive about such wishes, fearing that his castration or destruction will be the outcome of such competition. He views father figures as quite dangerous. But despite his fearfulness of father figures, Jim seems to want father's permission (and probably father's encouragement and support) in expressing himself in a more masculine way.

Apperceptive Techniques. These techniques require the individual to respond to less amorphous material by contributing some interpretation of his own. Figure 14-6 shows a picture from a series intended to assess parent-child relations (Alexander, 1952). The subject is asked to develop a story about a picture, explaining what led up to the scene, what is occurring, and what will happen. The story is to include the thoughts and feelings of the characters. Stories are then evaluated for the approach used to solve their problems, the nature of the emotional expressions conveyed, whether positive or negative, and the way in which the characters in them are viewed—as friendly or hostile. The following is an Alexander summary about an 11-year-old boy.

Ronald found thinking about the stimuli in the cards a threatening experience. He used only the main stimuli (mainly the figures) in the cards and added few stimuli in an effort to account for the ones presented. Emotional expressions were few in number and most of them were negative. Adults and parents are viewed as hostile and he has ag-

FIGURE 14-6   Sample picture from the Alexander Adult-Child Interaction test.

gressive and hostile feelings in return. He tries to solve his problems by avoidance and escape (Alexander, 1952, p. 18).

Incomplete sentences have been used to elicit children's attitudes and feelings toward people and toward other aspects of their environment. Stems of sentences are provided, which the child is required to complete. The following list of stems represents a test intended to assess parent-child relations (Hoeflin & Kell, 1959, p. 12). The responses are scored on the bases of how the child conceives of the parent and child relationship, whether it promotes growth or is autocratic, and of the positiveness or negativeness of feeling.

1. Our family	11. Discipline
2. As a child I enjoyed	12. Teen-agers
3. My mother	13. My father
4. Being a child	14. Making high grades in school
5. Obedience	15. Punishment
6. Children should not	16. As a child I disliked
7. If my father	17. A democratic family
8. When I was in high school	18. If my mother
9. I wish my parents had	19. Being at home
10. Being a (boy) (girl)	20. Making decisions in the home

Productive Techniques. As the wording implies, the child produces something in these tests which the examiner then interprets. Long before the formal beginnings of psychology, interest was shown in analyzing people's handwriting. Yet not much progress has been made through the years toward developing an objective analysis and valid interpretation of handwriting. Similarly, numerous difficulties are met in attempting to construct a valid measure of personality from children's drawings although several drawing tests are in current use. The rationale for relying on these tests is that children divulge important aspects of their personalities through the way they express themselves artistically.

Most widely used among children is the Draw-A-Person Test (DAP), a descendant of Goodenough's original Draw-A-Man Test (1926) which, as we saw, was designed to assess intelligence in young children. This method for evaluating children's drawings on the basis of hints of several personality traits was devised by Machover (1949). To her, the child's drawing of the human figure represented his image of himself in relation to his environment. Things noted about the drawing include the kinds of line employed, the part of the page covered, and the dimensions, proportions, and perspective of the figure. After the drawing has been completed, the examiner elicits from the child various associations he may have in connection with his picture. He is requested to describe the feelings and mood of the figure drawn and other such characteristics. There are no objective scoring norms for the DAP Test; its use is primarily as a clinical aid in understanding the individual child.

Several interesting findings emerged from a study that endeavored to develop a scale of sexual differentiation from the DAP Test (Haworth & Normington, 1961). Pairs of drawings, male and female figures, were obtained from 312 children ranging in age from seven through 12. Four levels of sexual differentiation were detected, from the lowest level of "figures nearly the same, no apparent sex," to the highest level of "each figure well differentiated as to sex," with such items as mustache or pants fly for the male and breasts and jewelry for the female. With age an increase in sex differentiation was noted, girls consistently showing greater differentiation than boys and also placing greater emphasis on figures of their own sex.

Objective Tests

Objective paper-and-pencil tests are perhaps the oldest approach to the assessment of personality. Their development related to the early success in constructing tests to appraise intelligence. Because these tests presumably provided valid assessments of intelligence, it was only natural that psychologists should make the effort to apply their technique to personality measurement. However, the relative value of objective and projective tests has generated lively controversy. Adherents of the projective approach contend that measurement of separate traits does injustice to the complexity of personality and to the interaction among personality factors. The opposite position notes the difficulty of scoring and interpreting the projective material obtained; without objectivity, it holds, a scientific assessment of personality can never be attained. Both views contain strengths as well as limitations. For the present, at least, adequate evaluation of a child's personality involves the use of a wide variety of instruments.

Personality Inventories. A personality inventory is expected to uncover a specific number of elements considered to be important by the builder of the test. Two of the tests used most commonly with children, the California Test of Personality and the Rogers Test of Personality Adjustment, have some validity. There is evidence (Smith, 1958) that both are significantly, and at the least, moderately, related to teacher and peer nomination of well- and poorly adjusted children (see Chapter 12). Because of the nature of objective tests, they obviously cannot be used below the seven- or eight-year level, although in the California Test the questions can be read to children by the examiner.

California Test. The California Test of Personality has various forms appropriate for use from kindergarten through the adult level. Its organization has been described in the following way by its authors (Thorpe, Clark, & Tiegs, 1953):

<table>
<tr><td rowspan="3">1. Self Adjustment:
Based on feelings
of personal security</td><td>A. Self-reliance</td></tr>
<tr><td>B. Sense of personal worth
C. Sense of personal freedom
D. Feeling of belonging
E. Freedom from withdrawing tendencies
F. Freedom from nervous symptoms</td></tr>
</table>

1. Self Adjustment:
   Based on feelings
   of personal security

    A. Self-reliance
    B. Sense of personal worth
    C. Sense of personal freedom
    D. Feeling of belonging
    E. Freedom from withdrawing tendencies
    F. Freedom from nervous symptoms

Life Adjustment:
A balance between
self and social
adjustment

    A. Social standards
    B. Social skills

2. Social Adjustment:
   Based on feelings
   of social security

    C. Freedom from anti-social tendencies
    D. Family relations
    E. School relations
    F. Community relations

The test is comprised of a series of questions that are answered by checking blanks marked "yes" or "no." The test's primary purpose, said its authors, is to indicate the extent to which a child is adjusting to the problems confronting him and to which he is developing a well-adjusted, socially effective personality. Fifteen raw scores, for which keys are provided, are converted into percentiles based on norms in order to be plotted on so-called *profile* sheets. Examination of a child's profile aids the teacher in ascertaining specifically where guidance or remedial effort is needed. The following items are typical of those contained in the primary series, kindergarten to grade three.

Is it hard for you to look out for yourself?	YES NO
Do the children forget to ask you to play with them?	YES NO
Do you feel bad because you can't do things well enough?	YES NO
Does your stomach ache often?	YES NO
Do you feel that some of the teachers have it in for you?	YES NO

Rogers Test. The Rogers Test of Personality Adjustment (Rogers, 1931), designed for children from nine through 13, is one of the oldest personality tests available for youngsters. From it, four scores and a total score can be derived. A personal inferiority score indicates the degree to which the child perceives himself as physically or mentally less capable than his peers. The score of social maladjustment is an index to the child's feelings about his social relations with other children. The family-relations score represents the child's reports of conflict and dissatisfaction in his relations with his parents and siblings. The daydreaming score reflects the child's indulgence in fantasies and unrealistic thinking. The total score indexes the seriousness of the child's maladjustment. As the intent of the items, as a rule, is rather concealed, the responses are probably more meaningful and valid than if the test simply required yes or no answers.

The Rogers Test of Personality Adjustment was administered to 256 fifth-graders from small towns and rural areas in the Midwest. In general, children from higher social-class backgrounds showed fewer signs of personality maladjustment than children from lower-class homes. However, those children whose fathers had the highest educational achievement showed greater maladjustment than many of the children whose fathers were less well educated. Pressures for achievement exerted by high-achieving parents on their children may be detrimental to healthy personality development (Burchinal, Gardner, & Hawkes, 1958).

Self-Ratings. Self-ratings or check lists, while less objective than personality inventories, reveal the way the individual sees himself. Information thus obtained about the concept of the self helps a youngster to a better understanding of himself. The Mooney Problem Check List (Mooney & Gordon, 1950) represents an instrument designed for this purpose. Its form for junior high school consists of 30 items in each of seven problem areas: health and physical development; school; home and family; money, work, and the future; boy and girl relations; relations to people in general; and self-centered concerns. The youngster underlines items that he feels cause him some personal concern and circles the number of items that he considers as serious problems for himself.

Parental Report

Many of the more formal personality tests used with some success among adults are unsuitable for children, especially at the younger age levels, because of the young child's inability to read and write and respond in a manner relevant to the questions posed to him. However, information acquired from persons intimate with the behavior of children is frequently of great value in appraising a child's approach to people and to his environment in general. Clearly, parents are in a position to furnish such information. Although data of this type are obtained indirectly and parental impressions of a child may not be entirely unbiased or objective, a parent's perception of the young child exposes a great deal about the youngster's personality and about the kind of psychological environment in which the child's personality is formed. Parental report may vary from freeflowing discussions to the use of objective instruments.

Interview. As a technique for appraisal, the interview can provide information about a child that is obtainable in no other way. The child's reaction to intimate interactions and situations within the family, the events that have been important in the shaping of his current level of adjustment, his characteristic mode of response to frustration and stress—all these and more may be discerned most directly from parental interviews. The alert interviewer will endeavor to separate facts from attitudes toward them. Both are valuable, perhaps equally so, but as the main interest is an appraisal of the child's personality, knowledge of a parent's attitude toward the child may help to explain rather than to assess his personality.

An interview may be totally unplanned, in which the interviewee is free to pursue any topic he wishes or it may be confined to a predetermined list of questions. Each type has its advantages and disadvantages and, in actual practice, the interview is seldom completely one or the other. Frequently in the initial stages of an interview, rapport is established by letting the parent discuss those areas he selects; later the interviewer may wish to dig further into certain points or to obtain information where gaps exist.

Since the information gathered through interviews is not easily quantified, except through the tedious procedure of rating the transcript of the taped interview, examiners frequently employ more objective methods of assessing the child's personality as revealed through parental report. Two of these are the *semantic differential* and the *Q-sort* techniques. The semantic differential technique was designed originally as a device for measuring the meaning of various concepts (see Osgood, Suci, & Tannenbaum, 1957). As its name implies, the technique helps to discern the differences in meaning that an individual holds toward two concepts. The individual discloses his attitude toward a concept or the meaning the concept has for him by rating it on a number of polarized scales. The discrepancy between an individual's ratings of two separate concepts is taken as representative of the extent to which their meanings differ to him.

In a study of the relation between maternal self-acceptance and maternal acceptance of her child, Medinnus and Curtis (1963) asked 56 mothers of preschool children to describe "My child (as he is)" by rating him on 20 bipolar scales. Then the mothers were asked to repeat the procedure, now describing "My child (as I would like him to be)." The item-by-item discrepancy in their ratings of the two concepts was taken as a measure of maternal acceptance of the child. Moderate and statistically significant correlations were obtained between two measures of maternal self-acceptance and adjustment, and the "semantic differential" measure of child acceptance. As we have already seen, the mothers who were most accepting of their children were those who scored highest in self-acceptance. These were some of the bipolar scales used:

friendly____:____:____:____:____:____:____hostile
trustful____:____:____:____:____:____:____suspicious
deliberate____:____:____:____:____:____:____impulsive
submissive____:____:____:____:____:____:____assertive
sociable____:____:____:____:____:____:____shy
mature____:____:____:____:____:____:____infantile
emotionally

The Q-sort of technique elicits an individual's view of himself or of others through a rating-type approach. Originally developed by Stephenson (1935), the technique requires the person to sort a large variety of descriptive phrases along a continuum from, say, "most like myself" to "least like myself." Rogers (1951) used this technique to obtain a picture of an individual's self-perceptions before and after therapy, as well as of his view of the "ideal self." The technique is particularly productive in collecting parental descriptions of their child and conceptions of the "ideal child." The latter sorting uncovers interesting information on the kinds of behavior and characteristics to which the parent attaches greatest significance. Moreover, discrepancy between two parents in their descriptions of their child and of the ideal child sheds some light on certain aspects of the psychological atmosphere in which the child is raised.

Thirty-eight sets of parents of five-year-olds sorted two pools of 42 items each to describe their own child and the ideal five-year-old (Medinnus, 1961b). Parental agreement was higher for the "real sort" describing their own child than for the "ideal sort," indicating that parents agree more in their perceptions of their children than in their expectations and goals for them. There was generally greater agreement between parents of boys than of girls. The item ranked as most important for the ideal five-year-old was: "is in good physical condition; is usually healthy."

OTHER APPRAISAL METHODS

Several further methods of gaining information about the child's behavioral development warrant brief mention, either because of general usefulness or because they attempt to appraise areas of behavior often overlooked in discussions of personality development.

Vineland Social Maturity Scale

Working with mentally retarded children, Doll observed great differences in the social competence of children of the same intellectual capacity. And since social competence is of particular importance to children of inferior intellectual ability, as we have seen, Doll recognized the need for a practical instrument to assess this area. First published in 1935, the Vineland Social Maturity Scale (Doll, 1935) consists of a series of items of growing difficulty representing progressive social independence in the following areas of behavior: self-help (eating, dressing), self-direction, locomotion, occupation, communication, and social relations.

Through interviews with parents, information about a child's behavior and development is obtained. The child is given a plus or minus for each item based on his ability to perform the task in question. The total score, representing the sum of the items passed, is translated into a Social Quotient (SQ) by converting the total score into a "social age" figure and dividing this by the chronological age of the child. The SQ, similar in computation to the IQ, compares the child's social competence with others of his chronological age. Thus a child of average social maturity for his age level would receive an SQ of 100. These are items contained in the three- to five-year levels (Doll, 1953):

III–IV	IV–V
Walks downstairs one step per tread	Cares for self at toilet
Plays cooperatively at kindergarten level	Washes face unassisted
Buttons coat or dress	Goes about neighborhood unattended
Helps at little household tasks	Dresses self except for tying
"Performs" for others	Uses pencil or crayon for drawing
Washes hands unaided	Plays competitive exercise games

Sociometric Tests

A child's acceptance by and popularity among his agemates is an important part of his behavior and adjustment. Although adjustment to peers is only one facet of a child's personality, his relationship with others serves well as a measure of his general adjustment. Children who rank low in popularity frequently exhibit, as we have observed, a variety of maladaptive and maladjusted behaviors.

It would be rare, especially in elementary schools, for teachers to have no notion of how well a child is accepted by his peers. However, as an additional aid, data furnished by a sociometric measure specify quite clearly how any child is accepted by his peers. The Guess Who method also discloses information about how a child is perceived. Is a particular child seen as possessing primarily positive, acceptable qualities or characteristics? Or are the characteristics attributed to him by his peers largely negative?

Peer ratings spot areas of strength and weakness in any child's behavior as perceived by his agemates. This information assists a teacher in her efforts to manipulate a child's social environment to produce positive changes in his behavior. It also helps her to establish in the classroom an atmosphere that is conducive to the development of healthy psychological adjustment in all the children. Among older children, the teacher or counselor may use the information gained from sociometric tests and Guess Who devices to aid the child in gaining insight into his behavior, especially with regard to those characteristics that impede his acceptance by his peers.

The Children's Manifest Anxiety Scale, the Children's Self-Concept Scale and a sociometric ranking were administered to 111 fourth, fifth, and sixth graders. The less popular children tended to be more anxious and they tended to hold poorer self concepts. These findings were true for both sexes and for the three grade levels. However, the low magnitude of the correlations suggested that the interrelations are complex and that other variables are of considerable importance in affecting a child's sociometric standing (Horowitz, 1962).

School Anecdotal Records

As a trained person, the teacher is in a particularly advantageous position to observe a child's behavior in a variety of day-to-day situations. Both in the formal classroom setting and on the informal playground, the child displays his general response to his environment. Specifically, he demonstrates his response to frustration, his resourcefulness in meeting new situations, his level of persistence, his attitudes of independence, his sense of responsibility, and his social and emotional adjustment.

Anecdotal records keep track of these behaviors. They are diary-like accounts of crucial observations and impressions of a child's performance. Frequently the incidents entered into the record are highly significant in understanding the personality and adjustment of a particular child. The usefulness of these records depends, however, on the objectivity of the recorder and his observations, and on the relevance of the incidents recorded. When anecodotal records are accumulated over a period of time, they present a rich, factual, detailed picture of the child. Recurring patterns of behavior can be noted and a broad understanding can be gained of a child's characteristic manner and level of functioning. The following entries in an anecdotal record of a youngster kept by her third-grade teacher illustrate the types of information generally included in such accounts.

March 1: Reading group three was in the front of the room having its phonics lesson while the other two reading groups were working at their desks. Debbie had volunteered to divide a word into syllables on the chalkboard. Julie, seated in the reading circle behind Debbie, repeatedly swung her crossed leg, hitting Debbie's posterior. Julie's behavior ceased when I remonstrated with her. (Julie's behavior was caused apparently by her jealousy of Debbie who this time won their ceaseless struggle to sit next to me in the reading circle.)

March 17: Julie and her best friend, Paulia, quarreled over a problem related to a difficulty between the two families while entering the school grounds in the morning. Characteristically, Julie impulsively and in anger slapped Paulia forcefully in the face. This provoked a battle between the two girls requiring intervention by the yard teacher.

April 4: Jimmy, on courtesy patrol in the hall outside of Julie's third-grade room, reported to me an incident which had occurred between him and Julie. When Jimmy attempted to prevent Julie from running in the hall, she refused to comply and when Jimmy attempted to enforce his command, Julie added insult to injury by defiantly calling him "stupid."

April 23: By actual count, Julie left her seat to socialize with other children ten times in the space of one hour this morning—this despite the fact I ordered her to return to and to remain in her seat each time. (Little wonder that she seldom completes her seatwork satisfactorily!)

June 3: This morning it was Julie's turn to be in charge of one of the balls during recess. She agreed to play "four square" with a small group of children. When Julie was "out" she became angry and upset and took the ball and ran to an isolated section of the playground. (One of the playground rules of our school forbids the breaking up of a school game.)

Ann came to me in tears during afternoon recess because Julie pushed her out of the line of children waiting to jump rope. (Though Julie desperately needs friends, the two incidents today illustrate her negative approach to others which antagonizes her classmates and makes an adequate social adjustment for Julie seem even more remote.)

SUMMARY

Three main areas of appraisal have been explored: infant assessment, assessment of intellectual ability, and assessment of personality. Despite the fruitless efforts of psychologist to predict future ability from tests administered to infants, Gesell's methods for measuring rate of general development in infancy have value in assessing developmental progress.

The mental testing movement originally developed IQ tests to discern levels of academic ability. Although intelligence tests have been charged with failing to assess a wide range of characteristics, such tests continue to predict adequately a child's level of performance in the school setting, the purpose for which they were originally intended.

Four broad techniques for appraising personality were examined: observational methods, projective measures, objective tests, and parental report. For a number of reasons the techniques devised to evaluate personality have not proved as satisfactory as those used for appraising the intellect. Even though each technique falls short of adequate assessment of the dynamic interrelation and interaction among an individual's personality traits, in the actual practice of diagnosing personality a number of the techniques described supplement one another. The result is that a fairly distinct picture of the child's personality structure unfolds.

REFERENCES

Alexander, T. The Adult-Child Interaction Test. *Monographs of the Society for Research in Child Development,* 1952, **17,** No. 2 (Serial No. 55).

Allport, G. W. *Pattern and growth in personality.* New York: Holt, 1961.

Anderson, J. E. The limitations of infant and preschool tests in the measurement of intelligence. *Journal of Psychology,* 1939, **8,** 351–379.

Bayley, N. *California First-Year Mental Scale.* Berkeley: University of California Press, 1933. (a)

Bayley, N. Mental growth during the first three years. A developmental study of sixty-one children by repeated tests. *Genetic Psychology Monographs,* 1933, **14,** No. 1. (b)

Binet, A., & Simon, T. The development of the Binet-Simon scale. In W. Dennis (Ed.), *Readings in the history of psychology.* New York: Appleton-Century-Crofts, 1948. Pp. 412–424.

Burchinal, L., Gardner, B., & Hawkes, G. Children's personality adjustment and the socio-economic status of their families. *Journal of Genetic Psychology,* 1958, **92,** 149–159.

Cattell, P. *Cattell Infant Intelligence Scale.* New York: Psychological Corporation, 1947.

Doll, E. A. A genetic scale of social maturity. *American Journal of Orthopsychiatry,* 1935, **5,** 180–188.

Doll, E. A. *The measurement of social competence.* Minneapolis: Educational Test Bureau, 1953.

Escalona, S.   The use of infant tests for predictive purposes.   *Bulletin of the Menninger Clinic*, 1950, **14**, 117–128.

Frank, L. K.   Projective methods for the study of personality.   *Journal of Psychology*, 1939, **8**, 389–413.

Frostig, M., & Horne, D.   *The Frostig program for the development of visual perception.*   Chicago: Follett, 1964.

Frostig, M., Maslow, P., Lefever, D., & Whittlesey, J.   *The Marianne Frostig Developmental Test of Visual Perception.*   Palo Alto: Consulting Psychologists Press, 1964.

Gesell, A.   *The first five years of life.*   New York: Harper, 1940.

Gesell, A., & Amatruda, C. S.   *Developmental diagnosis.*   New York: Hoeber, 1947.

Gilliland, A. R.   The measurement of the mentality of infants.   *Child Development*, 1948, **19**, 155–158.

Goodenough, F. L.   *Measurement of intelligence by drawings.*   Tarrytown-on-Hudson, N. Y.: World Book, 1926.

Goodenough, F. L.   *Mental testing.*   New York: Rinehart, 1949.   (a)

Goodenough, F. L.   The appraisal of child personality.   *Psychological Review*, 1949, **56**, 123–131.   (b)

Griffiths, R.   *Griffiths Mental Development Scale.*   London: University of London Press, 1954.

Haggerty, M. E., Olson, W. C., & Wickman, E. K.   *Haggerty-Olson-Wickman Behavior Rating Schedules.*   Yonkers, N. Y.: World Book, 1930.

Hartshorne H., & May, M. A.   *Studies in the nature of character.*   I.   *Studies in deceit.*   New York: Macmillan, 1928.

Haworth, M. R., & Normington, C. J.   A sexual differentiation scale for the D-A-P Test.   *Journal of Projective Techniques*, 1961, **25**, 441–450.

Hoeflin, R., & Kell, L.   The Kell-Hoeflin Incomplete Sentences Blank: Youth-Parent Relations.   *Monographs of the Society for Research in Child Development*, 1959, **24**, No. 3.

Hofstaetter, P. R.   The changing composition of "intelligence": A study in T technique.   *Journal of Genetic Psychology*, 1954, **85**, 159–164.

Horowitz, F. D.   The relationship of anxiety, self-concept, and sociometric status among fourth, fifth, and sixth grade children.   *Journal of Abnormal and Social Psychology*, 1962, **65**, 212–214.

Ilg, F., & Ames, L. B.   *School readiness.*   New York: Harper & Row, 1964.

Ilg, F., Ames, L. B., & Apell, R.   School readiness as evaluated by Gesell developmental, visual, and projective tests.   *Genetic Psychology Monographs*, 1965, **71**, 61–92.

Illingworth, R. S.   *The development of the infant and young child.*   London: Livingston, 1960.

Jordan, F., & Massey, J.   *School readiness survey.*   Palo Alto: Consulting Psychologists Press, 1967.

Knobloch, H., & Pasamanick, B.   A developmental questionnaire for infants forty weeks of age: An evaluation. *Monographs of the Society for Research in Child Development*, 1955, **20**, No. 2.

McCarthy, J., & Kirk, S. *The construction, standardization and statistical characteristics of the Illinois Test of Psycholinguistic Abilities*, 1963.

Machover, K. *Personality projection in the drawing of the human figure.* Springfield, Ill.: Thomas, 1949.

MacRae, J. M. Retests of children given mental tests as infants. *Journal of Genetic Psychology*, 1955, **87**, 111–119.

Medinnus, G. R. An investigation of school readiness and first grade adjustment. Unpublished manuscript, 1961. (a)

Medinnus, G. R. Q-sort descriptions of five-year-old children by their parents. *Child Development*, 1961, **32**, 473–489. (b)

Medinnus, G. R., & Curtis, F. The relation between maternal self-acceptance and child acceptance. *Journal of Consulting Psychology*, 1963, **27**, 542–544.

Metropolitan Achievement Tests. Yonkers, N. Y.: World Book, 1959.

Mooney, R. L., & Gordon, L. V. Mooney Problem Check List: 1950 Revision. New York: Psychological Corporation, 1950.

Murphy, L. B. *Personality in young children.* Vol. 1. *Methods for the study of personality in young children.* New York: Basic Books, 1956.

Osgood, C., Suci, G., & Tannenbaum, P. *The measurement of meaning.* Urbana: University of Illinois Press, 1957.

Patterson, G., Littman, R., & Bricker, W. Assertive behavior in children: A step toward a theory of aggression. *Monographs of the Society for Research in Child Development*, 1967, **32**, No. 5.

Rafferty, J. E., Tyler, B. B., & Tyler, F. B. Personality assessment from free play observations. *Child Development*, 1960, **31**, 691–702.

Rogers, C. R. Measuring personality adjustment in children nine to thirteen years of age. *Teachers College Contributions to Education*, 1931.

Rogers, C. R. *Client-centered therapy.* Boston: Houghton Mifflin, 1951.

Smith, L. M. The concurrent validity of six personality and adjustment tests for children. *Psychological Monographs: General and Applied*, 1958, **72**, (4), 1–30.

Stephenson, W. *The study of behavior.* Chicago: University of Chicago Press, 1935.

Stott, L. H., & Ball, R. S. Consistency and change in ascendance-submission in the social interaction of children. *Child Development*, 1957, **28**, 259–272.

Sullivan, E. T., Clark, W. W., & Tiegs, E. W. California Short-Form Test of Mental Maturity. Level 2. Monterey, Calif.: California Test Bureau, 1963.

Terman, L. M., & Merrill, M. A. *Measuring intelligence.* Boston: Houghton Mifflin, 1937.

Thorpe, L., Clark, W., & Tiegs, E. California Test of Personality. Primary, Form B. Los Angeles: California Test Bureau, 1953.

Tiegs, E. W., & Clark, W. W. California Achievement Tests. Complete Battery. Junior High Level, Form W. Los Angeles: California Test Bureau, 1957.

Wechsler, D. *Wechsler Intelligence Scale for Children.* New York: Psychological Corporation, 1949.

Wechsler, D. *Manual for the Wechsler Preschool and Primary Scale of Intelligence.* New York: Psychological Corporation, 1967.

Weener, P., Barritt, L., & Semmel, M. A critical evaluation of the Illinois Test of Psycholinguistic Abilities. *Exceptional Children,* 1967, **33**, 373–384.

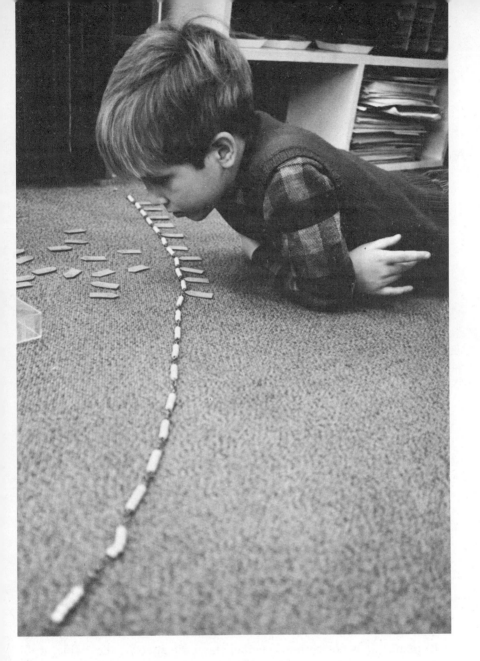

15

Personality Development

Perhaps no concept in psychology is as important or as elusive as personality. Like intelligence, personality might be thought of as a "hypothetical construct." Psychologists observe an individual's behavior and on the basis of their observations draw inferences about his personality. However, too often personality is more than a descriptive concept; it becomes explanatory.

"Susie stays apart from the other third graders because she has an introverted personality." Thus, the child's behavior has been explained by assuming that it reflects her "basic nature" and by attaching a label to it. Further, she can be linked with other children who are introverts. She has been typed, pigeonholed. Her behavior has been elucidated. This, of course, is one of the perils of employing the concept of personality. Inferences are drawn from selected observations of behavior in which attention is focused on only one aspect or characteristic. The notion of personality, however, is really thought to include all aspects of the individual.

To understand this child more fully necessitates rating her on many different bases. It is not enough to consider just her tendency to remain apart from others in a group situation. This neither explains her behavior nor describes her personality. Nor will a summation of her characteristics constitute a portrait of the individual. The interaction among these characteristics, their organization, and the unique manner in which each modifies and alters the others is what truly matters.

For the purposes of this chapter, personality may be defined as the distinct and unique organization of traits in an individual as reflected in how he reacts to himself and others and in how they react to him, and also in how he meets frustrations and conflicts—that is, in how he adjusts to his environment. The chapter is divided into three general areas: first, a reprise of the antecedents of personality; second, an analysis of the self concept and of self-consistency; and third, a treatment of those phases of personality that appear to be of particular significance in development.

Many attempts have been made to describe stages in personality development. It is not certain whether there are specific, inevitable, well-defined stages, but one assumption concerning their existence is worth attention. This assumes that an individual can move on to the next, more mature stage only after having successfully completed the demands of the previous stage or having satisfactorily met its requirements. For understanding the personality development of children, this is invaluable. It also has far-reaching implications for understanding adult behavior and adjustment.

550

Erikson (1950) described the following eight stages in personality development, each with its own distinctive goal normally to be attained in that period.

Infancy:	a basic sense of trust
Early childhood:	a sense of autonomy
Play age:	a sense of initiative
School age:	industry and competence
Adolescence:	personal identity
Young adult:	intimacy
Adulthood:	generativity
Mature age:	integrity and acceptance

The advanced stages of psychological maturity cannot be approached unless the goals of the preceding period have been met successfully. For example, a sense of trust is necessary before a child feels sufficiently secure to strive for autonomy. This is a trust in both the reliability of people and the satisfaction of basic physiological and psychological needs. Security gives freedom. The child who is led to mistrust others and his universe may be wedded forever to a need to seek the security he lacks.

In the normal progression to personality adjustment as a mature adult, an individual may be more vulnerable to certain influences during some periods of his life than during others. For example, some say, as noted earlier, that the effects of maternal deprivation are more severe in the second half of the child's first year. Perhaps in general a child cannot move on to a new and higher phase of personality development until he has achieved a certain amount of personality integration at his current level. Perhaps also the appearance of a more mature phase may be blocked or retarded by the interference of some event with the child's present degree of adjustment. The same principles apply as the child grows. Not just the first year or two of his life but the entire period from infancy through adolescence lays the groundwork for adult personality.

PERSONALITY ANTECEDENTS

In a sense, the entire book to this point could be considered as composed of antecedents of personality: maturation, learning, cultural factors, the home and family setting, including parental and sibling influences, the peer society, and finally, aspects of community. It may be argued, however, that the influences that occur earliest in a child's life tend to have the broadest impact on the individual's personality because they are the first incorporated into it and thus play a part in determining the effects of subsequent experiences.

Because personality is conceived of as the product of interaction between hereditary and environmental factors, let us examine both areas of influence. Since from birth onward, heredity and environment interact, it is impossible even at the age of two to say how much of a child's personality is attributable to one or the other. A child may inherit an irritable temperament from his father, but it is his mother who reacts to it, with resulting consequences for the child's personality.

Innate Predispositional Factors

An infant, as we have noted in Chapter 9, is an active energy system that affects its environment and in turn is affected by it. Flexible and resilient, the infant selects those aspects of the environment to which he responds. Innate characteristics determine both this selectivity and the infant's initial responses to the environment.

Endocrine and Nervous System. Malfunctioning of the endocrine glands produces deviant behavior in only a limited number of individuals. Nevertheless, there is a link between behavior and glandular secretion. An underactive thyroid, for example, causes a low rate of metabolism, resulting in sluggish behavior and lack of endurance. Contrarily, too high a rate of thyroid secretion engenders restlessness and "nervousness."

Hormonal secretion from the gonads, though it can be changed by environmental factors, stems primarily from innate sources. The sex hormones influence a number of behaviors and characteristics. Secondary sex manifestations, such as lower voice pitch, facial hair growth, and growth in musculature appearing in boys at puberty, exert broad influences on personality and adjustment. Further, the rate of sexual maturation, which is largely determined by hereditary forces, bears an important relation to certain personality tendencies at adolescence.

Findings from the California Adolescent Growth Study indicate that the girl who matures early and the boy who matures late both encounter problems of adjustment (Bayley & Tuddenham, 1944). Marked behavioral differences were noted by Jones and Bayley (1950) between boys who matured early and those who matured late. Late maturers persisted in childlike patterns of activity, eager and animated. Their peers considered them restless, talkative, and attention-seeking while viewing early maturers as popular and as having older friends, a sense of humor about themselves, and good appearance. Quite clearly the

rate of maturity relates to several aspects of adolescent personality because of the premium on "maturity" at this age level.   Thus we have
an excellent example of the interplay between innate factors—maturity
level—and environmental factors—social responses based on values and
social expectations—which then affects personality adjustment.   Moreover, while age of reaching puberty is unimportant in itself in adulthood, its effect on adjustment at adolescence may leave long-lasting
consequences.   A longitudinal follow-up of the subjects in the California Adolescent Studies found differences in favor of the early as
compared with the late maturer.   On a standard personality test administered at age 30, early maturers described themselves as able to
make a good impression, as poised, responsible, achieving in conformity
to society's expectations, and as relatively free from neurotic symptoms
(Jones, 1957).   By their late thirties, the late maturers showed ability
to cope with various situations, although their adaptability was accompanied by some fearfulness and vulnerability to threat (Jones, 1965).
Though the late maturer was in a less favorable position at adolescence,
his striving for social acceptance (which the early maturer was readily
accorded) resulted in a certain adaptability and flexibility later.   Thus
the effects of age of maturation may diminish with age but are apparent
even in adulthood; however, the advantages are not wholly on the side
of the early maturer over the long run.

Among infants the differences in the reactive tendencies of their nervous systems influence both their responses to their environments and the
manner in which the significant individuals in their environments
respond to them.   Newborns differ widely in level of activity, irritability,
and general emotional excitability—all of which reflect differences in
nervous systems.   Whether or not these particular characteristics have
long-term consistency in the individual, their influence on the child's
psychological surroundings and, in turn, on his personality at one point
in his development suggests they have some importance.   For example,
Stewart (1953) concluded from her observations of crying behavior in
infants that too much crying tended to generate insecurity in the mother
which, in turn, is transmitted back to the offspring.

There is no doubt that emotionality, the physiological portions of emotional experience, has a base in the autonomic nervous system.   This
is borne out by a study by Gottesman (1960) in which identical twins
resembled one another more than fraternal twins, especially with respect
to sociability versus withdrawal.   It does not mean, however, that differences among adults in emotional behavior are due exclusively to
constitutional factors.   Environmental factors play a tremendous part.
Nevertheless, infants and children differ in th~ functioning of their auto-

nomic nervous system, thus occasioning differences in emotionality and in the responses of adults (see Wenger, 1947; Jones, 1960).

Finally, any trait or characteristic based on the structure and operation of the nervous system is hereditary in origin. Admittedly, research has hardly scratched the surface in detecting relations between behavior and organic structure. But there seems to be enough evidence to conclude, for example, that intelligence has a physiological source in the central nervous system whereas such a trait as selfishness almost certainly has not.

Body Structure and Physical Abilities.   The child's basic physique is primarily a product of heredity. Despite a history of efforts to link type of body to personality and temperament, present evidence indicates only a slight relationship between physical and psychological make-up. Sheldon, the leading protagonist of the body-type theory of personality (Sheldon, Stevens, & Tucker, 1940), devised a scheme for ascertaining the portion of each of three body types in an individual's physique: *endomorphic*—a roundish build weak in bony and muscular development; *mesomorphic*—large bones and muscles with an athletic physique; and *ectomorphic*—long, slender extremities, lacking in muscular development. In addition, three basic types of temperament were described, each associated with one of the body types: with the endomorphic, *viscerotonic*—sociable, relaxed, love of comfort, slow reaction; with the mesomorphic, *somatotonic*—need for activity and action, assertive, courageous, energetic; and with the ectomorphic, *cerebrotonic* —restrained, inhibited, tense, preferring solitude.

The Gluecks found at least twice as many mesomorphic physiques among delinquent boys as among nondelinquents (Glueck & Glueck, 1956). Another investigation observed some differences in IQ test performances of seven-year-old boys grouped into the three categories of body types (Davidson, McInnes, & Parnell, 1957). In addition, more signs of emotional disturbance in the boys were reported by mothers of the ectomorphic group. Support for Sheldon's original contention was obtained in a study of high-school senior boys and a sample of college girls (Cortes & Gatti, 1965). Endomorphs rated themselves significantly more often as kind, relaxed, warm, soft-hearted; mesomorphs as confident, energetic, adventurous, enterprising; and ectomorphs as detached, tense, shy, and reserved. Mesomorphs were found also to demonstrate a higher need for achievement than the other two body types (Cortes & Gatti, 1966).

In an extensive study linking body build and behavior (Walker, 1962), 125 preschool children were rated by their teachers on 64 behavior items. The somatotyping used Sheldon's classification system. With regard to the relations between the behavioral and physique data, many more of the predictions were confirmed for boys than for girls, suggesting that physical factors are more important in affecting the behavior of boys. Certainly our cultural stereotypes and expectations concerning physique and behavior are more firmly established for males (despite the popular concern for female measurements). The meso- morphic body build showed the strongest relationship to the behavioral ratings, especially for boys.

> Characteristic of both boys and girls high in mesomorphy is a dominat- ing assertiveness (leader in play, competitive, self-assertive, easily angered, attacks others, etc.), high energy output, openness of expression, and fearlessness. The girls combine this assertiveness with socialness, cheer- fulness, and warmth. The boys' items give more suggestion of hostility (quarrelsome, revengeful, inconsiderate) and of an impulsive, headlong quality to their activity (daring, noisy, quick, accident prone, self-confi- dent, etc.) (Walker, 1962, p. 78).

Some relationships were evident for the ectomorphic physique:

> In common for both sexes are items suggesting a certain aloofness. . . . For boys, the items in general define a cautious, quiet child, not self- assertive, hesitant to give offense, looking to adults rather than to children for approval, sensitive, slow to recover from upsets. He appears lacking in energy reserves. . . . For girls, the composite picture is similar but tends more to indicate a somberness of outlook—unfriendly, tense, not gay or cheerful, irritable (p. 78).

Some additional support for the relation between personality and body type was obtained from mothers' ratings of these same children (Walker, 1963).

Digman (1963) demonstrated that excitability and "outgoingness" were related only minimally to parent attitudes, whereas other traits, such as empathy, and clusters of traits, such as meeting cultural de- mands, were closely related to them. Possibly excitability and out- goingness result more from genetic factors—perhaps body type—than from strictly social forces.

Some physiques more than others permit an individual to perform certain motor and physical behaviors successfully. Competence in the motor area is an important attribute in childhood, especially among boys (see Hardy, 1937; Sanford et al., 1943). The competence of the mesomorph wins favorable reaction from the group. This leads him to solicit further approval in the particular area of activity; thus, an assertiveness induced by social considerations may emanate from the self-confidence he develops. Similarly, a child who is unsuccessful in the motor area will seek rewarding experience elsewhere. Success in the classroom may compensate for failure on the playground.

A second and related factor is social expectation. The stereotypes of the jolly, plump individual, the thin bookworm, and the aggressive mesomorph may not be scientifically derived, but they establish certain expectations of behavior for children of these body types. For example, a father is less likely to spur an ectomorphic son than a mesomorphic son to athletic prowess. These cultural stereotypes are adopted early by children. Boys as young as six to 10 years of age agree closely in assigning personality traits to body types (Staffieri, 1967). All the behavior adjectives assigned to the mesomorph (which was the preferred body build) were positive, while those assigned to the ectomorph were unfavorable and of a generally socially submissive nature.

Attractive appearance has been seen to have some relation to popularity among children (Tryon, 1939; Hardy, 1937). Although popularity may be a result rather than a cause of an individual's personality, the extent to which a child is accepted by his peers, as noted in Chapter 11, exerts some influence on his self-acceptance. This, in turn, affects his subsequent personality development.

Intelligence. To consider intelligence as an innate predispositional factor is not to imply that intellectual functioning is entirely inherited. Indeed, it is an excellent example of the continual interaction of hereditary and environmental factors. Yet it is probable that heredity, by determining an individual's central nervous structure, imposes limits within which environmental influences work.

It is not easy to determine the precise role of intelligence in the development of personality. Despite the conclusion from a survey of 200 studies that no uniform relation exists between intelligence and emotional and personality traits (Lorge, 1940), there is evidence that shows a tie between intelligence and adjustment. Anderson (1960), in studying prediction of adjustment over a seven-year span, found IQ to be a significant prognosticator of adjustment and concluded: "Our results can be interpreted either as showing how difficult it is to separate out an intelligence factor from the complex of personality characteristics with which we are dealing when we talk about adjustment, or as indicating how important intelligence is in the adjustive process" (p. 64). Through factor analysis of various personality ratings and measures of analysis, Cattell (1945) has shown intelligence to correlate highly with self-control, reliability, industriousness, emotional independence, conscientiousness, and perseverance—all of which are traits of character.

Intelligence was less closely associated, however, with basic emotional integration and adjustment.

Several explanations account for the relation of intelligence to adjustment in American society. First, brighter children have brighter parents who handle the emotional problems of childhood more wisely, thus establishing a sounder psychological foundation in childhood. Second, brighter children perceive social expectation more accurately and conform accordingly. Their behavior is rewarded, which leads to good adjustment to the demands made of them. Third, brighter children are more resourceful in meeting social expectations and demands; therefore, they are more likely to be successful. Fourth, a moderate relation exists between intelligence and ingenuity, curiosity, and creativity, traits that abet popularity and adjustment in peer society. Fifth, a closer relation between intelligence and adjustment may be postulated for middle-class than for lower-class children because of middle-class emphasis on academic achievement and educational progress.

Just as intelligence exerts a broad and complex influence on personality development, aspects of personality affect intellectual functioning. In a longitudinal study of mental growth and personality development, children who gained or lost in IQ during elementary-school years were seen to differ significantly in the following personality traits: independence, aggressiveness, self-initiative, problem solving, anticipation, and competitiveness (Sontag, Baker, & Nelson, 1958). And in Terman and Oden's 20-year follow-up (1947) of a group of highly gifted children, comparisons were made between successful and unsuccessful male adults, the measure for success being the extent to which an individual has made use of his superior intellectual ability. The successful received higher ratings on perseverance, self-confidence, integration toward goals, and absence of inferiority feelings, leading to the conclusion that the two groups differed markedly in achievement drive and all-around social adjustment.

To be sure, the interaction between intellect and personality is complex, and a great variance in personality adjustment exists at all levels of intelligence. Certain problems of emotional adjustment are more frequent at the lower intellectual levels, yet highly endowed individuals are not entirely immune from personality difficulties. Thus it is apparent that even if there is no clear-cut tie between aspects of intellect and personality, intelligence does influence an individual's interactions with other people; it also affects adjustment to the demands of the environment.

Environmental Factors

What a child brings to a situation helps to shape the responses of others to him in the situation. This, in turn, determines how he will approach future situations. Let us deal here, then, with the social influences that bear on personality development. These include social expectations for child behavior as well as some cultural differences in expectations for behavior and personality. First, we should mention several nonpsychological factors that have some potential psychological bearing.

Organic Factors. Anything that affects the individual's willingness or ability to respond to his environment is certain to influence his view of himself and his interaction with others. For example, vitamin deficiencies may be reflected in such psychological symptoms as depression and irritability. More important perhaps is the lowered vitality of a child suffering from general nutritional deficiency. Illness, injury, and physical handicap undoubtedly impede the child's personality development. Yet research that has sought to find the precise impact of these factors on personality development is largely inconclusive.

To begin with, information concerning the child's personality development prior to illness or injury is seldom available. This limits the extent to which certain aspects of a child's personality may be attributed to them. The use of a control group, of course, would be advantageous, but it is difficult to obtain an adequate one suitably matched with the experimental group. Furthermore, present instruments for assessing personality are largely inadequate in this area of research. The children on whom personality measures were standardized are not comparable with, say, children with physical handicaps. Comparisons are therefore inappropriate. Similar responses by a healthy and a handicapped child on a personality inventory may have entirely different meanings for the two.

Prolonged illness reduces the child's contact with the environment and his interaction, which results in decreased stimulation. Coupled with increased bodily concern, this induces the child to withdraw his interest from the world about him and focus it upon himself. Egocentricity, selfishness, and undue concern with himself follow. Because illness handicaps, feelings of helplessness and dependency are born. These, together with parental resentment, rejection, overconcern, or overprotection, may have long-range effects on the child. Beverly (1936) found, for example, that an overwhelming majority of hospitalized children whom she interviewed answered the question, "Why do children get sick?" with the assertion, "Because they are bad." Indeed such an attitude can pervade the child's concept of himself and his sense of self-worth.

In discussions of the effect of physical injury or handicap on personality the notion of *body image* has often been invoked. An infant gradually becomes aware of his physical self through a variety of physical sensations. At first the distinction between *me* and *not me* is not a sharp one. Then experience furnishes countless clues that assist in the process of self-differentiation. Later, psychological attitudes toward the physical self develop out of the child's social interaction with others so that ultimately the most significant aspects of one's body image are those psychological attitudes that involve evaluation and consequent acceptance or rejection.

Because of the circular nature of an individual's attitude toward himself and the attitude of others toward him, there is not necessarily a close correspondence between the objective aspects of one's physical composition and the psychological attitudes associated with it. In any case, the image of one's physical self becomes increasingly consistent throughout childhood. For this reason any alteration in one's body requires some adjustments in body image. Perhaps one of the most difficult and yet most imperative adjustments is acceptance of the changed physical condition. This requires acknowledgment of dependency on others when physically handicapped and recognition of the fact that participation and achievement in some areas of life are impossible (Mussen & Newman, 1958). Realization of this avoids needless frustration.

Acceptance. Too frequently physical handicap engenders resentment and frustration in the child. Deviation from normality, especially if it restricts and curtails the child's active participation with his peers, can affect personality development. So can parental nonacceptance of the child and his handicap, which is particularly damaging to the child's sense of self-worth. The underlying psychological mechanism of this nonacceptance is complicated. Parents blame themselves for abnormality in their offspring. This was the case, for example, with mothers of children with cleft palate (Tisza, Selverstone, Rosenblum, & Hanlon, 1958). Actually, any condition in the child that adds to child-care responsibilities often irks the parent. This irksomeness is bound to affect the parent's attitude toward the child. The point is that parental acceptance or rejection, as we have seen in Chapter 10, influences the child's attitude toward himself, which is a significant factor in personality development.

Similarly, peer acceptance is an important element in self-acceptance, though it is not always clear which causes which. Perhaps the child's lower self-acceptance may generate hostility and resentment that reduce his acceptance by his peers. Sociometric studies have shown that children with speech defects are chosen less often than children without them when play and friendship are the bases for selection (Woods & Carrow, 1959), and that children with defective hearing are not as acceptable among peers as those whose hearing is normal (Elser, 1959).

Case studies spotlight strong differences in the degree to which physical handicaps become psychological burdens among children. What causes these differences? The major factor is doubtless the parent's attitude toward the child—the extent to which they accept him prior to and then with a handicap. Though bodily injury or physical handicap may exacerbate and complicate a previously hostile, nonaccepting parent-child relationship, it is doubtful whether a real acceptance of the child for his own sake would be substantially altered by such an occurence. One five-year-old, severely afflicted with cerebral palsy, was light-hearted, gay, and full of mischief. With much effort and exertion he would manage to propel himself up the ladder of a slide and then slide down, screaming with delight, to land at the bottom, arms and legs twisted appallingly. Every day at 5:30 his father came to fetch him at the day care nursery center, engulf the child in his arms, and wipe away the boy's uncontrolled saliva as the youngster jabbered on about the day's events. He would never watch his son hit a home run or score a touchdown, but, because of his acceptance of the boy, he would be able to see him grow and develop into a fine, worthwhile young man.

Sociocultural Factors

The differences among cultures are so strong and pervasive that *modal* personality types are often noted by anthropologists. They use the adjective *modal* to signify "common" or "fashionable" as in a la mode. This modal type may be essentially paranoid and suspicious, as among the Dobuans studied by Fortune (1932), or open and guileless, as were some of the Dobuans' neighbors studied by Malinowski (1922). It has been suggested that there is a modal American personality, which is changing largely as a result of technological, educational, and economic development within the culture. The specific behavioral pattern of an individual, based on his unique biological composition and social experience, takes form within the range of behaviors deemed acceptable by the culture.

Behavior and personality vary among individuals within a culture. Some of this variance results from social class, occupation, racial background, and place of residence. These broad sociological variables, as previously noted, have considerable bearing in the creation of individual differences in personality and behavior. Also contributing to the shaping of an individual's web of responses are various aspects in the family setting.

The biological forces on one side and the social forces on the other fix the limits within which parents and others in intimate association with the child may mold character and personality. Parental personality, attitudes, and behavior all influence the developing child. The development of dependence or independence, of activity level, and of ability to resist stress result, in part, from the child's interaction with his parents.

THE SELF CONCEPT

The term *self concept* has many definitions, sometimes conflicting. For the purpose of this discussion, we shall call the self concept an individual's attitude toward his physical self and his own behavior. In recent perusals of literature concerning the self concept (e.g., Hall & Lindzey, 1957; Wylie, 1961; Shlien, 1962), investigators have hit upon two bases for it: the social roles and attempts to synthesize them; and the body image, "the body as a psychological experience . . . the individual's feelings and attitudes toward his own body" (Fisher & Cleveland, 1958, p. x). In the pages that follow we shall dwell on these two aspects of the self and then turn to the relation of the self concept to behavior.

Role Theory

"All the world's a stage, and every man's a player." Centuries after Shakespeare, the scientific study of roles and the use of role theory as an explanatory device had its beginnings in the work of such sociologists as Durkheim and Tonnies. Their thoughts were first elucidated clearly by Cooley (1902), to be further developed in the social psychology of George H. Mead. Mead did not publish his ideas himself; after his death, his lecture notes were edited by his students (see Strauss, 1956).

Cooley originated the notion of the social or "looking glass" self. To him, man's ideas about himself were reflections of how others saw him. Mead divided personality structure into the *I* and the *me*. The *I* was the part of the self that was partly—perhaps largely—genetic in origin, the continuing part of personality present in every special situation. The *me* was basically social, a reflection of society's demands. Each individual was made up of many *me's*, as many as he had distinct social roles. The expectations and demands of all social groups of significance to the individual influenced his behavior at all times, but their relative influences shifted with the behavioral situation and the roles it required.

The *me* that is in the forefront at any time depends on the composition of the group toward which an individual's behavior is directed. For example, a boy in a Little League game has his teammates as his main *reference group*. They provide him with the most accurate information about how he is playing his particular role as baseball player. The Little League loses its power as a reference group as the boy's role changes to son, brother, or pupil, while other groups such as family, teachers, or classmates gain in influence.

Whiting (1960) suggests that we most adequately learn and portray the roles of people whom we envy or admire—often those people, usually our parents, who control the resources in the environment when we are children. It appears that Whiting's position may explain some types of role learning, such as "like father, like son," but does not adequately explain the learning of other, maladaptive roles, such as "stutterer" or "delinquent." Role assignment has much to do with personality. This has been clearly shown at many points throughout this book; individuals have a strong disposition to perform the roles assigned to them, even when the roles are damaging to self-esteem, as in the case of the stutterer, or to adjustment. As noted in Chapter 8, one major problem of members of minority groups is that, having been assigned roles as inferiors, they often accept such roles and attempt to live up to them.

A wide range of social and biological factors, as well as chance, enters into the roles assigned to an individual. Once he has had his roles assigned, however, the individual tends to respond in terms of these roles. This makes for regular, consistent behavior, as long as the roles are clearly defined and do not clash too sharply. Across those situations the *I* aspect of personality persists. And a good thing, too! One can see that the individual whose behavior is determined only by the demands of the social group would be the ultimate of the other-directed person, with no core of personal integrity. To use Freudian terms, this type of person would have an "externalized superego": a conscience dependent only on the values of the group to which he belongs at the time.

The roles assigned to an individual determine a fair portion of his behavior; when roles are central and significant and yet conflict directly with one another, there is behavioral disturbance. *Romeo and Juliet* is a classic example of role conflict in which romantic love and family honor collide; it is of little significance today, since family honor means less now than it did to individuals in Shakespeare's day—and perhaps the same is true of romantic love. *Crime and Punishment* is more pertinent to us because Raskolnikov's conflict between conventional upper-middle-class values and those of the poverty-stricken, amoral student world is more immediate in contemporary life.   The classic primary-group tragedy involving a clash of central roles still exists, and along with it in contemporary industrial society goes the problem of nonexistent roles and a loss of personal identity.   The breakdown occurring as a result of ambiguous role definitions has been well described by Dunham (1959) and forms the basis of most contemporary literature. Kafka's heroes, on trial for some unnamed crime, or changing overnight into a gigantic cockroach, are the ancestors of Beckett's and Sartre's existential men—individuals without a governing set of roles and values. Whereas having clear and conflicting roles is one basis for tragedy, the tragic nature and emptiness of a life in which one has no roles to play is doubtless greater.

The Body Image

Awareness of the physical self and its separation from the nonself comes about, in part, from body movements, internal changes such as hunger, and such things as laryngeal activity in which the infant feels movement simultaneously with hearing sound (Schilder, 1935).   It also comes from observing the effects of one's behavior on the external world (Piaget, 1954).

Degree of awareness of one's own body appears to be related to sex, with males being more aware of certain aspects of the physical self, and making greater use of such things as body orientation to structure the environment (Witkin, Dyke, Faterson, Goodenough, and Karp, 1962).

Generally the body image is assumed to be closely tied to physical reality; distortions in it relate to psychological disturbance.   In the following case a distorted body image seemed to be the source of some otherwise inexplicable behavior.

Rudy was a man in his early twenties.   He was 5′ 4″ tall and weighed about 135 pounds, and had an athletic body build.   He did not seek trouble to any noticeable extent, but certainly did nothing to avoid it. He had had his nose broken twice and his upper front teeth knocked out in fist fights with fellows who outweighed him by about 100 pounds. These fights could have been avoided without "losing face."   The writer wondered why Rudy did not do so, and why he continued to get into difficulties of this sort, until one day the writer noticed something.   Rudy always stooped when he went through a doorway.   Watching Rudy maneuver about made one fact obvious.   Rudy thought he was 7′ tall, and no number of losses made him the least concerned over someone a mere 6′ 2″. Occasionally distortion of body image can be discerned in an individual and explain behavior that appears highly unreasonable and illogical. Hence, body image exists—though not tied as closely to the physical self as is widely assumed.

Attempts to assess body image in a scientific manner and to predict behavior from it have not always been successful. Frequently, individuals are requested to draw a human figure; it is assumed that they will project into the drawing their own ideas about their physical selves. These drawings are then interpreted. If, for example, the individual draws his figure with hands concealed behind the back, he is believed to disclose a feeling of impotence, of inability to deal with problems. Perhaps the individual feels impotent only in the fine art of drawing hands! Very few individuals represent their own bodies when instructed to draw a person, suggested Swensen (1957). Even when they do, the interpretations of their drawings seem largely based on conjecture (Levy, 1950).

Other approaches to the measurement of the body image have been used less frequently, but have proved more useful. Fisher and Cleveland (see Fisher, 1958) were concerned with measuring the boundaries of the body exterior (does the individual view his body self as merging into the environment surrounding the body self, or as rigidly separated from the nonself?) through the analysis of Rorschach (see p. 532) responses. They hypothesized that persons whose psychosomatic symptoms involved the body interior (ulcers, etc.) would perceive their bodies merging with the environment and as being easily penetrated, while those whose symptoms involved a body exterior (skin disorders, etc.) would conceive of their bodies as surrounded by a rigid protective barrier that would "protect them from the world." Their data strongly supported their beliefs. In another approach to the measurement of the body image, Secord and Jourard (1953) developed a test aimed at measuring satisfaction with the physical self. Secord (1953) also developed a measure of concern for the physical self. He used homonyms —words such as *mole, trunk,* and *graft,* which have two or more meanings, one of which associates the word with a body part or function. The number of times that the body meaning is used in defining homonyms is an index of concern for one's own body. From the Secord and Jourard measures we can obtain some knowledge of the individual's interest in and attitude toward the physical self that does allow us to make predictions about such things as reactions to mutilation of the body, as in operations (Shaub, 1967). Further, these measures have been used to demonstrate that individual's valuation of the body and of the self tend to be commensurate (Secord, 1953). The Secord and Jourard measures seem to be the best presently available measures of the body image that can be scored objectively. Results obtained from studies in which these scales have been used generally support the belief that the body image is an important determinant of behavior.

One further point on body image. If body image determines behavior, and especially the self concept, which promotes consistency in behavior, then the behavior of individuals should become more variable as the physical self changes more rapidly. This is what happens in adolescence; rapid shifts in children's behavior often baffle parents. And, of course, data cited earlier on the relation of physical maturity to social adjustment are themselves suggestive of the impact on adjustment of the physical self and one's attitudes toward it.

The Self Concept and Adjustment

To many who are interested in psychotherapy (see, e.g., Rogers, 1951; Shlien, 1961), the self concept plays a vital role in adjustment. They say that the fundamental problem of the neurotic is that he is self-rejecting. The objective of their therapy is to cause him to come to terms with himself and adjust his behavior and perception of himself to the point at which he is able to accept himself. Raimy (1948) demonstrated that successful cases in psychotherapy enabled patients to acquire a more favorable view of themselves, whereas unsuccessful cases did not.

The overwhelming evidence from Wylie's (1961) review of the literature on the self suggested that self-acceptance was related to adjustment. A high regard of the self generally meant a high level of adjustment, except in a few cases where high self-esteem worked as adversely as self-rejection. In general, moreover, those individuals who were self-accepting were seen to be accepting of others (e.g., Wylie, 1957). What this means, of course, is that the individual who can accept himself can withstand aggression and disparagement from others; his personal psychological security grants him an objective view of the behavior of others and an understanding of the bases for their behavior. Such an individual can also sustain adversity better than a self-rejecting person. He can return aggression directly toward others, if necessary. He therefore need not develop neurotic defenses or take out his hostility on innocent victims.

Quite obviously it would be to the benefit of the culture to raise children who are self-accepting. From McCurdy's (1957) work on extremely creative individuals as well as from the researches of those directly concerned with the self concept (Maris, 1958), it would appear that individuals who are regarded highly by their parents, who are aware of this regard, and who enjoy a great deal of parental contact are most accepting of themselves. They are best able to face the possible rejection stemming from their own creative efforts that are considered deviant from the majority standpoint, and are presumably more accepting of others.

Consistency and the Self Concept

Personality presupposes consistency. Without consistent patterns of response, behavior would be chaotic and unpredictable. Since personality refers to persisting, continuing, predictable, social aspects of the self, there can be no personality without consistency.

There are many reasons to expect consistency. Man remains the same biological entity throughout life, and many determinants of personality, as we know, are biological in character. To the degree that man's biological composition does not change over a lifetime, consistency may be expected. No matter what else may change in the course of development, humans carry around the same physical self, and with it, their own responses and the responses of others to it.

Consistency would also be expected from what is known of the incorporation of social roles into the concept of the self as well as from what is known about identification. Role assignment is sufficient cause to play a social role. The performance of a role leads to increased expectancy on the part of others that the performer will not relinquish it. These firmer and more explicit expectancies impel one to act even more consistently in harmony with them. Since roles even in childhood have some constancy and with age become more constant as well as invariable and sharply defined, *some* consistency is foreseen at all ages, more in later than in earlier years.

A recent psychological theory, Festinger's *theory of cognitive dissonance* (1957), is based on the notion that humans fundamentally need to maintain consonance or consistency among various aspects of the self, and between the self and the outside world. These are some examples of dissonance: an individual believes that his children deserve the best possible education. He regards federal aid to education as creeping socialism. The school district, which operates on a skimpy tax base, cannot finance an adequate school system. There is a dissonance between two sets of social attitudes; if the individual has enough ability he will recognize the dissonance in himself and attempt to resolve it. The dissonance may occur between two aspects of the self, as in the foregoing illustration, or it may arise between behavior and belief. This is exemplified in the parent who believes that his children should make their own decisions, yet refuses to allow them to do so because errors may entail grave consequences.

There is evidence that the need for consonance, consistency, or the synthesis of conflicting values increases with age, and among children is also associated with IQ (Gollin, 1958). This need for self-consistency plays a major part in achieving consistent behavior. Yet if people were completely consistent, life would be extremely dull, and change, as in psychotherapy, would be difficult if not impossible to achieve. To what degree, then, are humans consistent?

Trait Consistency. At one time psychologists studied types, such as introvert versus extrovert. But as research findings failed to support predictions based on type psychology, many personality theorists abandoned types and turned to traits. Admitting that type psychology had not worked out, these theorists assumed that personality was composed of a set of consistent, continuing traits. This assumption was soon subjected to experimental test, and this test, the Hartshorne and May (1928; Hartshorne, May, & Shuttleworth, 1930) study of honesty, had a profound effect on psychology.

The objective of Hartshorne and May was simple: to find out if there were a general and consistent trait of honesty. If there were, individuals should be consistently honest from one situation to the next. Those who lied should also cheat and steal whereas those who were honest in one instance should also be honest in the other two. Testing a large number of schoolchildren in a wide selection of real-life situations involving cheating, stealing, or lying, they interpreted their findings as indicating only a very minor zone of common response to all three areas of honesty. Nor could they predict behavior in one situation from knowledge of the individual's behavior in other situations similarly involving honesty. Their results indicated there was no general trait of honesty. This meant presumably that any assumption of trait consistency was unwarranted and argued against a notion of human consistency altogether. If correct and applicable to broader situations, the Hartshorne and May conclusions would lead to the belief that the study of personality should be abandoned. Actually, this general hypothesis, based on their data, gave the Hartshorne and May study great significance, for it led to a series of investigations and critiques of trait consistency.

From a brief but general interview, MacKinnon (1938) predicted whether college students would be honest on tests modeled after those used by Hartshorne and May. His predictions were more accurate than would be expected by chance; this pointed to a general trait of honesty whose existence was rather easily discernible. Furthermore, he had much greater success in predicting honesty than dishonesty. His dishonest subjects fell into two groups: one that appeared basically honest but yielded to temptation and a second that was generally dishonest. For *most* of these individuals, honesty or dishonesty seemed to be the result of a general and consistent trait; for some, their behavior seemed largely determined by the stimulus of the moment. In general, MacKinnon's findings and conclusions appeared to contradict those of Hartshorne and May, perhaps because he used a brighter and older group of subjects, and individual consistency apparently increases with age and IQ (Hartshorne, May, & Shuttleworth, 1930).

Yet even the Hartshorne and May data, though interpreted as showing inconsistency, really represented a substantial degree of consistency. Burton (1963) analyzed the same data and concluded that they disclosed the existence of a moderately general and consistent trait. Other studies (Grinder & McMichael, 1963; Johnson, Ackerman, Frank, & Fionda, 1968), also indicate that honesty is sufficiently consistent as a trait for one to predict children's responses on measures of different aspects of conscience development and to anticipate behavior from paper-and-pencil tests.

But investigations of consistency in traits have not been limited to honesty. Murphy (1937) found consistency in sympathetic responses to others among three-year-olds though not among two-year-olds. Kagan and Moss (1960) reported on the stability of passive and dependent behavior in childhood and adulthood. Part of a longitudinal study to which we shall return presently, their findings supported the notion that much trait consistency existed among different behavioral situations at any time in an individual's life history. They obtained reliable measures of subtle aspects of personality even at preschool ages—and reliability implies consistency. How much consistency will be found depends on the effectiveness of the measuring device, the characteristics of the individuals measured (older and abler persons show greater consistency), and probably on the complexity of the social forces bearing on the trait in question.

Consistency over Time. To what extent does the individual remain consistent and how much does he change in time? One of the first studies of this question was conducted by Bühler and her students (reported in Murphy, Murphy, & Newcomb, 1937). They divided infants into four types: those easily stimulated by both pleasant and unpleasant stimuli; those easily stimulated by pleasant but not by unpleasant stimuli; those easily stimulated by unpleasant but not by pleasant stimuli; and those not easily stimulated by either. The results of the study suggested that most children remained in the same category, at least up through middle childhood.

Cited often among studies of consistency and change is Neilon's (1948). After a 15-year interval, she followed up the individuals who had been studied by Shirley (1933; see also Chapter 1) from birth to the age of two. Shirley's personality sketches of the 13 male and six female infants were published with pseudonyms; although Neilon and her associates knew the names of the children who had participated in the original study, they did not know which child was represented in each of Shirley's published biographies. Neilon collected rather full autobiographical sketches of 15 of the original 19 children at the age of 17—10 boys and 5 girls. She then requested a panel of judges —faculty members and graduate students—to match the 6 infant sketches with the 5 adolescent sketches of girls and the 13 infant sketches with the 10 adolescent sketches of boys. Ten judges matched the girls, five the boys. Shirley's original data were then consulted to find out the real names of the children associated with each infant sketch so that the accuracy of the matching could be seen. The judges succeeded in matching the girls to an extent that could be obtained by chance less than once in a million times; with the boys, a somewhat more difficult task, they were correct to an extent that could occur by chance only once in 4000 tries. Although considerable individual difference existed among individual children, one girl being matched correctly by all 10 judges and another by none, it was evident that there was much consistency in personality over a period of time; accurate matching occurred much more often than would be expected by chance.

Several subsequent studies have corroborated the idea that an individual's personality is usually consistent over time. These include Stott's (1957) study of a stability of ascendance and submission in children, in which he found that 82 per cent of a group of 106 youngsters disclosed a consistent pattern in this area from nursery school into adolescence. Escalona and Heider (1959) predicted behavior at the age of five from observation of infants in the first year of life. At five, they found their predictions correct much oftener than by chance but saw that prediction was more accurate in some areas, such as motor skill and sex-role interests, than in others, such as shyness and striving for achievement. Tuddenham (1958), following up individuals studied as adolescents 19 years earlier, observed a significant stability in more than one-third of the traits studied, despite the low reliability of ratings in adolescence and adulthood. The stablest trait for men was aggressive motivation, with a correlation of $+.91$ between ratings; for women, it was a desire for social prestige, with a correlation of $+.81$. In another longitudinal study, Martin (1964) demonstrated that children, in general, show a high degree of stability over time in amount and type of social behavior.

The most extensive recent study of consistency over time was undertaken by Kagan and Moss (1960, 1962) who analyzed the Fels longitudinal data (see Chapter 10). In general, they found that consistency was greater up to the age of 10 than thereafter. It seemed likely, as noted in reference to Burks' study of a single pair of identical twins (see Chapter 2), that a person could be "more himself" at later ages when parental pressures played less of a role in shaping behavior. Perhaps the lessening relationship between earlier and later personality, on the one hand, and between adolescent and adult behavior, on the other, stemmed in part from the greater independence from parental influences in later years. Even with this qualification, correlations between childhood and adulthood were generally substantial. Where the correlations were minimal, the shifts in societal pressures seemed most accountable. For example, dependent behavior in females was permissible throughout life, whereas extreme pressures were imposed on males from adolescence onward to become independent, hence the high correlation in female and low correlation in male dependency between childhood and adulthood. The reverse is true of aggression.

PRINCIPAL COMPONENTS OF PERSONALITY IN CHILDREN

Personality seems to gain complexity and consistency as the years pass. It grows more complex because the number and range of its antecedents increase, producing more intricate interactions. It increases in consistency because, as physical growth terminates, the body image becomes stable and roles played become clearer, more consonant with one another, and more tightly incorporated into the self concept.

Considerable research has been amassed on particular components of personality that seem to be central in the personality fabric of childhood, yet relatively independent of one another. These are dependence-independence, aggression, anxiety, conscience development, dominance-submission, and social acceptability. We propose to explore each in some detail, with emphasis on their antecedents.

Dependence-Independence

Dependency is the condition of the human infant. The infant is *instrumentally* dependent on his mother. Because he associates her with the satisfaction of his basic biological needs, the infant also develops a rewarding *emotional* dependence on her (Heathers, 1955b). How then does independent behavior develop? It comes about through maturation and learning. The young child grows increasingly capable of functioning independently.

Moreover, independent behavior is in itself rewarding to the child because of the satisfaction gained from exploring and manipulating the environment and from interacting with peers. Normally, therefore, there is an increase in independent behavior with age (Steth & Conner, 1962). In nursery school, children exhibit less behavior reflecting infantile reliance on adults and a shift toward a more active, assertive dependence on peers (Heathers, 1955a). However, emotional or psychological independence does not invariably accompany physical or instrumental independence. Further, some children manifest greater independence of behavior than others.

A Cultural Phenomenon. The concern of American psychologists over dependence versus independence reflects the importance attached by society to the development of independent behavior. The individual who is able to operate as an independent agent is regarded as a mature adult. However, anthropologists have shown that American emphasis on early independent training is not shared by all other cultures. Take this illustration, for example, of the attitude and behavior of parents in a New Guinea tribe.

> When the child begins to walk the quiet continuous rhythm of its life changes somewhat. It is now becoming a little heavy for the mother to carry about with her on long trips to the garden, and furthermore it can be expected to live without suckling for an hour or so. The mother leaves the child in the village with the father, or with some other relative, while she goes to the garden or for firewood. . . . As the child grows older, it is no longer confined so closely to the care of its own parents. Children are lent about. An aunt comes to visit and takes home the four-year-old for a week's stay, handing him on to some other relative for eventual return to his parents. This means that a child learns to think of the world as filled with parents, not merely a place in which all of his safety and happiness depend upon the continuance of his relationship to his own particular parents. . . . There is no insistence at all upon children's growing up rapidly, or acquiring special skills or proficiencies, and there is a corresponding lack of techniques for training

them physically. . . . The result is that the child grows up with a sense of emotional security in the care of others, not in its own control over the environment (quoted in Whiting & Child, 1953, from Mead, 1935).

Similarly, a study of child-rearing practices in Puerto Rico (Landy, 1959) found little parental encouragement of independent behavior in the young child. Children are not given regular tasks to perform and little is expected of them. This stems partly from the culture's view of the child: *sin capacidad*—without capacity.

Symptoms and Causes. What are the earmarks of dependent behavior? Of independent behavior? To Beller (1955) the following behaviors were signs of dependency: seeking help, seeking physical contact, seeking proximity, seeking attention, and seeking recognition. These were the behaviors denoting independence: taking initiative, trying to overcome obstacles in the environment, trying to carry activities to completion, getting satisfaction from work, and trying to do routine tasks by oneself. By and large, dependent behavior is characterized by reliance on someone else for assistance and assurance. A child is said to be dependent when he manifests behavior that, at his age level, should have been superseded by independent behavior. The six-year-old who does not dress himself alone, the four-year-old who does not feed himself, the five-year-old who does not play with his peers unattended by his mother all exhibit dependency.

Why does dependent behavior persist? No single explanation accounts either for dependence in children in general or its occurrence in any one child. All explanations, interestingly enough, have focused on various aspects of the parent-child relationship. An early study (Heathers, 1953) concluded that dependent behavior resulted from maternal overconcern; the mother was not only permissive about dependency behavior but also encouraged it. This view was reached by identifying independent and dependent behavior in children and then applying Fels ratings to the psychological atmosphere of their homes. The homes of the dependent youngsters rated higher on child-centered and babying counts. Others (Gavalas & Briggs, 1966) have argued that the extent to which dependency persists in a child is a function of the degree to which parents reward dependent behavior and fail to reward competent (achievement-oriented) behavior.

Widely held at the present time is the view that dependency increases and is intensified when the parent does not adequately meet the dependency needs of the child. Frustrated through lack of parental warmth, nurture, and affection, the child cannot proceed to greater emotional independence. This notion has supporting evidence, even though the results of various studies are not in full agreement. In an experimental study with preschool children, an increase in imitative behavior was noted in children who exhibited greater dependency behavior after an adult withdrew of nurturance and attention (Stein & Wright, 1964). This suggests that one reason for children's imitation of adults is to relieve dependency anxiety; incorporation of the adult behavior provides some measure of security. This interpretation is supported in a study showing strong similarity in values between mothers and sons when the mother trains the child early in independence (Rosen, 1964). Presumably, the early independence training arouses anxiety in the boy that is reduced by internalizing the mother's expectations and values.

In an extensive study of the antecedents of dependency and aggression (Sears, Whiting, Nowlis, & Sears, 1953), the amount of dependent behavior in nursery-school children correlated positively with the severity of their weaning in infancy. However, no such relation was found with respect to toilet training. And even the weaning finding was not supported by data obtained in the Pattern Study (Sears, Maccoby, & Levin, 1957). Conceivably the extent of the frustration of a child's early dependency needs is not adequately assessed through the mother's feeding and toilet-training practices.

Some Conclusions about Dependency Antecedents. To begin with, there is probably a curvilinear relationship within the normal range of dependency behavior between how parents meet or frustrate a child's early dependency needs and the persistence of such needs in the child. If the parent strongly rewards dependent behavior and takes a permissive attitude toward it, preventing or discouraging independence, dependency persists. Similarly, frustration of the infant's needs for dependence might intensify the yearning for dependency. The Pattern Study, for example, found dependency increased in children whose mothers punished them for such behavior; the same thing applied to children of homes where rejection was evident and withdrawal of love was used as a disciplinary technique. Parental conflict and rejection of the child were prominent in the family backgrounds of extremely dependent boys (McCord, McCord, & Verden, 1962). Low parental esteem for one another and for the child pervaded their homes. From this point of view dependent behavior was a manifestation of feelings of insecurity in the parent-child relationship. Gewirtz (1956) noted a high frequency of attention seeking in children when the adult was relatively unavailable. Thus dependence on adults appeared to increase when the children perceived them as psychologically distant.

Finally, the curvilinear relation between dependency and the extent of frustration by the parent may actually hold for only the broad normal range. If parents or parent-substitutes show a nearly complete absence of nurture, or if parental rejection exists to a pathological degree, the child may develop an intense independence. This is dramatically illustrated by six German-Jewish orphaned refugee children who spent the first two or three years of their lives in a concentration camp. The children had been reared together with a minimum of adult nurture. When transferred to a rehabilitation center, they were excessively distrustful and wary of adults. Their hostility toward adults was replaced by positive feelings only after a long period of time (Freud & Dann, 1951).

Among a group of aggressive adolescent boys, Bandura and Walters (1959) found their fathers to have been rejecting and to have punished early dependent behavior after the affection of their mothers had established a motive for dependency. Thus anxiety over dependency developed. The aggressive behavior, Bandura and Walters reasoned, was born in the early frustration of their dependency needs. Treatment of this antisocial behavior was hampered by the boys' suspicion and fearfulness of establishing a dependency relationship in therapy.

Although the socialization process is characterized ordinarily by increasing independence in the child, certain parental attitudes impede this development. Stendler (1952) maintained that there are critical periods during the early years when overdependency may result. The first of these occurs toward the end of the first year of life when the child becomes aware of his dependence on his mother. Recognizing her importance, the child tests her to see if he can really depend on her. Separation at this time might produce a child low in ego strength and toleration of frustration. The second critical period appears between the ages of two and three. At this time the pressure of the culture for independent behavior increases on the child. Disturbances in his relation of dependency with his mother during this period might touch off attempts to cope with the resulting anxiety by developing an extremely strong conscience. To support this notion of a critical period, Stendler (1954) showed that a larger number of discontinuities in personality adjustment turned up in dependent children than in others. Moreover, her data corroborated those of Bandura and Walters in noting the importance of paternal influence in the learning of dependency.

Two further considerations merit brief attention. First, because independence grows out of dependence, the two must not be considered distinct from each other. Several studies (Beller, 1955; Heathers, 1955a) have observed that despite a negative correlation between the amount of independent and dependent behavior shown by nursery-school youngsters, the two are not entirely inversely related. That is, even though some children display generally less dependent behavior than others, some of both kinds of behavior can be seen in all children.

Second, long-term consistency in dependent behavior is of great concern to child psychologists interested in predicting behavior. In their study of the display of passive and dependent behavior in 54 adults, Kagan and Moss (1960) collected information on how much dependency these individuals had shown as children between the ages of 3 and 10. Comparisons of the two sets of data indicated that passive and dependent behaviors remained stable over the years among women but not necessarily among men. Kagan and Moss inferred that passive and dependent behavior was punishable in males while perhaps actually being encouraged in females. More males proportionately than females shifted from high dependency in childhood to independence in adulthood, implying a sex difference in the extent to which pressures for independence are applied in America. Even in adolescence, girls enjoy less independence than boys.

Dependency and Other Behaviors. Is independent or dependent behavior related to other aspects of behavior? Among preschool children a negative connection has been shown between dependence on adults and popularity among peers (Marshall & McCandless, 1957; McCandless, Bilous, & Bennett, 1961). Actually, those children depending most on adults participate least with peers. Thus dependence on adults presumably hinders a child's interaction with his peers, whereas independence seems to be a valued trait even at the preschool level. In adolescence, independence and popularity go together; however, the inverse relation between dependence on adults and popularity is by no means a simple one. Dependent boys were seen in the McCord study (McCord et al., 1962) to display heightened anxiety and internal stress, which perhaps interfered with peer relations.

Independence relates to achievement and motivation for achieving. High-achieving nursery-school children depended less on adults for help and emotional support than did children lower in achievement in a study conducted by Crandall, Preston, and Rabson (1960). Furthermore, children who rated high in emotional independence from parents showed increases in IQ during preschool years (Sontag et al., 1958). One might infer that independence as a sign of security enables the child to function autonomously and apply effort toward personal accomplishment and attainment of goals.

Aggressive Behavior

Our culture seems uncertain as to how aggressive behavior should be regarded. During childhood aggression is discouraged; attitudes toward it are highly restrictive. Yet aggressiveness carries a premium in adult society. The ambitious, hard-driving, aggressive male represents the epitome of success in the competitive, free-enterprise system. His quiet, contemplative, introverted opposite is outdistanced in the race to the top. Aggressiveness appears to be approved in covert, sophisticated forms, but frowned upon in the overt, primitive, physical sorts that characterize children's behavior, except in such formalized events as athletic contests and war.

Aggression may be defined as any act or behavior that is intended to harm or injure. Thus defined, it is inimical to friendly, social intercourse. The rights and wishes of others are ignored or abridged. In this sense, aggressive behavior is maladaptive. There is also evidence that the behavior of highly aggressive children is inflexible and stereotyped (Dittmann & Goodrich, 1961). The implication is that children evincing a great amount of aggression have failed to develop inner controls and have not learned more appropriate, adaptable, and acceptable types of behavior.

The social interaction of young children is marked by aggressive, conflict-ridden behavior. Anger, hostility, quarrelling, and combativeness are observable frequently in children's relations with each other. It is impossible to determine how early these aggressive feelings appear in the child. However, the infant lashes out very early at the source of events that frustrate, restrict, or irritate him. The child uses any means at his command to eliminate unpleasant and undesirable stimuli. In the young child this usually means crying, screaming, and direct physical attack.

As children grow older overt aggression decreases. Inner controls are learned. More effective and more socially acceptable ways of solving conflicts are developed, and rules governing the rights of property become incorporated. However, at every age there are wide disparities among individuals in the amount of aggressive behavior, and in some children a marked persistence of aggression pervades a great number of behaviors.

Among the notions advanced to explain aggression in children, three stress various aspects of the parent-child relationship. In the first, *frustration-aggression,* any situation, condition, relationship, or experience that produces frustration in an individual is seen to generate aggression. The second notion emphasizes the *parent as a model* for the child; identifying with the parent, the child models his own behavior after the parent's. Third, parental *permissiveness of aggression* is said to increase the child's tendency to behave aggressively. Clearly all three notions are centered in the environment since these stress the child's learning experiences, particularly as they occur in the family setting.

There is also an argument for a biological basis for aggression. Diamond (1957), who examined studies among animals, found strain and sex differences in aggressiveness and concluded that genetic factors were influential in determining aggressive behavior, even though learning experiences were important. However, reviewing some of the same research, Berkowitz (1962) saw no evidence of an instinctive drive to hostility or aggression in animals. He accounted for the relatively rare occurrence of spontaneous aggression by frustration or through prior learning that rewarded aggressive behavior.

Although environmental factors contribute heavily to the appearance of aggressive behavior, it would be a mistake to overlook inherent differences in individuals that might indirectly increase their tendency to react aggressively to environmental events. Certain innate characteristics, then, may determine the kinds of learning experience to which the child is exposed and these, in turn, influence behavior and personality. Among nursery-school children, Walker (1962) obtained significant correlations between mesomorphic type and clusters of behavioral traits labeled "energetic-active" and "aggressive-assertive." He concluded that "variations in physical energy, in bodily effectiveness for assertive or dominating behavior, and in bodily sensitivity appear as important mediating links between physique structure and general behavior" (p. 79). Whereas no cause-and-effect statements can be drawn from studies showing a relationship between physical factors and personality, it is not possible to ignore entirely the role such factors play in molding responses to the environment.

Frustration-Aggression. Most people experience frustration in the course of a day's events. Goals are blocked. Rewards are not received. Desires remain unfulfilled. Developed by the Yale group (Dollard, Doob, Miller, Mowrer, & Sears, 1939), the frustration-aggression hypothesis holds that aggressive behavior is the typical response to frustration. Support for the hypothesis appears in experimental studies as well as in observation. To mention one briefly (Otis & McCandless, 1955), 63 preschool children were exposed to eight consecutive repetitions of a mildly frustrating situation. Observed and recorded for manifestations of aggressiveness, the children displayed an increase in aggressive conduct from the first four to the last four trials. Quite likely this finding is particularly significant in supporting the Yale group's hypothesis because the frustration was mild and the children were not greatly involved in the situation. Certainly plausible, then, are findings that point out the severe consequences of parental frustrations of the child's emotional needs.

The findings of several parent-child research studies concur in noting a bond between aggressive behavior in children and punishment for aggression. The Pattern Study explained this relationship along the following lines: the child receives some reward in resorting to aggression through the satisfaction realized from hurting others or expressing anger. But when this aggressive behavior incurs punishment, great frustration is felt, which incites the child to further aggression. Moreover, the Pattern Study noted a tendency for severe punishment of aggression toward parents to be one aspect of general strictness in child-rearing.

One study relating parental behaviors to aggressiveness in school children (Eron et al., 1961) found aggressive boys likely to have fathers who severely punished aggressive deportment in the home. That there was no significant correlation between aggression at school and maternal punishment of aggressive behavior at home suggested that fathers, more than mothers, were an important source of frustration in the home, especially for boys.

So much for restrictive and autocratic techniques producing frustration. As we have seen, the young child is totally dependent on his parents. When one or both parents fail him, frustration results. Hostile, aggressive behavior appears. In their book on adolescent aggression, Bandura and Walters (1959) attributed the development of aggressive behavior to disruption of the child's dependency relation with his parents. Their thesis is corroborated by the findings of another study of family correlates of aggression in nondelinquent boys (McCord, McCord, & Howard, 1961). Here, 95 per cent of the aggressive boys come from homes in which at least one parent was emotionally rejecting.

Thus there seems to be evidence for the frustration-aggression hypothesis. It is clear, however, that frustration does not lead inevitably to aggression. Depending upon the nature of the frustration, it may lead to an inhibition of aggressive behavior, especially if the frustration is seen by the child as punishment for aggression (Kuhn, Madsen, & Becker, 1967). While frustration may well lead to an intensification of hostile feeling, this may not be translated immediately into action. However, whether the frustration stems from a rejection of the child's need for dependency and affection or from a restrictive home atmosphere, the effects on the child's personality development are harmful.

The Parent as a Model. The parent serves as a model for the child, who adopts his parent's values and imitates his behavior, irrespective of whether such behavior is rewarded or expected. In general, adults set examples for children. Logically, then, it would seem that the more aggressive the adult's behavior, the more aggressive the child's. This view is supported by several studies (Bandura & Huston, 1961; Bandura, Ross, & Ross, 1961) in which preschool children imitated or reproduced the behavior of the conductor of the experiment, who was their model. An aggressive model elicited a greater amount of aggressive behavior than a nonaggressive model (see Figure 15-1).

Interestingly enough, boys show more aggression than girls after exposure to an aggressive *male* model. In the development of aggressive behavior the father plays a particularly pivotal role, just as he is a more important source of frustration than the mother. Indeed, a correlation of +.33 was obtained by Eron et al. (1961) between ratings of paternal aggression and child aggressiveness at home. And Winder and Rau (1962), in a study of the parental attitudes of deviant preadolescent boys, found parents of the aggressive boys to score higher in aggressiveness than parents of nonaggressive counterparts.

In one study pertinent to the notion that parents serve as models for a child's aggression, it was observed that children most closely identified with their parents displayed the most aggression in the doll-play sessions (Levin & Sears, 1956). This was particularly true for boys whose fathers did the punishing. Since boys from homes in which the father was absent showed less aggression in doll play than boys from intact homes (Sears, 1951; Bach, 1946), boys might be thought less likely to act aggressively in the absence of an aggressive male model. In similar manner, more aggression is evident in lower-class children than in those from the middle class (McKee & Leader, 1955) because the lower-class male who serves as the model is seen as typically aggressive, at least in the overt physical mannerisms that might prove most significant.

While the discussion here has focused upon parents as models, everyday observation indicates that the child may imitate others in his environment as well. Siblings, peers, and other adults may serve as models. In fact, one experimental study with preschoolers (Hicks, 1965) showed that exposure to aggressive behavior in a peer model is highly effective in eliciting imitative aggressive behaviors. It seems that, in

FIGURE 15-1 (By permission of the American Psychological Association and Albert Bandura.)

general, the more the child is exposed to aggressive behavior in others, the more likely he is to manifest such behavior himself.

Permissiveness of Aggression. This notion rests on the fact that aggression is more likely to occur when it is permitted. An increase in doll-play aggression in a permissive situation has been observed from session to session. This has been taken to signify that in a permissive atmosphere the child's fear of punishment for aggressive behavior diminishes and his inhibitions concerning the show of aggression lessen. The accepting, nonreproachful attitude of the adult is perceived by the child as granting him permission to exhibit aggression.

However, another interpretation is plausible. The amount of session-to-session aggression manifested by pairs of seven- to 10-year-old boys in a permissive, free-play situation was observed under two conditions (Siegel & Kohn, 1959): the presence of a permissive adult and the absence of any adult. Under the former condition, the typical increase of aggression in playing with dolls was noted from one session to the next. Under the latter condition, however, there was a drop in aggressive behavior from the first session to the second. Thus when an adult is present the child presumably tends to transfer certain ego functions, such as control of disapproved or punishable behavior, to him. In the absence of the adult the child must exercise his own self-control.

The Fels studies (Baldwin, 1948) indicated that one effect of democracy in the home was to raise the child's activity level. Since there is a connection between sheer level of activity and aggressiveness, this helps to explain the greater aggression noted in children from democratic or permissive homes. Democratic parents incline toward tolerating all child behaviors, including quarreling, activeness, and aggression. In the Pattern Study a slight relationship was seen between aggressive conduct in the child and the mother's permissiveness of aggression. Sears argued that maternal permissiveness signaled the child that aggressive behavior was acceptable; it was not punishable and was expected by the mother to occur. Yet Lynn (1961), in testing the Pattern Study's finding, could not discover such a link between aggression in children and maternal permissiveness of aggressive behavior. However, Lynn did observe a relationship between scores of a mother's extroversion and both her tendency to be permissive and her child's aggression in school. Lynn suggested the existence of a genetic factor since other studies also found a connection between extroversion and aggression.

The case for the notion that aggressiveness in children is abetted by a permissive atmosphere in the home is not clear-cut. The idea does not explain the original onset of aggression. Possibly, however, parental reluctance to punish various sorts of child behavior tacitly encourages such behaviors when their exercise is rewarding to the child. Regarding aggression, a child's frustrations are relieved by striking someone interfering with or interrupting his activity. If this behavior is allowed by parents, the tendency for aggressive behavior to recur in similar situations is reinforced.

Sex Differences. That boys are more aggressive than girls appears early in life and can be observed in a variety of settings and situations. Besides, children themselves perceive boys as the more aggressive of the sexes. Studies of the middle childhood years (Winder & Rau, 1962) and also of adolescence (Eron et al., 1961) show peers nominating boys oftener than girls as deporting themselves aggressively. It is likely that the sources of this greater male aggressiveness are both environmental and biological.

The boy's identification with his father signifies association of himself with a relatively aggressive model for his eventual role. Moreover, at least in America, it is the cultural expectation that boys will display more aggressiveness than girls. Indeed, aggression is tolerated and often urged on boys; their show of aggression is reinforced. And in the Pattern Study mothers appeared to be less permissive of aggression in girls than in boys. Following up the five-year-olds of the Pattern Study when they were 12, Sears (1961) rated boys higher in antisocial aggression and girls higher in anxiety over aggression. Apparently the unwillingness to permit aggressive behavior in girls gave them greater anxiety over its exhibition.

Kagan and Moss (1962) in their longitudinal study from childhood to adulthood reported greater long-term stability of aggressive conduct in males than females. Conceivably aggression is allowed in boys during their developmental years, but not in girls; it does not fit the cultural cliché of feminine, ladylike deportment. Whether the frustration-aggression hypothesis applies here is uncertain. The higher activity level of boys may engulf them in more frustrating situations. This might explain Fite's (1940) assertion of a relationship between aggression and level of activity. Then, too, the fact that parents in general and fathers in particular have greater expectations for their sons than for their daughters may produce frustration in boys.

The point was made that biological determinants of aggression cannot be ignored. Activity level rests in part on the nervous system. Greater nervous irritability may be typical of the male. Sex differences in longevity and in incidence of certain illnesses suggest that males may be more susceptible biologically to environmental pressures. Thus a complex interaction of biological and environmental forces may cause sex differences as well as individual differences in behavior—including aggressive behavior.

Aggression and Popularity. The hostile feelings underlying aggression do not promote positive social exchange. Aggression is likely to incur counteraggression. Not surprisingly, the relation between popularity and aggression throughout childhood and adolescence is negative (Winder & Rau, 1962; Eron et al., 1961). Among lower-class fifth- and sixth-graders, Lesser (1959) gathered Guess Who nominations for five categories of aggressive activity; *provoked physical aggression*—to attack or injure physically upon provocation; *outburst aggression*—to explode in an uncontrolled temper tantrum; *unprovoked physical aggression*—to attack or harm physically without provocation; *verbal aggression*—to attack or damage verbally; and *indirect aggression*—to attack or injure through some other person or object. Between popularity and provoked physical aggression the correlation was positive; the relation of popularity to the other four categories was negative. Most disapproved was indirect aggression, with verbal, unprovoked physical, and outburst aggression following in that order.

Too much aggressive behavior implies some basic maladjustment. Either the child has not learned better ways of responding to environmental forces or his need for aggression is so strong that he cannot behave otherwise. However this may be, it is not looked upon with favor by the child's peers.

Anxiety

This has been called the "age of anxiety." Commemorated in Auden's verse, intoned in Bernstein's music, encapsulated in Robbins's choreography, it has also received a great amount of attention in popular literature as well as in the writings of psychologists, sociologists, and philosophers. Modern man is beset by intense feelings of anxiety that arise from a plethora of causes ranging from the threat of nuclear annihilation to the insecurities resulting from the breakdown of the family as a social unit. The main concern here are the signs, symptoms, and antecedents of anxiety in children.

Psychological Theories. Freud made a distinction between fear and anxiety (see May, 1950). In fear, the individual's concern is drawn to the threat arising from a specific object. Anxiety, on the other hand, may be considered a generalized fear, which is a condition within the individual. Freud further distinguished objective anxiety from neurotic anxiety. The former is a reaction to external dangers, a protective, self-preservation mechanism, whereas neurotic anxiety appears in the absence of any apparent danger and is anticipatory in nature. Freud held that although the capacity for anxiety is innate, its appearance is the result of learning—learning stemming primarily from the child's early emotional relations with the parents. Describing a number of causes of anxiety, Freud stressed the importance in neurotic anxiety of the child's fear of loss of or separation from the mother.

To Rank, best known for his notion of *birth trauma,* anxiety arises from the individual's fear of the endless number of separations that occur from early childhood onward in the process of acquiring autonomy, independence, and individuality. The beginning of school may be one such threatening experience, involving as it does a partial disruption of the child's previous closeness with the mother.

Adler, in a sense, equated anxiety with neurotic feelings of inferiority that arise from the child's evaluation of himself as weaker and less competent than others. Basic anxiety, according to Horney, is a product of the child's conflict between dependence on parents and hostile feelings toward them. In general, anxiety arises from any threat to the individual's security. Sullivan thought that such threats originate in the infant even before the development of conscious awareness and result from his fear of disapproval from the important persons in his interpersonal environment. Because approval, especially from the mother, is of such crucial importance to the child, he tends to mold his behavior to conform to her demands and expectations. Anxiety arises whenever there are tendencies that may bring disapproval from others. These tendencies are therefore repressed, and such repression imposes a restriction on the child's awareness and on his developing sense of the self. As Sullivan saw it, anxiety is antithetical to emotional health, which denotes personal awareness and personal growth.

Finally, in his early work with the notion of anxiety, Mowrer saw anxiety as a conditioned form of reaction to pain. It is a strong motivating force for behavior since the organism seeks to reduce the level of anxiety and reinforces any behavior serving that purpose. Later Mowrer cited the origin of anxiety as repressed fears and the guilt associated with them.

Thus anxiety that arises initially in infancy or early childhood is an outgrowth of the child's relations with his parent. Whereas fear is a response to specific environmental danger, anxiety is a reaction to a pervasive threat to the individual's security. Certain fears are normal and desirable in the growing child. Anxiety, however, is restrictive rather than constructive.

Signs of Anxiety. Two broad types of behavior indicating anxiety can be discerned in children. In the first, the child avoids a large number of situations and experiences as though each possessed some potential danger. His world becomes restricted as a result; he retreats from life and his conduct becomes rigid and stereotyped. In the second type, the child's demeanor resembles "flight reaction"; he is restless, hyperactive, nervous, and uneasy. In both types, attention to the task at hand, persistence of a constructive nature, and interpersonal relations are all disrupted and impaired. Such children, of course, remain in a state of emotional conflict.

Characteristics of Anxiety. Evolving from the Taylor Manifest Anxiety Scale (Taylor, 1953) for identifying the strength of the anxiety drive in adults, several scales have been devised to assess the characteristics of anxious children. One of these, consisting of 53 items, requires the child to respond either "yes" or "no" to such statements as the following:

It is hard for me to keep my mind on anything.
I worry most of the time.
My feelings get hurt easily.
Often I feel sick in my stomach.
I have bad dreams.
(Castenada, McCandless, & Palermo, 1956, pp. 318–319)

Another test was designed expressly to detect the amount of anxiety experienced by children in a school test situation (Sarason, Davidson, Lighthall, & Waite, 1958a). Subsequent studies have examined various characteristics differentiating children who score high and low on an anxiety scale.

The effects of anxiety on intelligence and learning have received considerable attention. Despite some contradictory results, there has been a consistent negative correlation between anxiety and both intelligence and school achievement at the elementary-school level (McCandless & Castenada, 1956; Feldhusen & Klausmeier, 1962) and also at the senior-high level (Sarason, 1963). It is likely that anxiety impairs a child's intellectual functioning—as though so much of his attention and effort is diverted to coping with his problems that he cannot apply himself sufficiently to other tasks. In this sense the child is certainly emotionally handicapped. Several reports of a longitudinal study examining the relation between test anxiety and IQ and school achievement are now available (Sarason, Hill, & Zimbardo, 1964; Hill & Sarason, 1966). Though the findings are complex, several patterns emerge clearly: (1) The negative correlation typically obtained between test anxiety and both IQ and school achievement increases in magnitude throughout the elementary-school years, indicating that the effects of anxiety become increasingly detrimental to adequate school performance throughout this period; (2) extreme shifts in anxiety are related to reciprocal changes in IQ and achievement, so that, for example, a child who decreased markedly in anxiety level over time showed a corresponding increase in IQ and school achievement; (3) anxiety depresses reading achievement more noticeably than it affects scores on arithmetic subtests, suggesting that more emphasis and pressure are placed on the child by parent and teacher in the area of reading than in other academic skills.

Experimental studies on the relation of anxiety to learning have concluded that school children high in anxiety—that is, in motivation—surpass those low in anxiety on simple tasks but prove inferior on complex ones (Castenada, Palermo, & McCandless, 1956). This does not appear to be the case, however, in studies of college students (Buskirk, 1961; Sarason, 1961). From these investigations, the conclusion was reached that anxious subjects did not necessarily perform less well on complex tasks but that their performance was inferior on tasks entailing threats to their feelings of adequacy. This fits with the position that anxiety results from any threat to individual security. Clearly, therefore, in a school situation children, particularly anxious ones, function best in a secure, nonthreatening atmosphere.

Research relating anxiety to other personality characteristics falls into a consistent pattern. Highly anxious children are less popular with peers than children of low anxiety (McCandless, Castenada, & Palermo, 1956). They have less positive self concepts (Lipsitt, 1958; Horowitz, 1962); they express more dissatisfaction with themselves and others (Phillips, Hindsman, & Jennings, 1960); and in general they express more negative feelings than less anxious children (Barnard, Zimbardo, & Sarason, 1961). At the middle elementary-school level significant correlations have been obtained between scores on the Children's Manifest Anxiety Test and teacher ratings of adjustment as well as scores of the California Test of Personality (Iscoe & Cochran, 1960; Cowen, Zax, Klein, Izzo, & Trost, 1965). The more anxious children were rated as more maladjusted by their teachers who, in part, defined maladjustment on the basis of restlessness, lack of attention, and inability or unwillingness to "settle down."

In classroom observations, highly anxious boys show less orientation toward tasks than boys of low anxiety; they also display greater insecurity in their relation with their teacher. Among girls, however, the highly anxious are less distractible and evince a stronger need for achievement than those low in anxiety (Sarason, Davidson, Lighthall, & Waite, 1958b). Apparently anxiety operates in different ways with respect to sex. Psychoanalytic writers have argued that boys and girls handle anxiety differently. Girls are said to employ *autoplastic* defenses—defenses involving the individual herself, as in daydreaming—whereas boys handle anxiety through *alloplastic* defenses—defenses in which the individual turns outward toward other persons or objects, as in rebelliousness. Covert versus overt behavior may distinguish between boys and girls in this respect. Consistently, girls score higher on anxiety scales (Castenada, McCandless, & Palermo, 1956), implying that in American society it is easier for females than males to admit they are anxious (Davidson, Sarason, Lighthall, Waite, & Sarnoff, 1958; L'Abate, 1960). Nervousness is a woman's prerogative, whereas it is the man who develops an ulcer.

The idea that anxiety exerts a constricting influence on behavior is buttressed by studies indicating that the more anxious children score higher on scales measuring "rigidity of thinking" (Kitano, 1960). These children also show greater rigidity in their drawings (Fox, Davidson, Lighthall, Waite, & Sarason, 1958) and in their behavior (Smock, 1958); and they prefer familiar rather than novel stimuli (Mendel, 1965). Related to this is the finding that dependency characterizes the behavior of anxious children (Sarason, Davidson, Lighthall, & Waite, 1958b). Since dependency is often a sign of insecurity, anxiety, dependency, and insecurity are interrelated causally. They constrict and restrict the child's behavior and his world.

Parental Antecedents. Not much has been turned up so far in research regarding parental antecedents of anxiety, perhaps partly because mothers of highly anxious children have taken a highly defensive stance in interviews (Davidson, 1959). They are less frank in their responses and are less willing to divulge information about themselves. Possibly they are themselves anxious and insecure or they may be defensive for reasons of guilt over nonacceptance of their children. Mothers of children low in anxiety indicated that their children were free to express feelings of anger and aggression (Davidson, 1959). That family influences on the development of anxiety in children merit intensive examination was emphasized in a study (Adams & Sarason, 1963) that found significant correlations between anxiety test scores of high-school students, especially girls, and their mothers. Apparently anxious mothers establish the kind of home atmosphere that produces anxiety in the children. Anxiety may well be contagious.

Conscience Development

Conscience is sometimes defined with tongue in cheek as "that which keeps us from doing what we shouldn't do even when no one is looking." Indeed, this definition lights upon a major element in the idea of conscience: inner controls based on an individual's acceptance of values concerning right and wrong behavior. Yet there are other kinds of control of behavior. Control may be external in origin, resting in the prohibitions and demands of others. In Chapter 7 the distinction was noted between *guilt* and *shame* cultures, the latter controlling behavior by shame—fear of punishment, ridicule, ostracism, retribution—and the former by internalizing society's standards. One other point about conscience: inner controls are learned, as are the values to which they relate.

Between the Hartshorne and May (1928) study and the late 1950's, little concern was shown over conscience development in children. Matters of values and conscience were apparently not thought to be appropriate topics for scientific research. Then Sears (1960) noted that the identification of the child-rearing antecedents of inner controls and sanctions signified "one of the most important problems facing students of personality development today" (p. 97). Miller and Swanson (1960) saw moral standards in terms of inner conflict. Three reasons were advanced for this approach: moral needs, that is, internalized standards, are frequently the cause of conflict within the individual; the manner in which these conflicts are resolved depends on the particular moral values held by the individual; and each individual employs characteristic ways of resolving conflicts, and these are thought of as his "character structure."

Among adults, some are faced more frequently than others with conflicts over moral issues. Such conflicts are likelier, however, to involve a position taken on some moral issue than overt behavior, as in childhood. For example, is racial discrimination in public housing acceptable? Is nuclear war justified? Can unfair business competition be condoned? Most likely the mature adult resolves such issues in a rather consistent manner, and when he does employ defenses such as rationalization to avoid facing a conflict, they are a stable part of his personality. No wonder an understanding of conscience is essential to an understanding of human behavior.

Antecedents. There are three principal elements that affect the development of conscience. First, a culture's values or standards form an important part of the legacy transmitted to a child by his parents; one culture may discourage aggressiveness, another emphasize self-effacement, a third espouse personal recognition. The second factor is the child's intellectual development. An older, more intellectually mature child is better able to perceive what is expected of him; he can understand the reasons for certain restrictions and standards; he is able to generalize a principle and apply it to a variety of situations. More than a younger child, the older one can comprehend some of the abstract concepts behind social issues—unselfishness, equality, justice, truth. Third is the child's relations with his parents. Several research techniques have been used to study parental influences on development of conscience. In the Pattern Study, mothers were asked to indicate signs of conscience in their childhood. Two criteria were used; the child's tendency to "act the parental role," that is, his attempt to teach parental standards to siblings and friends; and the child's behavior following a wrongdoing, that is, his attempts to confess, apologize, or make amends. Evidence of the development of a conscience was rated on the following scale (Sears, Maccoby, & Levin, 1957, p. 381):

1. No evidence. Child hides, denies, does not seem unhappy when naughty.
2. Little evidence of conscience.
3. Moderate conscience development. May not confess directly but looks sheepish; seldom denies.
4. Considerable conscience.
5. Strong conscience. Child feels miserable when naughty; always confesses; never denies; strong need for forgiveness.

The concept employed most frequently to explain the child's internalization of adult standards is identification. Factors producing a strong identification with the parent tend to encourage development of conscience. Kindergarten boys who were highly masculine, presumably because of identification with their fathers, were also high in conscience development (Mussen & Distler, 1960). There is some experimental evidence that in a temptation situation children will imitate a model who yields to temptation (Stein, 1967). This suggests that parents serve rather directly as models for their children with regard to moral behavior. Research has dealt with two factors in particular regarding this antecedent of conscience development: the type of parental discipline and the warmth of the parent-child relationship.

As to disciplinary activity in the home, the Pattern Study indicated that psychological or love-oriented techniques exemplified in praise, isolation, and withdrawal of love aided the development of conscience more than the materialistic or physical methods embodied in tangible rewards, deprivation, and physical punishment. MacKinnon's (1938) investigation of college students found that those who transgressed prohibitions in an experimental setting were likelier to be children of fathers whose disciplinary tactics had been physical rather than psychological. Yet a study of four-year-olds (Burton, Maccoby, & Allinsmith, 1961) on resistance to cheating did not support these findings. In this investigation, scolding and physical punishment were more closely related to resistance to temptation than were psychological punishments or use of reasoning. Direct, physical techniques seemed most effective in the young child, although psychological techniques encouraging identification with the parent took over as the child grew older and gained in cognitive development.

Similar to the distinction between physical and psychological disciplinary methods is the differentiation between techniques of *induction* and of *sensitization* (Aronfreed, 1961). Reasoning with the child, ignoring or rejecting him, and explanation are all inductive techniques. They elicit in the child reactions to his own transgressions that may become independent of the original source of punishment. For instance, reasoning with a young child and explaining the consequences of an act should encourage him to examine his actions and to accept responsibility for them. Further, this technique activates the child's capacity for empathy by pointing out to him the harmful consequences of his behavior for his parents and for others. Sensitization techniques include physical punishment and scolding. These may simply make the child extremely susceptible to fear of external punishment following transgression and attach importance to the demands and expectations of others. Through use of a story-completion technique among sixth-graders, a relation was found between the child's type of moral response and the mother's disciplinary technique. Children whose mothers used inductive techniques were more prone to include notions of reparation and acceptance in their stories, whereas those whose mothers relied on a technique of sensitization oftener introduced external consequences of transgression in theirs.

Again concerned with parental disciplinary techniques, Hoffman (1963) distinguished between *power assertive* and *non-power-assertive* discipline. The former involves physical punishment and material deprivation, resulting in an externalized moral orientation based on fear of detection and fear of punishment. Non-power-assertive techniques include love-withdrawal and induction types of discipline, producing an internalized moral orientation characterized by strong guilt. Hoffman and Saltzstein (1967) found research support for their prediction that of the two types of non-power-assertive approach, induction would lead to stronger conscience development than love withdrawal. The latter technique fails to focus the child's thinking on the pain that he causes others by his misbehavior; the awareness of others' feelings and the realization that one is the causal agent of another's discomfort should serve to produce strong inner controls.

In the Pattern Study, love-oriented techniques characterized most middle-class mothers; physical types of discipline were used by most lower-class mothers. In the Aronfreed study, induction was the predominant choice of middle-class mothers and sensitization the major choice of lower-class mothers. The physical types of discipline espoused in lower-class homes, however, neither encourage identification nor produce inner controls.

Most efforts to link conscience development to specific child-rearing practices, such as the age and severity of toilet training, have not borne fruit (Grinder, 1962; Burton, Maccoby, & Allinsmith, 1961). Perhaps, as noted in the chapters on parental influences on children, the general psychological atmosphere of the home may be more important. In the Pattern Study, the threat to withdraw love, a psychological device, had little effect if the mother was relatively cold and rejecting. Conversely, it proved most effective when the child's relationship with his mother was warm and accepting. Thus the nonaccepted child has little to lose by displaying disapproved behavior. Only 18 per cent of the rejected children covered in the Pattern Study were judged as having "high conscience," compared with 31 per cent of the accepted group. And in support of the MacKinnon (1938) finding about the import of the kind of discipline practiced by the father, stronger consciences were observed in boys with accepting fathers than boys with fathers who tended to reject them. No such difference was detected, however, in girls.

Two major family qualities are tied to a strong superego in children, that is, to the "presence of an effectively behavior-guiding conscience" —consistency and a combination of mutual trust and approval (Peck, 1958). Logically, a consistent pattern of parental control and expectations provides a clear-cut setting for the development of positive conduct. In addition, an atmosphere of mutual trust inspires the child to absorb his parents' values and standards, which the child accepts for his own.

Development of conscience, then, needs to be understood in order to understand the development of personality, for the manner in which the individual resolves a moral conflict is a stable aspect of his personality. As significant as are the cultural lessons transmitted by parents, the child's own intellectual growth, and also his identification with parents, which leads to adoption of their values and to acquisition of inner controls, nothing counts as much as an atmosphere of warmth in the relationship between parents and child. Mutual trust, acceptance, and consistency combined with warmth are likely to assure strong conscience when childhood gives way to adolescence.

Dominant-Submissive Behavior

A hierarchy of behavior ranging from dominance to submissiveness has been seen many times in the social interaction of a wide assortment of organisms including rats, dogs, monkeys, domestic fowl, and humans. Implied in this pecking order is the jockeying for position, the maneuvering for power that is virtually an integral part of all social interaction, regardless of species. Here, too, we see the structure of groups, whose members can be ranked with respect to dominance and submission.

Factor analyses of personality tests and ratings almost invariably find a factor designated ascendance, or dominance, or assertiveness both at child (Cattell & Gruen, 1953; Cattell & Coan, 1957) and adult (Cattell, 1957) levels. In the paragraphs that follow we shall summarize some of the early studies that contributed methodologically to the investigation of ascendant behavior in children, and then turn to the antecedents of dominance and submissiveness and to the characteristics of leadership.

Experimental Studies. A noteworthy study is Jack's (1934), which sought experimentally to modify behavior. Jack observed four-year-olds in pairs in a room supplied with a sandbox and three types of toy. The following eight types of behavior were used in defining ascendance.

1. Verbal attempts to secure play material.
2. Forceful attempts to secure play materials.
3. Success in securing material from companion's possession.
4. Defense and snatching back of materials taken from one's possession.
5. Verbal attempts to direct behavior of companion.
6. Companion compliance with direction.
7. Forbidding, criticizing, reproving companion.
8. Providing pattern of behavior which companion imitates.

Concluding that the most significant difference between ascendant and nonascendant children was degree of self-confidence, Jack applied special training materials in her effort to modify the behavior of the five least ascendant youngsters. Later, when she paired them again in the experimental room, the ascendance scores of these particular youngsters showed significant gain.

Page (1936) achieved similar results among three- and four-year-olds. Yet Page noted that teacher ratings of ascendance away from the experimental setting did not change as a result of the modification of the children's behavior through training. Therefore she questioned whether the results of the training spread to the environment beyond the training room. Though lacking data on long-term effects of training, psychologists find it significant that by increasing a child's self-confidence through developing certain skills and proficiencies in him, they can alter his behavior in a social situation.

Similar modification of behavior was reported by Chittenden (1942). She provided special tutelage to 10 preschool children who were most dominating in their relations with other children. Conflicts involving dolls were analyzed, with the social and emotional consequences of certain kinds of behavior emphasized. Tests conducted after the training disclosed that these children had increased their cooperative behavior.

An interesting study (Blum & Kennedy, 1967) found that dominative behavior can be increased through reinforcement. Children were rewarded when the choice made by the nondominant member of a pair prevailed. Subsequently, the nondominant member made an increasing number of dominant responses. While the early studies emphasized training in dominative or assertive behavior, it appears that administering reinforcement (reward) for dominative behavior is effective in increasing its likelihood of occurrence, thus modifying a child's behavior on this dimension.

Dominant-Submissive Antecedents. Dominant behavior is observable in children at least as young as three years of age. It is also observable in lower organisms. Conceivably, therefore, constitutional factors predisposing an individual to dominance play a role in such behavior. Nevertheless, this does not eliminate the role of environmental antecedents.

Part of the problem of identifying the antecedents of ascendant behavior results from a confusion in nomenclature. Jack clearly did not differentiate between acceptable and unacceptable kinds of behavior in the types she selected to define ascendance. This distinction largely appeared later. Chittenden (1942) embraced both dominating and cooperative behavior in the term "assertiveness." Anderson (1937, 1939, 1946), it will be recalled, distinguished dominating from integrating behavior. In a similar vein, Parten (1932) described two types of leader: the bully, who used brute force and bossing, and the diplomat, who used artful and indirect suggestion. Finally, Mummery (1947) spoke of socially acceptable and socially unacceptable behavior.

Various distinctions between socially positive and socially negative types of domination aid in resolving some of the disagreement over parental antecedents of dominating behavior. From some of the Fels studies, Baldwin (1948, 1949) concluded that democracy in the home, especially an actively democratic home, tended to produce an active, aggressive child, likely to be a leader. Children from restrictive, controlled homes tend to be unaggressive and fearful. Baldwin reasoned that freedom in the home encouraged active exploration of the environment and a high degree of social participation. In agreement with the Fels data, Miles (in Anderson, 1946) noted that parents of adolescent leaders were less restrictive in handling their children. The child enjoyed the freedom to make his own decisions and judgments and to experiment with new opportunities.

These findings, however, contradicted those of an investigation by Meyer (1947) who, in rating homes of 29 preschool children on the 30 Fels Parent Behavior Scales, found significant negative correlations between their dominating responses under experimental conditions and such home atmosphere as democracy of policy, readiness of explanation, understanding of child's problems, and rapport with child. The homes of the dominant children were characterized by disciplinary friction and general discord. Similarly, Radke (1946) reported that children from autocratic homes tended to dominate their companions more readily than children from democratic homes. They were also less considerate of their peers. To Mummery (1954) the chief effect of democracy in the home was perhaps to influence the child's self concept in terms of self-acceptance and self-confidence. Because democratic parents respect the individuality of the child, it is likely that he will show respect for his peers in social situations. If such a child displays assertive behavior it will generally be socially acceptable, integrating, and cooperative in nature.

Leadership Behavior. Although not synonymous with dominating behavior, leadership has much in common with it. Leadership implies the successful use of techniques to guide and direct the behavior of others toward an agreed goal. Dominating behavior, on the other hand, may or may not succeed and may or may not involve a shared goal. Whether children who are dominating in the preschool period assume leadership in elementary-school years is not certain from the scant evidence at hand. Equally sparse is evidence relating to the transferability of leadership from one group to another.

Yet leadership is a topic of interest to social psychologists who deal with adult behavior. In general, there are two approaches to the subject (Allen, 1952). *Structuralists* regard leadership as a trait or a set of traits. *Functionalists* view it as a function of the situation. The two positions may be synthesized if leadership is considered in terms of role theory and role expectancy. It is likely that children who later become leaders possess in childhood the earmarks of leadership. The inclusion of leadership capacities in the child's concept of the self results from the successful use of these characteristics in opportunities to lead. Effective leadership in one situation inspires the child to assert it in others. Through repeated successes the notion of leadership becomes an integral part of the self concept. Furthermore, as others expect an individual to continue to lead, this contributes to further exhibition of leadership demeanor. Reputation occasions the repeated display of specific behaviors in children even if the repute is undeserved.

Having reviewed the available data on the qualities inherent in leaders, Stogdill (1948) listed these characteristics in which leaders surpassed the average members of their groups: intelligence, scholarship, dependability in exercising responsibilities, activity and social participation, socioeconomic status, initiative, persistence, knowing how to get things done, self-confidence, alertness to and insight to situations, cooperativeness, popularity, adaptability, verbal facility, athletic ability, originality, desire to excel, judgment, humor, chronological age, height, weight, appearance, energy, dominance, integrity, and mood control. These factors, Stogdill (1948, p. 64) concluded, could probably be classified under the following headings.

1. Capacity (intelligence, alertness, verbal facility, originality, judgment).
2. Achievement (scholarship, knowledge, athletic accomplishments).
3. Responsibility (dependability, initiative, persistence, aggressiveness, self-confidence, desire to excel).
4. Participation (activity, sociability, cooperation, adaptability, humor).
5. Status (socio-economic position, popularity).
6. Situation (mental level, status, skills, needs and interests of followers, objectives to be achieved, etc.).

As much as the traits seem to support the structuralist approach to leadership, Stogdill pointed out that the qualities and skills enabling an individual to function as a leader depended on the demands of the group and the situation. In preschool years, mere activity level is enough to determine leadership (Parten, 1932); in late elementary-school years and throughout adolescence, athletic ability and physical prowess are the important requisites for leadership among boys (Partridge, 1934); in college empathy is the key to leadership (Bell & Hall, 1954). Since the functionalists are also correct, leaders are made as well as born.

Social Acceptance

Social psychologists who contend that Americans place too much emphasis on sociability, adjustment to the group, and "other-directedness" support their complaint by pointing to the amount of research on social acceptance in the field of child psychology. Yet there are a number of reasons to believe that a child's degree of acceptance by his peers is of more than fleeting or superficial significance. Children not well accepted by their peers tend to express less positive feelings toward them (Lippitt & Gold, 1959), and it is reasonable to consider positive feelings toward others as one sign of mental health. In the classroom, poor pupil-to-pupil relationships is one indication of an unfavorable climate for learning and for positive group interaction (Spector, 1953).

The second reason for attaching importance to peer relationships is that early adjustment to peers is a good barometer for adjustment in adult life. Roff (1957, 1960, 1961) has been able to predict the adjustment of individuals to military service from comments made about them years before concerning their childhood relations with their peers. Early detection of difficulties in adult adjustment is possible, Roff held, from knowledge of the attitudes and opinions of an individual's associates regarding him. Undoubtedly, a vast number of persons who are not highly accepted by their peers in childhood make an adequate adjustment to adult life. There is a difference, though, between lack of acceptance and active rejection. The Roff data seem to indicate that it was active rejection to which he referred.

Finally, it is important to find the personality correlates of social acceptance because knowledge of them may make it possible to help children develop better relations with their peers. We have seen the negative correlations between social acceptance and aggressiveness, anxiety, and dependence. How can these aspects of personality be altered, modified, or altogether prevented?

Correlates of Social Acceptance. Efforts to isolate the factors bearing on social acceptance go back to the 1920's and the early 1930's. Furfey (1927) noted a tendency among preadolescent boys to elect chums of the same size, age, intelligence, and maturity as themselves. Challman (1932) found preschool children to be similar to their friends in chronological age, sociability, and physical activity. Similarities in mental age, height, extroversion, attractiveness of personality, IQ, and frequency of laughter mattered little in preschool choices of friendship. Lippitt (1941) noted cooperation in routines to be most clearly related to popularity in a group of preschool youngsters. Other correlates of social acceptance in children included socioeconomic status, school achievement, responsibility, cooperativeness, freedom from fears and anxieties, good health, attractiveness of appearance, and empathy. Interestingly enough, the social desirability of a child's first name appears to be related to popularity (McDavid & Harari, 1966). Favorable or unfavorable connotations become attached to personal names, so that a child bearing an unpopular or unpleasant name may be handicapped in his social interactions with peers. Sex difference is also important, since there is an increasing separation by sex in friendship choices throughout the early elementary-school years. Further, girls receive higher social acceptance scores than boys. Table 15-1 lists the traits designated by a group of 13- to 15-year-old boys as characterizing their most acceptable peers.

In contrast to earlier studies, the more recent ones have tried to single out the antecedents causing different levels of social acceptance. For example, studying family influences on adjustment to peers, Hoffman (1961) noted that children from homes dominated by the mother experienced difficulties in their relations with the opposite sex. This was equally true for boys and girls. Influential as was an affectional relationship with the father on the adjustment of both boys and girls to peers, it was especially so for boys. An affectional relationship with the mother augured well for her daughter's adjustment to peers.

The rejected, unpopular child is often shy, recessive, socially disinterested, and self-centered. Even if he is noisy and energetic, his attempts at social acceptance by his agemates go unheeded. This may be because the behavior of such children is motivated by strong needs for attention and social approval. Usually they are unable to share, to take turns, and to comply with rules and regulations, thus disclosing an underlying insecurity. Whether lack of acceptance or unacceptable behavior comes first is hard to ascertain. It is likely that both are causes and both are effects: undesirable behavior leads to unpopularity, which leads to more undesirable behavior. The importance of therapeutic intervention by a trained adult is obvious.

The following two personality sketches are drawn from a study that investigated the personalities of five popular and five unpopular chil-

TABLE 15-1 *　Correlates of Social Acceptance in 13- to 15-Year-Old Boys

Identifying Number	Name	Illustrative Terms
1	Intelligent	Intelligent, keen, bright vs. Dumb, stupid
2	Sociable	Friendly, sociable vs. Unfriendly, too quiet, stiff
3	Minds own business	Minds own business vs. Annoying, pest
4	Plays fair	Good sport, plays fair vs. Poor sport, plays unfair
5	Quiet	Quiet vs. Loud, noisy, overtalkative
6	Witty	Humorous, witty, good joker vs. Not humorous, no sense of humor
7	Athletic	Athletic, ball player vs. Not athletic
8	Helpful	Helpful vs. Not helpful
9	Unconceited	Humble, doesn't show off vs. Conceited, stuck up
10	Good company	Good company, fun to be with vs. No fun, poor company
11	Serious	Serious, not silly vs. Silly, foolish
12	Conscientious	Conscientious, good worker vs. Lazy, listless
13	Masculine	Real man, has guts vs. Sissy, helpless, girlish, fairy
14	Stays out of trouble	Stays out of trouble vs. Always in trouble
15	Talks well	Can talk, talks well vs. Can't talk
16	Honest	Honest, doesn't cheat vs. Dishonest, cheats, lies
17	Clean	Clean, neat vs. Sloppy, dirty
18	Doesn't fight	Doesn't fight vs. Always fighting
19	Kind	Kind, considerate vs. Unkind, not considerate, mean
20	Trustworthy	Trustworthy, keeps his word vs. Unreliable

*Feinberg, M. R., Smith, M., & Schmidt, R. (1958).

TABLE 15-1   (*Continued*)

Identifying Number	Name	Illustrative Terms
21	Gets along well with others	Gets along well with others vs. Can't get along
22	Leader	Leader vs. Not a leader
23	Cheerful	Cheerful vs. Grumpy, complains
24	Cooperative	Cooperative vs. Not cooperative
25	Good scholar	Good scholar, student vs. Poor scholar, student
26	Common interests	Same interests vs. Not same interests
27	Interesting	Interesting vs. Not interesting, dull
28	Good manners	Good manners vs. Poor manners
29	Pleasant, agreeable	Pleasant, agreeable vs. Argues, insults
30	Can take a joke	Can take a joke vs. Can't take a joke
31	Mature	Mature, grownup vs. Immature, babyish
32	Generous	Generous, unselfish vs. Tight, selfish
33	Good-looking	Good-looking, clean cut vs. Ugly
34	Good character	Good character vs. Poor character
35	Understanding	Understanding vs. Not understanding
36	Participates in activities	All around vs. No activities, doesn't take part
37	Calm	Calm, doesn't get excited, easy-going vs. Bad tempered, gets excited
38	Sincere	Sincere, means what he says vs. Insincere
39	Well dressed	Good dresser, sharp clothes vs. Poor dresser
40	Other specific terms used infrequently	
41	General nonspecific terms	Swell, good friend vs. No good, real drip

dren. Their contents will add meaning to this discussion of the correlates of social acceptance.

David is about average size for his age, and is quite good-looking. Always neat and clean, but not fussy or overly nice in appearance. Has a happy expression which radiates friendliness and good humor.

David is outstanding in friendliness and social interest. He is "smooth" in inter-personal relationships; carries on a conversation with ease and poise. Shows more initiative than most children in meeting new-comers who enter the room. Goes out of his way to make them feel welcome, and to show them around the building. Never snubs anyone, but still he does not try to establish intimate relationships with those to whom he is not especially attracted. Would never consciously hurt anyone. Is always very courteous in his relations with both teachers and children. Shows more sympathetic concern for others than most children of his age. Sometimes he asks the teacher to allow him to help another child who has difficulty in his school work. Also, he has been observed to pull a larger boy off a smaller one on the playground when his sense of fairness has been violated. As a patrol leader in the halls, he has shown a marked interest in aiding the smallest children. In spite of these characteristics, it must also be stated that David is described as "egocentric" and "bull-headed" at times. One of his most frequent companions states that he has lots of quarrels with David because "David gets mad if you disagree with him." Also, David does not usually react very well to criticism. He shows some resentment and acts like he considers it unwarranted, but seldom says anything.

David has a number of abilities which bring him group recognition. Is outstanding in dramatics. Often takes leading roles. Always knows his lines perfectly, and helps carry the entire performance. Also sings very well. Is a member of the school choir. Enjoys entertaining others. Likes to be before his public. Sometimes acts as an announcer. Has frequently been elected to class offices. He takes these obligations seriously and performs his duties well. As a patrolman in the sixth grade, he has been especially watchful and has shown marked ability in directing others and in getting them to do the right thing without antagonizing them. Is not bossy or dominating.

In classroom academic work, David is not especially brilliant, but his work is nearly always better than average. He makes good contributions to class discussions. Is very dependable in having his written work in on time. Takes pride in doing good school work and in making good grades. Also, he likes to please the teacher. Although David's application to his academic work is generally steady and conscientious, he seldom shows any initiative or originality. Prefers to be told what to do. Neither does he show much drive in trying to overcome problems that are very difficult. Is inclined to quit, and wait for the teacher to help him.

David conforms well to school regulations, but is not a perfectly behaved child. In the fourth grade he was paddled a number of times for impertinence to the teacher. This trait has not been much in evidence since. He is mischievous at times, both in the classroom and on the playground, but he never does anything of serious proportions and always does things above-board rather than pulling tricks behind the teacher's back. Never sneaking or under-handed. When caught in some kind of mischief, he readily confesses and does not try to shift blame to others (Bonney, 1947, pp. 14–16).

Eugene is a sturdy type of boy about average height. His appearance is somewhat marred by blackheads which he frequently picks at. Has a pleasant, but weak facial expression. His ambling gait, poor carriage, and lackadaisical manner cause others to think of him as a boy who has never taken life or its obligations very seriously. Does not appear unhappy, but he gives the impression of being insecure and uncertain of himself.

Eugene's personality structure is primarily that of an effeminate boy. He has never engaged in out-door boyish activities and refuses to play aggressive group games. He participates a little in simpler games like dodge ball or chase, but does not do well in these. Has a "don't care" attitude in respect to all playground activities. He is not uncoordinated or physically weak; he just doesn't identify himself with such things. When left alone at play period, he plays on the teeter-totter, swings, or teases the girls. When forced to participate in a group game such as baseball, he "puts on an act," tries to be cute, does a lot of irrelevant talking, and makes an "out" every time. The other boys laugh at him to his face, and deride him, but he shrugs it all off and pretends not to care. Never fights, never gets angry or argues about a point, and never attacks others. Has a minimum of courage and daring.

Eugene is characterized by emotional instability and immaturity. He is frequently restless in class, does quite a lot of "doodling," jabbers under his breath, and sometimes annoys other children by putting his arm on their desks. Is seriously lacking in persistency of effort. He will work very well at a task which he likes, but not for long. Once he was given an important part in a play, but he never learned his lines, even though he had much help and urging from the teacher. He got some of his lines right, but he improvised so much that the other players had a hard time catching their cues from him. This disgusted the other children. He did, however, show good dramatic sense and entered into the spirit of his part exceptionally well.

Eugene's emotional and social immaturity is emphasized by several other traits. One of these is his strong persistency in wanting his own way in group projects, club meetings, or indoor games. He does not take "no" for an answer from the teacher or the group, but will argue, cajole, or plead for hours to have what he wants. Another evidence of his emotional immaturity is his very naive identification with certain strong, capable boys. One day he told his special reading teacher with obvious elation how he had sat next to one of these admired boys in the picture show the day before. The fact that his sitting next to this boy was purely accidental made his mention of it all the more significant—and pathetic. Additional evidence of Eugene's inadequate social development is found in his excessive eating and in his playing with children much younger than himself. Several investigations have emphasized the relation between excessive eating and social inferiority. Eugene's eating certainly fits the diagnosis of a substitute pleasure for social failure. He frequently brings a mid-morning lunch in addition to eating a big lunch at noon. That there is some degree of unconscious compulsion in his eating is indicated by the fact that several times he said to his sixth grade teacher, "I feel better today; I didn't eat so much."

Eugene has a number of abilities which could be developed into real assets except for his inadequate personality structure. As previously stated, he has unusually good dramatic sense. Also he draws and paints quite well, but he will seldom work at anything long enough to achieve a praise-worthy product. At times he makes interesting and unusual contributions to class discussions. He may come forth with some rare bit of information which he has picked up from the radio or other sources, or he may see unusual, significant relationships in material being discussed in class; but these performances are very irregular (Bonney, 1947, pp. 46–48).

Constancy of Social Acceptance. Several factors indicate the likelihood of relative constancy in social acceptance from one group to another and one time to the next (Northway, 1946). First, Bonney (1943) found that a child's social position in grades two, three, and five was as constant as his intellectual and academic achievement throughout the elementary-school years. Years later, upon interviewing 25 first-grade children throughout the school year, Medinnus (1962) obtained correlations of about $+.85$ between scores of social acceptance from one interview to the next. Thus there is certainly short-term constancy in social acceptance. Second, a number of studies concur on the personality characteristics associated with acceptance and nonacceptance. Further, researches into children's friendships report an increasing constancy in friendship choices throughout childhood and adolescence (Horrocks & Thompson, 1946; Thompson & Horrocks, 1947; Horrocks & Buker, 1951). Before school age, constancy probably results from the restricted range of choices imposed by limitations in mobility. Later it may be accounted for by the increasing consistency of personality. In adolescence, friends are chosen on a deeper basis—on aspects of personality that are fairly stable.

That social acceptance is fairly constant while growing up points to its influence on the child's personality and adjustment. As awareness of social position increases with age (Ausubel, Schiff, & Gasser, 1952), a long-term pattern of acceptance and nonacceptance exerts direct and indirect influence on behavior, until knowledge of one's social status becomes an important part of one's self concept.

Modifying Social Acceptance. If social rejection reflects basic maladjustment of personality, raising the level of an individual's social acceptance is not easily accomplished. Because of the role of antecedent parent-child relationships in social acceptance, changes may involve the entire family. But this may be true only of extreme social rejection. For children in the intermediate zone, it may be profitable to concentrate on the self concept. Increasing their self-confidence, self-assurance, and self-esteem is most desirable. Children who manifest unacceptable behaviors usually know that they elicit unfavorable reactions from others but are unable to change. Feelings of inadequacy interfere with behavior and lead to deeper feelings of inadequacy. Somehow the treadmill must be stopped. And it is likely that modifications in self-feelings and in behavior are best achieved in the early elementary years.

The prime responsibility for assisting the child to more positive and acceptable social relations is the parents'. In the case of a boy, since athletic skill plays so great a role in his acceptability, the father can increase the child's self-confidence by practicing various games with him. This also serves to increase the boy's feeling of parental acceptance. In fact, the child's problems in acceptance by his peers may have their genesis in parental nonacceptance.

The teacher also has a role. An alert, sensitive teacher can do much to create a classroom atmosphere of mutual assistance, mutual understanding, tolerance, and acceptance of others. However, as children advance through the grades, teachers become less able to estimate acceptance by peers. Either they judge from criteria differing from those employed by peers or have little knowledge or awareness of children's social interactions. In any event, unless a teacher tries, through use of sociometric techniques, to identify those children who are not accepted by their peers, help for individual children will be impossible.

SUMMARY

The first part of this chapter recapitulated to a large degree material discussed in earlier parts of the book, which was brought together here in order to deal in one place with references to the relation of specific antecedents to that continuing and unique pattern of traits called personality. Differences in personality are evident at birth as a result of hereditary and congenital forces, and these early behavioral tendencies are responded to by the social forces impinging on the child.

The notion of personality implies consistency. Evidence points to the moderate consistency of human behavior, with consistency obtained earlier in some traits than in others, but with younger individuals generally showing less consistency than older ones. The existence of the self concept is often posited as a major basis for consistency. The self concept is composed, in part, of the body image—ideas about and acceptance of the physical self. With age and a decreased amount of bodily change, a relatively stable body image develops, which, in turn, increases stability of behavior. The self concept also includes social roles. Through reward, people tend to play roles more frequently and with greater degrees of accuracy. If possible, contradictory roles are resolved and an emotional commitment to the roles played is developed. As roles are better defined and better played, consistency increases.

Finally, the chapter examined six areas of personality that appear to be major in childhood and for which considerable information is available. These are: dependence-independence, aggression, anxiety, conscience development, dominance-submission, and social acceptance. In each of these areas we have attempted to trace the emergence of these personality characteristics to psychological conditions in the home and to the child's relations with his parents.

REFERENCES

Adams, E. B., & Sarason, I.   Relation between anxiety in children and their parents. *Child Development*, 1963, **34**, 237–246.

Allen, P. J.   The leadership pattern. *American Sociological Review*, 1952, **17**, 93–96.

Anderson, H. H.   Domination and integration in the social behavior of young children in an experimental play situation. *Genetic Psychology Monographs*, 1937, **19**, 341–408.

Anderson, H. H.   Domination and social integration in the behavior of kindergarten children and teachers. *Genetic Psychology Monographs*, 1939, **21**, 287–385.

Anderson, H. H.   Socially integrative behavior. *Journal of Abnormal and Social Psychology*, 1946, **41**, 379–384.

Anderson, J. E.   Parents' attitudes on child behavior: A report of three studies. *Child Development*, 1946, **17**, 91–97.

Anderson, J. E.   The prediction of adjustment over time.   In I. Iscoe & H. Stevenson (Eds.), *Personality development in children.*   Austin: University of Texas Press, 1960.   Pp. 28–72.

Aronfreed, J.   The nature, variety and social patterning of moral responses to transgression.   *Journal of Abnormal and Social Psychology,* 1961, **63,** 223–240.

Ausubel, D. P., Schiff, H. M., & Gasser, E. G.   A preliminary study of developmental trends in sociopathy: Accuracy of perception of own and others' sociometric status.   *Child Development,* 1952, **23,** 111–128.

Bach, G. R.   Father-fantasies and father-typing in father-separated children.   *Child Development,* 1946, **17,** 63–80.

Baldwin, A. L.   Socialization and the parent-child relationship.   *Child Development,* 1948, **19,** 127–136.

Baldwin, A. L.   The effect of home environment on nursery school behavior.   *Child Development,* 1949, **20,** 49–61.

Bandura, A., & Huston, A. C.   Identification as a process of incidental learning.   *Journal of Abnormal and Social Psychology,* 1961, **63,** 311–318.

Bandura, A., Ross, D., & Ross, S. A.   Transmission of aggression through imitation of aggressive models.   *Journal of Abnormal and Social Psychology,* 1961, **63,** 575–582.

Bandura, A., & Walters, R. H.   *Adolescent aggression.*   New York: Ronald, 1959.

Barnard, J., Zimbardo, P., & Sarason, S.   Anxiety and verbal behavior in children.   *Child Development,* 1961, **32,** 379–392.

Bayley, N., & Tuddenham, R.   Adolescent changes in body build.   In *National Society for the Study of Education, 43rd Yearbook, Part I, Adolescence.*   Chicago: University of Chicago Press, 1944.

Bell, G. B., & Hall, H. E.   The relationship between leadership and latency.   *Journal of Abnormal and Social Psychology,* 1954, **49,** 156–157.

Beller, E. K.   Dependence and independence in young children.   *Journal of Genetic Psychology,* 1955, **87,** 25–35.

Berkowitz, L.   *Aggression: A social psychological analysis.*   New York: McGraw-Hill, 1952.

Beverly, B. I.   The effect of illness on emotional development.   *Journal of Pediatrics,* 1936, **8,** 533–544.

Blum, E., & Kennedy, W.   Modification of dominant behavior in school children.   *Journal of Personality and Social Psychology,* 1967, **7,** 275–281.

Bonney, M. E.   The relative stability of social, intellectual, and academic status in grades II to IV, and the interrelationships between these various forms of growth.   *Journal of Educational Psychology,* 1943, **34,** 88–102.

Bonney, M. E.   Popular and unpopular children, a sociometric study.   *Sociometric Monographs,* No. 9.   New York: Beacon House, 1947.

Burton, R.   The generality of honesty reconsidered.   *Psychological Review,* 1963, **70,** 481–500.

Burton, R., Maccoby, E. E., & Allinsmith, W.   Antecedents of resistance to temptation in four-year-old children.   *Child Development,* 1961, **32,** 689–710.

Buskirk, C. V.   Performance on complex reasoning tasks as a function of anxiety.   *Journal of Abnormal and Social Psychology,* 1961, **62,** 201–209.

Castenada, A., McCandless, B., & Palermo, D.   The children's form of the Manifest Anxiety Scale.   *Child Development,* 1956, **27,** 317–326.

Castenada, A., Palermo, D., & McCandless, B.   Complex learning and performance as a function of anxiety in children and task difficulty.   *Child Development,* 1956, **27,** 327–332.

Cattell, R. B.   Personality traits associated with abilities.   I. With intelligence and drawing abilities.   *Educational and Psychological Measurement,* 1945, **5,** 131–146.

Cattell, R. B.   *Personality and motivation structure and measurement.*   Yonkers, N. Y.: World Book, 1957.

Cattell, R. B., & Coan, R. A.   Child personality structure as revealed in teachers' rating.   *Journal of Clinical Psychology,* 1957, **13,** 315–327.

Cattell, R. B., & Gruen, W.   The personality structure of 11-year-old children in terms of behavior rating data.   *Journal of Clinical Psychology,* 1953, **9,** 256–266.

Challman, R. C.   Factors influencing friendships among preschool children.   *Child Development,* 1932, **3,** 146–158.

Chittenden, G. E.   An experimental study in measuring and modifying assertive behavior in young children.   *Monographs of the Society for Research in Child Development,* 1942, **7,** No. 1.

Cooley, C. H.   *Human nature and the social order.*   New York: Scribner's, 1902.

Cortes, J., & Gatti, F. M.   Physique and self-description of temperament.   *Journal of Consulting Psychology,* 1965, **29,** 432–439.

Cortes, J., & Gatti, F. M.   Physique and motivation.   *Journal of Consulting Psychology,* 1966, **30,** 408–414.

Cowen, E., Zax, M., Klein, R., Izzo, L., & Trost, M.   The relation of anxiety in school children to school record, achievement, and behavioral measures.   *Child Development,* 1965, **36,** 685–695.

Crandall, V., Preston, A., & Rabson, A.   Maternal reactions and the development of independence and achievement behavior in young children.   *Child Development,* 1960, **31,** 243–251.

Davidson, K.   Interviews of parents of high anxious and low anxious children.   *Child Development,* 1959, **30,** 341–351.

Davidson, K., Sarason, S., Lighthall, F., Waite, R., & Sarnoff, I.   Differences between mothers' and fathers' ratings of low anxious and high anxious children.   *Child Development,* 1958, **29,** 155–160.

Davidson, M. A., McInnes, R. G., & Parnell, R. W. The distribution of personality traits in seven-year-old children: A combined psychological, psychiatric and somatotype study. *British Journal of Educational Psychology*, 1957, **27**, 48–61.

Diamond, S. *Personality and temperament.* New York: Harper, 1957.

Digman, J. M. Principal dimensions of child personality as inferred from teachers' judgments. *Child Development*, 1963, **34**, 43–60.

Dittman, A., & Goodrich, D. A comparison of social behavior in normal and hyperaggressive preadolescent boys. *Child Development*, 1961, **32**, 315–327.

Dollard, J., Doob, L. W., Miller, N. E., Mowrer, O. H., & Sears, R. R. *Frustration and aggression.* New Haven, Conn.: Yale University Press, 1939.

Dunham H. W. *Sociological theory and mental disorder.* Detroit: Wayne University Press, 1959.

Elser, R. The social position of hearing-handicapped children in the regular grades. *Exceptional Children*, 1959, **25**, 305–309.

Erikson, E. H. *Childhood and society.* New York: Norton, 1950.

Eron, L. D., Banta, T. J., Walder, L. O., & Laulicht, J. H. Comparison of data obtained from mothers and fathers on childrearing practices and their relation to child aggression. *Child Development*, 1961, **32**, 457–472.

Escalona, S. K., & Heider, G. M. *Prediction and outcome.* New York: Basic Books, 1959.

Feinberg, M., Smith, M., & Schmidt, R. An analysis of expressions used by adolescents at varying economic levels to describe accepted and rejected peers. *Journal of Genetic Psychology*, 1958, **93**, 133–148.

Feldhusen, J., & Klausmeier, H. Anxiety, intelligence, and achievement in children of low, average, and high intelligence. *Child Development*, 1962, **33**, 403–409.

Festinger, L. *A theory of cognitive dissonance.* Evanston, Ill.: Row-Peterson, 1957.

Fisher, S., & Cleveland, S. E. *Body image and personality.* Princeton, N. J.: Van Nostrand, 1958.

Fite, M. D. Aggressive behavior in young children and children's attitudes toward aggression. *Genetic Psychology Monographs*, 1940, **22**, 151–319.

Fortune, R. F. *Sorcerers of Dobu.* New York: Dutton, 1932.

Fox, C., Davidson, K., Lighthall, F., Waite, R., & Sarason, S. Human figure drawings of high and low anxious children. *Child Development*, 1958, **29**, 297–301.

Freud, A., & Dann, S. An experiment in group upbringing. *Psychoanalytic Study of Children*, 1951, **6**, 127–168. Reprinted in W. Martin & C. B. Stendler (Eds.), *Readings in child development.* New York: Harcourt, Brace, 1954.

Furfey, P. H.   Some factors influencing the selection of boys' chums.   *Journal of Applied Psychology*, 1927, **11**, 47–51.

Gavalas, R., & Briggs, P.   Concurrent schedules of reinforcement: a new concept of dependency.   *Merrill-Palmer Quarterly*, 1966, **12**, 97–121.

Gewirtz, J. L.   A factor analysis of some attention-seeking behaviors of young children.   *Child Development*, 1956, **27**, 17–36.

Glueck, S., & Glueck, E.   *Physique and delinquency.*   New York: Harper, 1956.

Gollin, E. A.   Organizational characteristics of social judgment: A developmental investigation.   *Journal of Personality*, 1958, **26**, 139–154.

Gottesman, I. I.   The psychogenics of personality.   Unpublished doctoral dissertation, University of Minnesota, 1960.

Grinder, R. E.   Parental childrearing practices, conscience, and resistance to temptation of sixth-grade children.   *Child Development*, 1962, **33**, 803–820.

Grinder, R. E., & McMichael, R. E.   Cultural influence on conscience development: Resistance to temptation and guilt among Samoans and American Caucasians.   *Journal of Abnormal and Social Psychology*, 1963, **66**, 503–507.

Hall, C. S., & Lindzey, G.   *Theories of personality.*   New York: Wiley, 1957.

Hardy, M. C.   Social recognition at the elementary school age.   *Journal of Social Psychology*, 1937, **8**, 365–384.

Hartshorne, H., & May, M. A.   *Studies in the nature of character: Vol. I. Studies in deceit.*   New York: Macmillan, 1928.

Hartshorne, H., May, M. A., & Shuttleworth, F. K.   *Studies in the nature of character: Vol. 3. Studies in the organization of character.*   New York: Macmillan, 1930.

Heathers, G.   Emotional dependence and independence in a physical threat situation.   *Child Development*, 1953, **24**, 169–179.

Heathers, G.   Emotional dependence and independence in nursery school play.   *Journal of Genetic Psychology*, 1955, **87**, 37–57.   (a)

Heathers, G.   Acquiring dependence and independence: A theoretical orientation.   *Journal of Genetic Psychology*, 1955, **87**, 277–291.   (b)

Hicks, D.   Imitation and retention of film-mediated aggressive peer and adult models.   *Journal of Personality and Social Psychology*, 1965, **2**, 97–100.

Hill, K., & Sarason, S.   The relation of test anxiety and defensiveness to test and school performance over the elementary-school years.   *Monographs of the Society for Research in Child Development*, 1966, **31**, No. 2.

Hoffman, L. W.   The father's role in the family and the child's peer-group adjustment.   *Merrill-Palmer Quarterly*, 1961, **7**, 97–105.

Hoffman, M. L.   Childrearing practices and moral development: Generalizations from empirical research.   *Child Development*, 1963, **34**, 295–318.

Hoffman, M. L., & Saltzstein, H.   Parent discipline and the child's moral development.   *Journal of Personality and Social Psychology*, 1967, **5**, 45–57.

Horowitz, F. D. The relationship of anxiety, self-concept, and sociometric status among fourth, fifth, and sixth grade children. *Journal of Abnormal and Social Psychology,* 1962, **65,** 212–214.

Horrocks, J. E., & Buker, M. E. A study of the friendship fluctuations of preadolescents. *Journal of Genetic Psychology,* 1951, **78,** 131–144.

Horrocks, J. E., & Thompson, G. G. A study of the friendship fluctuations of rural boys and girls. *Journal of Genetic Psychology,* 1946, **69,** 189–198.

Iscoe, I., & Cochran, I. Some correlates of manifest anxiety in children. *Journal of Consulting Psychology,* 1960, **24,** 97.

Jack, L. An experimental study of ascendant behavior in preschool children. In L. Jack, E. M. Manwell, I. G. Mengert, et. al., Behavior of the preschool child. *University of Iowa Study in Child Welfare,* 1934, **9,** 7–65.

Johnson, R. C., Ackerman, J. M., Frank, H., Fionda, A. J. Resistance to temptation, guilt following yielding, and psychopathology. *Journal of Consulting Psychology,* 1968, **32,** 169–175.

Jones, H. E. The longitudinal method in the study of personality. In I. Iscoe & H. Stevenson (Eds.), *Personality development in children.* Austin: University of Texas Press, 1960. Pp. 3–27.

Jones, M. C. The later careers of boys who were early- or late-maturing. *Child Development,* 1957, **28,** 113–128.

Jones, M. C. Psychological correlates of somatic development. *Child Development,* 1965, **36,** 899–911.

Jones, M. C., & Bayley, N. Physical maturing among boys as related to behavior. *Journal of Educational Psychology,* 1950, **41,** 129–148.

Kagan, J., & Moss, H. A. The stability of passive and dependent behavior from childhood through adulthood. *Child Development,* 1960, **31,** 577–591.

Kagan, J., & Moss, H. A. *Birth to maturity.* New York: Wiley, 1962.

Kitano, H. Validity of the Children's Manifest Anxiety Scale and the Modified Revised California Inventory. *Child Development,* 1960, **31,** 67–72.

Koch, H. I. Popularity in preschool children: Some related factors and a technique for its measurement. *Child Development,* 1933, **4,** 164–175.

Kuhn, D., Madsen, C., & Becker, W. Effects of exposure to an aggressive model and "frustration" on children's aggressive behavior. *Child Development,* 1967, **38,** 739–745.

L'Abate, L. Personality correlates of manifest anxiety in children. *Journal of Consulting Psychology,* 1960, **24,** 342–348.

Landy, D. *Tropical childhood.* Chapel Hill: University of North Carolina Press, 1959.

Lesser, G. S. The relationships between various forms of aggression and popularity among lower-class children. *Journal of Educational Psychology,* 1959, **50,** 20–25.

Levin, H., & Sears, R. R. Identification with parents as a determinant of doll play aggression. *Child Development,* 1956, **27,** 135–153.

Levy, S.   Figure drawing as a projective test.   In L. E. Abt & L. Bellak (Eds.), *Projective psychology.*   New York: Knopf, 1950.

Lippitt, R.   Popularity among preschool children.   *Child Development,* 1941, **12,** 305–332.

Lippitt, R., & Gold, M.   Classroom social structure as a mental health problem.   *Journal of Social Issues,* 1959, **15** (1), 40–49.

Lipsitt, L.   A Self-Concept Scale for Children and its relationship to the children's form of the Manifest Anxiety Scale.   *Child Development,* 1958, **29,** 463–472.

Lorge, I.   Intelligence and personality as revealed in questionnaires and inventories.   *National Society for the Study of Education, 39th Yearbook,* 1940, Part II, 275–281.

Lynn, R.   Personality characteristics of the mothers of aggressive and non-aggressive children.   *Journal of Genetic Psychology,* 1961, **99,** 159–164.

McCandless, B. R., Bilous, C. B., & Bennett, H. L.   Peer popularity and dependence on adults in preschool-age socialization.   *Child Development,* 1961, **32,** 511–518.

McCandless, B., & Castenada, A.   Anxiety in children, school achievement, and intelligence.   *Child Development,* 1956, **27,** 379–382.

McCandless, B., Castenada, A., & Palermo, D.   Anxiety in children and social status.   *Child Development,* 1956, **27,** 385–391.

McCord, W., McCord, J., & Howard, A.   Familial correlates of aggression in non-delinquent male children.   *Journal of Abnormal and Social Psychology,* 1961, **62,** 79–93.

McCord, W., McCord, J., & Verden, P.   Familial and behavioral correlates of dependency in male children.   *Child Development,* 1962, **33,** 313–326.

McCurdy, H. G.   The childhood pattern of genius.   *Journal of the Elisha Mitchell Scientific Society,* 1957, **73,** 448–462.   Also in R. A. King (Ed.), *Readings for an introduction to psychology.*   New York: McGraw-Hill, 1961.   Pp. 269–278.

McDavid, J., & Harari, H.   Stereotyping of names and popularity in grade-school children.   *Child Development,* 1966, **37,** 453–459.

McKee, J. P., & Leader, F. B.   The relationship of socioeconomic status and aggression to the competitive behavior of preschool children.   *Child Development,* 1955, **26,** 135–142.

MacKinnon, D.   Violations of prohibitions.   In H. A. Murray et al., *Explorations in personality.*   New York: Oxford University Press, 1938.

Malinowski, B.   *Argonauts of the western Pacific.*   New York: Dutton, 1922.

Maris, M.   Personal adjustment, assumed similarity to parents, and inferred parental evaluations of the self.   *Journal of Consulting Psychology,* 1958, **22,** 481–485.

Marshall, H. R., & McCandless, B. R.   Relationships between dependence on adults and social acceptance by peers.   *Child Development,* 1957, **28,** 413–419.

Martin, W. S.   Singularity and stability of profiles of social behavior.   In C. B. Stendler (Ed.), *Readings in child behavior and development.*   (2nd ed.)   New York: Harcourt, Brace, 1964.   Pp. 444–465.

May, R.   *The meaning of anxiety.*   New York: Ronald, 1950.

Mead, M.   *Sex and temperament in three primitive societies.*   New York: Morrow, 1935.

Medinnus, G. R.   An examination of several correlates of sociometric status in a first grade group.   *Journal of Genetic Psychology,* 1962, **101,** 3–13.

Mendel, G.   Children's preferences for differing degrees of novelty.   *Child Development,* 1965, **36,** 453–465.

Meyer, C. T.   The assertive behavior of children as related to parent behavior.   *Journal of Home Economics,* 1947, **7,** 77–80.

Miller, D. R., & Swanson, G. E.   *Inner conflict and defense.*   New York: Holt, 1960.

Mummery, D. V.   An analytical study of ascendant behavior of preschool children.   *Child Development,* 1947, **18,** 40–81.

Mummery, D. V.   Family backgrounds of assertive and nonassertive children.   *Child Development,* 1954, **25,** 63–80.

Murphy, G., Murphy, L. B., & Newcomb, T. M.   *Experimental social psychology.*   (Rev. ed.)   New York: Harper, 1937.

Murphy, L. B.   *Social behavior and child personality.*   New York: Columbia University Press, 1937.

Mussen, P., & Distler, L.   Child-rearing antecedents of masculine identification in kindergarten boys.   *Child Development,* 1960, **31,** 89–100.

Mussen, P., & Newman, D.   Handicap: Motivation, and adjustment in physically disabled children.   *Exceptional Children,* 1958, **24,** 255–260, 277–279.

Neilon, P.   Shirley's babies after fifteen years: A personality study.   *Journal of Genetic Psychology,* 1948, **73,** 175–186.

Northway, M. L.   Sociometry and some challenging problems of social relationships.   *Sociometry,* 1946, **9,** 187–198.

Otis, N. B., & McCandless, B. R.   Responses to repeated frustrations of young children differentiated according to need area.   *Journal of Abnormal and Social Psychology,* 1955, **50,** 349–353.

Page, M.   The modification of ascendant behavior in preschool children.   *University of Iowa Study in Child Welfare,* 1936, **12** (3), 69.

Parten, M. B.   Leadership among preschool children.   *Journal of Abnormal and Social Psychology,* 1932, **27,** 430–440.

Partridge, E. D.   Leadership among adolescent boys.   *Teachers College Contributions to Education,* 1934, No. 608.

Peck, R. F.   Family patterns correlated with adolescent personality structure.   *Journal of Abnormal and Social Psychology,* 1958, **57,** 347–350.

Phillips, B., Hindsman, E., & Jennings, E.   Influence of intelligence on anxiety and perception of self and others.   *Child Development,* 1960, **31,** 41–46.

Piaget, J. *The construction of reality in the child.* New York: Basic Books, 1954 (originally published in English in 1937).

Radke, M. J. The relation of parental authority to children's behavior and attitudes. *University of Minnesota Child Welfare Monographs,* 1946, No. 22.

Raimy, V. C. Self reference in counseling interviews. *Journal of Consulting Psychology,* 1948, **12,** 153–163.

Roff, M. Preservice personality problems and subsequent adjustments to military service: The prediction of psychoneurotic reactions. *USAF School of Aviation Medicine Report,* 1957, No. 57–136.

Roff, M. Relations between certain preservice factors and psychoneurosis during military duty. *Armed Forces Medical Journal,* 1960, **II,** 152–160.

Roff, M. Childhood social interactions and young adult bad conduct. *Journal of Abnormal and Social Psychology,* 1961, **63,** 333–337.

Rogers, C. R. *Client-centered therapy.* Boston: Houghton Mifflin, 1951.

Rosen, B. Family structure and value transmission. *Merrill-Palmer Quarterly,* 1964, **10,** 59–76.

Sanford, R. N., Adkins, M. M., Miller, R. B., Cobb, E. A., et al. Physique, personality and scholarship: A cooperative study of school children. *Monographs of the Society for Research in Child Development,* 1943, **8,** No. 1.

Sarason, I. The effects of anxiety and threat on the solution of a difficult task. *Journal of Abnormal and Social Psychology,* 1961, **62,** 165–168.

Sarason, I. Test anxiety and intellectual performance. *Journal of Abnormal and Social Psychology,* 1963, **66,** 73–75.

Sarason, S., Davidson, K., Lighthall, F., & Waite, R. A Test Anxiety Scale for Children. *Child Development,* 1958, **29,** 105–113. (a)

Sarason, S., Davidson, K., Lighthall, F., & Waite, R. Classroom observations of high and low anxious children. *Child Development,* 1958, **29,** 287–295. (b)

Sarason, S., Hill, K., & Zimbardo, P. A longitudinal study of the relation of test anxiety to performance on intelligence and achievement tests. *Monographs of the Society for Research in Child Development,* 1964, **29,** No. 7.

Schilder, P. *The image and appearance of the human body.* London: Kegan, Paul, 1935.

Sears, P. S. Doll play aggression in normal young children: Influence of sex, age, sibling status, father's absence. *Psychological Monographs: General and Applied,* 1951, **65,** No. 6.

Sears, R. R. The growth of conscience. In I. Iscoe & H. W. Stevenson (Eds.), *Personality development in children.* Austin: University of Texas Press, 1960. Pp. 92–111.

Sears, R. R. Relation of early socialization experiences to aggression in middle childhood. *Journal of Abnormal and Social Psychology,* 1961, **63,** 466–492.

Sears, R. R., Maccoby, E. E., & Levin, H. *Patterns of child rearing.* Evanston, Ill.: Row, Peterson, 1957.

Sears, R. R., Whiting, J. W. M., Nowlis, V., & Sears, P. S. Some child-rearing antecedents of aggression and dependency in young children. *Genetic Psychology Monographs,* 1953, **47,** 135–234.

Secord, P. Objectification of word association procedures by the use of homonyms in a measure of body cathexis. *Journal of Personality,* 1953, **21,** 479–495.

Secord, P., & Jourard, S. The appraisal of body cathexis: Body cathexis and the self. *Journal of Consulting Psychology,* 1953, **17,** 343–347.

Shaub, R. R. Kidney donors: Body image and psychopathology. Unpublished master's thesis, University of Colorado, 1967.

Sheldon, W. H., Stevens, S. S., & Tucker, W. B. *The varieties of human physique.* New York: Harper, 1940.

Shirley, M. M. *The first two years: A study of twenty-five babies.* Vol. 3. *Personality manifestations.* Minneapolis: University of Minnesota Press, 1933.

Shlien, J. A client-centered approach to schizophrenia: first approximation. In A. Burton (Ed.), *Psychotherapy of the psychoses.* New York: Basic Books, 1961.

Shlien, J. The self concept in relation to behavior: Theoretical and empirical research. *Religion Education, Research Supplement,* 1962, **17,** S111–S127.

Siegel, A. A., & Kohn, L. G. Permissiveness, permission, and aggression: The effect of adult presence or absence on aggression in children's play. *Child Development,* 1959, **30,** 131–141.

Smock, C. Perceptual rigidity and closure phenomenon as a function of manifest anxiety in children. *Child Development,* 1958, **29,** 237–247.

Sontag, L. W., Baker, C. T., & Nelson, V. L. Mental growth and personality development: A longitudinal study. *Monographs of the Society for Research in Child Development,* 1958, **23,** No. 68.

Spector, S. I. Climate and social acceptability. *Journal of Educational Sociology,* 1953, **27,** 108–114.

Staffieri, J. A study of social stereotype of body image in children. *Journal of Personality and Social Psychology,* 1967, **7,** 101–104.

Stein, A. Imitation of resistance to temptation. *Child Development,* 1967, **38,** 157–169.

Stein, A., & Wright, J. Imitative learning under conditions of nurturance and nurturance withdrawal. *Child Development,* 1964, **35,** 927–938.

Stendler, C. B. Critical periods in socialization and over-dependency. *Child Development,* 1952, **23,** 3–12.

Stendler, C. B. Possible causes of over-dependency in young children. *Child Development,* 1954, **25,** 125–146.

Steth, M., & Connor, R. Dependency and helpfulness in young children. *Child Development,* 1962, **33,** 15–20.

Stewart, A.   Excessive crying in infants—a family disease.   In M. Senn (Ed.), *Sixth conference on problems of infancy and childhood.*   New York: Josiah Macy, Jr., Foundation, 1953.   Pp. 138–160.

Stogdill, R. M.   Personal factors associated with leadership: A survey of the literature.   *Journal of Psychology,* 1948, **25**, 35–71.

Stott, L. H.   Stability in ascendance-submission.   *Merrill-Palmer Quarterly,* 1957, **3**, 145–159.

Strauss, A. (Ed.).   *The social psychology of George Herbert Mead.*   Chicago: University of Chicago Press, 1956.

Swensen, C. H., Jr.   Empirical evaluations of human figure drawings.   *Psychological Bulletin,* 1957, **54**, 431–466.

Taylor, J. A.   A personality scale of manifest anxiety.   *Journal of Abnormal and Social Psychology,* 1953, **48**, 285–290.

Terman, L. M., & Oden, M. H.   *The gifted child grows up.*   Stanford, Calif.: Stanford University Press, 1947.

Thompson, G. G., & Horrocks, J. E.   A study of the friendship fluctuations of urban boys and girls.   *Journal of Genetic Psychology,* 1947, **70**, 53–63.

Tisza, V. B., Selverstone, B., Rosenblum, G., & Hanlon, N.   Psychiatric observations of children with cleft palate.   *American Journal of Orthopsychiatry,* 1958, **28**, 416–423.

Tryon, C. M.   Evaluation of adolescent personality by adolescents.   *Monographs of the Society for Research in Child Development,* 1939, **4**, No. 4, p. 88.

Tuddenham, R. D.   Studies in reputation.   III. Correlates of popularity among elementary school children.   *Journal of Educational Psychology,* 1951, **42**, 257–276.

Tuddenham, R. D.   The constancy of personality ratings over two decades.   *Genetic Psychology Monographs,* 1958, **60**, 3–29.

Walker, R. N.   Body build and behavior in young children: I. Body build and nursery school teachers' ratings.   *Monographs of the Society for Research in Child Development,* 1962, **27**, No. 3.

Walker, R. N.   Body build and behavior in young children: II. Body build and parents' ratings.   *Child Development,* 1963, **34**, 1–23.

Wenger, M. A.   Preliminary study of the significance of measures of autonomic balance.   *Psychosomatic Medicine,* 1947, **9**, 301–309.

Whiting, J. W. M.   Resource medication and learning by identification.   In I. Iscoe & H. W. Stevenson (Eds.), *Personality development in children.*   Austin: University of Texas Press, 1960.

Whiting, J. W. M., & Child, I.   *Child training and personality.*   New Haven, Conn.: Yale University Press, 1953.

Winder, C. L., & Rau, L.   Parental attitudes associated with social deviance in preadolescent boys.   *Journal of Abnormal and Social Psychology,* 1962, **64**, 418–424.

Witkin, H. A., Dyke, R. B., Faterson, H. F., Goodenough, D. R., & Karp, S. A.   *Psychological differentiation.*   New York: Wiley, 1962.

Woods, F. J., & Carrow M. A.   The choice-rejection status of speech-defective children.   *Exceptional Children,* 1959, **25,** 279–283.

Wylie, R. C.   Some relationships between defensiveness and self-concept discrepancies.   *Journal of Personality,* 1957, **25,** 600–616.

Wylie, R. C.   *The self concept: A critical survey of pertinent literature.* Lincoln: University of Nebraska Press, 1961.

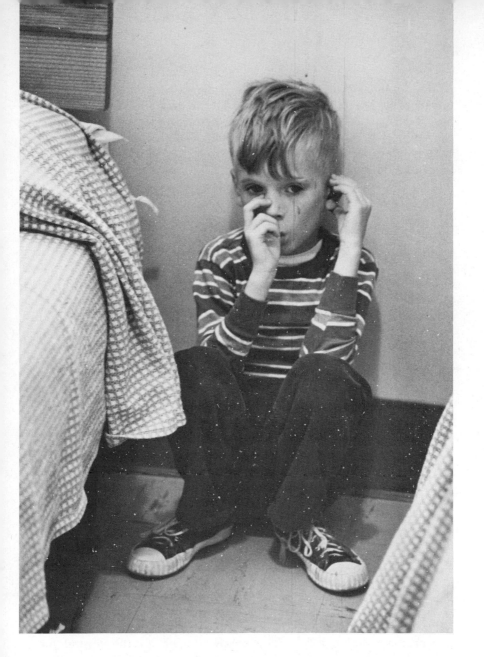

16

Disturbances in Development

As development progresses psychological problems often emerge. Disturbances set in motion problem behavior. How such behavior is caused, how it is diagnosed, how it is treated, and the probability of its cure constitute the substance of this chapter. These subjects will be considered under four general headings: causes, diagnosis, treatment techniques, and prognosis.

CAUSES OF BEHAVIORAL PROBLEMS

Only rarely do we find a disturbed individual with one specific form of maladjustment and no other symptoms. Oftener a patient will have a dominant set of problems accompanied by other, less well-developed signs of disturbance. So, too, with causation. Seldom can we say about any one problem of any one patient that this and only this aspect of his background produced the disturbance. Far more frequently a variety of factors contribute to the production of a given kind of problem.

A fine illustration of the diversity of factors that may be seen in the background of an individual appears in the autobiography of Carryl Chessman (1955), a robber who was convicted and executed for kidnapping. Chessman attributed his long record of crime to having been reared in a Los Angeles slum and to overcompensation for being a small, picked-on child. Although he placed no emphasis on the fact, Chessman did have a severe attack of encephalitis as a child, a disease that frequently produces undesirable behavioral changes in its victims. Thus all those who believe in sociological forces, feelings of inferiority, or organic factors as the prime cause of problem behavior are satisfied by Chessman's explanation of his deviant behavior. In addition, certain aspects of his family relationship support a Freudian interpretation of his conduct.

Although numerous forces combine to produce many behavioral problems, the effect of any one force differs from behavior to behavior. Hence the statement that "Problem A has much more of an innate physiological component, and is less influenced by the social milieu of the patient than Problem B." The relative import of the several forces believed to cause specific problem disorders can be, but seldom has been, determined.

Genetic Factors

Many problem behaviors relate to affective, or emotional, maladjustment. The individual may "feel too much" and be devastated by

618

events that bring no concern to others. Or he may "feel too little" and not have much attachment for others, in which case he is not greatly affected by social approval or disapproval and shows incompetence at learning social roles. The disturbed, fearful, neurotic youngster and the psychopathic delinquent have one thing in common: neither is influenced by the attitudes of others toward them or by inner standards in the same way that better-adjusted children are influenced. Individual differences in emotionality and emotional stability have a fairly substantial genetic base (Vandenberg, 1967). In this broad sense, genetic forces may underlie many varieties of problem behavior.

More specifically, the role of heredity is evident in many cases of schizophrenia. If one of a pair of siblings becomes schizophrenic, the chances are roughly one in seven that the other will become so. For fraternal twins the probability is the same. For stepbrothers and sisters growing up in the same home, the probability is approximately one in 50. Among identical twins, it is seven in eight. Although these findings by Kallman and by others (reviewed by Rosenthal, 1962) have been attacked for various reasons (Pastore, 1949; Jackson, 1964), their general conclusions appear to have been upheld, though more current studies (Gottesman & Shields, 1966; Kringlen, 1966) show a lesser influence of heredity than did Kallman's research. As noted above, not all twin pairs, even among identicals, are concordant (alike) in the sense that either both members of the pair are normal or else both members are schizophrenic. Rosenthal (1959) studied pairs of concordant (both schizophrenic) and discordant (only one schizophrenic) identical (MZ) twins. Differences in family structure and in the treatment of the twins were found between the two groups. Further, schizophrenics from discordant pairs (in which schizophrenia was presumably more a result of environmental pathology than it was among concordant schizophrenic twins) had a later onset and more favorable prognosis than did members of concordant pairs. Rosenthal's (1963) study of the "Genain" quadruplets, all of whom were schizophrenic, should be mentioned here. The intensive study of these four young women led to the conclusion that susceptibility to schizophrenic breakdown is genetically determined, but that the severity of the manifestations of the disturbance, for each of the quadruplets, was determined chiefly by the amount of environmental stress. As discussed in Chapter 2, the tendency to approach or withdraw from stimuli, as well as general emotionality and activity level, seem to be rather strongly determined by heredity. Since these aspects of personality are related to schizophrenic behavior, it is not surprising that at least some types of schizophrenic disturbance have a strong hereditary component.

Congenital Factors

As discussed in Chapter 3, it is difficult to separate hereditary from congenital factors, since symptoms of both become apparent at birth or some time after it. As noted in Chapter 3, the most thorough study so far of the connection between congenital factors and problem behavior was undertaken by a group headed by Pasamanick. Kawi and Pasamanick (1959) stated that there was within the uterus a continuum of maldevelopment "with a lethal component consisting of abortions, still births, and neonatal deaths, and a sublethal component consisting of cerebral palsy, epilepsy, mental deficiency, and behavior disorders in children." A frequent sequel to malnutrition and to complications in pregnancy is hyperactivity, confusion, and disorganization in the children (Pasamanick, Rogers, & Lilienfeld, 1956), symptoms that might often be confused with certain hereditary disorders or with postnatal brain injury. Negro-white differences in the frequency of malnutrition and of inadequate prenatal care may well account for any remaining variance in Negro-white IQ after sociological factors have been taken into account (see pp. 73–74). Malnutrition and inadequate prenatal care vary across race to such a degree that nonwhites have approximately twice as high a frequency of fetal, neonatal, and infant deaths as compared with whites (U. S. Bureau of the Census, 1967, p. 56). The data presented by Pasamanick and his associates are so strong and compelling that it seems clear that problems of retardation and of behavior pathology could be reduced markedly by increased federal or local efforts in this area of social welfare.

Postnatal Physical Factors

After 12 years of no untoward problems, a boy developed a number of symptoms. He refused to go to school, saying it gave him a headache. He demanded to be allowed to sleep with his parents because he had dizzy spells in bed. In addition, there were a number of other hypochondriac complaints. His parents took him to a private clinic, where a clinical psychologist and psychiatrist concurred that the youngster would benefit from therapy. Treatment had commenced when the parents decided to play it safe and consult a physician specializing in diagnosis. After learning of the symptoms, the internist measured the electrical potentials of the boy's brain by electroencephalograph and concluded that the youth had a brain tumor. Surgery confirmed the internist's diagnosis; a benign tumor was found and removed. The case illustrates the importance of being fully aware of the patient's physical condition before diagnosis.

Brain injury suffered in the uterus, at birth, or after birth appears to produce deviant behavior as well as mental deficiency, as Kawi and Pasamanick (1959) observed. Since brain injury results not only from tumors but also from diseases, such as encephalitis and meningitis, and from physical damage, it is a factor of relevance in the study of behavioral problems. On the other hand, it is the favored cause in diagnoses made by parents. *All* children have bad falls and high fevers; hence parents with a problem child can always assuage their guilt by blaming a fall or a fever rather than their own behavior. Although brain injury may be a valid cause and must be considered a possibility during diagnosis, unsubstantiated parental statements of injury or pressures to attribute the problem to it call for a wary attitude in the diagnostician.

The influence of biological factors in postnatal life is reinforced by Hebb's citation (1949, p. 262) of evidence that shows neurotic or psychotic behavior to have been associated, at least on occasion, with a large number of physical diseases. Whether inherited, congenital, or postnatal, physical conditions are obviously related to behavior disorders. For this reason it is not redundant to emphasize again the necessity of determining the physical state of the youngster who is referred to a social agency or clinic as a "problem child."

Family Factors

Ever since Freud's day, it has been believed that the basis of pathology lies in the family setting. Contemporary theory attributes pathology in the child to the behavior of the parents, especially that of the mother. It is rather surprising to find parental guilt and responsibility increasingly emphasized at the same time that the person with the problem, whether child or adult, is absolved of responsibility. Although, in many cases, parental deviations contribute to problem behavior in their children, these parental behaviors should be judged on the same basis as the child's problems—as being caused.

Further defense of the parents lies in the fact that the cause-and-effect relationship between parental behavior and child problems is often unclear. For example, "three-month colic," a term used by parents to describe a disorder in which the infant howls, in apparent agony, for roughly 20 out of every 24 hours in its first three months of life and then suddenly ceases without reason, illustrates the difficulties of attributing cause and effect to parental influences on child behavior problems. Lakin (1957) found that mothers of colicky infants, in contrast to mothers of noncolicky infants, were less accepting of the female role, felt less adequate, were less happy with their husbands and with their parents, and were less motherly in their attitudes. He concluded that these attributes of mothers produced the colic in their infants. However, could it not be that having an infant cry for 20 out of 24 hours for a few months might have produced the differences in attitude?

Similarly, several studies (e.g., Heilbrun, 1960; Kohn & Clausen, 1956) have shown mothers of schizophrenics to be both harsher and more overprotective than mothers of normal children. Aside from the obviously important fact that these judgments usually occur *after* the schizophrenic onset, there is still the matter of cause and effect. Fish (1959) produced evidence to corroborate Bender's (1947) contention that certain characteristic deviations of behavior were observable at or shortly after birth in a child who would later become schizophrenic. Other evidence indicates that a child who will later succumb to schizophrenia suffers no more traumatic experience than normal siblings, but will more probably react pathologically to any change in the environment and *invite a special response* from parents that further impairs an innately weak capacity to resist stress (Prout & White, 1956). Although it is unpopular to attribute pathological behavior to hereditary factors, genetic sources cannot be easily dismissed.

In some behavioral problems, however, parental pathology seems clearly to be the primary cause, as illustrated in this case reported by Bender (1952, pp. 214–216) and in Figure 16-1.

> Morris was a 10 year old boy. When he came to us he was a pathetic child. He had a neurological condition especially in his legs which made them feeble and produced chorea-like movements. Before admission it was said that at times the movements were so severe that he had to be carried about, and on occasion they became so intense that they were thought to be epileptic fits. This diagnosis seemed reasonable especially since his mother had epilepsy and was being cared for in an institution for epileptic patients. Morris had been living in an orphan home which was thought to be inadequate to care for a boy with such difficult problems. Morris had had some very unhappy experiences. Even before his mother had been separated from him, she would often become psychotic and at such times she would chase Morris with a knife and threaten to cut off his feet, saying his feet were not any good and were making him have fits like hers. He told us that on one occasion he hid under the bed just in time to avoid losing his feet.
>
> When he came to the hospital his legs were weak, clumsy, and awkward. There was definite evidence of a slight choreiform disability and poor

FIGURE 16-1   (*a*) Joe Palooka, by Morris (crayon).   (*b*) Tight-rope walker by Morris (pencil and water color) (Bender, 1952, p. 215).

muscular development, especially in the left leg.   There was however never any indication of epilepsy.   Morris was very self-conscious of his disability and tried to conceal it by clowning.   He tried to play the role of Charlie Chaplin.   But among the children he felt very inferior and could not compete in their active play and fights.

When asked to draw pictures of a man, he drew a one-legged man and called it Joe Palooka.   When he was given the miniature toys which we used for psychotherapeutic work, he always had his soldiers riding to battle in trucks, because he said they did not want to walk.   During the weeks that he spent with us he was given active orthopedic treatment and physiotherapy for his legs, psychotherapy by play technique, as well as group work in the art class. We could follow the progress of his improvement in his art work. Soon his men had two legs instead of one, although at first they were still always riding in carts. Later, they were walking on the ground, and soon they were climbing ladders. Finally when Morris was ready for discharge we got the picture where a man is walking a tight rope between two buildings. When Morris left he was not secure on his feet and in his ability to compete with other boys in active play. He was placed in a boarding home and arrangements were made for further orthopedic care and psychotherapy which utilized his ability to express himself in art. He joined a boys' club where he participated in an art class and a class in jujitsu. His physical condition, posture and gait improved steadily. At 15 he returned to the home of his father's family, together with his father, while his mother was still in the institution. With his growing motor coordination and interest in sports he developed good social success despite his limited intellectual endowment.

As Ackerman (1958) pointed out, the parent often produces a kind of pathology in the child that fills certain parental needs. A clear illustration of this "secondary" gain by the parent is seen in cases in which the parent has a dislike for authority figures, yet cannot bring this dislike out into the open. By providing subtle reinforcement, the parent produces a rebellious child. It does not take much talent or imagination on the part of the youngster to recognize a green light when a parent laughs and says, "Oh, you shouldn't have hit the high school principal in the nose." Verbal protest notwithstanding, the parent finds hitting an authority figure to be a rather pleasant prospect.

In other instances, parents produce deviation by providing the child with a deviant behavior model. Roebuck and Johnson (1964) show that individuals who as youths and adults have operated as "con men" have learned from parents a life style centered on deceit. As one con man related:

> I learned from my mother that "front" and how you carry yourself is the main thing with the marks (suckers). She'd buy $10 worth of groceries and while I held them walk up to the man and give him a rubber check for $50. She talked fast, smooth, and bold. You know, like she had a million. Of course she always dressed the part. She had such a way about her that the clerks in stores where she stole dresses were afraid to question her though they had a good idea she had their "rags" under her coat. She always said, "son if you get in the life (life in the underworld) get a soft hustle. No rough stuff" (Roebuck & Johnson, 1964, p. 241).

This is clearly an example of imitation and direct social learning, not so much of one type of criminality but a way of life predicated on cheating. Another life style learned in much the same manner is that of hypochondria. Observing a parent using a certain style of response to life, the child sees that the behavior pays and adopts it as his own.

In other instances of psychological disturbance caused by family circumstances, the fault is not so much in the individual family members as it is in the pattern of interaction within the family.

One aspect of interaction is the "double bind," in which the child is told, in essence, that if he behaves in way X, he will be punished, and that if he does not behave in this way, he'll also be punished. Here is a case in point:

> A young man who had fairly well recovered from an acute schizophrenic episode was visited in the hospital by his mother. He was glad to see her and impulsively put his arm around her shoulders, whereupon she stiffened. He withdrew his arm, and she asked, "Don't you love me any more?" He then blushed, and she said, "Dear, you must not be so easily embarrassed and afraid of your feelings" (Bateson, Jackson, Haley, & Weakland, 1956, p. 259).

Other patterns of communication that are said to produce psychological disturbance include "disconfirmation," in which the parent or parents respond to the child's behavior as though the behavior is irrelevant, and "disqualification" (Haley, 1959), as illustrated below:

> Typically in these families the mother tends to initiate what happens, while indicating either that she isn't, or that someone else should. The father will invite her to initiate what happens while condemning her when she does. Often they suggest the child take the lead, and then disqualify his attempts (Haley, 1963).

These are only several of the many theories of family interaction. It should be noted that, although the two examples above show the mothers to be the villains, these theories have to do with the entire family—the father, mother, and siblings.

Disorders in communication within the family may well be important sources of confusion for the child. Yet it seems entirely possible that all families have frequent disorders of this sort, and, for that matter, that all other groups do, too. Schofield's and Balian's (1959) research, showing that highly normal males have as many supposedly pathological factors in their home environment as do institutionalized patients, suggests that many phenomena, such as the double bind, are relatively common experiences for all of us. If so, they do not in themselves produce psychological disturbance. Rather, they produce disturbance in *some* people, and our problem is to determine why these people are so severely and adversely affected.

One further important aspect of the family situation is the role of the parent as diagnostician. The only common element in all behavioral problems is that they diagnosed by someone. Every clinician sees many children whose behavior is representative of children in general, yet who are viewed as severe problems by parents or, less often, by teachers. Other children seen as "holy terrors" by the world at large are angels to their parents. In this respect, an item on the "Lie" scale of a well-known personality test rests on the fact that nearly all adults confess to having indulged in petty theft at some time during childhood; thus, in a statistical sense, this behavior is normal. The same thing may be said for the findings of the Kinsey reports (1948, 1953) in which most children admitted to indulging in many varieties of sexual behavior at some time in development prior to reaching maturity. Yet if any of these behaviors are detected by parents and made to symbolize an evil nature, the child may well accept the parental diagnosis of being evil or delinquent and live up to the role thus assigned him.

A final illustration of a problem created primarily by diagnosis is found in feeding. Clinical psychologists are familiar with the maternal complaint: "He hasn't eaten anything for two days and he never does more than pick at his food. I'm afraid he'll become ill if he doesn't eat more." The starving child who accompanies her to the consultation nearly always turns out to be highly active, healthy, and obviously well nourished. The mother's diagnosis, though clearly having no foundation in reality, is certainly of great concern to her.

The high frequency of feeding problems (25 per cent of all children are diagnosed as feeding problems by someone, usually parents, according to Kanner, 1957) is associated with aspects of the culture as well as of the mother-child relationship. Most of the world goes to bed hungry, whereas Americans, as a nation, have more than enough. Because of this affluence, food is urged on children and its consumption is heavily emphasized. Advertising and other social forces make a fetish of nutrition in what is perhaps the best-fed society of all. This becomes an area of parental concern when many children shift from having a remarkable appetite (in the parent's view) for the first few years of life to a much reduced food intake at three and after as growth rate slows down and a high peak of metabolic efficiency is attained. The parent is concerned; the child feels it. The parent assigns the role of feeding problem to the child and the child accepts it. Since feeding problems occur only in food-rich societies, it seems likely that they do not originate with the child but with parental responses to the child's eating habits.

The problem in all these examples is more in diagnosis than in child behavior. Yet once the diagnosis has been made the child is treated differently and may accept the "problem child" role and become a genuine problem. The child judged doomed to perdition begins to think that he might as will live up to the reputation. The child diagnosed a stutterer stutters; the child considered a dullard may become a nonachiever (see Lecky, 1945), and the one deemed a feeding problem very likely becomes one (see Kanner, 1957, pp. 470–477). Adults should, therefore, exercise extreme caution in diagnosis.

One final point regarding the role of family factors in producing behavior problems. Why is it that the mother is so frequently viewed as being the cause of the child's problem? The child, terror though he may be, is treated as the victim of a pathological mother. She, on the other hand, is seen as pathological not because of environmental forces acting on her, but because of her own free will and accord. Some of Roe's (1953) data suggest that social scientists generally have grown up in a mother-dominated home. (Physical and biological scientists, on the other hand, have grown up in father-dominated homes.) Further, social scientists generally have had a rather stormy relationship with their mothers. As Roe points out, it may be that social scientists' theories of pathology, generally emphasizing maternal causes of disturbance, do not reflect reality with regard to the world at large so much as they reflect the social scientist's own life situation, in which a major influence is a dominative and difficult mother. It may be, however, that theories implicating the mothers as the chief causal agent in the production of neurotic disturbance are correct, even though the theories have been developed, in part, for the wrong reasons. Data (Medinnus, 1965; Brigham, Ricketts, & Johnson, 1967) suggest that psychopathic acting-out problems among boys are associated with poor father-son relationships, but that more neurotic kinds of disturbance are associated with poor mother-son relationships.

Sociological Factors

Sociologists have argued that most delinquents are psychologically "normal" but that they come from slum areas in which certain operative forces dispose an individual to become involved in illegal behaviors. Among children from depressed and criminal slum environments, it hardly seems necessary to seek strictly psychological forces to account for delinquency, and the subcultural delinquent is perhaps the commonest sociological problem.

Social class and subcultural differences in values frequently may cause lower-class children, especially from minority groups, to behave in ways that cause them to be judged as deviant by members of the majority culture.

The causes for any type of behavior problem are multiple, often interacting with one another. Yet careful study of prior conditions leading to problem behavior will, for many types of problem, yield discrete categories, as we shall presently observe, each with its own major cause and each with its own treatment.

DIAGNOSIS

The term *diagnosis* comes from the Greek and means to "know one from another." As the term itself indicates, the task of the diagnostician is to observe the symptomatic behavior closely and to establish the particular type of disorder most probably associated with the evident symptoms. Psychotherapists have not succeeded well in fulfilling this task. Sometimes they believe the challenge to be insurmountable. Yet medical doctors have faced and largely mastered the same problem.

Differential Diagnosis in Medicine

There are a number of varieties of fever, just as there are a number of varieties of mental deficiency and, probably, of schizophrenia. Fever, mental retardation, and schizophrenia have one thing in common: each has a single dominant symptom—high temperature, inability to learn adequately, and dissociation, respectively. Beneath the surface similarity of high temperature, closely observing physicians discerned secondary symptoms that allowed them to differentiate types of fever within the broad phenotype of fever. Malaria began with chills accompanied by blueness of the skin and cyclical vomiting, then showed high fever followed by normal or subnormal temperature until the next paroxysm. Typhoid showed some similarity to malaria in early symptoms, since chills are common to both. Unlike malaria, however, typhoid also produces early symptoms of tiredness and loss of appetite; as the disease advances, there are pains in the limbs and severe headaches. The cyclical quality of malaria is missing. Later, in typhoid, lethargy increases, pulse rate rises slightly, and temperature climbs higher. There is nervousness and delirium, and a rash on the chest and abdomen. Recovery is gradual.

A third fever, yellow fever, resembles typhoid in many respects, since early symptoms of both include severe headaches. However, victims of yellow fever feel pain in the back and neck rather than in the limbs, and the pulse rate drops rather than rises. In its early stages, yellow fever also resembles malaria; vomiting is a symptom of each. But jaundice accompanies yellow fever, as compared with the blueness of malaria.

By observing *all* the symptoms, one can detect a specific configuration that accompanies each disorder and allows for a clear differential diagnosis—a "telling one from the other." This diagnosis *could not* be arrived at by observing only the dominant symptom, fever, nor by observing most of the individual secondary symptoms. One can differentiate these fevers from one another and note the effectiveness of specific treatment techniques on each. Since no treatment suffices for all of them, any treatment is necessarily a failure in most cases until the subspecies of fever are distinguished so that one of them susceptible to a particular type of treatment can be singled out from the rest. Causes can then be discovered and steps taken for prevention as well as cure. The same point applies to psychological problems.

Differential Diagnosis and the Medical Model of Psychological Disturbance

Disorders that show considerable similarity in their manifest symptomatology may differ markedly in causation, in how they are most effectively treated, and in prognosis. Therefore it would seem highly advantageous to differentiate superficially similar sets of symptoms in order to find effective treatment techniques for each.

Arguments can be raised against differential diagnosis: Many attempts at developing systems of differential diagnosis have proved fruitless; different psychological problems are not caused by different physical agents (as is the case with physical disorders and "germs"), and may seem to be caused by the same kind of psychosocial problems (e.g., feelings of estrangement from others); all kinds of psychological disturbance may basically be one, though the symptoms vary somewhat, and therefore may be expected to yield to the same treatment procedures. For these reasons many psychologists believe that differential diagnosis is futile and without value. Each of these arguments is dealt with, in turn, below.

Attempts at developing systems of differential diagnosis *have* proved fruitless, but usually because the systems are based almost entirely on the symptoms present when the diagnosis is made. These symptoms frequently change from day to day and from examiner to examiner. Other, more recent systems for the differentiation of problem behaviors have proved to be of value. A system of differential diagnosis presently in use, in which schizophrenic disturbances are divided into two major categories (process and reaction), has shown that problems in the process category show a greater genetic component and a longer period of onset than in the reaction category. Individuals in the former category have a tendency to blame others for their problems, a longer period of institutionalization, a lower likelihood of release, and a poorer prognosis. In the same fashion, an awareness of subtle phenotypical differences between groups has allowed for a distinction to be made between childhood schizophrenia and autism (see Rimland, 1964), two disorders with differing probable causes (etiology), differing treatment possibilities, and differing prognosis. Other examples of the utility of differential diagnosis are given below.

It is true that psychological disturbances are not all caused by their own highly specific agents, as is the case with physical diseases. However, sometimes they are (e.g., phenylketonuria, caused by a pair of recessive genes), and sometimes it is possible to see the relative weighting of influence of different agents (as in hereditary and environmental factors in process and reactive schizophrenia). The fact that disorders sometimes can be separated from one another in terms of their causes, most effective therapies, and prognosis suggests that it is valuable to attempt to do so more often, to make use of the most effective treatment technique for a given kind of problem, to evaluate adequately the effectiveness of the technique, and to give the parents the most accurate statement of prognosis possible.

The whole concept of differential diagnosis is sometimes rejected because a therapist believes that his form of therapy is equally effective for all problems and therefore that diagnosis is pointless. In contrast, Eysenck (1961, 1965) has demonstrated in excellent reviews of the literature that about as many people who receive *no* therapy recover from their problems as people who do receive therapy. Eysenck's conclusion was that "talking therapy" has no positive value, and may even be harmful. An alternative conclusion that can be drawn from the data that Eysenck presents is that some people get worse, some are unchanged, and some gain from each variant of psychotherapy. If this latter conclusion is correct, our task is to discover what kind of person, with what kind of problem, benefits from each type of therapy—again a problem of differential diagnosis.

Other Instances of the Differential Diagnosis of Psychological Problems. Two groups of theories exist about the major causes of juvenile delinquency. Sociological theories stress the notion that a delinquent is usually a normal, well-integrated member of a subculture that accepts values judged to be delinquent by the majority culture. Psychological theories consider personal maladjustment as the basis for the delinquency. There has been little effort to fragmentize the broad category, delinquent, into various subtypes in order to determine the relative seriousness of each—how many remain delinquent and later become criminals, to what degree deviant behaviors are dangerous to others—or to learn whether specific varieties of delinquency respond better to one kind of treatment than another.

Johnson (1950) noted a phenotypical difference of some apparent significance among delinquents: solitary delinquents seemed to differ considerably from those who acted in concert with others. Further research (Randolph, Richardson, & Johnson, 1961) found that the simple division of delinquents into those who committed their delinquencies alone and those who did not was sufficient to uncover two distinct groups on the basis of background, however gross and simple this phenotypical classification might be. Solitary performers usually come from an ostensibly normal, middle-class environment. They report disturbed relations with both mother and father (Brigham, Ricketts, & Johnson, 1967). They are of average ability and disclose a very high degree of pathology in their responses to personality tests; they are *psychological* delinquents. Social delinquents generally come from lower-class homes in high-delinquency areas. They report disturbed relations with their fathers but generally normal psychological relations with their mothers (Medinnus, 1965; Brigham et al., 1967). They are usually dull to normal in ability and show few pathological signs on a standardized personality inventory; these are *sociological* delinquents.

The division is certainly a crude categorization, but far better than none at all. Solitary delinquents evince a much higher degree of *recidivism*—that is, a stronger tendency to be delinquent or criminal again in the future—indicating that solitary delinquency is a more serious problem. The psychological nature of the solitary delinquent's problems points to the advisability of some form of psychotherapy as a technique for treatment. Since the social delinquent's problems appear to be largely the product of a deviant crimogenic environment, direct manipulation of the setting, such as some form of placement outside the home, might serve more effectively as an ameliorating approach.

Another area in need of more adequate differential diagnosis is the separation of schizophrenia from mental deficiency in children and also, within the schizophrenic-type disturbances in childhood, the separation of various subtypes. Each of these types would be expected to have a distinctly different basis, a differing rate of spontaneous recovery without specific treatment, a differing accessibility to treatment, and would perhaps require a unique form of treatment. Without subdividing schizophrenia but separating it from mental deficiency, Schachter, Meyer, and Loomis (1962) characterized the schizophrenic child as follows:

1. Prolonged withdrawal reaction (physical, social and/or emotional).
2. Consistently and characteristically bizarre motility patterns.
3. Prolonged, seriously disturbed sleep patterns.
4. Extraordinary resistance to change.
5. Speech (where present) characterized by pronominal reversal, immediate or delayed cholalia, failure to be used for conventional communication, and bizarre associations.
6. Cataclysmic panic reactions.
7. Low spontaneity, affective flatness and/or inappropriateness.
8. Persistent marked negativism.
9. Absence of demonstrable organic brain damage.

They characterized the mentally defective child, on the other hand, in this manner:

1. Reasonably symmetrical general retardation in emotional and intellectual development to patterns more typical of younger children.
2. Speech development slow and appropriate to younger age period.
3. Absence of marked social withdrawal, negativism, bizarreness, or other evidence of psychosis.
4. Absence of demonstrable organic brain damage.

In a free-play situation, the mentally retarded children resembled a control group of normal children in their responses to people and resembled schizophrenics in their responses to objects. In contrast, the schizophrenics show a grave impairment in responses both to things and people. As might be expected, the schizophrenic children displayed more variability in performance on intelligence tests.

Differential diagnosis of mentally defective and of schizophrenic children is clearly possible. Although the two groups generally resemble one another in inability to benefit much from training and in being somewhat unresponsive, they differ in many ways. First, unlike most severely retarded children, schizophrenics have no apparent abnormalities of physical development. Second, they display a great deal of variability in level of ability; a 10-year-old may function like a 10-year-old in some test situations and like a two-year-old in others. Third, they exhibit movements typical of schizophrenics—whirling, walking in circles, and other perseverative motor habits. They are less interested in people than are more genuinely defective children. Yet there is a fair amount of misdiagnosis; children who are schizophrenic, or perhaps schizophrenic *and* retarded, are placed in mentally retarded programs, even though a number of easily observable symptoms might be used to differentiate the two groups.

Thus, despite the possibilities for relatively accurate differential diagnosis, it is not always made. Schizophrenic or schizoid children do not benefit as a rule from placement in mentally retarded educational programs and those programs suffer from their presence. Only through precise differentiation of two superficially similar problem groups can the genotype of each be ascertained and the most suitable treatment method be applied.

TREATMENT

While the medical model for differential diagnosis may not be entirely analogous to diagnosis of psychological problems, the data cited above strongly suggest that a separation of problem groups into sub-phenotypes, based on different causes, may improve the effectiveness of treatment. Perhaps we should act "as if" the medical model holds true.

Differential treatment, to be of maximal benefit, must be preceded by differential diagnosis. Diagnoses, of course, are made by many people, and those of parents and teachers are markedly different from those of clinicians with respect to the seriousness of behavioral problems. Even when parents or teachers recognize a bona fide problem, the evidence suggests that neither knows where to obtain help (e.g., Stendler, 1949). This section, therefore, describes various types of therapists and then considers various forms of therapy.

Quacks: How to Avoid Them

Charlatans, frauds, quacks, and crackpots abound in the field of diagnosing psychological disturbances and providing treatment for them (David, 1954; David & Springfield, 1958).

One reason for the prevalence of quacks is that many forms of therapy are in use and the relative efficacy of any one kind is hard to evaluate. With any luck at all, a quack who sets himself up as a therapist will find that at least half of his patients will improve, since there is evidence that, on the average, at least 50 per cent of neurotic individuals whose problems have no organic antecedent get well even without treatment (see Eysenck, 1961, pp. 697–725, especially 704–705).

That people often get well by themselves, have a *spontaneous remission,* works to the advantage of all therapists, including quacks.

Quacks fall into two main categories: commercial types in the business of therapy for money alone and single-minded crackpots who believe they have *the* answer to all of the world's ills but are being persecuted by better educated but jealous contemporaries. Both generally have college degrees of a sort, often from unaccredited institutions. Brophy and Durfee (1960) listed the various mail-order degrees purporting to qualify one for the practice of psychotherapy. In one of these diploma mills, they noted, four doctoral degrees—PsD, MsD, DD, and PhD—could be acquired in 20 months for $250. At this price, any quack could afford a doctor's degree. Some were not even graduates of elementary school.

One generally can avoid quacks by obtaining information regarding available legitimate professional help. The National Association for Mental Health in New York City publishes a directory of out-patient psychiatric clinics. The American Board of Psychological Services in St. Louis publishes a similar directory of psychological services. City or county medical associations can provide information regarding competent therapists. Many school systems now have their own staff psychologists and counselors. Numerous cities and counties have mental-health clinics, child-guidance centers, or family services where free or inexpensive treatment is obtainable.

Legitimate Therapists

Individuals engaged in legitimate mental-healing endeavors fall into four major categories; psychiatry, psychoanalysis, social work, and psychology. Their relative effectiveness, in terms of professional affiliation, generally is unclear (see Eysenck, 1961), as is that of more peripheral groups of trained psychotherapists such as pastoral counselors and pediatricians. The first three of the four major groups most frequently are involved in analytically oriented "directive" therapy; the last group, psychologists, in nondirective therapy and in behavior therapy.

Forms of Psychotherapy

However psychotherapists may differ from each other in professional affiliation, they all are confronted by the same problem: how to change the patient's behavior, or the behavior of the people interacting most closely with the patient, or both. The therapist's approach to this task depends on his conception of the role he can play and of the nature of problem behavior.

Directive Therapy. Directive or analytic therapists are most frequently psychiatrists and psychoanalysts. Since Freud, practitioners of this type of therapy have believed that if a problem is treated without finding its cause, the specific problem behavior that makes up the symptom may be "cured," but another symptom will take its place— as a nervous person who has been able to stop smoking may find himself gaining weight. Directive therapists generally believe that they know, within their own orientation or philosophy, the cause of a given problem. Whether their core of belief is around the Rankian birth trauma, the Freudian Oedipal complex, or some other concept that seems to them central as a cause of the behavior, their assignment is to direct the patient's flow of thoughts and associations in such a way that he also becomes aware of the cause. Once he has a conscious awareness, the patient need not expend psychic energy in repressing his feelings and can function normally.

Nondirective Therapy. The nondirective or client-centered therapist is usually a psychologist. He does not claim to know the cause of a disorder, but believes that in a supportive relationship with the patient he can reflect back to the patient the latter's own comments and behavior in a way that will help him to develop insight into his own problems. By understanding his problems, the patient will thus solve them.

Nondirective Play Therapy. Play is the child's commonest activity, and much treatment of children centers on play therapy. Although some play therapists are directive (see Kanner, 1957, p. 231), more commonly play therapy is nondirective. Axline's (1947) description of the theoretical basis and techniques of nondirective play therapy is classic. Like that of many contemporary therapists, her position was that the basis for problem behavior was in the environment, usually the home, and that the child's play often revealed the cause of the problem. Furthermore, in a nondirective atmosphere the child could resolve his problems. The therapist reflected back to the child the child's own statements so that the child could understand himself better. Play provided catharsis, an outpouring of feeling; this in itself was important. Finally, though the therapist was not essentially concerned with the learning of adequate social roles, this learning undoubtedly occurred, especially in a group play-therapy situation. The nondirective credo to the contrary, certain kinds of verbal and physical behavior are rewarded while others are extinguished through nonreinforcement during the therapy sessions, as shown by Truax (1966).

The patient in the following example of play therapy lived in an orphanage, was of somewhat better than average ability, but was doing poorly in school. She was rather unattractive and was aggressive toward both children and adults. The therapist had read extensive background material, but was inexperienced in play therapy.

First Contact—Individual. When Emma appeared for the first interview, she was told that she could come for forty-five minutes every Tuesday to play with the toys if she wanted to come. It was also explained that she could play with these toys in any way that she wanted to. The limitations were mentioned at this first meeting: She must stay inside the play area that had been marked off with chairs; she could not damage the walls or furniture; she could not take any of the toys out of the room. Otherwise she could do or say anything that she wanted to do or say while in the room with the therapist and the therapist would not tell anyone what she did do or say.

Emma stared at the therapist. Then she smiled her twisted smile and walked over to the drawing paper, picked up a piece of it and the crayons, brought them over to the table at which the therapist was sitting, sat down across from her and began to draw. She seemed very tense, and she certainly was silent. Not one word or glance in the direction of the therapist was forthcoming until the picture was finished. Then she glanced quickly at the therapist and looked away again.

Emma: This is my house. This is where I live at 7 Blank Street with my father, mother and sister. I have a sister older than me.

Therapist: Does you sister live here too?

Emma: Yes.

(Emma got up from the table, walked over to the bench where the paper dolls were, and brought them to the table where she had been drawing. Without a word she began to cut out the dolls—the father doll first, then the little girl, then the big girl, and lastly the mother doll. She began to cast more glances in the direction of the therapist. When she finished cutting out the family, she looked up and grinned. Then she cut out an evening dress for the mother.)

Emma (whispering): Is this *her* dress?

Therapist: Yes, that is the mother's dress.

(Emma continued cutting out dresses. She seemed completely absorbed with the task.)

Therapist: You like to play with the paper dolls.

Emma (making a face at the therapist): No, not very well.

Therapist: Would you rather play with something else?

Emma: I would rather color, but you don't have a color book.

Therapist: You wish I had a coloring book so you could color in it.

Emma: Yes.

(Emma continued to cut out dresses for each paper doll with the exception of the father. She picked him up and stared at him. Then quickly she piled them in a neat pile and put them away. She went back to the bench where the toys were laid out and looked at them. She turned suddenly and looked at the therapist.)

Emma (shortly): May I have a drink? (She pointed to the nursing bottle.)

Therapist: You may do anything with the toys that you want to do.

(Emma picked up the nursing bottle and drank from it, keeping her back turned to the therapist. Then she picked up the baby's rattle and shook it. Next she played quietly with the soldiers on the horses. She kept her back to the therapist all the time and so the therapist was unable to see what she was doing with the soldiers, but there seemed to be some kind of a quiet battle going on between the two soldiers. First one, then the other was knocked down. She muttered something that the therapist could not understand. She seemed very upset about something. She scowled, glanced back at the therapist, picked up the bottle again and began to drink from it, glanced back at the therapist, drank from the bottle, glanced at the therapist.)

Therapist: You like to drink from the bottle.

(Emma immediately put the bottle down. She picked up the gun, took it out of the hoster, whispered "Bang!" and put it back. Then she took the train out of the box and put it together. She pushed it along the bench for about two inches and then very suddenly crammed it back into the box. Then, still keeping her back to the therapist, she stood there and rubbed her hand along the edge of the bench.)

Therapist: Our time together is over for today, Emma.

(Emma came over to the table and stared at the therapist. The therapist smiled at her. Emma moistened her lips and smiled back with her lips only.)

Therapist: Do you want to say something, Emma?

Emma (whispering): Yes.

Therapist: What do you want to say? (Emma twisted her hands together, made faces at the therapist.)

Emma (whispering): I want to come back.

Therapist: You may come here by yourself every Tuesday, Emma. And you may come with a group tomorrow if you want to. (Then Emma really smiled. She walked over to the door.)

Therapist: Good-bye, Emma.

(No answer. Emma opened the door, went outside, looked back in, whispered "Good-bye!" and was gone.)

Comments. The picture which Emma drew during this first interview was a very conventional type of drawing, consisting of a square brown house, with three windows and a door. There were blue, red, and purple curtains at the windows. There was a big tree beside the house. A bit of blue sky was across the top of the picture, and a smiling blue sun with yellow lines radiating from it was in the left-hand corner. There were five bluebirds flying in the sky. This is mentioned in such detail because, as time passed, the art work produced by this child became more and more expressive. This first picture seemed a typical, formal type of picture. It also seems significant that she volunteered the information that she lived in this house with her father and mother and sister, although the child has been in the Orphans' Home for nearly three years. However, it is a part of her history that the mother is continually writing to the children and telling them that she is going to take them out of the Home. The mother has called them up many times and told them to get their things packed and she will come after them and take them away. The children get ready to go and the mother does not appear. The social worker had attempted to stop this practice, but had been unsuccessful up to the time of this report. Occasionally the mother does arrive for a brief visit, but seldom takes the children off the grounds with her.

The therapist's first response seems to be a very poor one. Emma had just expressed the crux of her problem—the broken home. The therapist responds with a question that takes the center of interest away from Emma and places it upon the sister. Quite naturally, Emma retreats. When Emma plays with the paper dolls, and contradicts the therapist when she suggests that Emma likes to play with paper dolls, the uneasy therapist tries to push Emma along with "Would you rather play with something else?" Emma names something that is not there. It would have been better in each instance if the therapist had followed along with the child.

The choice of uncut paper dolls for play-therapy material seems to be a poor choice, but in this case it seemed like good introductory material. The order in which she cut out the dolls is noteworthy. The fact that she cut out clothes for all except the father might be significant. At least it seems so in the light of what followed in later sessions when she played with the family of dolls.

Response by the therapist seems a bit meager in this interview, but it was a case of the therapist's not being quite sure of what to say and thinking that silence would be the best course to follow. Looking back over the interview, it seems that the therapist might have recognized the desire to drink from the bottle when Emma said, "May I have a drink?" rather than generalize on the permissiveness of the situation. When Emma apparently resented the comment from the therapist a little later to the effect that Emma did like to drink from the nursing bottle, the therapist might have recognized her resentment. Again, when Emma very quietly shot the therapist for her intrusion, the therapist might have recognized Emma's desire to shoot her. She might also have recognized the child's desire to come back again, rather than emphasizing the permissiveness of the situation (Axline, 1947, pp. 274–278).

Nothing highly dramatic happened during this session, yet the therapist gained some insight into Emma's problems. Emma achieved catharsis. Fourteen sessions with the child were reported, some individual, some group therapy. Although no one session produced remarkable change, Emma's feelings toward herself, other children, and adults became far more realistic and more positive as therapy progressed.

Behavior Therapy. The behavior therapist believes that his chief concern is with the patient's present behavior and not with the causes of the deviant behavior. To him, the symptoms *are* the disorder—these symptoms have been learned in the same way that all other behavior is learned, and the same rules operate in causing patients to stop manifesting their symptoms as operate in the extinction of any other behavior. This is a markedly different point of view from that of either the analytic or the nondirective therapist; if the behavior therapist changes the deviant behavior, he is satisfied.

It should be noted that some analytic and nondirective therapists do treat symptoms, but this is usually in conjunction with other efforts aimed at getting at the cause of a disturbance. We discuss behavior therapy at length here because it is currently receiving much attention from social scientists.

Behavior therapy developed gradually rather than all at once, but if it could be said to have one originator, he probably would be Wolpe. Wolpe was a Freudian when he first became a member of the South African contingent fighting Nazi Germany in the Libyan desert. With Pavlov as his chief source of reading material during the campaign, he emerged a behavior therapist within the Pavlovian tradition of conditioned reflex therapy (see Chapter 4). Wolpe's (1958) approach is concerned chiefly with reciprocal inhibition—basically, teaching the disturbed person to relax in tense situations, often through the use of Jacobson's (1938) *progressive relaxation* techniques, or else through the use of *desensitization,* which meant gradually exposing the disturbed individual to stimuli that progressively become more anxiety or fear producing as the means of causing anxiety reduction. Other kinds of behavior therapy involve causing the patient to model his behavior, in some adaptive fashion, after individuals in the environment (see Bandura, 1965; see also Slavson, 1952; Moreno, 1946; and Garland et al., 1962), and shaping behavior by reward, by punishment, or by a combination of reward and punishment or reward and nonreinforcement. The purpose of all types of behavior therapy is to change the frequency with which certain behaviors occur.

Examples of each kind of procedure are given below. Further case studies (many of them dealing with children) and discussions of the principles of behavior therapy can be found in Wolpe (1958), Eysenck (1960), Eysenck and Rachman (1965), Krasner and Ullman (1965), and Ullman and Krasner (1965). An example of the use of reciprocal inhibition as a therapeutic technique is found in Jones' (1924) work with her subject, Peter, in which social reassurance served as a tension reducer or counter-conditioning force and ultimately caused the disappearance of certain fears. Some form of supportive and affectional behavior often serves as the anxiety-reducing agent (and/or as a reward for performing the feared behavior) in younger children, sometimes in combination with desensitization procedures. Desensitization alone is used more frequently with older children.

Reciprocal inhibition through affection plus desensitization occurred in a study by Bentler (1962). An 11-and-a-half-month-old girl, Margaret, developed a strong fear of water, for reasons possibly associated with separation from the mother as well as from slipping and falling in the bathtub. The response strengthened and generalized (she feared handbasins, faucets, water, and a wading pool as well as the bathtub). She was treated through reciprocal inhibition of the fear response by associating the feared object with pleasure (favorite toys) and through desensitization (she was exposed first to the empty tub and then to the filled kitchen sink, then she was placed in the sink, then washed in the sink, and finally returned to being bathed in a tub). A number of experiences were required at each level of contact with the feared situation, but she recovered within approximately one month and again enjoyed bathing in the tub and playing in her wading pool. All symptoms of her phobic response to water disappeared and did not recur.

A more clear-cut use of desensitization therapy is reported by Greer (1964). A girl had a fear of becoming infested by lice. This fear reached the point that she could not bear physical proximity to others, and was unable to do such things as attend school. A hierarchy of anxiety-producing stimuli was developed (e.g., a stimulus situation low in the hierarchy would be "Imagine yourself looking through a microscope at a dead louse mounted on a slide"; one high in the hierarchy might be "Imagine that your arms, shoulders, and neck are covered with lice, all crawling up to get in your hair"). Once a hierarchy has been developed, the patient begins by visualizing the least anxiety-producing situation and continues to do this until the visualization of the imagined situation no longer produces anxiety, then visualizes the next most anxiety-producing situation, until finally even the most anxiety-producing situation can be imagined without fear. Often following, but sometimes simultaneously with the imagining, the patient also works through a hierarchy of behaviors (e.g., in the case mentioned above, an analogous behavioral hierarchy might range from dissecting a louse to allowing lice to crawl on her). Desensitization techniques seem more appropriate for fears and phobias than for other problems, but seem highly effective in this limited area and of fair value elsewhere.

The reciprocal inhibition and desensitization techniques described above are based, for the most part, on classical conditioning. Other kinds of behavior therapy have a close connection with the operant type of learning investigated by B .F. Skinner (see Chapter 4 for a discussion of operant and respondent learning). Behavior therapists of this latter persuasion are chiefly concerned with manipulating behavior through combinations of positive reinforcement, negative reinforcement, and nonreinforcement. An example of an emphasis on positive reinforcement for correct responses is found in a study by Neale (1963), in which a nine-year-old boy regained bowel control after being encopretic (soiling himself) for 18 months. First, the boy we encouraged to go to the toilet at four specified times each day. Success in defecation resulted in a variety of rewards. Later, he again learned to be aware of and to respond to a sense of rectal fullness, so the specified times were discontinued. Success in defecation in the toilet continued to be rewarded. Soiling of the clothes *never* was punished, once the training procedure had been initiated. Complete success was achieved within three months after treatment was begun.

An example of a technique emphasizing the use of negative reinforcement in order to produce a desired behavior is found in the work of Lovaas, Schaeffer, and Simmons (1965). Lovaas and his associates treat autistic children—children who do not respond socially or affectionally to other individuals. Briefly, Lovaas's original technique was to shock the autistic child through an electrified floor until he moved toward other people and until, somewhat later in training, he interacted in specified ways with other people. More recent work by Lovaas and his associates has placed less emphasis on negative reinforcement and more on reward.

Nonreinforcement of an undesirable response, leading to the extinction of the response, is illustrated by Williams (1959). A 21-month-old boy would cry and have tantrums if his parents left him in his bed before he went to sleep. One of the parents or an aunt who shared care of the child had to spend anywhere from one-half to two hours waiting in the bedroom each time he went to sleep. Treatment consisted of ignoring the crying and tantrums. When the child needed to be put to bed he was put to bed in a pleasant fashion and then the door was closed. The duration of crying on each successive occasion is shown in Figure 16-2. Two extinction series are shown, since the aunt rewarded his tantrum behavior on one occasion by remaining with him until he went to sleep. This re-evoked the behavior, but it was extinguished again through nonreinforcement. Most behavior therapists in the Skinnerian tradition use some combination of these three procedures—positive reinforcement of the desired behavior, negative reinforcement of the undesirable behavior, and nonreinforcement of the undesirable behavior.

The aim of behavior therapy is to eliminate socially undesirable behaviors ("symptoms") and to build in socially desirable behaviors. As noted above, other types of therapist generally believe that the undesirable behavior is a sign of some deeper psychic disturbance, and that if the symptom is eliminated without getting at the cause of the symptom, another problem will spring up in place of the one that was eliminated. However, Eysenck (1960, p. 9), a behavior therapist, says, *"Get rid of the symptom and you have eliminated the neurosis."* Further, according to Ullman and Krasner (1965, pp. 13–14), symptom

FIGURE 16-2   Length of crying in two extinction series as a function of successive occasions of being put to bed (from Williams, 1959, p. 269).

substitution does not seem to occur, Freudian theory to the contrary.

As a result of a concern for symptoms, of a high level of success in treating symptoms, and of finding no basis for the notion of symptom substitution, behavior therapists generally are opposed to the idea of differential diagnosis, as espoused in this chapter. However, behavior therapy is not universally effective in the treatment of any kind of disorder; it is less effective for some kinds of problem than for others; and, when effective inside the laboratory situation, it may or may not generalize to behavior in the larger social milieu. All these matters depend on the personality of the patient, the kind of psychological disturbance, and the relative weighting of the possible different types of behavior therapy used. Therefore, even though behavior therapy has proved to be far more effective than other approaches across a wide range of problem behaviors, the problem of determining what kind of disturbance benefits most from what kind of treatment remains a valid one.

Finally, with regard to behavior therapy, it should be noted that it is avowedly based on learning theory. It probably is true, as Breger and McGaugh say (see Breger & McGaugh, 1965; Rachman & Eysenck, 1966; Breger & McGaugh, 1966) that behavior therapy is based on overly simplified and, in part, inaccurate notions about the way that humans learn. Even so, behavior therapy seems effective. As in the case of many other human accomplishments, such as the prehistoric development of metallurgy, effective practice can precede complete theoretical understanding. Based on a set of testable ideas, behavior therapy appears to have the potential to develop into a still more effective procedure than it is at present.

PROGNOSIS

As noted in Chapter 15, humans show a good deal of consistency in their behavior. This consistency is undoubtedly related to the fact that, for any given individual certain behaviors lead to reward or positive reinforcement. This reinforcement may come from the self or from others who reward the individual's consistency because it makes behavior more orderly and predictable. Reinforcement may also take the form of "secondary gain" as, for instance, when an individual thinks to himself, "I feel less tense now that I've stolen a car."

So long as behaviors judged by society as deviant and maladaptive reward a specific individual, it is unlikely that change will occur. The therapeutic process, by rewarding a new class of behaviors, by extinguishing an old set through nonreinforcement, or by both, endeavors to reduce deviant behavior. Quite likely changes in age alone, without therapeutic assistance, produce new demands on the individual that reduce the rewards of certain deviant behaviors and increase the rewards of others. In considering prognosis—the probability of recovery—one attempts to distinguish the problems that persist over time, despite therapeutic aid and the shifts that accompany age, from those problem behaviors that are easily extinguishable through therapy or that disappear of their own accord as the patient grows older.

Looming large on the list of clinical referrals are problem behaviors that result largely from adult misunderstanding of child behavior—from judging normal acts to be atypical and deviant. These problems do not become problems until diagnosed. Next come the genuine problems that will decrease in severity or even disappear in most cases without any treatment whatsoever. Then there are the problems that are severe but transient and those that are mild but long-term. Finally, there are the severe, persisting problems that do not yield easily to treatment.

Physicians have long distinguished between chronic and transient disorders. Perhaps psychologists need to follow the example of medical practice. As long as therapists are in short supply, it would be of great value to have normative data on the duration and degree of debilitation of various problem disorders. Lacking this information, one cannot make a judicious use of therapy time. Without knowledge of how frequently various problems disappear by themselves, it is not possible even to evaluate the effects of therapy.

Acting Out and Withdrawn Behaviors

So broad a division of behavioral problems into acting out and withdrawal behaviors may not serve much purpose in permitting the prediction of severity or outcome of specific disorders. Yet the relative seriousness of each of these two broad categories warrants consideration, especially since the subject has aroused considerable controversy.

In one of the first studies aimed at finding the views of various individuals toward the seriousness of problems, Wickman (1928) found teachers and clinicians differing widely in their judgments of problem severity (see Chapter 12). From the rather large collection of problem behaviors rated, those judged as among the most serious by one group were often considered as among the least serious by the other. Although later studies (e.g., Beilin, 1959) have shown teachers and clinicians to be more in agreement nowadays than in Wickman's time, some of the differences he noted remain (Ritholz, 1959). The Ritholz study further demonstrated that parents and even children themselves agreed with the teachers. Whereas clinicians consider psychological conditions resulting in withdrawn behavior as the most serious, teachers, parents, and children are more concerned with actual conduct, generally aggressive in character.

In general the clinicians' assessment of problem seriousness appears correct, though incorrect in some particulars. The entire cluster of traits composing "withdrawal" seems to be a poor sign in prognosis. From among 73 children referred to a clinic, Brown (1960) took 20 who were doing well and an equal number who were doing poorly and compared them in symptoms exhibited at the time of original referral to the clinic. The worst cases manifested greater withdrawal in every respect. The best, on the other hand, oftener showed inhibition and caution—behaviors that have come to be associated with withdrawal. Whereas it might be argued that inhibited, cautious behavior will predict withdrawal, this is not true. These symptoms more accurately reflect a lesser frequency of the discharge of tension through total and diffuse motor behavior. Withdrawn behavior does appear to be quite serious, as clinicians maintain, but the clinicians seem wrong, in part, in their analyses of its constituent traits.

In the Wickman study, clinicians rated shyness as a rather serious problem. Some of them may have believed shyness itself to be pathological. Many more probably rated it as a serious problem because they believed that the shy, introverted individual was prone to schizophrenic disorders. This is questionable. The idea that the shy introvert is more susceptible to schizophrenia than the more extroverted individual is doubtful; both older (Ackerson, 1931) and more recent (Michael, Morris, & Soroker, 1957) studies indicate that shyness has a strong tendency to vanish of its own accord as an individual ages, and that it in no way predicts later schizophrenia. The withdrawn child who *can* relate to others, but does not do so, is withdrawn in a very different sense from the child who does not relate to others because of a general confusion and inability to respond. The latter kind of withdrawn behavior is more serious than acting out behaviors.

Despite the belief frequently held by therapists that acting out behaviors are more amenable to therapy than are neurotic or withdrawn behaviors, one of the most extensive follow-up studies of deviant children (Robins, 1966) shows that basically psychopathic or sociopathic acting out kinds of problems have by far the poorest prognosis of problem types. This, of course, is what we would expect from Mowrer's position (see Chapter 7).

In any broad category of behavior, certain subtypes have good prognosis and others are less promising of successful recovery. Table 16-1

TABLE 16-1   Behavior Problems and Their Probability of Remission

Investigator	High Probability of Remission	Low Probability of Remission
MacFarlane, Allen & Honzik, 1955 (an extensive longitudinal study)	Timidity Specific fears Tantrums Speech problems Enuresis Bad dreams Restlessness in sleep Poor appetite, "finicky" eating Thumb sucking Destructiveness Excessive demanding of attention Excessive activity Lying Masturbation	Excessive modesty Excessive dependence Oversensitiveness Nail biting Jealousy Somberness
Ackerson, 1931 (an extensive cross-sectional study)	Restlessness Shyness Distractibility Fearfulness Tantrums Finicky eating habits Negativism Cruelty to younger children	Depression Seclusiveness Unresponsiveness Oversensitiveness Daydreaming Sullenness Egocentricity Emotional lability Boastfulness Irritability Selfishness
Johnson, 1950	Social delinquent	Solitary delinquent
Michael, Morris, & Soroker, 1957	Shyness	
Bender, 1947		Childhood schizophrenia
Kanner & Eisenberg, 1955	Autism, if child verbal by age 5	Autism, if child still mute at age 5
Berkowitz, 1955	"Predelinquent" behavior (76% had no record as delinquents)	
Griffiths, 1952	Upper- and lower-class "delinquency-related" behaviors	Middle-class "delinquency-related" behaviors

lists behaviors ranging from simple problems of habit formation to relatively severe disorders. Accompanying them is evidence concerning their probability of remission—that is, recovery—in most cases, without treatment.

Only when it is known that individuals can recover by themselves from a number of problems can the effectiveness of therapy be determined. Some studies suggest that therapy is of little value (e.g., Levitt, Bieser, & Robertson, 1959; Robins & O'Neal, 1958). Other studies claim high rates of remission (e.g., Rexford, Schleifer, & Van Amerongen, 1956; Cunningham, Westerman, & Fischhoff, 1956). Either is hard to evaluate without knowing the frequency with which various problems arose among the children studied, the rate of spontaneous remission of these problems, and the type of therapy used.

SUMMARY

Hereditary, physiological, familial, and sociological factors all operate in the production of problem behavior. Their respective contributions vary from one disorder to the next. Moreover, as skill is developed in differentiating between superficially similar disorders, specific or relatively specific single causes may be found in the background of each of the subtypes of disorder composing a broad phenotypical category.

Clinicians differ from other individuals in their judgments of the seriousness of various disorders. Although perhaps incorrect about specifics, the clinicians seem generally correct in their assessment of problem severity. Unlike others who deal with children, the clinician uses systematic observation and is committed to scientific rules of evidence. Thus he is potentially capable of developing adequate diagnostic and therapeutic techniques.

In diagnosis, so far, emphasis on broad phenotypical categories has impeded the development of effective treatment methods. Differential diagnosis, based on observation of variation within the phenotype, leads to discovery of various genotypes and permits development of specific treatment aimed at one genotypical variety of problem.

As far as most problem behaviors are concerned, there are two general approaches to treatment of children—some form of play therapy or some form of behavior therapy. The value of play therapy is not entirely certain, while that of behavior therapy, in most of its aspects, seems well demonstrated. Fortunately, many problem behaviors disappear without treatment. Despite the present lack of knowledge of problem behavior and its treatment, there is reason to hope that present skills in treatment can be greatly improved.

REFERENCES

Ackerman, N. W. *The psychodynamics of family life.* New York: Basic Books, 1958.

Ackerson, L. *Children's behavior problems. I. Incidence, genetic, and intellectual factors.* Chicago: University of Chicago Press, 1931.

Axline, V. M. *Play therapy.* Boston: Houghton Mifflin, 1947.

Bandura, A. Behavior modification through modeling procedures. In *Research in behavior modification* (L. Krasner & L. P. Ullman, eds.). New York: Holt, Rinehart and Winston, 1965.

Bateson, G., Jackson, D. D., Haley, J., & Weakland, J. Toward a theory of schizophrenia. *Behavioral Science,* 1956, **1,** 251–264.

Beilin, H. Teacher's and clinician's attitudes toward behavior problems of children: a reappraisal. *Child Development,* 1959, **30,** 9–25.

Bender, L. R. *Child psychiatric techniques.* Springfield, Ill.: Thomas, 1952.

Bender, L. R. Childhood schizophrenia; clinical study of one hundred schizophrenic children. *American Journal of Orthopsychiatry,* 1947, **17,** 40–56.

Bentler, P. M. An infant's phobia treated with reciprocal inhibition therapy. *Journal of Child Psychology and Psychiatry,* 1962, **3,** 185–189.

Berkowitz, B. The Juvenile Aid Bureau of the New York City Police. *Nervous Child,* 1955, **11,** 42–48.

Breger, L., & McGaugh, J. L. Critique and reformulation of "learning theory" approaches to psychotherapy and neurosis. *Psychological Bulletin,* 1965, **63,** 338–358.

Breger, L., & McGaugh, J. L. Learning theory and behavior therapy: A reply to Rachman and Eysenck. *Psychological Bulletin,* 1966, **65,** 170–173.

Brigham, J. C., Ricketts, J. L., & Johnson, R. C. Reported maternal and paternal behaviors of solitary and social delinquents. *Journal of Consulting Psychology,* 1967, **31,** 420–422.

Brophy, A. L., & Durfee, R. A. Mail order training in psychotherapy. *American Psychologist,* 1960, **15,** 356–360.

Brown, J. L. Prognosis from presenting symptoms of preschool children with atypical development. *American Journal of Orthopsychiatry,* 1960, **30,** 382–390.

Chessman, C. *Cell 2455, death row.* New York: Pocket Books, 1955.

Cunningham, J. M., Westerman, Hester H., & Fischhoff, J. A follow up study of patients seen in a psychiatric clinic for children. *American Journal of Orthopsychiatry,* 1956, **26,** 602–611.

David, H. P. Phones, phonies, and psychologists. *American Psychologist,* 1954, **9,** 237–240.

David, H. P., & Springfield, F. B. Phones, phonies and psychologists: II. Four years later. *American Psychologist,* 1958, **13,** 61–64.

Eysenck, H. J. *Behavior therapy and the neuroses.* Oxford, England: Pergamon, 1960.

Eysenck, H. J. *Handbook of abnormal psychology.* New York: Basic Books, 1961.

Eysenck, H. J. The effects of psychotherapy. *International Journal of Psychiatry,* 1965, **1,** 97–144.

Eysenck, H. J., & Rachman, S. *The causes and cures of neuroses.* San Diego, California: Knapp, 1965.

Fish, B. Longitudinal observations of biological deviations in a schizophrenic infant. *American Journal of Psychiatry,* 1959, **116,** 25–31.

Garland, J. A., Kolodny, R. L., & Waldfogel, S. Social group work as adjunctive treatment for the emotionally disturbed adolescent: The experience of a specialized group work department. *American Journal of Orthopsychiatry,* 1962, **32,** 691–706.

Gottesman, I. I. Heritability of personality: A demonstration. *Psychological Monographs,* 1963, **77,** Whole No. 572.

Gottesman, I., & Shields, J. In pursuit of the schizophrenic genotype. Paper presented at the second Louisville conference on human behavior genetics. 1966.

Greer, J. H. Phobia treated by reciprocal inhibition, *Journal of Abnormal and Social Psychology,* 1964, **69,** 642–645.

Griffiths, W. *Behavior difficulties of children as perceived and judged by parents, teachers, and children themselves.* Minneapolis: University of Minnesota Press, 1952.

Haley, J. The family of the schizophrenic: A model system. *Journal of Nervous and Mental Disease,* 1959, **129,** 357–374.

Haley, J. *Strategies of psychotherapy.* New York: Grune & Stratton, 1963.

Hebb, D. O. *The organization of behavior.* New York: Wiley, 1949.

Heilbrun, A. B., Jr. Perceptual distortion and schizophrenia. *American Journal of Orthopsychiatry,* 1960, **30,** 412–418.

Hobbs, N. Helping disturbed children: Psychological and ecological strategies. *American Psychologist,* 1966, **21,** 1105–1115.

Jackson, D. D. *Myths of madness. New facts for old fallacies.* New York: Macmillan, 1964.

Jacobson, E. *Progressive relaxation.* Chicago: University of Chicago Press, 1938.

Johnson, R. C. Causal factors in the delinquency of fifty Denver boys. Unpublished master's thesis, Denver University, 1950.

Jones, M. C. A laboratory study of fear: The case of Peter. *Pedagogical Seminary and Journal of Genetic Psychology,* 1924, **31,** 308–315.

Kanner, L. *Child psychiatry.* Springfield, Ill.: Thomas, 1957.

Kanner, L., & Eisenberg, L. Notes on the follow-up studies of autistic children. In P. H. Hoch & J. Zubin (Eds.), *Psychopathology of childhood.* New York: Grune & Stratton, 1955.

Kawi, A. A., & Pasamanick, B. Prenatal and paranatal factors in the development of childhood reading disorders. *Monographs of the Society for Research in Child Development,* 1959, **24,** No. 4.

Kinsey, A. C., Pomeroy, W. B., & Martin, C. E. *Sexual behavior in the human male*. Philadelphia: Saunders, 1948.

Kinsey, A. C., Pomeroy, W. B., Martin, C. E., & Gebhard, P. H. *Sexual behavior in the human female*. Philadelphia: Saunders, 1953.

Kohn, M. L., & Clausen, J. A. Parental authority behavior and schizophrenia. *American Journal of Orthopsychiatry*, 1956, **26**, 297–313.

Krasner, L., & Ullman, L. P. *Research in Behavior Modification*. New York: Holt, Rinehart & Winston, 1965.

Kringlen, E. Schizophrenia in twins: An epidemiological clinical study. *Psychiatry*, 1966, **29**, 172–184.

Lakin, M. Personality factors in mothers of excessively crying (colicky) infants. *Monographs of the Society for Research in Child Development*, 1957, **22**, No. 1.

Lecky, P. *Self consistency, a theory of personality*. New York: Island Press, 1945.

Levitt, E. E., Bieser, H., & Robertson, R. A follow-up evaluation of cases treated at a community child guidance clinic. *American Journal of Orthopsychiatry*, 1959, **29**, 337–346.

Lovaas, O. I., Schaeffer, B., & Simmons, J. Q. Building social behavior in autistic children by use of electric shock. *Journal of Experimental Research in Personality*, 1965, **1**, 99–109.

MacFarlane, J. W., Allen, L., & Honzik, M. *A developmental study of behavior problems of normal children between 21 months and 14 years*. Berkeley: University of California Press, 1955.

Medinnus, G. R. Delinquents' perceptions of their parents. *Journal of Consulting Psychology*, 1965, **29**, 592–593.

Michael, C. M., Morris, D. P., & Soroker, E. Follow-up studies of shy, withdrawn children. II. Relative incidence of schizophrenia. *American Journal of Orthopsychiatry*, 1957, **27**, 331–337.

Moreno, J. L. *Psychodrama*. New York: Beacon House, 1946.

Mowrer, O. H. "Sin," the lesser of two evils. *American Psychologist*, 1960, **15**, 301–304.

Neale, D. H. Behavior therapy and encopresis in children. *Behavior Research Therapy*, 1963, **1**, 139–150.

Pasamanick, B., Rogers, M., & Lilienfeld, A. Pregnancy experience and the development of behavior disorder in children. *American Journal of Psychiatry*, 1956, **112**, 613–617.

Pastore, N. Genetics of schizophrenia. *Psychological Bulletin*, 1949, **46**, 285–302.

Pavlov, I. P. *Conditioned reflexes and psychiatry*. (Translated by W. H. Gant) New York: International Publishers, 1941.

Prout, C. T., & White, M. A. The schizophrenic's sibling. *Journal of Nervous and Mental Diseases*, 1956, **123**, 162–170.

Rachman, S., & Eysenck, H. J. Reply to a "critique and reformulation" of behavior therapy. *Psychological Bulletin*, 1966, **65**, 165–169.

Randolph, M. H., Richardson, H., & Johnson, R. C. A comparison of social and solitary male delinquents. *Journal of Consulting Psychology*, 1961, **25**, 293–295.

Rexford, E. N., Schleifer, M., & Van Amerongen, S. T. A follow-up of a psychiatric study of 57 antisocial young children. *Mental Hygiene*, 1956, **40**, 196–214.

Rimland, B. *Infantile autism.* New York: Appleton-Century-Crofts, 1964.

Ritholz, S. *Children's behavior.* New York: Bookman, 1959.

Robins, L. N. *Deviant children grown up.* Baltimore: Williams & Wilkins, 1966.

Robins, L. N., & O'Neal, P. The marital history of former problem children. *Social Problem*, 1958, **5**, 347–358.

Roe, A. A psychological study of eminent psychologists and anthropologists, and a comparison with biologists and physical scientists. *Psychological Monographs*, 1953, **57**, No. 2.

Roebuck, J. B., & Johnson, R. C. The short con man. *Crime and Delinquency*, 1964, **10**, 235–248.

Rogers, C. R. *Client centered therapy.* Boston: Houghton Mifflin, 1951.

Rosenthal, D. Some factors associated with concordance and discordance with respect to schizophrenia in monozygotic twins. *Journal of Nervous and Mental Diseases*, 1959, **129**, 1–10.

Rosenthal, D. Problems of sampling and diagnosis in the major twin studies of schizophrenia. *Journal of Psychiatric Research*, 1962, **1**, 116–134.

Rosenthal, D. (editor). *The Genain quadruplets.* New York: Basic Books, 1963.

Schachter, F. F., Meyer, L. R., & Loomis, E. A., Jr. Childhood schizophrenia and mental retardation: Differential diagnosis before and after one year of psychotherapy. *American Journal of Orthopsychiatry*, 1962, **32**, 584–594.

Schofield, W., & Balian, L. A comparative study of the personal histories of schizophrenic and nonpsychiatric patients. *Journal of Abnormal and Social Psychology*, 1959, **59**, 216–225.

Slavson, S. R. *Child psychotherapy.* New York: Columbia University Press, 1952.

Stendler, C. B. How well do elementary school teachers understand child behavior? *Journal of Educational Psychology*, 1949, **40**, 489–498.

Truax, C. B. Reinforcement and nonreinforcement in Rogerian psychotherapy. *Journal of Abnormal Psychology*, 1966, **71**, 1–9.

Ullman, L. P., & Krasner, L. *Case studies in behavior modification.* New York: Holt, Rinehart & Winston, 1965.

U. S. Bureau of the Census. *Statistical Abstract of the United States: 1967.* 88th ed., Washington, D. C., 1967.

Vandenberg, S. G. Hereditary factors in normal personality traits (as measured by inventories). In *Recent advances in biological psychology*, Vol. 9. New York: Plenum, 1967. Pp. 65–104.

Wickman, E. K.   *Children's behavior and teacher's attitudes.*   New York: Commonwealth Fund, 1928.

Williams, C. D.   The elimination of tantrum behavior by extinction procedures. *Journal of Abnormal and Social Psychology,* 1959, **59**, 269.

Wolpe, J.   *Psychotherapy by reciprocal inhibition.*   Stanford, California: Stanford University Press, 1958.

SECTION VI
ADOLESCENCE

Cultural factors determine whether adolescence is considered to be a stage in the life cycle. Adolescence is viewed as a separate stage of development in most of Western culture. We believe that the period of adolescence begins with physical changes that occur in the individual and ends when the individual has assumed adult roles. This section consists of three chapters. The first of these (Chapter 17) deals with physical, intellectual, and personality development. The second (Chapter 18) is a discussion of social behavior in adolescence. Chapter 19, the final substantive portion of the book, centers on various kinds of problems faced by adolescents.

17

Physical, Intellectual, and Personality Development in Adolescence

Adolescence, as a time period, may be defined in several ways. In terms of physical development, an individual's adolescent period may be said to have begun at the time that he or she shows the first signs of making the transition to sexual maturity, and to have ended when physical growth has ceased or almost ceased at about age 17 or 18. The period may also be defined in terms of social responses, beginning with the increase in interest in the other sex that usually accompanies sexual maturity and ending with the attainment of social and financial independence from the parents. Although the beginning of the adolescent period is not defined in legal terms, the ending of it is; a person is legally an adult in some respects at age 18, legally adult in all respects at age 21.

An approach to the study of the adolescent period is determined, at least in part, by the particular defining characteristics used. Our own view is that adolescence begins when signs of sexual maturity begin to occur in both physical and social development, and ends when the individual has assumed adult roles and is accepted in most ways as an adult by his reference group—those persons toward whom he refers his behaviors for approval. It has a physical basis, but in order to be considered as a period of separate developmental interest it must be viewed by the culture as a distinct stage, so that adolescents act and are treated differently from both children and adults of the culture.

Adolescence as a stage of life is not a universal phenomenon, and it is historically recent in origin. The Greeks and Romans did not view it as a separate stage, except for that short (one- to two-year) period when the actual physical change from sexual immaturity to sexual maturity occurred. The Roman Emperor Claudius was believed by all of his relatives in the Claudian and Julian families to be downright dull and slow in developing. Yet Claudius was married at 12 and a high priest at 13. This jump straight from childhood into adulthood is typical of classical cultures, and of the way of life in the Middle Ages and Renaissance as well. Aries (1962) notes that in the 1300's and 1400's, boys, even five-year-olds, went to school armed, and often had to take off their swords before they were allowed to attend class. Age was not a criterion in deciding what the individual should be taught; thus at Caen, France, in 1677, pupils in the primary grade ranged in age from nine to 17, and those in the highest grade ranged from 12 to 20 (Aries, 1962, p. 219). Cultures were not age graded. For both those who went to school and those who did not, the age of seven was considered to be the age of adulthood in most of Western culture. After seven, a person was legally responsible for his crimes, and could be hung if the offense warranted it. After this age children went to work if they were of the working classes, and all children were free to take part in all of the activities of adult society. Young children working in mines and mills in England and the United States in the 1800's must be viewed in this context. (See Cooper, 1842, in Kessen, 1965, for a report on child labor in England.)

It is only recently that the period of dependence has been extended beyond the age of sexual maturity. Tocqueville, one of the first Europeans to visit and to write about the newly independent United States, and one of the few to like what he saw, pointed out the ease of transition once found in the United States (brought to the writers' attention by a quotation in Douvan & Adelson, 1966):

> But as soon as the young American approaches manhood, the ties of filial obedience are relaxed day by day; master of his thoughts, he is soon master of his conduct. In America there is, strictly speaking, no adolescence: at the close of boyhood the man appears and begins to trace out his own path.
>
> It would be an error to suppose that this is preceded by a domestic struggle in which the son has obtained by a sort of moral violence the liberty that his father refused him. The same habits, the principles, which impel the one to assert his independence, predispose the other to consider the use of that independence as an incontestable right. The former does not exhibit any of those rancorous or irregular passions which disturb men long after they have shaken off an established authority; the latter feels none of that bitter and angry regret which is apt to survive a bygone power (Tocqueville, 1954, pp. 202–203; originally published in 1840).

Not all wealthy cultures recognize adolescence as a separate period of life (e.g., Imperial Rome did not), yet it seems that only a rich culture can afford to allow an extended period of adolescence in which a young person does not earn his own living and is dependent upon his parents. Even today, adolescence as a social phenomenon is often absent in entire cultures. As noted in Chapter 7, within hunting cultures childhood ends by age eight, and within agrarian cultures by age 10 to 12 (Landis, 1945). It is only in present-day industrial culture that the period we call adolescence is an extension of childhood dependency.

If adolescence can best be viewed as beginning at sexual maturity and ending at the point when the individual is independent from parental control, it appears that adolescence is lengthening in the Western culture and in segments of other cultures. As we discuss in the next section, sexual maturity is occurring earlier today than previously, and, as noted above, dependency continues until a later age. These changes are most apparent within the United States, but may be seen in industrial cultures throughout the world (e.g., see Gottlieb, Reeves, Ten Housen, 1966). For well over 100 years Europeans found considerable joy in pointing out the deficiencies of American child-rearing practices, which, they said, caused, in part, the hedonistic and somewhat criminal peer culture of American adolescence. Now, with "hooligans" in Red Square, Swedish motorcycle gangs throwing beer cans at the Upsala police, and English "mods" and "rockers" emulating Marlon Brando and his "wild ones" in their gang fights at Brighton, Europeans have small cause to jeer. The technical advances of Europe have made the employment of large numbers of adolescents unnecessary. Free from work and with money in their pockets, Europe's young people are now much more like our own, both in positive (seldom mentioned) and in negative ways. Student activities in India, Japan, and other countries suggest that there, too, in urban industrialized areas, adolescence as a social phenomenon has come into existence and is recognized as a separate developmental stage both by adolescents themselves and by their elders.

PHYSICAL CHANGES IN ADOLESCENCE

It should be recognized that although adolescence is a period of rather rapid physical change, there is still a clearly discernible continuity between a given individual's physical development in childhood and his development in adolescence. Persons who are tall as children tend to be tall in adolescence and adulthood (Shuttleworth, 1939). Body types (ectomorph, mesomorph, endomorph) remain relatively constant over time (Sheldon, Stevens, & Tucker, 1940). The person undergoing the changes associated with adolescence brings with him a long history of physical development, and the pattern of this development remains discernible during the rapid changes of adolescence.

The preadolescent growth spurt is the first harbinger of the changes that occur in the individual during adolescence. Rapidity of growth results from complex interactions of various endocrine glands. As may be seen in Figure 17-1, lymphoidal tissue (for the most part, the thymus gland) is most prominently present among the various kinds of body tissue during the period immediately preceding the rapid increase in genital tissue. It is during this period that growth is most rapid, as can be seen in Figure 17-2. The growth of genital organs, with associated changes in glandular secretions, slows and ultimately halts growth.

The individual undergoing the changes that lead from sexual immaturity to sexual maturity is said to be in the pubertal stage of development. It is extremely difficult to say exactly when a person has become

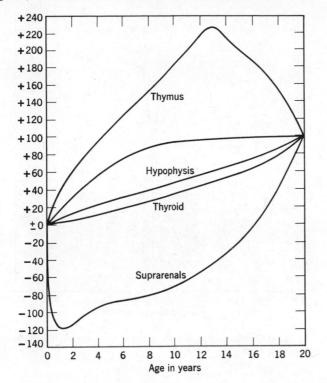

FIGURE 17-1   Differential growth trends in the weight of several endocrine organs, total increment from birth to maturity expressed as 100 per cent. Observe the radical differences.   From Harris, Jackson, Paterson, & Scammon (1930).

sexually mature (has passed through the age of puberty) but a number of different indices are used.   These are discussed below.

General Indices of Development

Each person, before becoming completely mature, is at a number of ages at any given moment in time.   We usually think of our age as our chronological age (CA).   But the person who is chronologically 13 may be more or less than 13 according to a number of other measures.   The idea of mental age (MA) and the associated concept of IQ are well known.   The person of CA 13 might have an MA of 15, or, for that matter, of 6 or of 8, depending on what age group he is nearest in terms of intellectual functioning.   In the same fashion, this 13-year-old may

FIGURE 17-2   Distribution of ages at maximum growth in standing height, by sex (Shuttleworth, 1939).

be a number of different ages in terms of physical development. Some 13-year-olds are almost fully adult in various kinds of physical development, while others are children who have not yet become pubescent.

Probably the most frequently used index of physiological maturity is skeletal age. As we develop from infancy to maturity, predictable and orderly changes occur in our skeletal structure. Many bones are not yet bone at all in infancy and early childhood, but consist of cartilage (gristle) that with age turns to bone. The number of bones present in the body (about 270 at birth, 350 at puberty, and 206 at adulthood) varies as bones form and later fuse together. While this change in absolute number goes on, individual bones change from cartilage and osteoblasts (areas within the incipient bone from which ossification proceeds) to bone. These changes in number of bones and in ossification of given bones are orderly and sequential, so that by determining where an individual is in this developmental sequence, we determine his skeletal age. Several ossification indices exist, but the one most commonly used at present is that developed by Greulich and Pyle (1959), which makes use of X-ray photos of the hand and wrist. The degree of ossification revealed in the picture of a given child or adolescent is compared with standard photos in the Greulich and Pyle atlas for each sex at different ages. The X-ray within the atlas that most resembles the subject's X-ray allows the categorization of this subject in terms of skeletal age. If a 13-year-old is skeletally 11 years and 1 month old, we know with a high degree of certainty that puberty will be quite late as compared with agemates and that growth in height will continue for a longer period of time. We can expect that this individual, if male, will have problems in adjustment associated with late development; we may wish to intervene by treating the individual with sex hormones in order to hasten sexual maturity. A similar set of developmental norms has been developed for changes in dentition (Carlos & Gittelsohn, 1965) so that we also can measure physiological maturity in terms of "dental age."

Willard C. Olsen (1949) has proposed that we assess an individual's developmental status by making use of a number of ages—mental age, reading age, height age, weight age, dental age, and skeletal age. He suggests that these ages usually run together (e.g., a person of CA 15 usually is about 15 years old on these other indices of age) but that a look at deviations across these various ages is of value. For example, compare subjects A and B in Figure 17-3. Longitudinal measures of A suggest that he is developing at a normal rate according to all physical measures of age, but is developing a good deal more slowly with regard to the two cognitive indices of age. B, on the other hand, is equally retarded in all measures. Since all of us finally reach physical maturity, B will too, though more slowly; it also may be that B will more slowly

FIGURE 17-3   Growth of a boy at a low level.

reach the level of normal adults in intelligence. If Olsen is right, B is a good deal better bet than A for sooner or later reaching a normal adult intellectual level because all his "ages" are developing at about an equal rate. In the same way, deviations of one or more of the physical measures of age allow us to make predictions about ultimate outcomes, and sometimes to decide on whether some sort of therapeutic intervention is necessary.

In summary, these physical measures of age (especially skeletal age) allow us to determine more accurately than we can from CA the level of physical development that an individual has reached.

Sexual Indices of Development

Internal and external changes of the primary (sex organs themselves) and secondary (body hair, breast development, larynx, etc.) sexual characteristics of young people are the chief indices of sexual maturity.

Sexual Changes in Girls. A number of changes occur as sexual maturity is reached by girls. For example, breast development can be classified into one of a number of stages, ranging from the "bud"—an enlargement and protrusion of the nipple, to the fully mature breast— and changes in amount and type of body hair can be chronologically ordered. However, the most frequently used measure of sexual maturity for girls is an either-or one: has she reached *menarche,* the age of first menstruation, or has she not? Menarche is a single point along a continuum, and is not a sign that a girl is completely sexually mature, since a period of sterility of a year or more in duration typically follows menarche (Montagu, 1950). It is a convenient marking point that serves as an operationally defined criterion of sexual maturity. Differences in age of menarche within any one generation are large, and have considerable impact on the personality and social adjustment of those who are most deviant from the mean. Reasons for this high degree of variability in age of menarche are not entirely known. A hereditary factor seems to be involved, since there is a substantial mother-daughter (Gould & Gould, 1932) and sister-sister (Popenoe, 1928) correlation in age of menarche. Further, the age of menarche of identical twin girls is far more similar than that of fraternal twin pairs (Tanner, 1960, pp. 43–45). Nutritional factors also play a role, but probably are less important today than they were a few generations ago, since social-class differences in diet probably have decreased in the last two decades. Body build also may exert influence. It seems clear that early maturers are shorter and broader than are late maturers, but it is not clear whether differences in body type cause differences in age of menarche or vice versa, or whether they both are caused by a third factor. Even with the influence of all of these factors combined, much of the variance is left unaccounted for. The social significance of out-of-step development is discussed in a later section.

There is substantial evidence that the age of menarche is decreasing across generations. In the 1830's and 1840's, Robertson (see Dennis, 1946, pp. 642–643) collected data on the menarcheal age of such varied groups as English, Hindu, and Laplander girls, and a large number of studies have been done since that time. Most of the studies done in the middle 1800's yield a mean menarcheal age of about 15.5 years. Engelmann (1901) obtained a mean menarcheal age of 14.20 for a sample of 5552 American girls. Data reported by Shuttleworth (1939) bring the mean age down to below 14. One of the authors obtained anonymous reports on age of menarche from 127 female college students in several large classes at the University of Colorado. He also obtained information concerning paternal occupation. These data must be viewed with some caution, since errors in recall undoubtedly occurred, and since the sample is not representative of the population at large. However, these college girls (the vast majority aged 19 to 22) reported a mean menarcheal age of 11.86, with no significant differences between occupational groups. The same finding of no socioeconomic differences is reported concerning English and Scots girls by Tanner (1968). The age of menarche thus seems to have decreased by nearly four years in the last century. A similar but slightly smaller downward shift in age of menarche (though the absolute ages are somewhat higher) is shown by Tanner (1968) in his discussion of the trend toward earlier maturation, and is illustrated in Figure 17-4. Since early studies (e.g., Engelmann, 1901) found social-class differences, with the earliest age of menarche being found in the highest social class, and crosscultural differences, with age of menarche being lowest in the richest culture (e.g., lower in England than in India) it is likely that nutritional factors have produced this remarkable acceleration of development, which has considerable social significance. The age of adolescence and problems associated with adolescence have been extended downward.

Parents complain that dating, dancing, interest in the other sex, and the wearing of more mature clothing and of cosmetics is beginning earlier and earlier. As noted in Chapter 11, a comparison of the Tryon (1939) and Tuddenham (1951) studies of the degree of popularity assigned different social roles by adolescents is only one of the pieces of evidence that demonstrate parents to be correct. In the Tryon study, 12-year-olds valued the rather prim, demure, somewhat "goody-goody" girl; 15-year-

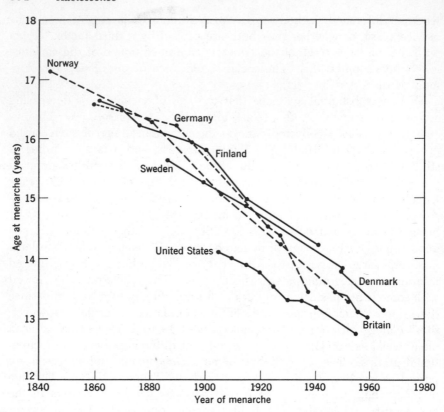

FIGURE 17-4   Age at menarche, or first menstrual period, has declined in the United States, Britain and Europe. Girls are estimated to begin menstruation between 2.5 and 3.3 years earlier on the average than a century ago. The age of menarche is an index of the rate of physical maturation (from Earlier Maturation in Man by J. M. Tanner. Copyright 1968 by Scientific American, Inc. All rights reserved).

olds rejected this style of life and preferred either the buoyant good sport or else the femme fatale.   Tuddenham's study, conducted a comparatively short time later, showed that the direction of changes in role acceptability remained constant, but that the whole sequence had shifted downward by several years.   Our personal hunch is that the 10-year-old girl of today is similar, in terms of values, to the 15-year-old of the years immediately preceding World War II.   Not all of this shift can be attributed to the earlier maturity of today's girls, but a fair proportion of it can.   We know that the age at which sexual maturity is attained has moved downward rather sharply, and interests have been demonstrated (Stone & Barker, 1939) to be much more closely tied to sexual maturity than to chronological age.

Sexual Changes in Boys. There is no such single useful marker as menarche in the investigation of sexual maturity in males. The Crampton criteria (Crampton, 1908a, 1908b) most frequently are used to place males along a continuum of sexual development. These criteria have to do with the maturity of the pubic hairs and involve three major stages, unpigmented (prepubescent), pigmented but straight (pubescent) and pigmented and kinky (postpubescent). There is no one-to-one correspondence between stages of development according to the Crampton criteria and the ability to produce spermatozoa, so that the exact age at which the average male reaches sexual maturity cannot be stated with accuracy. However, since boys are slightly more than two years behind girls in other areas of development, such as age of maximum increment in height (as shown in Figure 17-2 above), it seems likely that the present average age of sexual maturity for males is somewhere between 13.5 and 14.0 years, with a rather wide range of variation (e.g., from about age 9 to 16) around this mean among completely normal and healthy persons.

Sexual Maturity and Sexual Behavior

Freudian theory (see Freud, 1953) has as one of its tenets the belief that when a child is attempting to resolve the Oedipal situation by rejecting the opposite-sex parent and identifying with the same-sex parent, he comes to reject all members of the opposite sex for the time interval, called the latency period, beginning at about age five and ending at puberty. Thus at the time that the Oedipal situation is resolved, the child rejects all members of the opposite sex; at the end of latency the young person presumably becomes aware that the incest taboo does not apply to all members of the opposite sex. If all has gone well during previous developmental stages, he becomes sexually interested in the opposite sex.

The Kinsey reports on the sexual behavior of males (Kinsey, Pomeroy, & Martin, 1948) and females (Kinsey, Pomeroy, Martin, & Gebhart, 1953) remain the major empirical studies of human sexual behavior. These reports clearly demonstrate that there is no such thing as a latency period. Sexual behavior of a number of varieties occurs all through the "latency" time interval. There is, however, a marked increase in sexual behavior once sexual maturity has been reached. The average male is more sexually active when he is 16 years old than he will ever be again, in terms of frequency of sexual climax. As might be predicted, since heterosexual outlets are infrequent, the majority of orgasms are reached by masturbation. Since masturbation is a far less frequent sexual outlet for girls, and since cultural prohibitions concerning heterosexual activity are strong for girls, adolescent girls are less sexually active than adolescent boys. Nevertheless, they are more sexually active than had been believed before the Kinsey studies, and they are certainly sexually active throughout the so-called latency period.

The Effects of Out-of-Step Development

There is close to a 10-year range in age, for each sex, in the time that sexual maturity is reached by normal individuals. The peer group demands adherence to its own timetable for the achievement of various privileges (e.g., being allowed to date) and social skills (e.g., being able to dance), and those who are too far out of step in physical development do not meet this demand.

The effects of early or late physical development are greater for boys than for girls. Athletic prowess is the single most important determinant of peer acceptance for American males. The early maturer is taller, heavier, and stronger than his peers during adolescence, although late maturers do finally catch up and, in fact, probably surpass early maturers in height (Jones, 1957). Because of his physical superiority, the early maturer is a better athlete, and better accepted by his peers for this reason. Further, early maturers, when compared with late maturers, are more relaxed, more matter-of-fact, and less affected in their behavior— all positive traits to peers—presumably as a result of their early maturity (Jones & Bayley, 1950). The converse also is true, of course; Jones and Bayley have demonstrated that late maturers are less well liked by their peers, judged to be less attractive, and differ in a negative direction from early maturers on a number of personality ratings. A more recent study by Weatherley (1964) also shows late maturers to be less well adjusted, but finds few differences between early and average maturers.

The effect of early versus late maturity on the adjustment of girls is less well understood. Certainly, the effects are less marked than for boys (Jones, 1949; Weatherley, 1964), probably because the differences in athletic prowess associated with differing rates of physical development that are so important for boys are of no social consequence for girls. H. E. Jones (1949) originally believed that late-maturing girls had some social advantage over early-maturing girls. In his study, late maturers were judged to be more outgoing, assured, confident, and animated. However, analysis of Thematic Apperception Test (TAT) responses

(Jones & Mussen, 1958) of early- and late-maturing girls shows a reversal: late maturers are slightly less well adjusted. Weatherley's study (1964) also suggests that late-maturing girls are slightly less well adjusted than are early maturers, since late maturers are somewhat lower in academic achievement and are more anxious.

The early-maturing girl, with interests accompanying her sexual maturity, may be considered odd by her agemates. For that matter, a tall, relatively heavy, mature girl of 11 may even be a bit frightening, just in terms of size and strength, for her prepubescent male classmates. The late-maturing girl may be out of step, too—not really interested in boys and the activities associated with boys to the same degree as her peers. However, girls in general appear to have a talent for dissimulation (see Douvan & Adelson, 1966), so that any value differences resulting from retarded physical development usually are well concealed.

There are a number of experiences that seem to have considerable impact on individuals at the time they occur, but less of an effect over time. Being deviant in rate of physical development may be an experience of this sort. Jones (1957) obtained data that she interpreted as showing early maturers to remain better adjusted than late maturers into middle adulthood. Late maturers are shown to be more rebellious and impulsive as well as more succorant (helpful), to be less responsible and dominant, and to be less concerned with making a good impression than are early maturers, according to objective personality tests. Their life histories show less job stability and they are less often executives. Jones concluded that the early maturers were better adjusted even in adulthood. If the best-adjusted person in our culture is a dominative, insensitive, successful young executive, then the early maturers are better adjusted, but we find it difficult to accept these criteria. If a concern for others, a need for close social ties, and an interest in intellectual matters and social issues is indicative of adjustment, then the late maturers appear better adjusted. We find these criteria easier to accept. Tangential evidence supporting our opinion comes from Mussen's (1962) finding that men who had more masculine interests during adolescence [and most early maturers probably fell in the masculine-interest group from Jones' & Bayley's (1950) description] were less happy and less well adjusted in middle adulthood than were those who had more feminine interests (probably most of the late maturers) during adolescence.

So far as girls are concerned, the effect of differing rates of physical development is only a slight one during adolescence. Therefore it is not surprising that differences between early and late maturers also appear to be minimal during adulthood (Weatherley, 1964).

In summary, out-of-step development appears to have a considerable influence on the social adjustment of boys during adolescence, with late maturers being at a considerable disadvantage. Differences between early and late males still are discernible in adulthood, but are reversed in at least some areas. Differences are far less marked in the case of girls, and vary between traits and between studies. Only slight differences may be discerned in early adulthood between early- and late-maturing females.

ADOLESCENCE AND IDENTITY

Who am I? What things do I do? These are the questions of our time that each of us has to answer to obtain self identity, and typically we seriously begin to seek these answers during adolescence. The task is more difficult than in previous eras since now each person is more alone—he cannot define his identity in terms of his group memberships or in terms of family, as people once did, but must develop a more individual identity out of the many roles available to him.

Erik Erikson writes of the "eight ages of man," each having to do with the mastery of a specific developmental task (Erikson, 1963, pp. 247–274). The task of the adolescent is to develop a sense of personal identity.

In puberty and adolescence all samenesses and continuities relied on earlier are more or less questioned again, because of a rapidity of body growth which equals that of early childhood and because of the new addition of genital maturity. The growing and developing youth, faced with this physiological revolution within them, and with tangible adult tasks ahead of them are now primarily concerned with what they appear to be in the eyes of others as compared with what they feel they are, and with the question of how to connect the roles and skills cultivated earlier with the occupational prototypes of the day.

. . . The danger of this stage is role confusion. Where this is based on a strong previous doubt as to one's sexual identity, delinquent and outright psychotic episodes are not uncommon. If diagnosed and treated correctly, these incidents do not have the same fatal significance which they have at other ages. In most instances, however, it is the inability to settle on an occupational identity which disturbs individual young people. To keep themselves together they temporarily overidentify, to the point of apparent complete loss of identity, with the heroes of cliques and crowds. This initiates the stage of "falling in love," which is by no means entirely, or even primarily, a sexual matter—except where the *mores* demand it. To a considerable extent adolescent love is an attempt to arrive at a definition of one's identity by projecting one's diffused ego image on another and by seeing it thus reflected and gradually clarified. This is why so much of young love is conversation (Erikson, 1963).

Sociologists, as well as students of medieval history, generally believe that the problem of developing a sense of *self* identity first became a problem only at the time of the Renaissance and the Reformation. The man of the Middle Ages appears to have developed a sense of identity in terms of his social groups (e.g., I am a member of the tailor's guild; I am a citizen of Nuremberg) rather than a personally oriented sense of identity. A person's behaviors were clearly defined in terms of the behaviors considered appropriate for his social groups and his position in the hierarchical scheme of things. Even after the relatively static world of medieval man became less fixed, so that a person no longer had only one church, one city, or one rural district to call home, and so that he had more than one limited area of vocational choice, he still could have a sense of identity in terms of his family. Shakespeare, writing in the Elizabethan Age, a period of change almost as rapid as our own, certainly did not view individuals as members of a given group whose behaviors were determined by this group; whatever a man's group or rank, he was viewed as being capable of nobility or baseness, and of all the rest of the infinite variety of behaviors of which we humans are capable. But, far more than contemporary writers, Shakespeare viewed men's behavior as being a consequence of their family membership.

The extreme physical mobility of our culture has destroyed the bases of interaction and loyalty of the extended family (grandparents, parents, aunts, uncles, cousins). The nuclear family (parents and children) remains, and may, in fact, have gained in influence in the last century, but no longer provides an adequate basis for the development of a concept of self identity. Parents are unwilling to prescribe a set of behaviors and social roles consonant with a "family tradition," since the world is changing too rapidly for even the most insightful parent to accurately predict behaviors and roles that will be useful and adaptive a generation later. Even if parents were willing to predict and prescribe, most young people would not accept these behavioral and role prescriptions, since by adolescence they have encountered numerous other value systems that differ vastly from those of their parents and yet appear to be equally valid.

Body Change and the Self Concept

The self concept consists of an individual's evaluations of various aspects of the self and his ideas about himself. For most psychologists, one element of the self concept consists of *social roles*, as discussed in Chapter 15 and in the next section.

Another major aspect of the self concept is the development of the *body image*—an individual's awareness of and acceptance of his physical self. The rapid physical changes of adolescence produce a rapid change in body image, and typically lead to a rejection of the physical self as well. It is rare that an adolescent is accepting of his physical self. Something is always wrong; height, weight, degree of physical maturity, pimples, hair, or a multitude of other possible subjective defects become central concerns and lead frequently to self-rejection. Beliefs about and degree of acceptance of the physical self influence behavior. For example, a beautiful girl who believes herself to be plain, if not actually ugly, will probably act differently in a wide variety of social contexts than an equally beautiful girl who is more favorably disposed toward her physical self.

The physical self remains constant across a wide variety of situations that may involve very varied role demands, so that a consistent body image is generally a cause of behavioral consistency. Role demands change rapidly in adolescence, and so does the body image during this period of rapid physical development; thus both of the major elements of the self concept dispose an adolescent to variable and inconsistent behavior. Further, since it is generally found (e.g., see Fisher & Cleveland, 1958; Wylie, 1961) that acceptance of the body image is associated with behavior that could be termed "mentally healthy," and since it is known that many of the physical changes (in proportion, in height, in complexion) in adolescence lead to a rejection of the physical self by most adolescents, at least for some time, it seems reasonable to believe that some of the behavioral deviance associated with adolescence results either from this rejection of the body image or else from efforts to remold the body image in such a way as to make it acceptable. The hair dyeing, hair styling, clothing fads, and other such phenomena of adolescence may be viewed as attempts on the part of adolescents to develop consistent and acceptable body images.

Sooner or later each of us does come to terms with his physical self, and thereby acquires a consistent physical self identity. Usually, too, we come to have a more positive attitude toward our physical selves—perhaps because we get used to our own physical being. But the development of a consistent, favorable body image is a long and often unhappy process that may last all the way through adolescence and into adulthood before it is completed, even for individuals who appear to an outsider to be not only normal but attractive in appearance. Since physical attractiveness is the chief criterion of social acceptability in adolescence and young adulthood (Walster, Aronson, Abraham, & Roltman, 1966), the person who is not attractive or who has some physical defect understandably has difficulty in accepting the physical self. He may, however, come into his own in later years, when other aspects of the self, such as personality traits and intelligence, become more important than physical attractiveness.

The Self Concept as Related to Roles

Our social roles are assigned us, and role assignments begin early. Male-female, competent-incompetent, and many other roles are assigned, and, as discussed in Chapter 15, we have a tremendously strong tendency to play out those roles. Roles become more clearly defined and specified with age, and, as they continue to be played, self-consistency generally increases. Since adolescence is a time when a good deal of conscious seeking of self identity occurs, consistency in behavior appears to increase sharply as the period of adolescence progresses. The identity that the adolescent accepts is likely to be his, with relatively little modification (except for those compromises that most of us make when ideals are confronted with reality), from that time forward (e.g., see the data on consistency of personality traits over time in Kagan & Moss, 1962). It is necessary that adults provide young persons with the proper ingredients, in terms of roles needed for self-acceptance and acceptance of others, before the identity crises of adolescence.

Identity and the Sex Role

Like the body image and social roles, the sex role is a problem for each of us at some time in our development. Each of us has the task of learning to behave in ways sufficiently appropriate to our sex so that we are not markedly deviant. In our culture, males are supposed to be dominant, aggressive, independent, competitive, active, and not too conforming in their behavior, while women are supposed to be passive, submissive, dependent, uncompetitive, and conforming. The learning of one's sex role is, in the more fundamental ways, a task of childhood rather than of adolescence, but it is during adolescence that this learning is completed and that both adequate and inadequate learning are made more readily apparent.

Freudians believe that identification with the proper sex occurs as a result of the resolution of the Oedipal situation. In the first stage, the child loves the opposite-sex parent and, at a relatively low level of awareness, wishes his rival—the same-sex parent—dead. The child ultimately comes to think, "If I feel that way about him (or her), and wish him dead, then maybe he feels the same about me. And he's bigger, so he could transform thought into action." The child fears the same-sex parent, and as a result of this fear gives up the opposite-sex parent as a love object and identifies with (feels himself to be like, tries to act like) the same-sex parent. When identifying with the same-sex parent the young child also identifies with society as a whole, and develops a superego (part of which is analogous to the "conscience"), so that he now accepts society's rules as right and just, attempts to follow these rules, and feels guilt when he violates them. Boys fear both death and castration, and girls fear death but not castration from the same-sex parent. Because of the boys' greater fear, they more adequately resolve the Oedipal situation than do girls, and as a result have more highly developed superegos.

If the Freudian explanation of sex identification is correct, we would expect boys whose fathers are absent during the Oedipal period (approximately age three to five) to have weaker superegos than boys whose fathers are present during this period, since father absence should greatly reduce the possibility for the Oedipal situation to be resolved adequately. Data generally support this prediction. Father absence is associated with a relatively inadequate sex-role identification, producing either "feminine" boys (e.g., see Sears, Pintler, & Sears, 1946; Stolz, 1954) or a delinquent or psychopathic *compensatory* masculinity (Lynn & Sawrey, 1959; McCord, McCord, & Thurber, 1962; Seigman, 1966). Which kind of role inadequacy the boy will show appears to depend on the age at which the father absence occurs (Hetherington, 1966) and also, seemingly, on the age at which the father-absent boy is studied, since the studies showing father absence to produce femininity generally have to do with prepubescent boys; those that show an exaggerated compensatory masculinity generally deal with postpubescent boys. While these data are generally what we would expect from Freudian theory, other explanations also are possible. A number of theorists (e.g., Bandura & Huston, 1961; Kagan, 1964; Lynn, 1962; Mowrer, 1950) view identification as a learning phenomenon similar to other varieties of learning and subject to the same influences (e.g., amount of positive and negative reinforcement); thus the Freudian theory of sexuality is superfluous in explaining identification. It would seem that the relative reinforcing effects of each of the two parents, in terms of some combination of amount of contact, amount of nurturance, and amount of power of each parent determine the adequacy of identification of the offspring (Mussen & Distler, 1959; Mussen & Rutherford, 1963). These findings fit more closely into a learning theory than into a psychoanalytically oriented framework. Further, from the Freudian position we would expect to see little or no sex-role differentiation of boys and girls during the "pre-Oedipal" stage. Yet we know that whether as a result of genetic differences, of differential treatment, or of differential task demands (since girls can imitate their mothers, while boys must consciously break this maternal imitation and decide what is masculine), a fair amount of differentiation does occur even at age two or three. Whatever the basis for sex-role identification, it does exist, and the degree to which an adequate identification is achieved is related to adjustment.

For boys, a relatively high degree of masculine identification appears associated with good adjustment. As Heilbrun (1964) says, "Extensive empirical support can be found . . . that young males who are highly identified with their fathers are better adjusted." As noted earlier in this chapter, a high degree of masculinity in youth is not associated with good adjustment in middle adulthood, by which time interests associated with femininity, such as sociability and friendliness, are more indicative of good adjustment (Mussen, 1962). For women, on the other hand, whether in adolescence or adulthood, close identification with the mother and with the female role either is unrelated or negatively related to adjustment (Gray & Klaus, 1956; Heilbrun, 1964). The probable reason for this sex difference in the relation of identification to adjustment is that the female role prescribed in our culture is not a highly favorable one—passive, dull, and dependent. While all of us show strong tendencies to fulfill the roles expected of us, it seems reasonable to believe that it often is more adaptive to rebel against an inadequate and unfulfilling role than to play it out. For boys, inadequate masculine identification leads either to a culturally rejected femininity in behavior or else to a compensatory masculinity that often is legally delinquent in character. For girls, a rejection of the female role leads to increased intellectual achievement, creativity, and academic and vocational success. Adjustment depends not only on the degree to which an individual makes the proper sex-role identification but also on the adequacy of the sex role with which that person is expected to identify.

Each sex has its unique problems: boys have relatively little opportunity to practice an adequate set of role behaviors; girls have ample opportunity to practice the behaviors that form their role, but the behaviors themselves (except for sensitivity to others' feelings and needs) are not particularly desirable ones in terms of adjustment or of achievement.

Responses to the opposite sex are only one aspect of masculinity and femininity, yet it is this aspect—involving putting one's sex role "on the firing line"—that is a principal concern of adolescence. Cross-sex interactions in adolescence do not involve masculinity or femininity itself so much as an empirical test to which each of us subjects himself in order to test the validity of his sex-role definition. The actual nature of the adolescent's peer relations, aimed at determining the adequacy of his or her sex role, is discussed in Chapter 18.

Identity, Awareness of Competence, and Locus of Control

Just as each of us must develop a sex role, each of us must develop some awareness of his competence, of what tasks he is capable of performing. Feelings of competence become sharply apparent during adolescence. Unfortunately, actual competence and perceived competence vary considerably, and such factors as race and social class serve to decrease the self-perceived competence of a high proportion of minority-group and of low-economic-group adolescents (and these two groups overlap to a very considerable degree). On the other hand, the pressures of the society toward upward mobility if possible, and certainly against downward mobility at all costs, cause a rather large number of individuals to overestimate their potential. These persons, if their performance is sufficiently inept as to result in downward mobility, often become extremely prejudiced and authoritarian (Bettelheim & Janowitz, 1950), since it is far easier to blame others for one's own failure than to blame oneself.

The dominant tendency (at least on paper, at a fairly superficial level) is to overestimate ability in terms of vocational aspirations (Douvan & Adelson, 1966, p. 59). Realistic self-evaluations tend to increase with age, since with increasing experience young people are better able to evaluate their general competence as well as their specific areas of greatest and least competence.

A special aspect of the individual's feeling of competence is that of perceived internal as opposed to external locus of control of reinforcement. As Lefcourt (1966, p. 207) defines these loci of control,

> Internal control refers to the perception of positive and/or negative events as being a consequence of one's own actions and thereby under personal control; external control refers to the perception of positive and/or negative events as being unrelated to one's own behaviors in certain situations and therefore beyond personal control.

Individuals who believe in an internal locus of reinforcement—who believe that the rewards and punishments that they receive result from their own actions—also are those individuals who achieve more (Crandall, Katkovsky, & Preston, 1962), who are more willing to delay gratification and work toward long-term goals (Phyphers, 1968), and who attempt to change their environments in certain adaptive ways. For example, students in southern Negro colleges who are involved in the civil rights movement believe more in internal control than students not so involved (Gore & Rotter, 1963). A belief in internal control of reinforcement is a belief in personal competence to run one's own affairs. It has been demonstrated that individuals from lower economic groups are less internal in orientation than persons from middle economic groups, and that Negroes believe less in internal control than whites (Battle & Rotter, 1963). A belief in external control may be completely in tune with reality. For example, southern Negroes, as a group, probably do not run their own affairs or receive reinforcements on the basis of their competence to the same degree as do middle-class whites. Both lower-class and minority-group members often are realistically external in orientation, since luck, fate, and other people do appear to play a considerable role in determining the quality of reinforcements. However, whether reality-oriented or not, a belief in external control of reinforcement leads to apathy, fatalism, unwillingness to work for long-term goals, and feelings of incompetence. If it is of value to the culture to inculcate a desire for upward mobility, with its attendant achievement orientation and willingness to delay gratification, then special learning experiences may have to be devised in order to create a belief in internal control of reinforcement in low-income and/or minority-group youngsters, and by so doing, cause them to develop feelings of personal competence.

INTELLECTUAL CHANGES IN ADOLESCENCE

Many experts in developmental psychology would argue that most of the intellectual growth of a child occurs in early childhood (Goodenough, 1954; Bloom, 1964, p. 68). As noted in Chapter 6, both factor-analytic studies and longitudinal studies of the correlations across various ages of given children's intelligence indicate that it does not change markedly between childhood (e.g., age seven) and adulthood.

In opposition to the position presented above, Jean Piaget posits the occurrence of qualitative changes in mental activity during adolescence. Of chief concern at this point is Piaget's concept of a transition from concrete to abstract thought that supposedly occurs at about the beginning of adolescence. As noted in Chapter 6, concrete thought is the ability to form concepts involving "operational groupings concerning objects that can be manipulated or known through the senses" (Piaget, 1952, p. 123); a stage in development that lasts until it is superceded by abstract thought. "From 11–12 years and during adolescence, formal thought is projected and its groupings characterize the completion of reflective thought" (Piaget, 1952, p. 123).

In common with a number of other European theories, Piaget's theory has as a major premise a belief in the existence of qualitative differences in thought between different groups of people. In various of these theories, young children, schizophrenics, brain-injured individuals, and primitive peoples are contrasted to adolescents and adults, to persons who are not schizophrenic, to persons who are not brain-injured, and to people of industrial-technological cultures; the first groups are "concrete" in thought, the latter groups "abstract." Whenever this position is put to a rigorous test (e.g., see Johnson, Weiss, & Zelhart, 1964; Williams, 1964, for two such tests regarding schizophrenia) it is shown to be invalid. The writers know of no compelling evidence supporting the position that marked or qualitative change occurs in intelligence at the time of adolescence that might be viewed as comparable to the rapid changes in physical development discussed earlier.

VALUES

The culture, as mediated by the parents for the most part, conveys a set of values to each of its new members. Many of these values are not fully articulated and seldom are verbalized by those adults holding them, yet they are conveyed in subtle and pervasive ways to the young person. Parents choose, from among all of the values of the culture, those that they will emphasize most, as for example, individuality as opposed to conformity, obedience as opposed to independence. Whatever values are conveyed to the young person seem to be accepted without question for a time. In adolescence, however, perhaps as a part of the quest for identity, the young person faces squarely the task of developing a set of personal values. According to Douvan and Adelson (1966):

> *Adolescence is a decisive period* for the fate of personal morality. The youngster must accomplish two major tasks: consolidate his pattern of internal controls and move toward new values. While the tasks are related to each other, they are by no means equivalent. In the first case, the adolescent must learn to meet and live with heightened impulses; he must find a balance between desire and constraint which will allow enough to each side. In the second case, the youngster must construct an individual moral philosophy, a system of values and moral conduct which, however tacit, is his own, his own in the sense that it is not a simple copy of what he has been told to believe, but rather a guide to conduct and valuation appropriate to his own circumstances (p. 79).

There are a number of reasons why the adolescent is required to achieve a satisfactory personal code of values.

First, with increasing independence from parents, the adolescent can no longer accept ready-made the values he has received from them. Reasons and explanations that may have been sufficient at one time are no longer adequate. A southern white adolescent may ask himself, "But why must I consider the Negro to be inferior?" An adolescent reared in an orthodox Jewish home may not accept the reason for eating meat and cheese from separate dishes. A middle-class adolescent may rebel against his parents' social-class biases.

The adolescent frequently discovers that his parents do not always "tell it like it is." The idealistic attitudes of youth cause adolescents to view with alarm and disgust individuals for whom there is evidence that expediency rather than principles has dictated their behavior. The hero worship of preadolescence gives way to a certain cynicism. The adolescent's careful observation of adults (parents, teachers, community and national leaders) reveals flaws where previously he saw none. Perhaps part of the adolescent's occasional delight in discovering that his saint has feet of clay (and parents, at times, are more vulnerable and insecure than adolescents) involves a kind of leveling effect: the achievement of adult status is not beyond his reach; the distance between him and adults is not all that great. Unfortunately, too wide a discrepancy between an adult's stated beliefs and convictions and his actual conduct may cause the adolescent to reject out-of-hand all adult standards as mere pretensions. When the credibility gap becomes too great, the adolescent feels betrayed.

The adolescent's achievement of autonomy involves a certain amount of friction between him and his parents, and some of this friction centers around attitudes and values. But this is not to imply that the adolescent's relationship with his parents is fraught with disagreement over such issues. Several qualifications are necessary. First, since the adolescent is dependent upon his parents for a longer period of time today than formerly, it seems likely that a search for personal values is delayed. Thus today's college student may not be required to make certain decisions that an independent, self-supporting 17-year-old made 30 years ago. Second, there appears to be an important sex difference in the establishment of inner controls (Douvan & Adelson, 1966): ". . . moral development in girls moves from a rather passive, childlike acceptance of parental authority to an identification with the point of view of that authority" (p. 109). The "transitional period of defiance" seems characteristic of adolescent boys but not of girls. Boys, far more than girls, are forced to deal with impulse control, especially in the areas of sex and aggression. As a consequence of this, moral integration is a more salient issue for boys than for girls. Boys show more defiance over the imposition of parental rules and restrictions. And as these rules become less binding, the boy must develop his own rules, his own controls, and his own guidelines.

The adolescent's increased intellectual development accounts also for his concern with values and beliefs. It permits him to deal with such abstractions as "truth," "beauty," "immortality," "justice," and "equality." He develops a sense of perspective. While a young child may view with awe the immutable rules of the adult, an adolescent knows that rules are man-made and that they can change and have changed to fit new situations and new times. The adolescent's intellectual capacity permits him to examine the basis for beliefs and attitudes; his changing status in relation to adults requires that he do so. Seldom, however, does he adopt an entirely new set of beliefs; rather, he develops a different rationale for old beliefs. Whether it involves church attendance, matters of dress, or alcoholic consumption, the adolescent feels obligated to question adult rules, to consider the pros and cons, and then to make his own decision. When adults refuse to let this process occur, they hamper and discourage the adolescent's search for identity and maturity.

The adolescent's wider and more diverse experiences, both social and intellectual, also prompt him to examine his own set of values. Exposure to values and beliefs different from, and at times in contradiction with, those he has learned at home cause the adolescent to make comparisons, contrasts, and evaluative judgments. Interactions and discussions with peers from different racial, religious, and social-class backgrounds frequently stimulate the kinds of searching questions for which adults have no answers. Occasionally (unfortunately, not frequently enough) the adolescent is exposed to new ideas and new points of view in readings assigned in school. When permitted, frank and earnest discussion of political and moral issues can do much to help the adolescent establish his own basis and rationale for his beliefs.

We shall now turn to a brief examination of the adolescent's attitudes and beliefs in three areas: religious, political, and racial.

Religious Values

An example of the questioning of the values imposed by others is found in the area of religious belief. As noted earlier, in Chapter 13, G. Stanley-Hall (1882) and his followers (e.g., Starbuck, 1899) believed that religious conversion was an almost necessary part of adolescence. This belief was supported by an examination of the records of itinerant evangelists, which showed a high frequency of adolescent conversions. It seems apparent today that adolescence is not a time of religious conversion. It does, however, seem to be a time of deep questioning of and concern for various religious beliefs. Most adolescents doubt many or even most of the religious beliefs of their church and of their parents (Landis, 1960; Middleton & Putney, 1962). Teenagers come increasingly to reject the *form* of religion, but at the same time begin to show further concern for the *substance* of religion—for developing a decent and humane way of life. Since much of doctrinaire religious belief, with its ideas of the elect and the damned, strikes many as bigoted and lacking in any broad concern for humanity, and since there is ample evidence indicating that the most common type of churchgoer, who attends for reasons of social conformity, is prejudiced, narrow, and authoritarian (e.g., see Jones, 1958; Stouffer, 1955; Wilson, 1960), adolescent idealism itself works against involvement with formal religion.

It seems ironic that church attendance declines markedly at the very time the adolescent is searching for answers to religious and philosophical questions. At times, more so than in the past perhaps, the church has been unable to answer these questions to the adolescent's satisfaction. The autocratic inflexibility of doctrinaire religious beliefs does not appeal to adolescents. Nor has organized religion dealt sufficiently with relevant issues that are of urgent importance to the adolescent.

It is to the credit of most adolescents that, when faced with the problem of deciding which of the societal religious values they have been exposed to will become their own values, they reject the narrow aspects of religion and incorporate those aspects that dispose an individual to tolerance and humanism.

It seems that until recently the majority of adolescents identified more closely with the overt behaviors of our culture, rather than with the values that are believed basic to our culture yet are contradicted by our behavior. Now, for the first time, persons in their late teens and early twenties have taken our expressed values seriously and have made apparent the contradictions between our values and our behavior. Hence we have the student "rebels," who believe that we should live according to the basic humanitarian values of our culture.

Political Values

The reasons for the development of a set of standards described at the beginning of this section account in large part for the adolescent's growing interest in political ideas: independence from parents, increased intellectual development, and wider experiences. Concern with political issues is far less intense among adolescents in our society than it is for other values and attitudes. In part this reflects a general apathy among adults with regard to political ideology. Second, because of the relative isolation of the United States, adolescents are not exposed to political beliefs or forms of government that differ to any appreciable extent from our own.

In general, the adolescent's political convictions do not vary markedly from those held by his parents. As we have noted elsewhere in this chapter, the same is true for racial and religious attitudes, suggesting the absence of any profound adolescent rebellion—or at least such rebellion is not reflected in these areas. For example, Lane (1959) concluded that rebellion against parents typically is expressed in nonpolitical terms.

Middleton and Putney (1963) found some confirmation for the hypothesis that rebellion against parents will be expressed in the political area if the parents are interested in politics and if the adolescent perceives parental discipline as extreme. Students whose political views differed from their parents perceived parental discipline as extremely strict or extremely permissive; this was combined with an interest in political matters on the part of the parent. While, in general, it seems unlikely that political differences produce alienation between parent and child, there are cases when this does occur. More typically, conflict between parent and adolescent is on a deeper psychological level, which is expressed occasionally in disagreement over political philosophy.

In an interesting study of the growth of a broadly defined sense of community (Adelson & O'Neil, 1966), 120 adolescents were interviewed, 30 each at the ages of 11, 13, 15, and 18. The interviewer posed the following situation: "Imagine that a thousand men and women, dissatisfied with the way things are going in their country, decide to purchase and move to an island in the Pacific; once there, they must devise laws and modes of government" (p. 295). Subsequently, questions were asked on a number of hypothetical issues, such as the form of government, proposed laws, and the reciprocal obligations of citizens and state.

The clearest progress in ability to deal with abstract political concepts occurred between the ages of 11 and 13. The 11-year-olds were unable to deal with these matters on other than a concrete level; their perspective was personal and limited. The following are excerpts from interviews in response to the question, "What is the purpose of government?"

11-year-olds:

11A. To handle the state or whatever it is so it won't get out of hand, because if it gets out of hand you might have to . . . people might get mad or something.

11B. Well . . . buildings, they have to look over buildings that would be . . . um, that wouldn't be any use of the land if they had crops on it or something like that. And when they have highways the government would have to inspect it, certain details. I guess that's about all.

11C. So everything won't go wrong in the country. They want to have a government because they respect him and they think he's a good man.

Now the 13-year-olds:

13A. So the people have rights and freedom of speech. Also so the civilization will balance.

13B. To keep law and order and talk to the people to make new ideas.

13C. Well, I think it is to keep the country happy or keep it going properly. If you didn't have it, then it would just be chaos with stealing and things like this. It runs the country better and more efficiently (p. 297).

While 11-year-olds emphasized the negative and coercive functions of government, the 13-year-olds stressed the positive functions. The older adolescents were better able to deal with the future; they anticipated the long-range consequences of present decisions. Older children (15 years and over) are able to provide explanations for their positions. They are able to reason logically and sequentially, following a course of action through to its possible outcome. Further, they can deduce specific approaches from general principles. Younger adolescents often assume an authoritarian position on issues, probably due in part to their own subservient position in relation to their parents. With increasing age adolescents come to understand some of the finer points involved in issues concerning the rights of the individual versus the needs of the community.

In summary, the adolescent's political allegiances stem largely from those held by his parents. Rebellion against parents seldom takes the form of political disagreement except when the parents show strong concern with political matters. Increased intellectual development throughout adolescence permits a more mature understanding of political and governmental affairs.

Racial Attitudes

Racial attitudes are learned. The primary basis for this learning is the home. The prejudices of the parent reflect the particular ethnic, social-class, and geographical group with which he identifies. Later, conformity to prevailing peer group attitudes influences specific attitudes held by the adolescent.

While no sharp changes in racial attitudes are apparent throughout adolescence, there is evidence for some increase during adolescence in stereotyped thinking with regard to racial and religious groups (McNeil, 1960). That such attitudes remain relatively stable during this age period suggests that they are well established by late childhood or early adolescence.

Although early studies supported the contention, described in *The Authoritarian Personality* (Adorno, Frenkel-Brunswik, Levinson, & Sanford, 1950), that the child's relation with his parents lays the basis for prejudicial attitudes, this must now be qualified. The statement may apply in regard to middle-class individuals, in whom stereotyped thinking may reflect a basically rigid personality structure. In lower-class adolescents, however, such thinking is probably based on acceptance of general stereotyped attitudes prevailing in the lower class (Livson & Nichols, 1957; McCord, McCord, & Howard, 1960). The course that attitudes learned early in the home will take for any particular individual depends on a variety of factors. Is the adolescent at least moderately successful in his schoolwork and other activities? Is he accepted by peers? Does he relate well to adults? Are his family relations satisfactory? Undoubtedly some prejudice is due to a scapegoating phenomenon in which the individual blames others for his frustrations and failures.

Several implications for education can be drawn from the above discussion. Schools must attempt to provide the kinds of experiences for each child that will give him a feeling of self-worth and of self-acceptance, so that projection of blame and of negative characteristics will not be necessary. Second, schools can stimulate the kind of careful thinking that dispels irrational prejudice and restrictive stereotypes. Needless to say, the example set by the teacher is of great importance.

SUMMARY

Adolescence, as a stage in life, begins with physical and behavioral change and ends when the individual has assumed adult roles. Adolescence is a period of rapid physiological change. The individual (particularly a male) who is out of step in development is typically at a considerable social disadvantage during adolescence, but recovers from this negative experience in adulthood. Evidence suggests that the dramatic change in the physical self is not mirrored by a change of the same variety in the area of intellectual performance. The nature of intelligence appears unchanged from childhood through adulthood; rather, those changes that do occur appear to result from a gradual accretion of information, not from any qualitative change in level or kind of intellectual functioning.

A major developmental task of adolescence is the acquisition of a sense of personal identity.   The young person, exposed to many social roles and values, decides which ones he will accept and use as a basis for behavior.   Because of their need to sort out and to accept or reject roles and values, adolescents question the roles and values of the culture, and become aware of the gap between the values that adult members of our culture claim to hold and the behavior they display.   Despite the fact that they may be viewed negatively by adults, an increasing number of adolescents point out this divergence between the values and the behaviors of adults; they opt for the humanistic values of the culture rather than modeling their behavior after that of most of the adults. However, the vast majority of adolescents still come to be far more like than unlike their parents in values, and conform to the prevailing social mores.

REFERENCES

Adelson, J., & O'Neil, R.   Growth of political ideas in adolescence: The sense of community.   *Journal of Personality and Social Psychology*, 1966, **4**, 295–306.

Adorno, T. W., Frenkel-Brunswik, E., Levinson, D. J., & Sanford, R. N.   *The authoritarian personality*.   New York: Harper, 1950.

Aries, P.   *Centuries of childhood* (translated by R. Baldic).   New York: Knopf, 1962.

Bandura, A., & Huston, A. C.   Identification as a process of incidental learning. *Journal of Abnormal and Social Psychology*, 1961, **63**, 311–318.

Battle, E., & Rotter, J. B.   Children's feelings of personal control as related to social class and ethnic group.   *Journal of Personality*, 1963, **31**, 482–490.

Bettelheim, B., & Janowitz, M.   *Dynamics of prejudice*.   New York: Harper, 1950.

Bloom, B. S.   *Stability and change in human characteristics*.   New York: Wiley, 1964.

Boehm, L.   The development of independence: A comparative study.   *Child Development*, 1957, **28**, 82–92.

Carlos, J. P., & Gittelsohn, A. M.   Longitudinal studies of the natural history of caries.   I. Eruption patterns of the permanent teeth.   *Journal of Dental Research*, 1965, **44**, 509–516.

Crampton, C. W.   Anatomical or physiological age versus chronological age. *Pedagogical Seminary*, 1908, **15**, 23–237.   (a)

Crampton, C. W.   Physiological age.   *American Physical Education Review*, 1908, **13**, 144–154; 214–227; 263–283; 345–358.   (b)

Crandall, V. J., Katkovsky, W., & Preston, A.   Motivational and ability determinants of young children's intellectual achievement behaviors.   *Child Development*, 1962, **33**, 643–661.

Dennis, W. The adolescent. In L. Carmichael (Ed.), *Manual of child psychology*. New York: Wiley, 1946. Pp. 633–666.

Douvan, E., & Adelson, J. *The adolescent experience*. New York: Wiley, 1966.

Engelmann, G. J. Age of first menstruation on the American continent. *Transactions of the American Gynecological Society*, 1901, **26**, 77–110.

Erikson, E. H. *Childhood and society*. (2nd Ed.) New York: Norton, 1963. Pp. 247–274.

Fisher, S., & Cleveland, S. E. *Body image and personality*. Princeton, N. J.: Van Nostrand, 1958.

Freud, S. *Three essays in sexuality*. London: Hogarth, 1953.

Goodenough, F. L. The measurement of mental growth in childhood. In L. Carmichael (Ed.), *Manual of child psychology*. (2nd Ed.) New York: Wiley, 1954. Pp. 459–491.

Gore, P. M., & Rotter, J. B. A personality correlate of social action. *Journal of Personality*, 1963, **31**, 58–64.

Gottlieb, D., Reeves, J., & Ten Housen, W. D. *The emergence of youth societies. A cross-cultural approach*. New York: Free Press, 1966.

Gould, H. N., & Gould, M. R. Age of first menstruation in mothers and daughters. *Journal of the American Medical Association*, 1932, **98**, (16), 1349–1352.

Gray, W. S., & Klaus, R. The measurement of parental identification. *Genetic Psychology Monographs*, 1956, **54**, 87–114.

Greulich, W. W., & Pyle, S. I. *Radiographic atlas of skeletal development of the hand and wrist*. (2nd ed.) Stanford, Calif.: Stanford University Press, 1959.

Hall, G. S. The moral and religious training of children. *Princeton Review*, 1882, **10**, 26–480.

Harris, J. A., Jackson, C. M., Paterson, D. G., & Scammon, R. E. *The measurement of man*. Minneapolis: University of Minnesota Press, 1930.

Heilbrun, A. G. Conformity to masculinity-femininity stereotypes and ego identity in adolescents. *Psychological Reports*, 1964, **14**, 351–357.

Hetherington, E. M. Effects of paternal absence on sex typed behaviors in Negro and white pre-adolescents. *Journal of Personality and Social Psychology*, 1966, **4**, 87–91.

Johnson, R. C., Weiss, R. L., & Zelhart, P. F. Similarities and differences between normal and psychotic subjects in responses to verbal stimuli. *Journal of Abnormal and Social Psychology*, 1964, **68**, 233–236.

Jones, H. E. Adolescence in our society. In *The family in a democratic Society: Anniversary papers of the Community Service Society of New York*. New York: Columbia University Press, 1949. Pp. 70–82.

Jones, M. B. Religious values and authoritarian tendency. *Journal of Social Psychology*, 1958, **48**, 83–84.

Jones, M. C. The later careers of boys who were early or late maturing. *Child Development*, 1957, **28**, 113–128.

Jones, M. C., & Bayley, N.   Physical maturing among boys as related to behavior. *Journal of Educational Psychology,* 1950, **41,** 129–148.

Jones, M. C., & Mussen, P. H.   Self conceptions, motivations, and interpersonal attitudes of early- and late-maturing girls.   *Child Development,* 1958, **29,** 491–501.

Kagan, J.   Acquisition and significance of sex typing and sex role identity. In M. L. Hoffman & L. W. Hoffman (Eds.), *Review of child development research* (I), New York: Wiley, 1964.

Kagan, J., & Moss, H. A.   *Birth to maturity.*   New York: Wiley, 1962.

Kessen, W.   *The child.*   New York: Wiley, 1965.

Kinsey, A. C., Pomeroy, W. B., & Martin, C. E.   *Sexual behavior in the human male.*   Philadelphia: Saunders, 1948.

Kinsey, A. C., Pomeroy, W. B., Martin, C. E., & Gebhart, P. H.   *Sexual behavior in the human female.*   Philadelphia: Saunders, 1953.

Landis, B. Y.   Religion and youth.   In E. Ginzberg (Ed.), *The nation's children. Vol. 2, Development and education.*   New York: Columbia University Press, 1960.   Pp. 186–206.

Landis, P. H.   *Adolescence and youth.*   New York: McGraw-Hill, 1945.

Lane, R.   Fathers and sons: Foundations of political belief.   *American Sociological Review,* 1959, **24,** 502–511.

Lefcourt, H. M.   Internal versus external control of reinforcement.   *Psychological Bulletin,* 1966, **65,** 206–220.

Livson, N., & Nichols, T.   Social attitude configuration in an adolescent group. *Journal of Genetic Psychology,* 1957, **91,** 3–23.

Lynn, D. B.   Sex role and parental identification.   *Child Development,* 1962, **33,** 555–564.

Lynn, D. B., & Sawrey, W. H.   The effects of father absence on Norwegian boys and girls.   *Journal of Abnormal and Social Psychology,* 1959, **59,** 258–262.

McCord, W., McCord, J., & Howard, A.   Early familial experiences and bigotry.   *American Sociological Review,* 1960, **25,** 717–722.

McCord, J., McCord, W., & Thurber, E.   Some effects of paternal absence on male children.   *Journal of Abnormal and Social Psychology,* 1962, **64,** 361–369.

McNeil, J.   Changes in ethnic reaction tendencies during high school.   *Journal of Educational Research,* 1960, **53,** 199–200.

Middleton, R., & Putney, S.   Religion, normative standards, and behavior. *Sociometry,* 1962, **25,** 141–152.

Middleton, R., & Putney, S.   Political expression of adolescent rebellion.   *American Journal of Sociology,* 1963, **68,** 527–535.

Montagu, M. F. A.   The existence of a sterile phase in female adolescence. *Complex,* 1950, **1,** 27–30.

Mowrer, O. H.   Identification: A link between learning and psychotherapy.   In O. H. Mowrer, *Learning theory and personality dynamics.*   New York: Ronald, 1950.   Pp. 573–616.

Mussen, P. H.   Long term consequences of masculinity of interests in adolescence.   *Journal of Consulting Psychology*, 1962, **26**, 435–440.

Mussen, P. H., & Distler, L.   Masculinity, identification, and father-son relationships.   *Journal of Abnormal and Social Psychology*, 1959, **58**, 350–356.

Mussen, P. H., & Rutherford, E.   Parent-child relations and parental personality in relation to young children's sex-role preferences.   *Child Development*, 1963, **34**, 584–607.

Olson, W. C.   *Child development.*   Boston: Heath, 1949.   Pp. 174–187.

Piaget, J.   *The origins of intelligence in children.*   New York: International Univ. Press, 1952.

Popenoe, P.   Inheritance of age on onset of menstruation.   *Eugenic News*, 1928, **13**, 101.

Phyphers, J.   Interpersonal trust, locus of control, and ability to delay gratification.   Unpublished manuscript, University of Colorado, 1968.

Sears, R. R., Pintler, M. H., & Sears, P. S.   Effects of father separation on preschool children's doll play aggression.   *Child Development*, 1946, **17**, 219–243.

Seigman, A. W.   Father absence during early childhood and antisocial behavior.   *Journal of Abnormal Psychology*, 1966, **7**, 71–74.

Sheldon, W. H., Stevens, S. S., & Tucker, W. B.   *The varieties of human physique: An introduction to constitutional psychology.*   New York: Harper, 1940.

Shuttleworth, F. K.   The physical and mental growth of girls and boys age six to nineteen in relation to age at maximum growth.   *Monographs of the Society for Research in Child Development*, Series 22, 1939, **4**, No. 3.

Starbuck, E. D.   *Psychology of religion.*   New York: Scribner's, 1899.

Stolz, L. M., et al.   *Father relations of war-born children.*   Stanford: Stanford University Press, 1954.

Stone, C. P., & Barker, R. G.   The attitudes and interests of premenarchial and post menarchial girls.   *Journal of Genetic Psychology*, 1939, **54**, 27–71.

Stouffer, S.   *Communism, conformity, and civil rights.*   New York: Doubleday, 1955.

Tanner, J. M.   Genetics of human growth.   In J. M. Tanner (Ed.), *Human growth*, Vol. III.   Oxford: Pergamon Press, 1960.   Pp. 43–58.

Tanner, J. M.   Earlier maturation in man.   *Scientific American*, 1968, **218**, 21–28.

Tocqueville, A.   *Democracy in America*, Vol. 2.   New York: Vintage, 1954 (originally published in 1840).

Tryon, C. M.   Evaluation of adolescent personality by adolescents.   *Monographs of the Society for Research in Child Development*, 1939, **4**, No. 4.

Tuddenham, R. D.   Studies in reputation: III. Correlates of popularity among elementary school children.   *Journal of Personality and Social Psychology*, 1951, **42**, 257–276.

Walster, E., Aronson, V., Abraham, D., & Roltman, L.   Importance of physical attractiveness in dating behavior. *Journal of Personality and Social Psychology*, 1966, **4,** 508–516.

Weatherley, D.   Self perceived rate of physical maturation and personality in late adolescence.   *Child Development*, 1964, **35,** 1197–1210.

Williams, E. B.   Deductive reasoning in schizophrenia.   *Journal of Abnormal and Social Psychology*, 1964, **69,** 47–61.

Wilson, W.   Extrinsic religious values and prejudice.   *Journal of Abnormal and Social Psychology*, 1960, **60,** 286–288.

Wylie, C.   *The self-concept: A critical survey of pertinent literature.*   Lincoln, Neb.: University of Nebraska Press, 1961.

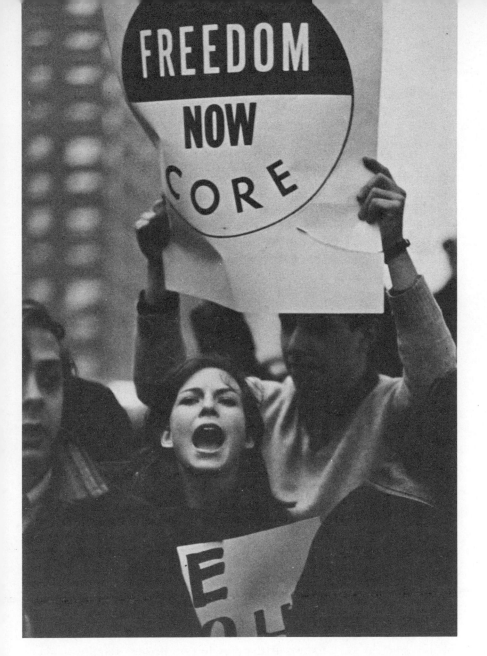

18

Social Behavior in Adolescence

As we have said, the major task of adolescence is the development of personal identity. We have considered some aspects of this personal identity in Chapter 17. Other aspects are so closely associated with social interactions and with the social norms of parents and of peers that they should be discussed within the context of social behavior. These aspects of the self are the development of independence and the development of self-imposed constraints or controls upon behavior, based on a personally held set of values. The interactive effects of parents and peers on the adolescent usually cause these two kinds of development to occur at roughly the same rate, so that they are complementary to one another. However, if one of these develops without the other (e.g., if an adolescent is emancipated from parental values and moral dicta, yet has not developed any set of inner constraints on behavior or value system to serve as a guide to behavior), or if the development of one is stunted as compared with the other, problem behavior is likely to occur. This situation typically involves pathogenic parent-child relations, peer relations, or both.

The American "youth culture" was the first of its kind (Denney, 1961), and as such probably has had marked influence on the international youth culture that now is discernible. American parents and their response to present conditions of adolescence may presage worldwide shifts in parent-child interactions.

PARENT-ADOLESCENT RELATIONS

In addition to the biological changes marking the beginning of adolescence and the adolescent's attachment to his peer group, the child's changing relationship with his parents during this age period is one of the areas receiving major attention in any consideration of adolescence. This latter concern is inherent in the meaning of adolescence in our society. Part of the important process of developing a sense of identity involves forming new kinds of interpersonal relations. A different basis for the adolescent's relationship with his parents must be established. While earlier the parent assumed a dominant role and the child a submissive one, the very nature of the growing up process requires a more equalitarian relationship. A study of personality needs of adolescents (Lucas & Horrocks, 1960) revealed a factor labeled "Independence and dominance in relationships with adults." This was described as involving the need for "independence from adult supervision as well as emancipation from the role of a child especially in the family setting." The parent must be mature and flexible enough to recognize and adapt to this important need of the adolescent period. The demands on both

690

parent and adolescent made by this changing relationship produce conflict and friction. A number of terms have been used to describe this situation: departure, emancipation, rebellion, disengagement, struggle for autonomy, and independence demands.

For purposes of discussion, let us look separately at the parent and the adolescent in terms of the meaning of this age period for each.

Parent Concerns

It has been said that adolescence comes at a particularly poor time for the parent. This may well be the case. Depending, of course, upon the age of the parents when they began their family, typically they are between the ages of 40 and 50 when their child is coping with adolescence. While 40 marks no crucial milestone or crisis in our society, it does denote the beginning of "middle age," with all that may imply. For the father, the onset of middle age may involve a painful reappraisal —perhaps an unpleasantly objective review of his status in relation to his goals. He may never reach the position of foreman or company executive to which he had once aspired. While the late-adolescent boy is first searching for his place in the occupational world, the father may be searching again for his. This time, however, his attitude is colored by frustration and a desperate awareness that in reality the future holds no great promise.

Although the problems are dissimilar, both father and son face adjustment in the sexual sphere. The father's adjustments do not involve the heightened expectation felt by the son; once again the two are widely separated on the continuum ranging from growing up to growing old. The father may regard his son with a certain amount of jealousy, in the sexual area and in other areas as well. Unfortunately this presents another obstacle to communication and understanding between the two.

Despite frantic efforts, a 40-year-old woman can never recapture her youth. Cosmetology, including plastic face lifting, cannot really erase the wrinkles of aging. The artificialities of appearance produced by such attempts can be seen for what they are—artificial. As a woman who had just turned 40 remarked, to her this meant the end of her dream of having an affair with the ski instructor. The inability of Mrs. Robinson in the movie "The Graduate" to adjust to her life at middle age caused her to seek an affair with her daughter's boyfriend; the consequences were bitterness and despair.

The child's growing maturity forces the parent to face the fact that he, too, is getting older. The mother plays the major role in child rearing. When children are young, the demands are great. So are the satisfactions; the mother's role is at once demanding and rewarding. At adolescence, however, the child's growing allegiance to the peer group implies a decline in reliance on the parent. The mother must face the time when her child-rearing role is at an end: she will no longer be needed in the same way; she may be haunted by a fear of emptiness and aimlessness; she must adjust to a different role in relation to her children.

Some of the problems faced by the adolescent may reawaken in the parent awareness of conflicts he encountered at adolescence which remain unresolved. Thus the parent's attempts to deal with his child's difficulties may be hampered by a rearousal of anxiety concerning his own adolescent difficulties. While experience may be a great teacher, the lessons it teaches seldom are complete. Because the parent's evaluation of his adolescent's behavior inevitably involves a certain amount of projection based on his own adolescent experience, some writers (Johnson & Szurek, 1952) have speculated that children's antisocial behavior, for example, sexual adventures of an adolescent daughter or a son's delinquent defiance of authority, may be an acting-out of the unconscious wishes of the parents.

The young child idealizes his parents, whom he sees as superhuman, trusts, and relies upon without reservation. Growing intellectual development and social awareness permit the child to evaluate and judge individuals, including his parents, on a more objective basis. The adolescent is alert to the strengths, weaknesses, and failures of peers, parents, and teachers, and frequently this objective appraisal poses a threat to parents. An analysis of children's essays concerning "The Kind of Person I Want To Be" revealed that children choose different models as they grow older (Havighurst, Robinson, & Dorr, 1946). The ideal person described by a young child is his parent. Later, the parent is replaced partially by romantic and glamorous figures. In late adolescence, the admired figure is a composite of respected individuals in the community. The first displacement, on a fantasy level, does not threaten the parent; the later displacement does. The parent cannot escape the fact that his child's evaluation of him is now on a realistic rather than an idealistic basis. Coupled with this threat is the adolescent's strong affiliation with peers, which the parent may view as partial rejection of the family.

Because ours is a rapidly changing society, a gap between generations in a number of areas seems inevitable. Certain aspects of values and beliefs have undergone change; they have become more relative and less absolute. Standards of conduct and behavior are not static. Economic conditions have undergone marked fluctuations. Philosophy of child rearing with respect to the relation between parent and child has changed noticeably in the last several decades. An emphasis on parental authority has given way to a more equalitarian, democratic approach that perhaps places greater demands on the parent, especially if he had been reared in a more structured atmosphere. While it seems unlikely that the family as a social institution is disintegrating, its role and function in relation to society have been altered. All of these changes produce a certain amount of parental vulnerability. Not wanting to appear old-fashioned and out-of-date, parents may yield too readily to their adolescent's demands. In a sense the adolescent forces his parents to re-examine their own beliefs and the basis for their own values and attitudes. This may be accompanied by uncertainty, resentment, and, at times, increased rigidity and inflexibility. The adult's values have been shaped through long years of experience, both bitter and sweet, and change does not come easily.

In summary, the emancipation and independence of the adolescent from his parent is necessary and inevitable. Yet, for a variety of reasons, both conscious and unconscious, the parent may be unwilling or unable to grant this independence. As Ausubel (1954) has noted, "The most important single cause of parent-youth conflict is the perseveration of parents' attitudes that interfere with the adolescent's greatly expanded need for volitional independence" (p. 226). As Douvan and Adelson (1966) point out in their excellent study of a large number of adolescents, there is a curvilinear relation between parental involvement with the child and the child's developing autonomy. Too much and too little involvement both hamper the adolescent's achievement of autonomy. If the parents manifest too little involvement, the security necessary for autonomy is not developed; too much involvement creates a dependency that is antithetical to emancipation.

Adolescent Concerns

As we discussed above, the adolescent's need for autonomy and independence from parents and other adults is a vital one. Perhaps a sense of identity (Who am I? Where and how will I fit in to society?) can be achieved only as a consequence of this pervasive struggle for independence. While the adolescent's need to become an individual in himself cannot be questioned, his perception of his goal, which is maturity and adulthood, occasionally is faulty. To the adolescent, an adult is a completely free agent. He can do what he wants when he wants. He can stay out as late as he pleases. No one nags at him about his school grades, hanging up his clothes, showing respect to elders, and closing the refrigerator door. Actually, of course, perhaps the single most important criterion of a mature adult is a deep sense of responsibility—to himself, to his family, and to the larger society. Creative use of independence requires maturity and responsibility. The adolescent must ask himself, "Freedom for what?"

Douvan and Adelson (1966) furnish evidence that specific issues involved in the adolescent's striving for autonomy depend upon his age. When questioned about disagreement with parents, the early-adolescent girl mentions items related to personal grooming such as clothing and lipstick. Such disagreements peak in early adolescence while aspects concerned with social activities (dating, choice of friends) are most prominent in middle adolescence (14 to 16 years). Later, conflict with parents is greatest over matters related to beliefs and attitudes. As issues at each level are resolved, others become more important.

Undoubtedly part of the cause of the conflict between parent and child during adolescence is that to the adolescent parents represent adult society and adult authority. And it is this authority that prevents him from regulating his own life as he sees fit. Justifiably or not, the adolescent feels that adults depreciate teenagers. In a study in which adolescents were instructed to rate "teenagers from the viewpoint of adults" (Hess & Goldblatt, 1957), they expected to be rated by adults as impulsive, impatient, inconsistent, spoiled, frivolous, irresponsible, and wild. Actually, parents rated teenagers in a mildly favorable manner. Moreover, adults rated "average teenagers" in much the same way as the adolescents rated themselves. We might speculate that the phenomenon of "self-fulfilling prophecy"—in which the adolescent unconsciously lives up to the expectations he believes adults have of him—operates to the disadvantage of the youth.

Lest it appear that the adolescent is bent on a single-minded pursuit of independence from parents, we should point out that the need for independence and the need for dependence are not mutually exclusive. Adolescence is best characterized by a shifting balance between these two urges. At times the adolescent actually seeks a closer relationship with his parents. Unfortunate consequences often result when the parent overinterprets the adolescent's need for independence and withdraws his emotional support. Perhaps the child never fully outgrows a need for parental acceptance and reassurance, and this provides an important emotional linkage between generations.

Gradually the adolescent's emotional involvement with the family and his participation in family affairs shifts to the peer group. Conformity to peer-group demands supplants conformity to parental demands. Brittain (1963, 1966) developed the Cross-Pressures Test, which assesses the adolescent's disposition toward parent conformity versus peer conformity. The following is an example of the type of item included in the test:

> For the past several weeks Martha has been dating two boys. One of them is Jack and the other is Frank. Jack is good-looking and intelligent. He is not especially talkative, but he can hold up his end of the conversation, and he is friendly. Frank is in some ways different from Jack. He is not especially good-looking, but he is more talkative than Jack, and he has a good sense of humor. Frank dresses with good taste. Both Frank and Jack have asked Martha to go steady. Many of her girl friends are going steady, and she would like to. But she isn't sure which she would rather go steady with—Frank or Jack. She has put both of them off about an answer because she can't make up her mind. Martha's mother and father haven't tried to tell her whom to date, but Martha can tell that they like Frank. But that is not the way Martha's girl friends feel. They like Jack better than Frank. Her friends would rather see Martha go steady with Jack.
>
> Can you guess what Martha decided to do?
> ———— Go steady with Frank
> ———— Go steady with Jack
>
> (Brittain, 1966, p. 710)

Whether the adolescent chooses the verdict of parents or peers depends upon which is seen as the more competent guide in a particular situation. In difficult situations he is likely to defer to parental judgment. He conforms to peer decisions in choices that may result in separation from them, and in order not to appear different from them. Clearly, peers serve as a reference group for the adolescent. He identifies with them and, in turn, they provide emotional support in his conflict with parents over various issues. Probably one of the most important reasons for the adolescent's conformity to peer demands and his involvement with peers is that this identification facilitates his emancipation from parents.

Sex of Child and Sex of Parent

In early childhood the mother assumes primary responsibility for child rearing. Later, the father plays an increasingly important role, especially in relation to an adolescent boy. He participates actively in matters of discipline and control involving the boy, while the mother continues as the primary socializing agent for the girl (Bowerman & Elder, 1964). In general, adolescent girls report their mothers and adolescent boys report their fathers as the principal decision maker in the family (Bronfenbrenner, 1961). In a study of adolescents' perceptions of parental resource control (Grinder & Spector, 1965), ninth- through twelfth-graders were asked to designate which parent would be most likely to make decisions affecting them in a number of different areas. The following five questions illustrate the situations covered:

1. Which parent would have more control over giving you permission to go out at night—for example to a party or to the movies?
2. Which parent would have more control over your choice of a career?
3. Which parent would you go to for consolation if you were unhappy?
4. Which parent would control the amount of privacy you could have—regarding your relations with friends, telephone conversations, etc.?
5. Which parent would be more influential in planning the use of the family's leisure time?

(Grinder & Spector, 1965, p. 340)

As a group, adolescents tended to perceive the relative power of their parents as nearly equal. However, girls viewed their mothers as having more control, and boys, their fathers.

A great deal of evidence has accumulated with regard to effect of an affectionate father-son relationship on the boy's adjustment in adolescence. An interesting crosscultural study of a group of adolescent boys in Rome, Florence, Palermo, and Boston (Mussen, Young, Gaddini, & Morante, 1963) found that boys who experience "insufficient paternal affection" were less secure, less self-confident, and less well adjusted socially than the group whose fathers showed sufficient affection.

In general, adolescents of both sexes experience greater interaction with their mothers than with their fathers. This greater contact with the mother has both negative and positive aspects. The extent of friction between the adolescent and the mother as compared with the father depends in part on the child's age. In a projective study of 50 girls between the ages of 9 and 17, Liccione (1955) found that mother-daughter friction increased up to the age of 15 but dropped off at 17, while the reverse was true for the amount of friction between father and daughter. The initial friction between mother and daughter may reflect the daughter's desire for independence; the subsequent decline in conflict may indicate that the girl has reached a higher level of maturity in that she now accepts her female role and, consequently, her relationship with her mother becomes more harmonious.

From an analysis of the responses of 400 tenth-graders to a 100-item Parent-Activity Inventory, Bronfenbrenner (1961) drew the following conclusions about the interactive effects of sex of child and sex of parent:

Taken together, the results on sex differences in parental behavior suggest that, within the family, boys and girls find themselves in somewhat contrasting situations.   Girls receive more affection, attention, and praise than boys—especially from their fathers—whereas boys are subjected to greater pressure and discipline, again mainly from their fathers.   In other words, particularly in their relationship with fathers, girls find themselves in a more supportive context than boys.   From the point of view of minimizing pressure and maximizing affection, the boy is in a relatively better situation in his relationship with the mother than with the father. . . .

(Bronfenbrenner, 1961, p. 249)

Parent-Adolescent Research

In Chapter 10 we saw that a number of parent-child research studies can be ordered in terms of two principal dimensions: autonomy-control and love-hostility.   However, parent-adolescent research cannot be discussed readily within such a framework.   Many of these studies deal with specific aspects of the child's relationship with his parents, such as sources of conflict (Connor, Johannes, & Walters, 1954; Bath & Lewis, 1962).   Other studies deal with rather specific characteristics of the adolescent, and these are related to variables in the home.   As a whole, research at this age level certainly is less voluminous than at the child level; by and large it is less well designed; and it seems less concerned with broad, theoretically important dimensions.   Thus it is frequently impossible to coordinate the parent-adolescent research findings with those dealing with the childhood period.

The Fels Studies.   The longitudinal studies conducted at the Fels Research Institute and at the University of California Institute of Human Development have been described elsewhere in the book.   In both studies repeated evaluations were made of the mother's behavior toward the child over an extended period of time.

Some of the significant correlations from the Fels report (Kagan & Freeman, 1963) between early maternal behaviors at ages two to four and four to seven and several adolescent variables are listed in Table 18-1.   The mother's willingness to justify her child-rearing policies to the child through explanation and reasoning was conducive to the adolescent's concern with intellectual mastery.   Clearly, the type of mother who believes in her child's capacity to comprehend the reasons for the discipline employed also emphasizes his intellectual capacity in other areas as well.

Sex differences in antecedents of conformity to adult demands were apparent.   Conformity in adolescent boys seemed to be produced by a cluster of traits suggesting high maternal nurturance.   For girls, on the

TABLE 18-1   Relation between Selected Adolescent Interview Variables and Selected Maternal Child-Rearing Practices *

Adolescent Variable: Intellectual Mastery

Maternal Variable (Males)	r	Maternal Variable (Females)	r
Acceleration (4–7)	.51		
Justification (2–4)	.51		
Justification (4–7)	.54		

Adolescent Variable: Conformity

Maternal Variable (Males)	r	Maternal Variable (Females)	r
Babying (4–7)	.45	Acceleration (2–4)	−.66
Protection (4–7)	.44	Protection (2–4)	.52
Acceptance (4–7)	.52	Restrictiveness (4–7)	.60
Affection (4–7)	.59	Severity (4–7)	.50
Criticism (4–7)	.47		

Adolescent Variable: Dependence Mother

Maternal Variable (Males)	r	Maternal Variable (Females)	r
Affection (2–4)	.43	Acceleration (2–4)	−.52
Acceptance (2–4)	.48	Severity (4–7)	.52

Adolescent Variable: Dependence Father

Maternal Variable (Males)	r	Maternal Variable (Females)	r
		Protection (2–4)	.50
		Restrictiveness (4–7)	.73
		Severity (4–7)	.58
		Coerciveness (4–7)	.77

Adolescent Variable: Task Withdrawal

Maternal Variable (Males)	r	Maternal Variable (Females)	r
Justification (2–4)	−.44	Acceleration (4–7)	−.50
Acceleration (2–4)	−.37	Acceptance (4–7)	.54
Acceleration (4–7)	−.41	Affection (4–7)	.68

Adolescent Variable: Social Withdrawal

Maternal Variable (Males)	r	Maternal Variable (Females)	r
Criticism (4–7)	.42		
Affection (4–7)	.38		

* From Kagan and Freeman (1963).

other hand, excessive severity of discipline and restrictiveness by the mother resulted in conformity at adolescence. Such behavior on the part of the father led to dependency in the girl.

The California Studies. In the California research (Schaefer & Bayley, 1963), maternal behavior from birth to three years showed a closer association with boys' behavior at adolescence than with girls'. Early ratings of maternal behavior on the love-hostility dimension were related to boys' behavior up to the age of 12 but not during adolescence. The reverse was found for the autonomy-control dimension. Thus early control variables (concern about health, excessive contact, fostering dependency, and emotional involvement) correlated positively with the following behavior variables of the adolescent boy: friendly, social, independent, bold, irritable, and rude.

Figure 18-1 shows relations between maternal behavior and three per-

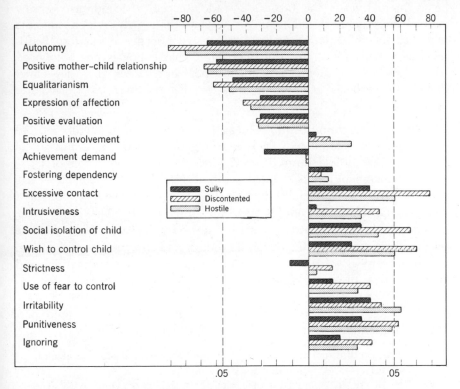

FIGURE 18-1   Correlations of maternal behavior between 9 and 14 years with daughters' sulky, discontented, and hostile clusters at adolescence.

sonality ratings for adolescent daughters. In general, both the hostility and the control variables were related to maladjusted behavior of daughters at adolescence. Negative correlations were obtained between daughters' ratings on a cluster of variables including defiant, hostile, sulky, and discontented and ratings of the following maternal variables: equalitarianism, positive mother-child relationship, autonomy, maternal sociability, cooperativeness, marital happiness, estimated intelligence, positive emotional state, and communicativeness. Taken together, this suggests that excessive control on the part of a mother, as well as her own poor adjustment, is detrimental to the daughter's personality adjustment at adolescence.

Several reasons may account for the fact that early maternal behaviors are related to certain aspects of boys' adolescent behavior, whereas for girls maternal behavior at adolescence is more important. First, the father plays an increasingly important role in affecting the boy's adjustment, so that we would not expect the mother's behavior to be as predictive as the father's by adolescence. Second, as we saw earlier, boys achieve independence earlier than girls, which suggests that they are influenced less than girls at adolescence by maternal attitudes and behavior. This does not imply that a boy is not influenced by various of his mother's characteristics, but rather that her effect diminishes earlier for the boy than for the girl in relation to other influences.

The Peck—Havighurst Study. In an intensive study of factors related to character development (Peck & Havighurst, 1960), a group of 34 children were studied from 10 to 17 years of age. Five levels of character development were defined: amoral (infancy), expedient (early childhood), conforming and irrational-conscientious (later childhood), and rational-altruistic (adolescence and adulthood). The latter type, considered the most mature, describes an individual who "has a stable set of moral principles by which he judges and directs his own action; he objectively assesses the results of an act in a given situation, and approves it on the grounds of whether or not it serves others as well as himself" (p. 8).

In order to assess the relation between character structure and personality the children were rated on the following variables:

P1, Moral Stability: The tendency to follow the established moral code, willingly and with genuine satisfaction.

P2, Ego Strength: A complex of capacities to react to events with accurate perception, appropriate emotions, and insightful, rational judgment; all proceeding from a well-integrated personality system. (This

system permits autonomous behavior, and at the same time it includes
a positive, ethical attitude toward other people.)

P3, Superego Strength: The degree to which behavior is directed by, or
in accord with, a set of internalized moral principles—a conscience.
These principles must be present within the person and they must
also influence his behavior effectively.

P4, Spontaneity: The tendency to express feelings and wishes directly in
action. (Positive feeling and empathy for other people are linked with
this, it turned out.)

P5, Friendliness: A generalized attitude of warm liking for other people.
Its polar opposite is a generalized attitude of hostility.

P6, Hostility-Guilt Complex: A complex of intense feelings of hostility,
linked with strong feelings of guilt about inner impulses.

(Peck & Havighurst, 1960, p. 86)

In addition, ratings were made of the families on the following four
vectors: F1, Consistency in family life (regularity in the home, consistency of parental control, common participation in activities); F2, De-
mocracy-autocracy (sharing in family decisions); F3, Mutual trust and
approval among family members (good interparental relations, confi-
dences shared with parents by child, parental trust and faith in the child,
parental approval of child, parental approval of child's activities); F4,
Parental severity (severity of parental control).

The results indicated that Mutual trust and Consistency were related
to the development of healthy Ego strength and Moral stability. These
same two family characteristics also showed the highest association with
the children's Maturity of character scores. In general, it appeared that
the mother was more influential than the father in affecting the children's
character development.

Bronfenbrenner's Study. A final study (Bronfenbrenner, 1961) examined family correlates of responsibility and leadership in a large group
of tenth-graders. The children were rated by their teachers on these
two variables, and they completed a 100-item questionnaire designed to
measure 20 different dimensions of parent-child relations.

It was found that three parental behavior variables were related to
the trait of responsibility: rejection, neglect, and affiliative companionship. Thus "the adolescent receiving lowest ratings in responsibility describes his parents as most likely to complain about and ridicule him,
compare him unfavorably with other children, spend little time with
him, and avoid his company" (p. 254). A marked sex difference was
observed, however. Responsibility in boys was associated with nurturance, affection, and companionship, especially from the mother, and with
relatively high amounts of discipline and authority from the father. All

of these variables were negatively related to responsibility in girls, for whom strong paternal discipline was deleterious to a high rating on responsibility.

The antecedents of leadership were not too different from those related to responsibility, except that parental overprotectiveness seemed to undermine an adolescent's successful attempts at leadership in the group. Again, a marked sex difference was apparent. "Specifically, affiliative companionship, nurturance, principled discipline, affection, and affective reward appear to foster the emergence of leadership in sons but discourage it in daughters" (p. 256).

This sex difference in antecedents of the two traits suggests that achievement of a high level of responsibility and leadership means something different for the girl than for the boy in terms of personality needs. In our culture both of these characteristics are an important part of the stereotyped male sex role but not the female. Thus attainment of these traits suggests an antifeminine reaction in the girl, which does not occur when she receives a great deal of parental affection and nurturance (i.e., acceptance for being herself and for assuming her "appropriate" sex role).

Summary

The ability of the parent to cope successfully with his child's adolescent period may, indeed, be a real test of his own adjustment to life. Because the problems faced by his adolescent may rearouse in the parent some of his own unresolved conflicts that occurred during that period, he must deal simultaneously with his child's problems, his own adolescent problems, and the problems he presently encounters at middle age. The adolescent should try to show patience and understanding toward his parents!

While in general the mother is the most influential figure for both boys and girls at adolescence, with increasing age boys are affected more by their relationship with their fathers and girls by their mothers. This is not surprising since appropriate sex-role identification is an important aspect of the development of a sense of identity at adolescence.

THE ADOLESCENT AND THE PEER GROUP

The two types of peer organization that have received the most attention from social scientists are cliques and gangs. Both types of group involve a high degree of acceptance of members by one another and a rejection of nonmembers by members. Cliques sometimes have been differentiated from gangs on the basis of sexual composition; that is, cliques generally are thought to consist of members of both sexes, gangs to be exclusively masculine. Gangs, but not cliques, are believed to be antisocial in nature. We believe that the groups are similar in most ways and that they differ chiefly in social class: a lower-class clique might be called a gang; an upper-middle-class gang might be called a clique. Cliques and gangs both begin as unisexual groups and by middle adolescence usually are bisexual in character; both engage in a fairly high proportion of behaviors that violate adult laws or mores. Cliques certainly are less at odds with the adult culture than are gangs, and commit violations of a different sort—for example, they may get drunk at the country club rather than roll a "wino" to get money for alcohol. *Clique* sounds better than *gang,* and we reserve the former term for middle-class groups, despite considerable similarity between them and the lower-class peer groups. The major differences between cliques and gangs are these: the membership of a clique is determined, for the most part, by clique members' adherence to adult (parental) standards such as social class, while acceptance within a gang is determined by personal attributes such as skill and daring, which are not class-related and may not be valued positively by adults. Therefore cliques support the status quo, while gangs do not.

Cliques

The best single study of cliques is found in Hollingshead's book *Elmtown's Youth* (1949). Elmtown (a fictitious name) is a small Midwestern county seat, with no other towns very near it. There had been very little migration to Elmtown for about a generation before Hollingshead's study; and the last newcomers had been an easily identifiable, ethnically distinct group, brought in as strikebreakers. Everyone knew everyone else; everyone could be graded easily and reliably in terms of social class. The top group (Class I) consisted of the wealthy descendants of the original settlers. Class II consisted of most of the professional, business, and upper managerial people. Class III consisted of some professional and business people as well as farmers and salaried employees. It was less easy to distinguish between Classes II and III than between other classes; nevertheless the two could be defined in terms of income and education as well as in style of life. (Class II was the "Country Club" set; Class III centered its activities around certain business groups, such as the Lion's Club, and church activities.) Class IV was made up of the working class—laborers, mill hands, craftsmen, store clerks. Class V included the criminal, the work-shy, and the very poor and uneducated.

The entire social system of the town, including the schools, was geared to the task of making relatively certain that a given adolescent stayed within his proper social sphere. The leading cliques within the high school consisted of the "G.W.G." (God We're Good) girls' clique and the "Cadets" boys' clique. The members of these cliques interacted with one another to the point that they formed a super-clique. These two cliques had the approval of the parents and the school, and from the data that Hollingshead presents it is clear that their function was to maintain the status of the families (almost all members of Class I or II) of clique members as well as the status of the members themselves. It appears that another major function of the cliques was to separate equals (potential marriage partners) from inferiors. Many other cliques existed —all aware of their inferiority to the G.W.G. and the Cadets—but few of them crossed more than one class line, as can be seen in Table 18-2. Dating followed class lines, as shown in Figure 18-2.

When dating crossed more than one class line, there was talk, both among the young people and among the adults and teachers. Ziggy Moran, the most socially successful girl in Class IV, is a case in point.

"Ziggy" Moran was one of 3 class IV girls who crossed two class lines successfully; she participated almost exclusively in a clique composed of girls from classes II and III. She also dated 1 of the 4 class I boys in school, much to the consternation of the boy's parents. They were afraid

TABLE 18-2 Percentage of Clique Relations Observed within and between Classes, by Sex *

	Boys			
Class	I and II	III	IV	V
I and II	*49*	38	13	0
III	11	*61*	27	1
IV	5	33	*60*	2
V	0	13	31	*56*

	Girls			
Class	II	III	IV	V
II	*56*	26	18	0
III	7	*64*	28	1
IV	4	21	*70*	5
V	0	4	36	*60*

* This table must be read across the rows. The figures in italic type are the percentages of choice within one's own class (from Hollingshead, 1949, p. 214).

Class of person dated	Boys				Girls			
	I and II	III	IV	V	I and II	III	IV	V

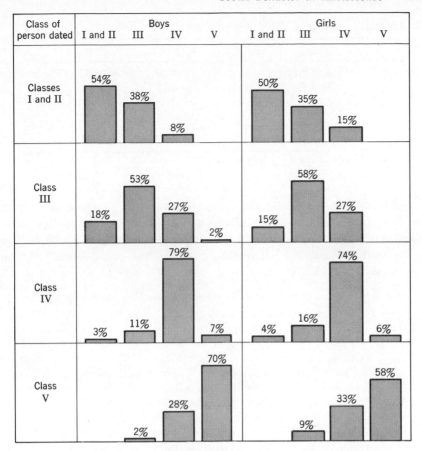

FIGURE 18-2   Intra- and interclass dating patterns of boys and girls (Hollingshead, 1949, p. 231).

"something would happen," as it had years before with "Ziggy's" older sister in a similar situation. "Ziggy's" success was so unusual that Elmtown adults and teachers often spoke of her as being "out of her element." Such remarks as, "She is flying too high," "After high school she is going to take a bad fall," "Ten years from now she will be taking in washing like her sister on Beacon Street," were common (Hollingshead, 1949, p. 213).

The class-clique system was actively abetted by the school. Scholarships and honors went to Class I or II adolescents, even when others were more deserving. Grades were assigned along social-class lines, as shown in Table 18-3, with this bias being present even when class differences in IQ were controlled for.

TABLE 18-3   Percentage with Mean Grade of:

Class	85–100	70–84	50–69
I and II	51.4	48.6	00.0
III	35.5	63.2	1.3
IV	18.4	69.2	12.4
V	8.3	66.7	25.0
Total	23.8	66.3	9.9

* From Hollingshead, 1949, p. 172.

The school board, the teachers, the parents, and the upper-class clique members combined to make high school an unhappy place for the lower-class youngsters. Small wonder that most of them quit, went to work in the mill, and retained their low place in the social order. As one girl (Class IV) said:

Frankly, for a lot of us there is nothing here, but just going to classes, listening to the teacher, reciting, studying, and going home again. We are pushed out of things. There is a group of girls here who think they are higher than us. They look down on us. I won't mention any names, but they are a group of girls from the higher families. They have a club that is supposed to be outside of school, but it's really in the school. They just go from one club to the other and hog all of the offices. They're in all the activities. They talk about what they're doing, what they're going to do, and they won't pay any attention to us. They snub us and they won't talk to us. Some of them will speak to us sometimes, but most of the time they must ignore us. I'd like to be in the school activities and the school plays, go to the dances, and things like that, but they make us feel like we're not wanted. I went to some of the activities when I first started high school. Last year, I was in the Home Makers' and the Cheer Club, but they ignored me. Now I'm not in anything. If we go to the high school dances, nobody will dance with us. They dance among themselves and have a good time and we're nobody. If we go to the football games, it's the same way. Those Cheer Club girls are supposed to sit together at a game and root, but they don't. They break up into little groups and, if you're not in one of the groups, you're left out of things (Hollingshead, 1949, pp. 202–203).

Reading *Elmtown's Youth* today takes the reader back to another era; it reads like one of John O'Haras' social histories in novel form, such as *Appointment in Samarra* (1934). It sounds, comparatively, like an age of innocence. For a parent whose daughter goes to school in a high school in which there are young entrepreneurs making stag movies with strictly local talent, and where LSD trips are a rite of passage in some circles, the "God We're Good" clique sounds pretty harmless. Cliques still exist in high schools, but it is unlikely that they frequently exert the high degree of control that they did in *Elmtown*. Cliques, to be as effective as they were, had to exist in a stable environment where people could be "pegged" in terms of their status. Further, there had to be agreement regarding the criteria used in assigning status, both between the young people themselves—so that those accepted into upper-status cliques were duly appreciative of acceptance and conformed to high-status clique rules, and those rejected were aware of their in-feriority—and between the young people and adults, so that the upper-status cliques conformed to adult values and thus received adult support.

Many facets of contemporary American life operate against cliques having the strength that they once had. The high school with which one of the writers is most familiar has a 33 per cent turnover rate during a given school year in each of its grades. Under these conditions, most youngsters do not know much about whom they should envy, and prob-ably do not sense any pain in being excluded from that school's equiv-alent of the "God We're Good" or "Cadet" cliques, even if they are aware that the cliques exist and that they are excluded. Further, the values that make for high peer status today are (unlike Elmtown) not as closely tied to family position or to adult values. Parents may still seek to use the peer group as a means of reinforcing parental values—espe-cially in separating out inappropriate sex partners—but the peer group, as is discussed below, seems to value accomplishment in certain areas plus the ability to think up and do exciting, interesting, or new things. Since this kind of accomplishment and ability is not tied to social class, class-oriented cliques appear to have lost much of their influence. Phys-ical and social mobility has created uncertainty and anomie but has broken the rigidity and smugness of the small town as well. While cliques continue to exist, they more often are based on mutual interests or abilities than on family status, and certainly are less well structured and more fluid in terms of membership than those of a generation ago.

The Older Type of Gang

We see differences as well as similarities between cliques and gangs. As noted above, clique is the term used most often to denote middle- and upper-class peer groups; the gang, in traditional usage, refers to lower-class groups. The gang has not had the open and tacit support from parents and other adults that cliques have had. Whereas cliques have rested on aspects of the adult world such as parental social status, gang membership and particularly gang leadership has depended much more on personal attributes and skill. Perhaps because lower-class youngsters have been excluded from cliques on the basis of parental occupation, lower-class boys, and to the degree that parents permit it, lower-class girls, have become involved in gangs, where personal attributes and skills override such things as family income.

Gang membership is a normal part of adolescence to most boys, and is not an exclusively lower-class phenomenon. Gangs engage in delinquent behavior, but also, even in the most criminal of gangs, in a large amount of shared nondelinquent behavior. Gangs, in the traditional sense, arise in economically deprived areas and have as members young people from minority groups (first-generation Americans with immigrant parents, or Negroes, or Spanish Americans in many cases). These groups have special needs (a rejection of old-world values and a need to learn "American" ways on the part of the immigrant youth; a need to develop a sense of masculinity on the part of Negro boys raised in a matriarchy; a need of Spanish boys to be viewed as adult males by their fathers) and general needs common to all adolescents (a need to do interesting things and to be active, a need for recognition) that are met by gang life more than by any other force within the slums. Further, the at least partially criminal nature of most slum gangs allows the members to make economic gains denied to them elsewhere. Finally, gang membership, in some areas of big cities, is necessary to escape beatings and blackmail. Small wonder that the gang has been an important social force in slum life. Yet if other avenues toward status, self-acceptance, and interesting and meaningful activity are available, even slum-dwelling adolescents are not likely to be deeply involved in gangs.

While many of the economic bases of gang life have lessened, the social-psychological ones remain—the need on the part of adolescents for activity, for interesting diversions, and the need to prove themselves competent at meaningful activities. With the decrease in some of the bases for gang membership, and the increase in others, the nature of the adolescent group has changed.

THE CONTEMPORARY PEER GROUP

The youth culture has spread geographically from California to the rest of the United States. Since the American youth culture is the oldest in the world, it has spread from here to England (returning somewhat embellished by Edwardian garb), to Red Square, to Copenhagen and Stockholm, and to urban Japan. It reaches from Los Angeles to the heartland of America in Oshkosh, Wisconsin, and Yankton, South

Dakota. It spreads downward across age groups, so that what once was an aspect of university-student culture at Berkeley now is known and acted on in most of the high schools, and even some junior highs, in the country. It spreads upward across age groups, too (suggesting a basic weakness in the adult culture), so that fashions for the young and not-so-young matron are based on the body build of an underdeveloped 14-year-old.

Why does the adolescent peer culture succeed? It succeeds because it is dangerous and exciting and it requires real skills, as in surfing or in the motorcycle riding of Hell's Angels; because it is *not* based on such things as class distinctions, which are contrary to our expressed adult value system but not to our actual behavior; because it *is* based on the idea that the individual should be judged in terms of personal attributes and accomplishments; because it is in many ways more humane and accepting of individual differences than adult cultural values; because it is concerned with expanding self-awareness at a time when people have few means of discovering themselves; because it is against sham; and because it fulfills the needs of young people better than does the adult culture. If parents provide more than the peer culture does, in terms of meeting the needs of their offspring, or if the society provides the same meaning, challenge, and test of skills, as (ideally) does the Peace Corps (see Kauffman, 1961), then aspects of the peer culture emphasizing delinquency or alienation will not prevail. Activism, however, may remain, since change is necessary in a growing culture. If our society lives up to its promise, in terms of social ethics, and is meaningful and interesting to its members, then effects of the peer culture will decrease in impact. If our culture does not move forward in these ways, then the more active and hedonistic elements of peer culture will prevail, as they do in Burgess's terrifying view of the future, *A Clockwork Orange* (1962).

SUMMARY

The major task of adolescence is to acquire a sense of personal identity. This identity is acquired, to varying degrees, from parents and peers. Certain aspects of the culture such as discontinuity in role demands make adolescence a difficult period. If coupled with the presence of a separate youth culture, role discontinuity results in the development of a separate set of adolescent values. In previous years, some peer organizations (cliques) served to reinforce parent values, while other peer organizations (gangs) ran counter to the standards of the dominant adult value system. For a number of reasons, cliques have lost in power, so that the peer group less often reinforces the adult value system. The gang once consisted of the rejected and disaffected; it persists in a somewhat altered form. Once usually delinquent in character, the gang now may be delinquent, activist, or alienated in character, or any combination of the three. The adult culture provides few opportunities for establishing self-understanding, for proving one's own competence, or for doing interesting things. The adolescent peer group does, and hence is gaining in strength. If this trend is to be reversed, the adult culture must change.

REFERENCES

Ausubel, D. *Theory and problems of adolescent development.* New York: Grune & Stratton, 1954.

Bath, J., & Lewis, E. Attitudes of young females toward some areas of parent-adolescent conflict. *Journal of Genetic Psychology,* 1962, **100,** 241–253.

Bowerman, C., & Elder, G. Variations in adolescent perception of family power structure. *American Sociological Review,* 1964, **29,** 551–567.

Brittain, C. Adolescent choices and parent-peer cross-pressures. *American Sociological Review,* 1963, **28,** 385–391.

Brittain, C. Age and sex of siblings and conformity toward parents versus peers in adolescence. *Child Development,* 1966, **37,** 709–714.

Bronfenbrenner, U. Some familiar antecedents of responsibility and leadership in adolescents. In L. Petrullo & B. Bass (Eds.), *Leadership and interpersonal behavior.* New York: Holt, Rinehart & Winston, 1961. Pp. 239–271.

Burgess, A. *A clockwork orange.* London: Heinemann, 1962.

Connor, R., Johannes, T., & Walters, J. Parent-adolescent relationships: I. Parent-adolescent conflicts. *Journal of Home Economics,* 1954, **46,** 183–186.

Denney, R. American youth today: A bigger cast, a wider screen. In E. H. Erikson (Ed.), *Youth: Change and challenge.* New York: Basic Books, 1961. Pp. 131–151.

Douvan, E., & Adelson, J. *The adolescent experience.* New York: Wiley, 1966.

Grinder, R., & Spector, J. Sex differences in adolescents' perceptions of parental resource control. *Journal of Genetic Psychology,* 1965, **106,** 337–344.

Havighurst, R., Robinson, M., & Dorr, M. The development of the ideal self in childhood and adolescence. *Journal of Educational Research,* 1946, **40,** 241–257.

Hess, R., & Goldblatt, I. The status of adolescents in American society: A problem in social identity. *Child Development,* 1957, **28,** 459–468.

Hollingshead, A. B. *Elmtown's youth.* New York: Wiley, 1949.

Johnson, A., & Szurek, S. The genesis of antisocial acting out in children and adults. *Psychoanalytic Quarterly,* 1952, **21,** 323–343.

Kagan, J., & Freeman, M. Relation of childhood intelligence, maternal behaviors, and social class to behavior during adolescence. *Child Development,* 1963, **34,** 899–911.

Kauffman, J. F. "Youth and the Peace Corps." In E. H. Erikson (Ed.), *Youth: Change and challenge.* New York: Basic Books, 1961. Pp. 152–160.

Liccione, J. The changing family relationships of adolescent girls. *Journal of Abnormal and Social Psychology,* 1955, **51,** 421–426.

Lucas, C., & Horrocks, J. An experimental approach to the analysis of adolescent needs. *Child Development,* 1960, **31,** 479–487.

Mussen, P., Young, H., Gaddini, R., & Morante, L. The influence of the father-son relationships on adolescent personality and attitudes. *Journal of Child Psychology and Psychiatry,* 1963, **4,** 3–16.

O'Hara, J. *Appointment in Samarra.* New York: Random House, 1934.

Peck, R., & Havighurst, R. *The psychology of character development.* New York: Wiley, 1960.

Schaefer, E., & Bayley, N. Maternal behavior, child behavior, and their intercorrelations from infancy through adolescence. *Monographs of the Society for Research in Child Development,* 1963, **28,** No. 3.

19

Current Problems and Programs

In this chapter we discuss five salient problems of the adolescent in present American society: delinquency, alcohol and drugs, early marriage, school dropout, and student activism. In addition, we describe several government programs designed for youth. While it is fashionable to focus on the problems of the adolescent period, too little attention is given to the positive aspects of youth and to the functions served by this age period in affecting society—in helping to change outworn ideas and traditions and in stimulating a careful re-examination of our goals and values. Nevertheless, concern with the problems of youth is appropriate, since these problems pinpoint and reflect the problems of society.

DELINQUENCY

The legal definition of delinquency often refers to the delinquent as a person (usually under the age of 18) who "requires the protection of the court"; that is, less euphemistically, is made a ward of the court or is in the custody of the court. Unlike adult criminal law, which centers in specific committed acts, juvenile delinquency often has to do with general, unspecified characteristics such as being "incorrigible," and with acts of omission (such as not going to school) as well as acts of commission. It is difficult, if not impossible, to develop any comprehensive theory explaining such diverse varieties of adult crime as con games, armed robbery, and embezzling; it is even more difficult to find any single theory of causation that can explain all forms of legally defined delinquency, which range from truancy to organized gang activities that would be, for adults, felonious in nature.

Delinquency, as a social problem, appears to be on the increase. Some of this increase results from a general increase in population; some of it results from the even greater increase among 12- to 18-year-olds as compared to the population at large; and some of it results from the fact that an increasingly high proportion of the population, including adolescents, lives in urban or suburban rather than rural environments. (The probability of being declared delinquent depends in part on the number of police available; rural youngsters are not often legally declared to be delinquent, not because they do not commit delinquent acts, but because no law enforcement agency becomes officially aware of these delinquent acts.) However, even if these factors are taken into consideration, delinquency still seems to be on the increase. This increase must be examined in terms of the various causes for delinquency, and in terms of the changing force that these antecedents have on the adolescent.

714

Delinquent Types

There are many types of delinquent, and some of these types have very little in common with one another. So long as we look at delinquency as a whole, it seems unlikely that any single explanation is going to be true or that any specific treatment is going to be effective for any large number of delinquents.

One way of separating out delinquent types is in terms of type of offense. It seems reasonable to believe that young persons declared delinquent as a result of continued truancy differ from those declared delinquent for running away from home, and that each of these two groups differs from drunk rollers, car thieves, or shoplifters in terms of the relevancy or importance of the different causes or reasons underlying their delinquency, and probably in terms of the most effective treatment of the problem behavior or behaviors. Roebuck and his associates (Roebuck, 1962, 1963; Roebuck & Cadwallader, 1962; Roebuck & Johnson, 1962a, 1962b; Roebuck & Johnson, 1964) have used this approach with adult criminals, but it has not been used systematically with juveniles.

Another approach to categorizing delinquents is to compare lower-class with middle-class, social with solitary, or sociopathic with neurotic delinquents. The categories lower-class, social, and sociopathic overlap to a fair degree, as do middle-class, solitary, and neurotic, as discussed in Chapter 16. As discussed in Chapter 16 also, it appears that the causes of delinquency vary between these types of delinquent; the solitary delinquent, usually from an ostensibly normal home environment, shows signs of considerable psychological disturbance and is apparently acting out delinquently as a result of deeper psychological needs, whereas the social delinquent, generally from a lower-class, slum environment, has minimal psychological disturbance and acts out delinquently chiefly because his subcultural values accept this acting out.

Other typologies are available; those presented above merely serve as examples of the fact that there are many kinds of delinquent, and that the cause or causes of delinquency probably vary across delinquent types.

Causes of Delinquency

Genetic Factors Associated with Delinquency.   Let us examine one area of research that suggests a genetic basis for at least some delinquency and crime. Humans generally have two sex chromosomes: XX in the case of females, XY in the case of males. Sex-chromosomal anomalies occur, however. Some females have only one X chromosome, and are designated XO sex chromosome; Turner's syndrome. Some males, typically with incomplete sexual development, are XXY, Klinefelter's syndrome. Of relevance to delinquency and crime are XYY males—supermales, one might say. XYY males are big, dull, and highly aggressive. Not surprisingly, they often are delinquent and/or criminal, and are found in considerable numbers in prisons and in hospitals for the criminally insane (Jacobs, Brunton, Melville, Brittain, & McClemont, 1965; Price & Whitmore, 1967). This genetic anomaly produces predictable behavior deviations. (Incidentally, the XYY male presents an interesting problem in criminal law: Is one responsible for his acts when his genes are awry? One can hear the offender say to the judge, "Sorry, your honor, but I'm not responsible for my destructive behavior. After all, I'm an XYY sex-chromosome type.") Other genetic factors may be involved, although less consistently and directly than the XYY syndrome, in delinquency and crime. For example, comparisons of MZ and DZ twin pairs (see Shields, 1954, for a review of this literature) suggest that polygenic genetic influences also are operative in disposing an individual to crime.

Physiological Factors Associated with Delinquency. As noted in Chapter 15, Glueck and Glueck have shown an association to exist between body type and delinquency, with mesomorphic (athletically built) individuals being over-represented in the delinquent group. This may be a result of social expectations. Mesomorphs may be expected to be active (and acting-out) in their behavior. However, mesomorphs may actually differ along dimensions relevant to delinquency. For example, there may be differences between persons of different body types in their optimal level of arousal (see Chapter 4). Both early (Thrasher, 1927) and more recent (Cohen, 1955) discussions of gangs note that a major function of gangs, and of delinquency, is to provide excitement (high arousal). It may be that persons who differ, either innately or as a result of experience, in optimal level of arousal also differ in probability of becoming delinquent, with those whose optimal level of arousal is high being the most stimulation-seeking and most active, hence most prone to becoming involved in delinquent activities.

Psychological Factors Associated with Delinquency. A tremendous variety of psychological factors have been investigated. Psychoanalytically oriented individuals look to such things as early (e.g., below age three; often in the first year of life) deprivation of mother love (Goldfarb, 1945; Karpman, 1951). The larger number of psychologists, whose ties are less analytic, also have centered their interests on parent-child relations, but generally somewhat later in the developmental span. Some studies have been directed toward discovering the psychological characteristics of delinquents and nondelinquents (Wirt & Briggs, 1959); of neurotic (personality problem), delinquent (conduct problem), and normal (no problem) children (Peterson, 1967); and of different varieties of delinquents (Randolph, Richardson, & Johnson, 1961). All of these kinds of study reveal highly significant differences in personality scores between groups, as measured on standardized personality tests. The origin of at least some of these differences appears to be in the family situation. For example, delinquents, as a group, appear to have extreme difficulties with male authority figures when compared with closely matched controls (Medinnus, 1965). Basically neurotic, solitary delinquents exhibit disturbed relations with their mothers as well, while the majority of delinquents do not (Brigham, Ricketts, & Johnson, 1967). Comparisons of delinquents with nondelinquent siblings show delinquents to be more emotionally disturbed (Richardson & Roebuck, 1965), possibly (though this proposition has not been tested) because of more disturbed relations with one or both parents before the delinquent career.

Other aspects of the parent-child relationship have been investigated. Hoffman and Saltzstein (1967) demonstrate that conscience development is weak (presumably disposing toward delinquency) in children of families in which parents frequently use "unqualified power assertion"— telling the child, in effect, "I'm not going to tell you why I want you to do this; you obey me because I say so." Conscience consists of at least two essentially unrelated elements, resistance to temptation and guilt after yielding to temptation (Johnson, Ackerman, Frank, & Fionda, 1968). Of the two, a lack of resistance seems the more closely associated with delinquency. Unfortunately, the separate effects of parent behaviors on these two different dimensions of conscience are not yet established.

The association between psychological aspects of the environment and delinquency clearly is substantial, but probably only for some varieties of delinquent. Other types of delinquent may be more frequently the result of sociological or cultural factors.

Sociological Factors Associated with Delinquency. Father absence, as a basically sociological social-class and ethnic variable, seems to be an important dimension of environmental variation influencing a number of domains of behavior. Lynn and Sawrey's (1959) and Siegman's (1966) data show that father absence, at least before age five, produces a compensatory, often delinquent masculinity in adolescence. Since father loss is associated with social class and with ethnicity, with lower-class Negroes showing the highest proportion of father loss, it is not surprising that this group shows the highest delinquency rate.

Consider Duke Custis, a product of the Negro lower-class matriarchy, and his attitudes toward the mild, the conventional, and the feminine:

. . . Once or twice a year my Aunt May come over from Brooklyn where she live to see us. She a big woman not skinny like my mother an when she come up the steps she puff like an engine. She always stand at the door with her hand on her heart. She say, "When you folks gonna move to a projeck with a elevator?"

My mother say. "Soons the City let us in. If I had as many kids as you Id a been in a long time ago. But I only got the one child you know May."

Aunt May look at me. "An just look at him." She say. "Just you look at him." She take an pull me over to her and look at my face. "He one of us all right." She say smilin at me. "He a Custis sure enough."

"He whut GOD give us." Gramma say.

"Got his fathers bones." My mother say.

Aunt May tell me. "Boy I surely do hope you have got you full growth. You get any taller an we wont be able to see you face no more."

"I aint so tall. Theys boys my age taller than me."

"How old you now Richard? Fourteen?"

"He was 14 las month." My mother say. "On the 8th."

"I make it out to be the 7th day." Gramma say.

"I guess I know when my own and only child was born." My mother say.

Gramma say. "You dint know nothin that day Girl."

"How you do in school Richard?" Aunt May ask me.

"Jabberin an cryin. Cryin and jabberin. That all you know that day." Gramma sayin.

"It o.k. I be glad when it over an I can get a job."

"Un huh." Aunt May say.

"Man at the liquor store give me a promise. He gonna give me a job soon as I gradjuate." I tell her. She believe anything.

"That nice clean work Richard." She say. "Clerkin in the liquor stores is nice clean work."

Clerkin in the liquor stores. Oh Man. Dont she know who she talkin to. Duke Custis. War Lord of the Royal Crocadiles. I been knifed 7 times and I got 9 stitches in my head from where a sonofabitch Wolve bastard hit me with a radio aireal off a car. From behind. Aunt May live aroun here and not way the hell over in Brooklyn she know I have a rep!

hen I come walkin down the street the people say. "Here come Duke. He cool. He got heart."

An on a Friday night Friday night is a big night people watch me

walkin down the street. They see me strut. They know a rumble on.
They know we are goin down on the Wolves.

"Tonight the night Duke Man?" They ask me.

I just smile and keep movin bouncin on my heels.

"You goin down on the Wolves tonight Duke?"

"You give it to em Duke."

"Kill em Duke."

Someday I come walkin down the street they all look at me with respect
an say. "There goes a cold killer. Here come Duke Custis. He a cold
killer." Then evrybody pay attention—an listen when I talk—I be the top
of the heap an when I push they stay push.

I keep movin. Some time I wave a hand to em. The coolies look at
me. Coolies dont swing with the gang. They are out an by themselves
alone. It make em mad to see me when I strut. Screw them. Aint no
place for coolies in this world.

Keep walking. My rumble strut. Everybody know somethin is cookin.
Here come Duke. He got a rep Man. Man he got heart. I swingin with
the gang tonight. They all waitin for me. Duke Custis. The War Lord
of the Royal Crocadiles.

Aunt May an Gramma Custis an my mother talkin about the old days
in Alabama. Shitman I just turn off when they off on that kick.

Before she leave Aunt May she look aroun an she say to my mother.
"Dolly. I dont see any indications that you have a husband anymore."

"Fred walk out?" Aunt May ask her.

"Oh him. That Fred. I threw him out long ago."

"The Lawd frowns his eyes on a man whut gambles and drinks."
Gramma say.

"Well whut husband you without now anyway?" Aunt May ask.

My mother say. "Charles Osborne his name."

"He walk out?"

"It aint so much he walk out as so much that he never come back."
My mother say.

"How long he been away?" My Aunt May ask at the door.

"A week today."   ✱

"Almos 2 weeks." Gramma say. "I make it closer to 2."

"Well maybe he still come back." Aunt May sayin.

"Oh I dont have a single solitary doubt about that." My mother say.
"He be back all right."

Oh Man. I set there a laughin in side. He aint comin back. When
a Man go he *go* (Miller, 1959, pp. 7–11).

Such things as father absence may deepen a given adolescent's involvement with the gang. However, as Duke says "Ain't no place for coolies
in this world." Therefore, in the slum, the majority of young males
belong to gangs. They must, for self-protection. Further, whereas
cliques are established with their structural basis resting on aspects of

the adult world such as parental social status, gang membership, and particularly gang leadership has depended much more on personal attributes and skill. Perhaps because lower-class youngsters are excluded from cliques on the basis of parental occupation, lower-class boys, and to the degree that parents permit it, lower-class girls, become involved in gangs, where personal worth over-rides such things as family income.

Excellent early research on gangs was conducted by Thrasher (1927) who studied large numbers of Chicago gangs, by Whyte (1943), who studied one gang of Italian "corner boys" (their name comes from hanging around street corners) intensively over a fairly long time interval, and by Shaw and his associates (e.g., Shaw, 1930; Shaw & Moore, 1931). Fictional accounts of the influence of the gang include Miller's *The Cool World,* cited above, and James T. Farrell's classic *Studs Lonigan* trilogy (1935).

Perhaps a major reason for contemporary public concern regarding delinquency is not that it has increased, but rather that sociological factors such as social class seem to be playing a lesser role as causative agents. Delinquency appears to be more and more randomly distributed across the population; middle-class delinquency appears to be increasing far more sharply than is delinquency in general. This sharp increase suggests that the culture is changing in ways that increasingly dispose its members toward crime and violence. Some of these cultural factors are discussed below.

Cultural Factors Associated with Delinquency. Paul Goodman (1960) suggests that ours is a fairly sick culture. Goodman says that we have close to full employment, but that most jobs are neither interesting nor useful. They are make-work projects.

> Consider a likely useful job. A youth who is alert and willing but not "verbally intelligent"—perhaps he has quit high school at the eleventh grade (the median), as soon as he legally could—chooses for auto mechanic. That's a good job, familiar to him, he often watched them as a kid. It's careful and dirty at the same time. In a small garage it's sociable; one can talk to the customers (girls). You please people in trouble by fixing their cars, and a man is proud to see rolling out on its own the car that limped in behind the tow truck. The pay is as good as the next fellow's, who is respected.
>
> So our young man takes this first-rate job. But what when he then learns that the cars have a built-in obsolescence, that the manufacturers do not want them to be repaired or repairable? They have lobbied a law that requires them to provide spare parts for only five years (it used to be ten). Repairing the new cars is often a matter of cosmetics, not me-

chanics; and the repairs are pointlessly expensive—a tail fin might cost $150. The insurance rates therefore double and treble on old and new cars both. Gone are the days of keeping the jalopies in good shape, the artist-work of a proud mechanic. But everybody is paying for foolishness, for in fact the new models are only trivially superior; the whole thing is a sell.

It is hard for the young man now to maintain his feelings of justification, sociability, serviceability. It is not surprising if he quickly becomes cynical and time-serving, interested in a fast buck (Goodman, 1960, pp. 19–20).

So our culture is phony; a sense of meaning and a feeling of self-worth often are lacking. Further, as Goodman notes (1960, pp. 42–43), most of what the adolescent has to do is uninteresting.

The adult culture provides little opportunity for doing meaningful and interesting things. Therefore the peer culture does what it can to fill the gap. The adolescent who can provide the group with things to do, and can himself do things, or who tells the adult culture that the things it wants are dumb or dull, is the "culture hero" of adolescents and young adults. Delinquency *was* the chief form of doing exciting things, as well as demonstrating one's own rejection of the adult culture. Other responses to the adult culture, such as activism, now are becoming more frequent and more socially visible.

Alienation, as a negative response to our culture, has come into prominence. The alienated person, according to Seeman (1959), feels powerless in dealing with society, has no strongly developed set of norms against which to judge his own behavior or the behavior of others, feels isolated and apart from others, and also is estranged from himself. (For a full discussion of alienation, and for an excellent case history, that of "Inburn," see Keniston, 1965.) The delinquent generally does not meet all of these criteria; he does, for example, have norms by which he can judge behavior. However, by other criteria, such as a feeling of powerlessness (Marwell, 1966), delinquents are alienated—and the more troublesome they are, the more powerless they appear to feel themselves to be (Wood, Wilson, Jessor, & Bogan, 1966). Although in most ways delinquents are alienated individuals (Jessor, Graves, Hanson, & Jessor, 1968), one can be alienated without being delinquent. The "beatnik" movement and the more recent "hippie" movement appear to reflect a more pure form of alienation, meeting all of Seeman's criteria set forth above.

A sense of personal meaning is becoming more difficult to achieve. Violence, at least, is an affirmation of one's existence, a way of telling the world that one is alive and important. And with a cultural tradition of violence, this is a route that many individuals take. Offenses against others become more frequent, perhaps because values become less clearly defined.

As noted in Chapter 7, Mowrer (1961) has argued that the conventional character typology, a la Freud, is one in which persons are arrayed, in order of severity of socialization, from low to high, psychopath–normal–neurotic, but that actually the order of groups of individuals along the socialization continuum is psychopath–neurotic–normal. Peterson's (1967) empirical research supports Mowrer's position, since he found that neurotics are less well socialized than normals, rather than having excessively severe superegos, as predicted from Freud's theories. Of relevance here to an analysis of the sickness or wellness of our culture is the fact that the distribution of individual scores obtained by Peterson is that given in Figure 19-1.

FIGURE 19-1   Socialization scores of three groups of children. Scores are obtained from the Socialization scale of the California Personality Inventory (Gough, 1957). The figure is from Peterson (1967, p. 464).

Mowrer suggests that as the distribution of personality types forming the J curve shown in Chapter 7, Figure 2, becomes more and more like a normal curve, the culture is becoming a sick one. If so, Peterson's data indicate that the culture already is quite sick.

Alienation, delinquency, and relatively low socialization all suggest that cultural forces are at work to produce a general trend toward deviancy that is superimposed on such individual specific factors as level of arousal or parent-child relations and such group specific factors as minority-group status and social class.

The Treatment of Delinquency

The conventional treatment for delinquency is confinement. Confinement, per se, has little to recommend it, though remedial education classes plus some vocational classes may be useful. Perhaps the only certain change that occurs along with confinement is that the person confined gets older. This in itself may account for the fact that at least some people appear to benefit behaviorally from confinement. Crime is a young man's game. Most delinquents do not become criminal adults. Glueck and Glueck demonstrated long ago (1934, 1940) that few persons criminal as young adults remain criminal at age 40. So time itself is on the side of society. Once a man has a job and a family he does not have as much time or energy to expend at hot-wiring cars or getting into fights.

Conventional types of psychotherapy have been attempted with delinquents. Not all delinquents—in fact, a minority—show substantial psychological disturbances (Randolph, et al., 1961); of those who do show such disturbance, most are solitary middle-class delinquents. Since there is a substantial social-class bias in who receives psychotherapy, with middle-class people receiving therapy more often (Hollingshead & Redlich, 1958), it seems likely that a substantial proportion of those delinquents who are emotionally disturbed do receive psychotherapy. It seems less likely that psychotherapy generally influences behavior positively. Jacobson and Wirt (1968) report a carefully executed long-term study of the effects of group therapy on prisoners. Looking at those treated, as a whole, there was no evidence that therapy had any positive effect. Within the therapy group, it was apparent that basically neurotic prisoners gained, and that more psychopathic or sociopathic prisoners actually got worse as a result of therapy. This finding again supports our position taken in Chapter 16, that no treatment is equally effective for all people, and that our job is to discover the particular subgroups that benefit from each of a number of treatments. Jacobson's and Wirt's data suggest that until this is done as many persons will be harmed as helped by many present forms of psychotherapy.

Operant shaping procedures have been used with young offenders; for example, extensive programs are now under way in many federal facilities for delinquents and young offenders. The immediate positive reinforcement of desirable behaviors can do much to improve behavior within this institutional setting. However, the best available present evidence suggests that the improvement of behavior does not transfer from the institution to the free environment (Fairweather, 1964, 1967).

Another therapeutic approach that is now increasing in use is the superego-building kind of therapy. Rather than centering on an understanding of the patient's motivations, and causing the patient to understand these motivations, this form of therapy attempts to get the patient to accept the fact that he is responsible for his behavior and that only he can change it. Mowrer's work (1961; 1964; 1967) probably got this movement going, but many others are involved. The material most directly relevant to delinquency is Glasser's (1965) *Reality Therapy*. It is too early to evaluate this movement accurately. However, what can be established, as from Glasser's evaluation of the effectiveness of his approach, is most encouraging.

If, in fact, the culture is absurd, to use Goodman's term, it is only by helping the delinquent find meaning and a sense of personal worth and personal responsibility that treatment can be expected to exert much positive influence on behavior.

ALCOHOL AND DRUGS

Alcohol

The use of alcohol, even to a degree that most individuals would agree to be excessive, is a common phenomenon. Adolescent drinking is viewed with disfavor by the parents of adolescents and by the majority of adolescents themselves (Campbell, 1964; Maddox & McCall, 1964, p. 74), yet the use of alcohol is a relatively common phenomenon among high-school students (Jessor, Graves, Hanson, & Jessor, 1968, pp. 183–185). Amount of alcohol use is associated with other forms of deviancy (e.g., see Jessor et al., p. 413), and, as in the triethnic (Anglo, Spanish, Indian) study conducted by Jessor et al., is itself a major social problem that increases in severity and frequency as legitimate access to desirable social goals decreases and the number of deviant role models increases.

Excessive use of alcohol probably is a far more frequent problem among both adolescents and adults than is drug addiction. Yet it is the topic of drugs, not drink, that makes headlines and brings forth editorial comments. This emphasis on drugs rather than alcohol may result from the fact that excessive alcohol use is not new and not uncommon, while drugs are both. But other factors may be involved in the differential disapproval of drugs versus alcohol. Roebuck (1962) has demonstrated that somewhat different personality types are involved in alcohol as opposed to drug use. Alcohol is chosen more often by active, aggressive, and outgoing people; drugs are chosen more frequently by relatively shy and withdrawn types. Perhaps our cultural emphasis on activity, aggression, and extroversion makes alcohol seem a more "normal" thing than drugs. At least, this is what Roebuck's data suggest—that the alcoholic does not diverge as far from the cultural norm as does the drug addict, since we can understand aggression more easily than passivity; outgoingness more easily than withdrawal. As Laurie (1967, p. 37) notes, "It is interesting that in parts of the East, where passivity is preferred, the approved drug is *cannabis*,* another pacifier, and alcohol is held in the same horror as we hold heroin."

Drugs

Perhaps the increased attractiveness that drugs now hold for many young people is a result of a greater feeling of helplessness and alienation. Drugs have a number of effects, some of which have appeal even to the most active, so that even that most active of all groups, Hell's Angels, was "turned on" to LSD (Thompson, 1966, pp. 292–303). But the members turned right back off again, for the most part; LSD did not, apparently, fit their psychological makeup. It may be, in general, that aggressive people try drugs, but quit; passive people more often stay with drugs, once started.

Drug usage is a social event. One learns to use drugs from people already using drugs. Becker's (1953) classic paper "Becoming a Marijuana User" details the amount of social learning involved, not only in getting a source of supply, but in learning to inhale correctly, learning how one is supposed to feel when one "gets high" and learning to enjoy this feeling.

Different kinds of drug usage are learned in different social contexts, produce different sets of sensations, and appeal to different groups of people. We shall discuss heroin, amphetamines and barbiturates, marijuana, and LSD.

Heroin. For a discussion of the beginnings of widespread use of heroin within a cultural enclave, see Claude Brown's *Manchild in the Promised*

---

* Marijuana.

Land (1965). Back in the early 1940's, in Harlem, fighting gangs were at their peak. By the late 1950's, the fighting gangs were almost dead; everyone was on heroin—"the stuff"—instead (Brown, 1965, p. 271) and Brown makes the reasons clear: first of all, the general despair of Harlem; second, and more immediate, the use of heroin as a way of escaping from membership in fighting gangs. No one expected anything from a junkie; they were—and are—so bizarre and so unreliable that they were excused from life as well as from gang duties. As activism has increased, and the feeling of helplessness decreased, the use of heroin also has decreased. Heroin, as a drug, may be the "hardest," most damaging, and most addictive. However, other drugs are far more important in terms of their rate of increase.

Barbiturates and Amphetamines. Barbiturates (sleeping pills) and amphetamines (pep pills) such as Benzedrine, used singly or in combination with one another, are probably the most common addictive drugs in use in the Western world. But as Laurie (1967, p. 61) says with regard to barbiturates, "here abuse, addiction, and suicide are taken as normal events of domestic life." Laurie suggests that barbiturates, in particular, are more often used by the middle-aged and the middle-class. Since this is the group that makes the laws and shapes public opinion, it is not surprising that the group's own preferred drug or drugs are not looked on as being as evil as those used by criminals, minority-group members, or hippies. Yet barbiturates lead to depression (Eysenck, 1964) and amphetamines to paranoid symptoms (Eysenck, 1964). These paranoid feelings often occur not only during drug use, but also during the period of letdown after the immediate effects of feeling alert and energetic have worn off. Despite the high frequency of use, little is known about the long-range effects of barbiturates and amphetamines, perhaps because they are so common that they are not looked on as being dangerous.

Marijuana. Marijuana is both notorious, as is heroin, and common, as are the drugs discussed immediately above. The marijuana plant appears able to grow anywhere, and the leaves may be dried and smoked in the same way as tobacco. Marijuana got its start in the Arab world, but now seems to have a worldwide distribution. As noted above, it appears that the symptoms associated with marijuana usage are learned. Within our culture, the mental effects are:

(a) dulling of attention, (b) loquacious euphoria of variable duration, (c) usually some psycho-motor activity and affective lability coloured by the underlying personality [i.e. emotional reactions are likely to become misplaced or misdirected—an example with another drug, alcohol, would be flirtations at a cocktail party], (d) perhaps some distortion of perception and time sense, depending on the dose, (e) perhaps some lassitude culminating in deep sleep if the dose is sufficient (Laurie, p. 82).

Like alcohol, it does not make the user euphoric, but intensifies his original mood, whatever that is. Like alcohol, it decreases the level of functioning at the same time that it makes the user feel particularly bright and witty.

A serious and open-minded investigation of marijuana, that of Mayor LaGuardia's Committee (1944), suggests that marijuana is not itself addictive and does not lead to addiction to "hard drugs" such as heroin. However, since the sensations felt are learned, to a substantial degree, and also depend on one's mood state when using marijuana, it would seem that reactions to it are unpredictable. If, as both Roebuck (1962) and Chein (1964) suggest, the typical drug user is a rather introverted and withdrawn person, it seems likely that, to the degree that marijuana users are representative of addict types, active and aggressive behavior will not occur as a result of marijuana usage. But given a different personality or momentary mood state on the part of some users, criminal behavior might well result from their use of marijuana, or a marginally adjusted personality might disintegrate still further.

LSD. Hallucinogens, especially LSD, form the hottest area of present debate concerning drugs. As shown in the curiously titled book, *Mushrooms, Russia, and History* (Pavlovna & Wasson, 1957), the use of hallucinogenic mushrooms was a sacred rite in Europe as well as in many other parts of the world. Peyote cactus buttons still form the sacrament of the Native American Church of America (an amalgam of American Indian and Christian beliefs). But mushrooms and peyote have given way to the synthetic LSD-25, d-lysergic acid diethylamide. *Newsweek* magazine (1966) estimated that at least 10,000 students at the University of California have tried LSD.

The prime presenting symptoms of an LSD experience are increased sensory awareness, hallucinations, a sense of unreality, and a feeling of cosmic awareness—of knowing the whole of the universe, and the purpose behind the universe. Here is a description of part of an LSD experience.

I got a black plastic plate and a knife, and cautiously cut the corner off the sugar cube. We split it, and ate; I expected Hofman's first instant reaction. Of course, nothing. After half an hour, we ate the rest, made some self-pitying jokes about buying sugar at £300 a box, and went to bed. . . .

We turned on the bedroom light and waited for visions. All that happened at first was that the room looked less white, colder and crooked. It is in fact white all over with a pleasant fluted wallpaper put in by the interior decorator who had it before us, with heavy white Victorian cornices and white blinds. Normally it's a pleasant, soft, diffuse box for sleeping in. The walls weren't pure white any more—yellowish. . . . I picked up a box of little disk magnets the children had been given; there was a tube of iron filings with them. If you poured the filings on the magnets, they clustered furry and curved in on themselves, they looked like space monsters. As you pulled the two disks apart the filings stretched out in knobbly arms, then fell back like the petals of a flower. When they came together again the petals reached out to each other, and near enough they stroked each other, some petals growing longer by the contact. We could hear the rustle of the filings over each other as the moving magnetic fields rearranged them.

I felt things were beginning to look odd, but only out of the corners of my eyes. If I glared, they immediately looked all right. Then I scratched the back of my head. This definitely was odd. There was a tremendous noise of threshing wheatfields. I could feel hair roots bending, knotting the scalp. There were the feelings a field gets being harrowed—by my finger-nails I supposed. I was fairly sure someone was scratching someone's head, and that someone's head seemed to be being scratched; but it was difficult to be sure whose or by whom.

It was as if inside one's head there were an alert observer, who at moments like this would have said: "The scratching sensations from fingers and scalp correlate with your arm and head positions; you are scratching your head." The drug had retired him; I had to solve the problem by sheer intellectual effort. My children, when they were small, used to reach up, grasp an ear, then they would burst into tears because someone was pulling it. Suddenly I could understand their predicament.

Barbara was holding her left arm before her face. "It's like an old film; it lurches," though she was holding it still. I tried with a hand, and it writhed slowly like the tentacles of a sea anemone (apparently the eyeball wriggles all the time to shift images onto fresh bits of retina; this movement is invisible until LSD knocks out the compensating mechanism, so one sees things moving slowly). It had taken quite a long time to get this far—the use of the word "trip" for an LSD experience is quite appropriate, though not in the sense one might imagine of strange lands and romantic experiences. For us it was very like going on a modern journey by aeroplane, say: a little fear, homely surroundings, aches, staying awake all night, dirtiness, more fear, the flat garish light of indoors at four in the morning. I became conscious of how badly made the house was; each particle of dust on the floor stood out like an overdone TV commercial for washing powder. Colours were richer—the old varnished floorboards escalated from being just old varnished boards to a rich, cynical *House and Garden* honey colour, but the effect wasn't particularly pleasant. . . .

Sounds became clearer—we could clearly hear someone winding up a watch next door; and we could hear every breath of a strange baby crying in some house down the street. Barbara seemed to sleep, then sat up, looked about her carefully, and said: "How many pairs of gloves am I?" She said afterwards that she'd been standing in High Street, Kensington, wondering who she was; she'd had to make an inventory round the room: "Who do I know who owns that pair of shoes, that dress? It must be Barbara Laurie."

Although I felt so odd, I found I could write legibly, and wrote down some fairly full notes. Thinking about it afterwards, it seems obvious that we had split a fairly small dose; anything larger would have precluded notetaking. Just as well. We could see very clearly the predicament we were in, like travellers stranded in some bizarre place. Often it seemed funny. We had been some months before to see Villa 21, a free-range unit for young schizophrenics in a mental hospital to the north of London. Barbara said now: "Someone, somewhere, must be able to make sense of all this," and we both giggled nervously, because one of the boys there had sat about conspicuously saying: "What's the meaning of it all? Someone must know?"

We turned the light off again. I began to feel frighteningly sure that this was madness; being roller-coastered inside your own head, knowing it was all illusion, yet unable to stop or control it. Time went unbearably slowly, and often seemed to slip backwards, so that the precious five minutes won towards release would slither away again in a whirl of sparks. I thought of the plight of madmen in their narrow hospital beds, with not just the problem of winning through until morning, when it would all— I sincerely hoped—go away, but through tomorrow and tomorrow and the next day and the next night, until when? Worse than a prison sentence because you would have no peace. It was like being locked up . . . with a lunatic who wouldn't stop letting off fireworks. . . .

I found I could smell now: with a little practice I could distinguish the smell of my left armpit from my right and each finger had a different, rich, gamey scent. Our two-year-old daughter, who is very fat and self-confident, came into the bed for a while. We both clung to her because she was so sane and normal. Barbara made us laugh by sitting up and theatrically declaiming: "So onward they slept, wearily gnashing their multi-coloured teeth." She drifted off to sleep, and dreamt that the iron filings were cream she had to swallow, and were coagulating in her throat; then later about two unhealed burns on her finger: she could see into the red pit, right into the cell structure and the quivering walls of protoplasm (Laurie, 1967, pp. 105–109).

The LSD experience may be mind-expanding, as LSD fans claim; LSD may not be so much mind-expanding as standards-lowering. We know of one person who, during an LSD experience, finally understood the meaning of the world. Throughout the rest of his experience he kept repeating what he had learned, so that he could bring back this marvelous information to enlighten the world. He came out of his hallucination saying over and over again, "A stitch in time saves nine." So much for cosmic insights. More reasonable is the idea that psychosis is characterized by hallucinations and delusions. What better way to dispose oneself toward psychosis than by getting practice at having hallucinations and delusions?

Treatment of Addiction

The physical symptoms of addiction can be overcome in a few weeks. The psychological needs that led the addict to the drug are not changed, and the Federal treatment centers at Fort Worth, Texas, and Lexington, Kentucky, have not been remarkably effective. The Federal facilities remove the physical, but not usually the psychological needs. Addicts do not seem to respond well to conventional psychotherapy, but do seem to respond to a more authoritative approach. Both Daytop Village (Shelly & Bassin, 1965) and Synanon (Yablonsky, 1962, 1965) have had a high degree of success in treating addicts. Like Mowrer (1964), and Glasser (1965) discussed above, the people involved in these movements take the position that the deviant person (in this case, the addict) is himself responsible for his deviancy, and cannot be cured until he quits blaming, for example, a rejecting mother, for his deviancy, and accepts personal responsibility for his actions. Within these groups the addict associates with former addicts who have become free of addiction. These former addicts cannot be fooled by the addict, and, further, form a peer group that shows the addict that he *can* quit. Status within the group depends on acting in a lawful and responsible way. Here is part of the case history of Frankie, an addict who became a member of Synanon.

> Of course, when he first arrived at Synanon, Frankie attempted to gain a "rep" by conniving and making deals in accord with his old mode of relating. He was laughed at, ridiculed and given a "hair-cut" (a verbal dressing down) by other "old-time con men" members of the organization. He was accused of "shucking and sliding" (simply not performing adequately). The old-time Synanists were ferocious about keeping the organization, which had literally saved their lives and given them a new life status, operating smoothly.
>
> Frankie found that "rep" was acquired in this social system (unlike ones he had known) by truth, honesty, and industry. The values of his other life required reversal if he was to gain a "rep" at Synanon. These values were not goals per se which someone moralized about in a mean-

ingless vacuum; they were means to the end of acquiring prestige in this tough social system with which he now intensely identified.

In the small *s* synanons, three nights a week, Frankie participated in a form of leaderless group psychotherapy. In these synanons the truth was viciously demanded. Any system of rationalizations about past or current experience was brutally demolished by the group. There was an intensive search for self-identity.

In the process the individual attempted to learn what goes on beneath the surface of his thoughts. For Frankie this was the first time in his life that he discovered others had some idea about what he was thinking underneath. He had . . . therapy in prison—but there he could "con" the therapist and most important, "I said what I thought they wanted to hear so I could hit the street sooner."

Most important Frankie began to get some comprehension of what others thought in a social situation. The fact of empathy or identifying with the thoughts and feelings of others became a significant reality.

Frankie was at first empathic in his usual pattern of sociopathic self-centered manipulation. However, a new force was introduced into the situation—he began to care about what happened to others at Synanon. This was at first selfish. Synanon was for him a good interesting way of life. He had identified with the system and learned "gut level" that if any Synanon member failed, he too was diminished and failed. . . .

In the status system, Frankie's rise to the role of coordinator was not quick nor easy. He moved from the "dishpan" to serving food at the kitchen counter.

After several months he was allowed to work outside on a pickup truck which acquired food and other donations. With two other individuals who worked with him on the truck a group decision was made one day "that one shot wouldn't hurt." One individual knew a "connection" on the route. They went to his home. All they could get were some pills.

When they arrived back at Synanon their slightly "loaded" appearance immediately became apparent to the group ("they spotted us right away") and they were hauled into the main office and viciously (verbally) attacked to tell all ("cop-out") or get out of the building. A general meeting was called and they were forced to reveal "all" before the entire group. Frankie was back at work on the dishpan that evening.

Such "slips" often come out in the synanon. In a sense, in addition to other forces of growth from the synanon it serves as a form of "first-aid" therapy. If anyone reveals a minor "slip," the personal wound is examined and cleaned up by the group before a serious act of misbehavior occurs. (The synanon situation has some of the characteristics of an underground organization operating during wartime. If any member "falls," it may entail the destruction of the entire organization.)

The norms of synanon society are the reverse of the criminal code. On one occasion Frankie, with two other members of Synanon, went for a walk into town. One individual suggested buying a bottle of wine. (No drinking is permitted.) The other two (including Frankie) smashed the idea. However, no one revealed the incident until 2 days later it came up in a synanon. The group jumped hardest on Frankie and the other individual who did not reveal the potential "slip," rather than on the transgressor who had suggested the wine. Frankie and the other "witness" were expected to report such "slips" immediately, since the group's life depended on keeping each other "straight." For the first time in his life Frankie was censured for "not squealing." The maxim "thou shalt not squeal" basic to the existence of the usual underworld criminal culture was reversed at Synanon and just as ferociously sanctioned. An individual could get "kicked out" of Synanon for *not* being a "stoolie." . . .

As a consequence of living in the Synanon social system, Frankie developed an increasing residual of social learning and ability. His destructive pattern of relating to others withered away because it was no longer functional for him within this new way of life. Synanon developed his empathic ability, produced an attachment to different, more socially acceptable values, and reconnected him adequately to the larger society within which Synanon functioned as a valid organization (Yablonsky, in Mowrer, 1967, pp. 567–568).

As noted on the preceding pages, Synanon and Daytop Lodge are part of a hard-line, superego-oriented, moral treatment approach to mental disturbance. This type of therapy was long ago demonstrated to be effective in the treatment of mental illness (Dain, 1964), but fell out of fashion. It presently seems to be coming into being again as a therapeutic technique for such widely disparate groups as neurotics, delinquents, and drug addicts. It seems to be effective and sometimes, as in the case of drug addiction, seems to be the only approach that is effective.

EARLY MARRIAGE

The adolescent period places a number of demands on the individual. Personality integration requires adjustment to one's appropriate sex role; the young person's relationships with parents and other adults are changing; vocational concerns and general concern for the future become important. Any additional demands both reflect and exacerbate problems existing within the individual. Moreover, coping with such demands frequently serves to retard rather than hasten normal personality development. Within this framework it is apparent that pregnancy and early marriage create an unusually severe crisis for the adolescent.

Frequency of Early Marriage

Several trends in frequency of early marriage are apparent from Table 19-1. First, it is clear that the rates of early marriage are not increasing. Little, if any, increase occurred between 1950 and 1960; in fact, there was a decrease for nonwhite females. Second, young marriages primarily involve females. Third, the rates have been consistently higher for nonwhites than whites, except in 1960, when there is no noticeable difference between the two groups. Figures on marriage rates as of March 1967 (Current Population Reports, 1968) show that 0.8 per cent of white males 14 to 17 years of age are married, and 6.9 per cent of 18- and 19-year-olds are married. Comparable figures for white females are 3.3 and 23.0. Among 14- to 17-year-old nonwhite males 0.9 per cent are married, as are 4.1 per cent of 18- and 19-year-olds. For nonwhite females these figures are 4.2 and 26.7.

Burchinal (1960, 1965) examined a number of factors frequently mentioned as affecting decisions for early marriage.

1. The insecurity of our times, which has created needs among young people to find someone with whom they can have unquestionable loyalty and love.

2. The cult of personal happiness and the rejection of intellectualism and achievement.

TABLE 19-1 Percentage of Any Age Level among the 15- to 18-Year-Old Population Who Were of the Married Status during the Given Year by Sex and Color *

	Females											
	White						Nonwhite					
Age	1910	1920	1930	1940	1950	1960	1910	1920	1930	1940	1950	1960
15	1.1	1.3	1.1	1.0	1.0	2.3	2.1	2.7	2.9	2.6	2.8	2.9
16	3.4	3.8	3.9	3.4	5.6	5.6	6.6	7.8	8.8	7.6	8.1	6.8
17	8.1	9.1	9.1	8.0	12.7	12.0	13.0	17.9	18.7	16.4	17.3	13.6
18	15.9	17.9	17.7	16.2	23.2	24.5	24.4	32.2	32.7	28.9	29.3	23.6
	Males											
15	0.1	0.2	0.1	0.1	0.6	0.6	0.1	0.3	0.2	0.3	0.4	0.7
16	0.1	0.3	0.2	0.3	0.6	0.9	0.2	0.6	0.4	0.6	0.4	1.1
17	0.3	0.8	0.6	0.6	1.2	1.9	0.9	1.6	1.4	1.4	1.8	2.1
18	1.2	2.4	1.9	1.9	3.4	5.4	3.0	5.3	4.2	4.2	4.8	5.3

* Adapted from Bureau of Census, Population Characteristics, for the respective years. Burchinal, 1965.

3. The bandwagon effect: one marriage contributes to another, and soon "everybody is doing it."

4. The impact of World War II, the Korean War, and the continuation of the draft.

5. An escape from an unhappy home, school, or community situation.

6. An attempt to resolve personal or social adjustment problems.

7. The reduction of economic risks in marriage as a result of current prosperity.

8. Encouragement from romantic and glamorous images of marriage and the corresponding unrealistic overevaluation of marriage.

9. Acceleration of adult status as reflected in advanced levels of heterosexual interaction at younger ages.

10. Stimulation of sexual drives by sex appeals and intense physical expressions of affection in mass media, with the result that premarital pregnancy becomes a precipitating factor in many if not most youthful marriage decisions.

(Burchinal, 1965, pp. 245–246)

Some adolescents who marry early feel that the ambiguity, uncertainty, and marginal status of this age period can be terminated by marriages. For the girl, a "Mrs." in front of her name gives her a feeling of importance; she is an adult. For the boy, he is now a man around his friends. Unfortunately, the adolescent's false perception of adulthood frequently means that he anticipates the privileges but ignores the responsibilities that it involves.

While the above factors tend to operate in favor of early marriage, there are conditions in current society that may have the opposite effect. First, attainment of higher educational levels should tend to reduce early marriage rates, since there is an inverse relation between age of marriage and educational level. Second, rising rates of employment among women suggest that many girls will want to prepare themselves for a vocation and pursue this vocation for several years before marriage. Increasingly, too, they will want their husbands to show some promise occupationally.

Problems of Early Marriage

A whole host of problems are encountered by adolescents who marry early: financial insecurity, poor job prospects, adjustment to a new status —from dependency on parents to independence, change of status in relation to peers, and thwarted educational ambitions. High-school dropout rates for married students are high. Estimates vary from 50 to 75 per cent. This means a boy is doomed to a low-level, largely unskilled job, yielding a low income that he is unprepared to budget wisely. The resentment he feels concerning his occupational inadequacy frequently is directed toward his wife and children.

Lack of experience and lack of perspective contribute to the difficulties. When the probable financial problems were pointed out by the high-school counsellor to a young man contemplating marriage, the student replied, "Oh, I've thought of all that. I've got seventy-five dollars in the bank." An unrealistic conception of marriage frequently leads to disappointment and disillusionment. In an interview study (LaBarre, 1968) of a small group of married, pregnant adolescent girls, a recurring theme of isolation and loneliness was evident. The girls had lost contact with their former high-school classmates, and their relationships with their families had altered.

Approximately one-third to more than one-half of young marriages involve premarital pregnancy, which requires additional adjustment. Medical evidence indicates that complications of pregnancy among adolescent girls are three to four times those of women in their twenties (Israel & Wouterez, 1963).

The task of establishing an identity—knowing who you are, why you are what you are, what your values are, what your goals are—should be achieved before an attempt is made to establish a durable relation with another person. Until an individual knows himself and can live with that self, it is difficult for him to know and live with someone else.

Several studies (Martinson, 1959; Moss & Gingles, 1959; Havighurst, 1961) agree in showing that adolescents who marry early are less well adjusted emotionally and socially than those who marry later. Moreover, they score lower on intelligence tests and receive lower grades than unmarried students. Havighurst interpreted his findings as indicating that "it is more accurate to say that people with the poorest chances of making a good marriage are most likely to marry early than to say that early marriages cause failure in marriage" (p. 46).

Outcomes

Divorce rates among early married couples exceed by two to four times those among couples who marry after 20 (Monohan, 1963). Further, since a fair percentage of the former group involves premarital pregnancy, this means that children are affected by the divorce and its aftermath. Thus the higher percentage of failure among early marriages leaves its mark on the children of such marriages. At the time of divorce the mother is young, frequently unskilled, poorly educated, and unable to cope with the demands placed upon her. The children do not fare well.

Approaches to the Problem

Since there are multiple causes for early marriage, no single solution exists. However, from the above discussion, several approaches seem clear. First, steps must be taken to clarify and to make meaningful the role of the adolescent in our society, since early marriages are in part a reflection of the uncertainty of this age period. Involvement in and commitment to the larger community through programs that capture the energy, the interest, and the imagination of young people are important. Second, since those who marry early are less well adjusted, do less well in school, and generally come from lower social classes, special attention must be given to this group of young people at the high-school level to alleviate these negative characteristics. Meaningful curricula and tutorial and remedial programs should be developed. Finally, courses in family life and personal growth should provide much-needed insights into the problems involved in the transition from adolescence to mature adulthood.

SCHOOL DROPOUTS

The school-dropouts project of the National Education Association defined a school dropout as:

> . . . a pupil who leaves a school, for any reason except death, before graduation or completion of a program of studies and without transferring to another school. The term *dropout* is used most often to designate an elementary or secondary school pupil who has been in membership during the regular school term and who withdraws from membership before graduating from secondary school (grade 12) or before completing an equivalent program of studies. Such an individual is considered a dropout whether his dropping out occurs during or between regular school terms, whether his dropping out occurs before or after he has passed the compulsory school attendance age, and, where applicable, whether or not he has completed a minimum required amount of school work (NEA Project: School Dropouts, 1965).

Characteristics of Dropouts

A majority of school withdrawals occur at the age of 16, which coincides with the end of compulsory school attendance in most states. Boys are more likely to drop out than girls, and they tend to be somewhat older when they drop out. Low reading achievement tends to be associated with school withdrawal, but the significant factor here is the low self concept that accompanies reading failure. In a comparison of 60 poor readers who dropped out of school and 60 who graduated, Penty (1956) found that the former group held more negative attitudes toward themselves. School dropouts have a history of poor grades, nonpromotion, and absenteeism. They are less likely to participate in extracurricular activities than nondropouts. Bell (1967) found that only 32 per cent of dropouts participated in such activities, while 96 per cent of the nondropouts participated.

Cervantes (1965) listed the following 20 characteristics commonly found among youth who are potential or actual school dropouts:

School

1. Two years behind in reading or arithmetic at seventh grade level. Majority of grades are below average.
2. Failure of one or more school years (1st, 2nd, 8th, 9th grades most commonly failed; 85% of dropouts behind one year; 53% two or more years).
3. Irregular attendance and frequent tardiness. Ill-defined sickness given as reason.
4. Performance consistently below potential.
5. No participation in extracurricular activities.
6. Frequent change of schools.
7. Behavior problems requiring disciplinary measures.
8. Feeling of "not belonging" (because of size, speech, personality development, nationality, social class, family disgrace, retardation in school, dress, lack of friends among schoolmates or staff, etc.).

Family

9. More children than parents can readily control (e.g., only child for divorced and working mother; five or more for non-divorced and working mother of blue and lower white-collar class).
10. Parents inconsistent in affection and discipline.
11. Unhappy family situation (common acceptance, communication, and pleasurable experiences lacking; family solidarity minimal).
12. Father figure weak or absent.
13. Education of parents at eighth grade level.
14. Few family friends; among these few many problem units (divorced, deserted, delinquents, dropouts).

Peers

15. Friends not approved by parents.
16. Friends not school oriented.
17. Friends much older or much younger.

TAT (Psychological orientation)

18. Resentful of all authority (home, school, police, job, church).
19. Deferred gratification pattern weak.
20. Weak self-image.

(Cervantes, 1965, pp. 198–199)

Although it is easy to stress the identifying characteristics of the drop-out, we should keep in mind facts indicating that 60 per cent of youth from low-income families do graduate from high school, while 30 per cent of all dropouts come from families in the white-collar class (Miller, 1964). Although inadequate finances and low IQ have been reported to be two important reasons for school dropouts, these do not appear to be the major causes. Although more dropouts than nondropouts are delinquent, a majority (80–90 per cent) of the dropouts have no record of delinquent behavior.

Technological Revolution

The phenomenon of school dropouts is not new, but the problem is. A generation and more ago unskilled and semiskilled jobs were numerous. Useful jobs not requiring a great degree of education were available. This is not true today. Indeed, there is no room at the bottom. Paradoxically, even if a young man completes high school today, there may be no jobs open to him. In other words, if every young man completed high school because of the promise of a better job, society could not come through with a job for all (Friedenberg, 1964).

Causes

While it is popular to construct long lists of reasons for school drop-out, it is likely that a majority of the reasons stem from the nature of the school, the nature of society, and from family and individual problems, some of which reflect the problems inherent in present-day society.

School-Related Factors. For a variety of reasons the school seems not to be meeting adequately the needs of all our youth. As Goodman (1964) notes:

> Many poor youth, herded into a situation that does not fit their disposition, for which they are unprepared by their background, and which does not interest them, simply develop a reactive stupidity very different from their behavior on the street or ball field. They drop behind, play truant, and as soon as possible drop out. If the school situation is immediately

useless and damaging to them, their response must be said to be life preservative.

Cervantes (1965) found that 62 per cent of the school dropouts he studied said their school experiences were definitely unfavorable, while 76 per cent of the graduates said their experiences were definitely favorable. With regard to specific reasons given, 79 per cent of the dropouts expressed criticism in the areas of curriculum, staff, and school activities, while an equal percentage of graduates expressed approval of aspects included in these areas. Although schools and school counselors give different reasons for school withdrawal than the dropouts themselves, and different reasons are given by the dropouts at the time of withdrawal than later, still, dissatisfaction with the school is one of the major reasons for dropping out.

Community Factors. In a study of dropouts in large cities, Dentler and Warshauer (1965) found a multiple correlation of .87 for whites between dropout rate and the following eight variables: percentage of labor force in white-collar occupations, percentage of white families with incomes of less than $1000, white adult functional illiteracy rate, percentage of overcrowded housing units, percentage of white families with incomes between $1000 and $1999, percentage of population under five years of age, increase in total population from 1950 to 1960, and nonwhite dropout rate. It is apparent that factors that raise the standard of living of people in a community, in terms of general education, welfare, and health, serve to reduce the school dropout rate. Communities that neglect these conditions of human welfare raise the dropout rate.

Family and Individual Factors. A number of family characteristics have been found to be associated with school dropout rates. The situation is a complex one, however, and it is unlikely that these characteristics are directly and causally related to school withdrawal. Moreover, many of these factors reflect more basic aspects of the family that militate against success and persistence in school. The most general family characteristic related to school dropout is that of socioeconomic status. Children from middle- and upper-income families are much less likely to drop out of school than those from low-income families. Basing family status on occupation of father, type of house, area of residence, and source of family income, Bowman and Matthews (1960) found that while only 4.7 per cent of the youth from upper and upper-middle classes dropped out of school, nearly one-third of the upper-lower- and nearly one-half of those from lower-lower-class families withdrew. Moreover, the parents of school dropouts are less well educated than the parents of those who graduate. Van Dyke and Hoyt (1958) found that 67 per cent of the parents of school dropouts, but only 38 per cent of the parents of graduates, had not completed high school. Another study (Williams, 1963) showed that 79 per cent of the mothers and 80 per cent of the fathers of dropouts had themselves not graduated from high school.

In an extensive study comparing dropouts and nondropouts (Cervantes, 1965), the child's perception of his relationship with his family was revealed by the following questions:

> Would you say that your whole family both understands and accepts you?
> And would you say that you both understand and accept them?
> Did your family encourage and help you in your plans for a good job or in your school plans?
> Did your family talk things over with each other very often?
> If your whole family had some free time how would they usually spend it?
> And at home, how many were there that you could say accept you, and you like to confide in, and you enjoy being with?

From an analysis of the responses of the dropouts, the following picture emerged. The overwhelming majority saw their family members as failing to accept each other as individuals. There seemed to be little communication and understanding among the family members. The family lacked solidarity and congeniality, and in general it was perceived by the dropout as an unhappy one. Cervantes argues convincingly that the nuclear family is of critical importance in shaping a child's attitude toward himself and toward school. Without the security that comes from support, encouragement, and acceptance from his family, a child experiences difficulty in coping with the problems encountered in the school situation.

On the basis of an examination of the projective data (stories elicited using the Thematic Apperception Test), Cervantes concluded that the primary factor differentiating between the dropouts and the nondropouts was that of hostility. The dropouts revealed a great deal of hostility against authority and against adult controls of all type.

Solutions to the Problem

The causes of school dropout are complex; they reflect some of the very basic problems inherent in our society. Consequently the solutions cannot be simple ones; they must be broad, bold, and imaginative. Most of the solutions that have been suggested focus on the school and its curriculum. For example, Cassel and Coleman (1962) offer the following suggestions: conduct an effective guidance and counseling program; provide broader instructional offerings; make more careful selection and preparation of teacher personnel; assure increased student involvement in cocurricular activities; solicit involvement of total community resources; maintain closer liaison and articulation with apprenticeship training; maintain closer liaison with juvenile authorities; make continuous evaluation and investigation of local retention. The following are included among the innovative suggestions by Goodman (1964): schools be decentralized into small units; community adults should be involved in the school program; for some classes, learning should take place in the community—"the streets, cafeterias, stores, movies, museums, parks, and factories" (p. 53)—rather than in the school building; and class attendance should be made optional. Other suggestions proposed include: involve business and labor in establishing work-study types of program; provide counseling for those who have dropped out of school; and enlist the aid of volunteer community groups in tutoring students who are experiencing academic difficulties.

The increasing number of preschool enrichment programs for disadvantaged children potentially can do much to prevent early academic failure. Since high-school learning problems frequently can be traced to academic difficulties as early as first and second grade, individual attention in these early years can prevent failure later. Of extreme importance is the development of initially favorable attitudes toward school, toward learning, and toward oneself in terms of academic competency and success. Failure is defined by society; it is not inherent in the individual. Every child can and must experience success. But this will require new approaches and a rethinking of the goals and values of education on the part of the teacher, the school, and society.

STUDENT ACTIVISM

Erikson (1963) has succinctly described the phenomenon of student activism and protest as the unique intersection of life history with history. Growing up involves change, and this is accelerated at adolescence physiologically, socially, and emotionally. When these changes within the individual coincide with rapid social changes, each facilitates, defines, and brings into focus the other. For example, the 1954 Supreme Court decision with regard to school integration stimulated the early idealism of the Negro youth who later initiated the first student sit-in at a lunch counter in Greensboro, North Carolina. An examination of some of the characteristics of current youth movements reveals a remarkable similarity between these and generally described characteristics of adolescence.

Common Characteristics of Adolescence and Activism

Identity.   The adolescent's search for identity has been discussed in previous chapters.   The transitional and marginal nature of the adolescent period requires an evaluation of earlier-held values, beliefs, and attitudes.   This is true for individuals as well as for societies that are in a state of flux and transition.   Plans are made; goals are set; and strong effort is made to reach stability and certainty.

Commitment to social action, especially when this involves attempting to change the structure created by adults, plays an important role in the development of identity at adolescence.   Participation in a group dedicated to the achievement of certain goals furnishes the individual with some measure of identity, which helps to overcome feelings of powerlessness and facelessness in our automated and impersonal society.

Idealism.   Adolescents frequently take strong idealistic and altruistic positions on various issues.   This is also a basic theme of current youth movements.   Inequities and injustices in society are condemned.   Adult society is accused of flagrant hypocrisy.   Verifying instances of this hypocrisy or phoniness gives the young person a feeling of moral superiority over adults.   Many adolescents feel that they have been betrayed, that the values they were taught as children are not really adhered to by adults—that equality in our democratic society does not ring true. Thus the "establishment" is distrusted; our current social institutions are criticized.   In part, too, the relativity of values found in modern society permits and encourages diversity of values.   The adult is unable to furnish evidence that the values he espouses are superior to those advocated by the adolescent.   Racial inequalities, large-scale poverty, cruel and confusing wars are impossible to justify; they bear convincing witness for the adolescent's position.   One participant in the 1962 student demonstrations in Washington, D.C., explained her purpose as follows: " 'To demonstrate that we as students and future intellectual leaders of our communities feel *there is a better way to live,* mankind can live in peace. . . . If I feel there's another way aside from war and bombs, it's my duty to tell others' " (Solomon & Fishman, 1964, p. 60).

Need for Independence.   Part of the undercurrent of youthful protest is the desire for autonomy of action and decision.   Young people are markedly affected by society but they cannot participate in its decisions.

Drafting 18-year-olds but not permitting them to vote is an example of this. Through participation in protest activities the adolescent feels he can influence adult decisions. Or, at the very least, his voice is heard in the council of peers. Student activists enjoy strong group support, which serves as a "vehicle for accelerating the break with family" (Fishman & Solomon, 1964). The rebellious nature of student protest movements reflects a more general rebellion against adults that characterizes the adolescent period.

Need for Recognition. Adults cannot relegate to obscurity a group of demonstrators. Public displays of protest demand attention. While such behavior may be passed off as immature or attention-seeking, it must be dealt with in some manner. An autocratic attempt to stifle such dissent is self-defeating. The plea, "Please take us seriously," must be heard. A dogmatic response serves only to justify the protesters' belief in the inflexibility of adult society.

Search for Stable Values. The transitional nature of adolescence, combined with a complex and rapidly changing society, produces many uncertainties and ambiguities that must be reduced. Thus many youth movements involve an adoption of simpler modes of life. Folk traditions are glorified. The writings of Thoreau are read with great earnestness. Though the concept is idealistic and romantic, the past is viewed as being less fraught with anxiety and conflict. People of the past are seen as truer to their beliefs, operating with fewer deceits, closer to their roots. If continuity can be established between the past and the present, some meaning and significance is derived from the individual's attempt to alter inconsistencies in modern society.

Characteristics of Student Activists

While student unrest and revolt appear widespread, it seems likely that only a very small percentage of students are involved in such activities. In a follow-up of 10,000 high-school graduates, only a small proportion of the 40 per cent who entered college became politically active (Trent & Craise, 1967). However, the relatively small group of student activists do differ in significant ways from nonactivists.

Questionnaires were administered to 218 students who participated in the 1962 Washington, D. C., student peace demonstration; in-depth interviews were conducted with an additional 29 participants (Solomon & Fishman, 1964). While one-fourth of the students described their homes as politically conservative or reactionary, a majority of them came from politically liberal backgrounds. With regard to academic objectives, two-thirds were majoring in the humanities or social sciences, with few in the physical or biological sciences or in preprofessional courses. This is in sharp contrast with the career objectives of a group of "counter-pickets" from student conservative groups, a majority of whom were planning careers in business or law.

A number of interesting differences were obtained in a study comparing a group of student activists with a group of nonactivists, all living in the Chicago area; the parents of the students were also interviewed (Flacks, 1967). The activists tended to come from upper-income, frequently professional families. The mothers were well educated and often were employed. While only 6 per cent of the fathers of the nonactivists described themselves as politically liberal, 60 per cent of the fathers of the activists designated themselves so. Differences between the two groups on specific issues are given in Table 19-2.

In a comparison on a personality test of a national group of college seniors, a group of Berkeley seniors, and a group of Free Speech Movement members who were arrested in demonstrations (Trent & Craise, 1967), the activist students scored higher than the other two groups on the following scales: Thinking introversion, Complexity, Estheticism, Autonomy, Impulse expression, and Religious liberalism. In general this can be interpreted as indicating that the politically committed students exceeded the other groups in interest in intellectual inquiry, tolerance for ambiguity, objectivity, and independence of thought. Further, they

TABLE 19-2   Students' and Fathers' Attitudes on Current Issues

	Activists		Nonactivists	
Issue	Students	Fathers	Students	Fathers
Percentage who approve:				
Bombing of North Vietnam	9	27	73	80
American troops in Dominican Republic	6	33	65	50
Student participation in protest demonstrations	100	80	61	37
Civil disobedience in civil rights protests	97	57	28	23
Congressional investigations of "un-American activities"	3	7	73	57
Lyndon Johnson	35	77	81	83
Barry Goldwater	0	7	35	20
Full socialization of industry	62	23	5	10
Socialization of the medical profession	94	43	30	27
N	34	30	37	30

From Flacks (1967), p. 67.

showed greater independence from established religious traditions, and they were more concerned with esthetic matters and abstract thinking. Other studies of Berkeley student activists show them to demonstrate high levels of flexibility (Watts & Whittaker, 1966) and high intellectual orientation (Heist, 1965).

A majority of the studies of student activists have dealt with liberal or leftist groups. This is probably because in general students holding beliefs falling on this end of the political spectrum are more active and more vocal. Issues concerning peace (anti-Vietnam and draft-card burning) and civil rights are the most important ones in many liberal protest movements in the last half of the 1960's. However, conservative student groups have become increasingly active, as evidenced during the 1964 Goldwater campaign. In a questionnaire and interview study of a small group of conservative college students in New England (Schiff, 1964), approximately two-thirds showed a conversion to this political ideology, suggesting that the conservative point of view appeals to certain needs within the individual. For these students, the transition from high school to college frequently produced uncertainty, loss of identity, and disequilibrium. Parental domination involving ambitious expectations for the child was a consistent pattern in their backgrounds. Dissonance resulting from failure to conform to these expectations was resolved by becoming an "obedient rebel," a dutiful child who aligned himself with parental values. The choice of conservative ideology seemed to be motivated by a need for authority. The high prestige value and traditional morality of conservatism seemed to hold special appeal for these individuals. Adherence to these values, combined with the intellectual simplicity and achievement-orientation of the conservative philosophy, furnished these students with a sense of stability and much-needed ego enhancement.

Although student activism has been most apparent at the college level, high-school students have shown increased appreciation of the power of group cohesiveness and protest. Perhaps more than at the college level, the issues of concern to high-school students reflect clearly some of the developmental needs of adolescence such as independence and autonomy from adults and the need for recognition. Less concern is shown with such broad national issues as the draft or the rightness of United States' foreign policy and more with personal issues revolving around school rules concerning grooming and dress, smoking, and functions of student government. However, the following list of demands submitted to the school administration of a junior high school in California illustrates the concern shown by minority-group students for recognition and understanding.

WE, THE CHICANO STUDENT UNION,
DEMAND THE FOLLOWING FROM THE
R. JUNIOR HIGH SCHOOL ADMINISTRATION:

1. No student or teacher will be reprimanded for participation in Friday's walkout, as the event was the consequence of the frustration brought upon the participants by the racist attitudes at R. Junior High School.
2. Police officers should not be present at any school functions, as this is one more example of police harassment directed towards Chicano students.
3. Chicanos should not have to conform to the standards of dress that have been set up by the Anglo-Saxon culture; we have our own culture which we feel is equal to the Anglo culture, if not superior.
4. More Chicano teachers and counselors should be hired as many of our problems result from the lack of understanding shown by Anglo instructors.
5. Because we are young adults we feel we have the right to an open campus.
6. No derogatory remarks, particularly racist in nature (dirty Mexican, greaser, spic, etc.), should be used by the faculty in addressing the Chicano students. Instructors having used these remarks should be terminated.
7. Student body offices should be open to all students. A high grade point average should not be a prerequisite to eligibility.
8. Courses teaching the history and culture of "La Raza" should be added to the curriculum.
9. A student-parent committee should be established to review and if necessary after the existing racist policies.
10. The R. Junior High Administration should recognize our organization, the Chicano Student Union, as representative of Mexican-American students on campus.

GOVERNMENT PROGRAMS

In this section we discuss four government-sponsored programs: Job Corps, Neighborhood Youth Corps, VISTA, and the Peace Corps. Each has been designed for a different purpose to meet the needs of certain groups of young people.

Job Corps *

The Job Corps originated under the Economic Opportunity Act of 1964. National recruiting began in January of 1965. Young men and

---

* For an interesting account of the early stages of development of this program see C. Weeks. *Job Corps.* Boston: Little, Brown, 1967.

women from 16 to 21 years of age are eligible for the program. The general purpose is to provide education and job training for adolescents from impoverished families. As stated under Title 1-A of the 1964 Economic Opportunity Act:

> The purpose of this part is to prepare for the responsibilities of citizenship and to increase the employability of young men and women . . . by providing them in rural and urban residential centers with education, vocational training, useful work experience, including work toward the conservation of natural resources, and other appropriate activities (p. 135).

Section III of the *Job Corps Screening Handbook* states that applicants must be classified under four or more of the following conditions in order to be considered:

1. Family lives in substandard housing.
2. Family suffers from very poor nutrition.
3. Parent has a serious physical or mental health condition.
4. Place where he or she lives is included in an area currently designated eligible for assistance under the Area Redevelopment Act (ARA).
5. Primary wage earner in family is unemployed.
6. Family receives public assistance.
7. Living facilities are overcrowded.
8. Father or father substitute missing from home.
9. Both parents have less than an 8th grade education or cannot read or write in English (or Spanish, for a Puerto Rican resident).
10. Jobs held by parents have been largely unskilled.
11. Adult family members are share croppers or migratory or seasonal farm workers, or the inquirer is a rural immigrant from an urban area.
12. Inquirer has shifted residence several times during the past year.
13. Inquirer has not lived with his own parent(s) for more than 5 consecutive years out of the past 10.
14. A (For Females Only) Inquirer is or has been an unwed mother.
14. B (For Males Only) Applicant is a selective service rejectee.

A youth accepted by the Job Corps will be assigned to one of three types of training centers.

> (1) conservation centers, located on public lands operated by the U. S. Department of Interior and Agriculture; (2) urban centers for men, frequently located on demilitarized Federal Installations, operated by private firms or institutions under contract; and (3) urban centers for women, located in urban areas, usually on leased facilities and also operated under contract.
>
> (*Congressional Digest,* 1966, pp. 69–72)

The reading test given at the time an application is filed determines the individual's placement into either a rural or an urban center. Those with scores below sixth-grade level are sent to rural centers; those with higher scores are assigned to urban centers.

Each youth is given room and board, medical and dental care, clothing for work, and money for clothing. Each is paid a $30 living allowance and a $50 readjustment allowance for each month of satisfactory service. Of this, $25 may be sent to a qualified dependent, with the federal government matching this amount.

Rural Centers. In the rural conservation centers the Corpsmen work in groups under experienced employees of the Forest Service, National Park Service, Bureau of Indian Affairs, and the Bureaus of Land Management, Reclamation, and Sport Fisheries and Wildlife. The work projects include construction of roads and nature trails, erosion control, survey of property lines, construction of campground and other recreational areas, reforestation, logging, landscaping, and building. Some of the Corpsmen learn culinary, clerical, and service skills through on-the-job training in the operation and maintenance of the center.

Urban Centers. The urban centers offer specialized, more intensive vocational training in addition to basic education. Some urban centers specialize in specific occupational skills. For example, a facility with extensive automotive equipment may be used to train mechanics. Some of the skills taught are: office machine operator, appliance and automotive repairman, machine tool operator, sales clerk, accounting, shipping and file clerk, hospital technician, waiter, cook and counter worker, laundry and dry cleaning work, meat cutter, and custodial-maintenance jobs. These are skills for which there is a strong demand. Young women are given training in marketable job skills, in home and family life, and in the development of values and attitudes that will contribute to stable family relationships, and in health and recreation. Some of the occupational skills learned are those of bookkeeper, typist, office machine operator, cashier, hospital ward clerk, data processor, sales clerk, stock clerk and other retail jobs, dietitian's aide and other food-preparation and service jobs, beauty operator, nurse's aide, practical nurse, housekeeper service jobs.

Problems. As defenders of the Job Corps point out, the approximately one-third dropout rate is not higher than that during the freshman year in many colleges and universities. Moreover, the young people are dropouts of one kind or another when they enter the program. In any case, attempts are being made to reduce the proportion of dropouts.

Many communities have refused to permit the establishment of Job Corps centers in their areas, primarily because of the kinds of young people admitted to the program—minority-group members, poorly educated, and lower social class. In general, however, the anticipated difficulties have not developed, despite occasional problems. To improve their image in the community, many of the centers have become involved in community projects such as helping orphans and crippled children, developing recreational areas, and contributing to community emergency work (fires and floods).

Racial attitudes and attitudes toward work and education are not easily changed; consequently these have presented problems in many centers. While job training is extremely important, attitudes toward oneself, toward society, and toward the future must be dealt with as well.

Probably one of the most persistent problems has been the cost of maintaining the Corpsmen. While the first estimate was $4700 per year per enrollee, the actual cost, as determined in 1966, was $12,000, a figure that included the capital investment costs at each center. Although this seems exorbitant, clearly the long-run savings to the taxpayer are far greater than this in the case of each individual who learns a trade and becomes a stable wage earner.

Prospects. Although trainees are not guaranteed a job after graduation, they are given assistance by the center. At centers administered by corporations, job placement within that corporation is frequent. Of the 700 men and women who completed training in the last nine months of the first year of the program, 35 per cent were drafted or enlisted, 18 per cent returned to school, and the remainder found jobs. Of the latter, 90 per cent were still employed in January 1966.

Neighborhood Youth Corps

This program was established under the Economic Opportunity Act and is run by the Department of Labor with the guidance of the Office of Economic Opportunity. Its purpose is to provide ". . . part-time employment, on-the-job training and useful work experience for students from low-income families who are in 9th through 12th grade of school" or to provide ". . . unemployed individuals with useful work experience and on-the-job training combined where needed with educational training" (Economic Opportunity Act of 1964, p. 9). The NYC has its greatest appeal for high-school students who might not be able to continue schooling if it were not for a part-time job, but it also appeals to those who have already dropped out of school. To qualify, the youth must be from age 16 to 21 and be from a family that is receiving welfare payments. The jobs are designed to be useful to the community and to give the worker a sense of being needed. The work is in community service, libraries, schools, playgrounds, and city or private agencies. The federal government does not run the programs directly, but it must approve the agencies before money can be appropriated. It is left up to each community to find the appropriate jobs and to establish a good program for its particular use. Unlike the Job Corps, the NYC youth remain at home and work while attending school.

VISTA

Also established by the Economic Opportunity Act of 1964, Volunteers in Service to America (VISTA) is considered the domestic peace corps. Its purpose is "to enable and encourage volunteers to participate in a personal way in the war on poverty, by living and working among deprived people of all ages . . . to encourage individuals from all walks of life to make a commitment to combat poverty in their home communities . . ." (Economic Opportunity Act of 1964, as amended, 1966, p. 50).

Anyone 18 years of age and over is eligible to join VISTA. The only examination required is a medical one and even people who have physical disabilities are eligible if they can carry out their assignments. There are no maximum age limits, and no special education or experience qualifications are necessary. Volunteers are trained in workshops, discussion groups, and intensive field work. While in training volunteers are paid a $50 a month stipend plus living and medical expenses. At the end of six weeks of training they are sent to areas in the United States and its territories. The period of service lasts one year, and a second and third year may be requested. During this time they are paid a modest cost-of-living allowance. At the end of service they are paid $50 for every month of service.

Peace Corps

The purpose of the Peace Corps is:

. . . to promote world peace and friendship by making available to interested countries Americans who will:
  * Help the people of these countries meet their needs for trained manpower;
  * Help promote a better understanding of the American people on the part of the peoples served; and
  * Help promote a better understanding of other peoples on the part of the American people.

(*Peace Corps Factbook & Directory*, 1968, p. 2)

All qualified single Americans above 18 years of age or married couples with no dependents under 18 may serve as Peace Corps Volunteers. They are selected on the basis of merit. An application form and questionnaire plus six letters of recommendation must be submitted before a candidate is tested. A physical examination is necessary and certain personal traits that seem to promise success are evaluated.

After acceptance a Volunteer reports for a 10- or 12-week training session on a college or university campus. He must study at least 60 hours a week, learn one of the international languages and a local language as well, study the history, geography, culture, and customs of the country to which he expects to go, and engage in strenuous physical exercise. If he survives this training, he is sent to an advanced training center for field work. This offers him a sample of life as he will find it on the job. He is then sent to a country that has asked for Peace Corps members. He is trained to be a "doer" not an "advisor." Peace Corps Volunteers receive a modest cost-of-living allowance, and at the end of their two-year period of service they receive an amount equal to $75 for each month of service.

Some psychological research has been conducted, largely with regard to predicting success in the Peace Corps (e.g., Mischel, 1965; Guthrie & Zektick, 1967). Mischel found that those who scored high on an authoritarian and an anxiety scale were rated less favorably than those who scored low. The ratings of success in a teaching assignment in Nigeria covered the following dimensions: teaching effectiveness; person-to-person contacts (interpersonal behavior with Nigerians); appreciation of Nigerian culture; representation of American culture by (a) personal behavior and (b) by interpreting American culture to Nigerians; and adjustment to the assignment.

In an interesting study of a group of Peace Corps teachers in Ghana (Smith, 1966), two extensive interviews were conducted with the Volunteers during their two years of teaching. A number of factors emerged from an analysis of Q-sort ratings (for a discussion of this procedure, see p. 540 above) of these interviews. The factors are listed below together with some of the descriptive statements characterizing each.

Personality Factor P-1:
Self-Confident Maturity

Generally self-confident.

A genuinely dependable and responsible person.

The values and principles which he holds directly affect what he does.

Personality Factor V-5:
Controlling Responsibility

Control of his situation is important to him.

A genuinely dependable and responsible person.

Engages in "posturing" to self and others; concerned with maintaining "face."

Personality Factor V-6:
Self-Actualizing Search for
Identity

Feels his own life is important,
that it matters what he does
with his life.

Devotes much of his energy to a
deliberate program of self-improvement (creative activity,
study, etc.).

Intense, tends to involve self
deeply.

Performance Factor P-1
Competent Teaching in Africa

Committed to carrying out his job
as Peace Corps teacher to the
best of his ability.

Is, all-in-all, a good competent
teacher.

Values his Peace Corp assignment
as relevant to his career plans.

Performance Factor V-1:
Constructive Involvement with
Africa

His African experiences have increased his concern with race
relations in the United States.

Generally likes his students, treats
them with warmth and understanding.

Has established intimate, continuing relationships with adult Africans.

Performance Factor V-2
Exclusive Teaching Commitment

His whole life has centered on the
school compound.

Absorbed in his work.

Committed to carrying out his job
as Peace Corps teacher to the
best of his ability.

Because the interviews in the Smith study covered a two-year period it was possible to identify shifts in attitudes over time. In general, "the volunteers became more tough-minded and realistic, more autonomous and independent of authority, and much more concerned with the plight of the American Negro (Smith, 1966, p. 565).

With regard to motivation for joining the Peace Corps, Smith identi-fied two principal motivations. First, many of the volunteers were un-certain of their life goals so they welcomed a two-year period for reassess-ment and self-discovery. Second, during this period of introspection they wished to accomplish something worthwhile. Finally, adventure and foreign experience appealed to some.

Of the various programs described in this section, the Peace Corps has made the most favorable impression on the American public. It is at once idealistic and pragmatic, and it appeals to Americans' concep-tion of themselves as willing to help underdeveloped nations, especially on a person-to-person basis.

REFERENCES

Becker, H. S. Becoming a marijuana user. *American Journal of Sociology,* 1953, **59**, 235–242.

Bell, J. A comparison of dropouts and nondropouts on participation in school activities. *Journal of Educational Research,* 1967, **60**, 248–251.

Bowman, P., & Matthews, C. *Motivations of youth for leaving school.* U. S. Department of Health, Education, and Welfare, Office of Education, Co-operative Research Project No. 200. Quincy, Ill.: University of Chicago and Quincy Youth Development Project, 1960.

Brigham, J. C., Ricketts, J. L., & Johnson, R. C. Reported maternal and paternal behaviors of solitary and social delinquents. *Journal of Consulting Psychology,* 1967, **31**, 420–422.

Brown, C. *Manchild in the promised land.* New York: MacMillan, 1965.

Burchinal, L. Research on young marriage: Implications for family life education. *Family Life Coordinator,* 1960, **9**, 6–24.

Burchinal, L. Trends and prospects for young marriages in the United States. *Journal of Marriage and the Family,* 1965, **27**, 243–254.

Campbell, E. Q. The internalization of moral norms. *Sociometry,* 1964, **27**, 391–412.

Cassel, R., & Coleman, J. A critical examination of the school dropout, reluctant learner, and abler non-college student problem. *Bulletin of the National Association of Secondary-School Principals,* 1962, **46**, 60–65.

Cervantes, L. *The dropout: Causes and cures.* Ann Arbor: University of Michigan Press, 1965.

Chein, I. *Narcotics, delinquency, and social policy.* London: Tavistock, 1964.

Cohen, A. K. *Delinquent boys.* Glencoe, Ill.: Free Press, 1955.

Current Population Reports. Population characteristics. Marital status and family status: March, 1967. February 23, 1968.

Dain, N. *Concepts of insanity in the United States, 1789–1865.* New Brunswick, N. J.: Rutgers University Press, 1964.

Dentler, R., & Warshauer, M. *Big city drop-outs and illiterates.* New York: Center for Urban Education, Teachers College, Columbia University, 1965.

Economic Opportunity Act of 1964. Washington, D. C.: U. S. Government Printing Office, 1967.

Economic Opportunity Act of 1964, as Amended. Washington, D. C.: U. S. Government Printing Office, 1966.

Erikson, E. H. Youth: Fidelity and diversity. In E. H. Erikson (Ed.), *Youth: Change and challenge.* New York: Basic Books, 1963. Pp. 1–23.

Eysenck, H. J. *Crime and personality.* London: Routledge and Kegan Paul, 1964.

Fairweather, G. W. *Social psychology in treating mental illness: An experimental approach.* New York: Wiley, 1964.

Fairweather, G. W. *Methods for experimental social innovation.* New York: Wiley, 1967.

Farrell, J. T. *Studs Lonigan: A trilogy.* New York: Vanguard, 1935.

Fishman, J., & Solomon, F. Youth and social action: An introduction. *Journal of Social Issues,* 1964, **20**, 1–27.

Flacks, R. The liberated generation: An exploration of the roots of student protest. *Journal of Social Issues,* 1967, **23**, 52–75.

Friedenberg, E. An ideology of school withdrawal. In D. Schreiber (Ed.), *The school dropout.* Washington, D. C.: National Education Association, 1964. Pp. 25–39.

Glasser, W. *Reality therapy.* New York: Harper & Row, 1965.

Glueck, S., & Glueck, E. T. *One thousand juvenile delinquents.* Cambridge: Harvard University Press, 1934.

Glueck, S., & Glueck, E. T. *Juvenile delinquents grow up.* New York: Commonwealth Fund, 1940.

Goldfarb, W. Psychological privation in infancy and subsequent adjustment. *American Journal of Orthopsychiatry,* 1945, **15**, 244–257.

Goodman, P. *Growing up absurd.* New York: Random House, 1960.

Goodman, P. The universal trap. In D. Schreiber (Ed.), *The school dropout.* Washington, D. C.: National Education Association, 1964. Pp. 40–53.

Guthrie, G., & Zektick, I. Predicting performance in the Peace Corps. *Journal of Social Psychology,* 1967, **71**, 11–21.

Havighurst, R. Early marriage and the schools. *School Review,* 1961, **69**, 36–47.

Heist, P. *Intellect and commitment: The faces of discontent.* Berkeley: Center for the Study of Higher Education, 1965. (mimeo)

Hoffman, M. L., & Saltzstein, H. D. Parent discipline and the child's moral development. *Journal of Personality and Social Psychology,* 1967, **5**, 45–57.

Hollingshead, A. S., & Redlich, F. C. *Social class and mental illness.* New York: Wiley, 1958.

Israel, S., & Wouterez, T. Teenage obstetrics. *American Journal of Obstetrics and Gynecology,* 1963, **86**, 659–667.

Jacobs, P., Brunton, M., Melville, M. M., Brittain, R. P., & McClemont, W. F. Aggressive behavior, mental sub-normality, and the XYY male. *Nature,* 1965, **208**, 1351–1352.

Jacobson, J. L., & Wirt, R. D. MMPI profiles associated with outcomes of group therapy with prisoners. Minneapolis, Minn.: University of Minnesota, 1968. (mimeo)

Jessor, R., Graves, T. D., Hanson, R. C., & Jessor, S. L. *Society, personality, and deviant behavior.* New York: Holt, Rinehart & Winston, 1968.

Johnson, R. C., Ackerman, J. M., Frank, H., & Fionda, A. J. Resistance to temptation, guilt following yielding, and mental health. *Journal of Consulting and Clinical Psychology,* 1968, **32**, 169–175.

Karpman, B. (Ed.), Psychopathic behavior in infants and children. *American Journal of Orthopsychiatry*, 1951, **21**, 223–272.

Keniston, K. *The uncommitted.* New York: Harcourt, Brace, & World, 1965.

LaBarre, M. Pregnancy experiences among married adolescents. *American Journal of Orthopsychiatry*, 1968, **38**, 47–55.

Laurie, P. *Drugs.* Middlesex, England: Penguin Books, 1967.

Lynn, D., & Sawrey, W. L. The effects of father-absence on Norwegian boys and girls. *Journal of Abnormal and Social Psychology*, 1959, **59**, 258–262.

Maddox, G. L., & McCall, B. C. *Drinking among teenagers.* New Brunswick, N. J.: Rutgers Center of Alcohol Studies, 1964.

Main "Economic Opportunity Act" Programs. *Congressional Digest*, March, 1966, 69–72.

Martinson, F. M. Ego deficiency as a factor in marriage—A male sample. *Marriage and Family Living*, 1959, **21**, 48–52.

Marwell, G. Adolescent powerlessness and delinquent behavior. *Social Problems*, 1966, **14**, 35–47.

Medinnus, G. R. Delinquents' perceptions of their parents. *Journal of Consulting Psychology*, 1965, **29**, 592–593.

Miller, S. Dropouts—A political problem. In D. Schreiber (Ed.), *The school dropout.* Washington, D. C.: National Education Association, 1964. Pp. 11–24.

Miller, W. *The cool world.* Boston: Little, Brown, 1959.

Mischel, W. Predicting the success of Peace Corps volunteers in Nigeria. *Journal of Personality and Social Psychology*, 1965, **1**, 510–517.

Monohan, T. Does age at marriage matter in divorce? *Social Forces*, 1963, **32**, 81–87.

Moss, J., & Gingles, R. The relationship of personality to the incidence of early marriage. *Marriage and Family Living*, 1959, **21**, 373–377.

Mowrer, O. H. *The crisis in psychiatry and religion.* Princeton, N. J.: Van Nostrand, 1961.

Mowrer, O. H. *The new group therapy.* Princeton, N. J.: Van Nostrand, 1964.

Mowrer, O. H. (Ed.), *Morality and mental health.* Chicago: Rand-McNally, 1967.

National Education Association Project: School Dropouts. *Dropout studies, design and conduct.* Washington, D. C.: National Education Association, 1965.

Newsweek. May 2, 1966, p. 17.

Pavlovna, V., & Wasson, R. G. *Mushrooms, Russia, and history.* New York: Pantheon, 1957.

Peace Corps Factbook & Directory. Washington, D. C., 1968.

Penty, R. *Reading ability and high school drop-outs.* New York: Teachers College, Columbia University, 1956.

Peterson, D. R. The insecure child: Over-socialized or under-socialized? In

O. H. Mowrer (Ed.), *Morality and mental health.* Chicago: Rand McNally, 1967. Pp. 459–471.

Price, W. H., & Whitmore, P. B. Criminal behavior and the XYY male. *Nature,* 1967, **5078,** 815.

Randolph, M. H., Richardson, H., & Johnson, R. C. A comparison of social and solitary male delinquents. *Journal of Consulting Psychology,* 1961, **25,** 293–295.

Richardson, H., & Roebuck, J. B. Minnesota Multiphasic Personality Inventory and California Psychological Inventory differences between delinquents and their nondelinquent siblings. *Proceedings of the seventy-third annual convention of the American Psychological Association, 1965.* Washington, D. C.: American Psychological Association, 1965. Pp. 255–256.

Roebuck, J. B. The drug addict as an offender type. *Crime and Delinquency,* 1962, **8,** 36–43.

Roebuck, J. B. The Negro numbers man as a criminal type: The construction of a typology. *Journal of Criminal Law, Criminology, and Police Science,* 1963, **54,** 48–60.

Roebuck, J. B., & Cadwallader, M. L. The Negro armed robber as a criminal type: The construction and application of a typology. *Pacific Sociological Review,* 1961, **4,** 21–26.

Roebuck, J. B., & Johnson, R. C. The jack-of-all-trades offender. *Crime and Delinquency,* 1962, **8,** 172–181.   (a)

Roebuck, J. B., & Johnson, R. C. The Negro drinker and assaulter as a criminal type. *Crime and Delinquency,* 1962, **8,** 21–33.   (b)

Roebuck, J. B., & Johnson, R. C. The "short con" man. *Crime and Delinquency,* 1964, **10,** 235–248.

Schiff, L. The obedient rebels: A study of college conversions to conservatism. *Journal of Social Issues,* 1964, **20,** 74–95.

Seeman, M. On the meaning of alienation. *American Sociological Review,* 1959, **24,** 783–791.

Shaw, C. R. *Jack-roller: A delinquent boy's own story.* Chicago: University of Chicago Press, 1930.

Shaw, C. R., & Moore, M. E. *Natural history of a delinquent career.* Chicago: University of Chicago Press, 1931.

Shelly, J. A., & Bassin, A. Daytop Lodge—A new treatment approach for drug addicts. *Corrective Psychiatry,* 1965, **11,** 186–195.

Shields, J. Personality differences and neurotic traits in normal twin school children. A study in psychiatric genetics. *Eugenics Review,* 1954, **45,** 213–246.

Siegman, A. W. Father absence during early childhood and anti-social behavior. *Journal of Abnormal Psychology,* 1966, **21,** 555–566.

Smith, M. B. Explorations in competence: A study of Peace Corps teachers in Ghana. *American Psychologist,* 1966, **21,** 555–566.

Solomon, F., & Fishman, J. Youth and peace: A psychosocial study of student peace demonstrators in Washington, D. C. *Journal of Social Issues,* 1964, **20,** 54–73.

Mayor's Committee on Marijuana. *The marijuana problem in the City of New York: Sociological, medical, psychological, and pharmacological studies* ("The LaGuardia Report"). Lancaster, Pa.: Cattell Press, 1944.

Thompson, H. S. *Hell's angels.* New York: Ballantine, 1966.

Thrasher, F. M. *The gang.* Chicago: University of Chicago Press, 1963 (original publication, 1927).

Trent, J., & Craise, J. Commitment and conformity in the American college. *Journal of Social Issues,* 1967, **23,** 34–51.

Van Dyke, L., & Hoyt, K. *The drop-out problem in Iowa high schools.* U. S. Department of Health, Education, and Welfare, Office of Education, Co-operative Research Project No. 160. Iowa City: State University of Iowa and Iowa State Department of Public Instruction, 1958.

Watts, W., & Whittaker, D. Free speech advocates at Berkeley. *Journal of Applied Behavioral Science,* 1966, **2,** 41–62.

Whyte, W. F. *Street corner society.* Chicago: University of Chicago Press, 1943.

Williams, P. School dropouts. *NEA Journal,* 1963, **52,** 10–12.

Wirt, R. D., & Briggs, P. F. Personality and environmental factors in the development of delinquency. *Psychological Monographs,* 1959, **73,** 15, Whole No. 485.

Wood, B. S., Wilson, G. G., Jessor, R., & Bogan, R. B. Troublemaking behavior in a correctional institution: Relationship to inmates' definition of their situation. *American Journal of Orthopsychiatry,* 1966, **36,** 795–802.

Yablonsky, L. The anticriminal society: Synanon. *Federal Probation,* 1962, **26,** 50–57 (and in O. H. Mowrer (Ed.), *Morality and mental health.* Chicago: Rand-McNally, 1967. Pp. 561–571).

Yablonsky, L. *The tunnel back: Synanon.* New York: MacMillan, 1965.

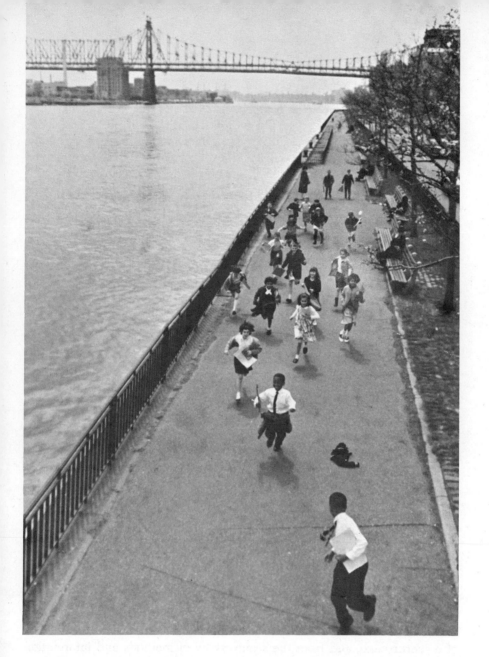

Summing Up

20

The aim of science is to understand natural phenomena. The scientist assumes that the universe is orderly and that natural phenomena, ultimately, are predictable and lawful. Understanding and prediction come from the use of the scientific method. The scientific method is merely a set of "rules" by which scientists attempt to eliminate bias from their observations and thus view nature as it is, not as they wish it to be.

Systematic observation of unbiased samples of the phenomenon under investigation is the key to an accurate understanding of the universe. Experiments are the form of observation most commonly used in science, since in experiments uncontrolled or unknown sources of variance are reduced to a minimum. Further, experiments, far more than naturalistic observation, may be directed to highly specific problems whose solution may provide the information needed to decide which of two or more conflicting theories is the most accurate portrayal of the relations between natural phenomena.

On the negative side, an emphasis on experimentation may cause the neglect, for the most part, of those natural phenomena that do not readily fit within conventional experimental design. This is illustrated in the psychology of learning; there is a plethora of experiments dealing with forms of learning common to all species but few dealing with those complex forms of cognition that set mankind apart from other species.

We observe, systematically and without bias. From this observation we attempt to understand, predict, and, at times, control the phenomena with which we deal. In psychology, especially in developmental psychology, there are grave ethical problems involved in scientifically controlling behavior. It seems reasonable to believe that the level of development of a science should be judged by the degree to which that science allows understanding and predictions.

This book has attempted to provide information about the known and the predictable in developmental psychology. In general, although at a lesser stage of development than the physical or biological sciences, developmental psychology has much to be proud of. It has steadily increased the rigor of its methods of investigation and the accuracy of its predictions. From the scattered anecdotes and unsupported folk beliefs of a century ago, and from the scanty array of methods and information available at the turn of the century, it has developed adequate research methods, a vast store of facts, and a few theories useful for knitting together at least some of the facts in an orderly fashion. Developmental psychology appears to be at the stage where theories more accurate and inclusive than those now available can be evolved and proved valuable rather than merely blinding people to natural events for which they cannot account.

The developmental psychologist has to deal with two major questions. First, in what ways are humans all alike, and why? Second, within this framework of similarity, how do individual differences arise? These are two of the problems that this book has attempted to deal with as best possible in the light of imperfect knowledge.

Two sets of forces work upon mankind, those that are biological-genetic, and those that are social. The biological-genetic forces are chiefly influential in producing a basic similarity among all humans; they also serve to produce a biological core of individual difference that is further increased by each individual's unique set of social experiences. Social forces also produce similarity among humans. We share the characteristic of growing up within some primary group, of being cared for by one or more parents or parent-surrogates; we all must face the challenge of moving from a position of dependence to one of comparative independence. Further similarity results from being brought up within one specific culture, with its own pattern of relieving social stresses. However alike humans may be as a result of the similarity in the way they are socialized, it is their unique social environment that greatly enlarges their individual differences that are hereditary in nature.

Humans are alike. We are bipedal, with stereoscopic vision and with sensitive hands, free to manipulate objects in the environment. We follow the same general course of growth and maturation. We share with all other animals certain ways of learning, such as operant and respondent learning, but are different from all nonprimates in other areas, such as in the ease of formation of learning sets. We are like one another, but unlike all other organisms, in the ease with which we deal with abstract concepts, delayed reactions, and complex and creative problem solving. This human uniqueness appears to be the result of the fact that only humans are capable of symbolic behavior. Language is again an inherited ability, causing humans to share a broad social heritage, built up across generations, and to show similarity in social and intellectual responses to the world. We are manipulative, curious, and arousal seeking. Within this framework of similarity individual differences occur.

We are different. Genetic inheritance makes individuals differ from one another in obvious ways, as in eye color, skin color, size, and physical attractiveness, and in less obvious but more significant ways, as in intelligence and in activity level. Certain innate differences are present, and these differences are enhanced by the environment.

The contemporary American child grows up in a rich, urban, industrial society in which there is little need for early economic productivity. This society is becoming milder in its approach to child rearing, although it may still be considered relatively harsh in some areas if judged by crosscultural standards. The child is less subject to parental pressures and more subject to the influences of such agents of socialization as his peers and the school. Although parental influences are probably somewhat less pervasive than previously at any given time in the child's early life, the period of dependency on parents has lengthened considerably.

Within these areas of similarity within the culture, forces producing diversity operate. The sex of the child, his ordinal position, the characteristics of his siblings, and the economic well-being and marital adjustment of the parents are all important factors producing differences in the way the child is treated within the family—and thus, in causing variation in personality, adjustment, and behavior, both in childhood and in later years. These sociological factors within the family setting, interacting with the child's innate characteristics and with parental personalities, attitudes toward child rearing, and behaviors, help make each child unique. The family, and especially the parents, plays the major role of shaping the child and producing that complex set of traits called personality.

Other agents of socialization also operate on the child. Certainly, for most individuals, agemates play an important role in socialization. Although the peer group is often viewed as a "bad" influence, it has a number of useful functions. It conveys information and value, provides the child with a source of identification and, perhaps most important of all, serves as a buffer and a normalizer of deviant parent attitudes.

The school is a second extrafamilial grouping that has considerable influence on the development of the child. Both information and values are transmitted. By exposing all children to a relatively uniform set of experiences, the school helps to produce a more homogeneous culture— one that is in some ways increasingly oriented toward a middle-class value system based on a belief in hard work, delayed gratification, and social mobility. The educational system engenders a drive for mobility and provides the formal education necessary for its achievement.

The community, religious institutions, and mass media of communication also have some influence on the socialization process. However, the effect of these last social forces appears to be less than is commonly believed. Further, the effects of the so-called "good" forces such as schoolbooks and religious instruction are not all good, nor are the effects of movies, television, and comics as uniformly pernicious as is often assumed. The effects are ambiguous and generally rather minor. Some few children, however, are deeply influenced by such things as community setting or television. These children appear to be young people whose parents have largely abdicated the responsibility of providing values and security, or are individuals with a fair degree of psychological disturbance, or both.

Although genetic inheritance sets the limits within which individuals vary from one another, it also produces a substantial portion of the resulting variation. Upon this genetic variation multifarious environmental forces act to make each of us unique. The complex and interactive play of environmental and hereditary forces, plus the interaction between the many environmental factors themselves, combine to produce the individual. Family and friends, community and school, and books and comic books are only a small sampling of the social influences encountered by a child. Influences may be short-term or long-range, gradual and mild, or sudden and traumatic. Further, the child is not merely a weak and passive recipient of stimulation but is a vigorous and active organism that determines, to a considerable extent, the kind of stimulation it is to receive and the degree of impact that stimuli will have in changing behavior.

From these crosscurrents of stimulation the child broadens his sphere of activity. He develops a personality—a unique set of traits. He develops a self concept—a set of ideas concerning the physical self and a set of self-expectations concerning behavior; this makes him relatively consistent and predictable in behavior. He tends to respond in ways consistent with this self concept and thus develops a more rigid and clearly delineated set of social roles with age.

Adolescence, as a separate developmental stage, may be said to begin at the time that signs of sexual maturity occur and end with the attainment of adult roles and adult independence. Our culture, as well as most other industrial cultures, has lengthened markedly the time interval between sexual maturity and social adulthood, thus causing adolescence to be a distinct and rather difficult stage of the life cycle. Physical changes of considerable magnitude occur during adolescence; and the person who is out of step developmentally in the timing of these changes is likely to have some difficulty in adjustment during adolescence. However, the effects of out-of-step physical development appear to dissipate in adulthood. Evidence supporting qualitative change in intellectual functioning during adolescence that is comparable to physical change seems lacking in strength. Social development during adolescence is determined largely by interacting, often conflicting demands of parents and peers. Problems result when these conflicting demands are inadequately resolved, usually because of defects in the parent-child relationship or else because of extremely strong peer influence. Problems also exist among adolescents because societally prescribed roles for adolescents often are dull and undemanding. Changes in the culture may be necessary if adolescence is to become less of a problem period of life.

The human, born weak, small, and totally dependent, masters his developmental tasks and emerges as a tough and strong organism, resistant to stress and capable of self-repair and of manipulating the environment to shape it closer to his heart's desire—social, yet independent; unique, yet part of the whole stream of human life.

We have attempted to map the course of child and adolescent development. The problems faced in understanding and predicting behavior are complex, and although some questions, such as the influence of maturation on physical development, have been largely answered, others, such as the bases of personality deviation in childhood, are far from solution. We believe that all scientific problems are potentially solvable, and hope that at least some of the *terra incognita* of developmental psychology will be mapped by students who have read this book.

PHOTO CREDITS

Author Index

Italic page numbers refer to citations in the references at the end of each chapter.

767

Subject Index